Beginning Visual Basic 6 Application Development

Ken Slovak
Diane Poremsky
Pierre Boutquin
Jason Bock
Matthew Reynolds
Kent Sharkey
Lee Whitney

Wrox Press Ltd.

Beginning Visual Basic 6 Application Development

11-20-00

Published by Wrox Press Ltd,
Arden House, 1102 Warwick Road, Acocks Green,
Birmingham, B27 6BH, UK
Printed in the United States
ISBN 1-861001-0-96

Trademark Acknowledgements

Wrox has endeavored to provide trademark information about all the companies and products mentioned in this book by the appropriate use of capitals. However, Wrox cannot guarantee the accuracy of this information.

Credits

Authors
Ken Slovak
Diane Poremsky
Pierre Boutquin
Jason Bock
Matthew Reynolds
Kent Sharkey
Lee Whitney

Additional Material
Marc Simkin

Technical Reviewers
Eleanor Baylis
Matthew Bortniker
Carl Burnham
Robert Chang
Ben Cops
Jon Duckett
Damian Foggon
Kate Hall
John Harris
Nathan Heine
Thomas Jones
Ron Landers
Rockford Lhotka
David Liske
Robert Oliver
Kathy Peters
Matthew Reynolds
David Schultz
Kenn Scribner
Marc Simkin
Jon Stephens
Don Udawattage
Warren Wiltsie
Donald Xie

Technical Architect
Ian Blackham

Production Manager
Laurent Lafon

Technical Editors
Alastair Ewins
Claire Fletcher
Lisa Stephenson

Category Managers
Chris Hindley
Joanna Mason
Dominic Lowe

Author Agents
Sarah Bowers
Sophie Edwards

Development Editor
Greg Pearson

Project Administration
Sophie Edwards
Jake Manning

Production Coordinator
Tom Bartlett

Additional Layout
Laurent Lafon

Figures
Tom Bartlett
William Fallon
Shabnam Hussain

Cover Design
Chris Morris
Shelley Frasier

Index
Martin Brooks

Proofreaders
Fiona Berryman
Christopher Smith

About the Authors

Ken Slovak

Ken Slovak is a consultant and developer who specializes in Outlook, MS Office, VBA and VB programming. He is a Microsoft Outlook MVP (Most Valuable Professional), a designation conferred on him by Microsoft in recognition of his support work for the Outlook community. He is the lead author of Professional Microsoft Outlook 2000 Programming, co-author of Programming Microsoft Outlook 2000, contributor to Professional CDO Programming, is a technical editor for a number of Outlook books, and is a columnist, author and technical reviewer for Exchange and Outlook magazine.

Prior to becoming a consultant he was chief engineer of an industrial instrumentation manufacturing company for 14 years, and he has been working with computers for more than 20 years. He has designed integrated Outlook/Exchange/Office applications, numerous instrumentation systems, and has developed desktop applications and embedded system software in many computer languages; including Visual Basic, Access, C, Assembly languages, and FoxPro. He has written many technical and operating manuals, and has also developed technical and sales literature for numerous computerized systems. Ken currently resides in Central Florida.

Dedication

This one is for the memory of Katie, one of the loves of my life, and the best dog I've ever known - Ken Slovak

Acknowledgements

To all the people at Wrox Press who have helped develop this book, I am very thankful. Special thanks go to Ian Blackham, Claire Fletcher, Lisa Stephenson, Alastair Ewins, Sophie Edwards, Eleanor Baylis, Dominic Lowe, Joanna Mason, and to all the technical personnel, technical reviewers and others who have brought this book to life. Your professionalism has been an inspiration to me. It has been an enjoyable experience working with all of you, and I hope to do it again. Also, thanks go to my co-authors on this book. I hope that our efforts have produced a book that will teach you something about developing distributed applications.

My thanks always go to my colleagues and friends in the Outlook and MVP communities: Sue Mosher, Randy Byrne, Sig Weber, Vince Averello, Jessie Louise McClennan, Diane Poremsky, Russ Valentine, Jay Harlow, Hollis Paul, Chris Burnham, Milly Staples, Ben Schorr, Steve Moede, and Bill Rodgers. Some of the many people at Microsoft I want to thank for their help, support and friendship are Abdias Ruiz, Ronna Pinkerton, KC Lemson and Scott Bradley.

Thanks and love go to the whole family; Mom and Ricky, Dad and Mom, Chris, Bobby and Donata, Sandie and Bruce. Special thanks go again to my co-author and good friend Diane Poremsky, now the whole world will finally know that she really doesn't have two heads. Finally, as always my gratitude goes to Susie, the love of my life and my best friend. And to Casey, my new chief assistant and dog, who worked side by side with me through many of the long hours writing this book.

Diane Poremsky

Diane Poremsky is a consultant who specializes in Microsoft Windows, Outlook and Office training and development. She is a Microsoft Outlook MVP (Most Valuable Professional), in recognition for her technical support of Microsoft Outlook. She is a technical editor for a number of computer books, and is a columnist, author and technical reviewer for Exchange and Outlook magazine.

Diane currently resides in East Tennessee with her family.

Dedication

To Chris and Becky – always remember that graduation should be a rest stop on the interstate of learning, not an exit ramp.

Acknowledgements

A big thanks to my friend and co-author, Ken Slovak, for his encouragement, support and guidance in my first major writing project. Special thanks to Ian Blackham for his exceptional patience and tolerance. You guys are the greatest. Thanks also everyone at Wrox Press who have helped develop this book, including Claire Fletcher, Lisa Stephenson, Alastair Ewins, Sophie Edwards, Eleanor Baylis, Dominic Lowe, Joanna Mason, and to all the technical personnel and others who have helped make this book great.

Love and thanks to my husband Phil and my daughters, Becky, Liz, Jessica and Cecilia, for their patience and understanding during the long hours spent at the computer. Their cooking skills showed remarkable improvement by the time I reached the end of the book. Chris, if you were not away at college you'd have learned to cook too.

Thanks also to the rest of my family: Mom and Dad, Carol, Kate and Tom, for your moral support and encouragement. You may not understand what it's about but you're getting a copy for Christmas anyway.

To my many online friends who provided welcome distractions and comic relief during long nights working, including the Beta Bros group and Peter Williams, thanks for reminding me that laughter is the best medicine.

Pierre Boutquin

Pierre Boutquin is a senior analyst in the corporate treasury of a major Canadian bank, where he helps develop leading-edge market risk management software. He has over a decade of experience implementing PC-based computer systems with in-depth knowledge of distributed systems design, data warehousing, Visual Basic, Visual C++, and SQL. He has co-authored many programming books besides the present book, most recently "SQL Unleashed 2nd Edition". He has also contributed material on COM+, XML and SQL for other books.

Pierre's spare time is mainly owned by Koshka and Sasha, his two adorable Burmese cats. While petting them, he often thinks how nice it would be to find more time and get back into chess or keep up with news from Belgium, his native country. You can reach him at boutquin@hotmail.com.

Acknowledgements

Much hard work goes into the creation of a book, and not just from the people mentioned on the cover of the book. I must especially thank the Wrox team and the co-authors of this book for their tremendous dedication to produce a quality book. The reviewers deserve a lot of credit for making me look like an accomplished writer.

Special thanks to Mildred Watts of Grand Bank, Newfoundland with whom I stayed while on a writing retreat. I would have lost contact with my editors without the generous use of one of the computers in the local library, of which Mildred is the librarian. As promised, I will not mention the can of milk on the dinner table.

I must also thank Kent Sharkey for writing the XML chapter and Margaret Fekete for her help with researching database design (material on compiling and linking will have to wait for another book!). Finally, this effort would not have been possible without the support from my family and friends: Sandra (thanks for the proofreading!), Andrea (keep sending these funny e-mails!), Jennifer, Tindy and Doel, and Marcel and Diana Ban.

Jason Bock

Jason Bock is a Senior Consultant for High Gear Inc., a consulting company focused on object-oriented development in distributed systems. He has worked on a diverse number of business applications using different object and component technologies (such as VB, Java, COM, etc.). He is also the author of *Visual Basic 6 Win32 API Tutorial*, published by Wrox Press, and he has written technical articles on VB and Java development. He has a Bachelors and a Masters degree in Electrical Engineering from Marquette University. He can be reached at jason.bock@high-gear.com.

Acknowledgements

I'd like to thank Liz for letting me "disappear" for a while as I wrote my chapter for this book.

Matthew Reynolds

Matthew Reynolds is an Internet consultant and evangelist specializing in building e-business solutions based on the Windows DNA platform. He lives in the UK and divides his time between working for established "dot coms" and enthusiastic startups through his consulting firm, RedPiranha.com. He can be reached at matthewr@wrox.com.

Acknowledgements

I'd like to thank pretty much everyone I know for his or her contribution to making this book possible! This includes: Alex, Darren, Edward, Vickie, Tim, Zoe, Faye, Clare, Paul, Claire, Jenni, Niamh, Steve, Natasha, Mark, David, Tom, James, Ollie, Chris, Alex B, Chris C, Neil, Nick, Amir, Gretchen, Benjamin, Brandon, Denise, Mum, Dad and apologies to everyone else that I've shamefully omitted.

Kent Sharkey

After many years grubbing in the dirt as an independent consultant and trainer, Kent evolved into a Technical Business Development Manager with Microsoft. At work, he spends his time helping companies learn how to apply emerging technologies to help their business. When not at work, he's often found hiking in the great Northwest, or discovering exactly what a hill means to a cyclist. He lives in Redmond with his wife, Margaret, and two cats, Tzeetzah and Squirrel.

Acknowledgements

I would like to first thank Margaret. Without your support and acceptance, I wouldn't get through my life. Second, my co-authors for giving me a forum to add to. Third, to the editorial team at Wrox to help mold my scribbling into something similar to writing. Finally, to my two writing assistants, Tzeetzah and Squirrel, whose scrambling across the keyboard late at night encouraged me to go to sleep occasionally.

Lee Whitney

Lee Whitney is a software designer and project manager for Computer Software Inc. in Chalfont, Pennsylvania and has nine years experience designing software applications. Lee is also a Microsoft Certified Professional in Visual Basic Desktop Applications and he teaches evening classes for schools in the Philadelphia area on Visual Basic, COM and SQL.

Acknowledgement

I would like to thank the Wrox staff for making my first professional writing experience not only painless but down right enjoyable. To my wife Doreen I give my thanks and love for her support and patience while I worked "two" jobs. Finally to my son Jack who brings love, joy and "Piz--ZA" to every corner of my life.

Marc Simkin

Marc Simkin is part of Cap Gemini Ernst & Young US LLC's New York Advanced Development Center, where he specializes in architecting and implementing large scale n-tier, multi-platform systems. Marc's current area of specialization is Windows development. Before joining CGE&Y, Marc spent more years than he cares to remember architecting and implementing systems for various investment banks.

Table of Contents

Introduction   **1**

   Who Should Read this Book   **2**

   How to Get the Most from this Book   **2**

   What's Covered in this Book   **2**

   Conventions Used   **3**

   Customer Support   **4**

   Source Code   **4**

   Errata   **4**

   P2P.WROX.COM   **5**

Chapter 1: Visual Basic Application Development   **7**

   Application Development   **8**
     Enterprise Applications   8
     Basic concepts   8
     Scalability, Reliability, and Availability   9

   Distributed Applications   **10**
     Client/Server Architecture   10
       The Fat and Thin Client Models   11
     3-Tier and n-Tier Architecture   11
       Benefits of n-Tier Development   12

   The Software Development Process   **13**
     Business Requirements and Analysis   14
     Modeling the Software   14

   Distributed Application Development using Microsoft Products   **15**
     Windows DNA   16
       Microsoft Transaction Server (MTS)   17
       Internet Information Server (IIS)   17
       Active Server Pages (ASP)   17
       Component Object Model (COM)   17
       Microsoft Message Queue Server (MSMQ)   17
       Universal Data Access (UDA)   18
       SQL Server   18
       COM+   18

Table of Contents

The WROBA Case Study   **18**

Software Requirements   **21**
Operating System Requirements   21
Visual Basic Versions   21
ActiveX Data Objects Code Libraries   21
MTS and COM+   22
SQL Server   22

Summary   **23**

Chapter 2: The Software Development Process   **25**

The Waterfall Method   **26**

Iterative Development Methodologies   **29**
The Microsoft Solutions Framework   30
Applying the MSF to Application Development   32
The Rational Unified Process   33
RUP Workflows   34
Applying the RUP to Application Development   35
RUP and the WROBA Case Study   36

Summary   **36**

Chapter 3: Introduction to Visual Basic Objects   **39**

What are Objects?   **40**
Objects have Properties   40
Objects have Methods   40
Objects have Events   41
Objects are Encapsulated   41
Objects have State   41
Objects have Scope   42
Objects are Instantiated   44
Objects have a Lifetime   44

Creating Classes in Visual Basic   **45**
Class Properties   47
Passing Parameters ByVal versus ByRef   49
Property Set   50
Add Procedure Dialogue   51
User-Defined Methods   53
Using Properties and Methods   54
Initialize and Terminate Events   54
Recap   56

Creating and Using Objects in an Application   **57**
Declaring an Object Variable   57
Creating an Instance of an Object   58
Early Binding versus Late Binding   59
Properties and Methods   59
Release Memory   60
Enumerated Properties   63
User-Defined Events   66

The Class Builder Utility   **68**

Object Browser   **75**

Optimization   **78**
    Object References   78
    Object Binding   79
    Variants   79
    Accessing Object Properties   80
    Using With   80
    Using Loops   81

Testing   **82**
    Breakpoints   83
    Watches   86
    Immediate Window   87
        Using Message Boxes   88

Summary   **88**

Chapter 4: Component Development   **91**

COM Components   **92**
    Specifications   92
    Services   92
    Advantages of COM   93
    COM Interfaces   94
    Implementing COM Interfaces in Visual Basic   95

ActiveX Controls   **100**
    In-process Servers   101
    Out-of-process Servers   101

Creating an ActiveX DLL   **101**
    Project Properties   106
        Threading   106
        Unattended Execution   109
        Version Compatibility   109
        Instancing   113

Creating Instances of ActiveX DLLs   **114**
    Calling our ActiveX DLL from a Client Application   114
    The Use of ActiveX Servers in WROBA   116
        Calling an ActiveX Server from Another ActiveX Server   116
        Error Handling in an ActiveX Server   117
        Creating Different Objects from Within the Same ActiveX DLL   119
        Summary   120

Registering COM Components   **120**
    Run the Component   121
    Regsvr32.exe   121
        The Package and Deployment Wizard   122
        The Visual Component Manager   128
        Retrieving Components   131

DCOM – Distributed Component Object Model   **132**
    DCOM Application Design   133

Summary   **136**

Table of Contents

Chapter 5: Microsoft Transaction Server   139

What is a Transaction?   140
The ACID Test   140
  Atomicity   140
  Consistency   140
  Isolation   141
  Durability   141

MTS: An Overview   141
Transactional Components   142
Object Management   142
Configurable Run-Time   143
Interception   143

Exploring MTS   144
MTS Packages   145
Roles   148
Monitoring Transactions   149

COM+   150
One Minor Annoyance in COM+   153

Creating Transactional Components in VB   154
The Logger Component   154
  Properties and Methods of the Logger Component   155
  Creating the VB Project   155
Transaction Modes   157
  Requires a Transaction (RequiresTransaction)   157
  Requires a New Transaction (RequiresNewTransaction)   157
  Supports Transactions (UsesTransactions)   157
  Does not Support Transactions (NoTransactions)   157
  How Transaction Modes Work   157
  Creating Instances of MTS Components   158
  Tying Transaction Objects Together   158

MTS Objects   160
The Context Object   161
  Transaction Voting   162
  New to COM+: ContextInfo   163
The SecurityProperty Object   163
The ObjectControl Interface   164
  Activate   164
  Deactivate   164
  CanBePooled   164
The AppServer Object   164
  GetObjectContext   165
  SafeRef   165
  New to COM+: IContextState   166

Implementing CLogger   167

Transactional Objects and State   **179**
Checking the Object's State   179
SetComplete, SetAbort, and Object Lifetimes   181
Why Does MTS Do This?   182
Maintaining State   182
Separating Transactional and Non-Transactional Aspects   182

Deploying MTS and COM+ Components   **189**
Exporting MTS Packages and COM+ Applications   189

Summary   **193**

Chapter 6: Beginning WROBA   **195**

The Requirements for the WROBA Case Study   **196**

Business Requirements   **196**
Determining Business Goals   196
The Importance of Good Communication   198
Identifying Tasks   198
Information Sources   198
Existing System   198
Business Community   199

WROBA Application Deliverables   **201**
Milestone 1 – Vision Statement Draft   202
Milestone 2 – Design Goals Draft   202
Milestone 3 – Use Case Diagrams   203
The Customer   204
The Administrator   204
Milestone 4 – Use Case Scenarios   205
Creating Scenarios   205
WROBA Scenarios   207

Technology Requirements   **224**
Performance   224
Maintainability   229
Extensibility   230
Scalability   230
Availability   231

Security   **232**

Summary   **232**

Table of Contents

Chapter 7: Unified Modeling Language   235

What is UML   236

Introducing the UML Diagrams   237
Use Case Diagrams   237
    Creating a Use Case Diagram   238
    Use Case Relationships   238
    Use Case Diagram Examples   239
Class Diagrams   241
    Creating Class Diagrams   241
    Class Diagram Example   244
Interaction Diagrams   245
    Sequence Diagrams   245
    Creating Sequence Diagrams   245
    Sequence Diagram Example   247
    Collaboration Diagrams   247
    Collaboration Diagram Example   248
Object Diagrams   248
Component Diagrams   249
Deployment Diagrams   249
Statechart Diagrams   250
Activity Diagrams   251
Package Diagrams   252
UML Summary   252

Visual Modeler   254
Creating Deployment Diagrams with Visual Modeler   266
Creating Component Diagrams with Visual Modeler   268

Summary   271

Chapter 8: Designing a Solution   273

Component Design   273
Component Performance in Distributed Applications   275
Component Relationships   277
    Ownership   277
    Containment   279
    Generalization   280
    Usage   284
Component Interaction Rules   285
    Own/Contain Rules   285
    Generalize Rule   286
Component Design Summary   288

Modeling Software Solutions   289
Logical Design   289
The UML Model Phases   290

Designing the UML Diagrams   **291**

The Domain Model Diagrams   291
The Transfer Funds Scenario   292
Looking for Nouns and Verbs – the Class Diagram   293
Assessing the Class Diagram   297
Further Work   299
The Sequence Diagram – An Event Timeline   299
The Design Model Diagrams   302
The Collaboration Diagram – Objects Working Together   302
The Statechart Diagram – External Events in Action   303
The Activity Diagram – Internal Events in Action   303

What Next – The Implementation Model Phase   **304**

Summary   **305**

Chapter 9: Database I – Design and Creation   **309**

Logical Data Model   **310**
Entities   311
Entity Attributes   312
Entity Identifiers   314
Entity Relationships   314
Normalization   316
Normalization in the WROBA Logical Design   317
Second Normal Form   319
Third Normal Form   319
Denormalization   320
The Logical Design for the WROBA Application   321

Physical Data Design   **323**
Defining the Database Schema   323
Data Types   324
Unique ID Creation Issues   326
NULLS and Default Values   326
Column Constraints   327
Referential Integrity (RI)   327
Indexes   328

Implementing the Database for WROBA   **328**
Adding Tables to the Database   330
Creating Relationships between Tables   333
Completing the Physical Design   336

Summary   **340**

Chapter 10: Database II – SQL and Stored Procedures   **343**

Using SQL   **344**

Data Definition Language – DDL   **344**
Creating Tables   345
SQL Scripts   349
Altering Tables   351
Deleting Tables   353

Table of Contents

Data Manipulation Language – DML   **354**
  Adding Data   354
  Modifying Existing Data   359
  Deleting Data   360
  Retrieving Data   361
    Composing Queries   364
    Joins   367
    Aliases   369

Stored Procedures   **370**
  Why Use Stored Procedures?   371
  Adding the Remaining Stored Procedures to WROBA   378
    Type 1 – Procedures for Deleting Rows   379
    Type 2 – Procedures for Inserting Rows 379
    Type 3 – Procedures for Selecting Rows 380
    Type 4 – Procedures for Verifying Rows 381

Summary   **382**

Chapter 11: Data Access and ADO   **385**

Data Access   **386**
  The ADO Object Model   387
    The Connection Object   388
    The Command Object   389
    The Recordset Object   392
    Cursors   392
  Events   395

Using ADO in Visual Basic   **396**

Summary   **410**

Chapter 12: Data Services Tier   **413**

The Stucture of WROBA   **414**

Data Services Tier – The Bank_DB component   **417**
  Coding the Data Tier   421
    The MHelpers Module   421
    The MContext Code Module   422
    The DBHelper Class Module   428
    The Account Class Module   433
    The Admin Class Module   437
    The Bank Class Module   448
    BankLocator Class Module   457
    The Payees Class Module   459
    Creating the ActiveX DLL   464
    An Aside – Logging Errors   465

Summary   **470**

Chapter 13: Business Services Tier — 473

Business Services Tier Code Categories — 474

Business Services Tier Implementation — 475

Coding the Business Tier — 478
The Bank Class Module — 478
The BankLocator Class Module — 487
The Payees Class Module — 488
The Transfer Class Module — 492
The Admin Class Module — 496
Creating the ActiveX DLL — 502

Summary — 503

Chapter 14: User Tier I – Customer Services — 505

GUI Design and Implementation — 506
GUI Design Principles — 509
GUI Implementation Principles — 510
Form Validation — 511

WROBA GUI and Customer Services — 514
WROBA GUI Implementation — 515
Shared Modules in the WROBA User Tier — 517
The MMain Code Module — 517
The CPayeeInformation Class Module — 518
The SharedProperties Class Module — 521
Logging into the WROBA Application — 523
Status Forms — 529
WROBA Customer Main Menu — 531
WROBA Customer Information Menu — 542
Displaying Account Details — 543
Adding a Payee — 551
Editing Payee Information — 557
Changing Passwords — 564
WROBA Customer Transaction Menu — 566
Paying Bills — 567
Transferring Funds — 575

Summary — 580

Chapter 15: User Tier II – Administration Services — 583

WROBA Administration — 584
WROBA Administration Code in Other Tiers — 585
Administration Logic Implementation — 585

WROBA Administrator Main Menu — 587
File Menu — 588
Help Menu — 588

Table of Contents

WROBA Administrator Cards Menu   **593**
    Adding a New WROBA Card   594
    Deleting a WROBA Card   600
    Unlocking a WROBA Card   604
    Locking a WROBA Card   607

WROBA Administrator Banks Menu   **610**
    Adding a New Bank   611
    Edit Bank   614

Security   **621**
    WROBA Security   622
    Distributed Application Security   622
    Additional Security   623

Reviewing the WROBA Implementation Process   **623**

Summary   **625**

Chapter 16: Testing, Deployment, and Maintenance   **627**

Testing   **628**
    Stabilizing Interim Milestones   628
    Integration Testing   629
    System Testing   629
        Creating Test Cases   629
    Severity and Priority Level Classifications   632
        Severity Level Definitions   632
        Priority Level Definitions   632
    Reaching the Release Candidate Milestone   632
    Post-Mortem Review   633

Deployment   **633**
    What is Deployment?   633
    Using the Package and Deployment Wizard   634
    Creating a Project Package   634
    Deploying an Existing Package   642

Deploying MTS and COM+ Components   **645**
    Automating the Import of MTS/COM+ Packages   647
    Importing MTS Components   647
    Importing COM+ Applications   650
    The Windows Installer   651

Maintenance   **652**
    Deployed Application Maintenance   652
    Changing Component Interfaces   653
    Version Numbering   660
    Visual SourceSafe   661

Summary   **662**

Chapter 17: Web-Enabling the WROBA Application   665

Web Development   666
The Web Server   667
     Web Server Software   667
     Getting Connected   667
"Hello, world!" in HTML   668
     A Basic HTML Page   670
     Some Other HTML Tags   672

Dynamic Web Sites   676
Active Server Pages   677
The Internals of ASP   679
     The Built-in Objects   681

Web-Enabling WROBA   683
Authentication   684
Presenting Accounts and Creating a Menu   690
Viewing the Account History   694
Transferring Funds   695
Other Functionality   702
Summary   702

Chapter 18: Inter-Application Communication Using XML   705

What is XML?   706
Applying XML   707

XML Structure   709
Elements and Attributes   710
DTD and Schemas   712
     XML Structure – Summary   714

Using XML in Visual Basic Applications   714
XML and 3-Tier Architectures   715
The Document Object Model   717
The MSXML Component   718
     Objects, Methods, and Properties in the MSXML Component   719

Using XML with the WROBA Application   722
     The Network Application   722

Further Considerations   735
     Transferring XML to Other Applications   735
     Other XML Standards   735
     BizTalk   735

Summary   736

Table of Contents

Appendix A: The WROBA Application   739

Creating the BigBank Database – SQL Scripts   739
Running the SQL Scripts   740
Building the Database – Schema.sql   740
    Resetting the Database to its Initial State   745
Populating the Tables – FillTables.sql   751
Error Logging – Logger.sql   754

Stored Procedures   755
Stored Procedures to Delete Rows   756
Stored Procedures to Insert Rows into Tables   757
Stored Procedures to Select Rows   759
Stored Procedures to Update Tables   762
Stored Procedures to Verify Information   766

The Visual Basic Project   767
Bank_DB   768
Bank_Bus   769
Bank_UI   770

Appendix B: Installing and Configuring MTS   775

Appendix C: ADO 2.1 and 2.5 Object Model   783

Objects   783
Command Object   784
    Methods   784
    Properties   784
Connection Object   785
    Methods   785
    Properties   786
    Events   787
Error Object   787
    Properties   787
Errors Collection   788
    Methods   788
    Properties   788
Field Object   788
    Methods   788
    Properties   789
Fields Collection   789
    Methods   789
    Properties   790
Property Object   790
    Properties   790
Properties Collection   790
    Methods   790
    Properties   791
Parameter   791
    Methods   791
    Properties   791
Parameters Collection   792
    Methods   792
    Properties   792

Record   792
    Methods   792
    Properties   793
Recordset   793
    Methods   793
    Properties   795
    Events   797
Stream   798
    Methods   798
    Properties   798
Method Calls – Syntax   799
    Command   799
    Connection   799
    Errors   799
    Field   800
    Fields   800
    Parameter   800
    Parameters   800
    Properties   800
    Record   800
    Recordset   801
    Stream   801

Appendix D: ASP 2.0 and ASP 3.0 Object Model   **803**

Objects   **803**
    The Application Object   804
        Collections   804
        Methods   804
        Events   804
    The ASPError Object   804
        Properties   805
    The Request Object   805
        Collections   805
        Properties   806
        Methods   806
    The Response Object   806
        Collections   806
        Properties   806
        Methods   807
    The Server Object   808
        Properties   808
        Methods   808
    The Session Object   809
        Collections   809
        Properties   809
        Methods   809
        Events   809
    The ObjectContext Object   810
        Methods   810
        Events   810

Index   **811**

Introduction

This book is aimed fairly and squarely at Visual Basic programmers who have a handle on the language itself but now want to advance their knowledge and see how to use VB in the development of large-scale solutions. This book is designed to act as a stepping-stone between introductory texts that just teach the basics of the language and more advanced treatments of specific topics.

We aim to show how you can leverage your core VB programming skills to address complex problems and provide sophisticated, scalable, maintainable, and extendable solutions. Apart from teaching or revising (depending on your knowledge) certain coding topics, like object-oriented coding approaches and use of transactions, this book will show you how to work from ground level in developing an application. Crucially, we'll be showing you how to analyze and model the solution, as well as implement the code.

To achieve this goal we're going to consider how we would go about providing an on-line banking application for a client bank. We're going to go from analyzing the business requirements of our hypothetical client through modeling the solution and a comprehensive coding of a desktop solution to the point at which we discuss deployment of the application to a number of geographically dispersed users. As a natural part of the study, we'll be covering topics such as software architecture and effective coding approaches.

To finish the book we'll show how the application design and the programming methods applied make it easy to extend our application, and we'll show how easy it is to take a well designed desktop type application and Web-enable it. Not only that, but we'll then show how we can use one of the hottest technologies around, XML, to enable our application to communicate with other applications.

Of course, to teach everything about all the topics touched on in the book would be impossible, but what we will do is show you how to approach application development and open your eyes to the technologies available to you as you become a more experienced programmer.

Who Should Read this Book

This book is a *Beginning....* series book, and is aimed at beginning programmers who have a grasp of the Visual Basic language and now want to see how this knowledge can be applied to providing enterprise application solutions within a distributed architecture. In short, we hope this book will teach you a lot about software development in the 'real world'.

This is obviously relatively sophisticated stuff, and to start this book we would expect you to have a certain knowledge of Visual Basic programming (say, familiarity with the level reached by the end of *Beginning Visual Basic 6, ISBN 1861001053*). Indeed, this book is part of the Wrox Visual Basic learning tree, and it's positioned as a link between the introductory material contained in *Beginning Visual Basic 6* and some of our more advanced and specialized books. Thus, after you've finished this book you should be in a good position to engage with some of our *Professional* texts.

How to Get the Most from this Book

The detailed software requirements for building the project are outlined in Chapter 1, which we advise looking at before you embark on the book, but as a short list we suggest:

- ❑ Either Windows NT 4.0 (SP 4 or greater) with the Windows NT 4.0 Option Pack, or Windows 2000

- ❑ Microsoft Visual Basic 6.0

- ❑ Microsoft SQL Server 7.0 (Desktop version)

The Windows NT 4 Option Pack can be ordered (or downloaded free) from Microsoft's web site at http://www.microsoft.com/ntserver/nts/downloads/recommended/NT4OptPk/default.asp

A downloadable evaluation version of SQL Server is available at http://www.microsoft.com/sql/productinfo/evalcd.htm

What's Covered in this Book

This book effectively breaks down into 4 areas:

- ❑ Introductory topics – Chapters 1 and 2

- ❑ Programming approaches – Chapters 3 – 5

- ❑ The **WRox Online Banking Application** (**WROBA**) – Chapters 6 – 16

- ❑ Extending the WROBA case study – Chapters 17 and 18

Chapter 1 introduces us to the whole area of application development and the different types of software architecture we may implement. Specifically, we focus on the 3-tier model and introduce the WRox Online Banking Application (WROBA) case study that we'll be using to illustrate application development. In **Chapter 2** we continue our introduction to this whole area by looking at how software is developed in the widest sense.

The next three chapters focus on teaching the programming technologies we'll utilize throughout the rest of the book; in **Chapter 3** we look at object-oriented programming in Visual Basic, in **Chapter 4** the topic of component based development using COM is discussed, while in **Chapter 5** we look at how to handle transactions in Visual Basic using Microsoft Transaction Server (MTS) or COM+. Here we illustrate the principles being discussed with simple, clear examples, so that when we get onto the case study you'll have a good grasp of the principles involved.

In **Chapter 6** we embark on the WROBA case study in earnest by looking at the business requirements of the hypothetical client we are working with, and begin to see what functionality they desire from our application.

Chapter 7 provides us with an introduction to the Unified Modeling Language, which gives us a basis for the modeling and design of the case study application. We build on this knowledge in **Chapter 8** when we start designing our software solution.

At this point we move towards implementation of the WROBA case study – since we have to use a linear presentation of the code, and to enable the solution to be built in a sequential manner, we have chosen to describe the implementation in a bottom-up style. So in **Chapter 9** we talk about design and creation of our database, while in **Chapter 10** we look at ways to programmatically populate and modify the database through the use of scripts, and describe the use of stored procedures in the application.

We then move onto the Visual Basic coding of the components involved in the WROBA application. **Chapter 11** discusses data access technologies and provides an introduction to ActiveX Data Objects, before we use the technology for real as we implement the data services tier component in **Chapter 12**. In **Chapter 13** we move onto the business services tier, while we finish off the implementation stage in **Chapters 14** and **15** when we look at the two interfaces presented in the user services tier

Chapter 16 completes the initial stage of the treatment of the WROBA application as we consider testing, deployment, and maintenance.

Chapter 17 starts our look at how we can easily enhance and modify a well-designed solution. In this chapter we provide a brief introduction to Internet technologies such as HTML and ASP, and show how to build a new front end for the application that allows it to be used over the Internet. We continue our theme of extending the application in **Chapter 18**, where we look at how our WROBA application may communicate with other applications through the use of XML.

Conventions Used

You are going to encounter different styles as you are reading through this book. This has been done to help you easily identify different types of information and to help you keep from missing any key points. These styles are:

> **Important information, key points, and additional explanations are displayed like this to make them stand out. Be sure to pay attention to these when you find them.**

General notes, background information, and brief asides look like this.

- ❑ Keys that you press on the keyboard, like *Ctrl* and *Delete*, are displayed in italics

- ❑ If you see something like, `BackupDB`, you'll know that it is a filename, object name or function name

- ❑ The first time you encounter an **important word**, it is displayed in bold text

- ❑ Words that appear on the screen, such as menu options, are in a similar font to the one used on screen, for example, the File menu

This is how code samples look the first time they are introduced:

```
Private Sub Command_Click
    MsgBox "Don't touch me"
End Sub
```

Whereas code that you've already seen, or that doesn't relate directly to the point being made, looks like this:

```
Private Sub Command_Click
    MsgBox "Don't touch me"
End Sub
```

Customer Support

We want to know what you think about this book: what you liked, what you didn't like, and what you think we can do better next time. You can send your comments, either by returning the reply card in the back of the book, or by e-mail (to `feedback@wrox.com`). Please be sure to mention the book title in your message.

Source Code

Full source code for the WROBA case study, extensions to the case study, and examples used in this book, can be downloaded from the Wrox web site at: `http://www.wrox.com`.

Errata

We've made every effort to make sure that there are no errors in the text or the code. However, to err is human, and as such we recognize the need to keep you informed of any mistakes as they're spotted and corrected. Errata sheets are available for all our books at `www.wrox.com`. If you find an error that hasn't already been reported, please let us know.

P2P.WROX.COM

For author and peer support join the Visual Basic mailing lists. Our unique system provides **programmer to programmer™ support** on mailing lists, forums and newsgroups, all *in addition* to our one-to-one e-mail system. Be confident that your query is not just being examined by a support professional, but by the many Wrox authors and other industry experts present on our mailing lists. At p2p.wrox.com you'll find two different lists specifically aimed at Visual Basic developers that will support you, not only while you read this book, but also as you start to develop your own applications. These lists are:

- ❑ **Beginning VB** – A heavily moderated list to make sure that questions that can stop you dead in your tracks at early stage of learning are answered quickly.

- ❑ **Pro VB** – A general discussion of VB topics. If there's something VB related you'd just like to know more about, or a completely baffling problem with no solution, then this is your forum.

Although this is a *Beginning...* series book, either list may be appropriate, depending on the question you have. Very specific questions about how the Visual Basic code works are best directed to the Beginning list, while more open ended questions about application development using Visual Basic are more suited to the Pro list.

To enroll for support just follow this four-step system:

1. Go to p2p.wrox.com.

2. Click on the Visual Basic button.

3. Click on the type of mailing list you wish to join.

4. Fill in your e-mail address and password (of at least 4 digits) and e-mail it to us.

Why this System Offers the Best Support

You can choose to join the mailing lists or you can receive them as a weekly digest. If you don't have the time, or facility, to receive the mailing list, then you can search our online archives. Junk and spam mails are deleted, and your own e-mail address is protected by the unique Lyris system. Any queries about joining or leaving lists, or any other queries about the list, should be sent to listsupport@p2p.wrox.com.

Visual Basic Application Development

Even if you've written only a few applications using **Visual Basic** (**VB**), you probably know how easy it makes creating small applications. VB's visual tools allow you to drag and drop user interface elements onto forms, and its integrated environment is superb for interactively writing the code that drives the application. Because there are only a few steps involved, only minimal planning is needed to successfully create an application.

However, building a large, distributed enterprise application is a complex undertaking, even when using VB. This book aims to show you how to build on your understanding of the VB language, and introduce you to the concepts and approaches required in the development of larger applications. We're going to cover a lot of ground over the next few hundred pages – we'll be showing you programming techniques, as well as introducing the systematic methods used to design, create and manage a distributed application throughout its life (the **software development life cycle – SDLC**).

Don't worry though; we're going to be breaking down the complexity into manageable steps. This whole book is based around developing an online banking application. We'll begin by giving you a thorough grounding in the programming approaches needed for such applications. These approaches will be demonstrated with clear, simple examples so that when we move on to the case study proper, you'll be familiar with the coding techniques used.

Initially we need to get a good handle on the differences between small VB programs, and distributed or enterprise applications. So, in this chapter, we'll look at the following topics:

- ❑ Application development
- ❑ Distributed applications
- ❑ Software development processes and why they are used
- ❑ Distributed application development using Microsoft products
- ❑ The WROBA case study
- ❑ The software requirements for making best use of this book

In particular, we'll be introducing the technologies that are used to build large, enterprise-class applications on the Windows family of operating systems. Each of these technologies will receive more detailed coverage in later chapters, so by the end of the book you'll have a clear understanding of how they are used.

Let's begin by clarifying what application development involves.

Application Development

Application development encompasses the full cycle involved in planning and building an application, from inception to maintaining the released application. As we mentioned earlier, this is often referred to as the software development life cycle (SDLC); a topic that's investigated in Chapter 2.

Enterprise Applications

Applications can be classified by the size of the target audience, for example:

- ❑ Desktop – 1 user
- ❑ Workgroup – 2-99 users
- ❑ Department – 100-999 users
- ❑ Division – 1,000-9,999 users
- ❑ Enterprise – 10,000+ users

Web applications may have hundreds of thousands of users and so, from a design and engineering perspective, are usually treated as **enterprise applications**.

In these definitions the number of users associated with each size is somewhat arbitrary, because the complexity of the application also has a bearing on its classification. The reason we mention these classifications is that each significant increase in target audience size also increases the challenges that must be overcome when building the application. For example, simply having a second user introduces the problem of having one user overwrite changes made by another.

Basic concepts

In this book, we'll study the concepts and skills required to successfully plan and build an enterprise application with Visual Basic. Not only will we show how to develop such an application, but we'll also show that the coding approach we take allows the solution to be easily extended and modified with the minimum of effort. To demonstrate this we'll show you how to Web-enable the application, and make use of new technologies to facilitate communication with other applications.

In order to make the most of this book, you should already be familiar with Visual Basic, and know how to build objects using Visual Basic. As we pointed out earlier, we're going to begin by exploring the programming tools that we'll need to develop enterprise applications. Thus, in Chapters 3 and 4 you'll find a refresher on Visual Basic object-oriented software and component development, while in Chapter 5 we'll discuss the services provided by Microsoft to manage our components.

> **If you need to brush up on Visual Basic, then try the book preceding this one in the Wrox VB learning tree –** *Beginning Visual Basic 6, ISBN 1861001053.*

As you'll quickly come to realize, over the course of developing an enterprise application you'll have to develop an awareness of a number of different technologies to complement your VB knowledge. For example, in Chapters 10, 11, and 12 we'll be using **ActiveX Data Objects** (**ADO**) and **Structured Query Language** (**SQL**) to communicate with a SQL Server 7.0 database.

The strategy we're going to adopt to make use of these potentially unfamiliar programming concepts is to investigate the theory, and then see how it works using a simple example. We'll then, at the appropriate time, extend these concepts and demonstrate how they are used in the case study.

> *The case study is a complex application, and it can be downloaded from the Wrox web site at* www.wrox.com. *Although we're not expecting that you'll type all the code in yourself, all the code in the application can be found either in the body of the book or in Appendix A, so if you wish you can build the application as you read.*

When we start to develop enterprise applications we need to pay attention to a variety of interesting issues, such as scalability, reliability and availability.

Scalability, Reliability, and Availability

Scalability is the capability of software to adapt to increases in its target audience with no changes in code. This is critical in creating applications that can run anywhere from the desktop level to the enterprise level. If each new size of target audience for an application requires code changes, the cost of the application will rocket, and maintenance of the application will quickly become a nightmare. Designing an application so that it can work with very large size target audiences is designing it for scalability. The application that we'll develop in our case study will run from the desktop level to the enterprise level with no code changes. It was designed with scalability in mind.

Reliability in this context relates to **atomic** operations (**transactions**) that can be **rolled back** to the original state if any failure occurs during the transaction process. The atomicity of a transaction means that either all or none of the actions of the transaction are completed – no partially completed actions are permitted.

For example, if a bank customer performs a transaction to transfer money between two accounts they hold, the process will involve at some point removing money from one account and adding it to the other. If the transaction *wasn't* atomic, and a fault occurred, the customer might find the money had disappeared from the one account but never made it to the other! However, in the case of an atomic operation, the transaction would be rolled back to leave the account status as it was before the transfer was attempted.

This transactional rollback capability comes with a performance penalty though, so the placement of processes under transactional control must be evaluated as a trade-off between speed and reliability. In our case study, although the business and data tier components are all placed under MTS (COM+ in Windows 2000) control, only a few processes are transactionally controlled. We'll be discussing the topic of transactions specifically in Chapter 5.

Availability is the ability of the software to keep running under adverse conditions, such as power failures, heavy loads of network traffic, peaks in the number of users, and hardware failures of components such as power supplies. Some things related to availability are out of the software domain, such as uninterruptible power supplies and standby power generators, hard drive **redundancy** (redundancy is the duplication of functions and services critical to application activities) and error correction, or redundancy of power supplies for servers.

Availability will be a concern within the software development process. For instance, we might need to provide access to the software no matter how many users it has, or under what conditions the user or software are operating. That could require us to design the application so that it can be run on multiple servers or clusters of servers.

We will look in more detail at designing for scalability, reliability and availability in Chapters 5, 6, 7 and 8.

Once we start developing enterprise applications to take account of factors such as scalability, reliability, and availability, we're going to want to consider the possibility of dividing the tasks that the software performs over a number of different machines. For example if we have a large database supporting an application, we've got to make sure everyone can use the same database, even though there are going to be a number of users on different computers working at the same time. This brings us onto the topic of **distributed applications**.

Distributed Applications

Although some of you may have developed VB applications in the past, chances are they were designed to run on *single* computers as monolithic applications. Distributed applications, on the other hand, are usually designed to be capable of running on *two or more* computers.

Client/Server Architecture

The most common model of a distributed application is the **client/server** application model:

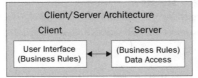

A client/server application runs the client processes separately from the server processes, usually on a different computer. The main points of a client/server application are:

- The *client* processes provide an interface for the user, and gather and present data, usually either on a screen on the user's computer or in a printed report. This part of the application is also called the **user tier** or the **presentation layer**.

- The *server* processes provide an interface with the data store. It is, for this reason, also called the **data tier** or the **data layer**.

- The *logic* that validates data, monitors security and permissions, and performs other business rules can be contained on either the client or the server, or split between the two.

This type of distributed application may be executed over more than one computer, although it doesn't have to be – both user tier and the data tier may be run on a single machine. The client/server model is often used with database programs where a *front end* program, often designed in Visual Basic or Microsoft Access, is used to present the user with data that is acquired from a database server.

A client/server application is an example of a **2-tier** distributed application. The logic for client/server applications can also be designed to form a separate **middle tier** instead of running either in the client or the server or being split between the two applications. This middle tier is often called the **business tier** or the **business logic layer**. Client/server applications that are designed this way have three *logical* tiers but run in two *physical* tiers. The middle tier may be contained in either the client or the server.

The Fat and Thin Client Models

Client/server applications that are designed to run the user and business tiers of the application on the client, and the data tier on the server are known as **fat client** applications.

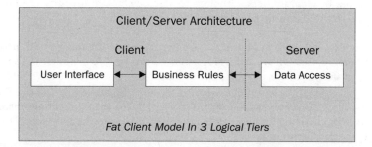

Fat Client Model In 3 Logical Tiers

On the other hand, client/server applications that are designed to run the user tier on the client and the business and data tiers on the server are known as **thin client** applications. As you can see, even though such applications may be intended to run on two computers, they may implement three logical tiers.

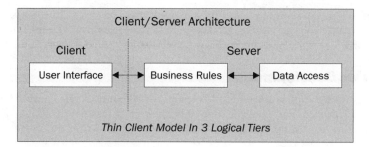

Thin Client Model In 3 Logical Tiers

3-Tier and n-Tier Architecture

The next logical step is to separate the tiers so that the application can be run on three separate computers. This implementation, where the user interface, business rules and data services are designed to run as three separate tiers, is known as a **3-tier** application (although all 3 tiers could, if we wished, be run on a single machine).

Chapter 1

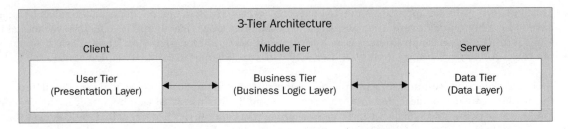

Further refinement of the application may lead to more than three tiers being implemented. For example, the administrative functions in the case study that's designed in this book can be implemented as a separate user interface tier, or a Web interface may be provided as an alternate interface to a client based interface.

Applications that are designed to run in two or more separate tiers are known as **n-tier** applications, where **n** is the number of separate tiers (although the term is most frequently used to refer to applications that are divided into three or more tiers).

It's important to understand these models if we are to appreciate the design and programming presented in this book, since the application we'll develop is based on the 3-tier model. Let's just recap on the structure of the standard model for a 3-tier application:

- ❑ **User tier** – This tier presents the **user interface** (**UI**) for the application, displays data and collects user input. This tier also sends requests for data to the next tier. This tier is often known as the **presentation layer**.

- ❑ **Business tier** – This tier incorporates the business rules for the application. This middle tier receives requests for data from the user tier, evaluates them against the business rules and passes them on to the data tier. It then receives data from the data tier and passes this back to the user tier. This tier is also known as the **business logic layer**.

- ❑ **Data tier** – This tier communicates directly with the data store (SQL Server database, other type of database such as Oracle, Exchange data store, Excel workbook, etc.) and passes data between the data store and the business tier. This tier is also known as the **data layer**.

Benefits of N-Tier Development

One benefit of separating applications into distinct pieces is that it enables **parallel development** of the different tiers of the application. For example, one developer (or a team of developers) can work on the user tier, while another writes the business tier, while yet another works on the data tier.

This separation also provides **encapsulation** for the different tiers and components, which can result in a more robust application. Each tier (or layer) is treated as a *black box* by the other tiers. Only clearly defined inputs and outputs from each tier can be seen by any of the other tiers.

Using these tiers also allows for easier maintenance and support, since it's easier to change and upgrade a single specific component than to make changes in a monolithic application. If the business rules of an n-tier application are changed, it's only necessary to change the software in the business tier on one server. In a monolithic application, a change in the business rules would mean updating the software on every computer that was running the application.

Most importantly, these logical layers offer the greatest flexibility in distribution, as the tiers could reside anywhere from a single desktop to servers and clients around the world (in other words, it's easy to turn the logical tiers into physical tiers). This enables the application to scale easily from the desktop or workgroup application level to the enterprise or Web application level. It also offers the side benefit of being able to place the different tiers on computers that are optimized for roles as servers or as clients, which enhances the performance of the application.

The principal benefit of a well-designed distributed application is an application that can scale well: handle more throughput with the same performance only by adding more hardware (so no code changes are required).

Developing complex applications is not a trivial undertaking, and several studies have shown that, unfortunately, the failure rate for large software projects is unacceptably high. Using a methodical approach to developing applications can reduce the failure rate. This kind of approach is called a **software development process**.

The Software Development Process

The concept underlying a software development process is simple but effective: document what works and what does not work for development projects. That way, success can be repeated by following what worked in prior projects, and prior mistakes can be avoided.

> **A software development process is a detailed description of the activities required to transform business requirements into a software product and, later on, to translate changes in these requirements into a new release of the software product.**

There are many different software development processes that can be used when developing an application. In this book we'll introduce three software development processes, the **Waterfall** and **Iterative** processes (an iterative process will be used to develop our case study application), and the **Microsoft Solutions Framework** (**MSF**).

- ❑ The Waterfall method was the earliest organized software development process. It arranges the stages of a software development process into a cascading, linear process that never revisits a stage once it is completed.

- ❑ The Iterative processes (there are many of them) were developed after, in virtue of its lack of flexibility, the Waterfall process proved unable to provide a solution to the problems of software reliability and cost. They also emphasize moving from one stage of a project to another. However, they allow for revisiting a previous stage of the process, when knowledge acquired in a later stage makes the output of the earlier stage obsolete or incomplete.

- ❑ MSF is based on Microsoft's experience in building enterprise level applications using an n-tier logical application model, an iterative methodology and a structured graphical modeling language called **Unified Modeling Language** (**UML**).

We'll discuss software development processes in Chapter 2, and UML in Chapter 7.

Business Requirements and Analysis

Whatever software development process we use, the most important part of the process is to understand the **business requirements**. A software business builds software for profit. It usually sells the finished product and hopes to make money. Other businesses must find another way to recover the costs of building software or having it built for them.

Business requirements describe the fundamental reasons why a customer wants to invest money to build a software solution. These requirements are specific to each business, and are not related to any functional requirements the software might have (like being able to hold vast amounts of data). They may include goals like reducing time spent, or increasing efficiency, for processes such as tracking order information, shipments, or cash flow. These goals lead to a **vision statement** for the software, which is the first part of the iterative design process.

Determining and analyzing business requirements for the software is crucial to the success of the software and its ability to perform the tasks for which it's designed. We will investigate the process of determining and analyzing business requirements for an application in Chapter 6.

Modeling the Software

There are many ways to model the software for a development project. One traditional way that you may be familiar with is the flow chart. A flow chart can be created at a high level, indicating the flow of the application from tier to tier, and among the modules and objects within a tier. Flow charts can also model the flow of execution within a module or object.

However, flow charts are really more suited to non-object-oriented, procedural code than to the object-oriented or stateless code we need to use for our application. Flow charts are best suited to modeling linear flow of program execution, because they can only indicate transitions of state or stateless behavior awkwardly at best, or to modeling complex algorithms. They are still used, but often at a level of modeling the behavior of methods or properties rather than modeling application or component behavior.

The modeling approach we'll take in this book is a leading object-oriented analysis and design notation, the Unified Modeling Language (UML). We'll look at how to model a distributed application using UML in Chapter 7.

> The Unified Modeling Language is a notation to help visualize, specify, document and construct software products. Its home page on the web is `http://www.rational.com/uml`.

Now we've got a handle on some of the underlying concepts we're basing the application development on, let's start to get practical and look at how these ideas can be physically realized. We're going to be developing an application for use on Windows operating systems using Visual Basic as our programming language, and thus the products we're going to be using are all from Microsoft. Indeed Microsoft makes it very easy for us to develop 3-tier applications.

Distributed Application Development using Microsoft Products

When we develop our 3-tier application in a Microsoft environment we'll effectively be developing using the **Windows Distributed interNet Architecture** (**Windows DNA**). This term refers to an n-tier logical application model, coupled with a framework designed to efficiently design and develop distributed applications. Crucially, it encompasses a number of tools and services that are enabling technologies – they make it possible to concentrate on the business requirements and code of a distributed application, and not have to worry too much about the plumbing of what goes where and how it works.

So, for example, some of the services make it simple to make certain parts of our project take part in transactions, and those services will control any transactions that take place. We just have to concern ourselves with deciding which parts of our project should take part in transactions, *not* how to control transactions in software.

The Windows DNA concept is now evolving into **Windows DNA 2000** which is both a marketing term devised by Microsoft to help promote the Windows 2000 family of operating systems and a reference to the development of the original tools and services into a complete development *platform*.

> *The Microsoft Solutions Framework (MSF) Application Model we referred to above consists of a logical 3-tier services-based approach to designing and developing software applications, using Windows DNA.*

The overall architecture looks very familiar. However, as we'll discover, the tools and services that underpin the whole architecture make developing complex applications quite straightforward:

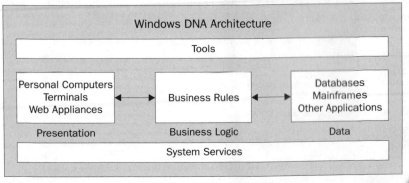

Let's overview the tools and technologies associated with this approach. We won't be [?] use of all these technologies (some of them are for more advanced development than we're doi[?] but we'll quickly introduce most of the names.

Windows DNA

Windows DNA, or, as it's becoming, the Windows DNA 2000 platform, is supported by a comprehensive set of application services on the Windows operating systems. As we said, the basic idea behind Windows DNA is to provide us, as developers, with a set of tools enabling us to easily create the application infrastructure, so that we can concentrate on the logic that's specific to the business problem being solved. These infrastructure services are covered in more detail in later chapters as we use them, but they include support for building Web-based applications, support for transactions, and a unifying component model.

With the release of Windows 2000 and associated products this area is in a state of transition, and the precise technologies you're likely to use to develop an application will depend on the platform your client is using. Of course there is an easy migration path between the different technologies, and in this book we'll show you how to develop for both Windows 9x/NT 4.0 and Windows 2000 platforms.

So, for 3-tier development in a Windows 9x/NT 4.0 environment the tools at our disposal include:

- **Microsoft Transaction Server (MTS)** – A rich set of integrated services that makes it easy to build multi-user server-side components and perform transactions across multiple data sources

- **Microsoft Internet Information Server (IIS)** – Web server software

- **Active Server Pages (ASP)** – A server-side scripting technology that makes it easy to build Web pages that are both dynamic and interactive

- **Microsoft Component Object Model (COM)** – A foundation for creating distributed applications built from components

- **Microsoft Message Queue Server (MSMQ)** – A flexible, reliable approach to communication between applications

- **Universal Data Access (UDA)** – A set of data access services, including an easy-to-use high-level programming interface **ActiveX Data Objects (ADO)**

- **Microsoft SQL Server 7.0** – A relational database management system for the Microsoft Windows platform

In Windows 2000 there are the following variations:

- MTS has been merged with COM and is part of **COM+**

- IIS is called Internet Information *Services*

With the exception of SQL Server 7.0, all these technologies are currently included with the Windows 2000 Server series of operating systems. However, the situation is slightly different for users of Windows NT 4.0. We'll discuss exactly what software you need to make the most of this book (and how to obtain it) at the end of the chapter.

Let's now expand slightly on what these technologies can do for us, and where we are likely to use them.

Microsoft Transaction Server (MTS)

Microsoft Transaction Server (**MTS**) delivers the *plumbing* for multi-user server applications, including transactions, scalability services, connection management, security contexts, and point-and-click administration. This provides us with an easy way to build and deploy scalable server applications, and to build single-user components that can be made multi-user merely by hosting them in MTS. MTS also provides a security context for the components that it manages, which enables the components to run in a required security context regardless of the security context of the client.

We'll be looking at MTS in detail in Chapter 5, and we'll use it within our case study to support the activities that form our Business and Data tiers.

In Windows 2000, MTS has been consolidated with COM into COM+, a unified programming model that we discuss in a moment.

Internet Information Server (IIS)

Microsoft's **Internet Information Server/Services** (**IIS**) enables the development of Web-based business applications that can be extended over the Internet or deployed over corporate intranets. Internet Information Server integrates with MTS and ASP, and this integration has introduced a new concept to the Internet–**transactional applications**.

We'll be using IIS (or one of it's close relations PWS) in Chapter 17 when we Web-enable our case study.

Active Server Pages (ASP)

Active Server Pages (**ASP**) is the critical technology for server-side scripting in Microsoft's web strategy. This technology is used to create and run dynamic, interactive Web server applications, and we'll make extensive use of ASP when we Web-enable the case study in Chapter 17.

ASP page scripts can be written using VBScript (the default), JavaScript, or other scripting languages. ASP pages are especially useful in creating dynamic interactive Web content that will run on any browser, as all the processing occurs on the server before the resulting Web page is served up to the browser.

Component Object Model (COM)

The **Component Object Model** (**COM**) is Microsoft's standard set of specifications that allows components to communicate with each other. It is language independent, so components created using Visual Basic can work with components coded in, say, C++. Of course, here we'll be building our components in VB, and we'll spend a lot of time in Chapters 12 and 13 coding components to act as our Data tier and our Business tier.

Microsoft Message Queue Server (MSMQ)

Message queuing is another feature of the Microsoft Windows Server operating systems. **Microsoft Message Queue Server** (**MSMQ**) helps to integrate applications by implementing a business event delivery environment where messages can be sent between applications. It also makes it easier to build reliable applications that will work over networks that may not be as reliable as we would wish.

This simple application, based on the Component Object Model, lets developers focus on business logic, not sophisticated communications programming. MSMQ, while being extremely useful, lies outside the scope of this book.

Universal Data Access (UDA)

Universal Data Access (**UDA**) provides high-performance access to a variety of information sources, including relational (from sources such as SQL Server, Access or Oracle) and non-relational data (such as data from Active Directory, Microsoft Exchange, etc.). UDA also provides an easy-to-use programming interface, **ActiveX Data Objects** (**ADO**) that works with all programming tools and languages that support COM.

We're going to be encountering UDA and using ADO in Chapter 11.

SQL Server

SQL Server is a relational database management system for the Microsoft Windows platform. SQL Server delivers a flexible, powerful platform that scales up to terabyte-size (a terabyte is 1,000 GB) databases and down to small business servers and laptop databases. This product is going to provide the data store for our case study, and we'll be working with it extensively in Chapters 9 and 10.

COM+

COM+ is an extension to the Component Object Model (COM), and is shipping as an integrated component in Windows 2000 operating systems. This technology enables us to create distributed components that can interact over any network using the language of our choice.

The COM+ services delivered in Windows 2000 are the next evolutionary step of COM and MTS. The consolidation of these two programming models makes it easier to develop distributed applications by unifying the development, deployment, debugging and maintenance of an application that used to rely on COM for certain services and MTS for others.

COM+ is mentioned in Chapter 4 and covered in more detail in Chapter 5.

Well, we've mentioned it enough times, so let's see what our case study actually consists of.

The WROBA Case Study

The **WROBA** (**WRox Online Banking Application**) case study used in this book uses a theme you may be familiar with – online banking. In fact, what we are going to develop during the first part of the book is a desktop based application – it still counts as online, in that it will enable a user sitting at their desk to carry out various banking activities, even though it will have a Visual Basic form type user interface.

The functionality of the case study was arrived at by careful analysis of the business requirements of a hypothetical client (Big Bank) and this is covered in Chapter 6. But so we're all clear about where we are heading, let's highlight some of the major parts of WROBA. There are two sides to the application; a customer side and an administration side.

The customer side will:

- ❑   Show the status of the users accounts (two accounts are permissible Checking and Saving, but only one of each per card)
- ❑   Allow previous transactions to be viewed

- ❑ Allow user passwords to be changed
- ❑ Allow users to add or edit payee details
- ❑ Allow users to move money between accounts
- ❑ Allow users to pay bills to payees

The administration side of the application offers a separate login for designated administrators, and allows the administrator to:

- ❑ Add and delete new accounts (as represented by cards)
- ❑ Lock and unlock cards that have fallen foul either of the login system (too many wrong login attempts) or the banking authorities
- ❑ Add and edit bank details (this feature is not fully implemented in our fledgling application)

Let's have a look at how this initial version relates to the 3-tier architecture we've previously looked at:

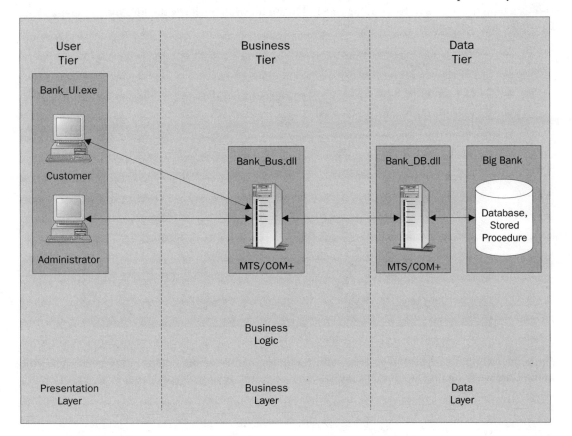

The data tier consists of two units – a SQL Server 7.0 database (called BigBank) that contains both data and stored procedures for accessing and operating on that data, and the Bank_DB.dll component. We'll be designing and creating the database in Chapter 9, developing stored procedures in Chapter 10, and coding the COM component in Chapter 12.

The business tier consists of one COM component – Bank_Bus.dll that we'll code in Chapter 13.

The user tier functionality is provided by Bank_UI.exe – although it could be split into two projects, we have dealt with it as one. We'll consider the customer side of the interface in Chapter 14 and the administration side in Chapter 15.

In terms of the Windows DNA model, we're using SQL Server 7.0 to manage the data, UDA as we code the Bank_DB.dll COM component, and MTS (or COM+ depending on the platform) to provide an environment for Bank_Bus,dll and Bank_DB.dll to operate in. We haven't talked about ASP and IIS here, but when we show how to extend the WROBA case study and Web-enable it in Chapter 17, those products will also make an appearance.

Since it's a mere case study, there is some simplification. There are areas, which we highlight, that the enthusiastic reader may like to improve upon. We've made no attempts to implement deposit and withdrawal functionality, since there is no cash drawer, and no electronic checks or credit card accounts are implemented.

Just as a taste of what we'll be building, the following illustration shows the Information menu of the customer interface part of the application:

As we said previously, if you want to work through the book and develop the application as you read along, that would be great. But you may also find it helpful to see the final working version, so you know what we're aiming at – if that's the case the code can be downloaded from www.wrox.com.

Software Requirements

The code examples and case study in this book require that you have the following software installed on a computer using the Windows NT 4 (SP4 or greater) or Windows 2000 operating systems. In summary the software requirements are:

Windows NT 4:

- ❑ Visual Basic 6 (SP3 recommended)
- ❑ SQL Server 7.0 (SP1 recommended)
- ❑ ADO 2.1 or ADO 2.5
- ❑ MTS 2.0 (Microsoft Transaction Server)

Windows 2000:

- ❑ Visual Basic 6 (SP3 recommended)
- ❑ SQL Server 7.0 (SP1 recommended)
- ❑ ADO 2.5
- ❑ COM+ Services

Operating System Requirements

Although the code examples and case study can be run on a computer running the Windows 95, Windows 98, or Windows 98 Second Edition operating systems, we strongly recommend the use of Windows NT 4 or Windows 2000 due to the reduced component functionality and lack of security in the Windows 9x series of operating systems. The illustrations and examples in this book were created on computers running Windows NT 4 and Windows 2000, although we mention how to accomplish the required tasks in Windows 9x where differences are present. No software changes are necessary if you use the Windows 2000 or Windows NT 4 operating systems.

Visual Basic Versions

The version of Visual Basic 6 we're using is the Enterprise Edition, although the Professional Edition may also be used. The Professional Edition lacks tools such as Visual Modeler, however, so some features or add-ins that the book uses may not be present if the Professional Edition is used. If tools are included only in the Enterprise Edition, we indicate this when they're discussed.

ActiveX Data Objects Code Libraries

The code examples will run with either version of ADO (ActiveX Data Objects); if you have ADO 2.5 installed instead of ADO 2.1 in either Windows NT 4 or Windows 2000, only a change to the project references from ADO 2.1 to ADO 2.5 is necessary.

ADO is Microsoft's preferred high-level data interface to data stores. It provides a reasonably easy to use object model that's easier to work with than lower level interfaces such as ODBC (Open DataBase Connectivity). Since this book works with Microsoft technologies, we'll use ADO exclusively for accessing the WROBA data in an SQL Server 7.0 database.

ADO is available as a Tools installation with VB, is installed by Office 2000, and is available for download at the Microsoft Universal Data Access (UDA) Web site.

> A downloadable version of ADO 2.5 is available as part of the MDAC 2.5 (Microsoft Data Access Components) download at `http://www.microsoft.com/data/download.htm`.

MTS and COM+

Database transactions are handled by Microsoft Transaction Server (MTS), which is an operating system component that is available as part of the Windows NT Option Pack installation. COM+ is a replacement for MTS in Windows 2000, and is automatically loaded as part of the Windows installation. A more limited version of MTS is available for the Windows 9x series of operating systems, and can be loaded from the VB 6 Enterprise Edition disks, the Windows NT 4 Option Pack, or can be downloaded from the Microsoft web site. The Windows NT 4 Option Pack contains a version of MTS that can be used by the Windows 9x series of operating systems, in addition to the version for Windows NT.

> A downloadable version of MTS 2.0 is available at `http://www.microsoft.com/ntserver/nts/downloads/recommended/NT4OptPk/default.asp`.

The Option Pack may be used to install MTS 2.0 in Windows NT or in Windows 9x and we discuss the installation and configuration of this product in Appendix B.

SQL Server

A free, 120 day evaluation version of SQL Server 7.0 may be downloaded from the Microsoft MSDN web site. A SQL Server 7.0 evaluation version CD can also be ordered at the same web site. Visual Basic 6 Enterprise Edition also includes a version of SQL Server 7.0 that can be used.

> A downloadable evaluation version of SQL Server is available at `http://www.microsoft.com/sql/productinfo/evalcd.htm`.

Summary

In this chapter, we've introduced many new concepts and terms. Don't worry if it all seems a little foreign and abstract at the moment, the purpose of this book is to show how these ideas translate into tangible applications.

We began the chapter by looking at the concept of application development, as being distinct from programming, and then moved on to look at client/server and 3-tier applications as examples of distributed applications. At this point, the idea of a software development process and software life cycle management was introduced.

We then moved away from the theoretical and started to look at the products we need to implement a distributed application using the Windows DNA platform. Then, to bring us right back down to earth, we introduced the WROBA case study, which we'll be using to illustrate 3-tier application development using Visual Basic, and summarized the software we'll be using to build our solution.

Before we move on, let's just recap on some of the major points of the chapter:

- ❑ Application development and software life cycle management encompass all the stages involved in planning and building an application, from inception to maintaining the released application.

- ❑ A software development process is a description of the activities required to transform business requirements into a software product and, later, to translate changes in these requirements into a new release of the software product.

- ❑ The 3-tier Application Model consists of a logical 3-tier services-based approach to designing and developing software applications utilizing user, business logic and data tiers where:

    - ❑ The user tier is responsible for the user interface and generates data requests to the business logic tier. This layer resides either on the user's computer (desktop Windows clients) or in IIS on a server (Internet-based clients).

    - ❑ The business logic tier is where the application-specific processing and business rules are maintained.

    - ❑ The data tier is focused only on getting data out of or putting data into the database.

Our next task is to understand a little more about the software development process prior to actually getting our hands dirty and starting on some programming.

The Software Development Process

As we said in the first chapter, developing large applications is a complex task and has been found to have rather high failure rates – in fact, a 1995 study by the Standish Group, a market research and advisory firm specializing in electronic commerce and mission-critical software (`http://www.standishgroup.com/msie.htm`), found that only 16% of all Information Technology (IT) projects were successfully completed. As application developers, we need to understand how to approach the whole process of solution development. It's not good enough to write a great piece of software that has wonderful functionality if it isn't delivered on time and doesn't meet customers' expectations.

In this chapter, we're going to look at the general approaches we can take to developing large applications, and we're going to see how we make use of one of these approaches in the development of the WROBA case study application. A professional developer is likely to work with formal development processes as tester, programmer, analyst, project manager and program manager. It's safe to say that no large application is developed by, or for, any major corporation these days without the benefit of a standardized software development process.

As we indicated previously, using a methodical approach to application development – a **software development process** – can increase the success rate of application development. To recap:

> *A software development process is a detailed description of the activities required to transform business requirements into a software product and – later on – to translate changes in these requirements into a new release of the software product.*

Software development processes aren't used just for developing code. They employ structured methods for software project management, testing, application maintenance, documentation, user training, and other things that are collectively called the **software development life cycle** (**SDLC**). Actually, a good software development process plays such a critical role in the success of application development that there are companies making a profit by selling software development methods.

There are many different software development processes that can be used when developing an application. This chapter will introduce you to three different approaches to the software development process:

❑   A straight line method known as the **Waterfall** method

❑   Two circular (or spiral) methods which fall under the heading of **Iterative** methods:

    ❑   The **Microsoft Solutions Framework (MSF)**

    ❑   The **Rational Unified Process (RUP)**

There are many iterative methods for software development, each of which utilizes somewhat different stages and terminology. The techniques that these iterative methods use to describe the project are different, but many of the latest methods use a design language called the **Unified Modeling Language (UML)**, which we will use in this book. UML is introduced in detail in Chapter 6, where we look at analyzing project requirements, and is described more fully in Chapter 7.

The two Iterative methods chosen for examination in this chapter, MSF and RUP, are closely related. They are also two of the most commonly used standard software development processes. Even if you use another software development process in your work, it will most likely be related to, or derived from, one of these two processes.

Milestones

A concept that we will encounter throughout this book, and in most of the documentation about software development processes, is that of a **milestone**. Milestones are used as checkpoints in the development process: places where either a set of deliverables for a project has been achieved, or internal project stages have been completed and are reviewed. If a milestone involves deliverables for a project, the deliverables are sent to the client and client approval marks the completion of that milestone.

> *A milestone in a software development process is similar to a milestone marker on a highway. Both mark off distinct places on a journey: locations where current progress and the distance left to go are measured.*

The Waterfall Method

The Waterfall methodology is the classic software development method. It was formalized in the mid 1970's by the United States Department of Defense as part of an effort to lower system development costs and increase the reliability of software systems. This became codified in a formal specification known as a **Mil Spec** (**Military Specification**).

The United States Department of Defense is such a large purchaser of software and computer systems that the issuance of Mil Specs, such as the one for the Waterfall method, creates an immediate market for products that follow the requirements of the Mil Spec.

The Waterfall methodology takes a linear approach to software development. In this approach, we proceed from a vision statement about the application right through to testing and delivery in a step-by-step fashion. When one step is completed, we go on to the next step. The name comes from the way the process advances, like water cascading down a set of rock steps in a waterfall.

History has shown, however, that because of its inflexibility and the large quantities of documentation it requires, this method cannot allow for changes and fails to solve software development cost and reliability problems, thus failing to deal with the problems it was intended to solve. Nonetheless, the Waterfall method sparked an interest in software development methodologies, and this led to the development of different types of development processes.

The Waterfall method uses a task-oriented approach, where each milestone in the development process must be met before the next set of tasks is approached. The tasks are often broken down into stages, such as definition, analysis, design, construction, test, transition and migration, and production. In a large development effort, these tasks may be performed by different teams and must be documented and passed on from one team to another. This approach to the software development process is very rigid, making changes difficult and expensive to implement, because once a task is finished, it is never revisited. The following diagram shows one possible task-milestone-based approach using the Waterfall process:

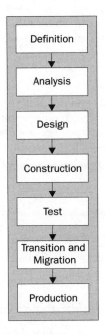

Let's examine the different stages that are outlined here:

Definition

Definition is the stage of the project where the goals for the project are decided. A vision statement, or mission statement, which defines the goal or goals for the project, is created in this stage. A business case for the project is also created, which provides the cost justification for the project.

Analysis

Analysis is the stage of the project when the requirements and goals for the project are examined. When involved in **analysis** it is important to remember that:

The business goals that drive the project are decided by the business community, and are derived from the needs of the business community.

Analyzing these needs and discovering the business rules that underlie how a process is performed are critical for the success of a project. If the analysis misses discovering some of the business rules, or confuses the needs of the customer with features that are desired, the project is guaranteed to fail.

Some developers feel this is the most critical stage of a project. Failure to discover all the business rules, or any incomplete analysis of the customer's needs, will result in an application that doesn't do its job properly. Attempts to fix this later in the project result in grafting on fixes that usually create bugs that are hard to find and fix.

While examining wish lists of features that seem attractive to the users, ensure that you don't omit features that are actually needed. Try to include as many features that are desired (not needed) as the project schedule and development resources allow, and allow for a path for later development of those features if they can't be added during this version of the application. This will help increase end user "buy-in" of the application.

During this stage specialists known as **subject matter experts** are often brought in to supplement the expertise available to the development team. These subject matter experts may be experts in the details of the business the project is designed for, or they may be specialists in specific technologies that are found to be required for the project.

Design

During the **design** stage, the business rules and needs of the business community are translated into a **logical design** for the project. This logical design may be diagrammed with flow charts or other methods of graphically depicting the program flow. Decisions are made at this point in the project about the user interface of the application, the "look and feel" that it presents to the user. The logical design is used as the input to the construction stage of the project, and is usually used as the basis for documenting the project and the application.

Construction

The **construction** stage is when the logical design is translated into the actual code. Specialty teams may be set up for specific aspects of the coding, such as database design, user interface design and designing algorithms that are specific to the business process being modeled.

Test

The **testing** stage is also critical. Modern practice is to use teams of testers: test specialists who are members of a test team that is part of the development group, and some of whom are members of the user community for the application. Bugs that are found are classified into levels of severity. Critical bugs that cause crashes, errors in the application's outputs or loss of data must be fixed. Fixing other less severe bugs may be postponed to later revisions of the application, if fixing them is too difficult or is likely to introduce other bugs. It would be nice to release an application that has no bugs, but in the real world that is rarely achievable in the time frame allotted for a project.

Transition and Migration

Transition and migration is when the application is deployed to the users. The process of training users on the application and replacing the existing process are when the most resistance to the project is usually found. In many cases, users are comfortable and familiar with existing processes, even when those processes are flawed or difficult.

Until the users are comfortable with the new application, they may prove resistant to using it, and may express unhappiness with it. This is when users need most help.

Production

This is the stage when the project is complete and the application is installed and running on the users' computers. If all the preceding stages of the project have been successfully completed, the users will be happy with the application.

The Waterfall method was an improvement on previous ways of developing software projects, most of which used bottom-up methods of software development that didn't lend themselves to rigorous analysis. However, experience showed that it failed to get a handle on rapidly rising software development costs, and also failed to make significant improvements in software reliability. The components of the Waterfall method are still in use today, but the rigid cascading approach to the development process has been largely discarded in favor of more flexible processes. In 1988, a theoretician named Barry W. Boehm proposed a **spiral model** for software development that is considered the beginning of formal iterative development methodologies. Let's now turn our attention to this.

Iterative Development Methodologies

There are many iterative development methodologies based on a spiral model – here we'll look at two:

- ❑ The **Microsoft Solutions Framework** (**MSF**)

- ❑ The **Rational Unified Process** (**RUP**)

Unlike the waterfall method, where each stage in the project leads in a straight line to the next stage, a spiral iterative method revisits previous stages as needed. This produces a spiral of progress through the stages of the project, as shown in the following diagram:

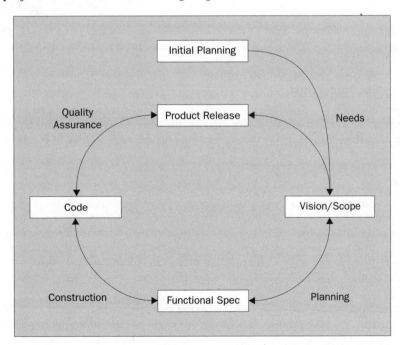

In this book, we'll be using RUP as the approach for developing the case study application. But let's first look at the process that Microsoft promotes, based on its experience in building enterprise level applications. This process isn't used to develop the case study, but it is closely related to RUP (and in fact is partially derived from RUP) and is one of the most prominent processes used today, especially in development environments using Microsoft products and tools.

The Microsoft Solutions Framework

> The Microsoft Solutions Framework (MSF) is a series of concepts, models, and best practices for planning, building, and managing software projects. Its home page on the web is http://www.microsoft.com/msf.

The core building blocks of MSF are its six major models, each of which characterizes a core set of concepts related to the development process as a whole:

- ❑ The Enterprise Architecture Model
- ❑ The Team Model
- ❑ The Process Model
- ❑ The Risk Management Model
- ❑ The Design Process Model
- ❑ The Application Model

Microsoft recently added a new model to the six core MSF models, the **TCO Model** (**Total Cost of Ownership Model**). The models can be used in combination, or independently, as needed. Let's look at these models in a little more detail.

The Enterprise Architecture Model

This model provides a set of guidelines for building a software enterprise architecture through the use of versioned releases (we'll talk about versioning during the case study). The model aligns information technology with business requirements through four perspectives: business, application, information, and technology.

The Team Model

A model that provides a structure for organizing teams on projects. This model does not take the place of an organizational hierarchy; instead it emphasizes six roles that provide responsibilities and goals for team members as a team of peers. Management of the team is determined by a separate organizational chart. The functions performed by each role in the team are clearly defined, and the membership of each role can be scaled to the requirements of the project by adding team members based on the size and scope of the project. The six roles are:

1. **Product Management** provides a vision for the product, acquires and analyzes customer requirements, develops and maintains the business case and manages customer expectations.

2. **Program Management** makes the decisions necessary to release the product. Program management owns the schedule, budget and features for the product, and coordinates the decision-making process for the team.

3. **Development** creates or implements a product that meets the specification and customer expectations. It is up to development to ensure that the product is compliant with the functional specification for the product.

4. **Testing** ensures that all issues are known before the release of the product. This does not mean that all issues or bugs are resolved by the release date, just that they are described and known, and that workarounds are described if such workarounds exist.

5. **User education** provides the documentation and training materials for the product. This team role also provides sample solutions as examples of using the product. Ideally, this education makes the product easier to use and more cost effective to implement.

6. **Logistics** ensures a smooth rollout, as well as installation and migration of the product to the operations and support groups.

The Process Model

This model consists of four phases, each of which ends with a major milestone being achieved. In chronological order we have:

1. **Envisioning** involves thinking about how the solution addresses not only the current need, but also issues that cause that need, similar issues in other departments, and potential issues that may be faced in the future. The Envisioning phase ends in the *VISION/SCOPE APPROVED* milestone. A **vision statement** describes the goals for the product and provides clear direction. **Scope** is the opposite of vision; it defines the limits for that version of the product.

2. **Planning** is when customers and the team agree on what is to be delivered, and how it will be built. The Planning phase ends in the *PROJECT PLAN APPROVED* milestone. The project plan contains both a functional specification and a schedule for the project. The functional specification provides the project team with enough detail to identify resource requirements and make commitments for development and following the schedule.

3. The **Developing** phase ends in the *SCOPE COMPLETE/FIRST USE* milestone. The development team sets a number of interim delivery milestones, each of which involves a full test/debug/fix cycle. At the *SCOPE COMPLETE/FIRST USE* milestone, customers and the team assess the product's functionality and verify that rollout and support plans are in place. All new development is complete, and deferred functionality (such as enhancements to the application) is documented for the next release.

4. The **Stabilization** Phase ends in the *RELEASE* milestone. Testing activities are performed concurrently with code development. During the stabilizing phase bug finding and fixing become the primary focus. At this milestone, the product is formally turned over to the operations and support groups. Typically, the project team either begins work on the next release or disperses to other development projects.

The Risk Management Model

This model provides a structured way for managing risk on projects. It provides us with a discipline and environment to assess what can go wrong, determine what risks are important, and implement strategies to deal with those risks. Risk is the possibility of suffering loss, whether from lowered product quality, increased cost, missed deadlines, or project failure. Risk management involves assessing and identifying the sources of risk and analyzing, tracking, and controlling those risks. MSF identifies five stages of risk management:

1. **Risk Identification**, including a risk statement that includes the risk sources and consequences.

2. **Risk Analysis**, including probability, impact, exposure and a top 10 risk list.

3. **Risk Action Planning**, including action and contingency plans to manage the risks.

4. **Risk Tracking**, including risk status reports.

5. **Risk Control**, which is the management of the risks based on the previous stages and the metrics chosen to measure and assess the risks.

The Design Process Model

This provides for three design phases that allow for a parallel and iterative approach to design. The **conceptual**, **logical**, and **physical** design phases provide three different perspectives for the user, team, and developers. Going from conceptual design to physical design shows the translation of **user-based scenarios** (**Use Cases**) to services-based components so the application features can be traced back to end-user requirements. This helps to ensure that the application is created to meet the business and user needs.

The Application Model

The application model provides a logical three-tier services-based approach to designing and developing software applications. The use of user services, business services, and data services tiers allows for parallel development of the software for each tier, easier maintenance and support, and maximum flexibility in distribution of the final product. We've already discussed such architectures in Chapter 1.

The TCO (Total Cost of Ownership) Model

This assesses the budgeted and unbudgeted costs of owning and maintaining software throughout the product life cycle.

Applying the MSF to Application Development

The MSF process uses relatively short iterative cycles, going through all the stages of the process with each iteration. Each model of MSF that is used in the development process is repeated for each cycle (with MSF you use some or all of the models, depending on the project requirements). As each cycle is completed, a new one begins until the product meets the functional specification for the project, and the final release of the product is achieved. Each new cycle uses the results of the previous cycle to refine the product and the specification. This seemingly endless process is kept under control by maintaining the schedule and keeping the specification focused on implementing the plan rather than adding new features to the product.

The implementation of the MSF process using its models is a development process as well as a management process. The development process is closely related to the Rational Unified Process, which we discuss next, and uses many of the same tools and disciplines that are used in the Rational Unified Process, particularly Unified Modeling Language (UML).

The Rational Unified Process

The **Rational Unified Process** (**RUP**) is a software development life cycle process, developed by a company called Rational Software, an Internet software development company that sells e-software, consulting services and design tools. RUP provides a regimented approach to assigning tasks and responsibilities within a project. Rational Software was founded by one of the pioneers of iterative design methodologies, Grady Booch, and is the company that is also responsible for the development of the **Unified Modeling Language** (**UML**), a graphical method of depicting and analyzing the components of software and software systems.

> *We will use UML in this book to analyze and model the WROBA case study. The coverage of UML begins in Chapter 6, when we analyze the requirements for the WROBA case study. Rational Software's Web site is located at:* `http://www.rational.com`. *There you can find useful whitepapers about RUP and UML.*

The goal of RUP is to ensure the delivery of high-quality software that meets the needs of users on a predictable schedule and budget. Of course, in any development process the goals of cost, quality and time are tradeoffs. It's almost never possible to achieve all three goals without compromises. An example is the release of software that is known to have bugs in it to meet product release deadlines. If the bugs are minor and the other goals of the project are met, release schedules may take precedence over the desire to eliminate all bugs from the software.

The Rational Unified Process relies heavily on the use of various object-oriented methods and techniques including:

- ❑ **Use Cases**, which describe the sequence of actions during an interaction of a user with a system.
- ❑ **UML**, which is used to model systems through different types of diagrams. The UML diagrams include:
  - ❑ **Use Case diagrams** – these model user interactions with the software system.
  - ❑ **Sequence diagrams** – these model the step-by-step sequences of a Use Case over time.
  - ❑ **Class diagrams** – these model the classes that are used as software building blocks.
  - ❑ **Statechart diagrams** – these model the dynamic states of a class in response to external events.
  - ❑ **Component based development** – this emphasizes the development of modular, reusable software components as the building blocks of software systems.

We look at UML diagrams in detail in Chapter 7. However, a brief introduction to types of UML diagrams will be useful in understanding RUP. We'll be discussing aspects of object-oriented programming in the next chapter.

There is no way that one chapter can explain RUP completely, and here we just aim to give a flavor of the approach. If you'd like more detail there are two good books on the subject: *The Rational Unified Process: An Introduction* by *Philippe Kruchten, ISBN 0201707101* and *The Unified Software Development Process* by *Ivar Jacobson, Grady Booch, and James Rumbaugh, ISBN 0201571692.*

So to understand a little more about RUP, let's look at the basic building blocks of the approach: workflows. Then we'll discuss how RUP is practically implemented.

RUP Workflows

In order to understand the components of RUP, we need to clarify two key terms: **artifact** and **workflow**:

❑ An artifact is a piece of information that is used as input or output to a step in the workflow. This piece of information can be a document (such as Use Cases, supplemental specifications, operating manuals, and glossaries), or a model (such as Use Case diagrams, Sequence diagrams and Statechart diagrams). These pieces of information should be under the control of some sort of version control software.

❑ A workflow is a series of steps that when performed in total will result in a noticeable change in value to the ultimate user. In this respect workflows are similar to the models used in the MSF process. You will see how workflows are used iteratively in the RUP after we define the workflows themselves.

There are 9 different workflows that make up the Rational Unified Process, divided into engineering and support workflows. These are:

❑ **Project Management Workflow** – a support workflow that concerns itself with guiding the project through its life by providing an approach to dealing with planning, staffing, executing, and monitoring the project while at the same time avoiding the risks that are normally associated with a project, such as missed deadlines, cost overruns or diminished product quality.

❑ **Business Modeling Workflow** – this is used to develop a business Use Case model as well as a business object model. This is done by understanding the structure and dynamics of the organization that has commissioned the project, while making sure all parties involved with the project have a common understanding of the goals and requirements of the project.

❑ **Requirements Workflow** – a workflow concerned with *what* needs to be done, *not* the details of *how* the needs will be implemented. The requirements of what the users or owners of a system expect the system to do are gathered and analyzed in a systematic fashion. This gathering of requirements defines the functionality of the system, which in turn provides the basis for the planning and costing of the system. At the end of this workflow, work is started on defining the look and feel of the system's user interface.

❑ **Analysis and Design Workflow** – is concerned with *how* things are to be done. The requirements gathered as part of the Requirements Workflow are compiled into a specification that describes how to implement the system. This workflow makes heavy use of UML and an appropriate modeling tool, such as the Visual Modeler. This is included with Visual Basic Enterprise Edition, and we'll make use of it later in this book. The application and infrastructure architectures are determined during this workflow.

- ❑ **Implementation Workflow** – is concerned with building the software. The specification from the Analysis and Design Workflow is implemented during this workflow.

- ❑ **Test Workflow** – concerns itself with testing the system that has been developed, or portions of the system. The system should fulfill the requirements determined during the Requirements Workflow, and the development of automated test procedures and performance of regression testing are important aspects of this workflow. It is very important to emphasize that the Test Workflow is performed on an ongoing iterative basis throughout the project life cycle, not just in one discrete phase of the project. The results of the Test Workflow are used to refine the other engineering workflows: Business Modeling, Requirements, Analysis and Design, Implementation, and Deployment.

- ❑ **Configuration and Change Management Workflow** – a support workflow that concerns itself with managing and tracking the changes to the code used to build the system as well as changes to the requirements. The documentation and code for the project are placed under control of version control software, such as the Visual Source Safe system that is included with Visual Basic. This version control software audits and tracks changes to the software and supporting documentation so that conflicting changes can be resolved and changes can be undone, returning to previous versions. This workflow also covers change request management, which is the management of reporting defects, managing changes through the software life cycle, and the use of defect data to track progress and trends.

- ❑ **Environment Workflow** – a support workflow that concerns itself with supporting the other workflows. This workflow is responsible for tool selection, to tool building, to training in the use of the tools.

- ❑ **Deployment Workflow** – a workflow concerned with getting the system into the users' hands. Things covered in this workflow include software packaging, distribution, installation, user training with the software, and formal acceptance testing.

It is important to emphasize that these workflows may appear similar to the phases of the Waterfall development process, but, crucially, in the iterative project life cycle, they are revisited repeatedly. The workflows are interleaved and repeated, with the results of each workflow refining the previously visited workflows. Each cycle of the iterative development process will emphasize different workflows, and the work for each workflow will be performed with varying degrees of intensity during each iteration. Importantly, the process is not the linear process that we saw with the Waterfall process.

Applying the RUP to Application Development

The RUP model is used in the following way: the product and project managers for the project set the direction and manage the daily tasks. The product manager is responsible for producing the Business Modeling Workflow. Once this is complete, it is given to the project manager to be used as a template for completing the Requirements Workflow. After the Requirements Workflow is complete for the current iteration, the project manager hands the requirements to the development team so they may complete the Analysis and Design and Implementation workflows.

While the developers are working, the project manager ensures the components and code they are creating are tested by the test team, and test results are fed back to the product manager (business model feedback), the project manager (requirements feedback), and development team (implementation feedback) so that another iteration might be generated, if required. The project manager is responsible for leading the Configuration and Change Management Workflow, which is used throughout the process.

The implementation team is responsible for the Environment Workflow, under the guidance of the project manager. In this workflow, the development team creates the tools that the test team requires to test aspects of the overall product, while the project manager is responsible for training aspects of the job. Ultimately, the product manager is responsible for the final product. However, it's the project manager, in conjunction with the development team, who manages the Deployment Workflow. This is done in conjunction with implementation.

RUP and the WROBA Case Study

This book uses RUP as the process for developing the WROBA case study application. As you read the book chapter by chapter, this may not always seem obvious, since it's hard to write a book so that it reads in an iterative fashion. Since some things, like database design, have to be explained in order to make other chapters that follow understandable, it may even seem like the case study is being designed in a bottom up way and not in a top down process. These things are due to the linear way that books are written and read, and do not affect the actual design process that was employed for the case study.

Summary

In this chapter we discussed software life cycle processes. These highly organized methods of developing and maintaining software are used to increase software reliability and reduce software development costs.

The Waterfall process, a linear process in which project development cascades from one phase to the next, was the earliest formal software life cycle process. The phases of the waterfall method are definition, analysis, design, construction, test, transition and migration, and production. We pointed out that the failure of the waterfall method to bring software development costs and quality under control led theorists to develop other methods for software development, the most common of which are now the iterative methods.

As part of the discussion on iterative methods we looked at the MSF (Microsoft Solutions Framework) and RUP (Rational Unified Process) spiral iterative methods, which both teach organized models or workflows that are revisited, often many times, in the software development process.

The MSF method uses a number of models to organize everything from the requirements analysis, to the composition of the project team, to the development, testing and ultimate deployment of the project. The RUP method uses 9 core workflows to organize the software development process. These workflows are revisited iteratively throughout the development process, refining the models that were created, and correcting errors and omissions in the business rules and implementation.

In the next chapters we cover the tools we need to develop distributed applications. In Chapter 3 we'll look at object-oriented software development. In Chapter 4 we move onto the development of components and COM (the Component Object Model), while in Chapter 5 our subject is Microsoft Transaction Server (MTS), which is used to provide management of components and transactions for our case study.

Once we've covered the necessary tools and technologies, we start the software development process in Chapter 6 with an analysis of the requirements for the WROBA case study.

Introduction to
Visual Basic Objects

OOP is an acronym that is bandied about with a lot of frequency these days. It stands for **Object-Oriented Programming** and it is the basis for many of the principles discussed in this book. OOP is a method of creating software using software objects. If you have coded a Visual Basic program then you have used object-based programming. A standard Visual Basic program starts with a form, which is an object. Each time we add a control (such as a textbox or a label) to our form we are adding objects to our application. We then write code to determine how these objects interact with each other in our application. Object-based programming is not OOP but it is a first step to understanding and using objects. Once we have a foundation in object-based programming we can then move on to creating and using custom designed objects and learning the Object-Oriented principles that govern these custom objects.

This is the first of three chapters that are going to teach (or revise) the programming approaches we need to develop distributed applications. Here we're going to examine objects in depth – we'll start by looking at the characteristics common to all objects. Classes, which are the foundation of objects, will then be introduced and we will learn how to build a class. We will also examine some of the tools at our disposal that make class building easier.

In this chapter, we'll be using simple examples to clearly show how these programming techniques are used. We won't be building any parts of the case study but some of our samples have distinct parallels in the WROBA code we encounter later. The purpose of the three upcoming teaching/revision chapters is to make sure we have all the programming skills we need when we hit the case study itself. To this end, we're also including here a quick discussion of some approaches for creating efficient code and a quick reminder of useful debugging techniques.

> *Creating classes and using objects is not unique to the Visual Basic language: many languages support these principles. This book, though, is meant to explain these concepts in Visual Basic terms: the way we implement objects in Visual Basic can differ greatly from the syntax used in other programming languages, such as C++ or Java.*

The main topics covered in this chapter are:

- ❑ What are objects?
- ❑ Creating classes in Visual Basic
- ❑ Creating and using objects in an application
- ❑ The Class Builder Utility
- ❑ The Object Browser
- ❑ Optimization
- ❑ Testing

As always, the code for this chapter can be downloaded from www.wrox.com.

What are Objects?

As we saw earlier, if you are familiar with Visual Basic, then you are already accustomed to working with objects. Each time we work with a form or a control, such as a text box or a command button, we actually work with an object. These are referred to as **intrinsic objects**, since they come packaged with Visual Basic. Double-click on the textbox icon in our toolbox and we get a textbox on our form, we didn't have to create the code to create the textbox. The beauty is that we don't need to know how the code for the textbox works to use the textbox: we just use it. As programmers, we want to be able to create objects that we can use and reuse in different applications, and objects that we can share with other programmers. These are called **user-defined objects** and we will learn how to create them a little later in this chapter.

Before we learn how to create our own objects let's examine some characteristics common to all objects. Below are listed eight characteristics that accrue to objects.

Objects have Properties

Properties are the characteristics of an object; they are the things that describe an object. Just as characteristics help to describe a person (a person is six feet tall, weighs 175 pounds, is left-handed), properties help to describe an object. Height and width are examples of properties of the Visual Basic textbox control. We cannot change what properties are available to us in an intrinsic object, although, of course, we can change their values. We will soon learn how to create properties for our user-defined objects.

Objects have Methods

Methods are things that an object can do; they are actions an object can take. Just as a person has things that he or she can do, such as run, walk, or speak, an object has things that it can do. What things an object can do are determined by what type the object is: all textboxes have the same methods (such as setfocus) whereas the listbox object has a different set of methods or things it can do (such as additem). Later we will see how easy it is to create our own methods.

Objects have Events

Events are things that happen to an object. People have events that can happen to them, for example, they can be hugged or slapped. Objects also have events associated with them. Let's look at our old friend the textbox: this object can lose focus, or change or receive a keypress, to name a few of its events. Anything that can be done to an object would be considered an event. As you may have guessed we can't add events to any of Visual Basic's intrinsic objects but we will learn how to create them for our own objects.

Objects are Encapsulated

Let's examine our textbox again – we may not know how to create properties, methods or events but we can still use the properties, methods and events of the textbox object without any problems. We don't have to know how the underlying code works to use the object. If we want our textbox to be 200 pixels in height, we don't need to know how to program our code to graphically draw our textbox that size, we just have to know that the height property of the textbox object is available and then set its value to 200. This is known as **encapsulation**.

Since objects are encapsulated they are often referred to as **black-box tools**. A black-box tool is a tool we can use without knowing its inner working. A good example of this is a stereo system. All we need to do to get sound is stack the black boxes, wire them as indicated in the installation instructions, select the tuner and push the power button. After we've located a radio station, we'll hear sound come from the tuner, whether or not we are familiar with the electronics contained in these black boxes. Objects can be thought of as the software equivalent of these black boxes: we can use objects without knowing what complex algorithms they contain.

Encapsulating our code within an object provides several advantages:

- ❑ We can easily use objects, as we don't have to know their inner workings, which aids in the speed and ease of the development process.

- ❑ It makes it easier to share our objects with other programmers.

- ❑ By creating a compiled object (referred to as a COM component, we cover this topic in depth in Chapter 4) we can share our object without ever letting anyone see the underlying code. This would be an advantage if we want to share our code with other developers, but don't necessarily want to share any complex logic that our source code would expose.

Objects have State

The **state** of an object is the set of all of the values of all of its properties. To say that an object has a height property and a width property is not state: just knowing what properties an object has does not describe the object, as we need to know the values of the object's properties. And we need to know the values of all the properties.

Let's go back to our people analogy – say we are reading the personal ads in our local paper and one of the ads reads "height – six feet tall". That's the entire ad: it doesn't give us a clear picture of that person, and it doesn't fully describe that person. Now if the ad said: "Divorced male, age 35, six feet tall, 180 pounds, professional Visual Basic developer", this is a much clearer description of the person. This is state. To apply this principle to our textbox, it has a `height = 375`, `width = 1215`, `forecolor = black` and `backcolor = white` and many more property values. All of these values combined make up the object's state.

Keep in mind that the state of one textbox can be very different from that of another textbox. Let's look at two textboxes named `Text1` and `Text2`. Both are textbox type objects, which mean they both have all of the same properties, but as we can see below they appear very different. That is because while they may have the same properties, the values of those properties (or their **state**) are very different.

Text1

Name	Text1
Height	375
Width	1215
BackColor	White
ForeColor	Black

Text2

Name	Text2
Height	495
Width	2775
BackColor	Black
ForeColor	White

We change the state of an object by changing the values of its properties.

Objects have Scope

The **scope** of an object defines what portions of a program have access to this object. Scope is a very important concept in object-oriented programming. It is important to only limit the portions of our program that need an object to be able to see the object. If we make the scope too narrow we may not be able to use an object that we created elsewhere. If we make our scope too broad we may accidentally change our object, which may yield unpredictable results. For example, we may have two very different objects used in different sections of our application but they could conceivably share the same name. If the scope of the two objects is the same then we might change one object when in fact we meant to change the other. Let's look at some specific types of scope and how they can affect our objects.

In Visual Basic, there are three types of scope:

❑ Procedure-level scope

❑ Module-level scope

❑ Global scope

Procedure-level scope makes the variable or object visible only in the sub or function where it is declared. Such a declaration is made within a sub or a function using the Dim keyword; we will examine the code to declare objects in much greater detail later in the chapter.

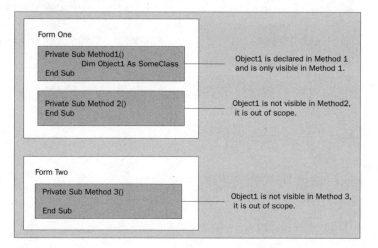

Module-level scope makes the variable or object visible in all the subs and functions in the module where it is declared. The variable or object is not visible outside of the module where it is declared. Such a declaration is made in the General Declarations section of a module or Form using the Private keyword.

Remember that a module is a section of code that can contain declarations and procedures. One or more modules make up a Visual Basic application. There are three types of Visual Basic modules: form (which has a .frm file extension), standard (.bas) and class (.cls).

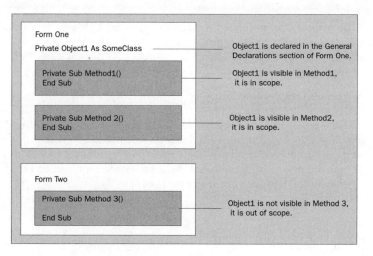

Global scope makes the variable or object visible to all Forms and modules in the application. Such a declaration is made in the General Declarations section of a code module using the Public keyword.

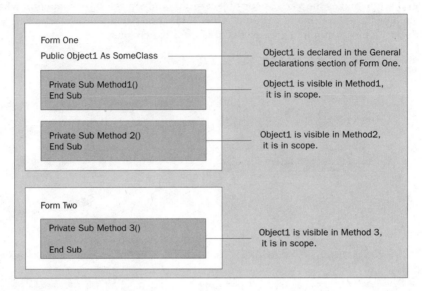

Objects are Instantiated

Before we can clearly explain instantiation we need to differentiate between classes and objects. When a home is built, an architect who creates a set of blueprints first designs it. From these blueprints a single house or many houses can be built. Visual Basic **classes** are the equivalent of the blueprints, whereas **objects** are the finished houses. When we code our Visual Basic application we will be creating **instances** of a class; these instances are our objects. The class determines what properties and methods the object will have.

We will delve into the code syntax necessary to create instances of objects later in this chapter, and will look at how to create classes in the next section.

Objects have a Lifetime

Unlike variables, which are created and destroyed automatically, we typically have control over the **lifetime** of an object, especially user-created objects. Each time an object is created – or, as we learned previously, instantiated – a piece of memory is allocated to that object. The more objects we have instantiated at a given time the more memory is used. As an application is required to use more and more memory, that application's performance will begin to deteriorate. As OOP developers we need to learn to use objects judiciously, creating them only when they are required and destroying them, hence freeing the memory they use, when they are no longer needed.

Creating Classes in Visual Basic

So now we've seen the theory of what classes and objects are, we will now learn how to create a class, and the user-defined properties, methods and events of our class. We will begin with an exercise that will create the shell for our class.

When we first started programming in Visual Basic we started with simple applications that consisted of a single form with code behind it. As we learned to write more complex applications we found a need to use multiple forms in our applications. Now we may have had several forms all running the same procedures resulting in duplication of code, so we learned to use standard (or .bas) modules. We are now going to learn how a class module will allow us to implement all the advantages of objects. In this exercise, we will create a slimmed down version of the SharedProperties class that we encounter later in the book.

In this chapter all the screen shots are from an NT platform, but as we've said before, all this will work perfectly well in Windows 2000.

Try It Out – Creating a Class Shell in Visual Basic

1. Start Visual Basic 6.0 and select Standard EXE:

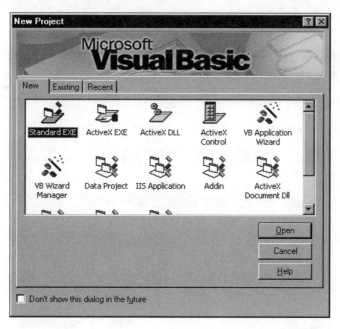

2. From the Visual Basic IDE (IDE stands for Integrated Development Environment; it's the main workspace for Visual Basic) choose Add Class Module from the Project Menu:

3. Select Class Module from the Add Class Module dialog box and click Open:

4. Rename the class by changing the name to `SharedProperties` in the property window. If the property window is not visible, right-click on the **Class** icon in the project window and select **Properties**:

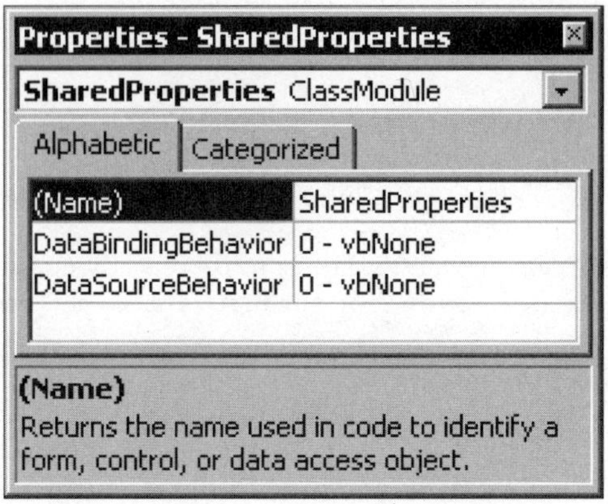

We now have the shell of a class module added to our project. We should now be able to see this in the Project Explorer Window:

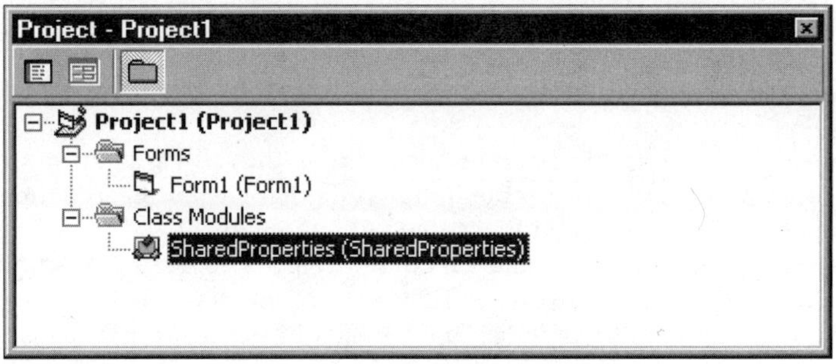

Now that we've created our class, we can go on to add some properties to it.

Class Properties

We can create user-defined properties for our class. Properties are really just Visual Basic variables that are encapsulated in a class. We then use property `Let` and `Get` routines, to read and write values to these variables. The variables are isolated from the user of the class.

5. This will bring up the **Property Builder** window. Enter the property name, `PayeeID`, the data type of String and click the radio button for **Public Property**. Click the **OK** button to proceed.

We should now see that the new property has been added to the class:

6. Repeat the above step to add our three additional properties. Follow the table below for the proper settings.

Property Name	Data Type	Public
BankID	Integer	Y
CardID	Long	Y
Amount	Currency	Y

7. To create our method either select File | New | Method from the menu or click the Add New Method button on the toolbar, making sure that the appropriate class is selected. This will bring up the Method Builder. Type in the method name, Init. We need to add some arguments for this method so click on the '+' sign.

8. This brings up the Add Argument dialogue box. Type in the argument name of PayeeID, a String data type, and click the ByVal checkbox. Then click OK. We will need to add three more arguments to the Init method using the same procedure. The argument's name and data type will be the same as the properties listed in the table in Step 6.

9. When you have added all the arguments the Method Builder should look as follows. Click OK to proceed.

10. We still have our event to add so choose File | New | Event from the menu or click the Add New Event button from the toolbar to bring up the Event Builder window. The Event Builder is very similar to the Method Builder only this time we do not have any arguments. Type `OnInit` in the name field then click OK.

11. Click on the All tab: your Class Builder Utility should now look like this. Our class, though, only exists in the Class Builder; it has not yet been added to our project. To do this, select File | Update Project from the menu.

12. The CPayeeInformation class has been added to our project. Open the code window for our new class and you will see that the following code has been generated. This is a fully functional class. The only tweaking of the code would be to add the RaiseError code to fire our event.

```
'local variable(s) to hold property value(s)

Private mvarPayeeID As String 'local copy
Private mvarBankID As Integer 'local copy
Private mvarCardID As Long 'local copy
Private mvarAmount As Currency 'local copy

'To fire this event, use RaiseEvent with the following syntax:
'RaiseEvent OnInit[(arg1, arg2, ... , argn)]
Public Event OnInit()

, Public Sub Init(ByVal BankID As Integer, ByVal PayeeID As String, _
ByVal CardID As Long, ByVal Amount As Currency)
End Sub

Public Property Let Amount(ByVal vData As Currency)
'used when assigning a value to the property, on the left side of an assignment.
    'Syntax: X.Amount = 5
    mvarAmount = vData
End Property
```

```
Public Property Get Amount() As Currency
'used when retrieving value of a property, on the right side of an assignment.
    'Syntax: Debug.Print X.Amount
    Amount = mvarAmount
End Property

Public Property Let CardID(ByVal vData As Long)
'used when assigning a value to the property, on the left side of an assignment.
    'Syntax: X.CardID = 5
    mvarCardID = vData
End Property

Public Property Get CardID() As Long
'used when retrieving value of a property, on the right side of an assignment.
    'Syntax: Debug.Print X.CardID
    CardID = mvarCardID
End Property

Public Property Let BankID(ByVal vData As Integer)
'used when assigning a value to the property, on the left side of an assignment.
    'Syntax: X.BankID = 5
    mvarBankID = vData
End Property

Public Property Get BankID() As Integer
'used when retrieving value of a property, on the right side of an assignment.
    'Syntax: Debug.Print X.BankID
    BankID = mvarBankID
End Property

Public Property Let PayeeID(ByVal vData As String)
'used when assigning a value to the property, on the left side of an assignment.
    'Syntax: X.PayeeID = 5
    mvarPayeeID = vData
End Property

Public Property Get PayeeID() As String
'used when retrieving value of a property, on the right side of an assignment.
    'Syntax: Debug.Print X.PayeeID
    PayeeID = mvarPayeeID
End Property
```

The Object Browser

We have another tool at our disposal that allows us to view information about our class definitions. This tool is named the **Object Browser**. The Object Browser is especially useful when working with large numbers of complex classes. It allows us to see each class and its members in a concise, easy to read fashion. Let's take a look. You can access the Object Browser by choosing View | Object Browser from the menu or by pressing *F2*.

Notice that the top left combo box contains <All Libraries>. The Object Browser is showing us not only the classes for our project but also all the classes and libraries that are provided with Visual Basic. Let's narrow our scope to just the classes that we created in this chapter: choose Bank App from the drop down list.

Notice that the left hand pane contains the classes we created in this chapter as well as our form. The class icon represents these.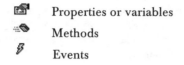

We will also see that `BankType`, our enumerated type, is shown in this pane. It is represented with this icon. 🖳

If we highlight a class in the left hand pane, its members (properties, methods and events) are displayed in the right hand pane. Information about the highlighted item is displayed in the bottom panel. The following icons are used to illustrate class members:

    🖻   Properties or variables

    🖎   Methods

    ⚡   Events

Highlight a class member and the bottom panel will display whether it is public or private, its data type, any parameters that might be required and which class it is a member of.

The left and right arrow buttons at the top of the Object Browser allow us to move to the next or previous member. The next button to the right, **Copy to Clipboard**, will copy the highlighted item to the clipboard. The next button, **View Definition**, will take us to the code where the item is declared.

We also have the ability to search for a class or member in the Object Browser. Type in the text of the item you are searching for in the lower combo box and click the button with the binoculars icon. A search results pane will then be displayed.

Now that we know how to create classes and use objects, let's turn our attention to how we can make sure that the code we place within our classes and objects is the best, most efficient code possible. This is going to become important as we build complex applications that will make demands on system resources.

We've come across some of these points previously, but let's just draw all of them altogether in one place as a bit of a summary.

Optimization

A user assesses the speed of an application in two ways: the perceived speed and the real speed. This section deals with ensuring the real speed of the application is as high as possible. Let's look at some techniques that will, in general, result in our code having less work to do. Less work to do will of course result in faster execution time. In particular, we will look at:

- ❑ Object References
- ❑ Object Binding
- ❑ Variants
- ❑ Accessing Object Properties
- ❑ Using `With`
- ❑ Using Loops

Of course, when thinking about optimization it is worth checking that any assumptions being made are valid for the specific situation being addressed (bearing in mind the need to have scalable, extensible code).

Optimization and Context

All assumptions need to be tested. This is especially true when it comes to optimization. As speed of execution depends on hardware as well as software, the many interrelated factors make it hard for any rules to be universally valid. You need to make certain that the rule applies to your case. Just because a method is slower than other methods, it doesn't mean it should never be used. There are times when the slower way happens to be the better choice for the situation at hand.

When measuring performance, you should try to use hardware that is similar to what your users will use. For a large target audience this typically means conducting several tests on, for example, a high-end, a low-end, and a medium configuration.

Object References

> **Speed Tip 1: Reduce the number of dots in object references.**

Using a temporary object may result in speed improvements when accessing properties or methods of objects within objects. So instead of using multiple instances of:

```
frmSomeForm.txtTextBox.Text = "Some Text"
```

which, as the two dots indicate, accesses properties of an object from within an object, it may be better to create a temporary object:

```
Dim txtTempTextBox as TextBox
Set txtTempTextBox = frmSomeForm.txtTextBox
```

and then set the property of this temporary object:

```
txtTempTextBox.Text = "Some Text"
```

As Visual Basic doesn't have to dig down into the object of an object, as it did previously, the procedure can be processed more quickly.

Object Binding

> **Speed Tip 2: Early binding makes code run more efficiently and faster.**

We have already covered the benefits of early binding. Objects are early-bound if a specific object type is assigned to a variable in the declaration statement. Object references are late-bound if the variables are declared as variables of the generic Object class. This means that Visual Basic has to decide what type of object would best suit each specific object at runtime, thus clogging up system resources and slowing down the processing time.

Variants

A Variant is a universal data type that can contain an Integer, a Double, a Date, a String, or even an Array or Collection. Similar to object references mentioned above, variables can be declared as a specific data type or left as the generic data type of Variant, with the exact data type to be determined by Visual Basic when the code is executed. However, this versatility causes slower performance.

> **Speed Tip 3: Avoid Variants.**

Variants are the Visual Basic default data type, so:

```
Dim SomeVar
```

is equivalent to:

```
Dim SomeVar As Variant
```

Instead, it's better to declare the appropriate data type for the variables, for instance:

```
Dim lngStatus As Long
Dim blnAdmin As Boolean
```

79

Accessing Object Properties

> **Speed Tip 4: Avoid unnecessary access to properties of objects.**

Accessing a property of an object is much slower than accessing a variable; a typical example is repetitively accessing a multi-line text box:

```
Private Sub InsideLoop()

    Dim intCount As Integer
    txtNumbers.Text = ""
    For intCount = 1 To 1000
        txtNumbers.Text = txtNumbers.Text & CStr(intCount) & vbCrLf
    Next intCount

End Sub
```

Adding a variable and accessing the Text property only once, as in the following code, will result in a dramatic speed improvement.

```
Private Sub InsideLoop()

    Dim intCount As Integer
    Dim strText As String

    strText = ""
    For intCount = 1 To 1000
        strText = strText & CStr(intCount) & vbCrLf
    Next intCount
    txtNumbers.Text = strText

End Sub
```

Using With

> **Speed Tip 5: Use the With object construct.**

This tip is related to the previous two. The With construct allows us to imply that the methods and properties starting with a dot apply to the object in the With statement. Consider, for example, the following snippet of ADO code (we'll be covering ADO in detail in Chapter 11). Notice that the last block of code sets properties for the same Command object:

```
Dim cmd     As ADODB.Command

    ' Create the ADO objects
    Set cmd = New ADODB.Command
```

80

```
                ' Init the ADO objects
                cmd.ActiveConnection = ConnectionString
                cmd.CommandText = StoredProcedureName
                cmd.CommandType = adCmdStoredProc

                ' Etc.
```

We could rewrite this code as follows:

```
Dim cmd        As ADODB.Command

    ' Create the ADO objects
    Set cmd = New ADODB.Command

    ' Init the ADO objects
    With cmd
        .ActiveConnection = ConnectionString
        .CommandText = StoredProcedureName
        .CommandType = adCmdStoredProc
    End With

    ' Etc.
```

This second version of the code is a bit easier to read, but, more importantly in the context of performance, it executes more quickly because it makes just one call to the cmd object. This is the approach that we have taken in the WROBA case study.

Using Loops

Speed Tip 6: Reduce the code inside loops as much as possible.

The classic example for this tip is the For...Next loop. At the end of each loop, the expression after the To needs to be evaluated, so Visual Basic can decide whether another iteration is needed. To make this expression run as quickly as possible one improvement that can be made is to use a variable. For example the following routine:

```
Dim intCounter As Integer

For intCounter = 0 To lstListBox.ListCount - 1
    Debug.Print lstListBox.ItemData(intCounter)
Next intCounter
```

would execute a lot faster if it were re-coded as:

```
Dim intCounter        As Integer
Dim intListCountMax   As Integer

intListCountMax = lstListBox.ListCount - 1
For intCounter = 0 To intListCountMax
    Debug.Print lstListBox.ItemData(intCounter)
Next intCounter
```

Each time the first version loops, it needs to determine the value of `1stListBox.ListCount -1`. Using the second version, the value of `1stListBox.ListCount -1` is assigned to `intListCountMax` and the code only needs to refer to that value as it goes through each loop.

So we've been through some fairly simple examples in this chapter and if you tried them and they didn't work right first time, no doubt you sorted out the problems pretty quickly. Of course, things get more problematical when a larger application doesn't work correctly. Since we're going to be doing a lot of coding during this book, let's have a quick refresher on testing and debugging.

Testing

At every stage of the development of an application, it is necessary to ensure that our code is free from bugs. However, at this point it is necessary to introduce testing procedures, as these form an essential part of the development process from its very earliest stages. When we have worked through the rest of the book, and have the complete case study, we will return to testing and discuss the issues of integration and system testing. However, at this stage, we will look only at **unit testing**.

Before a piece of code is added to the project, it is wise to carry out some form of unit testing. The purpose of unit testing is to ensure that we haven't overlooked some detail when coding a form, code module, or class module. Unit testing is performed at a very low level, sometimes even at the Subroutine/Function level. One of the benefits of Visual Basic is the ease with which we can test our code using the debugging tools provided, including breakpoints, watches and the immediate window. The immediate window is on the View menu; watches, breakpoints, and others can be found on the Debug menu. Some of these menu items are also on the Debug toolbar (View | Toolbars):

In this section, we will look at some debugging tools that Visual Basic makes available to us during unit testing. These include:

❑ Breakpoints

❑ Watches

❑ Immediate Window

So, let's start by looking at how to use breakpoints.

Breakpoints

During development, when we run our code to test the execution of it, it will break on errors, unless we have an error handling routine in place. We can also set break points before running our code. Since break mode halts the operation of the application, we can analyze its current state and make changes that affect how it runs. This would apply to almost any part of the code where we think there might be a problem, except non-executable lines, such as Dim statements and comments.

During testing, it is important that we test all execution paths of our code. Each time we write an If statement we have two possible **execution paths**. This is because the condition in the If statement can be either False or True. For a large amount of code, we probably need a tool to keep track of which execution path has been tested. For small amounts of code, we can set **breakpoints**.

A breakpoint is something that only applies within the development environment (as opposed to compiled applications), and instructs Visual Basic to stop execution of the code when reaching this point. We set a breakpoint by setting the cursor on the line of code where we want to stop, then pressing *F9*. Pressing *F9* again removes the breakpoint. Breakpoints can also be set and cleared using the Debug toolbar or menu.

In the next example, we will see how to use breakpoints and Debug.Assert statements to perform **coverage analysis**. Coverage analysis keeps track of which execution path has been tested. Assertions provide us with a method of testing for conditions that should exist at specific points within your code. Think of it as assuming your statement is correct: if it is, the Assert statement will be ignored; if the statement is wrong, Visual Basic will drop into break mode to alert us that we made a wrong assumption. We can use any expression that evaluates to either True or False and drop into break mode if the expression evaluates to False. For example, if vartest = 4, we will break on this statement: Debug.Assert vartest > 5; however, if vartest = 6, the code will continue to run because the statement is True.

> To ensure that every branch of the code has been tested, ensure that every **If** has an
> **Else** (if necessary, add an **Else** with a **Debug.Assert True** statement).
> Then, place a breakpoint after every **If** and after every **Else** to ensure that every
> branch has been tested.

Try It Out – Coverage Analysis Using Breakpoints

1. Open a new Standard EXE project. Remove the form (Project | Remove Form1.frm) and add a module (Project | Add Module). Add the following function and constants to the module:

```
Option Explicit

Private Const SLASH     As String = "\"
Private Const DOT       As String = "."
Public Function ShortFileName(strFileName As String) As String
' Returns fileName without extension.
' for example if you pass "c:..\name.ext", it will return "c:..\name"
```

```
    Dim intDotPos        As Integer
    Dim intSlashPos      As Integer

    If Len(strFileName) Then
        ' Search from back to front, in case there is
        ' more than one slash...
        intSlashPos = InStrRev(strFileName, SLASH)

        ' Again, search from back to front, in case there is
        ' more than one dot...
        If intSlashPos Then
           intDotPos = _
              InStrRev(Right$(strFileName, Len(strFileName) _
                      - intSlashPos), DOT)
        Else
           ' No SLASH in file name
           intDotPos = InStrRev(strFileName, DOT)
        End If

        If intDotPos Then
           ShortFileName = Left$(strFileName, intSlashPos + intDotPos - 1)
        Else
           ' No DOT in file name
           ShortFileName = strFileName
        End If
    Else
        Debug.Assert True
    End If
End Function
```

2. Add a second module and insert the following code:

```
Option Explicit

Private Sub Main()
    Debug.Assert _
        ShortFileName("") = ""
    Debug.Assert _
        ShortFileName("C:\SomeDir\SomeFile.ext") = "C:\SomeDir\SomeFile"
    Debug.Assert _
        ShortFileName("C:\SomeDir\SomeFile..ext") = "C:\SomeDir\SomeFile."
    Debug.Assert _
        ShortFileName("C:\SomeDir.ext\SomeFile.ext") = _
                              "C:\SomeDir.ext\SomeFile"
    Debug.Assert _
        ShortFileName("C:\SomeDir.ext\SomeFile") = "C:\SomeDir.ext\SomeFile"
    Debug.Assert _
        ShortFileName("SomeFile.ext") = "SomeFile"
    Debug.Assert _
        ShortFileName("SomeFile..ext") = "SomeFile."
    Debug.Assert _
        ShortFileName("SomeFile") = "SomeFile"

    MsgBox "ShortFileName passed all tests!", vbExclamation
End Sub
```

3. Set breakpoints at each different code branch as shown below, by positioning the cursor in the line and pressing *F9* or by clicking in the margin in front of the line we wish to add a break to. The line will be highlighted and a dot added in the margin where we clicked:

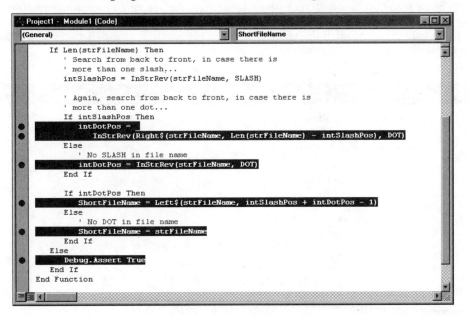

4. Run the project, removing each breakpoint (by pressing *F9* or clicking in the margin again) as you reach it. At the end of the run, you will notice that all breakpoints have been reached, which means that we have tested every possible execution path.

How It Works

As the `Main` Sub runs, each statement is tested against the `If...Then` statements in the `ShortFileName` function. This function removes the extension from the text assigned to the variable, `ShortFileName`, by counting the number of characters in the string and determining the position of the dot before the extension. Then the two strings in the statement are compared. If the variable assigned to `ShortFileName` does equal the string (from the `Main` Sub), then `Debug.Assert` is `True` and the code continues processing. Otherwise, it stops only when it gets to the breakpoints.

At this point, if we use **Step Into** (*F8*) rather than **Run** (*F5*), we can watch each statement execute. **Step Into** executes the current statement and breaks at the next line, even if it's in another procedure. In addition to **Step Into**, we also have **Step Over** and **Step Out**. **Step Over** executes the procedure called by the current line and breaks at the line following the current line. **Step Out** advances past the remainder of the code in the current procedure. This allows us to skip over parts of code that contain long loops or parts of code that we don't want to check at this time.

If a breakpoint is removed after the code has stopped on it once, then, when all breakpoints have been removed, it's apparent that each statement has been used. If any breakpoints are still set after the code finishes, then it's obvious that line is being skipped over during execution.

Watches

As we are debugging an application, a variable or expression may not produce the result we are expecting. Since many problems aren't easily traced to a single statement, we may wish to watch the behavior of the expression as the procedure is being executed. We can use the watch expression to automatically enter break mode if the value changes or is equal to a specified value. The value of the watch is displayed in the Watches window.

Try It Out – Using Watches

1. Open a new Standard EXE project and add a textbox to the form.

2. Name the textbox txtNumbers.

3. Enter this code into the form (View | Code):

```
Private Sub Form_Load()
    Dim intCount As Integer
    Dim strText As String

    strText = ""
    For intCount = 1 To 1000
        strText = strText & CStr(intCount) & vbCrLf
    Next intCount
    txtNumbers.Text = strText

End Sub
```

4. Highlight intCount and select Debug | Add Watch. Select 'Break When Value Changes', as shown in the following figure:

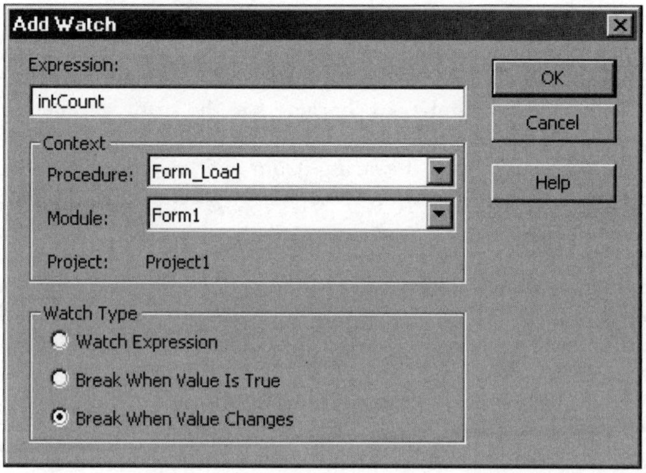

5. Add a watch for strText. Use the default watch type of Watch Expression.

6. Run the form (*F5* or **Start** button on toolbar). Continue a few times using the *F5* key. The values for the watched expressions change with each **Continue**.

7. Edit the Watch (right click on the watch in the **Watches** pane) and change the `intCount` expression to read `intCount = 15`. Set the Watch type to **Break When Value is True**.

8. Run the form again. When it breaks, adjust the width of the value pane if needed and you'll see that the value of the `strText` variable has ended at 14.

Watches				
Expression	Value		Type	Contex
intCount = 15	True		Boolean	Form1.F
strText	"1 2 3 4 5 6 7 8 9 10 11 12 13 14 "		String	Form1.F

Immediate Window

The **Immediate** window (**View | Immediate Window**) shows the results created by debugging statements in the code. We can also type commands directly into the window. The `Debug.Print` statement is used to return results to this window.

1. Add `Debug.Print strText` to the end of the procedure used in the Watch exercise above (select the existing watches and press *Delete* to remove them).

```
Private Sub Form_Load()
    Dim intCount As Integer
    Dim strText As String

    strText = ""
    For intCount = 1 To 1000
        strText = strText & CStr(intCount) & vbCrLf
    Next intCount
    txtNumbers.Text = strText

    Debug.Print strText

End Sub
```

The numbers from 1 to 1000 will be printed in a column in the **Immediate** window. They can be used to return variables, as in our example above, or to let us know we've reached a specific point in our code.

Using Message Boxes

Some people like to use message boxes (MsgBox) instead of Debug.Print to alert them when certain places have been reached in the execution.

To do this, it would be necessary to replace the Debug.Print strText line above with MsgBox strText.

Initially it seems like a reasonable idea. However, it has two distinct drawbacks:

❑ It is necessary to OK the message box for the procedure to continue.

❑ At compile time, it is necessary to remove all message boxes added for testing. Debug lines are removed automatically from the compiled code during the compilation process, but remain in the project code as we refine your code.

As you have learned, Visual Basic offers powerful, yet easy to use debugging methods using Watches and Debug statements. Both offer the ability to test your code using expressions. As the Debug statements remain in your source code, they are automatically used whenever your code is changed and retested in the development environment.

Summary

In this chapter, we took some of the important first steps in our journey to become Object-Oriented Programmers. We learned what an object is and we examined the characteristics that are common to all objects (Properties, Methods, Events, Encapsulation, Instantiation, State, Scope, and Lifetime). If you want to learn more about using objects in Visual Basic, we recommend another parallel book in the Wrox Visual Basic learning tree – *Beginning Visual Basic 6 Objects*, ISBN 186100172x, also by Wrox Press.

We then went on to discuss how classes are the foundation for creating objects. They are the 'blueprints' we use to build our objects. We learned how to create a class and add our own properties and methods. After building a class, we then learned how to instantiate it from a client application and expose its properties and methods. We then added a user-defined event to our class.

We also looked at a couple of tools we can use when working with classes. We used the Class Builder utility and saw how it helps make the process of creating classes (and their associate properties, methods and events) easier. We also explored how using the Object Browser can help us view information about classes. We then highlighted some ways in which we can optimize our code to make it more efficient, and make it run faster when it is processed.

Finally, we revised some essential methods for testing our code. In particular, we explored the use of breakpoints and watches. It is important to get into the habit of thoroughly testing code as the development process progresses. This can save a lot of trouble later on, and can be particularly important in the development of a large distributed application.

In the next chapter, we will move on to looking at component development, where we'll learn about COM and ActiveX, which will allow us to write components that are easy to maintain and that are built for reusability.

4

Component Development

In Chapter 3, we learned how to create and use classes in a Visual Basic project. Functions and subroutines allow us to write sections of code that can be called from multiple locations from within our application. Classes, such as those we learned to write in Chapter 3, take this concept a step further by making it easier to reuse code. This chapter will examine in detail **Component Object Model** (**COM**) components and their advantages in application development. We will concentrate on learning to create a specific type of COM component known as an **ActiveX server**. Delivery and management of COM components will also be introduced in this chapter. We will also take a brief look at the Distributed Component Object Model (DCOM).

As we saw in Chapter 1, COM became COM+ in Windows 2000 as it was merged with MTS. There are changes between COM and COM+, but they are outside the scope of this book. In this chapter, we will only refer to COM, although whatever we say will also apply to COM+. Any changes are not worth us worrying about in the context of this book; so relax!

In investigating the creation and use of COM, we will develop a small, self-contained application that we will call SampleCarApp. This can be downloaded from the Wrox web site. And in our discussion of ActiveX server, we will take a brief look forward at the WROBA case study. As pointed out earlier, this can also be downloaded from the Wrox web site.

Let's take a look at how this chapter will be structured:

- ❑ What is COM? Why should I use it?
- ❑ What is an ActiveX server? In-process versus Out-of-process servers.
- ❑ Creating an ActiveX DLL, including the instancing and threading options available.
- ❑ Creating Instances of ActiveX DLLs.
- ❑ Calling an ActiveX DLL from a Client Application.
- ❑ Raising Events.
- ❑ Registering COM components.
- ❑ Delivery of components via the Package and Deployment Wizard.
- ❑ DCOM.

This chapter will provide us with the solid foundation needed to create enterprise scale object-oriented applications, so let's dig in!

COM Components

So what exactly is the **Component Object Model** (henceforth referred to as COM)? Well, actually it is two things: first of all it is a well designed specification for creating objects, and secondly, it is a set of services that enable the creation and use of COM objects.

Specifications

The COM specification describes what rules have to be followed in writing code to create an object. These rules describe the way the object should look and how it can behave. In Chapter 3, classes were described using the analogy of blueprints for a house; while blueprints are used as a template for house building, so are classes used as the template for object building. However, before house blueprints can be created, there has to be a set of principles that need to be adhered to: the architect needs to know that a house requires, for instance, a foundation, a frame, and a roof, amongst other things. A COM programmer also needs to adhere to an underlying set of specifications before he or she sets out to create a COM component.

COM is a **binary standard**. A binary standard means that software written to the COM specification can be used without having any dependencies on the underlying source code. COM components also have the necessary mechanisms to communicate with other COM components as well as COM enabled applications. COM components are compiled into binary files and these files in turn can be distributed for use in COM-based applications. Since these files are in binary form, they can be used regardless of which language was used to create the component.

COM is rooted in **OOP** (object-oriented programming), which we explored in the previous chapter. We have client applications communicating with objects. The objects are created from classes that are defined in binary files known as COM components. This model allows for client applications to create and use objects created from classes that are contained in these binary files.

Services

COM is more than just a set of programming specifications. COM also includes a set of **library routines** that are a part of all Win32 operating systems. This does not mean that COM is limited only to Windows: it is available to other operating systems as an installable service. These COM services are largely transparent to the Visual Basic developer. The COM services are implemented from a set of **Dynamic Link Libraries** (**DLLs**); these DLLs perform the following functions:

- **Creation of COM component instances** – When the New keyword is invoked, or the CreateObject function used, COM services are being utilized.

- **Locator Services** – Since a COM component can reside at virtually any physical location accessible to an application, the COM locator services will find and keep track of that location.

- **Remote Procedure Calls** – COM provides a mechanism for one component to execute functionality in another component.

Advantages of COM

As a developer, you will always be looking for ways to make your work easier and more efficient. This can be accomplished by reusing code, creating easily maintainable routines, using code from others when applicable, or getting your applications to run on multiple platforms. These are just a few of the issues that face developers, and COM takes a giant leap in helping you to solve them.

Let's take a look at what COM can do for us:

- ❑ **Binary compatibility** – We discussed this when we looked at COM specifications. Any COM component can use any other COM component; the language used to create the component is irrelevant. So, if your friend who programs in C++ just created the perfect component, you can use that component in your Visual Basic application (with their permission, of course).

- ❑ **Encapsulation** – This is the "black-box" theory discussed in Chapter 3; you don't need to know anything about how the COM component works, only how to use its exposed properties and methods. Encapsulation goes hand in hand with binary compatibility: if the component is written in C++, or Java, or whatever, you don't need to know a lick of that language's syntax to use the component.

- ❑ **Portability** – COM components created for your application can easily be ported along with your application to another operating system that supports COM.

- ❑ **Location transparency** – Location, location, location – that's the golden rule of real estate but not something we want to be bothered with as developers. That's the beauty of COM; you can create a COM component and put it anywhere. Once you register it, the operating system and COM services keep track of where it is; all you have to do is call your component by its name and COM does the rest.

- ❑ **Code reuse** – Binary compatibility and encapsulation let us use others' code, even if it's written in another language. Visual Basic Classes take a step in the right direction in letting us reuse our own objects in different applications, but it certainly has it limitations. Let's say we created a class that makes a connection to a database. For each application we create, it is necessary to add a copy of that class to our project. It would then get compiled into the final application; it's almost just a sophisticated way to do the old "cut and paste". COM gives us true code reusability: if we use a COM component, it is necessary to compile and register it only once. Now any application that needs that database connection code can just access it by name.

- ❑ **Code maintenance** – No matter how much time we developers spend designing and testing there will always be bugs to fix and new features to be added. Lets take another look at our class with database connection code – suppose a fatal bug is discovered after all applications using this class have been installed. Well we not only have to fix the code in the class but also have to go back and recompile every application that uses that class. COM solves this problem for us: since the same COM component can be used by multiple applications, all we have to do is recompile our component and all applications accessing the component will reap the benefits of the new code.

COM Interfaces

Interfaces are an integral part of COM programming. Interfaces describe the methods and properties that are available in a class without describing how the methods or properties are implemented. If you are new to COM programming, this may be somewhat of an abstract concept, so let's try to clarify it somewhat.

Suppose we had a factory to make automobiles. All of the cars made in our factory would contain tires and engines (properties) and they could brake and accelerate (methods). These common properties and methods would constitute the car interface. Now, our factory would not make just one generic car – it would offer several models, such as sports cars and compact cars. The models would be the car classes. Each car class would implement the car interface, but each class's implementation of the interface could be very different. For example, while the sports car and the compact car both have engines, the type of engine would be very different.

The COM interface gives the client a common set of rules for all objects created from classes that implement the same interface. A driver of our car knows that whatever car he or she chooses will accelerate if he or she presses the gas pedal, and slow down when he or she presses the brake pedal. It would be very difficult to drive our cars if, in the sports car, we had to step on a brake pedal, but in the compact car, we had to press a stop button!

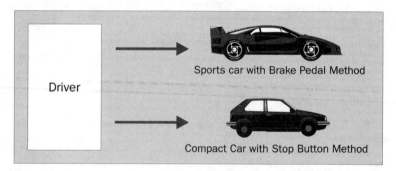

Even though the cars may use different methods to slow the vehicle, the user must be given the familiar brake pedal interface. Interfaces ensure that similar classes will all be accessed in the same manner. The use of interfaces also enforces encapsulation, as the interface is the only way in which we can access the object – we don't get to see what is happening inside the component.

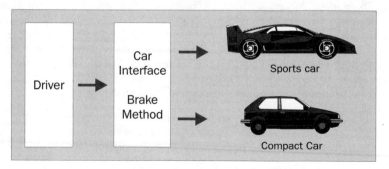

Implementing COM Interfaces in Visual Basic

A Visual Basic Interface is just a special type of Visual Basic class. Think of it as a shell of a class with no code within any of the property or method routines. Let's see how we could create our car interface in Visual Basic.

Try It Out – Creating a COM Interface

1. Initially, we need to add a class to a Visual Basic Project. Name it ICar, and add the following code:

```
Public Property Get Engine() As String

End Property

Public Property Let Engine(ByVal vNewValue As String)

End Property

Public Property Get Tires() As String

End Property

Public Property Let Tires(ByVal vNewValue As String)

End Property

Public Function Accelerate(ByVal Speed As Integer) As Integer

End Function

Public Function Brake(ByVal Speed As Integer) As Integer

End Function
```

Notice that we created Let and Get routines for our properties Engine and Tires, but that there are no variables to contain the property values, nor is there any code to set or retrieve the variables' values. There are also routines for our Accelerate and Brake methods, but again, no code to implement them. As you can see, this interface class isn't going to be very useful on its own. However, it is meant to be used in conjunction with other classes that need to implement the interface's properties and methods.

Let's take a look at a class that would use the ICar interface that we just created.

2. Add another class to your project and name it CSportsCar. The first thing we want to do in the code window of the CSportsCar class is to tell it that we want to use the ICar interface. We do that with the Implements key word. You simply add the following line of code:

```
Implements ICar
```

3. Notice that once you add this line of code the interface `ICar` becomes available in the left drop-down box of the class code window. Select `ICar` interface and its properties and methods are now available in the right drop-down box:

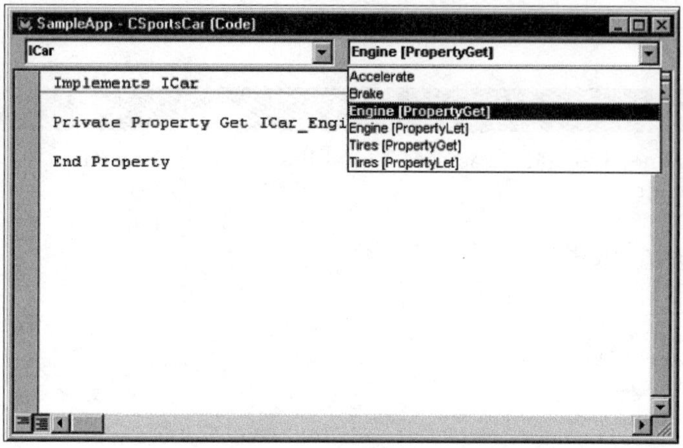

4. When the `Engine Property Get` routine is selected, the following code is placed in the `CSportsCar` code window.

```
Private Property Get ICar_Engine() As String

End Property
```

Notice that the property name is prefaced by the interface name. Another key distinction is that the property routine is private. This ensures that this class can only be accessed through the `ICar` interface. Later in this section we will look at why this is important.

5. We will now add the rest of our property routines and their implementation code. Refer back to Chapter 3 if you need a refresher on creating `Property Let` and `Get` routines. Our code should now look like the sample below:

```
Dim m_Engine As String
Dim m_Tires As String

Private Property Let ICar_Engine(ByVal RHS As String)
    m_Engine = RHS
End Property

Private Property Get ICar_Engine() As String
    ICar_Engine = m_Engine
End Property

Private Property Let ICar_Tires(ByVal RHS As String)
    m_Tires = RHS
End Property

Private Property Get ICar_Tires() As String
    ICar_Tires = m_Tires
End Property
```

6. We will also add code to the brake and accelerate methods. This code is very simplistic. The accelerate method increments the speed by 10 each time it is called, the brake method reduces the speed by 10, as illustrated by the following code:

```
Private Function ICar_Accelerate(ByVal Speed As Integer) As Integer
ICar_Accelerate = Speed + 10
End Function

Private Function ICar_Brake(ByVal Speed As Integer) As Integer
   ICar_Brake = Speed - 10
End Function
```

This implementation is specific to the CSportsCar class. If we now create a CCompactCar class, it will use all the code we have looked at in this section; only the implementation of the acceleration and braking speeds might be different, as shown below:

```
Private Function ICar_Accelerate(ByVal Speed As Integer) As Integer
   ICar_Accelerate = Speed + 5
End Function

Private Function ICar_Brake(ByVal Speed As Integer) As Integer
   ICar_Brake = Speed - 5
End Function
```

7. Let's now create a form from which we can call our class and interface. If you didn't delete Form1 that starts every standard Visual Basic project, use that; if you did, then just choose **Add Form** from the Visual Basic IDE **Project** menu. Our form will be quite simple, consisting of just a combo box, a label and two command buttons. In design view, add two entries to the combo box: **Compact Car** and **Sports Car**. Each time the user clicks the command button it will update the label with the new speed for the car specified in the combo box. Follow the illustration below to design your form:

Object	Property	Text to Enter
Form	Name	Form1
	Caption	Form1
Combo box	Name	Combo1
	List (first item)	Compact Car
	List (second item)	Sports Car
Command Button	Name	Command1
	Caption	Accelerate
Command Button	Name	Command2
	Caption	Brake
Label	Name	Label1
	Caption	blank

8. Type the following code into the code window of `Form1`.

```
Dim oSportsCar As ICar
Dim oCompactCar As ICar

Dim SportSpeed As Integer
Dim CompactSpeed As Integer

Private Sub Combo1_Click()
   If Combo1.ListIndex = 1 Then
      Label1.Caption = "You are driving " & CStr(SportSpeed) & " mph"
   Else
      Label1.Caption = "You are driving " & CStr(CompactSpeed) & " mph"
   End If
End Sub

Private Sub Command1_Click()
   If Combo1.ListIndex = 1 Then
      SportSpeed = oSportsCar.Accelerate(SportSpeed)
      Label1.Caption = "You are driving " & CStr(SportSpeed) & " mph"
   Else
      CompactSpeed = oCompactCar.Accelerate(CompactSpeed)
      Label1.Caption = "You are driving " & CStr(CompactSpeed) & " mph"
   End If
End Sub

Private Sub Command2_Click()
   If Combo1.ListIndex = 1 Then
      SportSpeed = oSportsCar.Brake(SportSpeed)
      Label1.Caption = "You are driving " & CStr(SportSpeed) & " mph"
   Else
```

```
        CompactSpeed = oCompactCar.Brake(CompactSpeed)
        Label1.Caption = "You are driving " & CStr(CompactSpeed) & " mph"
    End If
End Sub

Private Sub Form_Load()
    Set oSportsCar = New CSportsCar
    Set oCompactCar = New CCompactCar
    SportSpeed = 0
    CompactSpeed = 0
    Combo1.ListIndex = 0
End Sub

Private Sub Form_Unload(Cancel As Integer)
    Set oSportsCar = Nothing
    Set oCompactCar = Nothing
End Sub
```

How It Works

In the previous chapter we learned how to create an instance of an object from a class. There are some significant differences now that our class implements an interface.

Earlier in this section we created private Let and Get routines for our CSportsCar class. If we now declare an object of type CSportsCar and then instantiate an object from the class, there would be no exposed properties or methods.

```
Dim oSportsCar As CSportsCar
Set oSportsCar = New CSportsCar
```

Of course, we could have made the CSportsCar routines public but then it would infer that the properties and methods exposed were part the CSportsCar interface, not the CSportsCar class that implements the ICar interface. This is considered very poor coding practice so we avoid it by making the CSportsCar routines private.

We are able to expose the properties and methods by declaring an object of the interfaces type. We then create an instance of our object based on the CSportsCar class.

```
Dim oSportsCar As Icar
Set oSportsCar = New CSportsCar
```

In the General Declarations section of our form, we declare two variables for our SportsCar and CompactCar objects of type Icar. This is the interface. We also declare two integer variables to hold the speed of each car.

Upon loading the form, we instantiate each object variable from the appropriate car class as well as initialize the integer variables to 0.

The code behind the click event of Command1 checks to see which car type is specified in the combo box and then calls the Accelerate method from the appropriate object and updates the caption of Label1. The code behind the click event of Command2 operates in the same way, except that it calls the Brake method.

99

The form's Unload releases memory held by the object variables by setting them equal to nothing. There is also code behind the click event of Combo1 that updates the caption of Label1 with the speed of the selected car.

If you wish, you can download the SampleCarApp from the Wrox website to view a working model of classes and interfaces in action.

ActiveX Controls

COM components can take several different forms:

❑   The first COM component most Visual Basic programmers are exposed to is the ActiveX control. The textbox controls, the listbox control, and, in fact, all the controls available in the Visual Basic toolbox are examples of COM components called **ActiveX controls**. We can also create our own ActiveX controls or install custom ActiveX controls from another programmer (these are commonly referred to as third party controls). These ActiveX controls are compiled into files that contain a .ocx file extension.

❑   A second type of COM component is the **ActiveX Document**. More information about ActiveX Documents can be found in the Wrox book *VB Com.* ActiveX Documents are "mini" applications designed to run from within a container that supports them. A container is a host application designed to hold and expose the functionality of the child applications that it contains . For example, we might create a mortgage calculator in Visual Basic, and subsequently find that we need to use it as part of a Web site. Rather than have two separate sets of code, one Visual Basic code and the other Web based code (such as an ASP page, which we'll look at later in the book), we could have our Web browser call the mortgage calculator as an ActiveX document and share the same code., The most common ActiveX Document container is Microsoft's Internet Explorer.

❑   A third type of COM component, and the focus of this chapter, is the **ActiveX Server.**

> An *ActiveX Server* is a stand-alone binary file, which packages a collection of classes and interfaces. Client applications can instantiate objects from these classes and interfaces to expose their properties and methods.

The ActiveX server is one of the main tools we have as programmers to create n-tier client server applications. It is these ActiveX servers that allow us to take advantage of the power of COM components. Some common uses for ActiveX servers include:

❑   Managing Database Connections.

❑   Data Validation Rules.

❑   Collections of Common Data Properties.

❑   Business Logic.

You can create two different types of ActiveX servers with Visual Basic: in-process servers and out-of-process servers.

In-process Servers

An **in-process** server is also known as a **dll** (**Dynamic Link Library**) server because of the three character file extension it gets when compiled. An in-process server runs in the same process space (area of memory) as its calling application. It must be called by an application; it cannot be started and run by itself. The main advantage to using in-process servers is speed. Since they share the same memory space as an application, calls back and forth between the application and the in-process server's objects are very fast. This type of ActiveX server is limited in that the compiled in-process server (the .dll file) needs to reside on the same machine as the calling application(s).

Out-of-process Servers

This type of ActiveX server has a .exe extension. It runs in its own memory space; separate from any application that calls on it. The out-of-process server can be started on its own or started by a calling application. This type of server generally appears slower than an in-process server because of the added overhead of crossing process boundaries, and in some instances network boundaries. One advantage of this type of server is the ability for it to exist on a different machine to the application (hence the possibility of crossing network boundaries). Another advantage is its existence in its own memory space; if for some reason the out-of-process server would crash, it would not also crash the calling application.

This diagram illustrates the difference between in-process and out-of-process ActiveX servers.

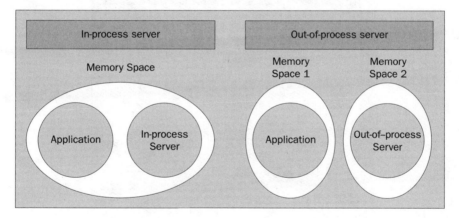

Creating an ActiveX DLL

Visual Basic makes creating ActiveX servers extremely easy. As we learned above, an in-process ActiveX server will be compiled and saved with a .dll extension, so henceforth we will refer to it as an ActiveX DLL. In the following exercise we will create our own ActiveX DLL for the SampleCarApp application that we looked at when we discussed interfaces earlier in this chapter.

ActiveX DLLs are created as separate projects in Visual Basic; as we learnt in our earlier discussion, an in-process server shares memory with its calling application. This can make debugging and trouble shooting your ActiveX DLL very difficult if you create it as a standalone project. We can overcome this obstacle if we create a Visual Basic **Project Group** that contains both our ActiveX server and our calling application. This allows us to step through the ActiveX DLL and the calling application as though they were a single project. Keep in mind that this project group is handy for development and debugging purposes, but in a real world solution the calling application and the ActiveX DLL will most likely be in entirely separate physical locations.

In the following example we will create the shell of an ActiveX DLL. During this exercise we will introduce the concepts of **threading**, **unattended execution**, **version compatibility** and **instancing**. Don't be concerned that we don't explain these during this exercise: they will all be explained in detail after it is completed.

Try It Out – Creating an ActiveX DLL

1. Start Visual Basic and open a new Standard EXE. Rename the project to SampleCarApp.

2. We now want to add another project. Select File | Add Project… and then select ActiveX DLL as the project type and click Open.

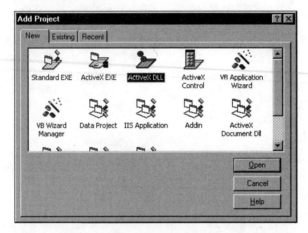

We now have a project group. Project Explorer should look like this:

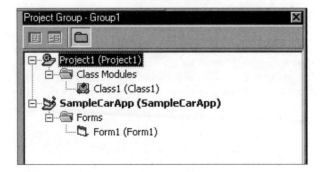

3. As we can see, we have now created a new project that is listed in the Project Explorer. It has the default name of `Project1`. Visual Basic has also supplied us with a default class named `Class1`. Let's give our new project a meaningful name and set some of its properties. We do this from the **Project Properties** dialog box. We access this dialog by right-clicking on Project1 in the Project Explorer and selecting **Project1 Properties** from the pop-up menu or select Project1 **properties** from the **Project menu**.

Change the **Project Name** to `Cars` and enter a description as shown. Ensure the **Threading Model** is set to **Apartment Threaded** and the **Unattended Execution** option is checked.

4. Next, move to the **Component** tab and select **Project Compatibility**, then click **OK** to close the dialog box.

5. As you can see, we have the shell of an empty class named `Class1` waiting for code. Let's use our interface code from the COM Interface section. Rename the class `ICar` and add the following code to the code window:

```
Public Property Get Engine() As String
End Property

Public Property Let Engine(ByVal vNewValue As String)
End Property

Public Property Get Tires() As String
End Property

Public Property Let Tires(ByVal vNewValue As String)
End Property

Public Function Accelerate(ByVal Speed As Integer) As Integer
End Function

Public Function Brake(ByVal Speed As Integer) As Integer
End Function
```

It is necessary to create our Interface class first, since we will need to utilize this interface in the creation of our subsequent class CSportsCar, which we will examine in the next step.

6. We also need to add our `CSportsCar` class. Make sure the `Cars` ActiveX DLL project is highlighted; then, from the **Project** menu choose **Add Class Module**. From the **Add Class Module** dialog box, select the **New** tab and highlight **Class Module**. Then click **Open** to proceed.

7. Rename the new class to `CSportsCar` and add the following code to the code window.

```
Implements ICar

Dim m_Engine As String
Dim m_Tires As String

Private Function ICar_Accelerate(ByVal Speed As Integer) As Integer
   ICar_Accelerate = Speed + 10
End Function

Private Function ICar_Brake(ByVal Speed As Integer) As Integer
   ICar_Brake = Speed - 10
End Function

Private Property Let ICar_Engine(ByVal RHS As String)
   m_Engine = RHS
End Property

Private Property Get ICar_Engine() As String
   ICar_Engine = m_Engine
End Property


Private Property Let ICar_Tires(ByVal RHS As String)
   m_Tires = RHS
End Property

Private Property Get ICar_Tires() As String
   ICar_Tires = m_Tires
End Property
```

8. Now we can save and compile our ActiveX DLL.

Highlight the `Cars` project and then from the **File** menu choose **Save Cars**.

If you are saving the ActiveX project `Cars` for the first time, you will get the **Save** dialog box. Note that we are saving it with a `.vbp` file extension. Our ActiveX DLL is still just Visual Basic project code at this point; it doesn't get the `.dll` file extension until we compile it.

Highlight **Cars**, and then, from the **File** menu choose **Make Cars.dll**.

We will once again get the **Save** dialog box asking for the location of where we want to save the compiled `Cars.dll` file. Recall that when we discussed the advantages of COM components, we said location didn't matter. The operating system keeps track of our ActiveX DLL location when we register it in the Windows system registry (it registers automatically when we compile, we will learn how to register components manually a little bit later). This means we can save the `.dll` file anywhere on our computer and it will work just fine (though life as a developer is much easier if we keep all associated DLLs in a central, easily accessible location).

9. There is still one more step before we can use our ActiveX DLL in our main project: we have to set a project reference to it. Make sure that the `SampleCarApp` project is now highlighted.

Select References from the Project Menu.

From the References dialogue box check Cars, then click OK.

We have now created our component. We will see how to utilize it a little later.

Project Properties

In running through this work, we've made some critical choices. In particular, we selected Apartment Threading, and chose Unattended Execution on the General tab of the Project Properties dialogue box. We also checked Project Compatibility on the Component tab of the same box.

We now turn to exploring these options in detail.

We will also take a look at **instancing**. Instancing determines the way in which a calling application can create instances of our class. We didn't encounter this in creating our class, as we left it set to its default setting; MultiUse. However, there would be circumstances in which we would want to control the ways in which instances of our class could be created, so it will be useful to explore this.

Threading

As we saw earlier, in the Project Properties dialogue box we ensured that we selected Apartment Threaded. Let's spend a short while investigating what threading is, and look at the two basic threading models that are available to us in constructing an **in-process** server. However, let's first look at some concepts that these models are built upon; specifically, threads and apartments.

Threads

When an application is run in a WIN32 environment, an instance of the application, called a **process**, is created. This gets an address space in virtual memory. Within each process are one or more schedulable pieces of execution called **threads**. It is also important to note that multiple processes cannot share threads. The operating system recognizes each thread and schedules each thread for execution by the processor.

Each thread is given an allotment of time; when the time allotment expires, the processor pauses the execution of the current thread and begins processing the next thread in line for its allotment of time. The processor then cycles through the schedule of threads, alternately processing and pausing execution. When a thread's execution is complete it is dropped from the processor's schedule; as new threads are created, they are, in turn, added to the schedule. This concept of alternately processing threads in small time increments creates the impression that a single processor computer is executing multiple tasks simultaneously. This is commonly referred to as **multi-tasking**.

Until version 6.0, any time a Visual Basic programmer created an instance of an application, it would create a process. This would contain a single thread of execution. This is known as a **single-threaded** application. We were blissfully unconcerned with the behind-the-scenes scheduling of threads by the operating system and processor.

On the other hand, C and C++ programmers have long had the ability to create additional threads (known as **multi-thread processing**) within the same process using the WIN32 API function, `CreateThread`. This powerful feature allowed C programmers to spawn a separate thread to handle background processes, such as the printing of a long report, while the main application continued to process. With this powerful feature comes the responsibility of avoiding the potential pitfalls of multi-thread processing. Global data in one thread has the potential to be accessed by another thread in that same process; this has the potential to create inconsistency or corruption. For example, let's say we have two threads and they both access data contained in the same global array. Suppose thread one is processing and it redeclares the global array; its very next step is to add data to the newly redeclared array, but just before it has the chance, its time allotment expires and the processor pauses execution. The processor begins processing thread two, which tries to access data in the global array (which is empty; remember, we just redeclared it in thread one) so of course it either generates an error or returns unpredictable results. C programmers then need to take these issues into consideration if they are to create solid and robust multi-threaded applications.

Apartments

As we just saw, there are two ways to write code (from a threading perspective, that is). You can write a single-threaded application, which isn't concerned with passing global data between threads (because there is only one thread), or you can write multi-threaded applications.

As COM components can be written using either method, this poses an interesting question. So, how do components using different methods communicate? The developers of COM overcame this dilemma by creating apartments. Apartments allow each component to behave as if every component they interact with uses the same type of thread management. COM has a strict set of rules that prohibits a thread in one apartment from directly accessing an object that resides in another apartment. COM does provide a special layer of communication between apartments, which provides a framework for passing method calls in a safe environment, avoiding the aforementioned pitfalls that can occur in a multi-threaded environment.

Keep in mind that threading is an advanced concept and would take an entire chapter or more to fully explain. The focus of this section is to give you an idea of the general concept of threading. A thorough discussion of the concept of threading may be found in the Wrox book *Beginning Components for ASP*, *ISBN number 1861002882*.

Now that we have discussed some of the underlying principles, let's look at the two ActiveX DLL threading options available:

Single Threading

If the **Single Threaded** option is chosen, all objects created from the ActiveX server will run on a single shared thread. The thread is created when the first object is created; all subsequent objects will share the same thread in sequence. There is no multi-tasking available within the process; the first task on the thread must complete prior to beginning the next task. All standard `.exe` projects (*not* ActiveX exe servers) run using single threaded execution.

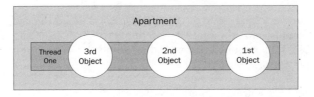

Apartment Threading

Visual Basic makes it very easy to create multi-threaded COM components. All that is required is that we choose the *apartment threading* option. The code that controls the threads and apartments is handled by the host application; no additional Visual Basic code is required.

Behind the scenes, each time an object is created, a new thread is created. This all occurs within the boundaries of a single apartment.

The apartment threaded or **multi-threading** option is essential when using ActiveX components with MTS (Microsoft Transaction Server). This is discussed in the next chapter. Even if you are not currently planning to run in an MTS environment, selecting this option allows you the freedom to use your component in an MTS environment in the future.

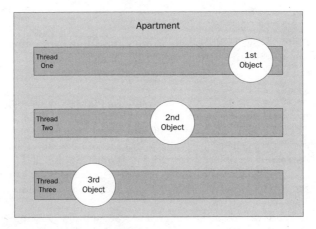

Threading with Out-of-process Servers

Before we proceed, let's discuss the threading options available with *out-of-process* or ActiveX EXE servers:

❑ **Thread per object** – If this option is selected, each object created from this ActiveX server will operate in its own thread of execution. This is very similar to the apartment-threaded option discussed for ActiveX DLLs.

❑ **Thread Pool** – With this option, we can specify the number of threads available for use. Then, as objects are created, they are assigned to each thread in turn. For example, if we set the number of threads to two and create three objects, the first thread creates and owns the first object, the second thread creates and owns the second object, the first thread then gets the third object and so on. This setting is usually employed when the application frequently creates many instances of the object creating a drain on system resources. Using thread pooling allows us to limit the number of resources at the application's disposal, while still retaining the benefits of a multi-threaded component.

It is important to point out that this option is not the same as load balancing, which is where you try to share the workload evenly. In the previous example, even if the second thread's object is not processing any objects, the first thread will continue to process its two objects. Setting the number of threads to one creates a **Single Use** component (Single Use is an instancing setting – we will be discussing instancing later in this chapter).

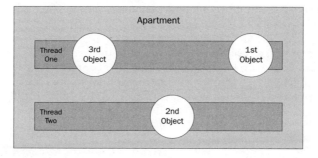

Unattended Execution

Selecting the Unattended Execution option tells the compiler that a component won't try to interact with a user directly. This is especially important in the realm of client/server applications where components may exist on separate machines.

Imagine a scenario in which a client machine calls a component on a server halfway around the world. That's no big deal, it happens all the time. Now if that component should create and display a message box or modal form then we are stuck at our client machine if there is no one with immediate physical access to the server. We have just inadvertently hung our application. Unattended Execution prevents this from occurring, because instead of displaying the MsgBox to the screen, the system will instead write out the function to the Windows Event Log (a general system log file).

Version Compatibility

Let's analyze a typical scenario that faces programmers in the development cycle. A typical client/server application would consist of a client application and several ActiveX DLL servers. We then discover that one of our ActiveX DLLs needs substantial changes. If we are not careful how we implement those changes it could adversely affect the ability of the client applications to communicate with the ActiveX DLL. **Version compatibility** is Visual Basic's way of guarding against changes that can potentially disrupt communication between components.

Before investigating compatibility, it will be necessary to investigate the means by which COM components are registered. To this end, we will now make a brief digression to become familiarized with **GUIDs**.

GUIDs

> **A GUID (Global Unique Identifier) is a computer-generated 128-bit number used to uniquely identify COM components, COM Interfaces and COM classes.**

Each interface or class that is created in a COM component is identified by a unique GUID. The GUID is a 128-bit integer that is usually expressed in Windows as a 32 character hexadecimal and is stored in the Windows registry. A sample of a GUID in the registry looks like this:

```
{A3456B11-56A3-11D1-8602-3D889C000000}
```

The actual GUIDs are created when the COM component is compiled and they are placed in the registry when the COM component is registered (we'll cover compiling and registering later in this chapter). This is done by means of an algorithm that uses the time and the machine ID from the network card to ensure that the number is unique, although Visual Basic hides the code that generates and references these GUIDs.

As Visual Basic programmers, all we have to do is refer to the user friendly name of the class or interface (such as `CSportsCar` or `ICar`) in the calling client application, and the system will then be able to find the corresponding GUID in the system registry. From the GUID, the client can find the appropriate COM component that contains our class or interface code regardless of where it is physically located.

While we as Visual Basic programmers don't need to be concerned with the underlying mechanics of how GUIDs are generated, a basic understanding of GUIDs is necessary when we discuss binary compatibility later in this chapter. Just as a primary key is used in a relational database for accessing information on a specific row of data, the GUID is used by COM to access information from the system registry.

The GUIDs associated with particular components may be accessed using the Registry Editor:

A basic understanding of GUIDs is necessary if we are to understand the issues associated with component compatibility. It is to this that we now turn.

The Version Compatibility field of the Component tab of the Project Properties dialog box, shown below, gives us three basic options. We'll now explore what these different options mean for us.

Project Compatibility

When an ActiveX server is compiled, it is identified to the operating system by an entry in the system registry. The existing GUIDs will be unregistered and replaced with a new set of GUIDs whenever the ActiveX server is compiled. The key here is that the component is unregistered, which removes the GUID from the system registry and prevents the registry from filling up with unnecessary GUID entries. Since the component is unregistered, we are also able to reregister it and retain the same name and preserve its identity, even though the GUID has changed. This option should be selected when we are in development, and do not yet have any production client applications accessing our ActiveX server.

No Compatibility

This option does not enforce version compatibility. New GUIDs are created when the ActiveX server is compiled as result of this option being selected. If we choose this option, then if we recompile the ActiveX server, it will also be necessary to recompile the client application. This is usually not a good choice for ActiveX servers, except in the case where you want to replace old software with an entirely new compiled version of the component as well as a new version of the client application, or when you are compiling a component for the first time.

Binary Compatibility

When we compile with this option selected, the compiler finds the ActiveX server registered with a matching GUID. It then compares all the methods from the existing version to the methods of the new version you are about to compile. If there have been any changes in these methods, it will provide us with a warning asking us to confirm how we wish to proceed. Let's briefly take a look at an example.

Supposing we had created and compiled a component that has one method, and that it's called `TestMethod`. Notice that `TestMethod` does **not** require any parameters:

```
Public Function TestMethod() As String
```

Now, suppose we want to change the function so that it requires a parameter and then recompile the ActiveX server.

```
Public Function TestMethod( TestParam As String) As String
```

Any previous applications that were using `TestMethod` would now return an error because their existing code would have calls to the method that passed no parameters, while the new version of our ActiveX server now requires a parameter.

Visual Basic helps protect against this type of conflict with the Binary Compatibility option. If the Binary Compatibility option has been set, then when we try to compile our component we will get the following warning:

If we choose the **Break Compatibility** option, a new GUID is created. Any compiled applications calling the ActiveX server will now encounter an error when they try to declare an object based on any of its classes or interfaces. This occurs because the GUID the application is trying to reference no longer exists. To recover, the client application must set a reference to the ActiveX server with the new GUID and then be recompiled.

If the **Preserve Compatibility** option is chosen, the ActiveX server is compiled as a new component, but retains the same GUID. Client applications will be able to create objects from your ActiveX server's interfaces and classes. However, the client application will encounter errors if it calls any of the conflicting methods that generated the compile warning. This option can be used when you know existing client application will not be using any of the conflicting methods.

To recover from client errors we have two choices; either we can fix the ActiveX server so that the method is compatible with the existing client application and recompile with this option, or we can fix the source code in the client application to call the revised methods correctly and recompile the client application.

Instancing

Instancing refers to how instances of this class can be created from calling applications.

The following choices are available for ActiveX DLLs:

❑ **Private** – A client application cannot create an instance of this class, nor can it use an instance of this class created within the server. This class is only visible from within the server itself.

❑ **PublicNonCreatable** – If the server has created an instance of this class then it can be used by a client application. A client application cannot however use the New keyword or CreateObject function to create an instance of this class.

❑ **MultiUse** – Client applications can use the New keyword or CreateObject functions to create objects from this class. Many instances of a class can be created within a single server process. This is the property's default setting, which is why we didn't look at this when creating our class.

❑ **GlobalMultiUse** – From an ActiveX server perspective, this is very similar to MultiUse; multiple objects can be created from a single instance of the class. The difference lies in the way the objects created from this class are treated in the client application. Rather than having to use the New keyword or CreateObject function the methods and properties exposed by the class are treated as global functions.

There are also two more properties available to ActiveX out-of-process servers. These are:

❑ **SingleUse** – Client application can use the New keyword or CreateObject functions to create objects from this class. Each time an object is created, a new instance of the class is created in a separate server process.

❑ **GlobalSingleUse** – Similar to single use in that a new instance of the class is created for every object, but the methods and properties of the class are treated as global functions, similar to that of GlobalMultiUse.

Creating Instances of ActiveX DLLs

Now we are ready to call our class from our client application. It is really no different to instantiating a class or an intrinsic Visual Basic library like ADO 2.5. This is the beauty and power of COM; once we create an object, they all look and operate in a similar manner. For example, all objects will be created, or more precisely instantiated, using the same techniques. The properties and methods of all objects are also accessed using the same techniques.

Initially, we will look at how to access the Car ActiveX server that we just made. Then, in looking at how one ActiveX server may access another ActiveX server, we will take a brief look at some code from the WROBA case study application. We will make a detailed exploration of how the case study is constructed in later chapters. For now, we will just see one of the ways in which ActiveX servers are utilized there.

Calling our ActiveX DLL from a Client Application

Let's take a look at some code from an application that will access the Car ActiveX server we just created. It is a simple application that will call the Accelerate method and then display the current speed in a label on a form.

Try It Out – Calling an ActiveX DLL from a Client Application

1. Go back to the project SampleCarApp that we started in the exercise from the Creating an ActiveX DLL section. Select Form1 in design view and add a label and a command button so that it resembles the diagram below.

2. Initially, it is necessary to declare our object variable in the general declarations section. Remember that we need to use the Interface, *not* the Class, when we declare our object variable. We also declare a variable of integer type:

```
Dim oCar As ICar
Dim  iSpeed As Integer
```

Notice when you are typing code in the Visual Basic IDE that as soon as you've finished typing the word 'As', IntelliSense should provide you with a drop down list of available objects. If ICar is not in that list go back and check to make sure you set a reference to it (Creating an ActiveX DLL: Step 9).

3. We still can't use our object, we've only declared a variable. Before using it, we need to instantiate it with the New keyword or the CreateObject function. We do that with the Form_Load event of our application. Now that we are instantiating our object, we use the class that implements the interface we just declared in the general declarations section:

```
Set oCar = New CSportsCar
```

4. In Form_Load we also set the initial values of our integer variable and our label:

```
ISpeed = 0
Label1.Caption = "Your speed is " & iSpeed & " mph"
```

Now our object's properties and methods are exposed and ready to be used. In this case we want to use the Accelerate method of our CSportsCar class. We will use this method to update the iSpeed variable each time the command button is clicked, so this code will exist in the Command1_Click event.

5. To access this method we must first indicate the object that contains the method, which is oCar. We cannot access the class directly. That's why we created an object variable and put an instance of the class in it. We also update our label in this event:

```
Private Sub Command1_Click()
    iSpeed = oCar.Accelerate(iSpeed)
    Label1.Caption = "Your speed is " & iSpeed & " mph"
End Sub
```

Notice that the Accelerate method takes a parameter just as if we were passing parameters to a regular subroutine or function.

6. The code that destroys our object is in the Form_Unload event of our application. By setting the object variable oCar equal to the Nothing keyword, we release the memory reserved for this object.

```
Private Sub Form_Unload(Cancel As Integer)
    Set oCar = Nothing
End Sub
```

It's not uncommon for an application to use dozens if not hundreds of objects while it is running. If all objects remained in effect for the life of an application this could bring performance to a crawl. Nobody wants to use a slow application, and nobody wants a programmer who writes slow code, so learn good habits early and make judicious use of your objects. In other words, when you are done using an object, destroy it to release any allocated memory.

How It Works.

This exercise was very similar to the earlier exercise on creating an interface class. Just as we did in that exercise, here when we click the command button, it calls the `Accelerate` method from the `oCar` object. The `Accelerate` method returns the new speed value, which we use to update the label that is displayed to the user.

The significant difference from the previous exercise is that we create an object from a class contained in a compiled ActiveX DLL. This exercise simulates a very simple client/server environment.

We will now look at ways that ActiveX servers are used in the sample Bank Application that accompanies this book.

The Use of ActiveX Servers in WROBA

In this following section, we take a look forward to some of the ways in which ActiveX servers are utilized in the WROBA case study. We will examine only selected sections of the case study, which illustrate how ActiveX servers are used in an enterprise solution. Later in the book, the case study will be examined from an application design viewpoint. In particular, this section will take a look at:

❑ Calling an ActiveX Server from another ActiveX Server.

❑ Error Handling in an ActiveX server.

❑ Creating Different Objects from within the same ActiveX.

Calling an ActiveX Server from Another ActiveX Server

As we have seen, once we have created an ActiveX DLL, using it is really no different to using a standard class or an intrinsic Visual Basic object. The whole idea of COM programming is to create modules of code that perform specific tasks, and if those modules need other specific tasks done then they in turn call other modules. A good example of this is illustrated in the `WROBAUnlock` method.

This `WROBAUnlock` method is part of the `Bank` Class of the `Bank_Bus` ActiveX server. As we can see, it makes a call to another ActiveX server named `Bank_DB`.

```
Public Sub WROBAUnLock(ByVal BankID As Integer, _
    ByVal CardID As Long)
'  Unlock the account

    Dim objBank As Bank_DB.Bank

    On Error GoTo ErrorHandler
```

```
        Set objBank = CtxCreateObject("Bank_DB.Bank")

        'Passthrough call to data tier
        objBank.WROBAUnLock BankID, CardID

        CtxSetComplete

  Clean_Up:
        Set objBank = Nothing
        Exit Sub

  ErrorHandler:
        RaiseError MODULE_NAME, "WROBAUnLock(" & CStr(BankID) & _
            ", " & CStr(CardID) & ")"
        GoTo Clean_Up
  End Sub
```

The lines of code that enable us to expose the methods and properties of the Bank class are slightly different to what we learned in our simple sports car exercise. This time we use the CreateObject Function rather than the New keyword (the **New** keyword does not allow us to indicate a remote location).

Also, when declaring the object and using the object, we preface the class name with the name of the ActiveX server. This is necessary because we have classes of the same name that reside in different ActiveX servers.

```
    Dim objBank As Bank_DB.Bank

    Set objBank = ctxCreateObject("Bank_DB.Bank")
```

We don't actually use CreateObject but, rather, we call a function called ctxCreateObject. This function, which is located in the MContext module, creates an instance of our object, but it also handles some things that are necessary for MTS (Microsoft Transaction Server). I am not going to try and explain MTS concepts now because they are looked at in depth in Chapter 5. Suffice it to say for our purposes in this chapter CreateObject and ctxCreateObject are essentially the same.

We have seen how one ActiveX server is called by another ActiveX server within the WROBA application; before we look at how different objects may be created from within the same ActiveX server, it will be worth our while taking a glance at how errors are handled within the WROBAUnlock method.

Error Handling in an ActiveX Server

The Err object keeps track of Visual Basic error numbers and descriptions. This can be pretty helpful within the framework of a single project that makes no calls to any outside components. However, in today's development environment of multiple COM components we need to know where the error occurred as well.

Suppose we have a client application that instantiates 3 different ActiveX DLLs, each of which in turn instantiates 3 more ActiveX DLLs, as illustrated overleaf:

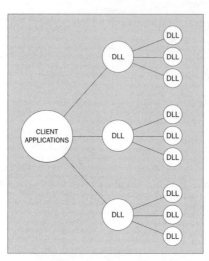

As we can see from the diagram, we have a total of twelve ActiveX DLLs and our client application.

Now, supposing that when our application is run, we were to be confronted by the following error:

This would be a nightmare to troubleshoot. Did the error generate from our main application or one of our ActiveX DLLs? If it was an ActiveX DLL, then which one was it?

We overcome this potential obstacle by creating an error handling function named RaiseError, which we call from the following code:

```
RaiseError MODULE_NAME, "WROBAUnLock(" & CStr(BankID) & ", " & _
    CStr(CardID) & _")"
```

Notice that we pass to the function two parameters. The first is a variable that will contain the name of the class or module where the error occurred. The second parameter is a string which contains the function or subroutine name, and the parameters that it received. The function will then return all the necessary information to troubleshoot and hopefully resolve the error. The diagram below illustrates the information that might be returned when an error occurs:

Later in the book we will examine exactly what information is returned to the user and how that information is gathered and displayed.

Creating Different Objects from Within the Same ActiveX

We have seen how a Client Application can create objects from ActiveX servers, and we have seen ActiveX servers create objects from other ActiveX DLLs. Now we will take a very brief look at how we can create different objects from within the same ActiveX DLL.

Within the case study, we create an ActiveX DLL called Bank_Bus.Bank. This has a method which instantiates an object called Bank_DB.Bank, and calls its WROBAUnlock method. The code for the WROBAUnlock method is as follows:

```
Public Sub WROBAUnLock(ByVal BankID As Integer, _
    ByVal CardId As Long)

    Dim objBankLocator As Bank_DB.BankLocator
    Dim strDSN As String

    On Error GoTo ErrorHandler

    ' Locate the selected bank and get the DSN for it
    Set objBankLocator = New Bank_DB.BankLocator
    strDSN = objBankLocator.GetBank(BankID)

    ' Run the stored procedure
    m_objDBHelper.RunSP strDSN, "sp_delete_TxLock", _
        Array("@BankId_1", adSmallInt, adSizeSmallInt, BankID), _
        Array("@CardId_2", adInteger, adSizeInteger, CardId)

Clean_Up:
    Set objBankLocator = Nothing
    CtxSetComplete
    Exit Sub

ErrorHandler:
    RaiseError MODULE_NAME, "WROBAUnLock"
    GoTo Clean_Up
End Sub
```

We won't go into an in-depth explanation of this entire routine, but will just focus on the part of the code pertinent to the creation and use of COM components.

From this method, we need to access a method from another class within this ActiveX DLL, namely, the class called BankLocator. As we can see, the code that achieves this is the same as that we would use if we were calling it from a client application, or from another ActiveX DLL.

Initially, we declare a variable to hold an instance of the object class:

```
Dim objBankLocator As Bank_DB.BankLocator
```

Then we create an instance of the object, this time with the New keyword:

```
Set objBankLocator = New Bank_DB.BankLocator
```

119

Now we have exposed the properties and methods of this class and we can use its methods; in this case GetBank:

```
strDSN = objBankLocator.GetBank(BankID)
```

As we can see, instantiating objects from the same ActiveX DLL isn't any different from instantiating from any other ActiveX DLL.

Summary

We have seen how one ActiveX server can call another ActiveX server; in our case, we saw how Bank_Bus calls Bank_DB. In particular, we have seen how the Bank class creates an instance of Bank_DB's Bank class.

After a brief digression on error handling, we saw how the Bank class within the Bank_DB ActiveX DLL creates an instance of its own BankLocator class.

We can see the sequence of events in this diagram:

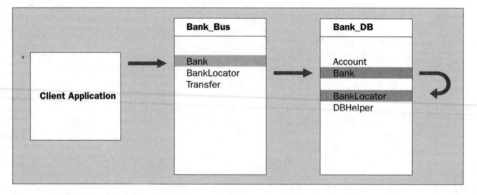

We have seen how to create COM components, specifically the ActiveX DLL, and how to put them to use in our application, and that, before they can be used, COM components need to be recognized by the operating system. We touched briefly on how this is done in our exercise.

Next we will explore in detail how we make the operating system aware of our COM components through registration.

Registering COM Components

We have learned so far how to create ActiveX servers and how to call them from other components. One item that yet needs to be discussed is registering components. At the beginning of the chapter we pointed out that one of the advantages of COM components is that they have location transparency. In other words, ActiveX DLLs or ActiveX EXEs can exist anywhere on a machine (or on another machine, in the case of ActiveX EXEs) and work just fine. It is not necessary to name a specific location. This location transparency is made possible by registering components. When we register a component, we put an entry in the system registry that tells the operating system the name of the component and where it exists.

In our previous examples we never specifically registered a component, because when we compiled our ActiveX DLLs, by using the project compatibility option from the component tab in project properties, they registered automatically as part of the compile. That's OK when developing components, but when we need to distribute components to end users, we will need methods of registering them.

Run the Component

If we have created a component capable of running on its own, such as an ActiveX EXE server, we can simply run the component. Since this type of component is a stand alone compiled object that runs in its own process, it will automatically register itself when it is started. For example, supposing we had developed an ActiveX EXE project and compile it into an ActiveX EXE server. The compiling process would register the component on your machine. But what happens if you want the component to run on another machine? We simply copy the ActiveX EXE server to the new machine and double-click it to run it; it will register automatically. It's that simple!

Regsvr32.exe

In the case of an ActiveX DLL server, which cannot stand-alone but needs to be started from another component, we need a utility to register our component. The name of the utility is regsvr32.exe. This is supplied with the Windows operating system and can be found in the Windows\System folder.

To use it, first make sure that your ActiveX DLL has been saved and compiled. You can then copy that DLL to another machine, and manually register it.

Regsvr32.exe is a command line utility that needs to be run from a DOS prompt, or the Command Prompt, if you are using Windows NT or Windows 2000. From the start button, select command prompt (Windows NT and Windows 2000) or the DOS prompt (Windows 95/98) and you'll be presented with a DOS screen in which you can enter the command. The regsvr32.exe file is located in the WinNT\system (or WinNT\system32 depending on which service pack you have installed) directory on Windows NT systems and the Windows\system folder on Win 95/98 systems.

Supposing we wanted to register an ActiveX DLL named deployme.dll that is located in the Wrox folder on the client machine (it doesn't matter whether the client has the ActiveX DLL on their hard drive, or on a network drive, or on any other drive – the method we look at next works for all destination locations). As illustrated, we can run the utility by typing regsvr32 (typing the .exe extension is optional) followed by the name and path of the component; in this case, we will use e:\wrox\deployme.dll as an example destination:

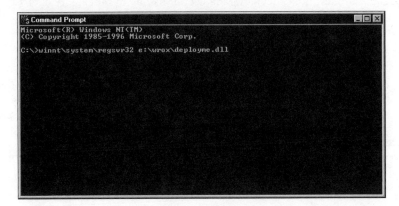

If the component registers successfully we should receive a message box indicating success as illustrated below.

Alternatively, we can run regsvr32.exe from the Run... prompt on the Start menu:

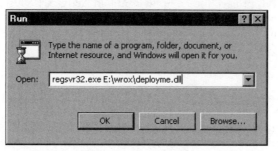

In this case, it is not necessary to specify the path of regsvr32.

There will be times when we need to unregister our components. We still use the same utility, regsvr32, only this time we add the command line parameter, /u. Our command line would then read as follows:

```
C:\>winnt\system\regsvr32 e:\wrox\deployme.dll /u
```

In fact there are several command line parameters we should mention:

❑ /u – Unregisters component – we have just covered this one.

❑ /c – Console output – the default parameter, this is what causes you to be alerted by a message box to the success or failure of the registration

❑ /s – Silent output – no message boxes will appear following a successful (or unsuccessful) registration. This parameter is often used when a batch file is created to register many components at once, thus alleviating the user of having to repeatedly click OK in response to each registration.

The Package and Deployment Wizard

Probably the most common way to distribute and register components is through the Package and Deployment Wizard. Most users of windows software are accustomed to installing software, upgrades and patches just by double-clicking a setup file. Well, this is exactly what the Package and Deployment Wizard will do for us; it creates a setup file, which we in turn supply to the user. The setup file then takes care of copying the ActiveX component to the desired location and registering it. Actually, the Package and Deployment Wizard handles client applications and database file reports, amongst other things. We examine its uses in depth in Chapter 15; for now we will only cover how it impacts component deployment.

Try It Out – Using the Package and Deployment Wizard to Create a Setup File

1. From the Visual Basic IDE choose Package and Deployment Wizard from the Add-ins menu.

2. If the Package and Deployment option is not visible the choose **Add-in Manager**, from the Add-in Manager dialog box, select **Package and Deployment Wizard**.

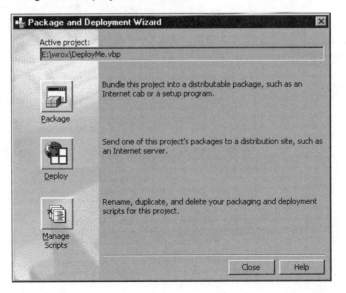

3. Make sure that the **Loaded/Unloaded** and **Load on Startup** boxes are checked. Then click **OK**.

4. Now go back to the **Add-ins Menu** and the **Package and Deployment Wizard** choice will be enabled.

5. Start the **Package and Deployment Wizard**.

6. Select the Package option. From the Package Type screen select Standard Setup Package and click Next.

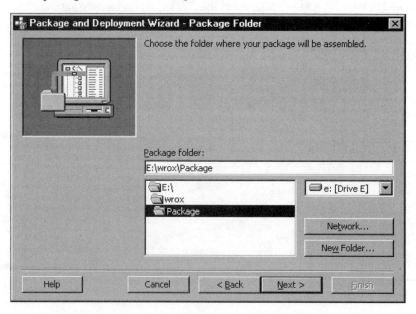

7. From the Package Folder screen we will choose the location on our computer where the setup file and all other necessary files for setup are to be created. For this example, we will locate our package at E:\wrox\Package. Click Next.

8. The next screen of our Wizard is very important because it allows us to specify which files will be contained in package, and will be deployed when the user runs the set-up routine. As we can see, our `deployme.dll` is one of the included files. There are also a number of files that the Wizard supplies to handle the deployment of our component. If we wanted to add more components to our package we would simply click the **Add** button and select the files from the standard file dialog. Click **Next** to continue.

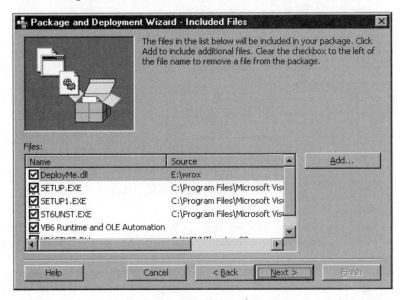

9. This screen allows us to create one large set-up file, or break it up to fit on several floppy disks.

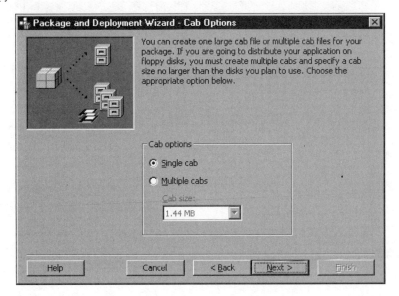

10. This screen asks for the title that will be displayed during installation.

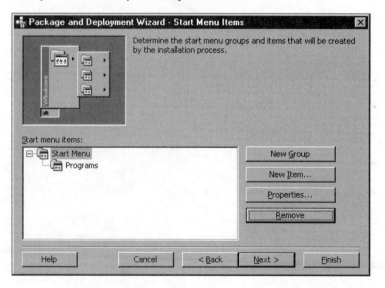

11. Here we specify the group where the installed files can be reached via the **Start** button. This is a limitation when using the Package and Deployment Wizard for stand alone ActiveX DLL files. Since they cannot be started by themselves, it doesn't make sense to give them a start button group and entry, but the Package and Deployment Wizard will not let us remove the group programs. Don't worry, having an ActiveX DLL in the start menu won't hurt anything and can be removed manually, it is just a trade off that you may choose to make for an otherwise easy installation of your component. Click **Next** to continue.

12. On the next screen we can specify where our component(s) will be located. Since our component can be located anywhere (remember location transparency) we could specify any location by typing a path name into the Install Location field. The default is the directory path that is used by the application or component, which is represented by the system variable, $(AppPath). We'll take the default and proceed by clicking Next.

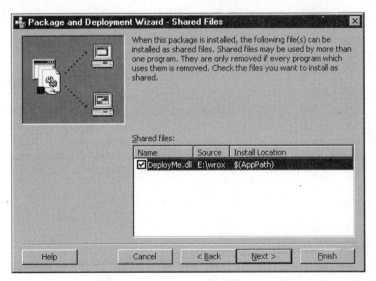

13. This is another important screen in regards to COM components. One of the major benefits of creating COM components is to allow more than one client access to the same component (Code reusability). If we check our ActiveX DLL as shared it won't uninstall our component unless every application using our component is uninstalled. Check the box next to our component and click Next.

14. The last screen allows us to name a script for the settings this Wizard used in case we need to rerun the Wizard using the same parameters. This way we can reference a previously saved script when we start subsequent uses of the Package and Deployment Wizard, and it will fill in all the screens for us. This enables us to run duplicate setup packages or make minor adjustments to an existing script. Accept the default and click Finish.

The Wizard will now create the cab file and place into the directory we specified in Step 3. We can now distribute the files in this directory for easy installation of our component.

The Visual Component Manager

In today's modular environment of component programming it won't be long until you accumulate quite a library of components. If your programming style is anything like mine you probably will end up with components scattered all over the place! Having a tool to help manage and implement these components would be quite useful. The **Visual Component Manager** is such a tool. You probably already have this, as it comes bundled with the Enterprise Editions of Visual Studio 6 and Visual Basic 6.

The Visual Component Manager is a repository for storing our components (and information about our components) and a front end for easy access to them. Now instead of scouring our hard drive for those .dll files, which, in any case, probably have fairly cryptic names, we can use the Visual Component Manager. It will not only have all our components in one place, but also supply us with descriptions and pertinent information about our component. The Visual Component Manager also makes it very easy to share components with other developers, even if those other developers are working remotely.

We need to learn two things to use the Visual Component Manager:

- ❑ How to Add components
- ❑ How to Find and Retrieve components

We will now turn to investigating how these two things are achieved.

Try It Out– Adding Components to the Visual Component Manager

1. Select Visual Component Manager (VCM) from the View menu of the Visual Basic IDE. (If this menu choice is not visible, use the Add-in Manager as described earlier in Step one of the Package and Deployment exercise).

2. Expand the Local Database folder. If you are opening the VCM for the first time you may get a message box asking you if you wish to import the VB templates. Click **Yes**; VCM will then set up a directory of empty folders for you. Otherwise you will have to create and name folders manually (not that you can't add additional folders if you see fit). We will now have a list of folders where we can store components of different types. In this exercise we will add our `Bank_DB.dll` component to VCM. We can use the VCM Publish Wizard to do this. This can be accessed in several ways:

❑ Right click the COM servers folder and choose **New | Component**.

❑ Select the COM Servers folder and click the Publish New Component button on the toolbar.

❑ Right click the component from Visual Basic and choose **Publish Component**.

3. Click **Next** at the introduction screen, which will bring us to the **Title** and **Properties** screen. Here we enter the Component Name, Primary File Name (with it's physical location), the component Type and the Author (the developer who created the component).

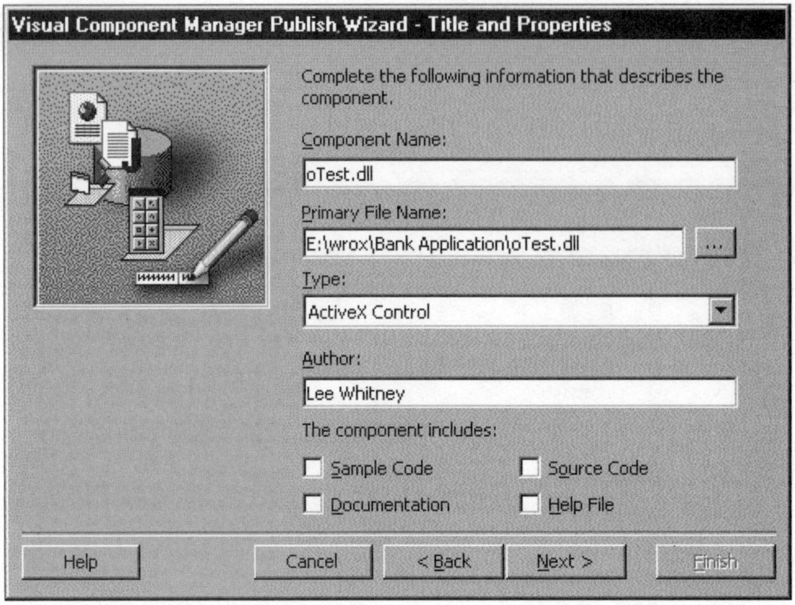

4. The next screen, More Properties, allows us to enter a description. It is important that we provide a detailed explanation of what this component contains, listing the types of properties and methods that it contains. We can also associate keywords with our component; this will help later on when we try looking for it.

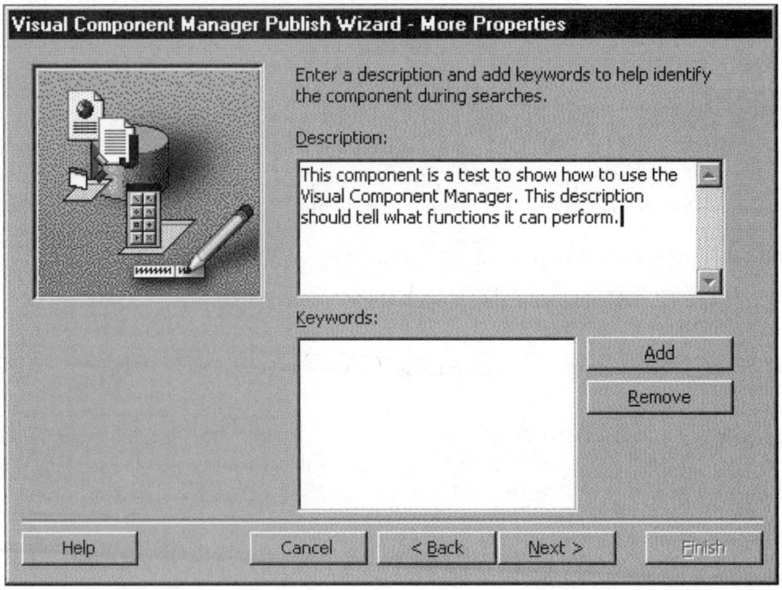

5. Finally, we will get to the COM registration screen. If you check the box next to the component, that tells VCM to automatically register that component for anyone who uses VCM to get copies of it.

6. You can now click Finish. Notice that the component has now been added to VCM's COM Server folder.

Retrieving Components

It wouldn't make much sense keeping a repository of components if there wouldn't be a need to get components for reuse in other projects. The Visual Component Manager (VCM) makes adding a component to projects fairly straightforward. Let's see just how easy it is.

Try It Out – Retrieving Components

1. Open VCM. This can be found in View | Visual Component Manager.

2. Locate the desired component. If you are not sure of its location, you can find it by clicking the search icon (the familiar binoculars). It will then bring up the Visual Component Managers Find dialog box.

3. From this dialogue you can specify the component's name, type or supply text. When you enter text the 'Containing text in:' frame becomes enabled and you can select one or more from the choices of Keywords, Description or Annotations.

4. Double-click the component.

That's all there is to it. The selected component should now have been added to our project.

So far we have learned how to create and register in-process components (ActiveX DLLs) and we've also explored some tools that make working with components a bit easier. Up to this point, we have focused mostly on COM components that are in-process components and run on the same machine as the calling application. Now let's take a look at how we can use remote COM components through a protocol known as **DCOM** – the **Distributed Component Object Model**.

DCOM – Distributed Component Object Model

DCOM seems to always be mentioned in the same breath as COM. This might lead the novice programmer to assume that DCOM is another model for creating components. Let's dispel this notion right now: DCOM is not a new set of rules for creating components, but rather a protocol for using the very same COM components we have discussed in this chapter in a network of two or more computers.

> **DCOM is not used in the WROBA application, and so it will not feature very much in this book. However, for completeness, we will take a brief look at DCOM here. A thorough investigation of DCOM may be found in the Wrox book *VB Com, ISBN number 1861002130.***

Up until now we have discussed component development for use on a single machine, as illustrated here:

DCOM allows us to work with components that exist on machines other than our client application. As we saw earlier, ActiveX DLLs exist in the same process (or memory space) as the calling application. Since we cannot have the same process span two machines, we need to use ActiveX EXE servers when working with DCOM.

DCOM Application Design

Suppose we have developed an application consisting of a Standard Visual Basic .exe client application that serve as the front end, and ActiveX DLL servers that handle validation, business rules and data access tasks respectively. Our application has been developed for a company, which, in order to accommodate a changing marketplace, is regularly updating its business rules. To accommodate these changes, we find we have to consistently upgrade the ActiveX DLL that handles our business rules, recompile it, and then redistribute it to all the client computers that used our application.

To make changing our business rules easier, we might decide to create a DCOM component to handle the business rules and place that on a single server that all the clients would access. This would make maintaining and distributing the business rules code much more efficient and manageable, for instead of having to update a number of machines with new components, we would simply update the DCOM component on the server.

This might seem like a reasonable way of dealing with our circumstances. However, while it might enable easy upgrading of the component, it would quite probably make the users of our application very unhappy. What we had not taken into consideration was the additional network traffic that would occur as the result of implementing a DCOM component. Now every time the clients reference one of our component's properties, it has to make a trip across the network, and, likewise, for every time it uses one of the component's methods. Our once speedy application would slow to a crawl by using DCOM.

As we can see, DCOM gives us some additional issues to consider when designing applications:

- **Network Traffic** – How many calls back and forth across the network need to be made? Don't make two trips across the network, each for one piece of data, if you can make one trip and get both pieces of data.

- **Bandwidth** – How fast can your network handle the passing of data back and forth? Is the network you're developing on indicative of the network used in a production environment?

- **Overhead** – Additional calls back and forth between the clients and servers are necessary to ensure that the network connections are still active. As the number of clients and servers grow, the overhead network traffic will increase exponentially.

Now that we have an overview of DCOM under our belts, let's try creating a simple DCOM component. Keep in mind that this exercise is to illustrate how a DCOM component works, but don't be fooled into thinking that creating real-world distributed enterprise solutions are anywhere near as straightforward.

Try It Out – Creating a Simple DCOM component

We will create a simple component that will do nothing more than create a simple message box. Running the component's method from the client will generate the message box on the server. Granted, this is a useless and potentially dangerous application of DCOM (because if nobody is at the server to reply to the message box it will hang the client application), but adequate for a simple demonstration.

1. Create a new ActiveX EXE project in Visual Basic and rename Project1 to DCOM_Test and rename Class1 to RemoteMsg.

2. Go to the Component tab of the DCOM_Test Properties Window (refer to our exercise of creating a COM component earlier in the chapter for a more detailed explanation of the Project Property dialog box). Check the Remote Server Files checkbox and click OK.

3. Add the following code to `RemoteMsg`.

```
Public Sub RemoteMsg()

   MsgBox "Test Successful"

End Sub
```

4. From the File menu select Make DCOM_Test.EXE... An ActiveX EXE that exists on the same machine would compile into a single `.exe` file, but since we chose the **Remote Server Files** property, the compile process not only creates a `DCOM_Test.exe` file but also two additional files; `DCOM_Test.TLB` and `DCOM.VBR`. The VBR (Visual Basic Registry) file contains a list of registry entries that will be added to the server machine; the TLB file is the **Type Library File**. The goal of DCOM is to allow us to program components without having to be concerned with the network overhead; that's what these files do for us.

5. Use the **Package and Deployment Wizard** from the **Add-Ins** menu to create a package for our component. The process will be the same as that described in the component registration section of the chapter. The only difference will be the addition of the Remote Server prompt which shows our `.VBR` file. Click **Yes** to proceed.

6. Run the `setup.exe` file created by the Package and Deployment Wizard on the server machine. This will install and register our DCOM component.

7. Create the client application by starting a new Standard Visual Basic Project.

8. Set a reference to our `DCOM_Test` component using the **References** dialog box.

9. Add a command button to your form and place the following code in the click event.

```
Private Sub Command1_Click()

   Dim oDCOM As clsRemoteMsg
   Set oDCOM = CreateObject("DCOM_Test.RemoteMsg", "ServerName")
   oDCOM.RemoteMsg
   Set oDCOM = Nothing

End Sub
```

Notice that the above code is very similar to the standard code for calling a COM component. The only substantial difference is that we need to instantiate our object using the CreateObject function and we need to pass it two parameters instead of one. We still pass it the type of object we are creating (in this case DCOM_Test.RemoteMsg) but now we also need to pass it the name of the server where the component is located. The New keyword cannot be used in place of CreateObject because it has no way of indicating a remote location. You will need to replace ServerName with the machine name of the server that is hosting your DCOM component.

How It Works

When we run the client application and click the command button on the client machine, a message box will be generated on the server machine. The Command1click event creates an object named oDCOM from a class named clsRemoteMsg located on a remote machine. We then call the oDCOM's RemoteMsg method to display a message on the remote computer.

From a user's standpoint not much is going on – click on a button and a different computer gets a message – but from a programmers standpoint we've had our first taste of the power of distributed components.

Summary

This chapter began with an explanation of COM components, and we discussed the advantages to COM in our applications. We then introduced the basic building block of COM components; the ActiveX Server. We noted that an ActiveX Server could be either an in-process server (ActiveX DLL) or an out-of-process server (ActiveX EXE), and the advantages and limitations of each.

Next, we walked through the process of creating an ActiveX DLL. In this exercise we examined the principles of threading, version compatibility and instancing. When we had completed the exercise we had created the ActiveX DLLs used in the companion Bank application.

We then saw how our Bank application created instances of the ActiveX DLLs. We also looked at error handling principles as they apply to COM components. Since we are creating an application of multiple components, these components need a way of communicating with each other and the client application, so we examined raising events.

Once we knew how to code COM components, we needed a way to register them for use by our application. We learned how to register them manually with the regsvr32 utility and how to automate the process using the Package and Deployment Wizard. We also used the Visual Component Manager to create a repository for our COM components.

We then briefly explored DCOM and undertook a simple exercise, before moving on to a discussion of optimization issues.

In the next chapter, we will move on to look at Microsoft Transaction Server (MTS) in more depth.

Microsoft Transaction Server

In this chapter, we'll become familiar with the essentials of **Microsoft Transaction Server** (**MTS**). As we mentioned in Chapter 1, MTS provides the plumbing for managing multi-user server applications.

In particular, we'll explore the following topics:

- ❑ Transactions
- ❑ The MTS Management Console
- ❑ COM+
- ❑ Creating transactional components in VB
- ❑ Installing and testing transactional components in MTS

To demonstrate how to go about creating and working with MTS components, we'll use the Try It Outs in this chapter to build a Logger component that creates application logs. We'll also be using MTS in our BigBank case study later in the book.

In the main body of this chapter, we'll be using MTS within NT. Within Windows 2000, the functionality associated with MTS is an integral part of COM+. For the benefit of Windows 2000 users, we'll be discussing the differences between using MTS and COM+ before we engage with creating our own transactional components.

It's not the intention of this chapter to cover every aspect of MTS in detail. Whole books have been written about MTS, and to try to convince you that I'm going to compress such knowledge down to a chapter and still make you a MTS expert would do you a disservice. Rather, I'll concentrate on covering the basics and help you understand the design issues that come with creating transactional components.

If you want more information about MTS, try Professional Visual Basic 6 MTS Programming, ISBN 1861002440, also by Wrox Press.

What is a Transaction?

Before we begin our tour of MTS, we need to understand just what a transaction is.

> **Basically, a transaction is an interaction between two or more parties in which objects are exchanged.**

I'm being very general here in that I'm not defining what these objects are. They can be coins, or stamps, or food items, or anything else that can be exchanged between the parties. The point is that there is something being moved from one party to another.

Let's suppose that Joe asks me if I'll give him my cold fusion reactor for his life savings of $1,000,000. If we both agree on the deal and make the exchange, we've just made a transaction. However, in the business world, transactions can get problematic. What happens if I give my reactor to Joe, but Joe doesn't have the money in return? Obviously, he shouldn't get the reactor. But what if I've agreed to give him the reactor *before* he gives me the money? Joe might decide to bail out and make a patent on a new source of power while I'm left stranded. This is a simplistic example of an incomplete transaction.

In a situation where we want to ensure that a transaction can't be left in this type of unsatisfactory state, we can demand that it must follow four basic rules. Let's look at how we can ensure that a transaction meets certain necessary conditions.

The ACID Test

To make sure that all members of a transaction, and those outside of the transaction, have a reliable view of the transaction, we need to ensure that it passes the **ACID** test. This test has four rules:

- ❑ Atomicity
- ❑ Consistency
- ❑ Isolation
- ❑ Durability

Let's take a look at each one in detail.

Atomicity

This rule states that either all of the actions in the transaction take place or none of them do.

Thus, if Joe didn't have the money, he couldn't leave the exchange with my reactor. Conversely, if he did have the money, I would have to give the reactor to him.

Consistency

This rule states that the results of the transaction must leave the system in a consistent state – that is, at the end of a transaction, the data involved in it must not be left in an invalid state according to any defined business rules.

Let's use an example to help clarify this. If Joe says he's given me $1,000,000 but I actually have $2,000,000 in my hand at the end of the exchange, the consistency rule was violated. Something went wrong somewhere. To satisfy the consistency rule, I need to be able to pocket exactly $1,000,000 – no more, no less.

Isolation

This rule states that no one should be able to see what is going on within our transaction until it's done. Isolation guarantees that multiple transactions can't modify the same data at the same time, and that changes made by one transaction can't be seen by another transaction until the first transaction has finished.

For example, suppose that Susan is involved as a broker between me and Joe. Joe gives Susan money in $100,000 installments. Once I get the entire sum, I hand over the reactor to Susan, who hands it to Joe. If Dan is sitting around waiting for us to complete the transaction in another room, he should never know that at one time, Joe had $400,000 left in his wallet. The only thing Dan can know is that Joe had $1,000,000 at the beginning of the transaction and that he left the transaction with no money but with a reactor in hand. How the transaction occurred is none of Dan's business – he's isolated from the inner workings of the transaction. Also, Dan can't pull anything out of my wallet until I am done talking with Joe and Susan.

Durability

This states that once the transaction is committed, it cannot be lost even if the entire system fails.

Let's say that Joe deposits the money into my bank account online. If the online banking system says that the transfer occurred, Joe should not be able to withdraw any more money from his account (since he's broke at that point). Even if the bank system crashed after the transaction committed, Joe should have a balance of $0.

Transaction programming can be complex and difficult – it takes time and effort to make a reliable transactional system. Thankfully, software development companies have taken the time to create transaction processing (or TP) systems like MTS, which makes the whole process of transaction programming fairly straightforward. So let's move on to discuss what MTS is all about.

MTS: An Overview

When MTS first broke out onto the COM world in 1996, the COM programming world (for the most part) didn't catch on right away. For one thing, the first version of MTS had a fair number of "features" (that is, bugs) and was difficult to work with.

The other, more intractable aspect of MTS, was figuring out what it did! Since it had the word "transaction" in its name, most programmers assumed that transactions were involved – and they were right. However, they were in for quite a surprise if they simply dropped their new components into MTS without taking the time to understand what the MTS environment is all about. MTS changed how COM programmers designed their systems, and it became important to understand just what this change was.

Thankfully, the fog has lifted. Most of the confusing issues, such as stateless programming, have been discussed over and over in newsgroups and articles. If you've never dealt with MTS before, you're probably coming in at a good time – you won't have to suffer the same headaches.

Before we delve into the guts of MTS, we'll take a look at its main selling points.

Transactional Components

So far, we've written components in VB that can act in concert with other components. However, what if we want to ensure that the work we've done in one component will only commit if all of the work done by some other component also commits? For example, you don't want to commit a withdrawal record from your checking account if the deposit to your savings account failed for some unknown reason.

We could try to handle this by ourselves, and we could probably come up with some environment to ensure that components are sound from a transactional standpoint. However, we'd probably end up creating something like MTS!

MTS works with your component to provide correct transactional semantics. It uses the **Distributed Transaction Coordinator** (**DTC**) to do this – a service that manages the transactional activity on your computer. The DTC is not part of MTS; rather, MTS uses the DTC to handle the communication between transactional components. The DTC deals with all of the messy transaction code necessary to ensure that transactional systems across multiple machines work correctly. Thankfully, MTS hides all of the DTC's communication from us, so we usually don't have to worry about the DTC's role.

Object Management

One of the unfortunate results of naming the MTS environment Microsoft **Transaction** Server is the heavy emphasis that places on the transactional nature of some systems. Granted, the ability to use transactions in components shouldn't be underestimated, but MTS is more than that. It also acts as an **Object Request Broker**, managing your component instances and services for your objects.

If you've ever tried to handle configuring an in-process DLL using a tool called DCOMCNFG.EXE, you'll come to appreciate how easy it is to make your in-process COM server available to other machines through MTS.

> In a nutshell, DCOMCNFG.EXE is a tool that was created by Microsoft to allow developers to configure a COM server on one machine, and allow it to be called by a client from another machine. Other than letting you set some security settings, it didn't do much more than that (and it's notorious for being a bit buggy in places). Thankfully, we now have MTS to manage and configure our objects.

Furthermore, MTS has always been designed to handle object pooling (although this feature wasn't enabled until COM+, and VB6 can't create objects that can be pooled in COM+ anyway, due to its threading model). Object pooling allows COM+ to keep a number of objects alive and ready for clients who want to use their services. Although MTS doesn't implement object pooling, it does manage the lifetime of your component, as you'll see shortly.

Configurable Run-Time

MTS is a great example of making a service such as transactional support relatively easy to add and configure at run-time. We'll see later on that you can change the transaction behavior of your object with a simple change of an option button.

In fact, MTS was such a good idea that COM+ made the COM run-time MTS-aware (we'll see why the COM run-time and MTS were separated pre-COM+ later on in the chapter). Thus, in COM+ you can configure services other than transactions at run-time too.

You can also handle security and object lifetime in MTS with ease. Being able to alter services like transactions and security is a great tool to have as a COM programmer.

Interception

Interception plays a critical role within MTS. To implement interception, MTS sets up what is known as a **Context Wrapper** around your object. The client never talks to your server-side component; it's all done through the Context Wrapper. A Context Wrapper mimics your object's interface and "tricks" the client into thinking that they have a direct reference to your object:

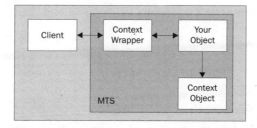

The advantage of this architecture in MTS is twofold:

- ❑ MTS can change the right side of the diagram with the client none the wiser, due to the Context Wrapper.

- ❑ MTS can provide the underlying object with something called a **Context object**. The underlying object can use this context object to find out such things as who created the object, or whether the current method call is in a transaction.

The Context Wrapper examines the class that the client wants to instantiate, and creates an intermediary interface layer that sits between the client and the actual object.

> **Every time an object is created by MTS, the Context object is also created.**

The Context object provides the MTS object with a way to communicate with the MTS executive, as well as being able to retrieve run-time information regarding the context where the object is running. This level of interception plays a big part in a transactional component – we'll see how later on when we deal with transactions and state.

Exploring MTS

We've gone over the basics of MTS, but before we start creating MTS components in VB, let's take a look at the MTS MMC snap-in environment. By covering the MTS environment from the GUI administration tool, you'll see how elements like roles and transactions are handled. We'll also define some of the terminology that we'll run into as we explore the administration tool.

We're assuming here that you've already installed MTS on your computer. If you don't have MTS installed, you can refer to Appendix B for detailed instructions on how to install it.

We're also assuming that, if you're running NT4, you've installed MTS from the Option Pack. If you've installed MTS using the BackOffice typical installation, you may not have the default packages that are present in these screen shots. If you're running Windows 2000, we'll be looking at how the terminology and the COM+ GUI differ from this shortly. The Windows 9x version also looks slightly different.

Try It Out – Navigating the MMC

1. First, start up the management console (or MMC – the first M is for Microsoft). If you're using NT, you can find it from the Start menu under **Programs | Windows NT Option Pack | Microsoft Transaction Server | Transaction Server Explorer**.

You can also type in MMC from the Run command line. If this is the first time you've used the MTS GUI, you'll have to add it by selecting Console | Add/Remove Snap-in.. | Add, and then selecting Microsoft Transaction Server from the dialog that appears.

You should see a screen something like this:

There are a number of ways to navigate through the console window. For example, in the previous window, we could use the Action menu to perform certain tasks related to the active node in the tree (**Microsoft Transaction Server** in our case), or we could right-click on the node and get a pop-up menu. Or we can click on the + sign next to the node to expand it.

2. Expand the Microsoft Transaction Server node until you reach the Packages Installed folder. Then left-click on the Packages Installed node – you should see the following screen:

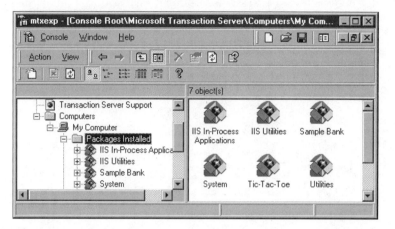

MTS Packages

A package is a container of components with similar characteristics.

We can create our own packages, or import pre-defined MTS packages. In essence, a package acts just like the icon illustrates: it contains objects. We can control security attributes for all of the components within the package.

Try It Out – Introducing the Packages Installed Node

1. Now right-click on the Packages Installed node, but don't select any of the menu options. Just take a look at the options available:

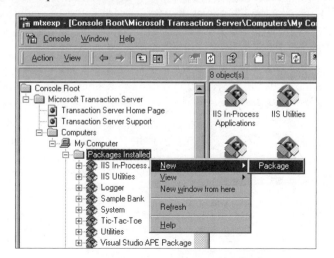

Note that you can add a new package by selecting the New menu option. We'll do that later on when we create our components. As you search the MTS environment, you might note that some of the nodes allow us to create new entities, such as things called roles and users that we'll look at later.

2. Now right-click the Tic-Tac-Toe package and select the Properties menu option to bring up the following dialog window:

```
┌─────────────────────────────────────────────────────────┐
│ Tic-Tac-Toe Properties                          [?][X]   │
├─────────────────────────────────────────────────────────┤
│ ┌General┐ Security │ Advanced │ Identity │ Activation │   │
│                                                          │
│   [icon]    │Tic-Tac-Toe                            │    │
│                                                          │
│   Description:                                            │
│   ┌──────────────────────────────────────────────┐      │
│   │                                                │      │
│   │                                                │      │
│   └──────────────────────────────────────────────┘      │
│                                                          │
│   Package ID:  {8481868B-A008-11D3-857C-000000000000}    │
│                                                          │
│                                                          │
│                                                          │
│                                                          │
│      [  OK  ]   [ Cancel ]   [ Apply ]   [ Help ]        │
└─────────────────────────────────────────────────────────┘
```

We won't investigate the tabs in detail here, but note that we can control package properties such as activation and security. For example, if we click on the Advanced tab, we'll see that it's possible to change the lifetime of the server process. Recall that we talked about the concept of interception in MTS – when we investigate the Context Wrapper in detail, we'll see that the shutdown time affects the lifetime of the context object.

3. Now drill down in the Tic-Tac-Toe package, and open up the Components node. You should see two components listed: tServer.Computer and tServer.Human. As the names imply, these are the ProgIDs of the classes.

We can include classes from different components in the same package if we want to, but we should make sure that members of a package have similar characteristics for consistency's sake. For example, we could add the Logger component that we create later on in the chapter to this package, but that wouldn't make much sense, as it doesn't have a lot to do with playing tic-tac-toe.

4. Now right-click on the tServer.Computer node and open up the Properties window:

This is the dialog box where you can control the transactional behavior of your component.

5. Open the Transaction tab:

We'll discover exactly what these four values mean when we create our own components, but for now just be aware that they specify to what extent the component supports transactions. The important thing to note is that we can change this value whenever we want, without having to recompile our COM server. If we need to alter the component's transactional behavior, all it takes is to change one option.

6. Cancel this screen, and drill down further into the tServer.Computer node. Here we'll find the Role Membership node, which exists off each Components node:

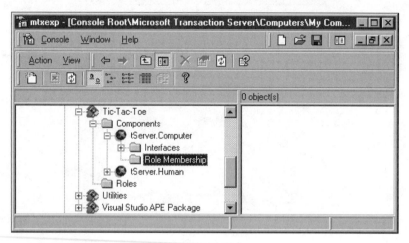

Let's take a look at what this node involves.

Roles

A role is a collection of users that have similar security characteristics.

Roles enable us to assign particular permissions to different groups of users. For instance, we could create two roles, Guest and PowerUser, and assign *everyone* in our organization to the Guest role, but only assign *specific users* to the PowerUser role. We would add these roles to the Role Membership node.

The Role Membership node is another collection – it's a collection of roles. Therefore, you could add the Group role to tServer.Human's Role Membership collection and the PowerUser role to tServer.Computer's Role Membership collection. The nice aspect about roles is that they enable us to grant permissions on a role-by-role basis. So, if you needed to remove a person from having access to your components, you simply remove them from a role. You don't have to hunt around in each component to remove the user.

Note that the Windows 9x version of MTS does not support role-based security.

Monitoring Transactions

Before we leave our quick tour of the MTS environment, let's take a look at two screens that can help us in figuring out the status and usage of our components.

Try It Out – Monitoring Transactions

1. Click on the Transaction List node, and the following list will appear on the right-hand side of the window:

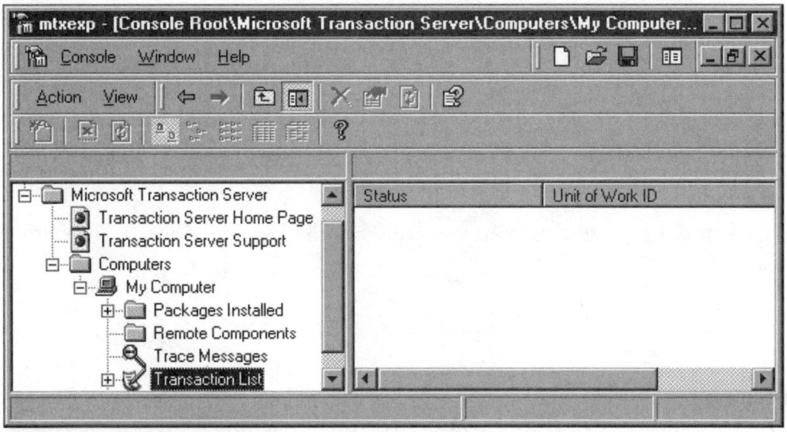

When components are running, we'll see a list of any current transactions and their status. However, as you can see, my computer wasn't very busy when I took the screen shot. Just remember that if we want to ensure that a transaction is currently running, we can refer to this screen.

2. The other screen of note is the Transaction Statistics screen, which you can view by clicking on the Transaction Statistics node:

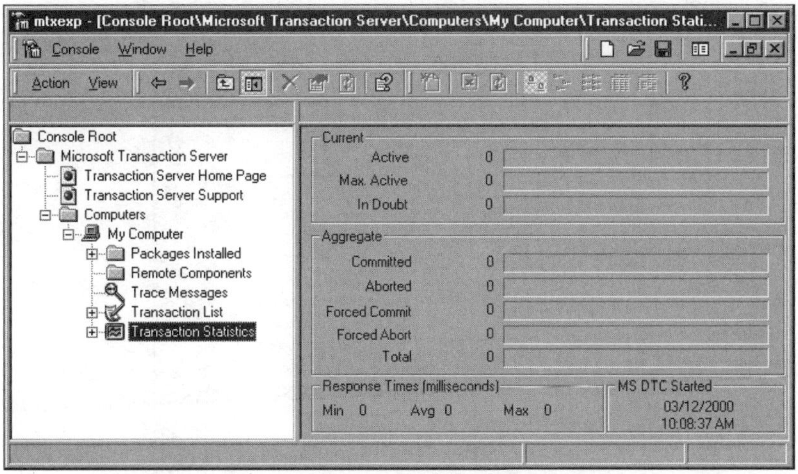

149

This screen isn't exhaustive in scope, but it does give you some interesting statistics. You can see how many transactions were created, committed and aborted since the DTC was started. You can also get a general feel for how fast your components are performing by looking at the Response Times statistics.

This was a very brief overview of the MTS environment, but we'll make more use of the MTS MMC as we move through the chapter.

> **There is one warning to give you if you start playing with the MTS settings. If you enable security on the System package and nobody is assigned to the Administrator role, you'll lock you and everyone else out from MTS. As you can guess, this is not a pretty situation to be in, so always make sure someone is in that role.**

Before going on to creating a transactional component, we'll take a quick look at using transactional objects within COM+. There are some important issues that COM+ users need to be aware of when following through the exercises below, and this is the time to get those preliminaries out of the way.

Users of NT impatient to get onto the exercises can skip the next section – unless you want to find out what you're missing.

COM+

In this whirlwind tour of COM+, we'll focus primarily on administrative issues. Some important terminology in COM+ has changed, so it will be worthwhile taking a brief look at what to expect when you move from development within NT to a Windows 2000 context.

Try It Out – The COM+ Administrator

The first thing that may throw us when encountering COM+ is that the MTS Administrator has been renamed **Component Services**.

1. It can be found by clicking the Start button and selecting Settings | Control Panel. Double-click the Administration tools, and double-click Component Services:

As you can see, there is still much in common between the MTS Administrator and the Component Services interface.

2. Expand the Component Services node until you reach COM+Applications. In COM+, an **application** is equivalent to an MTS package:

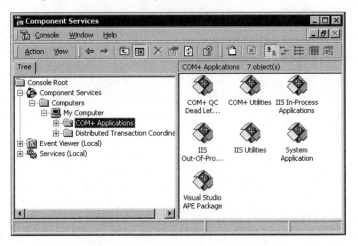

You may have seen the equation COM + MTS = COM+, and this screen shot illustrates that idea. Every COM server that we install through the Component Services administrator is a COM+ application, and every COM+ application now has a Context Wrapper and a context object.

3. Let's drill down into COM+ Applications – specifically, click on the Visual Studio APE Package:

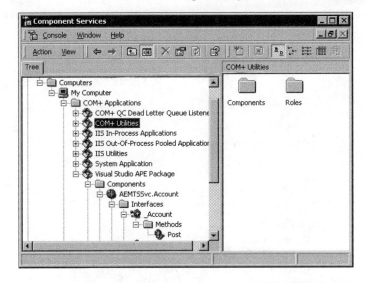

As you can see, COM+ applications show not only the components and the interfaces supplied by that component, it also shows the methods available for that interface.

151

4. Right-click on Post and select **Properties**. You'll get the following dialog window:

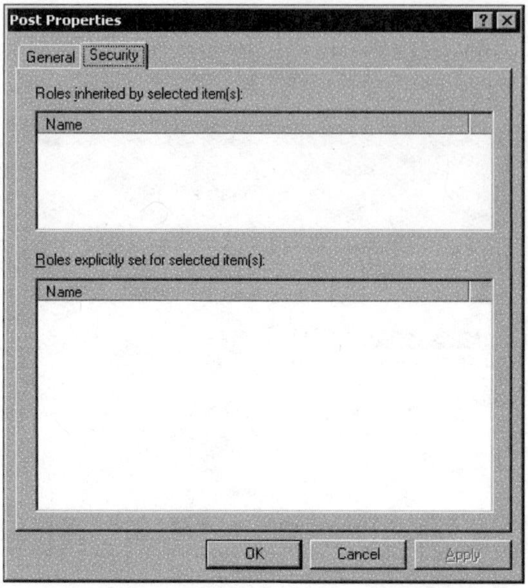

So we can set up security down to the method level in COM+. That's about as fine-grained as we can get – in the MTS world, security can only be enforced down to the interface level from the MMC. We can still perform security checks programmatically in each method in MTS, but COM+ removes that coding burden from you.

5. Let's take a brief look at the services that are available at the component level. Right-click on AEMTSSvc.Account, and select **Properties**:

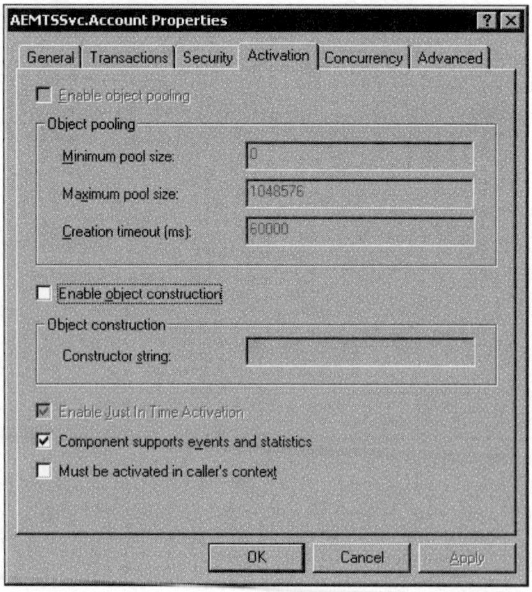

Notice that we have more to choose from. We still have the Transaction tab, but we also have Concurrency options and Object pooling parameters. We can even pass in a string to our object as a constructor value, so long as the object implements the IObjectConstruct interface.

6. Finally, if you're looking for the transaction statistics screens, they're now under the Distributed Transaction Coordinator node:

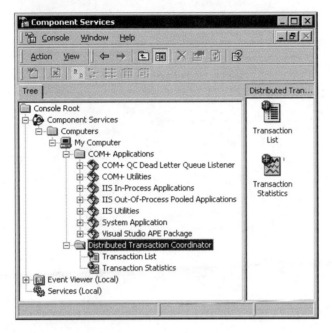

One Minor Annoyance in COM+

Before we leave the COM+ world, there is one thing that we should be wary about if we want to move components from MTS to the COM+ environment – that's the MTS type library name. For example, as we'll soon see, when using MTS it's necessary to declare, within VB, that we want to implement the ObjectControl. This is done in the following way:

```
Implements MTxAS.ObjectControl
```

This references the **Microsoft Transaction Server Type Library**.

However, if we open our COM server project in VB and take a look at the References screen, we might be in for a surprise – there is no Microsoft Transaction Server Type Library. Instead, we have the **COM+ Services Type Library**:

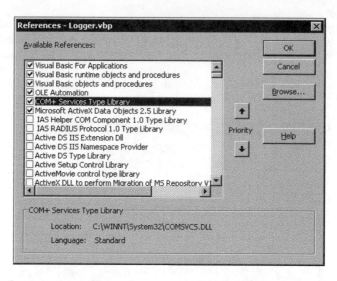

This may not seem that important. However, it means that the previous `Implements` statement no longer works! The code that we would have to use with COM+ is:

```
Implements COMSVCSLib.ObjectControl
```

Compiled components will still work, as the interface identifier hasn't changed. However, just be aware that if pre-COM+ applications are opened up in VB on a W2K machine, you'll get compilation errors.

It's beyond the scope of this section to cover everything, but as we can see, COM+ gives us significantly more to configure and control than MTS. COM+ has moved far beyond merely managing transactions.

Creating Transactional Components in VB

Now that we've taken a look at the MTS MMC environment, and made a brief exploration of COM+, let's dive in and create a transactional component in VB.

We'll describe the component we're going to be creating in this chapter, what its purpose is, and what the interface is to the component. We'll start by setting up the project in VB. Later in the chapter, after we've looked into the theory a little more, we'll code the component in VB, and add in the necessary code to ensure that our component is MTS-aware. By creating a transactional component in VB you'll become more familiar with some of the concepts and terms that we allude to throughout the chapter.

The Logger Component

Most of the time, we as VB developers are used to having a rich debugging environment to test our systems in. However, when our components are running in a production environment, we usually don't have the luxury to bring the server to a halt and use VB to debug the component. Therefore, one simple solution is to create a logging component that we can use in our server components to log certain events. We could use this component in our case study to log when we withdrew money from our account, or when a quarterly report was created.

Granted, we can use the LogEvent of the App object, but we are limited as to the information that can be added to the EventLog (assuming that our application is running on NT or W2K). We could use NT Event Application Programming Interface (API) functions to add a richer set of data, but using the APIs can be problematic. For simplicity's sake, it's useful to have a trace component hanging around to log system information.

So let's create a component to persist system event information. We'll allow the client to set information such as:

- ❑ The severity level of the message
- ❑ The name of the component that the message came from
- ❑ The method that the message was created in
- ❑ A timestamp
- ❑ The message itself

We'll also give the client a method to signal when the data should be persisted.

Properties and Methods of the Logger Component

Our class will have five properties:

- ❑ ClassName
- ❑ Message
- ❑ MessageCode
- ❑ MethodName
- ❑ Timestamp

We'll also include two methods

- ❑ Submit
- ❑ Reset

We'll use Submit to add our information to the log, and if we want to add another message we can call Reset, which will reset the state of the object. Submit takes one argument of type MessageLevel – this allows the client to specify the severity of the message, along with submitting a code value via MessageCode.

Creating the VB Project

Now that we have a good idea as to how the component is going to work, let's jump into VB and find out how we get MTS into the picture. We'll go through the setup first, and then we'll explore the steps in more detail.

Try It Out – Creating the Project

1. Start Visual Basic, and create a new ActiveX DLL project.

2. Name the project Logger, and name the current class module available in the project CLogger. Also, set the MTSTransactionMode property of the CLogger class to 2 – RequiresTransaction:

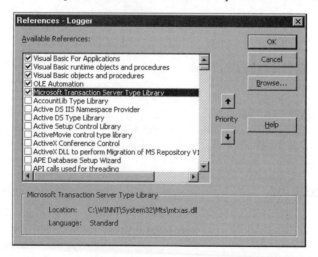

This means that the component will always run under a transaction (we'll explain what the values of MTSTransactionMode mean in the next section).

3. Select the References menu option under Project, and select the Microsoft Transaction Server Type Library list item (in Windows 2000 select the COM+ Services Type Library). This will allow us to implement interfaces in our component that MTS will use:

4. Select the Logger Properties menu option under Project, and select the Unattended Execution check box on the General tab.

Transaction Modes

We've seen four transaction values in the MTS MMC, and we just saw four very similar ones pop up in a VB class, so I think this a good time to actually explain what these values are. They determine how a component will behave in a transaction. Let's go through each one in detail (the VB keyword is the one in parentheses), and then we'll walk through some examples to illustrate how these settings affect component interactions.

Requires a Transaction (RequiresTransaction)

If a component is configured with this value, it will always exist in a transaction. If a transaction doesn't exist when this component is created, a new one is created for the component.

Requires a New Transaction (RequiresNewTransaction)

This option requires a component to always have a new transaction created when it's created, even if a transaction currently exists. This new transaction is completely isolated from any pre-existing transactions in the current call flow, and its finishing status (a commit or abort) does not affect the other transactions.

Supports Transactions (UsesTransactions)

If a current transaction exists, the component will jump right into it. If a transaction doesn't exist, it's no big deal – it'll work just fine without one and it will not create a new transaction.

Does not Support Transactions (NoTransactions)

If we want our component to run under MTS to obtain contextual information, but want it to be oblivious to the transactional semantics of the ACID test, then we should select this value. The component will never exist in a transaction, and nothing that happens within the component will affect the outcome of transactions involving other components in the application. In essence, this value should be selected for components that are not transactional.

How Transaction Modes Work

It's one thing to know what the values are; it's another thing to know how they work so you can design your systems correctly. So let's take a look at a few examples to show what happens when components call other components with different transaction mode values.

Let's suppose that we have four components; A, B, C, and D. A supports transactions, B requires a transaction, C requires a new transaction, and D doesn't support transactions. Now what would happen if A created B, which created C, which created D?

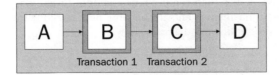

157

Since A supports transactions but no previous transaction was created, A doesn't exist in a transaction. But B requires a transaction, so MTS creates one. C, however, wants to live in its own world, so another, independent transaction is created. However, D doesn't care one whit about transactions, so MTS leaves it be. Note that if C fails but B succeeds, B's work is committed.

Now what would happen if both A and B require a transaction, C doesn't support transactions, and D requires a transaction, and we had the same call flow as before?

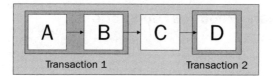

Since A requires a transaction, a new one is made. This time, A and B share the same transaction – since A calls B and B requires a transaction, B can share A's transaction. However, since C doesn't support transactions, D has to make a new one. As you can see, the transactional flow is cut off. If we wanted to ensure that A, B, and D either all succeeded or all failed, we would need to do one of two things; move D before C or make C support or require transactions (but not require a *new* one).

Creating Instances of MTS Components

As we saw in Chapter 3, there are two ways that we can create instances of objects from our VB code: the CreateObject function and the New Keyword. MTS provides us with another method: the CreateInstance function. The differences between these methods are subtle, but important.

If we use the CreateObject function or the New keyword, our object is created through COM, which doesn't recognize such things as Context Wrappers and the Context object. That's OK if we're just creating one instance of an MTS component, but what about the case where we're creating a new instance of a component within an existing MTS object. Then, the new object won't inherit the transactional and security information from the Context object of the existing object.

If we want the new object to inherit the context of the existing object, we need to use the CreateInstance function, which makes object creation requests to MTS rather than COM.

Tying Transaction Objects Together

We've just seen that the root object of the transaction determines the characteristics of the transaction flow across the objects. At first glance, this may not seem like a big deal, but consider the following circumstance.

We have two objects, A and B, and both require a transaction. Initially, they were not designed to work together, but in the course of business events it's become necessary for the two to meet. A client is using the two objects together as the following diagram shows:

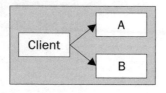

Here's the problem. When the client creates A, MTS will give A its own transaction. Similarly, when B is instantiated by the client, it will also get its own transaction. Therefore, if A decides to rollback the transaction, it will have no effect on what B decides to do. This isn't good if we want the two components to share a transaction – for example, in the case of a banking transaction involving a withdrawal and a subsequent deposit, it would mean a withdrawal can rollback, but the deposit may commit. Remember, it is the root object that determines the transaction flow as the previous transaction examples demonstrated. Since B was not instantiated by A, it doesn't share A's transaction:

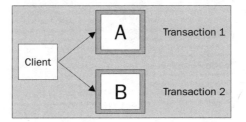

However, there is a way around this. MTS provides something called the **Transaction Context** object.

The TransactionContext Object

The `TransactionContext` object is part of the **Transaction Context Type Library** DLL (or the `txctx.dll` COM server if you prefer). We won't investigate this DLL in detail, but the nice thing is that the `TransactionContext` object gives you control over transactions.

The `TransactionContext` object requires a new transaction, so it will always have its own transaction. Furthermore, it has its own `CreateInstance` method, which will create objects for you in its transaction. The apparent beauty from the client's perspective is that it can control the transaction, as the following code snippet demonstrates:

```
Dim oTX As TransactionContext
Dim oA as A
Dim oB as B

Set oTX = CreateObject("TxCtx.TransactionContext")
Set oA = oTX.CreateInstance("SomeLib.A")
Set oB = oTX.CreateInstance("SomeLib.B")

' Do some work with oA and oB
' and commit their work.
```

Of course, if the work done by A or B isn't sucessful, the transaction will still fail. But if the client application isn't satisfied with the end results, it can call abort the transaction via the `TransactionContext` object.

However, as good as this appears, don't be tempted by this object! By using the `TransactionContext` object, you've added logic to your client that shouldn't be there. The client shouldn't determine the outcome of the transaction; that's the business object's job. There are other, more technical reasons not to use this approach, but I recommend that you avoid this approach.

The Wrapper Object

Rather than using the `TransactionContext` object, we can use a **Wrapper** object. This creates the transaction and delegates the business logic (that is, the calls to A and B) for you:

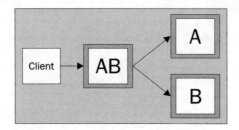

The `Wrapper` object resides in MTS and, if it's marked to get a new transaction, it will always have a transaction when it's called. In this case, our client code ends up as:

```
Dim oWrap as ABWrapper

Set oWrap = CreateObject("SomeWrapperLib.ABWrapper")
oWrap.DoWork
```

This is a much more elegant approach and eliminates the problems with the `TransactionContext` object.

Although these are theoretical examples, the results are important. We need to understand how transactions flow in a sequence of component calls, because subtle changes in the flow can adversely affect the outcome. I'll illustrate this point later on in the chapter.

Now that we've covered transaction modes and how they affect transactional flow, let's move on to the concept of how components vote for the success or failure of a transaction.

MTS Objects

The Microsoft Transaction Server Type Library defines four objects that we'll use in our programs when we're dealing with MTS:

- ❑   `ObjectContext`
- ❑   `SecurityProperty`
- ❑   `ObjectControl`
- ❑   `AppServer`

Let's discuss each of these in more detail.

The Context Object

The Context (or ObjectContext) object is set up for us by MTS to access context information. In MTS, this information ranges from the current transactional state to the name of the client that is really making the call on your object.

> *Note that the Context Object is different to the Context Wrapper. They are two different entities with different purposes. Just remember that the "thing" around your object is the Context Wrapper, and the "thing" beside your object is the Context Object*

The following is a list of the properties available from the Context object (we'll see in the next section how to get a reference to this object):

Property	Description
Count	Returns the total number of named properties available from the Context object.
Item	Returns the value of the given named property.
Security	Returns a reference to a Security object (discussed in the next section).

And the methods available from the Context object are as follows:

Method	Description
CreateInstance	Creates a new object with the current object's context. Do not use New or CreateObject within a MTS object if you want to preserve the context of the object.
DisableCommit	Lets MTS know that you're not satisfied with the current state of the work.
EnableCommit	Lets MTS know that you're satisfied with the current state of the work.
IsCallerInRole	Checks to see if the object's caller is in the specified role.
IsInTransaction	Returns True if the object is currently involved in a transaction.
IsSecurityEnabled	If the object is not run under MTS, this method returns False.
SetAbort	Lets MTS know you're done with your work and you don't want to commit it.
SetComplete	Lets MTS know you're done with your work and you want to commit it.

We can use some of these methods to let MTS know the outcome of a transaction. Let's see exactly how our object casts its vote for the success or failure of the transaction.

Transaction Voting

We just saw how objects can participate in transactions with other objects without knowledge of the other objects that are in the transaction. But how does MTS know if it should commit or rollback any changes that were made in the transaction? Well, MTS uses a voting scheme to determine the outcome of the transaction.

Basically, if all of the objects are satisfied with their work and vote for a commit, MTS will commit the work. If one or more objects are not satisfied with their work, MTS will roll back all of the changes. Pretty simple, isn't it?

Actually, MTS uses two bits to manage the object's status relative to the transaction. These are known as the **consistency bit** (which is set to `True` when the object is created) and the **done bit** (which is set to `False` on object creation). By calling the following functions, you manipulate the values of these bits so that the MTS executive knows what to do with your object's state. Let's take a look at how we can cast our vote.

SetComplete

This method says to MTS, "I'm done, and I'm satisfied with my work." If every object in the transactions calls this method, the transaction will commit. This sets the done and consistency bits to `True`.

SetAbort

This method says to MTS, "I'm done, and I'm not satisfied with my work." In this case, it doesn't matter what any other objects in the transaction vote – the transaction will be rolled back. This also sets the done bit to `True` but the consistency bit to `False`.

DisableCommit

This method says to MTS, "I'm currently not satisfied with the state of my work." If no other calls are made within the current transaction to the object in question or any other objects, MTS will rollback the transaction. However, if this object is called again, it can cast its vote to change the outcome of the transaction if it so desires. This method sets the consistency bit to `False`.

EnableCommit

This method says to MTS, "I'm currently satisfied with the state of my work." This is the opposite of `DisableCommit`: if need be, MTS can commit the transaction. This sets the consistency bit to `True`.

A Quick Note on the Bit Values

For each of the methods, we've described what MTS does and how the bit values are manipulated. It's important to note that the done bit is the only one that notifies MTS that you are done with everything you will do in the current transaction (we'll see how that affect the object lifeline later on in the chapter).

If a method finishes and the done bit is set to `True`, MTS inspects the value of the consistency bit. If it's `False`, the transaction will not commit. Remember that since this bit is set to `True` on object creation, it takes a call to either `SetAbort` or `DisableCommit` to flip the state of this bit to `False`. It only takes one consistency bit value from one of the objects within the entire transaction to be `False` for the whole transaction to rollback.

We'll use these methods later on in the chapter.

New to COM+: ContextInfo

COM+ gives you access to another object via the Context object's interface – the ContextInfo object, which you can access via the ContextInfo property from the Context object. This object allows you to get more information on the current transaction and the current activity.

Here is a list of the methods that are available from ContextInfo:

Method	Description
IsInTransaction	Indicates if the object is within a transaction.
GetTransaction	Returns a reference to an object that implements the ITransaction interface.
GetTransactionId	Returns the transaction identifier.
GetActivityId	Returns the activity identifier.
GetContextId	Returns the context identifier.

Note that GetTransaction returns yet another object that implements the ITransaction interface. Basically, this interface has three methods: Commit, Abort, and GetTransactionInfo. The third method takes a UDT as an argument to return information about the transaction to the caller.

As we're concentrating on functionality that's available to both NT and Windows 2000 users in this book, we won't cover this interface further. If you want to know more, swing by Microsoft's web site for further information on ITransaction.

Let's look at the other objects we'll come across with MTS.

The SecurityProperty Object

As you saw in the table above, the Context object has a property called Security. This is an object called SecurityProperty. This can give us all sorts of information about the client that is using our object.

Below is a list of all of the methods available from this object:

Method	Description
GetDirectCallerName	Returns the user name associated with the process that called the current method.
GetDirectCreatorName	Returns the user name associated with the process that created the object.
GetOriginalCallerName	Returns the user name associated with the base process that called the current method.
GetOriginalCreatorName	Returns the user name associated with the base process that created the object.

These methods are very helpful if you want to log who is calling your objects.

The ObjectControl Interface

During the lifetime of an object, we can receive notifications from MTS of certain events that have taken place by implementing the `ObjectControl` interface. When MTS creates our objects, it checks to see if they implement `ObjectControl`. If they do, it will call the interface's methods. These are:

- ❑ Activate
- ❑ Deactivate
- ❑ CanBePooled

Let's take a look at each method on the interface in detail.

Activate

This method is called when MTS has created the Context Wrapper around your object and has added information to the context object. MTS will not call any methods on an object until it has called `Activate`. Therefore, we can use this notification to grab a reference to the context object and perform any other initializations we want that are relative to any MTS-related activity.

As we mentioned, MTS calls `Activate` after it has created the context object. Therefore, don't try to get a reference to this object in `Class_Initialize`, because it won't be there. Similarly, don't use the context object in `Class_Terminate`; the context object is gone by that time.

Deactivate

This is the opposite of `Activate`. MTS will call this method when it's done with an object, but before it releases its reference to the object. Therefore, we can release any resources at this point, before the object is terminated.

CanBePooled

This method has been around since MTS 1.0. Even though the first (and second) version of MTS didn't support object pooling, it included this method in the interface contract for future compatibility.

However, as a VB6 developer, you should always return a `False` value for this method. The reasons are a bit technical for our discussion, but it has to do with threading, apartments, and how VB handles variables in a threading environment. If you were to return a `True` value, you may experience some very weird and unexpected behavior.

COM+ does support object pooling, but due to the limitations in VB up to version 6, you should still return a `False` value. However, there are substantial enhancements in the works for VB7, so you may be able to pool your VB7 objects.

The AppServer Object

`AppServer` defines two methods:

- ❑ GetObjectContext
- ❑ SafeRef

This is a **GlobalMultiUse** object, which is provided within the MTS environment – that means it's available anywhere within your project via the `AppServer` object reference and does not need to be created via the `New` operator or the `CreateObject()` method.

These return references to our MTS object from two different perspectives.

GetObjectContext

> `GetObjectContext` returns the current `Context` object for your object.

Just remember to avoid this call during initialization and termination of your object, because the `Context` object doesn't exist.

```
Set objContext = GetObjectContext
```

SafeRef

> `SafeRef` returns a reference to the Context Wrapper for your MTS object.

We can call `SafeRef` directly from our code. The following tells our MTS object to return a reference to itself:

```
Set oRef = SafeRef(Me)
```

We can also scope it with the `AppServer` object. The following returns the same reference:

```
Set oRef = AppServer.SafeRef(Me)
```

Recall that a Context Wrapper wraps each object in MTS, but that this wrapper is not part of the object itself. Thus, if we had a method on our object called `ReturnMe` that was implemented like this:

```
Public Sub ReturnMe() As CLogger

    Set ReturnMe = Me

End Sub
```

we would lose the Context Wrapper – as the Context Wrapper is not a part of our object's supported COM interfaces, we would have a normal `CLogger` object reference returned. This can lead to all sorts of problems, because MTS no longer has tabs on the calls being made to the object. Remember, the COM run-time is not aware of the MTS run-time, so whatever MTS is adding onto your object is above and beyond what COM knows about.

If we need to pass a reference to our object to the outside world, we can use `SafeRef`:

```
Public Sub ReturnMe() As CLogger

    Set ReturnMe = SafeRef(Me)

End Sub
```

Now the Context Wrapper is preserved.

> **SafeRef** should only be called when you want give a reference to your MTS object to code that is external to your object.

New to COM+: IContextState

When you call `GetContextObject`, you get an object reference back that implements the `IObjectContext` interface. If you're using COM+, you can also set the return value back from `GetObjectContext` to an `IContextState` interface, like this:

```
Dim objContextState As COMSVCSLib.IContextState
Set objContextState = GetObjectContext
```

`IContextState` has four methods that allow you to manipulate the values of the consistency and done bits independently. Recall that the `SetComplete` and `SetAbort` manipulate both bit values; `IcontextState` gives you the ability to manipulate either one.

Here's a listing of this interface's methods:

Method	Description
SetDeactivationOnReturn	Sets the done bit to either True or False.
GetDeactivationOnReturn	Returns the value of the done bit.
SetMyTransactionVote	Sets the value of the consistency bit to either True or False
GetMyTransactionVote	Returns the value of the consistency bit.

That's just about all we need to know in order to be able to get down to some serious coding in our MTS component.

Implementing CLogger

So let's move on to implementing our CLogger class.

Try It Out – Making CLogger MTS-Aware

1. Open up the CLogger class, and add the following code to the General Declarations section:

```
Option Explicit

Implements MTxAS.ObjectControl
' If using COM+ use Implements COMSVCSLib.ObjectControl

Public Enum MessageLevel
   Informational = 0
   Warning
   Critical
End Enum

Private Const LOG_FILE As String = "\logfile.txt"

Private m_dteTimestamp As Date
Private m_objContext As ObjectContext
Private m_strClassName As String
Private m_strMessage As String
Private m_strMessageCode As String
Private m_strMethodName As String
```

2. Select the ObjectControl member of the Object list in the code editor, and implement the three methods that are listed. Add the following code to these methods:

```
Private Sub ObjectControl_Activate()

    Set m_objContext = GetObjectContext

End Sub

Private Sub ObjectControl_Deactivate()

    Set m_objContext = Nothing

End Sub

Private Function ObjectControl_CanBePooled() As Boolean

    ObjectControl_CanBePooled = False

End Function
```

167

3. Now implement the `Get` and `Let` property methods for each property in the `CLogger` definition:

```
Public Property Get ClassName() As String

    ClassName = m_strClassName

End Property
```

```
Public Property Let ClassName(ByVal Val As String)

    m_strClassName = Val

End Property
```

```
Public Property Get Message() As String

    Message = m_strMessage

End Property
```

```
Public Property Let Message(ByVal Val As String)

    m_strMessage = Val

End Property
```

```
Public Property Get MessageCode() As String

    MessageCode = m_strMessageCode

End Property
```

```
Public Property Let MessageCode(ByVal Val As String)

    m_strMessageCode = Val

End Property
```

```
Public Property Get MethodName() As String

    MethodName = m_strMethodName

End Property
```

```
Public Property Let MethodName(ByVal Val As String)

    m_strMethodName = Val

End Property
```

```
Public Property Get Timestamp() As Date

    Timestamp = m_dteTimestamp

End Property
```

```
Public Property Let Timestamp(ByVal Val As Date)

    m_dteTimestamp = Val

End Property
```

4. Add the following code for the two methods, Submit and Reset:

```
Public Function Submit(ByVal Level As MessageLevel) As Boolean

    On Error GoTo Error_Submit

    Dim lngFile As Long

    lngFile = FreeFile

    Open App.Path & "\" & LOG_FILE For Append As lngFile

'   Write the data.
    Write #lngFile, "Time: " & CStr(m_dteTimestamp)
    Write #lngFile, "Class Name: " & m_strClassName
    Write #lngFile, "Method Name: " & m_strMethodName
    Write #lngFile, "Message Code: " & m_strMessageCode
    Write #lngFile, "Level: " & Level
    Write #lngFile, "Message: " & m_strMessage
    Write #lngFile, vbCrLf

    Close lngFile

    m_objContext.SetComplete

    Exit Function

Error_Submit:

    If lngFile <> 0 Then
     Close lngFile
    End If

    m_objContext.SetAbort
    Err.Raise Err.Number, "Submit", Err.Description

End Function
```

```
Public Sub Reset()

    ObjectReset

End Sub
```

```
Private Sub ObjectReset()

    On Error Resume Next

    m_dteTimestamp = Null
    m_strClassName = vbNullString
    m_strMessage = vbNullString
    m_strMessageCode = vbNullString
    m_strMethodName = vbNullString

End Sub
```

5. Compile the server as `Logger.DLL`. We've now created our transactional component. We'll explore how to implement it shortly.

How It Works

In the first step, we add the `MessageLevel` enumeration, which allows the client to define what kind of message we're adding to our log:

```
Public Enum MessageLevel
    Informational = 0
    Warning
    Critical
End Enum
```

We've also added a constant that defines what file we should add our messages to:

```
Private Const LOG_FILE As String = "\logfile.txt"
```

We also added some private member variables, which we'll use to hold the values that define the message, such as when the message was created (`m_dteTimestamp`) and what the message is (`m_strMessage`).

```
Private m_dteTimestamp As Date
Private m_objContext As ObjectContext
Private m_strClassName As String
Private m_strMessage As String
Private m_strMessageCode As String
Private m_strMethodName As String
```

In the second step, we implement the ObjectControl interface. We grab a reference to the context object in the Activate method:

```
Set m_objContext = GetObjectContext
```

and we release it in the Deactivate method:

```
Set m_objContext = Nothing
```

We also made sure we return a False value for CanBePooled:

```
ObjectControl_CanBePooled = False
```

In the third step, we create all of the Gets and Lets methods for CLogger's properties. To recap from earlier, these are:

❑   ClassName

❑   Message

❑   MessageCode

❑   MethodName

❑   Timestamp

Finally, in the fourth step, we implement the Reset and Submit methods.

Reset simply delegates the call to ObjectReset, a private method that resets the member variables to initial conditions:

```
m_dteTimestamp = Null
m_strClassName = vbNullString
m_strMessage = vbNullString
m_strMessageCode = vbNullString
m_strMethodName = vbNullString
```

Submit opens a log file and adds the object information to the file:

```
Dim lngFile As Long

lngFile = FreeFile

Open App.Path & "\" & LOG_FILE For Append As lngFile

' Write the data.
Write #lngFile, "Time: " & CStr(m_dteTimestamp)
Write #lngFile, "Class Name: " & m_strClassName
Write #lngFile, "Method Name: " & m_strMethodName
Write #lngFile, "Message Code: " & m_strMessageCode
Write #lngFile, "Level: " & Level
Write #lngFile, "Message: " & m_strMessage
Write #lngFile, vbCrLf

Close lngFile
```

If this all completes succesfully, we call `SetComplete`.

```
m_objContext.SetComplete
```

However, if an error occurs during `Submit`'s execution, we call `SetAbort` and then raise the error back to the client:

```
Error_Submit:

  If lngFile <> 0 Then
    Close lngFile
  End If

  m_objContext.SetAbort
  Err.Raise Err.Number, "Submit", Err.Description
```

Now that we have created a transactional component, we need to get it running under MTS. We also need a test client to see how the component is working. Let's tackle the installation problem first, and then we'll address the test client issue.

Try It Out – Installing the Logger Component

1. Initially, we want to create a package. Start the MTS MMC program, and drill down to the **Packages Installed** node. Right-click on that node, and select **New | Package**. (In COM+, drill down to **COM+ Applications**. Right-click and select **New | Application**. You'll see an additional splash screen – just click **Next** to get rid of it.) You should see the following dialog window:

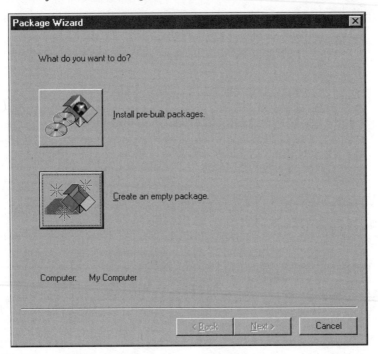

2. Select Create an empty package. You should get the following dialog box:

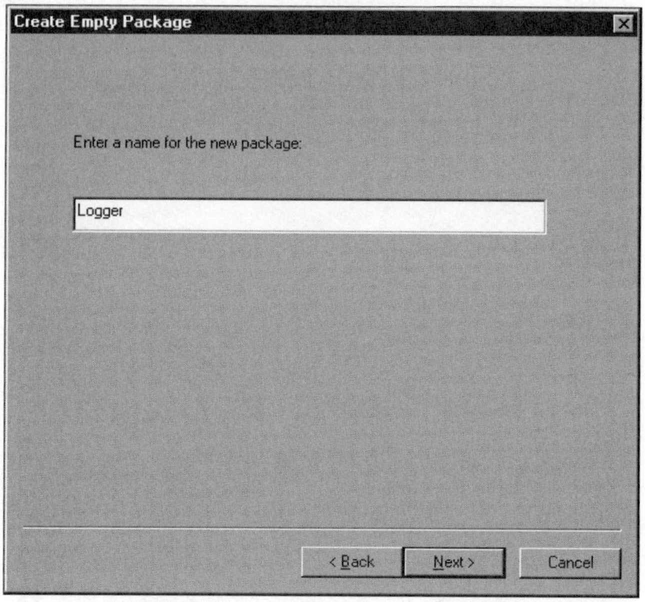

Create Empty Package

Enter a name for the new package:

Logger

< Back   Next >   Cancel

3. Name the package Logger. (In COM+ you'll be prompted for the Activation type – just leave this as the default Server application.) Now press the Next button – you'll get the following dialog window:

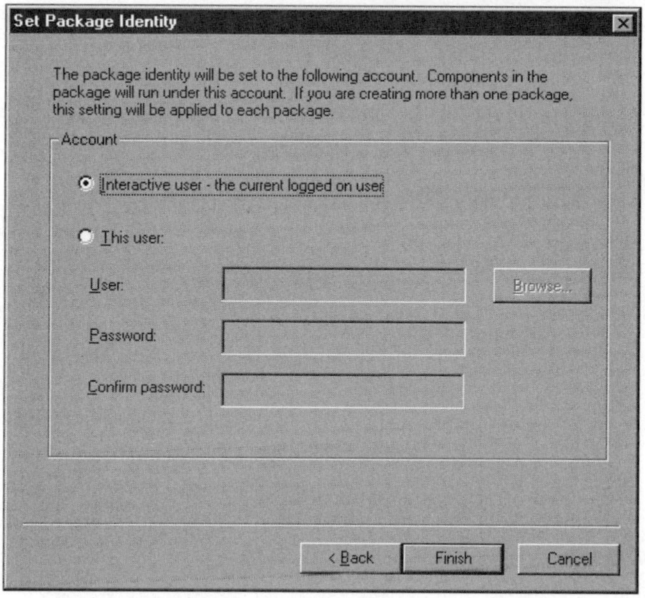

Set Package Identity

The package identity will be set to the following account. Components in the package will run under this account. If you are creating more than one package, this setting will be applied to each package.

Account

○ Interactive user - the current logged on user

○ This user:

User: Browse...

Password:

Confirm password:

< Back   Finish   Cancel

Leave the default selected (Interactive user – the current logged on user) and press Finish. That's all there is to creating a package.

4. Now add the `Logger` component to this package: drill down to the **Components** node in our new **Logger** package, right-click on it and select **New | Component**, which will display the following dialog box (again, with COM+ you'll get additional splash screens here):

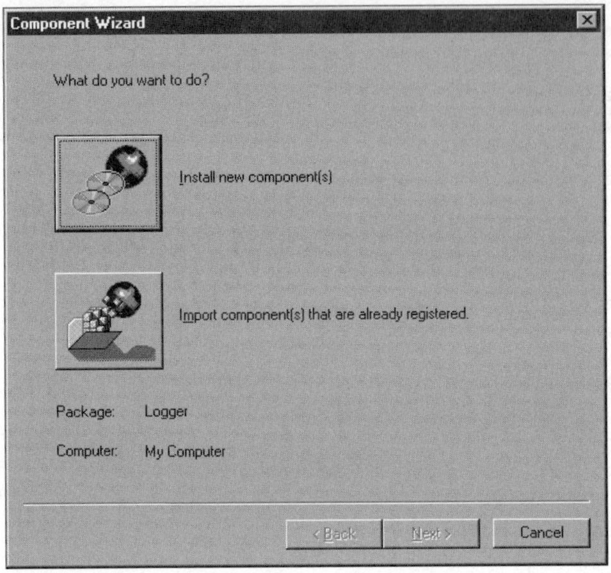

5. Press the **Import component(s) that are already registered** button. You should get a dialog window that lists all of the components registered on your machine that currently don't exist in a MTS package:

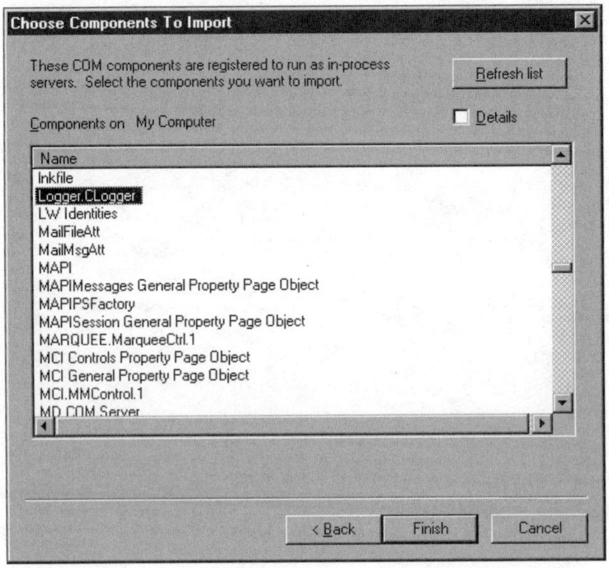

Select the **Logger.CLogger** component, and press **Finish**.

6. We now want to check the component properties. To do this, right-click on your new Logger.CLogger component in your Logger package, and select Properties. Select the Transaction tab on the dialog window:

Ensure that the value selected is Requires a transaction, and press the OK button.

How It Works

Initially, we created a new package called Logger, and, in the second step, we added the CLogger class from the Logger component to the Logger package. Note that we left the package identity as the interactive user. For our purposes, this will do, but when you publish a component in a production package you should select a specific user. Remember that on an NT server box, it's quite unusual to leave a user logged in, therefore, you won't necessarily have an interactive user, and your component won't launch!

In the third step, we verified that our transaction setting was correct. When you import a component that's already registered on the machine, MTS doesn't read the type library information for the component, and subsequently won't set the transaction value. If our Logger component wasn't registered on the machine, we could have let MTS install the component. In this case, MTS will register the component information correctly. However, it also imports every class in your component, which might not be what you wanted.

Now that we have our component running under MTS, let's make the test client to see that it is working properly.

Try It Out – Creating the Test Client

1. Create a new Standard EXE project in VB, name the project LoggerTest, and name the form frmLoggerTest.

2. Add one command button to the form, name it cmdLoggerTest, and set the Caption property to Test CLogger. Your form should look something like this:

3. Open the References dialog window, and make sure that our Logger component is selected:

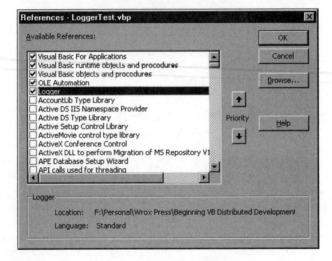

Then click OK.

4. Add the following code to your form:

```
Option Explicit

Private Sub cmdLoggerTest_Click()

   TestCLogger

End Sub
```

```
Private Sub TestCLogger()

  On Error GoTo Error_TestCLogger

  Dim oLog As Logger.CLogger

  Set oLog = CreateObject("Logger.CLogger")

  If Not oLog Is Nothing Then
   With oLog
     .ClassName = "frmLoggerTest"
     .Message = "Just a test message."
     .MessageCode = "1"
     .MethodName = "TestCLogger"
     .TimeStamp = Now
     .Submit Informational
   End With
   Set oLog = Nothing
  End If

  Exit Sub

Error_TestCLogger:

  MsgBox Err.Number & " - " & Err.Description

End Sub
```

5. Now save and run the project: but before you press the command button, take a look at the Transaction Statistics:

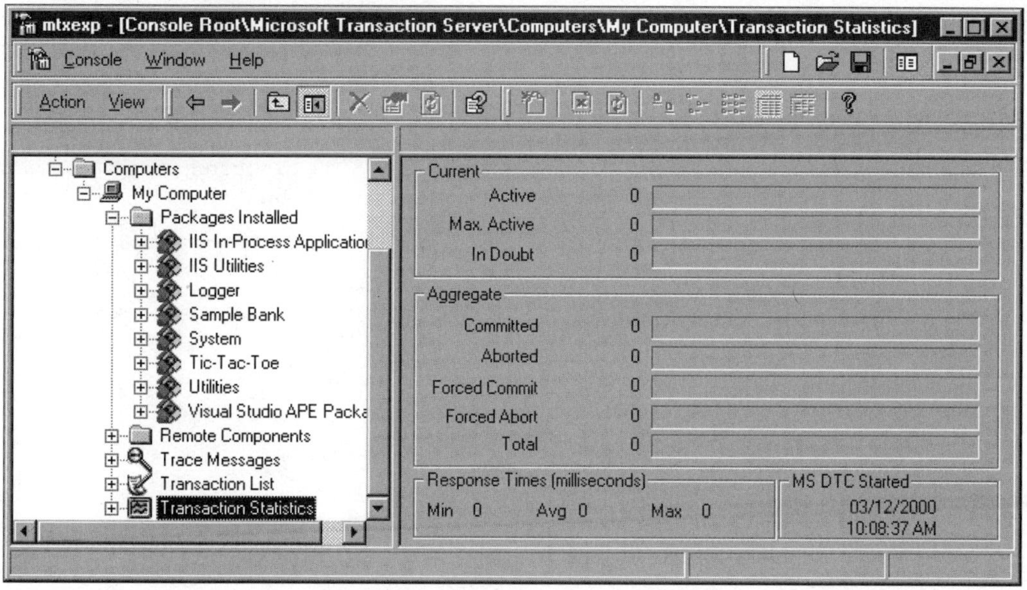

6. Press the button, and recheck your statistics:

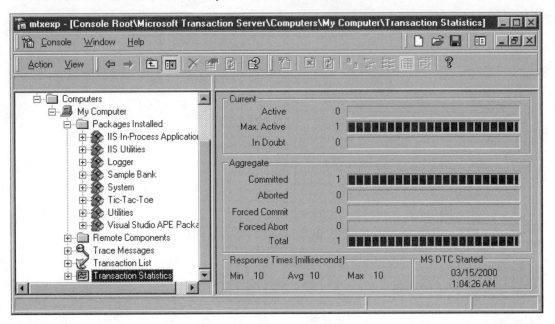

7. Also, take a look at the first entry in the log file (`logfile.txt`):

```
"Time: 03/15/2000 1:05:07 AM"
"Class Name: frmLoggerTest"
"Method Name: TestCLogger"
"Message Code: 1"
"Level: 0"
"Message: Just a test message."
```

How It Works

In our client, we've made a reference to our `Logger` component. We can therefore create an instance of `CLogger`, and we do this when the user presses the `cmdTestLogger` button:

```
Dim oLog As Logger.CLogger

Set oLog = CreateObject("Logger.CLogger")
```

Then, provided that the object has been created successfully, we create a test message by setting the values of our properties:

```
If Not oLog Is Nothing Then
  With oLog
    .ClassName = "frmLoggerTest"
    .Message = "Just a test message."
    .MessageCode = "1"
```

```
      .MethodName = "TestCLogger"
      .TimeStamp = Now
      .Submit Informational
   End With
   Set oLog = Nothing
End If
```

If you watch the transactional statistics while using the Logger client, you should see the statistics change when a new log entry is made – that means our component works and it's MTS-aware!

Transactional Objects and State

Now that we have a working Windows client that calls an MTS-aware COM server, we need to focus our attention on the importance of calling SetComplete or SetAbort. As we'll see, the lifetime of an object is not necessarily what we might expect it to be.

Checking the Object's State

Let's add a new button to our form that reads the value of ClassName before and after Submit is called. We'll display this information in a message box for simplicity's sake.

Try It Out – Checking the CLogger Object State

1. Add a new command button under the current **Test CLogger** button. Call it cmdTestObjectState, and set its **Caption** value to **Test Object State**.

2. Add the following code to the form:

```
Private Sub cmdTestObjectState_Click()

   TestObjectState

End Sub
```

3. And now add the following. This is virtually the same the testCLogger code, except that we're showing what the value of ClassName is. You might just want to copy and paste the code from there, and make the highlighted changes:

```
Private Sub TestObjectState()

   On Error GoTo Error_TestObjectState

   Dim oLog As Logger.CLogger

   Set oLog = CreateObject("Logger.CLogger")

   If Not oLog Is Nothing Then
     With oLog
```

```
      .ClassName = "frmLoggerTest"
      .Message = "Just a test message."
      .MessageCode = "1"
      .MethodName = "TestCLogger"
      .TimeStamp = Now
      MsgBox "Before Submit is called, the ClassName is " & .ClassName
      .Submit Informational
      MsgBox "After Submit is called, the ClassName is " & .ClassName
    End With
    Set oLog = Nothing
  End If

  Exit Sub

Error_TestObjectState:

  MsgBox Err.Number & " - " & Err.Description

End Sub
```

4. Save the project and recompile the DLL.

5. Run the project and click the **Test Object State** button. You should see one message box like this:

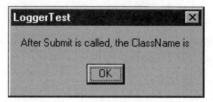

6. Then click OK. The second message box displays this message:

This might strike us as being quite unexpected. We might be forgiven for expecting the value of ClassName to have remained the same. So what happened to value of ClassName?

How It Works

Our first message box displays the value of ClassName as we just set it in our code:

```
      .ClassName = "frmLoggerTest"
  ...
      MsgBox "Before Submit is called, the ClassName is " & .ClassName
```

Nothing strange there. Then we call `Submit` and try to display `ClassName` again:

```
.Submit Informational
MsgBox "After Submit is called, the ClassName is " & .ClassName
```

But this time we seem to have lost the value of `ClassName`. We don't call `ObjectReset` in `Submit`, nor do we set `ClassName` equal to an empty string either. Why aren't we getting the same answer back?

What MTS is doing behind the scenes – more specifically, behind the Context Wrapper – is destroying, and then recreating, your `CLogger` object. That's why we get an empty string the second time we call `ClassName` – because we're referencing a new object, and the `ClassName` property has never been set for this object!

This behavior has caused much confusion for COM programmers, so let's make sure that we understand what's going on here.

SetComplete, SetAbort, and Object Lifetimes

To illustrate this further, let's take a look at a diagram. Before you call `Submit`, this is how the objects are set up:

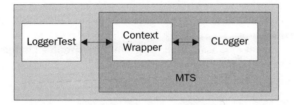

After `Submit` is called, MTS destroys your object, but the client still has a reference to the Context Wrapper.

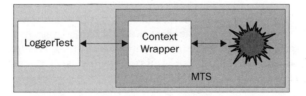

Thus, if the client makes a call to what it thinks is a live `CLogger` object, MTS has to crank up a new object – which is exactly what happens with our second message.

Why does MTS do this? It seems like an awful lot of work for nothing. MTS has to do this for one simple reason; to preserve transactional semantics.

Scenario #4

The **Add Payee** Scenario describes adding a new payee account to the list of authorized payees.

- ❑ **Name**
  Add Payee.

- ❑ **Summary**
  This Scenario involves creating payees to be used when selecting payees in the "Pay Bill" Scenario.

- ❑ **Assumptions**
  None.

- ❑ **Pre-Conditions**
  User is logged on and selects "Add Payee".

- ❑ **Steps**

User	System
User enters a unique payee description.	
User selects a payee card to pay to and validates the payee.	
	System verifies that payee is a valid card.
User initiates the creation of the new payee.	
	System adds the new payee.

- ❑ **Business Rules**
  - ❑ Payee descriptions must be unique for each payee.
  - ❑ Only one payee can be created for any WROBA card.
  - ❑ Each payee that is added is linked to one of the payee's card accounts.

- ❑ **Post Conditions**
  The newly created payee is available when selecting payees in the "Pay Bill" Scenario.

- ❑ **Exceptions**
  The new payee creation is aborted with a "Invalid account" message if the account number does not exist with the selected bank.

- ❑ **Open Issues**
  None.

Scenario #5

The **Edit Payee** Scenario describes the Use Case for changing the description and default payment amount for a payee, or deleting an existing payee.

- ❑ **Name**
  Edit Payee.

- ❑ **Summary**
  This Scenario involves editing the description and default payment amount for payees, and also deleting existing payees.

- ❑ **Assumptions**
  None.

- ❑ **Pre-Conditions**
  User is logged on and selects "Edit Payee".

- ❑ **Steps**

User	System
The user selects a unique payee description.	
The user edits the payee description and default payment amount, if changing the payee information is desired. If deleting the payee is desired, this step is skipped.	
The user initiates the saving of the edited payee or deletion of the selected payee.	
	System saves changes.

- ❑ **Business Rules**
  Payee descriptions must be unique for each payee.

- ❑ **Post Conditions**
  The newly edited payee is available when selecting payees in the "Pay Bill" Scenario.

- ❑ **Exceptions**
  - ❑ Saving the changed payee information is aborted with a "Invalid account" message if the account number does not exist with the selected bank.
  - ❑ If the payee is being deleted Step 2 is skipped.

- ❑ **Open Issues**
  None.

Scenario #6

The next Scenario, **Account History**, describes the retrieval and display of the transaction history of a selected account, either Checking or Saving.

- ❑ **Name**
  Account History.

- ❑ **Summary**
  This Scenario involves retrieving the account history of either a Saving account or a Checking account.

- ❑ **Assumptions**
  None.

- ❑ **Pre-Conditions**
  User is logged on and selects "Account History", which shows all recorded transactions for the selected account since the account was created.

- ❑ **Steps**

User	System
The user selects for which account (Saving or Checking) to show the history.	
	The account history is shown.

- ❑ **Business Rules**
  None.

- ❑ **Post Conditions**
  Account balances remain unchanged.

- ❑ **Exceptions**
  None.

- ❑ **Open Issues**
  None.

Scenario #7

The **Change Password** Scenario, the final customer-level Use Case, describes the changing of a user's password.

- ❑ **Name**
  Change Password.

- ❑ **Summary**
  This Scenario changes the login password for the logged on card.

- ❑ **Assumptions**
  None.

- ❑ **Pre-Conditions**
  User is logged on and selects "Change Password".

- ❑ **Steps**

User	System
The user enters a new password and confirms it.	
	The password is changed.

- ❑ **Business Rules**

  - ❑ A password must be at least three characters and no more than eight characters.

  - ❑ Passwords are NOT case-sensitive and may contain A-Z and 0-9.

- ❑ **Post Conditions**
  Account balances remain unchanged.

- ❑ **Exceptions**
  None.

- ❑ **Open Issues**
  None.

Scenario #8

The first of the administrator-level Use Case Scenarios, **Administrator Login**, describes the initial interaction of an Actor logging in as an administrator. The interaction is the same as that for an Actor logging in as a customer.

- ❑ **Name**
  Administrator Login.

- ❑ **Summary**
  This Scenario involves gaining access to the system by providing a unique WROBA administrator card number and a matching password.

- ❑ **Assumptions**
  None.

- ❑ **Pre-Conditions**
  Application is in initial state.

- ❑ **Steps**

User	System
User is identified to the system by entering a card identification number.	
User is authenticated by entering the matching password.	
	System determines that the login is for an administrator account. The card is locked out from further logins while the admin login is active.
The user is given a choice to:	
Add New Card	
Delete Card	
Unlock Card	
Lock Card	
Add New Bank	
Edit Bank	
Exit and Log Off	

❑ **Business Rules**

  ❑ A card identification number is a twelve-digit number.

  ❑ The first three digits of the card identification number are used to look up to which bank the account identified by the remaining nine digits belongs (although in the case study only the rightmost five digits are used and the full use of only one bank is implemented).

  ❑ A password must be at least three characters and no more than eight characters. Passwords are NOT case-sensitive and may contain A-Z and 0-9. The administrator password is "Admin".

  ❑ An account is locked after five consecutive unsuccessful logins.

❑ **Post Conditions**
The Administrator is logged in to the card account, and other logins to this card account are locked out while the administrative login is active.

❑ **Exceptions**

  ❑ The logon is aborted with a "Invalid ID or password" message if the ID does not exist or is not valid (for example, if it is less than 12 digits).

  ❑ The logon is aborted with a "Invalid ID or password" message if the ID and password do not match.

❑ **Open Issues**
None.

Scenario #9

The next Scenario, **New Card**, describes the creation of a new WROBA card. This card is immediately available for use.

- **Name**
  New Card.

- **Summary**
  This Scenario involves creating a new WROBA card.

- **Assumptions**
  None.

- **Pre-Conditions**
  User is logged on as administrator and selects "New Card".

- **Steps**

User	System
The administrator selects an account type to create (Checking or Saving).	
The administrator enters the initial card balance, overdraft limit and daily transaction limit.	
The administrator initiates the creation of the new card.	
	System creates a new card, and assigns it a card number and default password.
	System displays the new card number and password.

- **Business Rules**
  The daily transaction limit must be smaller than or equal to the sum of the initial balance and the overdraft limit.

- **Post Conditions**
  The new card is available for immediate login.

- **Exceptions**
  The card creation is aborted with a "Not sufficient funds" message if the daily transaction limit is larger than the sum of the initial balance and the overdraft limit.

- **Open Issues**
  None.

Scenario #10

The **Delete Card** Use Case Scenario describes the deletion of a WROBA card account. The card's transaction history will be retained in the database to provide an audit trail.

- ❑ **Name**
  Delete Card.

- ❑ **Summary**
  This Scenario involves removing an existing WROBA card account.

- ❑ **Assumptions**
  None.

- ❑ **Pre-Conditions**
  User is logged on as administrator and selects "Delete Card".

- ❑ **Steps**

User	System
The administrator enters a card account.	
The administrator validates the existence of the card account.	
	System verifies the existence of the card account.
The user initiates the deletion.	
	System removes the card account.

- ❑ **Business Rules**

  - ❑ The card account to be deleted must already exist.

  - ❑ The history of the account must be retained for an audit trail and records verification.

- ❑ **Post Conditions**
  The card account no longer exists. Account records are retained for audit trail and records verification purposes.

- ❑ **Exceptions**
  None.

- ❑ **Open Issues**
  None.

Scenario #11

The **Unlock Card** Scenario describes the interaction of an administrator with the system in issuing an unlock order for a WROBA card.

- ❑ **Name**
  Unlock Card.

- ❑ **Summary**
  This Scenario involves unlocking a locked-out WROBA card account.

- ❑ **Assumptions**
  None.

- ❑ **Pre-Conditions**
  User is logged on as administrator and selects "Unlock Card".

- ❑ **Steps**

User	System
Administrator enters an existing card account number.	
Administrator validates the existence of the card account.	
	System verifies the existence of the card account.
Administrator initiates the unlocking of the card account.	
	System unlocks the card account to enable logging into the account.

- ❑ **Business Rules**
  The card must be an existing card account.

- ❑ **Post Conditions**
  The newly unlocked card account is available for immediate login and use.

- ❑ **Exceptions**
  None.

- ❑ **Open Issues**
  None.

Scenario #12

The **Lock Card** Scenario describes the interaction of an administrator with the system in issuing a lock order for a WROBA card account.

- ❑ **Name**
  Lock Card.

- ❑ **Summary**
  This Scenario involves locking a WROBA card account from being logged into.

- ❑ **Assumptions**
  None.

- ❑ **Pre-Conditions**
  User is logged on as administrator and selects "Lock Card".

- ❑ **Steps**

User	System
The administrator enters an existing card account number.	
The administrator validates the existence of the card account.	
	System verifies the existence of the card account.
The administrator initiates the locking of the card account.	
	System locks the card account from being logged into.

- ❑ **Business Rules**
  The card account must exist.

- ❑ **Post Conditions**
  The newly locked card account cannot be logged into.

- ❑ **Exceptions**
  If the card account is logged into when the lock is applied, the card will be unlocked when the card user logs out.

- ❑ **Open Issues**
  Should card be logged out if it is in use when the lock is issued to preserve the lock?

Scenario #13

The **New Bank** Scenario describes the interaction required to add a new bank to the list of member banks in the WROBA card network.

- ❑ **Name**
  New Bank.

- ❑ **Summary**
  This Scenario involves addition of a new bank as a WROBA card network member.

- ❑ **Assumptions**
  None.

- ❑ **Pre-Conditions**
  User is logged on as administrator and selects "New Bank".

- ❑ **Steps**

User	System
Administrator enters the description and connection string for the new bank. (A connection string is used to connect to a database). Administrator initiates the creation of the new bank.	
	The system adds the new bank.

- ❑ **Business Rules**
  None.

- ❑ **Post Conditions**
  The new bank is immediately available for logging into and account retrieval.

- ❑ **Exceptions**
  None.

- ❑ **Open Issues**
  None.

Scenario #14

The **Edit Bank** Scenario describes the interaction for changing the description or connection string for an existing bank member of the WROBA card network.

- ❑ **Name**
  Edit Bank.

- ❑ **Summary**
  This Scenario involves changing the description and connection string of an existing bank.

- ❑ **Assumptions**
  None.

- ❑ **Pre-Conditions**
  User is logged as administrator on and selects "Edit Bank".

- ❑ **Steps**

User	System
The administrator makes the desired changes to the description and connection string.	
The administrator initiates saving the changes.	
	The system saves the changes.

- ❑ **Business Rules**
  A bank description must be unique.

- ❑ **Post Conditions**
  The changed bank immediately has the new description and connection string.

- ❑ **Exceptions**
  None.

- ❑ **Open Issues**
  None.

Scenario #15

The final Scenario, **Exit**, describes exiting from the WROBA application from either the user or administrator logins.

- ❑ **Name**
  Exit.

- ❑ **Summary**
  This Scenario involves exiting the application.

- ❑ **Assumptions**
  None.

- ❑ **Pre-Conditions**
  User is logged on and selects "Exit".

- ❑ **Steps**

User	System
User selects to exit.	
	The card is unlocked and the application is closed.

- ❑ **Business Rules**
  None.

- ❑ **Post Conditions**
  Card that is logged off is unlocked.

- ❑ **Exceptions**
  None.

- ❑ **Open Issues**
  None.

Technology Requirements

Just as with the business requirements, selecting the correct technology starts with gathering goal-oriented information. In a large organization, the technology and networking support people would typically be involved in this discussion, as broad expertise is needed to correctly assess all the elements that play a role. Of course, if you're working with a small organization you may well be expected to contribute significantly to the discussion regarding these issues!

Therefore, although these technology requirements are not part of the deliverables for the WROBA project, and are not strictly part of the software development process, they play a major role in how users perceive the responsiveness of the system. Thus for completeness in our discussion of application development we should consider them here.

The major areas we need to look at when assessing technology requirements are:

- ❑ Performance
- ❑ Maintainability
- ❑ Extensibility
- ❑ Scalability
- ❑ Availability
- ❑ Security

Let's take a look at each of them.

Performance

Every user wants programs to respond quickly and efficiently. Ensuring this is a performance issue. There are two types of performance: **real performance** and **perceived performance**.

Real performance is how quickly the operations are actually performed. Real performance is achieved through optimizing the design and the implementation.

Perceived performance gives the impression of real performance when operations take a little while. This can be achieved by keeping the user informed that something is going on. Examples of this are:

- ❑ Splash screens allowing an application to retrieve information at start up without having the user wonder what's going on
- ❑ Progress indicators giving feedback on the completion of a lengthy operation

When analyzing performance requirements, consideration needs to be given to the following:

- ❑ Transaction per time slice
- ❑ Bandwidth
- ❑ Capacity
- ❑ Interoperability with existing systems

- ❑ Peak versus average requirements

- ❑ Response time expectations

- ❑ Existing response time characteristics

- ❑ Server and Client hardware

- ❑ Barriers to performance

Transaction Per Time Slice

> **A transaction is one or more separate actions that are grouped together and executed as a single logical action. This single logical action either entirely succeeds or entirely fails.**

We encountered a more detailed definition of transactions in the last chapter. In order to assess the performance requirements of the application, we should find out how many transactions will occur over a given period of time. We can compute the **number of transactions per time slice** using the Scenarios we created earlier. For each Scenario, find out how often it will be executed by each user group. We'll use this information to calculate the bandwidth the application needs.

The standard time slice for SQL Server 7.0 operations is 100 milliseconds. This value can be changed, but changing it will impact the performance of all applications running on that computer. Unless transactions are timing out it's usually best to leave the time slice setting at its default value.

The number of transactions can be estimated by figuring out how many users the system is designed to handle concurrently, and how many transactions each user is likely to require per interval. For example, we might assume that each user will perform no more than 1 operation every 5 seconds, and there will be 10,000 concurrent users. That equates to 2,000 operations per second. If each operation were exactly 1 transaction, the result would be 200 transactions per time slice.

Bandwidth

> **Bandwidth is the capacity to carry information, measured in data capacity per unit of time (bits per second).**

Once we've determined the number of transactions per time slice, we can estimate the bandwidth requirements. For each transaction, we estimate the number of bytes that will be transferred. The following table estimates the requirements of each data type:

Type	Storage Requirement
Boolean	2 Bytes
Integer Number	4 Bytes
Decimal Number	8 Bytes
Character Information	2 Bytes per Character
Average String Length	30 Characters

The average string length can vary widely depending on the application involved – an application that retrieves archived magazine articles from a textual database will have a much longer average string length than the WROBA application.

Transmitting data over a network requires overhead, typically 4 bits of overhead per byte transmitted. So, counting the overhead, there are 12 bits in every byte being transmitted. This translates into the following formula:

> **Average bandwidth requirement (kilobits/seconds) =**
> **Average daily transaction requirement (bytes/day) ***
> **12 (bits/bytes) / 86400 (seconds/day) / 1024 (bits/kilobits)**

The transactions per time slice example above estimated 2000 transactions per second. Each transaction may involve the transfer of different amounts of data. For example, a transaction that passes a Long data value and returns a Boolean value will involve the transfer of 6 bytes. This transaction would require 72 bits, using the estimate of 12 bits per byte given above. A transaction that passed two Long data values and returned a database `Recordset` object might require many more bits, depending on the number of rows and columns returned in the recordset.

Deciding what number to use for the average daily transaction requirement (bytes/day) can be difficult. One method we can use is to run a performance monitor such as **PerfMon**, which comes with Windows, to monitor the running application in a development lab setting. Extrapolating from the actual amount of network traffic is one way to get preliminary estimates of the number of bytes per day the system will require.

For this example of the average bandwidth requirement, we will arbitrarily assume that the average number of bytes required for a transaction is 20 bytes. This will be the average of all the transaction types that occur in the system. This number is not derived from any metrics taken from the system; it's only an assumption for the purpose of illustrating the example. Using this assumption, the formula for deriving the average daily transaction requirements would be:

> **Average daily transaction requirement =**
> **2000 transactions per second * 86400 (seconds/day) * 20 bytes =**
> **3,456,000,000 bytes/day**

And from this, we can calculate the average bandwidth requirements using the following formula:

> **Average bandwidth requirement (kilobits/seconds) =**
> **3456000000 (bytes/day) * 12 (bits/bytes) / 86400 (seconds/day) / 1024 (bits/kilobits) =**
> **468.75 kilobits/second**

Using the examples above, the average bandwidth requirements for the WROBA application is 468.75 kilobits/second. Actual average bandwidth requirements will vary depending on the average number of concurrent users, average number of transactions per second and the average number of bytes transferred per transaction. The average number of concurrent users can usually be estimated fairly accurately, at least for the initial installation of an application. The average number of transactions per second can be estimated by observing users interacting with the system, but using a network traffic monitor is the best way to estimate the average number of bytes transferred per transaction.

Capacity

Once we've determined the bandwidth requirement, it's necessary to find out if our network has the necessary **capacity** to handle this workload. It's also useful to work out how many network licenses may be needed at this stage. If, for example, we estimate that we'll need 100 concurrent connections to a server, we need to ensure that we have the necessary licenses to allow for that many concurrent connections, drivers and licensed components, and budget accordingly.

Interoperability with Existing Systems

Of course, capacity planning will need to take interoperability with existing standards and systems, as well as legacy systems, into consideration. Our organization may also have specifications that dictate how certain elements of our application will interact with the existing systems. We've got to conform to these specifications to ensure that our application doesn't cause problems in existing systems.

Peak versus Average Requirements

The importance of peak versus average measurement becomes critical when planning to cross a river. An unfortunate soul who only measures the average depth of the river may very well drown while crossing. The same principle applies, albeit in a less dramatic way, to application design and planning.

While the **average requirements**, as measured above, are a very important measure, it's also necessary to take into account the **peak requirements**, to ensure our application doesn't break down under heavier workloads. The same formula for average requirements can be modified as follows to calculate the peak requirements:

> **Peak bandwidth requirement (kilobits/seconds) =**
> **Peak transaction requirement (bytes/hour) ***
> **12 (bits/bytes) / 3600 (seconds/hour) / 1024 (bits/kilobits)**

If this formula is used with the same numbers as we used in our average bandwidth requirement calculation, the results will be the same: 468.75 kilobits/second. So what's the use of the peak requirement then? The answer is that the number of transactions used for the peak number should be different from the average number of transactions.

The number of peak transactions will vary depending on the time of day, the time of the year and the nature of the business involved. For an application such as WROBA, the peak times might be just after a major shopping holiday like Christmas. Each business will have different peak periods. For such a peak, the number of expected users might be double that of an average period, or even more.

If we use a number for the peak transactions per hour that is triple that of the average number of transactions, our formula to calculate the peak hourly requirements will look like this:

> **Peak hourly transaction requirement =**
> **6000 transactions per second * 3600 (seconds/hour) * 20 bytes =**
> **432,000,000 bytes/hour**

And our formula for calculating Peak bandwidth requirement (in kilobits per second), like this:

> **Peak bandwidth requirement (kilobits/seconds) =**
> **432000000 (bytes/hour) * 12 (bits/bytes) / 3600 (seconds/hour) / 1024 (bits/kilobits) =**
> **1406.25 kilobits/second**

In this example, as we'd expect, when the peak number of transactions is triple that of the average number, the peak bandwidth requirement is triple the average bandwidth requirement. One thing to examine closely when calculating the peak requirement is the average number of bytes per transaction. This number may be different depending on the patterns of use during the peak periods.

When applying the peak bandwidth requirement, it may not be practical to design the system to supply the capacity to fully satisfy the peak demand. Monetary and other business requirements may necessitate accepting a lower number of peak transactions per second than the peak bandwidth requirement implies. This is evident in many systems where system response slows down during peak periods. The amount of slowdown that's acceptable will determine the balance that's required between peak demand and available capacity – maintaining reserve capacity for a peak that occurs once a day for 15 minutes and is triple normal demand may not be practical or financially possible.

Response Time Expectations

Response time expectations are a sub-section of performance. It's what users often have in mind when they talk about performance. The response time is the time an action takes to start displaying results on the screen. As with performance, a distinction can be made between real response time and perceived response time. Perceived response time may be used to make the real response time seem acceptable.

Existing Response Time Characteristics

Any new system will often be evaluated against **existing response time characteristics**. A new system with a response time of two seconds will seem very fast in an environment where the existing systems return responses in five seconds, but will seem extremely slow if existing systems return responses in under a second.

Server and Client Hardware

Server and client hardware is something that also must be evaluated before a new system is deployed. The system's requirements for RAM, processor speed, hard disk space and network bandwidth may necessitate upgrading or replacing client and server computers, network cards and cabling, routers or switches and other components. Dedicated database servers may be required. These requirements should be carefully evaluated; otherwise, the new system may not meet performance expectations (or even install or run).

Barriers to Performance

The degree to which we can realize our performance goals is governed by existing limitations. Such **barriers to performance** include:

- ❑ Hardware, including CPU, RAM and storage capacity
- ❑ Operating systems and other programs with which our solution works
- ❑ Network, including bandwidth capacity, network cards and modems
- ❑ Data access
- ❑ Number of users
- ❑ Application design

One thing to be aware of is that n-tier applications are inherently slower than legacy applications, which telnet into a mainframe computer and work with data on a textual basis. If the n-tier application has a graphical user interface, this will also make it slower than a text-based interface.

We'll see in later chapters how the choice of architecture type may impact the performance goals.

Maintainability

> **Maintainability is the capability of keeping the application in working order.**

We will need to consider these factors to determine the maintainability requirements:

- ❑ Breadth of application distribution
- ❑ Method of distribution
- ❑ Maintenance expectations
- ❑ Location and knowledge level of maintenance staff
- ❑ Impact of third-party maintenance agreement

Breadth of Application Distribution

The **breadth of application distribution** refers to the extent of the geographic distribution of an application. It also refers to the degree to which the application needs to scale – how many users will access the application simultaneously.

Method of Distribution

The method of distribution is affected both by the application breadth and by the amount of data that needs to be distributed. Centralized solutions, such as downloading from a web site or network location, can more easily handle a large number of users, but have difficulty coping with large amounts of data. The traditional distribution methods, such as CD distribution, can handle large amounts of data, but become awkward as the number of users increase.

Maintenance Expectations

Maintenance is a service, and a user's satisfaction with a service is measured by how well the service satisfies the user's expectation. It's therefore important to determine the user's expectations with respect to maintenance in the early planning stages of the project.

Location and Knowledge Level of Maintenance Staff

The location of the maintenance staff will have an obvious effect on the application design. If the maintenance staff are off-site, we may, for example, need to replicate the user's environment. The knowledge level will determine how much training is required.

Impact of Third-party Maintenance Agreement

In large organizations, some or all of the hardware or network maintenance may be outsourced to an outside company. This needs to be taken into account when planning a new system.

Extensibility

> **Extensibility is the ability of an application to go beyond its original design.**

We should design what's needed today, but also anticipate what will be required tomorrow. It's important to identify what areas of the application may need to be extended in the future, so that the application can grow with the needs of the users, without necessarily needing to create a new version of the product.

This would apply to things such as adding functions to the application, and in the case of the WROBA application, might include adding the capability to have more than one payee defined for a particular target card, or the ability to utilize databases located on the servers of other participating banks.

Scalability

Scalability is the ability of the system's design to maintain the same performance in response to growth. Scalability is a design characteristic and, as we'll see shortly, is often a direct result of the choice of architecture. The definition of scalability does not imply that the system must be able to accommodate growth without *any* changes. In particular, having to add additional hardware doesn't detract from a system's scalability.

Growth usually occurs in one of four ways:

- ❑ Growth of Audience
- ❑ Growth of Organization
- ❑ Growth of Data
- ❑ Growth in Cycle of Use

Growth of Audience

The audience refers to the number of users. Not only is it necessary to determine how many users will initially use the system, but we must also gather information on how the user base will evolve.

Growth of Organization

A system's user base may also grow through organizational growth, such as a merger. These differ from the previous type in that the user base normally grows gradually, while organizational growth may lead to a large, sudden growth.

Growth of Data

This growth area often needs careful consideration if the application has a database component. It is necessary to determine how much data the system will have at its initial stage and at what rate the data grows. To respond to this growth, we may need to determine when data can be archived or deleted, and implement the required system and procedures.

Growth in Cycle of Use

Another growth area is an increase of usage frequency. When a monthly report is printed daily, this obviously leads to a 30-fold increase in resource usage.

Availability

> **Availability is a measurement that specifies how much uptime the system must provide and how much downtime can be tolerated.**

Reaching the availability requirement depends on the application's reliability. A reliable application will have little, or no, unplanned downtime. Planned downtime may be necessary for such tasks as system backups, software upgrades, new software installation, or reconfiguring computer hardware. Availability is measured by the ratio of the uptime to the total time. For instance, one hour of downtime per day = 23 / 24 or 95.83% system availability. Achieving a high level of availability is a costly proposition, usually involving adding redundant components (both hardware and software).

We will need to consider these factors to determine the availability requirements:

- ❑ Hours of operation
- ❑ Levels of availability – how much time down is to be considered excessive? What is the service level required by the organization?
- ❑ Geographic scope
- ❑ Impact of downtime

Applications such as WROBA are required to be available on a 24-hour basis, 7 days a week. Systems designed for "24/7" operation are the most difficult to implement because they are expected to have no down time. While this is not always possible to implement, it provides the availability requirements for designing the system.

Hours of Operation

The **hours of operation** will determine when the solution will be used and is a key factor behind the availability levels.

Levels of Availability

It is necessary to determine the different levels of availability of our application. We may only have to provide limited availability outside of the hours of operation. The Scenarios gathered during the business requirement phase can be used to partition the application, and determine what parts of the application require what levels of availability.

Geographic Scope

Due to different time zones, geographic scope may have an effect on availability. If an organization has offices in New York and London, and both offices operate from 9 to 5, then with the five hour time difference, the hours of operation actually span 13 hours, instead of 8.

Impact of Downtime

Since achieving high levels of availability tends to be very expensive, a cost/benefit analysis must be performed. This involves quantifying the cost of downtime to balance against the costs of achieving certain levels of availability. Spending $200,000 to build a fault-tolerant system sounds futile when the daily cost of downtime is $1,000, but reasonable if the cost is $10,000.

Security

Security requirements are determined by grouping users into certain roles, which define the tasks they perform. For each role, it's necessary to determine which functions of the applications should be made available and which functions should be off-limit.

A good starting point for determining roles is the owner, user and operator classifications discussed previously. In the case of the WROBA application, there are 2 roles: customer and administrator. The use of roles in implementing and maintaining security was introduced in Chapter 5, when we learned about MTS. It will also be discussed in Chapter 12 when we cover implementing the business user logic.

Summary

In this chapter, we looked at how you set about starting a project to build an application for a client. We looked at the need to communicate carefully and clearly with a number of people within the client organization to clearly establish the parameters for the project.

We began by looking at how to gather and analyze the business requirements and tasks for a software project, and how to put together vision statement and design goals drafts. We then introduced Use Case diagrams, Use Cases, and Use Case Scenarios and showed how they could be used in understanding the functionality the WROBA application will need to satisfy the client.

We finished the chapter by looking at aspects of the technology requirements an application (or client) may require to give appropriate performance, maintainability, extensibility, scalability, and availability. Finally, the topic of security was briefly introduced.

Our next chapter concerns an introduction to UML, which is crucial for understanding how we have developed the WROBA case study.

Unified Modeling Language

In this chapter, we'll look at a leading object-oriented analysis and design notation, the **Unified Modeling Language** (**UML**). Although we can only offer an introduction to the basics of UML in this book, we hope that they'll provide a good, practical introduction to the topic and show why it is useful in application development.

> **A more extensive study of UML can be found in *VB6 UML Design and Development*, *ISBN 1861002513*, by *Wrox Press*.**

An important thing to remember is that UML is more than a technique for producing sketchy diagrams: a design process using UML is a rigorous process that requires just as much discipline as any other design process. What the UML diagrams provide, in a properly implemented process, is a set of blueprints that are used to architect the building of the software project, just as ordinary blueprints detail every step of building a physical structure.

In this chapter, we'll cover:

❑   What the Unified Modeling Language is and why it's so useful in application development.

❑   The diagrams UML makes available.

❑   How to use Visual Modeler to produce some types of UML diagrams.

This chapter is going to provide us with the background in UML we need to be able to effectively design the WROBA solution – inevitably this means there will be points in the chapter where we have to take examples from later in the book to illustrate the points we are making. If you're new to application development all this theory about modeling may come as a bit of a shock – be assured though, when creating sophisticated applications, being able to accurately analyze the problem to be solved is *essential* to the eventual production of a quality solution.

What is UML

> The Unified Modeling Language is a notation to help visualize, specify, document and construct software products. Further details and training aids can be found on the UML website at **http://www.rational.com/uml**.

UML was originally developed in the mid 1990's by Rational Software (who we encountered in our discussion of RUP in Chapter 2). UML has since been submitted as a standard under the auspices of the Object Management Group (a non-profit corporation with over 800 member companies such as Microsoft, Sun, Hewlett-Packard, and IBM, that creates and manages object specifications that help in the creation and distribution of standardized object software). Feedback from OMG members has resulted in the release of new versions of the UML. This book uses the current version (at the time of going to press) – UML version 1.3.

*UML, the Unified Modeling Language, is a language that uses a set of standard models and diagrams to **model** object-oriented programming projects. So, although it won't implement the models being described, it will help us to visualize the project by describing the problem that the project is being developed to tackle. In other words, through modeling our project in UML we'll get a much better feel for the various user requirements, build a better project design, and ultimately produce better code.*

Creating UML Diagrams

Many different software programs can be used to create UML diagrams. However, the programs that have specific UML design features often implement only a subset of the different UML diagrams and have different names for those diagram types. In fact, as we'll see in this chapter, different programs will create the same diagram types somewhat differently.

The diagrams here were originally drawn using the following programs:

❑ Visual Modeler – This program implements only the Class, Component and Deployment diagrams (we'll find out about these and other types of diagrams as the chapter progresses). It comes with VB 6 Enterprise Edition and can generate VB code from UML drawings, making class prototypes from the class diagrams that are created.

❑ Visio 2000 – This application (a set of Computer Assisted Design – CAD – programs) is now part of the Microsoft Office 2000 suite of applications and implements a wider variety of UML diagram types. The Professional Edition of Visio 2000, which includes UML diagram templates, is available for download if you are an MSDN (Microsoft Developer Network) Universal subscriber, or it may be purchased separately.

Both of these programs can reverse engineer existing code into a UML model.

Within this chapter, we'll be walking through an exercise using Visual Modeler and won't refer to Visio 2000 explicitly again. Before you think about skipping the chapter just because you don't own those applications, we'd like to reiterate what we first said:

UML won't implement the models being described, it will help us to visualize the project by describing the problem that the project is being developed to tackle.

Hence, we think it's valuable to gain an appreciation of UML before moving onto the coding of our solution. Reading this chapter and the next one will help you to have a greater appreciation of where the various elements of the project have come from. Not having the above applications will not preclude you from doing the VB coding (and indeed many elements of the UML modelling can be done with pen and paper), but may encourage you to gain access to them once you see their utility in application development.

OK, onto the main event

Introducing the UML Diagrams

In this section, we'll be looking at the types of diagrams used in UML. These diagrams show either **static** or **dynamic** views of the system, or are **container** diagrams (diagrams which reduce a project's visible complexity by packaging related subsets of a project together in one simplified diagram). The types of UML diagram are as follows:

- Use Case diagram (dynamic diagram)
- Class diagram (static diagram)
- Sequence diagram (dynamic Interaction diagram)
- Collaboration diagram (dynamic Interaction diagram)
- Object diagram (static diagram)
- Component diagram (static diagram)
- Deployment diagram (static diagram)
- Statechart diagram (dynamic diagram)
- Activity diagram (dynamic diagram)
- Package diagram (container diagram)

Use Case Diagrams

We came across **Use Case** diagrams in the previous chapter, but here we'll consider them in greater depth. Use Case models describe a set of user needs, so the diagrams we produce with them will describe the relationships between the Actors and the system, or at least parts of the system.

We defined some of the terms used with Use Cases and Use Case diagrams in the last chapter, but let's go over them again:

- An **Actor** is a human or other system that interacts with the proposed system.

- A **Use Case** or **Use Case Scenario** is an *Actor-centric* specification describing the sequence of actions, including alternatives to the sequence, during an interaction of an Actor with the system. A Use Case contains one major success scenario, and alternative scenarios derived from the Use Case.

- A **Use Case diagram** consists of a *graphical* depiction of the Use Cases and the Actors that participate in them.

- A **Use Case Scenario** consists of a *textual* description of the Use Cases and the Actors that participate in them.

The Use Case diagram is the roadmap for the application: it shows which tasks an Actor can accomplish. It isn't a very detailed diagram; it simply shows the relationships between the Use Cases. Detailed directions are contained in the Use Case Scenarios, which contain step-by-step descriptions for accomplishing each task in the Use Case diagram.

Creating a Use Case Diagram

Use Case diagrams use five notional elements:

- ❑ System Boundary
- ❑ System Name
- ❑ Use Case
- ❑ Actor
- ❑ Actor-Use Case interaction

The **System Boundary** is a rectangle showing what is part of the proposed system and what is not. The Actors are drawn outside the System Boundary, showing them as external to the system. The **Name** of the proposed system is written in the top part of the System Boundary rectangle. Use Cases are drawn using ellipses, with each ellipse representing one Use Case, with the name of the Use Case written inside the ellipse. A straight line from an Actor to a specific Use Case indicates that the Actor initiates the Use Case.

Putting this all together gives something like this:

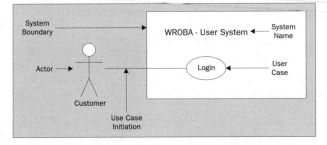

As we saw in the previous chapter, it's possible to express relationships between Use Cases. Let's look at this in some more detail.

Use Case Relationships

Although we only talked about two relationships in Chapter 6, UML 1.3 in fact defines three types of relationships between Use Cases: **include, extend**, and **generalize**.

The Include Relationship

The **include relationship** (which replaces the **uses relationship** of UML 1.1) is used to show that a Use Case occurs inside another Use Case. An example in the WROBA case study is the Main Menu Use Case that includes the Get Account Balances Use Case. The include relationship is shown by an arrowhead at the end of a line as seen in the figure. This is the same graphical notation as the extend relationship discussed in the next section, so the distinction is made by adding <<includes>> to the line:

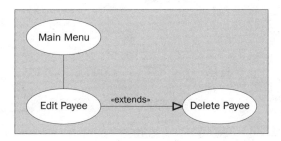

The Extend Relationship

The **extend relationship** allows us to show a Use Case that is executed only under certain circumstances or at a specific point (called the **extension point**). An example in the WROBA case study is the Delete Payee Use Case within the Edit Payee Use Case. This Delete Payee Use Case is executed in the specific case where the user issues a Delete command. The extend relationship is shown by an arrowhead at the end of a line as shown in the figure below, and to differentiate it from the include relationship <<extends>> is added to the line:

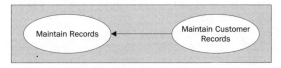

The Generalize Relationship

The **generalize relationship** was introduced only in UML 1.3 and allows a *child* Use Case to inherit behaviour and semantics from a *parent* Use Case. There aren't any real examples of this type of relationship in the case study, but a general example of this is supplied by considering a Maintain Customer Records Use Case that is a generalization of a Maintain Records Use Case. The generalize relationship is shown by an arrowhead at the end of a full line as seen in the figure below. The arrowhead is placed with the parent class.

Use Case Diagram Examples

The following Use Case diagram is similar (but stylistically different) to the WROBA User System Use Case diagram that was created in Chapter 6 as one of the project deliverables. It shows the set of interactions between an Actor – a Customer operator of the system and the system – and the interactions that occur *within* the system.

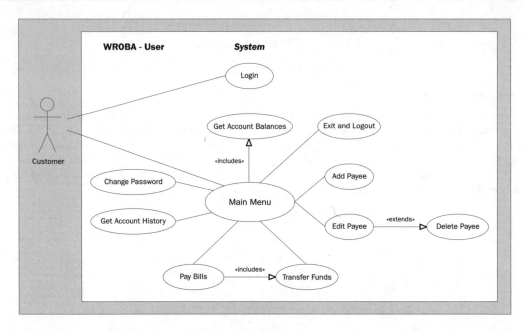

A Use Case diagram such as the one for the WROBA system can become hard to follow because of all the elements of the system that can interact with each other. Another style of Use Case diagram gives us a different view of the system. Such diagrams can be easier to follow, especially with systems that are even more complicated than the WROBA system.

Using this style, the interaction between the Actor and the system is depicted in one diagram, and the interactions between the elements *within* the system are depicted in other diagrams.

Below is a partial example of such a diagram. It isn't complete and depicts only the Actor-system interactions, and two of the internal system interactions. However, it does illustrate an alternate method of depicting the elements that make up the Use Case diagram.

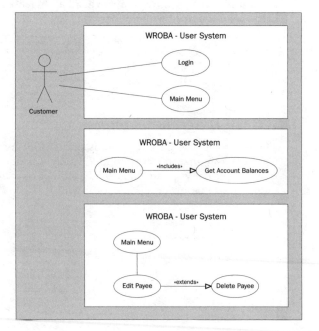

In some cases, this style is easier to follow than the standard Use Case diagram style. It does, however, have the drawback that the elements of the system are dispersed into multiple diagrams, and may not be as easily understood as a system as the unified style of the Use Case diagram.

Class Diagrams

The **Class diagram** is the key diagram that is used throughout the object-oriented analysis and design phase. The initial Class diagram is derived from the Use Case Scenarios and subsequently, it gets iteratively refined through the other types of diagrams. Things that are discovered when creating other types of UML diagrams are used to refine the class diagram until the system design is complete. We will learn how to derive class diagrams from Use Case Scenarios in Chapter 8, when we start designing the WRox Online Banking Application.

> **A Class diagram depicts which classes constitute the proposed software system, the relationships between these classes, and which methods and properties each class has.**

There are a number of topics discussed in this section, such as **ownership**, **aggregation**, and **generalization**, which we're going to introduce here, but will cover in more detail in Chapter 8. Let's start by taking a look at how a class diagram is constructed.

Creating Class Diagrams

Class diagrams are created with three notational elements:

- ❑ Classes
- ❑ Interfaces
- ❑ Relationships

A class is represented by a rectangle with three compartments: the top compartment is used for the class name, the middle one for properties (attributes), and the bottom one for methods. The name can be shown with or without the object that it belongs to. As we don't design the WROBA application until the next chapter, we're going to have to jump ahead of ourselves to provide an example of such a diagram.

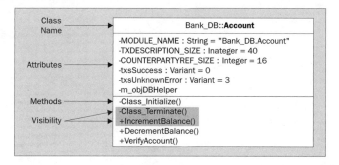

In this figure we show the Account class. The parent object Bank_DB (the data tier component) is shown with the name of the class. This is shown as: Bank_DB::Account. Attributes are shown with their data type (String, Integer, Variant, etc.) and their assigned value, in the case of constants.

The attributes and methods show their **visibility**. This corresponds to the **scope** of the attribute or method:

- ❑ Module level visibility is represented by a '−' (minus sign)
- ❑ Global visibility is represented by a '+' (plus sign)

There are different informational display options available in most UML-capable drawing systems – the class diagram we have here shows the visibility and name options. It shows that the `Class_Initialize` and `Class_Terminate` methods are private, as are all the attributes, whereas the `IncrementBalance` and `DecrementBalance` methods and the `VerifyAccount` property are public in scope.

The level of detail that is shown in the class diagram will increase as the diagram is updated throughout the development process. In the initial phases of the development process, a class diagram might only show a general class name with few or no other details.

Representing an Interface

An **interface** is represented by a "lollipop" attached to a class. Interfaces are the methods, properties and events that a class exposes to the outside world. Complex interfaces may be set to show detailed information about the interface in many UML design systems. In our example for the `BankLocator` class (of the business tier `Bank_Bus` component) we show an interface to the public read-only property `GetBank`:

Bank_Bus::**BankLocator**
-MODULE_NAME
+GetBank(in BankID : Long) : String

○ Interface

Representing Composition

The ownership relationship (called **composition** in UML) is represented by a line with a filled diamond at the end attached to the owner. Composition is a **parent/child** relationship, where the child (**contained class**) cannot exist without its parent (**container class**). The example of composition shown here indicates that each parent `Bank` class can have 1 or more child `Account` classes. Note the term `<<accessor>>` is shown next to the `Property Get` methods:

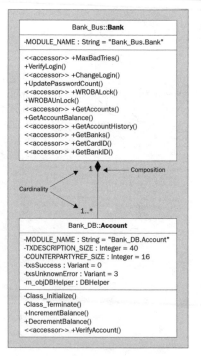

The numbers at each end of the line indicate the **cardinality** (or **multiplicity**) of the relationship; in other words, how many of each class can participate in the relationship. In this figure, the Bank class can have from 1 to an unspecified number of Accounts, but each Account class can only belong to one Bank. In this respect, the indication of cardinality helps clarify how the classes relate to each other.

Representing Simple Aggregation

The **containment** relationship (called **simple aggregation** in UML) is represented by a line with an open diamond at the owner's end. In a containment relationship the contained class's lifetime does not depend on the container class and the contained class has an existence independent of the container class. We can think of this type of relationship along the lines of the relationship between a car and its passengers. The car *contains* the passengers, but the passengers do not depend on the car for their existence; they can leave the car (the container class) without ceasing to exist. This is what distinguishes simple aggregation from composition. Cardinality is indicated in the same way as it is with the composition relationship.

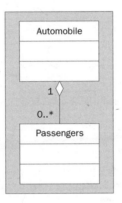

Representing Generalization

A **generalize** relationship is one in which one class inherits the implementation of another class, called the **base** class. To illustrate this, let's consider the hypothetical situation where there is a class, SavingAccount, which inherits the implementation of the more general Account class. A CheckingAccount would inherit the same Account implementation as the SavingAccount. The generalize relationship is represented by a line from the derived class to the base class with a large un-filled triangle where the line touches the base class.

243

Representing Usage

A **usage** relationship can be used either to represent a collaborative relationship between two or more classes, or a relationship which has yet to be refined to one of the other types of relationship. The using relationship is represented by a line between classes. In this case, by means of an identification number, the Bank class uses the BankLocator class to locate a particular bank. Notice that we have here chosen to show the term get adjacent to the Property Get methods:

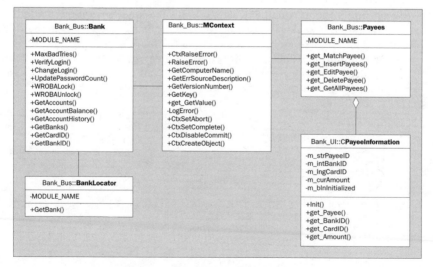

So, let's see how this may work for a number of classes in an application. Again, we'll have to look forward to the case study.

Class Diagram Example

The following class diagram shows the relationships among five classes (from all 3 tiers of our case study application): the Bank class has a usage relationship with the BankLocator class and MContext helper class; the Payees class has a usage relationship with the MContext helper class, and a simple aggregation relationship with the CPayeeInformation class:

Our next topic concerns interaction diagrams. We'll be coming across these in the next chapter and when we get down to implementing the WROBA application.

Interaction Diagrams

Interaction diagrams may be of two sorts – **sequence diagrams** and **collaboration diagrams**.

> Sequence diagrams and collaboration diagrams are semantically equivalent, which means that a sequence diagram can be transformed into a collaboration diagram (or a collaboration diagram into a sequence diagram), without losing any information. The difference is that sequence diagrams concentrate on the temporal flow, and collaboration diagrams concentrate on the objects.

Through the creation of interaction diagrams, the methods and properties of the class diagram are refined and validated.

To illustrate sequence and collaboration diagrams we're going to use the first Use Case Scenario we created in Chapter 6 – the Customer Login Scenario. This Scenario involves the customer identifying themselves to the system, being authenticated, and gaining access to a main menu.

Sequence Diagrams

Sequence diagrams are used to document the step-by-step sequences of a Use Case Scenario. The vertical dimension in a sequence diagram represents time, where sequences of events unfold downwards. The horizontal dimension represents different Actors or objects, such as Actors and parts of the system.

> A *Sequence diagram* shows the classes involved in a Use Case Scenario and depicts the sequential use of their methods and properties during this Use Case Scenario.

Creating Sequence Diagrams

Sequence diagrams are two-dimensional charts showing the interaction between Actors and the objects involved in a Use Case. Sequence diagrams are created with three notional elements:

❑   participants

❑   lifelines

❑   method calls

Let's see how we can represent each of these elements.

Representing a Participant

A **participant** in a sequence diagram is either an Actor, represented by the Actor symbol, or a **class instance,** represented by a rectangle.

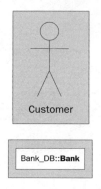

Representing a Lifeline

A **lifeline** is a vertical line representing the participation of the participant over time. The lifeline can show a **destructor**, represented by an "X", to indicate the end of the participant's lifetime. **Activations** can be placed on a lifeline, represented by a vertically oriented rectangle. This rectangle represents a period of time during which the participant is performing an action that activates another participant. In our example, we show an activation that sends a message to a second participant.

Representing a Method Call

A **method call** is an interaction between two participants. Activations can be shown on the lifeline of a participant to show when a second participant is activated, and **messages** can be sent between participants. Messages are represented by solid lines with filled arrowheads, with the arrowhead indicating the direction the message travels. **Return messages** are indicated by dashed lines with outline arrowheads. Messages can also be sent from a participant to itself, represented by a line and filled-in arrowhead that curves back on itself. These messages are also known as **recursive** messages.

The illustration here shows an example of how method calls are represented. It's important to remember at this point that the diagrams that are shown are not indicative of the final diagrams for the case study. The case study has not been refined to that level at this stage of the project.

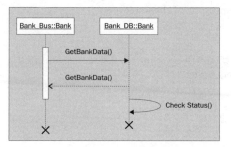

Sequence Diagram Example

The following sequence diagram depicts the Customer Login Scenario that we created in Chapter 6. This sequence diagram is a first iteration; further refinements will be made in the process of producing other UML diagrams, and as further analysis is made of the Use Case Scenario and the sequence diagram itself.

The diagram shows that the `Bank` and `BankLocator` classes and the `FLogin` form show destructors at the end of their lifetimes. The `SharedProperties` class and `FMainMenu` form are persistent from the time they are created through the timeline depicted by this sequence diagram. We will look at how to analyze Use Case Scenarios to produce sequence diagrams in Chapter 8.

Sequence Diagram for Use Case Scenario #1

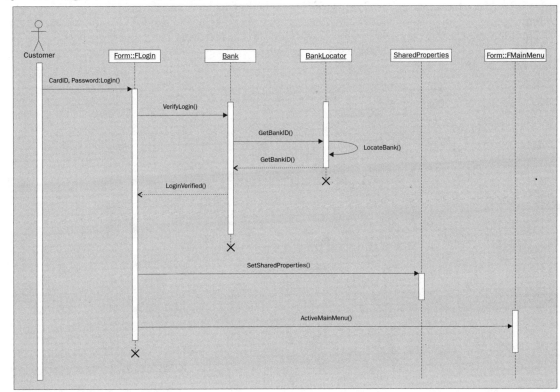

Collaboration Diagrams

> A collaboration diagram shows the classes involved in a Use Case Scenario and depicts the non-sequential use of their methods and properties during this Use Case Scenario.

Collaboration diagrams, which are a type of **Interaction diagram**, are used to depict how a group of objects collaborate for one system event defined by one Use Case. Unlike sequence diagrams, collaboration diagrams show relationships among object roles and do not represent time on one of the dimensions. Instead, the messages in a collaboration diagram are numbered to indicate the sequence in which they occur. Multiple messages from one class are numbered using a dot notation that indicates in which order the messages are sent, such as 2.1, 2.2 and so on. The interaction is the set of messages that are exchanged among the objects collaborating in the system event to achieve a result or perform an operation.

Collaboration Diagram Example

The following collaboration diagram shows the same system event shown in the previous sequence diagram. In this case, the diagram shows the set of messages exchanged during a system login. The initial message that initiates the system event always comes from outside the depicted system. In this diagram, the Actor initiating the login system event is shown, but in many cases the initiating message is simply shown as originating outside the boundaries of the system. We can see that the messages to and from the Bank class are numbered from 2, with subsequent messages using numbers that are subsets of 2. Messages to and from other classes use different base numbers, related to the order in which the messages occur.

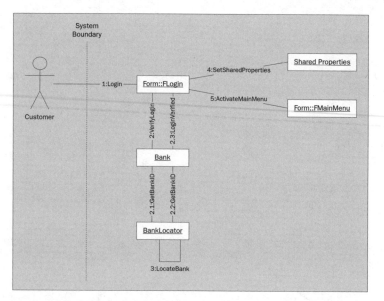

Object Diagrams

An Object diagram depicts a set of objects and their relationships.

Object diagrams, which are also known as **Instance diagrams**, represent a static structure of objects and links. They are primarily used to show an object in its context. Object diagrams are also used to refine the class diagram by helping us to think in concrete terms; that is, in terms of class instances. Object diagrams are used to discover or refine the methods and properties of the classes in the class diagram.

Object diagrams are simplified collaboration diagrams as we see here, where our previous example is re-represented in this new format. One major simplification is that they don't show the passing of messages among the classes. They show only the links and associations among the classes. Cardinality (multiplicity) of any associations is not shown in Object diagrams, only instances of classes and other objects:

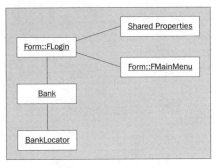

Component Diagrams

A Component diagram groups the classes identified in the class diagram into components.

The **Component diagram**, together with the Deployment diagram, discussed below, shows the physical structure of the application. The Component diagram shows in what physical executable deliverable (.EXE or .DLL) each class resides. As we do not yet know all the classes that we'll require, they are not shown inside the components.

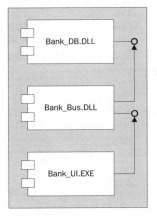

Deployment Diagrams

A Deployment diagram depicts on what hardware the components identified in the Component diagram will be deployed.

When drawing a **Deployment diagram** for a distributed application, we represent both the computers that act as servers and the computers that act as clients, and identify where each component on the component diagram will be deployed.

Data Services Server

Bank_DB.DLL

Business Logic Server

Bank_Bus.DLL

User Computer

Bank_UI.EXE

Statechart Diagrams

> A Statechart diagram models the dynamic state of a specific class: states, actions and transitions in response to external events.

Statechart diagrams represent the way in which an object's state changes as it responds to external events. The object may return to its initial state after responding to a particular event, or it may enter a new, different state.

In the following example, the statechart diagram represents an initial analysis of a menu window that waits for user input and executes an event in response to that input. After execution of the menu event, the object returns to its initial state (although this isn't explicitly shown in the diagram). The slash shown before the /MenuSelection message is one method of indicating the passing of a message from one state to another in the diagram.

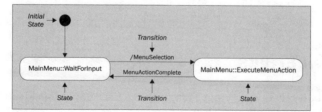

One example of a situation in the case study that could be represented by such a diagram is the Account History screen that we encounter in Chapter 14.

Activity Diagrams

> **An Activity diagram is a type of statechart diagram that models state changes in response to internally generated actions.**

An **Activity diagram** depicts the changes in object states in response to *internally* generated actions rather than *external* events (as was the case with ordinary statechart diagrams).

Activity diagrams are used to increase our understanding of complex class methods by specifying the internals of the method. They are also used to show the details of a complex method and help us to discover and document concurrent and parallel activities. They are often used for analyzing Use Cases, multi-threaded applications, and for modeling workflow.

Our example activity diagram shows the state and transitions that occur when the bank locator process is executed. The initial state transitions to the Find Bank state. A fork transition shows activities that occur in parallel, with the guard conditions indicating the condition that each transition is tested against. It is possible to think of guard conditions as the equivalent of the conditions tested for in If...Then or Select...Case code blocks. The Bank found guard condition leads to the Get Bank Connection String action state, while the Bank not found guard condition leads to the Set Blank Connection String action state. A join transition then occurs in the flow where both previous states transition to the Return Bank Connection String action state. The final state indicates that the activity that this activity diagram depicts is completed.

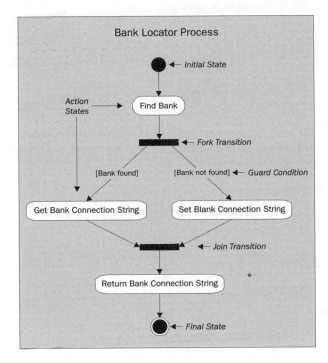

Package Diagrams

Package diagrams are used to divide models into smaller subsets. These packages are easier to work with than diagrams that show every detail of a subset of a model. They can contain other packages, individual diagrams, documentation, or almost anything that we want to place into the package subset of the model. Package diagrams are represented as manila folders, with a tab on the top of the folder.

We can use packages throughout the development process to group related objects. If any diagram becomes too large, it is possible to group elements of the diagram into a package diagram. Package diagrams can also be used to define system architectures.

The example package diagram shown (related to the Bank_UI.exe user tier component) contains three sub-packages: one each for code modules, classes and forms. The class sub-package is expanded to show the two member classes of the Classes package:

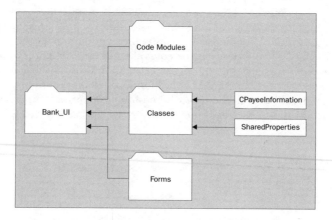

UML Summary

In the preceding sections we learned about UML and the types of diagrams it utilizes. We saw examples of many of the elements that make up the different UML diagrams, and the different types of UML diagrams. Let's just summarize all this information.

The UML diagrams that depict a static view of the system are:

- ❑ Class diagrams
- ❑ Object diagrams
- ❑ Component diagrams
- ❑ Deployment diagrams

The UML diagrams that depict a dynamic view of the system are:

- ❑ Use Case diagrams
- ❑ Sequence diagrams
- ❑ Collaboration diagrams
- ❑ Statechart diagrams
- ❑ Activity diagrams

Finally, the UML diagram used as a container to group diagrams, classes, objects and other elements of a project is:

- ❑ Package diagram

We have encountered quite a few symbols in the previous section that are used to indicate different UML relationships and connections between components. It's difficult to memorize these symbols until we become quite familiar with working with UML, so the following table will provide a recap on the use of these symbols, and a handy reference:

UML Meaning	Symbol
Generalize, Extend and Include Relations	 ◁———————
Transition	 ——————→
Message	Message10  ——→
Message Return	Message10  ←- - - - - -
Message Call	Message10  ——→
Dependency	 - - - - - - -→
Composition	 ◆———
Aggregation	 ◇———

There's a lot more to UML than we can cover in any great depth in one chapter; there are elements that can be used in UML diagrams that were not covered in this chapter, and won't be used in this book. However, we've covered enough UML here to be able to go to the next phase of the project, designing a solution.

Before we do that, we will take a look at using a UML tool that comes with VB6 Enterprise Edition – Visual Modeler. This will help us to begin to understand how to actually put UML to use in the design process.

Visual Modeler

Visual Modeler (**VM**) is a tool that is included with the Enterprise Edition of VB6. It can be started on its own, or from the Add-Ins menu in Visual Basic. VM can be used to create a subset of the UML diagrams that we learned about earlier in this chapter. The static UML diagrams we can create with VM are:

- ❑ Class diagram
- ❑ Component diagram
- ❑ Deployment diagram
- ❑ Package diagram

VM does not provide the shapes needed to create the dynamic UML diagrams such as Use Case, sequence, collaboration, statechart and activity diagrams. VM does, however, offer project **round-tripping** with VB. Round-tripping refers to the generation of class prototypes for VB from the VM diagrams we create; to reverse engineer the VB project back into VM. It includes the creation of code prototypes of the classes represented by the component classes in VM. This is particularly helpful when design iterations in the code and in the model must be synchronized.

In this little walk through we're going to look at how we can use Visual Modeler to create a class prototype for the BankLocator class of the business tier component.

Try It Out – Creating a Class

1. Open Visual Modeler by navigating the Windows Start menu to the Programs category, open the Microsoft Visual Studio 6.0 program group, open the Microsoft Visual Studio 6.0 Enterprise Tools program subgroup, and select the Microsoft Visual Modeler program shortcut.

2. Visual Modeler opens to show a blank 3-tier class diagram, with compartments labeled User Services, Business Services and Data Services, as shown in this screen shot:

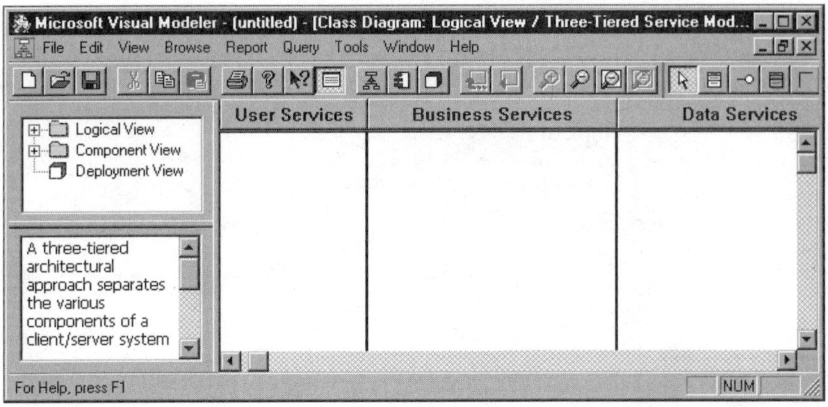

3. We'll use the Class Wizard to create the prototype of the new class and place it in the Business Services tier. Choose Class Wizard from the Tools menu.

4. Once the Class Wizard has opened its first screen, we can name the new class BankLocator:

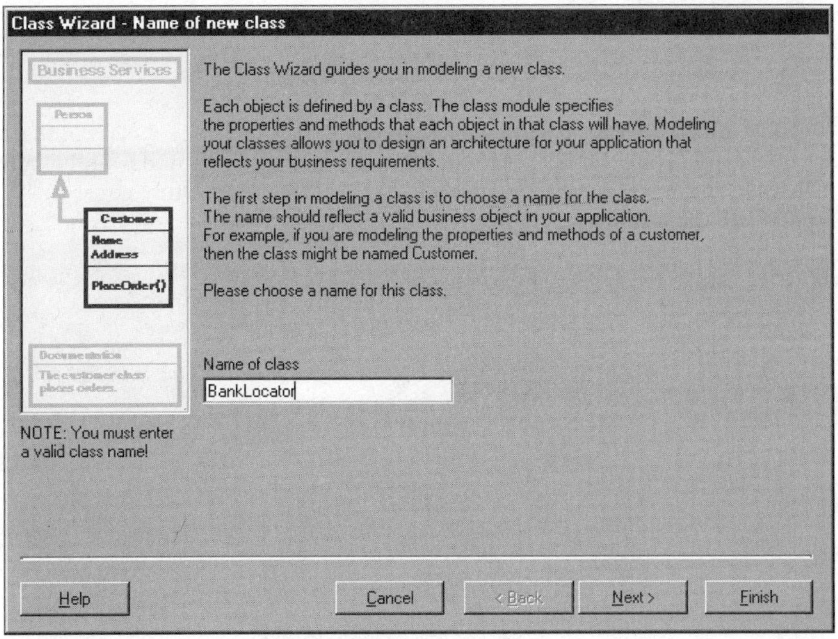

5. Press the Next button, and in the Class Wizard screen enter text documenting the responsibilities of the new BankLocator class module. This documentation will be preserved as comments in the class module when we generate code for the class prototype.

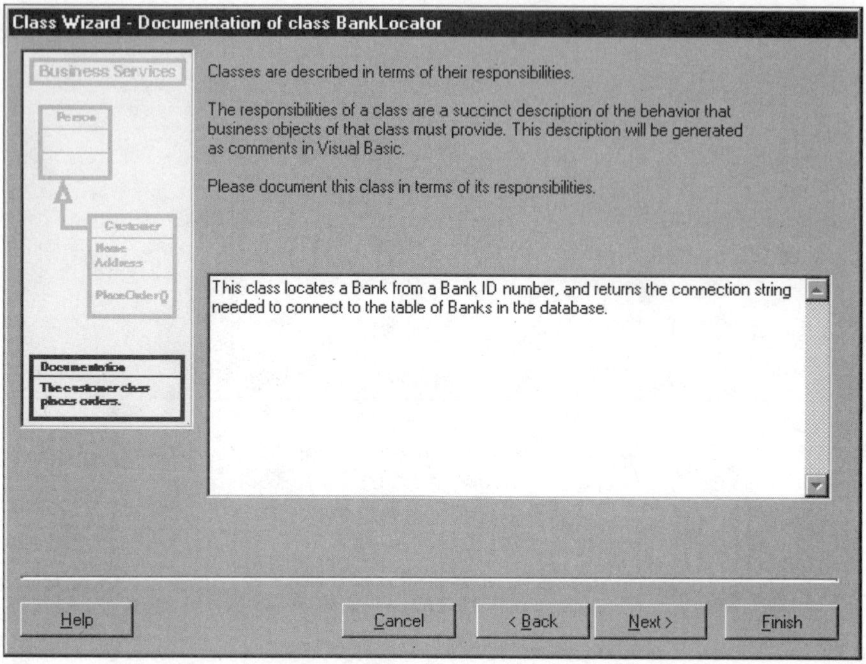

Class Wizard - Documentation of class BankLocator

Business Services

Person

Customer
Name
Address
PlaceOrder()

Documentation
The customer class places orders.

Classes are described in terms of their responsibilities.

The responsibilities of a class are a succinct description of the behavior that business objects of that class must provide. This description will be generated as comments in Visual Basic.

Please document this class in terms of its responsibilities.

This class locates a Bank from a Bank ID number, and returns the connection string needed to connect to the table of Banks in the database.

Help		Cancel	< Back	Next >	Finish

6. Click Next. In the next screen, choose to place the `BankLocator` class in the Business Services tier. Choosing Finish at any point will bypass the remainder of the Wizard screens. At this point the Wizard does not have enough information to fully construct the code, so continue with the following screens:

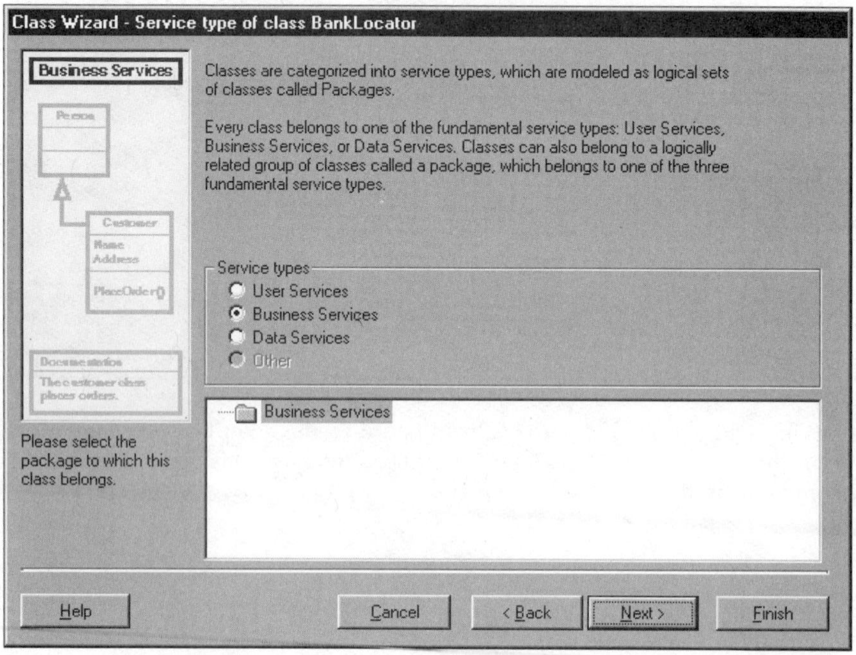

Class Wizard - Service type of class BankLocator

Business Services

Person

Customer
Name
Address
PlaceOrder()

Documentation
The customer class places orders.

Please select the package to which this class belongs.

Classes are categorized into service types, which are modeled as logical sets of classes called Packages.

Every class belongs to one of the fundamental service types: User Services, Business Services, or Data Services. Classes can also belong to a logically related group of classes called a package, which belongs to one of the three fundamental service types.

Service types
- ○ User Services
- ● Business Services
- ○ Data Services
- ○ Other

Business Services

Help		Cancel	< Back	Next >	Finish

7. The screen now brought up gives us the choice of whether or not to have the new class inherit the implementation and/or the interface of an existing class. In this case the class is new, so select No. Then click Next:

8. Now we get to add the methods of the class:

- ❑ Right-click in the Methods text area and select Insert.
- ❑ Click in the Name area of the General tab and name the method GetBank.
- ❑ Select a return type of String.
- ❑ Select the Arguments tab.
- ❑ Right-click in the Arguments area and select Insert to add an argument for the method.
- ❑ Name the argument BankID and select a Long data type for it.
- ❑ Make sure Visual Basic is selected as the language for the class.
- ❑ Now click Next.

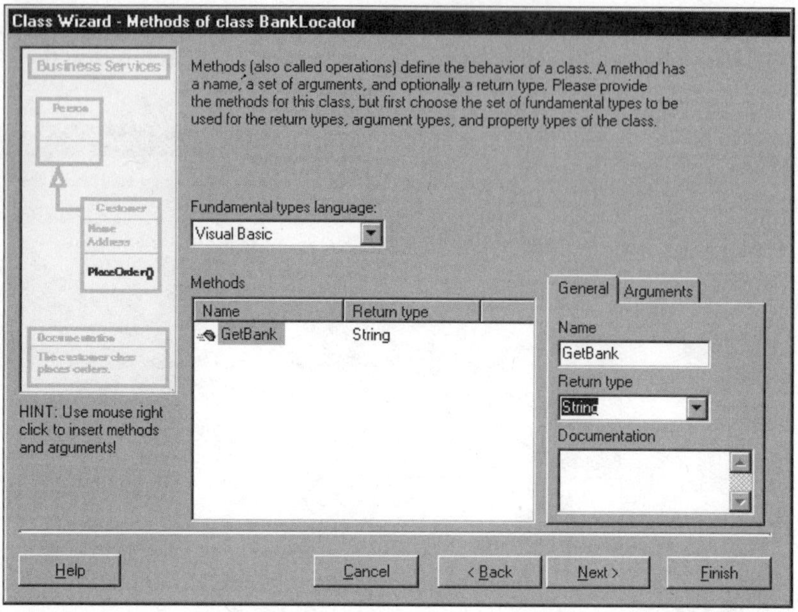

9. In the next screen, we add properties (attributes) for the class. We simply follow the same procedure as with methods: right-clicking in the Properties area to insert a new property and naming it MODULE_NAME. Set its type to String, and enter an initial value for it of "Bank_Bus.BankLocator".

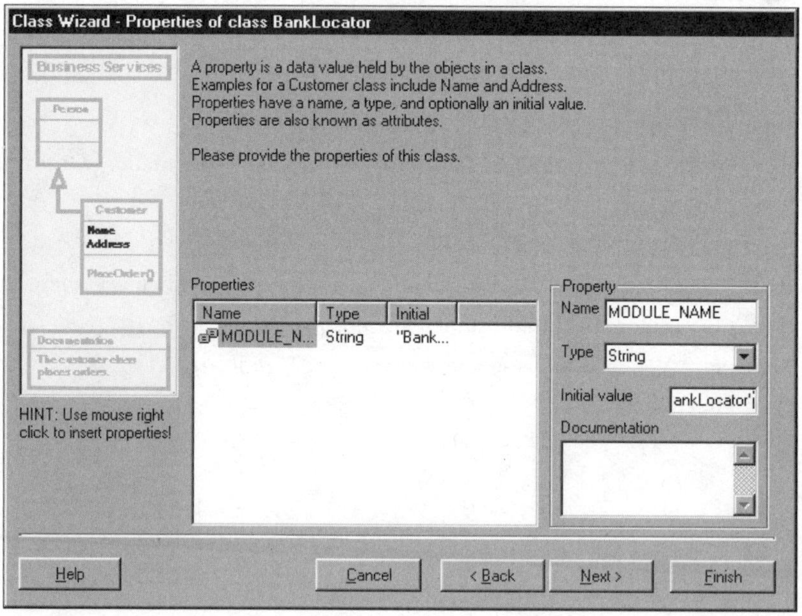

10. Click Next. The final screen shows a report of what the Class Wizard proposes to create as the new class. Press the Finish button and the Wizard will create the new class.

11. The newly created class is placed in the Business Services tier, and is illustrated like this:

BankLocator
⬦MODULE_NAME : String = "Bank_Bus.BankLocator"
◆GetBank()

12. We can choose to display the method's arguments by right-clicking on the class (in the Class Diagram window) and selecting Options | Show Method Arguments.

13. Then, set the visibility of the MODULE_NAME attribute (property) to Private by expanding the Browser. The Browser is the pane on the top left of the VM window. If the Browser is not open, it can be opened from the View menu. Expand the Logical View tree, and open the Business Services container and expand the BankLocator node. The Browser should look similar to the following illustration:

14. Now, right-click on the MODULE_NAME property to open the context menu, and select Open Specification. The Property Specification property page opens, where we can select the Private visibility option:

```
┌─────────────────────────────────────────────────┐
│ 🔍 Property Specification for MODULE_NAME  [?][X] │
├─────────────────────────────────────────────────┤
│ ┌─General─┐                                       │
│ │ General │                                       │
│                                                   │
│  Name:      [MODULE_NAME    ]  Class: BankLocator │
│                                                   │
│  Type:      [String        ▼]  ☑ Show classes     │
│                                                   │
│                                                   │
│  Initial value: ["Bank_Bus.BankLocator"        ] │
│                                                   │
│  ┌─Export Control────────────────────────────┐   │
│  │ ○ Public  ○ Protected  ● Private  ○ Implementation │
│  └───────────────────────────────────────────┘   │
│  Documentation:                                   │
│  ┌─────────────────────────────────────────┐▲    │
│  │ID_3                                      │      │
│  │                                          │      │
│  │                                          │      │
│  │                                          │▼     │
│  └─────────────────────────────────────────┘      │
│  [  OK  ]  [ Cancel ]  [ Apply ]  [Browse ▼] [Help]│
└─────────────────────────────────────────────────┘
```

15. Apply the change and close the Property Specification property page. The class should now look like this:

```
┌────────────────────────────────────────────────────┐
│                  BankLocator                        │
├────────────────────────────────────────────────────┤
│ 🔒MODULE_NAME : String = "Bank_Bus.BankLocator"     │
├────────────────────────────────────────────────────┤
│ ◆GetBank(BankID : Long) : String                    │
└────────────────────────────────────────────────────┘
```

The class now shows the method argument and return type, and the padlock symbol to the left of the MODULE_NAME property indicates that its visibility is private to the class. We are now almost ready to generate a code prototype of our new class in VB. Before we move onto that, however, we should just make sure that Visual Basic is set up in the right way to work with Visual Modeler.

Try It Out – Preparing Visual Basic

1. Start up Microsoft Visual Basic 6.0.

2. Select Cancel on the New Project screen.

3. From the Add-Ins menu, select Add-In Manager.

4. When the Add-In Manager appears, scroll down to find Visual Modeler Add-In and Visual Modeler Menus Add-In. Make sure that the Loaded/Unloaded and Load on Startup options are checked, then press OK.

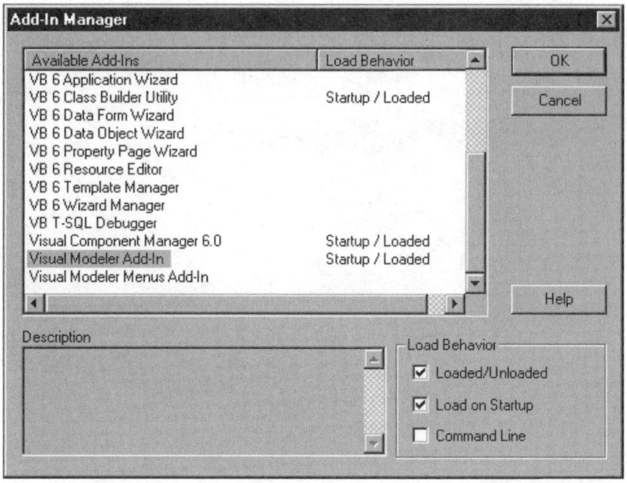

Add-In Manager

Available Add-Ins	Load Behavior	
VB 6 Application Wizard		**OK**
VB 6 Class Builder Utility	Startup / Loaded	
VB 6 Data Form Wizard		**Cancel**
VB 6 Data Object Wizard		
VB 6 Property Page Wizard		
VB 6 Resource Editor		
VB 6 Template Manager		
VB 6 Wizard Manager		
VB T-SQL Debugger		
Visual Component Manager 6.0	Startup / Loaded	
Visual Modeler Add-In	Startup / Loaded	
Visual Modeler Menus Add-In		**Help**

Description

Load Behavior
- ☑ Loaded/Unloaded
- ☑ Load on Startup
- ☐ Command Line

5. Visual Basic is now set up correctly to generate a code prototype from our new class.

Now we can move on to generating our code.

Try It Out – Generating Code

1. Return to Visual Modeler and click on the BankLocator class (in the Class diagram window) to select it, and then choose Tools | Generate Code. In the Code Generator's first screen, Assign to new Component, select Visual Basic DLL as the component type to create. Press OK to begin generating the code:

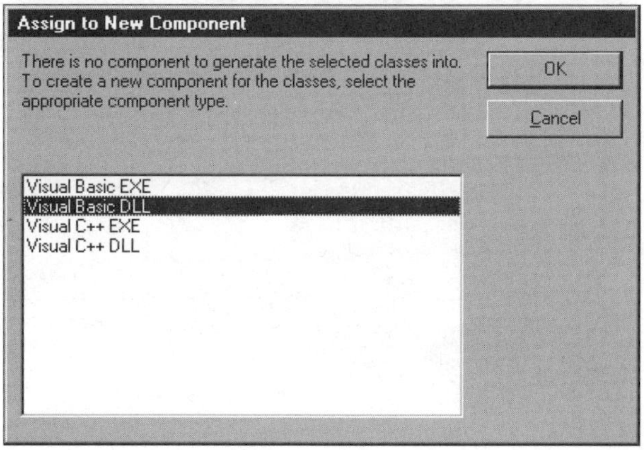

Assign to New Component

There is no component to generate the selected classes into. To create a new component for the classes, select the appropriate component type.

OK

Cancel

Visual Basic EXE
Visual Basic DLL
Visual C++ EXE
Visual C++ DLL

2. The Code Generation Wizard displays an informational screen, which we can choose not to display again, and the next screen shows that the BankLocator class is already selected for code generation. This screen enables us to add additional classes and other entities to the items for which code will be generated:

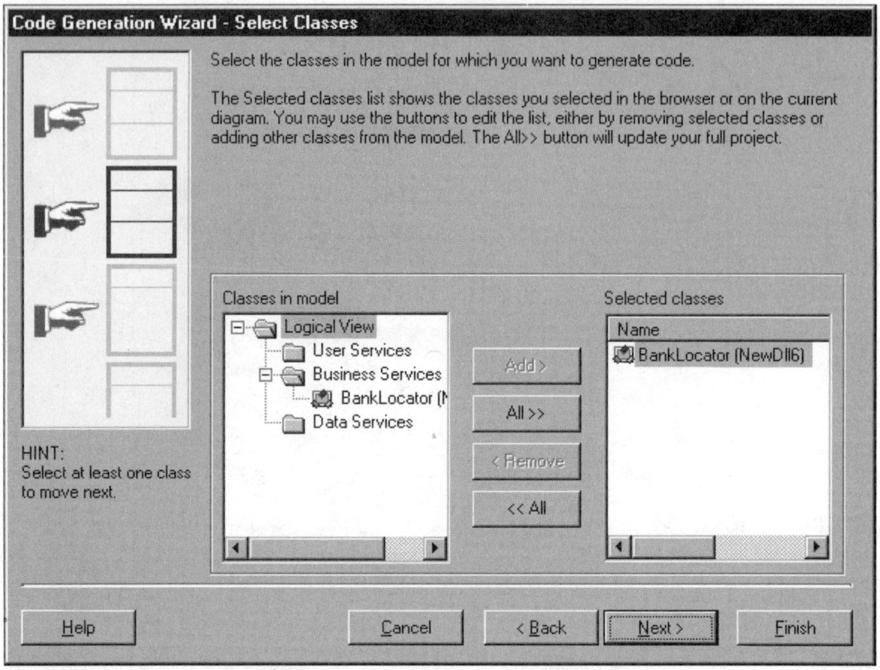

Code Generation Wizard - Select Classes

Select the classes in the model for which you want to generate code.

The Selected classes list shows the classes you selected in the browser or on the current diagram. You may use the buttons to edit the list, either by removing selected classes or adding other classes from the model. The All>> button will update your full project.

HINT:
Select at least one class to move next.

Classes in model

- Logical View
  - User Services
  - Business Services
    - BankLocator (N
  - Data Services

Add >

All >>

< Remove

<< All

Selected classes

Name

BankLocator (NewDll6)

Help   Cancel   < Back   Next >   Finish

3. The next screen enables us to preview the code that will be generated. If we want to preview the code, we click the Preview button, but before we do this, we'll need to set some of the properties of our class:

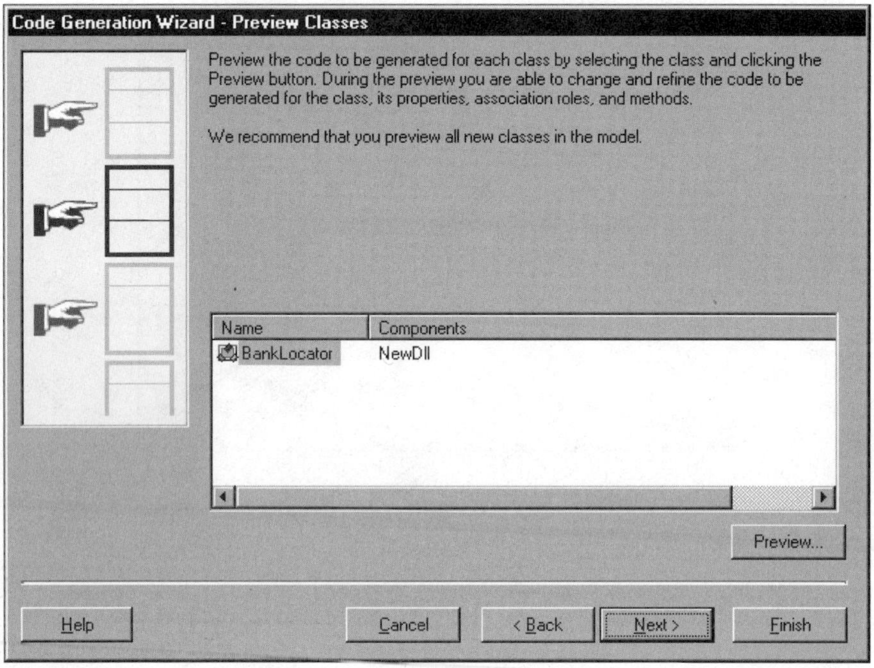

Code Generation Wizard - Preview Classes

Preview the code to be generated for each class by selecting the class and clicking the Preview button. During the preview you are able to change and refine the code to be generated for the class, its properties, association roles, and methods.

We recommend that you preview all new classes in the model.

Name	Components
BankLocator	NewDll

Preview...

Help   Cancel   < Back   Next >   Finish

4. Select Preview to bring up the first property page. This enables us to change the instancing of the class to any of the options offered by VB. In this case, set the Instancing option to PublicNotCreatable and leave the Collection Class option unchanged:

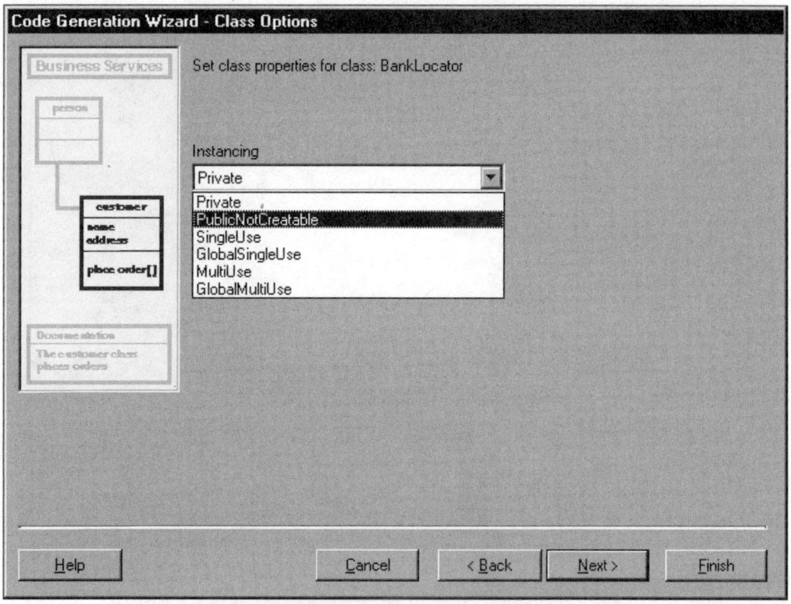

5. Next, we have a screen that enables us to set the properties of the property/attribute if required. Any changes we make are reflected in the code textbox at the bottom of the screen:

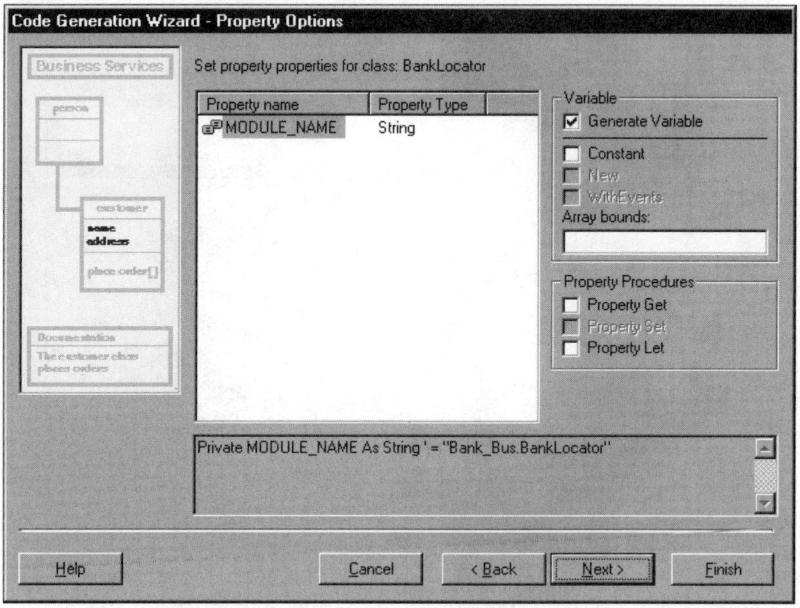

6. The next screen enables us to set properties for the associations and roles for the class in relation to other classes. Since our class has no associations or roles specified at this point, there are none listed. Click Next to continue.

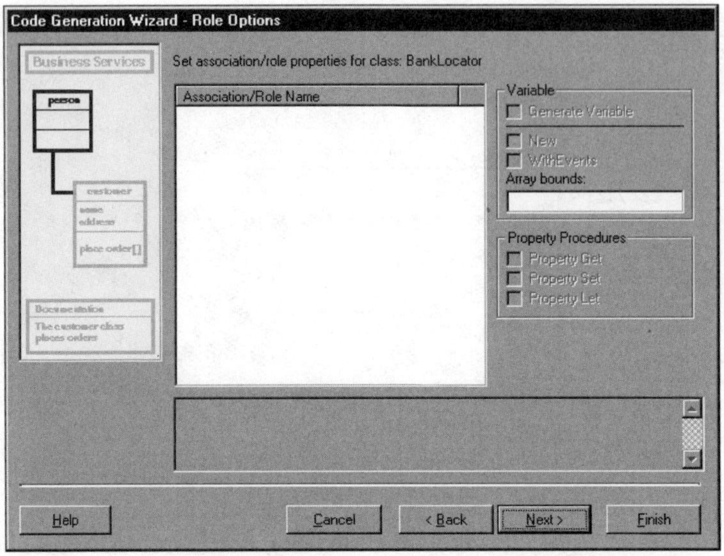

7. The next screen enables us to set model properties, which we can use to create object variables in the generated code. In the following screen we set the properties of the methods in the class. Set the Method Type to Property Get and press the Finish button to finish setting class properties.

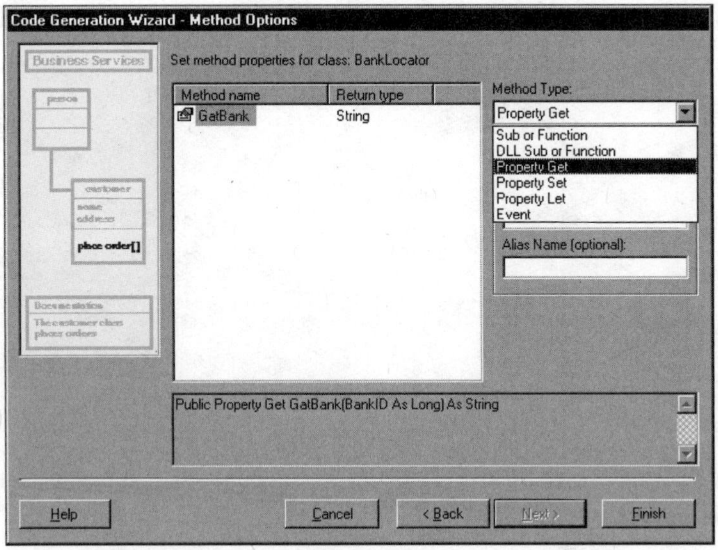

8. This will take us back to the screen in which we first opted to view the code. At this point, we need to click Next to move on to the next screen.

9. In this screen, we set the global options for the code generation. In this case, to simplify the generated code, clear all the checkboxes except for the Save model... and Include comments checkboxes:

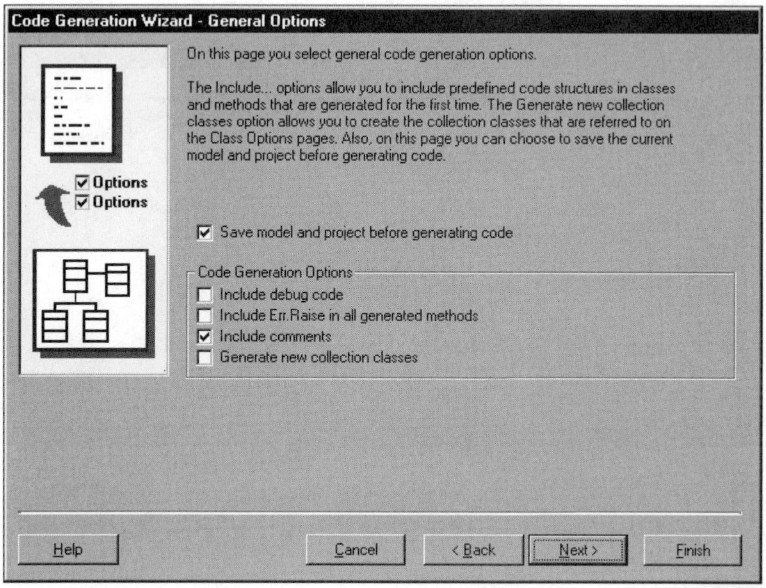

10. After another information screen, we arrive at the final screen where pressing Finish generates the code. This may take some time, so be patient. We may encounter a screen that enables us to remove components that have no correspondence in the model. Remove the Form1 component from the code and proceed with the code generation by pressing OK:

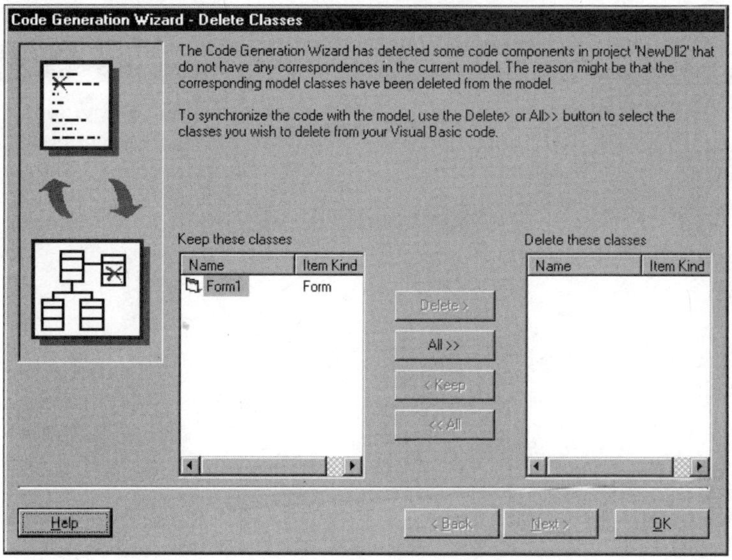

11. The code that is generated is shown in the VB project that is created and opened when the code generator finishes. Each attribute and method of the class is assigned a Model ID number that helps keep the code and the model in synch. Prototype methods are generated for the methods in the class and for the `Class_Initialize` and `Class_Terminate` events.

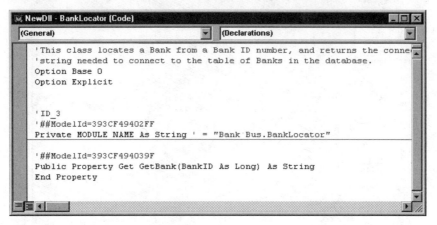

```
'This class locates a Bank from a Bank ID number, and returns the conne
'string needed to connect to the table of Banks in the database.
Option Base 0
Option Explicit


'ID_3
'##ModelId=393CF49402FF
Private MODULE NAME As String ' = "Bank Bus.BankLocator"

'##ModelId=393CF494039F
Public Property Get GetBank(BankID As Long) As String
End Property
```

Now that we have seen how to generate code from Visual Modeler, we will move on to look at one way in which we can integrate our new class within an application; by creating Deployment Diagrams using Visual Modeler.

Creating Deployment Diagrams with Visual Modeler

The Deployment diagrams that we can create with VM are simple diagrams with nodes representing instances of physical components of the system, such as computers, with processes that are contained in the node shown below the node.

Try It Out – Create a Deployment Diagram

1. In the Model Browser in Visual Modeler, double-click on the Deployment View to open a Deployment diagram. Right-click on the Deployment View and select New Node in the context menu. Repeat this process until there are a total of three nodes in the diagram.

2. Right-click on the first node and select Open Specification. In the General tab, name the node Data Services.

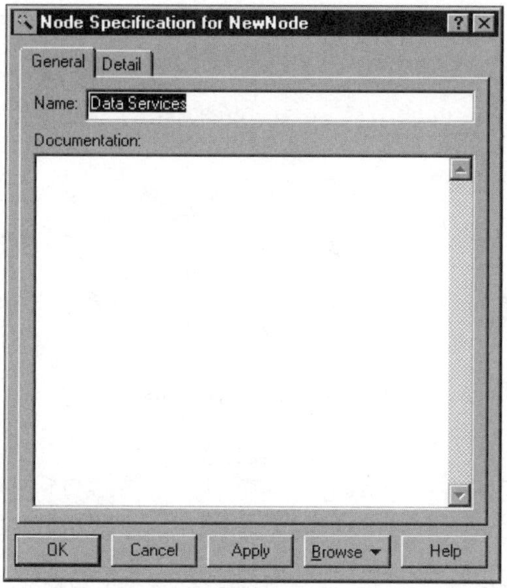

3. In the Detail tab, right-click and select Insert to insert a new process. Name the process Bank_DB.DLL:

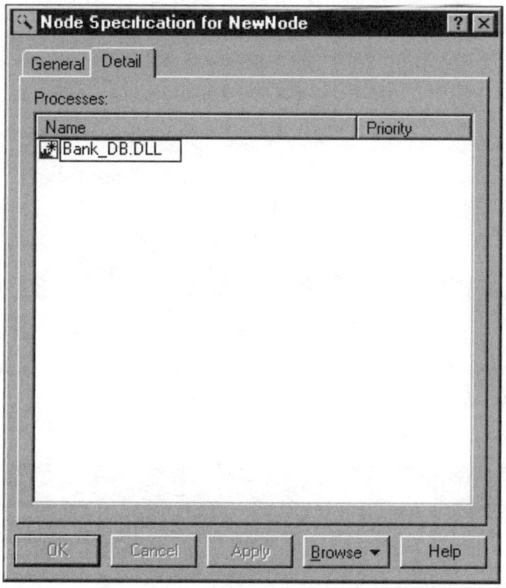

4. Press OK to apply the changes and repeat the process with the second node. Name it Business Services and insert a process named Bank_Bus.DLL.

5. Press OK to apply the changes and repeat the process with the third node. Name it User Services, and insert a process named Bank_UI.EXE.

6. Click on the Data Services node in the context menu and drag it into the Deployment View window. Repeat with the remaining two nodes.

7. Add a connection from the first tier to the next tier by choosing Tools | Create | Connection: click on Data Services and drag the mouse to Business Services: a line should appear that joins the two.

8. Repeat the process to make a connection between the Business Services and the User Services.

9. Right-click on Data Services and check the Show Processes option – repeat for the other two services.

10. Our Deployment diagram should now look like this:

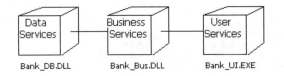

11. The Deployment diagram we have just generated depicts a system identical to that shown in the Deployment diagram example shown previously in this chapter.

Creating such Deployment diagrams can be a great help when constructing a large application. They help us visualize the ways in which the different components of our application interact with one another and which components belong in which tier.

We will now turn to another helpful visualization technique available in Visual Modeler; one for creating diagrams of *components*.

Creating Component Diagrams with Visual Modeler

The Component diagrams that we can create with VM are fairly simple, with only the capability of showing the executable components themselves. The classes that are contained in the components are not shown.

Try It Out: Create a Component Diagram

1. In Visual Modeler choose Browse | Component Diagram and choose to create a new diagram. Name the new Component diagram WROBA.

2. Choose Tools | Create | Component, then click anywhere within the new diagram. Repeat twice to add another two component packages to the diagram.

3. Right-click on the first component and choose Open Specification. Name the component Bank_DB.DLL and set the Stereotype to DLL. Set the language to Visual Basic.

Component Specification for NewComponent

General | Realizes

Name: Bank_DB.DLL

Stereotype: DLL   Language: Visual Basic

Documentation:

OK   Cancel   Apply   Browse ▾   Help

4. Repeat the process with the other two components and name them Bank_Bus.DLL (with a Stereotype of DLL) and Bank_UI.EXE (with a Stereotype of EXE). The diagram should look similar to this:

Bank_
DB.DLL

Bank_
Bus.DLL

Bank_
UI.EXE

5. Choose Tools | Create | Dependency. Click in the Bank_UI.EXE component and drag the mouse into the Bank_Bus.DLL component to create a dependency between the two components.

6. Choose Tools I Create I Dependency. Click in the Bank_Bus.DLL component and drag the mouse into the Bank_DB.DLL component to create a dependency between them. Our component diagram should now look like this:

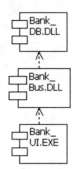

Visual Modeler can create only a subset of the possible UML diagrams, and the Deployment and Component diagrams it creates are limited. It is possible to add other elements to a diagram, such as notes. However, to really find out what Visual Modeler is capable of, it would be worthwhile experimenting with it. Although it isn't a fully-fledged UML design system, it does have powerful code generation and reverse engineering features that make it a useful tool.

In this section we have learned how to set up Visual Basic to integrate with Visual Modeler, and how to create Class, Component and Deployment diagrams with Visual Modeler. We've also learned how to use Visual Modeler to generate VB code from a Class.

Summary

Throughout this book, we'll build on the knowledge gained in this chapter. We started the chapter by looking at what the Unified Modeling Language (UML) is and pointed out that, although it might seem a difficult and slightly esoteric subject, it can be very helpful in aiding us in application development.

We then moved on to look at some of the major diagram types used within UML: we saw that there are two main types of diagram – ones that depict a static view of the system (like class diagrams) and ones that depict a dynamic view of the system (like Use Case diagrams). Additionally we have package diagrams that act as a container for some of the other types.

We finished up the chapter by looking at using Visual Modeler, the UML design tool included with VB6 Enterprise Edition, and saw how it can help us generate prototype code and UML diagrams quickly and easily.

All of this has given us a thorough introduction to the UML we use within this book. Although it is by no means a complete exploration of the language, it will serve to allow us to develop reasonably detailed analyses of customer needs.

UML is a tricky subject to get to grips with first off – until you experience how useful it can be in application development it is somewhat difficult to get a handle on. Hopefully, as you progress through the book (and especially with the next chapter) you'll see how UML is of great use. By the time you've ended the book and seen the case study in action (and how the 3-tier architecture is flexible and extensible) you may wish to revisit these chapters to gain a greater appreciation of the subject. Just like software development, learning sometimes benefits from an iterative approach.

In the next chapter, we will start using UML to design the WROBA case study application.

Designing a Solution

In this chapter, we're going to use the **deliverables** from the analysis phase of the project to begin designing the project. The deliverables are the Use Cases, Use Case diagrams and Use Case Scenarios. We will use UML diagrams to model these deliverables.

The design phase is an iterative process, just as the analysis phase was. During the design phase the analysis phase may have to be revisited, as new requirements are discovered or added, or requirements that were analyzed previously are discovered to be incomplete or in error. In this phase of the software development process we'll start at a generalized logical level and then proceed to specifics that begin the implementation phase of the project. As part of this process we'll learn more about using the different UML diagrams we introduced in the previous chapter.

Thus in this chapter we'll look at the topics of:

- ❑   Component design
- ❑   Modeling software solutions
- ❑   Using Use Case Scenarios to model the WROBA case study via **domain** and **design** model diagrams

This is going to be a chapter that introduces some new terms and concepts – again some of this material may seem quite complex at first glance, but don't worry all will become clear by the end of the chapter when we get stuck into designing the WROBA application.

Component Design

Let's kick off with a definition:

> **Component design is the task of designing the component interfaces and the component relationships. Component design is not concerned with component implementation.**

In Visual Basic, as an object-oriented programming language, classes implement interfaces. So the business of component design is that of defining a set of classes, and specifying which methods, properties and events these classes implement (through their interfaces, of course).

For a moment let's recap some of the material we covered in Chapters 3 and 4 as the difference between an interface and an implementation for a class can be unclear.

An **interface** is the set of properties and methods that a class exposes as public properties and methods. What this means for a **component interface** is a promise that from one version to another the properties and methods will be consistent. The way a property or method works inside the class may be changed, but that should not change how it is viewed from the outside world. New methods and properties may be added to a class, but none may be removed without breaking component compatibility.

When a component that uses an interface that is exposed by a library (such as a DLL) is created, an exposed method or property must be provided for each method or property in that interface. Each exposed method or property must be present in the interface, and must be defined in exactly the same way as in the interface, to properly represent that class.

Class inheritance, where a child class inherits the properties and methods of a parent class through an interface, is an important part of object-oriented programming (we'll come across the topic when we consider Generalization). Interestingly Visual Basic 6 does not implement class inheritance, (although there are workarounds that can simulate inheritance). True class inheritance will be a feature of the next version of this language (Visual Basic 7), according to the latest information from Microsoft at the time this book was written. As we saw in Chapter 4, in VB6 most of the uses of interfaces are for the early stages of class design, presenting black-box models of classes, and implementing classes that are exposed as skeletons in libraries such as DLL and TLB files.

Logical and Physical Design

Component design consists of a logical design phase and a physical design phase. During the **logical design**, the classes and their relationships are identified using the Use Case Scenarios from Chapter 6 as the starting point. In this chapter we'll learn how to derive the logical design. During the **physical design**, the components are allocated a location on the network, based on the architectural tier (presentation, business, or data in a 3-tier design) to which they belong. Physical design, which uses logical design as its starting point, is covered in Chapters 9 to 15.

Component design, as with many other design activities, is not a linear process, where there is a straight line from start to finish. Instead, it is an iterative process where successive refinements lead to a solution. These step-by-step refinements apply both within a design step (within logical design for example) and between design steps, such as between logical and physical design.

> **Design does not lead to a single, correct solution. Any solution must therefore be validated against the stated design goals.**

It must also be pointed out that there is often more than one solution that will correspond to a set of scenarios. Often it is impossible to logically decide which one is better solely by the virtues of each design. Therefore the design must be validated against the stated design goals, sometimes by building a proof-of-concept prototype.

In this section, we're going to look at how the techniques used for object-oriented analysis and design can be adapted to solve the challenges specific to component-based development. To do this we're going to discuss:

- ❑ Component performance issues
- ❑ Component relationships
- ❑ Component interactions

Component Performance in Distributed Applications

As we know from Chapter 1, in a distributed application components may run on different machines than the parent application.

Object-oriented techniques may be used successfully when designing with components, but must take into account the consequences of components running on different machines. This distribution of components across machines has a profound impact on design decisions because crossing machine boundaries is a very expensive operation in terms of time.

> A network trip, also called a network round trip or just a round trip, is an expensive operation that occurs each time a method or property of a remote component is called. A remote component is a component located on a different computer or server to the application using the component.

In the case of passing a parameter by reference, a second network trip is required to pass the resulting value back to the caller. Let's have a look at what this means in practice. Let's say we have a remote component (CCustomer), which contains the following code:

```
Dim m_strFirstName As String
Dim m_strLastName As String

Public Property Let FirstName(strName As String)
    m_strFirstName = strName
End Property

Public Property Let LastName(strName As String)
    m_strLastName = strName
End Property
```

Then, let's say we want to make calls to that class to set the FirstName and LastName properties:

```
' CCustomer is a remote component
Dim objCustomer As CCustomer
Set objCustomer = New CCustomer

' 2 calls = 2 network trips
ObjCustomer.FirstName = "Cecilia"
ObjCustomer.LastName = "Poremsky"
```

This causes two network round trips.

This may be avoided by sending all properties in one call, by using an `Init` method for the class. In this case the remote class would have the form:

```
Dim m_strFirstName As String
Dim m_strLastName As String

Public Sub Init(FirstName As String, LastName As String)
    m_strFirstName = FirstName
    m_strLastName = LastName
End Sub
```

and the calling code:

```
' CCustomer is a remote component
Dim objCustomer as CCustomer
Set objCustomer = New CCustomer

' 1 call = 1 network trip
ObjCustomer.Init FirstName:="Cecilia", _
    LastName:="Poremsky"
```

The `Init` method enables the same information to be set while using only one network round trip.

These code examples have passed arguments in the default `ByRef` calling format. Using `ByRef` arguments causes a network round trip, since the argument can be changed in the called remote class. The first half of the network round trip is to get the variable that is being passed, the second half is to write back the value even if it was not changed.

When arguments are passed `ByVal`, only the value of the argument is passed and it cannot be changed in the called remote class. So a network round trip is not required and the call only requires a one-way network trip:

```
Dim m_strFirstName As String
Dim m_strLastName As String

Public Sub Init(ByVal FirstName As String, ByVal LastName As String)
    m_strFirstName = FirstName
    m_strLastName = LastName
End Sub
```

Such optimizations are not often discovered in the first-cut design, and are one of the reasons a few iterations are often needed before a good design is achieved.

Considerations such as these come into play when designing distributed applications and are just not a concern in a monolithic application where all classes are in-process and run on the same machine. Optimizations such as the ones just illustrated will be more important as the design and implementation phases proceed, but it is good to be aware of them from the onset so that the decisions taken at the beginning of the design phase are consistent with the desired end results. It isn't worth spending too much time trying to optimize the performance of the solution at this point, but performance considerations such as network trips are issues we should remain aware of.

To have all the information needed to implement the classes for an application, we need to discover the relationships and interactions between the classes.

Component Relationships

The pioneers of object-oriented design have studied class relationships and classified these relationships into four categories:

- **Ownership**
- **Containment**
- **Generalization**
- **Usage**

We'll look at each category, and see how these relationships are typically implemented in Visual Basic. This is important because similar relationships exist in UML diagrams (as we saw in the previous chapter), and they will directly translate from the UML diagrams into the VB code.

Knowing how to implement these relationships gives us the skills that are needed when developing applications using a formal design process that includes the use of UML. Here we've repeated the UML depictions of these relationships just to reinforce the discussion.

Ownership

> **In an ownership relationship, the contained class cannot exist without its container.**

Ownership is closely related to **containment**, which is described in the next section. The difference lies in the life cycle of the contained class. In an ownership relationship, the contained class cannot exist without its container. A typical example of such a parent-child relationship is Bank/Bank Account. A bank contains one or more account items. An account item only exists in the context of a bank. The ownership relationship is called **composition** in UML, and in the UML diagram the filled diamond indicates the class that is the owner class:

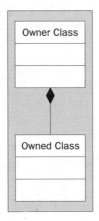

In Visual Basic, ownership is implemented via **membership**. Membership in this case means that the class that is created implements a specified class interface. One way of expressing this in VB code is to use the New constructor to instantiate a new instance of a defined class within another class.

The *owner* class contains one or more instances of the *owned* class. All the owned objects are created within the owner class and the owner class destroys all these owned objects when it is destroyed. That sounds complicated but the implementation is quite straightforward, for example a one-to-one ownership relationship (remember from Chapter 7 that these relationships have an associated multiplicity) could be implemented as follows:

```
' Bank class that owns an Account class item
Private m_objOwned As CAccountClass

Private Sub Class_Initialize()
    ' The owned object is created within the owner class
    Set m_objOwned = New CAccountClass
End Sub

Private Sub Class_Terminate()
    ' Destroy the owned object
    Set m_objOwned = Nothing
End Sub
```

The Initialize event of the owner class instantiates the module level class m_objOwned with the New keyword, and the Terminate event destroys the owned class by setting it equal to Nothing.

For a one-to-many ownership relationship a collection is created to hold instances of the owned classes in the Initialize event of the owner class, and a Public method of the class is used to instantiate instances of the owned class and add them to that collection. The Terminate event of the owner class is used to loop through the collection of owned classes, setting each one equal to Nothing to destroy it. Then the collection is destroyed by setting it equal to Nothing:

```
Private m_colOwnedObjects As Collection
Private m_objOwned As CAccountClass

Private Sub Class_Initialize()
    ' Create a collection to contain 1 or more member classes. The
    ' collection is a container for 1 to x number of owned items.
    Set m_colOwnedObjects = New Collection
End Sub

Public Sub AddOwned(strFirstName As String, strLastName As String)
' The arguments needed to create a valid instance of CAccountClass
' are passed to the AddOwned Sub. The instance is privately created
' inside the AddOwned Sub, and added to the collection of classes.
    Set m_objOwned = New CAccountClass

    m_objOwned.Init strFirstName, strLastName
    m_colOwnedObjects.Add m_objOwned

    Set m_objOwned = Nothing
End Sub
```

```
    Private Sub Class_Terminate()
    ' In the Class_Terminate Sub, the privately created instances
    ' of CaccountClass are released.

        For Each m_objOwned In m_colOwnedObjects
            Set m_objOwned = Nothing
        Next m_objOwned

        Set m_colOwnedObjects = Nothing
    End Sub
```

Containment

Containment implies that the contained class exists independently of the container.

As pointed out above, **containment** is closely related to ownership. Containment implies that the contained class exists independently of the container. A typical example of such a relationship is Airplane/Passenger. Passengers exist outside of the context of any specific airplane. UML refers to containment as simple aggregation, which is represented by an unfilled diamond at the connection point of the container class:

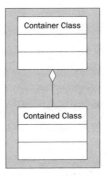

In Visual Basic, containment is also implemented via membership. The container contains one or more instances of the contained class. However, the contained objects are created and destroyed outside of the container. The following code shows how a one-to-one containment relationship is typically implemented – the contained class is passed as an argument to a `Property Set`:

```
    Private m_objContained As CSomeClass

    Public Property Set Contained(objContained As CSomeClass)
        ' The contained object is created (and will be released)
        ' outside of the container class
        Set m_objContained = objContained
    End Property

    Private Sub Class_Terminate()
        ' NOTE: m_objContained is NOT released in the container!
    End Sub
```

To implement a one-to-many containment relationship we could use code of the form:

```
Private m_colContainedObjects As Collection

Private Sub Class_Initialize()
    Set m_colContainedObjects = New Collection
End Sub

Public Sub AddContained(objContained As CSomeClass)
    ' The contained object is created (and will be released)
    ' outside of the class
    m_colContainedObjects.Add objContained
End Sub

Private Sub Class_Terminate()
    ' NOTE: The objects in the collection are NOT released in the class
    ' termination. Only the objects created in this class are released in
    ' the class termination. In this case, that is the collection object.

    Set m_colContainedObjects = Nothing
End Sub
```

A collection is created to contain instances of the contained classes within the container class, and a `Public` method of the container class is used to add the independently created instances of the contained class to the collection.

Generalization

Generalization, also known as implementation inheritance, occurs when a class, (called the derived class), inherits the implementation of another class, (called the base class). Interface inheritance is when a class inherits the interface, but not the implementation, of another class.

Generalization, sometimes also called **implementation inheritance**, is a relationship commonly expressed by an *is a type of* phrase: A Saving Account *is a type of* Bank Account. Inheriting the implementation means that changes in the base class are automatically used by the derived class. UML also uses the term generalization to refer to this relationship, which is represented as:

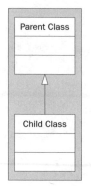

Interface inheritance is when a class inherits the interface, but not the implementation, of another class. With interface inheritance, the derived class ignores implementation changes in the base class.

Implementation inheritance requires a bit of work in Visual Basic and is achieved by combining interface inheritance with containment. Many academics and hard-core C++ programmers are unaware of this technique and use the lack of implementation inheritance as part of the argument of why Visual Basic is object-based instead of object-oriented. Since the benefits of implementation inheritance can be harvested in Visual Basic, this discussion is mainly an academic and political argument.

> *Implementing generalization is not straightforward in Visual Basic 6. On February 15th 2000, Microsoft announced direct support for implementation inheritance in Visual Basic 7.*

Although not trivial, let's see how we can implement generalization.

Try It Out – Implementing Generalization in VB6

1. Open Visual Basic and create a New Project – select Standard EXE as the project type.

2. Remove the default form by right-clicking on the form in Project Explorer and selecting Remove Form1. Then add a class module to the project by choosing Project | Add Class Module and selecting Class Module from the choices in the dialog box.

3. Name the new class BaseClass and add the following code to this class:

```
Option Explicit

Private m_strFirstName As String
Private m_strLastName As String

Public Sub Init(ByVal FirstName As String, ByVal LastName As String)
    m_strFirstName = FirstName
    m_strLastName = LastName
End Sub

Public Sub ShowNames()
    ' Show the first and last names, separated by a space
    MsgBox m_strFirstName & " " & m_strLastName, vbInformation
End Sub

Public Function SimpleFunction() As String
    ' Return a string made up of the first name followed by a _
    ' space, followed by the last name
    SimpleFunction = m_strFirstName & " " & m_strLastName
End Function
```

4. Add another class module to the project, name it DerivedClass and add the following code:

```
Option Explicit
' The derived class inherits the interface from the base class
' Note that we inherit the interface of a full-fledged class, not
' just some aspect of the interface.
Implements BaseClass

' We use a private member of the base class to be able to reuse
' the implementation of the base class.
Private m_objBaseClass As BaseClass

' -------- THE DERIVED CLASS OWNS A PRIVATE INSTANCE OF THE BASE CLASS --------
Private Sub Class_Initialize()
' Typically the base class is owned by the derived class,
' though containment is also possible.
    Set m_objBaseClass = New BaseClass
End Sub

Private Sub Class_Terminate()
    Set m_objBaseClass = Nothing
End Sub

' -------- PUBLIC METHODS AND PROPERTIES OF THE DERIVED CLASS --------
Public Sub Init(ByVal FirstName As String, ByVal LastName As String)
    BaseClass_Init FirstName, LastName
End Sub

Public Sub ShowNames()
    BaseClass_ShowNames
' Here you may add code specific to the derived class
End Sub

Public Function SimpleFunction() As String
' In this example we extend the SimpleFunction in the derived class
    SimpleFunction = "Miss " & BaseClass_SimpleFunction
End Function

' -------- ENSURE THE DERIVED CLASS INHERITS FROM THE BASE CLASS --------
' The private methods and properties of the interface are implemented
' using the private base class.
Private Sub BaseClass_Init(ByVal FirstName As String, ByVal LastName As String)
    m_objBaseClass.Init FirstName, LastName
End Sub

Private Sub BaseClass_ShowNames()
    m_objBaseClass.ShowNames
End Sub

Private Function BaseClass_SimpleFunction() As String
    BaseClass_SimpleFunction = m_objBaseClass.SimpleFunction
End Function
```

5. Add a code module (*not* a class module) to the project by choosing **Project | Add Module**. Name this module **MMain** and add the following code to the module to demonstrate generalization:

```
Option Explicit

Sub Main()
Dim objDerivedClass As DerivedClass

    Set objDerivedClass = New DerivedClass

    objDerivedClass.Init "Cecilia", "Poremsky"
    objDerivedClass.ShowNames
    MsgBox "SimpleFunction = " & objDerivedClass.SimpleFunction, _
      vbExclamation

    Set objDerivedClass = Nothing
End Sub
```

6. Choose **Project | Properties** and make sure that on the **General** tab the **Startup Object** is listed as **Sub Main** – if it isn't, select **Sub Main** in the **Startup Object** list box.

7. Save this project as **Derived Class Example**, and run it. As expected, the call to `objDerivedClass.ShowNames` in the derived class displays a dialog box showing **Cecilia Poremsky**, and the call to `objDerivedClass.SimpleFunction` in the derived class returns **Miss Cecilia Poremsky**:

8. Now, change the `SimpleFunction` in the **BaseClass** class module to return only the last name instead of the first and last names separated by a space:

```
Public Function SimpleFunction() As String
    ' Return a string made up of the last name
    SimpleFunction = m_strLastName
End Function
```

9. Run the project. This time, the `SimpleFunction` in the **DerivedClass** class module returns **Miss Poremsky**:

283

How It Works

The code is heavily commented and can be followed, but it is worth highlighting the use of the `Implements` keyword to declare that the derived class implements the public methods and properties of the parent base class:

```
' The derived class inherits the interface from the base class
' Note that we inherit the interface of a full-fledged class, not
' just some aspect of the interface.

Implements BaseClass
```

The code in the public methods and properties of the derived class (the implementation) may be different to that in the base class, but the interface is the same.

Through inheritance, we can have a derived class use code implemented in a base class and automatically change its behavior when this code is changed in the base class. In the sample project, we were able to change the behavior of the `SimpleFunction` function in the derived class by just changing the `SimpleFunction` function in the base class (leaving the `SimpleFunction` function in the derived class unchanged). This is why this is called implementation inheritance – the derived class inherits the implementation of the base class.

Usage

Usage is a relationship that implies that one class collaborates with another class. UML also refers to this relationship as usage. On one hand, this type of relationship is used as a generic class relationship, before a more precise type of relationship has been determined. On the other hand, not every instance of usage relationship needs to be transformed into another type. The UML diagram for this is:

An example of this is when a class is passed as a parameter in a method.

```
Sub SomeMethodInAClass(objSomeOtherClass As CSomeOtherClass)
    MsgBox "Last name is: " & objSomeOtherClass.LastName
End Sub
```

This may be left as a usage relationship, or we may determine that the relationship should be transformed into a containment relationship. This may require transforming the method into a property.

Component Interaction Rules

In this section, to help us design correct class models, we're going to look at the rules governing the interaction of classes, in particular we'll look at:

- ❑ Own/contain rules
- ❑ The generalize rule

Own/Contain Rules

Four rules, pointed out by Jake Sturm in his book *VB6 UML Design and Development, ISBN 1861002513,* also by *Wrox Press,* govern the relationship between a base class and the contained class in an ownership or containment relationship (here our discussion encompasses both relationships, but remember there is a distinction between them). Since implementation inheritance in Visual Basic must be implemented using containment, these rules also apply to inheritance. In the code fragments below, a class (from now on called the parent class), declares a member class, called the contained/owned class, as follows:

```
Private m_objSomeClass As CSomeClass
```

Rule 1: The parent class can pass information to the contained class by an `Init` method or by using properties.

An example of information being passed to the contained/owned class is:

```
Sub SomeMethodInTheBaseClass(lngSomeNumber As Long, strSomeText As String)
    ' Passing a single item of information with a property
    m_objSomeClass.Key = lngSomeNumber

    ' Passing a set of items with a method
    m_objSomeClass.Init lngSomeNumber, strSomeText
End Sub
```

As pointed out above, the use of an `Init` method is usually motivated by the desire to reduce network trips. If a set of properties were often used together, we would similarly create a method to pass this set in one trip, for example `SetName()` or `SetAddress()`. This optimization technique should be used even when the items being passed are not logically related.

Rule 2: The parent class can get the contained/owned class to perform a task by calling a method of the contained/owned class.

An example of the contained/owned class performing a task in the parent class is:

```
Sub SomeOtherMethodInTheBaseClass(lngSomeNumber As Long, _
        strSomeText As String)
    ' Some code here, maybe
```

```
        m_objSomeClass.PrintKeyAndName lngSomeNumber, strSomeText

    ' Some more code here as well, maybe
End Sub
```

There are two ways to perform a method call:

❑   A **synchronous** method call waits until all processing is done before calling the next line of code, which is the default behavior in VB.

❑   An **asynchronous** method immediately returns to the caller (likely after doing some quick initialization). The caller is then notified when the method is finished.

There are two notification mechanisms:

❑   Call-back methods

❑   Events

A call-back method is a method that will be called whenever the method has finished. This is implemented by passing the call-back method to the called method as a means of returning a notification. Call-back methods are used in some Win32 API calls (Win32 API referring to the set of DLL's available in 32-bit Windows systems that provide procedures for common OS related functions), and are more common in C++ than in VB, but they can be used in VB. An event notification is implemented by raising an event in the calling class to notify that class that the called method has finished. Event notifications are more common and are the preferred method of implementing notifications – see rule 4 below.

> **Rule 3: The contained/owned class has no direct access to the methods or properties of the parent class.**
>
> **Rule 4: The contained/owned class can pass information to the parent class by using events.**

Rules 3 and 4 dictate how information is passed up from the owned/contained class to the parent class – only by using events. This requires changing the declaration of the contained/owned class to:

```
    Private WithEvents m_objSomeClass As CSomeClass
```

The WithEvents clause in the declaration shown above notifies VB that the class will handle events raised by the contained/owned class.

Generalize Rule

The rule governing implementation inheritance is called the **Liskov substitution principle** and gives a framework to decide when implementation inheritance is appropriate.

> **The Liskov substitution principle is that the interface of the derived class must be substitutable for that of the base class (require no more, promise no less).**

This principle, also called **contravariance**, is specifically designed to facilitate **polymorphism**. Polymorphism, is a term used in object-oriented programming and refers to the ability to create objects that inherit the characteristics of a general object but implement specific individual functionality.

For example, a general Bank class will implement certain methods and properties such as Account. A SavingsBank class would implement all the methods and properties of the Bank class (like Account) but might add methods and properties for Loans, Money Market accounts and other specialized characteristics of a Savings Bank.

Strict adherence to this contravariance principle (first discussed, though not in the context of Visual Basic, by Barbara Liskov in a paper published in May 1988) allows us to use derived classes everywhere we expect base classes.

Implementing Polymorphic Behavior

When implementing polymorphic behavior, we use a base class as a container for derived classes, so the interface of the derived class must be substitutable for that of the base class. This does not mean that the *implementation* of the derived class must be identical to that of the base class. It only promises that the *interface* (public methods and properties) is the same.

For methods, this means that the incoming (`ByVal` and `ByRef`) parameters should not require more than what is required in the base class, while the outgoing (`ByRef`) parameters and return values (functions) should promise no less than what is promised by the base class. As `ByRef` parameters are both incoming and outgoing, their requirements in the derived class must therefore be exactly the same as in the base class. The requirements must be taken from the *specification* of the base class, rather than the *implementation* of the base class, which may be more specific.

That might sound a bit abstract so let's illustrate how these constraints work. In our hypothetical base class, a function requires its parameter to be odd, while it promises to return a number divisible by three:

```
Public Function SomeFunctionInTheBaseClass(ByVal lngSomeNumber _
    As Long) as Long
Dim lngResult As Long

    ' REQUIRE: lngSomeNumber is odd
    If (0 = lngSomeNumber Mod 2) Then
        Err.Raise vbObjectError + 100, "SomeFunctionInTheBaseClass", _
        "lngSomeNumber is NOT odd!"
    Else
        ' Some code here to compute lngResult

        ' PROMISE: lngResult is divisible by 3
        Debug.Assert (0 = lngResult Mod 3)

        SomeFunctionInTheBaseClass = lngResult
    End If
End Function
```

For the same function in the derived class, the function must not impose stronger requirements on its parameter (here the requirement is weakened – the function will accept an odd or even number), while it must not make a weaker promise (here a stronger promise is made – the function returns a number divisible by 21):

```
Public Function DerivedClass_SomeFunctionInTheBaseClass(ByVal _
    lngSomeNumber As Long) as Long
Dim lngResult As Long

    ' REQUIRE: lngSomeNumber can be any number

    ' Some code here to compute lngResult

    ' PROMISE: lngResult is divisible by 3 * 7 (21)
    Debug.Assert (0 = lngResult Mod 21)

    SomeFunctionInTheBaseClass = lngResult
End Function
```

The contravariance principle is most often applied with polymorphic collections – as seen in the code below:

```
Private Sub SomeMethod()
Dim objBaseClass As CBaseClass
Dim lngResult As Long

    For Each objBaseClass In m_colSomeCollection
        ' lngSomeNumber must be odd since objBaseClass may
        ' actually be a BaseClass
        lngResult = objBaseClass.SomeFunctionInTheBaseClass(17)

        ' Check Base Class PROMISE
        Debug.Assert (0 = lngResult Mod 3)

        MsgBox lngResult, vbExclamation
    Next objBaseClass
End Sub
```

This example illustrates the purpose behind the Liskov substitution principle. If the derived class had stronger input requirements, then a call to SomeFunctionInTheBaseClass using a parameter acceptable to the base class might fail. And if the derived class had weaker output promises, then the promise of the base class might not be fulfilled. "Require no more, promise no less" guarantees that derived classes are "call compatible" with the base class from which they are derived.

Now that section has introduced some important principles, but may have left you a bit dazzled by all the new terms so let's take stock.

Component Design Summary

We can break down the material covered into three areas – vocabulary, principles and skills. Firstly we can highlight the following important terms and phrases:

- ❑ **Logical design** is the design stage where the classes and their relationships are identified.
- ❑ **Physical design** is the design stage where components are allocated a location on the network – see Chapters 11 - 15.

❑   A **network trip** is an expensive operation that occurs each time a method or property of a remote component is called.

❑   **Component design** is the task of designing the component interfaces and their relationships.

❑   **Implementation inheritance** is when a class, called the **derived class**, inherits the implementation of another class, called the **base class.**

❑   **Interface inheritance** is when a class inherits the interface, but not the implementation, of another class.

❑   **Contravariance** promises that the interface of a derived class must be substitutable for that of the base class.

The important principles to remember here are:

❑   In a distributed application, components may run on different machines.

❑   Component design is an iterative process where successive refinements lead to a solution.

❑   Design does not lead to a single, correct solution. Any solution must therefore be validated against the stated design goals.

As with most areas, real skills aren't acquired until the subject is practiced. After reading this section we don't think you'll be skilled in the art of using these approaches, but you've got a great start in being able to:

❑   Identify the type of relationship between two classes.

❑   Implement one-to-one or one-to-many ownership (or containment) in Visual Basic.

❑   Implement implementation inheritance in Visual Basic.

❑   Implement a Use relationship or Collaboration in Visual Basic.

Modeling Software Solutions

We are now in the position of being able to consider progressing from the initial analysis phase of the software development process through the modeling phase. The two approaches we consider here are logical design and UML model phases. These methods are similar and related, and we will use an approach that utilizes both methods. First we look at logical design.

Logical Design

The first four steps of logical design, described below, are rarely executed in the order in which they're listed, with Step 2 starting only after Step 1 is fully completed. Instead the design evolves through several iterations of Step 1 through 4. This is expressed by the additional fifth step – revising and refining the logical design.

Step 1 – Identifying Business Objects

The first step in the logical design phase involves scanning the *nouns* used in the Use Case Scenarios. These nouns are listed and examined. First, the references to Actors and other entities that are not part of the system are thrown out. Then, a search for synonyms is done and some more nouns may be thrown out. In the end, we have class diagrams with just the class names filled in, where each class diagram represents one noun. It's important to remember that each class at this stage is a concept that represents something in the real world (a real world domain). The details of the implementation of the class are discovered later in the process. The search for nouns in the Use Case Scenarios (and the search for verbs in Step 2) is similar to the process we follow in Chapter 9 when designing the database for the WROBA case study.

Step 2 – Defining Interfaces

The second step in logical design involves scanning the *verbs* used in the Use Case Scenarios. Each verb is added as a method to a class. Since a method typically changes the state of a class, adding a method often also leads to the addition of properties to the class. These properties also help us to determine whether the method was added to the right class. If the properties changed by the method are inherent characteristics of the class, then we're doing the right thing.

Step 3 – Identifying Business Object Dependencies

During the addition of methods to the classes, we may sometimes find that the affected properties belong to more than one class – this means that a relationship has been highlighted. Connecting the class diagrams with associations that describe these relationships completes the class diagrams.

Step 4 – Validating Logical Design

The logical design is validated using sequence diagrams – it should be possible to model every scenario using the methods described in the class diagram.

Step 5 – Revising and Refining the Logical Design

It's extremely unusual, to get everything right the first time, so the design will generally be iterated several times before everything works and the design is accepted.

The UML Model Phases

The process of modeling a software solution using UML can be divided into four model phases:

- ❑ Use Case model
- ❑ Domain model
- ❑ Design model
- ❑ Implementation model

Each modeling phase uses different UML diagram types to model the software solution in progressively more detailed ways. The phases also seem to be consecutive, but really are iterative, with each phase occurring a number of times.

Use Case Model Phase

Use Cases are narrative descriptions of processes that are created early in a development cycle. They describe the interactions between external Actors and the system, and help us to understand the system requirements and the terminology used. During the Use Case phase, we create Use Case diagrams and scenarios (we developed these for the WROBA case study in Chapter 6).

Domain Model Phase

The domain model phase is focused on understanding the domain for which we're developing a solution. This is still an analysis phase, in which objects and relationships in the real world are considered, rather than about how to implement them using programming concepts. During the domain model phase, class diagrams, package diagrams, and sequence diagrams are created.

Design Model Phase

During the Use Case and domain model phases, the focus is on understanding the requirements and concepts related to the system under development. In the design phase, this understanding is applied and a programming solution is developed. To develop this solution, we use collaboration diagrams to determine how objects will communicate, and class diagrams to define the classes that will be implemented in the software. To understand the life cycle of an object, statechart or activity diagrams are used, in relation to a particular class or Use Case.

Implementation Model Phase

The implementation model phase focuses on the physical and component structure of the development environment. During the implementation phase, component diagrams and deployment diagrams are created.

Designing the UML Diagrams

At this point we can finally (at long last, you may say) take a Use Case and start designing the UML diagrams that we will use in the implementation phase. We mentioned above that class, package, and sequence diagrams are produced during the Domain Model phase, and we're going to start with the class diagram.

As we pointed out in the previous chapter, the **class diagram** is the key diagram throughout the object-oriented analysis and design phase. The initial class diagram is derived from the Use Case Scenarios and subsequently, this diagram gets iteratively refined through the other types of diagrams.

The Domain Model Diagrams

There are 15 Use Case Scenarios that were developed in Chapter 6 to represent the business requirements of the WROBA case study. We're not going to bore you by deriving every possible UML diagram for every Use Case Scenario, instead we'll just pick one Use Case Scenario and walk through the UML diagrams that are developed in the design phase of the project. The Use Case Scenario is Transfer Funds, Use Case Scenario #2. So that you won't have to thumb through the book looking for that scenario, it's repeated here:

The Transfer Funds Scenario

- **Name**
  Transfer Funds

- **Summary**
  This Scenario involves transferring funds from a Saving account to a Checking account and from a Checking account to a Saving account.

- **Assumptions**
  None.

- **Pre-Conditions**
  User is logged on and selects "Transfer Funds".

- **Steps**

User	System
The user selects from which account (Savings or Checking) to transfer funds.	
	System selects the other account as the destination of the funds transfer.
The user puts in the amount of the funds transfer.	
The user initiates the transaction.	
	System debits the source account and credits the target account.

- **Business Rules**
  - The amount to be transferred must be smaller than or equal to the sum of the account balance and the overdraft limit.
  - The daily withdrawal limit must not be exceeded.
  - The "to" account is verified as existing before the "from" account is debited.

- **Post Conditions**
  The "from" account is debited and the "to" account is credited with the amount selected by the user.

- **Exceptions**
  - The transaction is aborted with a "Not sufficient funds" message if the amount to be transferred is larger than the sum of the account balance and the overdraft limit.
  - The transaction is aborted with a "Daily limit exceeded" message if the daily withdrawal limit would have been exceeded.

- **Open Issues**
  None.

Looking for Nouns and Verbs – the Class Diagram

After removing the synonyms, the nouns in this Use Case Scenario are:

❑ *Accounts*

❑ *System (Bank)*

❑ *Transfer*

❑ *Message*

We will add another noun for the form in which the user selects the source account, destination account, and the amount to transfer:

❑ *Form*

In the next section we will create the class diagram that our nouns describe using Visual Modeler (a tool included in Visual Basic Enterprise Edition). Again don't be perturbed if you don't have the application – following the discussion through will help understanding of the case study and indicate how useful this tool can be.

Try It Out – Creating Class Diagrams with Visual Modeler

1. Open Visual Modeler (Start | Programs | Microsoft Visual Studio 6.0 | Microsoft Visual Studio 6.0 Enterprise Tools | Microsoft Visual Modeler). A new, untitled diagram should be opened with columns for User, Business and Data Services tiers. The diagram will look similar to the following:

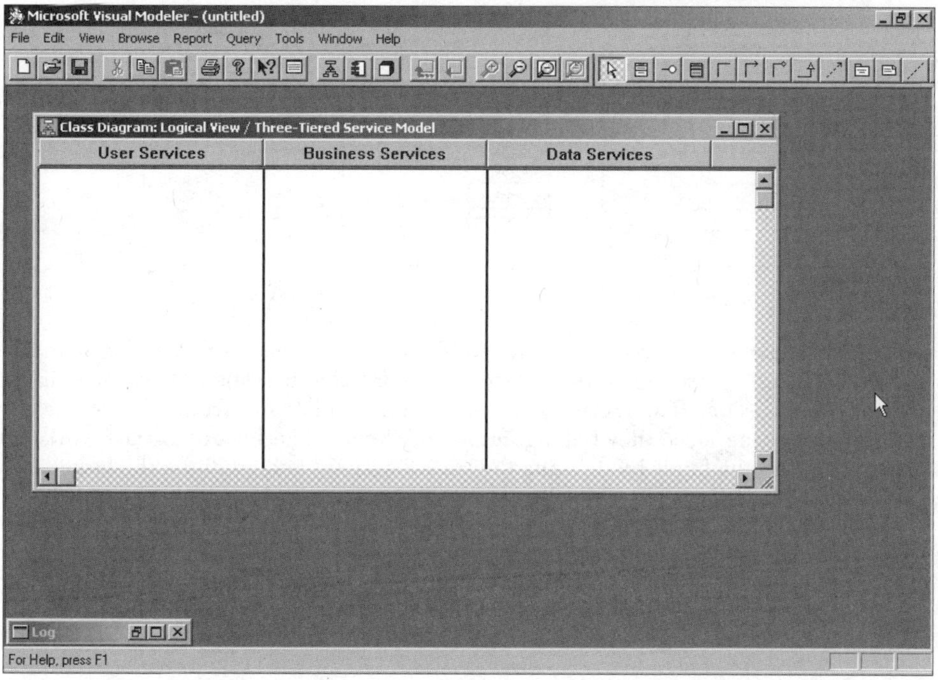

2. Add a class to the User Services tier by choosing Tools I Create I Class and then clicking in the User Services section to give:

3. Rename the new class (NewClass) as Form by typing over the highlighted name. If the class isn't selected, highlight the name by double-clicking in the class to open the Class Specification dialog, and change the name in the Name text box on the General tab.

4. Add another class to the User Services tier and name it Message, then add two classes to the Business Services tier (by choosing Tools I Create I Class twice and clicking in the Business Services tier each time). Name these classes Bank and Transfer.

5. Add a class to the Data Services tier by choosing Tools I Create I Class and clicking in the Data Services tier – name this class Accounts. We should now have something like:

How It Works

The classes (nouns) have been tentatively assigned to the three service tiers. The Form and Message classes are obviously user or presentation service classes. Bank and Transfer are placed in the business logic or business services tier. These classes will locate and validate the accounts, and evaluate the business rules of the scenario, so they belong in the middle tier. The Accounts class works directly with the database to transfer the funds by debiting the source account and crediting the target account, so it belongs in the data services tier.

The next thing to do is discover the verbs in the scenario, which become methods of the classes. These verbs are:

- ❑   *Select* source
- ❑   *Select* target
- ❑   *Enter* amount
- ❑   *Perform* transfer
- ❑   *Transfer* funds
- ❑   *Debit* account
- ❑   *Credit* account
- ❑   *Display* message

In the next section we'll create the methods that our verbs describe. The first four of these verbs obviously belong to the Form class, which is collecting user inputs. So we will add them as methods of the Form class. The next, Transfer funds, belongs to the Transfer class in the business services tier. The next two, debit and credit account, belong to the data services class Accounts. The final verb, display message, belongs to the Message class.

Try It Out – Creating Methods with Visual Modeler

1. Double-click on the Form class in the diagram from the previous section to open the Class Specification dialog.

2. Click on the Methods tab and right-click on the empty list of methods to open the context menu:

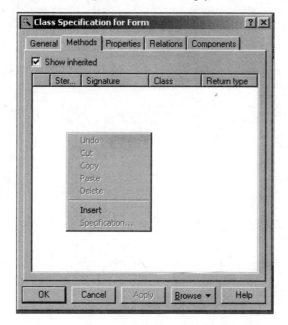

3. Select Insert to create a new method. Double-click on the NewMethod method to open the specification and name the method SelectSource.

4. Add three other methods to the Form class and name them SelectTarget, EnterAmount and PerformTransfer. Now the User Services tier of the class diagram should appear as:

5. Now we have to repeat the process for the other classes, starting by opening the specification for the Transfer class in the Business Services tier and adding a method named TransferFunds.

6. Next, for the Accounts class in the Data Services tier add methods named DebitSourceAccount and CreditTargetAccount.

7. Lastly, for the moment, for the Message class in the User Services tier add a method named DisplayMessage.

8. To indicate an association from the Form class to the Message class for displaying a message, choose Tools | Create | Association and click in the Form class. Drag the mouse to the Message class and release the mouse button.

9. Once you've done that repeat the procedure to create associations from the Form class to the Bank and Transfer classes and from the Transfer class to the Accounts class. We should now have:

Assessing the Class Diagram

As yet we have just looked at the steps in the Use Case Scenario, looking at the verbs that implement the business rules gives us the following:

- ❑   *Verify* target account exists

- ❑   *Test* daily withdrawal limit

- ❑   *Verify* funds available

The first one of these will be added as a method to the data services tier while the remaining verbs will be implemented as **constraints** on tables or as **stored procedures** in the database.

Constraints and stored procedures will be discussed in Chapters 9 and 10, but briefly; it might be helpful to point out that constraints implement guard conditions on a database table (such as "data in this column must be unique"), while stored procedures are scripts that are methods or queries that execute directly in the database.

Implementing business rules in table constraints or stored procedures is good practice, both from a point of view of distribution and centrality as well as performance. Since constraints and stored procedures execute or exist directly in the database, revisions have to be distributed to a small base of installations and there are fewer network trips than implementing business rules in the business logic tier. The only network trips involved in business rules or data logic implemented as constraints or stored procedures are when the database is called and when it returns a result.

Examining the class diagram carefully at this point is a checkpoint to see if we have left anything out of the class diagram or the underlying Use Case Scenario. It's often far easier to visualize where nouns and verbs (classes and methods) are missing from a class diagram than from studying a Use Case or Use Case Scenario. Things we find have been omitted will lead us to revise the Use Case and the Use Case Scenario as part of our iterative process.

In this Use Case Scenario we seem to be missing a means of determining which bank and accounts to look for. This can be taken care of by adding a ReadState method to get the user's bank number and WROBA card ID. This information is needed by most of the WROBA scenarios, so it should be stored in a global instance of a user properties class when the user logs in. So let's add a class named SharedProperties to the class diagram (in actual fact, if we were working through all the scenarios in order, this class would have been created in the class diagram for Use Case Scenario #1, Login).

Try It Out – Completing the Class Diagram

1.   The first thing to do is to add the method identified by analysis of the business rules – add a method named VerifyAccount to the Accounts class in the Data Services tier. Double-click on the new method to open its specification and in the Stereotype combo box type the word Get. Press OK to accept the new stereotype (in the context of Visual Modeler a stereotype of a class, or another object, is a mapping from the object in Visual Modeler to the corresponding Visual Basic object like a Form or a Get for a property).

2.   Next, we need to add the information we discovered through the iteration – add a method named ReadState to the Form module in the User Services tier.

3. Then, add a new class named SharedProperties to the User Services tier, and, to this class, add two methods named GetCardID and GetBankID. Open the specifications for the methods and set the stereotypes to Get.

4. To show the difference between the form and the classes, set the stereotype for Form by opening the Class Specification dialog for Form and in the stereotype combo box type the word Form.

5. Open the specifications for all the other classes and in the stereotype combo box type the word Class. Note, that after the stereotype is created for the first time, it will be remembered and will become available for selection through the combo box.

6. The class diagram is getting pretty detailed, but there are a few more things to do with it. The Bank class is in the Business Services tier, but it is doing nothing so far. That class will be called to get account information; add a method called GetAccounts.

7. It also would be nice to label the associations that have been added between classes, add some more associations, and indicate direction for some of the associations. To label an association, right-click on it and choose Open Specification from the context menu – so for the association between Form and Bank, carry out the process and name the association Get User Accounts.

8. Right-clicking on an association and clicking on the Navigable choice in the context menu will allow us to bring up an arrowhead to indicate the direction of the association. The arrowhead will always appear pointing to the class that was clicked first when the association was created. If the arrowhead points in the wrong direction, delete the association and create a new one by clicking first in the class to which the arrowhead needs to point.

9. To finalize the class diagram, more associations, labels and directional indications are required; to save tedium we won't list these but will instead just show the finished article:

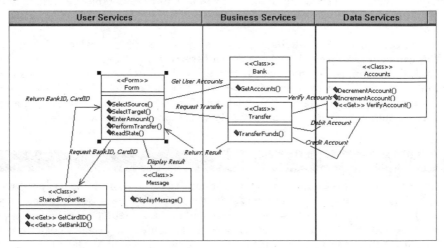

10. To save the class diagram select File | Save As and name it TransferFunds.

Further Work

We've begun to get into some detail about the classes at this stage of the process. If we've discovered business requirements that were missed previously we can go back to the Use Case and the scenario and add those items. Although our development process is iterative, it is good practice to try to be as thorough at each stage of the process as possible. An iterative process is no excuse for sloppy or half-hearted work. In fact, an iterative process usually takes longer than a non-iterative process, but will produce a product that is better thought out, documented, and has fewer bugs and errors of omission when it is performed properly.

Although we haven't done it here, the class diagram could be further refined by classifying the general usage associations that are drawn among the classes into composition (ownership), simple aggregation (containment), and generalization relationships (we'll consider this again when we discuss collaboration diagrams).

Visual Modeler can be used at this point to generate code from the class diagram. It will generate templates for all the classes, methods and properties that are selected in the diagram. This code can be used as the starting point for the implementation of the project. The class diagrams for each Use Case can be used to generate code that can be added to previously generated code. If new methods or properties are added to the code, they can be reverse engineered into an updated master class diagram.

Although code can be generated at this point it is worth being patient and creating a few more diagrams first. The Transfer Funds Scenario may be simple enough to be modeled fully with only a class diagram; however, other Use Cases will require further work before the process has been analyzed and modeled sufficiently to generate code.

The Sequence Diagram – An Event Timeline

A simple class diagram such as the one for Transfer Funds can easily be drawn using Visual Modeler. However, Visual Modeler is not capable of drawing the next diagram that our project calls for, the **sequence diagram**. As in Chapter 7 we originally used Visio 2000 Professional to create the sequence diagram.

This diagram depicts the sequence of actions and messages that occur over time for the Transfer Funds Scenario. It depicts all the classes that are involved in the scenario, and shows the messages passed between the classes. The lifetimes of the classes are shown, where time moves in a vertical direction down the drawing.

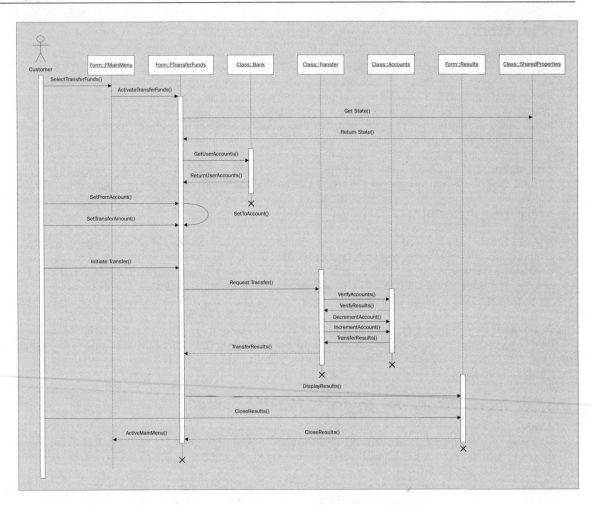

When the timeline represented by a sequence diagram is read, time starts at the top of the diagram. The progression of time is indicated by following the diagram from top to bottom. Interactions that occur at the same time are indicated at the same vertical place in time, but at different horizontal places.

The interactions of the sequence diagram have the following time sequence:

1. The Customer activates Funds Transfer in the FMainMenu form.

2. The Funds Transfer form (FTransferFunds) activates.

3. The Funds Transfer form requests the user's Bank ID and Card ID from SharedProperties.

4. The Funds Transfer form reads the user's Bank ID and Card ID from SharedProperties.

...ere the focus is on discovering and documenting ...ithin methods. These micro model diagrams of methods ...workflows of a single method. The following activity ...TransferFunds method of the Transfer class:

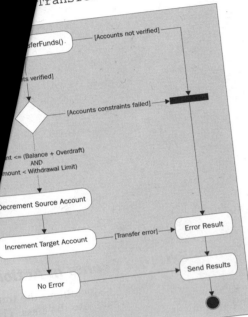

The Implementation Model Phase

...we'll learn to use logical design and modeling techniques to design the project ...eate the UML diagrams for the implementation model phase in Chapters 12 – 15, ...ating the code to implement the WROBA case study project.

...that none of the previous model phases are completely finished. The diagrams that were ...this chapter are always subject to further iteration and refinement as we progress through ...t design process.

5. The Funds Transfer form requests the user's WROBA card accounts from Bank.

6. Bank returns the user's WROBA card accounts to the Funds Transfer form.

7. The Customer picks a source account.

8. The Funds Transfer form sets the destination account.

9. The Customer sets a transfer amount.

10. The Customer initiates the transfer.

11. The Funds Transfer form requests a transfer from Transfer.

12. Transfer requests a verification that the destination account exists before decrementing the source account from Accounts.

13. Transfer requests a decrement of the source account by the transfer amount from Accounts.

14. Transfer requests an increment of the destination account by the transfer amount from Accounts.

15. Accounts returns the error code signifying success or failure of the transaction to Transfer.

16. Transfer returns an error code to the Funds Transfer form.

17. The Funds Transfer form sends a message to the Results form (Results) to display the results.

18. The Customer closes the Results form.

19. The Results form notifies the Funds Transfer form that the Customer has closed it.

20. The Funds Transfer form activates the MainMenu form and closes itself.

The sequence diagram depicts the sequence of interactions that occur during the user's (or any Actor's) interaction with the scenario, and it helps to clarify the messages and notifications that are needed for those interactions. This in turn helps discover any additional methods that are required for the scenario. The sequence diagram not only refines the class diagram, it can lead to further iterations of the class diagram, Use Case diagram and Use Case Scenario.

A **package diagram** can be created for the Use Case, class and sequence diagrams created so far for each service tier. These packages, which are used to organize subsets of a project, can also include the Use Case Scenarios, documentation and any generated code for each of the user, business logic and data services tiers.

It is often worthwhile striving to break down attributes into as many components as possible, since it makes returning just one specific part of the data much easier. A good example of this is when working with addresses: we would usually break the address attribute down into street, street number, mail stop, city, region (state or province), postal code and country. This way we can easily find out how many customers live in a particular city, without having to write code to extract the city from the address string.

Let's walk through some scenarios to see what information we can extract.

❑   When the first attempt to logon is made, the identification number and password are verified. If the number and password are valid, access is granted; otherwise, the invalid password counter increments and the user is given a second chance to enter the correct password. Identification number, password, and password counter describe the characteristics used by the WROBA card.

❑   After a successful logon, the user is shown their account information. This information comes from the bank account entity, which is characterized by the attributes account number, the account type (Checking or Saving), the current balance, the daily withdrawal limit, the overdraft protection limit, the date of the last withdrawal and the daily withdrawal limit remaining today.

On running through this process we can flesh out our first diagram by adding some attributes to the entities previously identified:

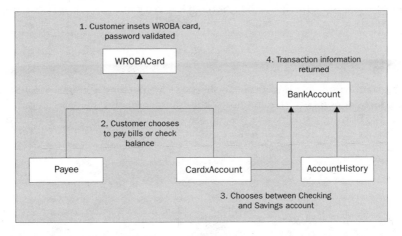

The words in the noun list don't necessarily match those used in the diagram. This is because it's a good idea to use short but descriptive names that don't contain spaces, to replace longer words or phrases. So, identification number becomes `CardId`, and account number becomes `AccountId`. Notice that all numbers that are used to identify entities are renamed with the suffix `Id`. Although any name could be used, it's good practice to use an understandable naming convention when naming elements, so anyone can look at the tables and understand what has been done. Transaction date, amount, type and description are similarly named like this using the abbreviation `Tx` for transaction.

One of the other important points of the diagram is that some of the attributes are underlined – these attributes are the entity identifiers for the entities they are associated with. This is our next topic.

Entity Identifiers

Entity identifiers are database objects that uniquely identify each record in a table. Just as each person has a unique identifier (for example, their social security number), so do entities. This unique identifier is known as a **primary key**. A primary key is a field whose value uniquely identifies each record in a table. Hence, in the previous diagram, the primary keys are the underlined attributes.

> **A primary key is a set of entity attributes (often just one attribute) that uniquely identifies each instance of an entity.**

A *natural* primary key is a primary key that is also a real-world characteristic of the entity, for example a bank account number. Other entities do not have a natural primary key (invoices, for example), and it is necessary to create a system-generated primary key. We'll see how this is done below, but conceptually it involves nothing more than generating a sequence of unique identifiers (for example, sequential numbers).

> **A foreign key is a primary key of one entity that is referenced by another entity.**

Rows in some tables are dependent on one or more rows in another table. The dependency between the rows is identified by the use of **foreign keys**. A foreign key is a column (or set of columns) in one table that references the primary key of another table. These inter-table dependencies are known as relationships.

Entity Relationships

Consider a bank transaction detailing a transfer between a Checking account and a Saving account – it will contain the account numbers, the amount of the transaction and the date. In our design, the account number (AccountId) is the primary key (PK) in the BankAccount table and is the foreign key (FK1) in the AccountHistory table, in which the transaction number (TxId) is the primary key. We can illustrate this as:

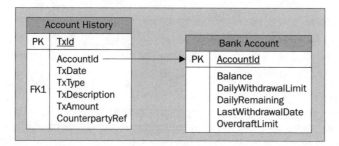

> **A relationship defines how two tables are associated.**

A relationship is a link between tables that references the primary key in one table to a foreign key in another table and there are three types of entity relationship:

- ❑ One-to-one
- ❑ One-to-many
- ❑ Many-to-many

Let's consider these in turn.

One-to-one Relationships

A **one-to-one relationship** means that a single instance of an entity is associated with at most one instance of another entity. Such relationships are rare and are often an indication that we should combine the two entities involved in the relationship. Combining the two entities is most strongly suggested by a true one-to-one relationship where every single instance of an entity is associated with exactly one instance of another entity.

The most common use for one-to-one relationships is to place data in a separate table, often out of performance or space considerations. We don't have an example of such a relationship in the WROBA case study so we'll have to hypothesize for a moment. In the WROBA case study there is only one Saving and one Checking account per card (account). Now let's say the bank moves, cautiously, into the credit market and allows each card (account) to apply for just one credit card. Since such a conservative bank may have equally conservative customers, it is likely that not all depositors would take up this offer. If the credit card information were contained in the `BankAccount` table, we would find many empty tables in that table. As the credit card account data would not be accessed as often as the Checking and Saving accounts, it helps to improve database speed by having it in a separate table.

One-to-many Relationships

A **one-to-many relationship** exists between two tables in which a single row in the first table can be related to one or more rows in the second table, but a row in the second table can be related only to one row in the first table. For example, a WROBA card can have both a Checking and a Saving account connected to it, but each account can only have one WROBA card:

WROBACard	Account Number	AccountType
10001	20001	Checking
10001	20002	Saving
10002	20003	Checking
10002	20004	Saving

Many-to-many Relationships

A **many-to-many relationship** means that each instance of an entity is associated with one or more instances of another entity and that each instance of the latter entity is associated with one or more instances of the former entity.

For example, a payee (bill collector) may have more than one account paying them and an account can have several payees. Many-to-many relationships cannot be physically created in a database. In order to create the physical model, many-to-many relationships are **resolved** into two one-to-many relationships by creating a new table, called a **link entity** (or **junction table**), which contains the primary keys from each of the involved tables.

In the bill-paying example mentioned above, we would have to create a `PayeexAccounts` link entity containing the `AccountId` (the primary key for the `Accounts` entity) and `PayeeID` (the primary key for the `Payee` entity). In fact, in our database, the other elements of the design mean this is not needed.

Our next task is to refine our logical design through the processes of **normalization** and **denormalization**.

Normalization

We can summarize normalization as follows:

> **Normalization is the process of eliminating duplicated data from the database by refining tables, columns, and relationships to create a consistent database design.**

A normalized database generally contains a lot of narrow tables (few columns), while an un-normalized database typically contains a few wide tables (more columns). An un-normalized database often contains duplicated data, which makes the database larger than it should be. Worse still, if data is updated in one location, but not in the other locations, then the database will become inconsistent. Preventing database corruption by creating a normalized database is easier than correcting the errors later.

Normalization is carried out in stages, called normal forms. At each stage the underlying assumption is that all requirements from the prior stages have been fulfilled.

In the **first normal form** (**1NF**) each attribute only stores one value, rather than a list of values, in a given table. This is because if lists are stored in a single column there is no simple way to manipulate the values, making it difficult to retrieve data. All the data in the table should be related and a primary key assigned. 1NF also prohibits repeating attributes in multiple columns – these repeating data groups should be put in a new table with a new primary key.

The **second normal form** (**2NF**) builds on the first normal form and here every non-key column is fully dependent on the entire primary key.

With **third normal form** (**3NF**) all non-key columns are mutually independent.

As we said previously, every higher normal form is a superset of all lower forms. If an entity is in second normal form, it is already in first normal form. If an entity is in third normal form, it is already in second normal form.

There are some further normal forms, with such exotic names as Boyce-Codd normal form (BCNF), fourth normal form, and fifth normal form, but in practice it is rare that going beyond the third normal form will give any further benefit. This is partially due to the big effort involved in getting entities normalized beyond the third normal form. We'll limit ourselves to examining the first three normal forms and leave detailed coverage of the remaining normal forms for the specialized literature on database design.

In order to visualize these three normal forms, we'll return to our WROBA case study for the data, but for the purposes of demonstration will have to take some liberties with the initial tables we see.

Normalization in the WROBA Logical Design

The WROBA design has addressed some aspects of normalization already, so as our starting point for this illustration, let's consider what would happen if we had just tabulated some account information. Conceivably we might have generated the following un-normalized set of information:

AccountId	Account Type	Account TypeDesc	Balance	TxType	TxType Desc	TxAmount
20001	1	Checking	$254.00	1	ATM Transfer	($20.00)
				2	Pay Bill	($20.00)
20002	2	Saving	$2,376.00	1	ATM Transfer	$20.00
				2	Pay Bill	($20.00)
20003	1	Checking	($56.00)	1	ATM Transfer	$60.00
				2	Pay Bill	($100.00)
20004	2	Saving	$3,236.00	1	ATM Transfer	$140.00
				2	Pay Bill	($200.00)

For the purposes of this example, let's begin our analysis by designating the primary key to be **composite** (consisting of two or more attributes); say, AccountId and AccountType. Admittedly, this is hypothetical, but the BigBank does have examples of composite primary keys – see the CardxAccount table later.

We obviously have a problem with multiple values in certain fields. To address this we could think about storing the repeating transaction information in columns with numbered names such as TxTypeDesc1, TxTypeDesc2 and TxTypeDesc3 (with corresponding associated TxType1, TxAmount1, TxType2, TxAmount2 columns). However, repeating information like this is not ideal because we have a built-in limit on how many transactions one account can contain. We could choose to allow a high number of transactions per account by setting up the tables with a large number of columns, but that would waste a lot of space and slow down data retrieval. The first normal form solves this by forbidding such repetition.

First Normal Form

As we pointed out initially, a table in 1NF has attributes that store only one value and does not have repeating attributes in multiple columns. Additionally we have a problem in the above table that logically the transaction information and the account information do not belong together.

In our example shown above, we have multiple values in the TxType, TxTypeDesc, and TxAmount columns. If we split the information into multiple columns we would then have case of repeating groups of TxType, TxTypeDesc and TxAmount columns. In order to achieve 1NF, we move these attributes from the original entity into a separate entity and assign a primary key. This approach also separates the account data and the transaction data.

BankAccount

AccountId	AccountType	AccountTypeDesc	Balance
20001	1	Checking	$254.00
20002	2	Saving	$2,376.00
20003	1	Checking	($56.00)
20004	2	Saving	$3,236.00

AccountHistory

TxId	AccountId	TxType	TxTypeDesc	TxDate	TxAmount
1	20001	1	TSF	3/19/2000	($20.00)
2	20001	2	BIL	3/20/2000	($20.00)
3	20002	1	TSF	3/19/2000	$20.00
4	20002	2	BIL	3/19/2000	($20.00)
5	20003	1	TSF	3/20/2000	$60.00
6	20003	2	BIL	3/19/2000	($100.00)
7	20004	1	TSF	3/19/2000	$140.00
8	20004	2	BIL	3/20/2000	($200.00)

Sometimes, business requirements will dictate that the sequence is important within the groups. In such a case, the database designer may add a column to the new 1NF entity to track this sequence within the group – here we have the TxDate column added. Additionally, the TxId column has been added to provide a primary key for the entity (there being no obvious natural one). The data is related through the AccountId, which is the foreign key in the AccountHistory table. Remember that for the case of this walk through we still have a composite primary key in the BankAccount table.

These tables are now looking very much like the ones we currently have in our logical design for WROBA (the main difference being that the ones shown here are missing a few attributes compared to our main design ones).

This design is superior to the un-normalized design in two ways: firstly, there is no design limit as to how many transactions each account can initiate; secondly, if we need to add additional items concerning transactions, such as transaction time, only one column needs updating. However, this is still not an effective design. The account description (AccountTypeDesc) is repeated in the Accounts entity, as is the transaction description (TxTypeDesc) in the Transactions entity.

Let's see what moving to second normal form does for us.

Second Normal Form

Second normal form builds on the first normal form. To achieve 2NF the tables should be in 1NF and all non-key fields must depend on all fields in the primary key.

In the case of a composite key (a key composed of two or more attributes), an attribute is fully dependent on a composite key if that attribute requires *all* attributes of the composite key to determine its value. In other words, each non-key attribute must depend on all the parts of the composite key. If any attributes do not require all attributes of the composite key, they must be split into their own entity along with the part of the composite key on which they depend.

In our current example, `AccountTypeDesc` does not rely on the `AccountId` part of the `BankAccount` composite primary key but is in fact just related to the `AccountType` part. Thus, logically we can split this table into two new tables:

BankAccount

AccountId	AccountType	Balance
20001	1	$254.00
20002	2	$2,376.00
20003	1	($56.00)
20004	2	$3,236.00

AccountType

AccountType	AccountTypeDesc
0	Administrator
1	Checking
2	Saving

Now `AccountId` and `AccountType` can exist as separate primary keys with `AccountType` as the foreign key in the `BankAccount` table.

Incidentally, at this point we don't have to concern ourselves with the new `AccountHistory` table as that has a single attribute primary key and is already in 2NF.

Third Normal Form

Finally, for our analysis, we come to third normal form. A 2NF entity is in third normal form if, and only if, every non-key column does not depend on any other non-key column. A 2NF entity is in third normal form (3NF) when every non-key attribute is dependant only on the table's primary key. If any attribute depends on another non-key attribute within the entity, it must be split into its own entity along with the attribute on which it depends.

So here, when we inspect the `AccountHistory` table we notice that the `TxType` and `TxTypeDesc` columns are related. Thus, it's easy to envisage a situation where due to faulty data entry a row may contain a value of 1 for the `TxType` but something other than TSF for the `TXTypeDesc`. To solve this problem we need to create another two tables:

AccountHistory

TxId	AccountId	TxType	TxDate	TxAmount
1	20001	1	3/19/2000	($20.00)
2	20001	2	3/20/2000	($20.00)
3	20002	1	3/19/2000	$20.00
4	20002	2	3/19/2000	($20.00)
5	20003	1	3/20/2000	$60.00
6	20003	2	3/19/2000	($100.00)
7	20004	1	3/19/2000	$140.00
8	20004	2	3/20/2000	($200.00)

Transaction Types (TxType)

TxType	TxTypeDesc
1	TSF
2	BIL

Here, `TxType` is a foreign key in the `AccountHistory` table.

The `BankAccount` and `AccountType` tables are both in 3NF already so we don't need to worry about them further.

Following this work the design now has the minimum of duplication required to capture all the order information. For example, updating an Account description (for example, changing Checking to Cheque) will be reflected in all the entries containing account type 1. Similarly, if the transaction type needs to be changed from `TSF` to `Transfer`, only a single record needs to be updated. This is an indication of a correct database design: the number of records that are affected reflects the number of real-world entities that are affected. That is, only one product or client changes its name.

You may now understand why we had to artificially set up the original `BankAccount` table with a composite primary key – if we had used the single attribute primary key of `AccountId` first off, we wouldn't have had an example to demonstrate the 1NF to 2NF step!

After a database design is in third normal form, experienced database designers may decide that they can improve performance by breaking the normalization rules – a process termed **denormalization**.

Denormalization

Denormalization can improve efficiency and works by reducing the complexity of the database. The designer may select to split a table with a huge amount of rows into several tables. Another reason for denormalization is because the users ask for it, usually because they feel that denormalization makes data entry easier by combining two tables that are often used together. A few of these denormalization practices are so common that reference books forget to mention that an entity is actually in violation of 3NF. The most typical example of this is a US zip code included in an address. The zip code depends on the city and street and should be placed in a separate entity to achieve 3NF. For most applications, this has few benefits and harms performance.

The Logical Design for the WROBA Application

Before we reveal the final logical design we've produced for the WROBA case study let's recap on the steps we've taken to arrive at the design:

1. We determined the purpose and data requirements of the database.

2. We identified the entities by examining the business requirements.

3. We identified the attributes associated with each entity.

4. We identified the primary keys that uniquely identify each entity.

5. We identified relationships between the entities.

6. We normalized the entities we had decided on.

Of course the steps may not be performed exactly in the order listed. And again, there will be iteration throughout the design process. Typically, when an entity is discovered, its attributes are listed and a primary key chosen. The primary key identifies each individual record stored in the database table, such as the `AccountID` or `BankID` from our model. No two records will have the same primary key. The relationship of each entity with the others is also determined as the entities are created.

The following diagram shows the completed logical database design.

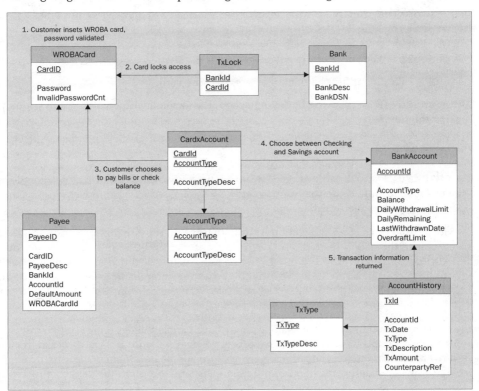

As we can see, a few more tables have appeared since the last diagram – the normalization process has added the `AccountType` and `TxType` tables, while consideration of the security needs of the bank lead to the `TxLock` and `Bank` tables.

Let's follow this last topic up by re-considering the login. From the Use Case Scenario in Chapter 6, we know the object of the login process is to gain access to the system by providing a WROBA card number and a matching password. We also know a card is locked after five consecutive unsuccessful logins, or after a successful login, and only one user may be logged into a card at a time. The scenario also specifies the makeup of the card identification number. The first three digits of the card ID number identify the bank and the last nine digits represent the account number. This information helps us design three tables used in the database, `WROBACard`, `TxLock` and `Bank`. The `WROBAcard` table keeps track of the password and the number of attempts to logon with an incorrect password. The `TXLock` table prevents the account from being accessed from another location at the same time.

Let's see how our design matches up against another scenario. Consider the action of transferring funds from a Saving account to a Checking account and from a Checking account to a Saving account. The amount to be transferred must be smaller than or equal to the sum of the account balance and the overdraft limit. The daily withdrawal limit must not be exceeded. The `CardxAccount` table allows us to choose the account we want to transfer funds from, the `BankAccount` table contains the account information we need to test the balance conditions, and the `AccountHistory` table stores the completed transaction information.

Un-normalized Behavior in the WROBA Logical Design

Let's consider the `Payee` table – it contains the following columns and descriptions:

- ❑ `PayeeId` – The primary key; it uses `uniqueidentifier` to assign a number.

- ❑ `CardId` – The WROBA card number.

- ❑ `PayeeDesc` – The name of the payee.

- ❑ `BankId` – This identifies the bank that provides the card.

- ❑ `AccountId` – The Checking or Saving account associated with the card from which we are taking the funds.

- ❑ `DefaultAmount` – The default amount assigned to the payee – if no amount is entered, this amount is used.

- ❑ `WROBACardId` – With `WROBACardId` stored, we know who created the payee and can limit the payees shown to those that were created by the logged in cardholder. Without this, all payees are visible to all cardholders.

It actually violates the rules of normalization – while there is no repeating information in the table, unfortunately not all the data is related. `PayeeId`, `PayeeDesc` and `DefaultAmount` are directly related but `WROBACardId` is related to the `PayeeId` and the `CardId` that created it. It would have been better to have created a new `PayeeType` table (with the columns `PayeeId`, `PayeeDesc`, and `DefaultAmount`) together with a smaller `Payee` table (with the columns `PayeeID`, `CardId`, `BankId`, `AccountId`, and `Payee`).

If we started the application from scratch again, we may have handled things slightly differently. However, this provides a solid example of what the iterative process of database and application design is all about – making improvements to the original design as we work through the development process. The `WROBACardId` was added during the iterative process and its presence starts the iterative process once more.

An Aside – OLTP and OLAP

At the outset of the logical design we made some fundamental decisions about the functionality of the database we were designing, based on an understanding of the business requirements we had previously identified. In fact we have designed an **online transaction processing** (**OLTP**) application. OLTP gives us the ability to have large numbers of users adding and modifying data concurrently. The result is that the database is constantly being updated with real-time data and response time can deteriorate quickly due to competition for available resources. A well-designed database is very important for optimal performance and in this type of application, where we are required to insert new data online, the process of normalization can help us achieve an optimal design. Apart from banks, other industries that would require OLTP applications include airlines and hotels who run reservations systems.

There is another online processing type called **online analytical processing** (**OLAP**). In OLAP applications, the data is loaded at regular intervals (for example daily, weekly or monthly) and the bulk of the processing involves reporting on this loaded data, which is read-only. OLAP would be used to prepare historical reports, for example, showing how many banking transactions over a certain dollar value were processed on any previous day. Sometimes these applications are also called **Decision Support Systems** (**DSS**). This gets into the area of **data warehousing** (data warehouses are repositories of historical data) and dimensional modeling, which is a subject for more advanced texts so we won't be mentioning OLAP again in this book.

Physical Data Design

Once we have spent the time normalizing our entities, transforming the logical design onto a physical design is fairly straightforward.

> *There is a SQL script file, available for download from* http://www.wrox.com, *that can be used to create the database (see Appendix A for more details). Although this is very tempting, working through the chapter and manually creating the database won't take much effort and will help you to understand the concepts more thoroughly, and lead to a greater knowledge of the case study.*

Defining the Database Schema

Once we have created the normalized entity-relationship diagram for the logical data model, we need to build the corresponding physical structure. This is called the database **schema**. The following rules are used to map the logical model to a physical database:

1. Entities in the logical model become tables.

2. Entity attributes become columns in the table.

3. Entity identifiers become primary and foreign keys.

4. Entity relationships are mapped to relationships among tables.

In order to be able to do this mapping properly we need to understand a little bit about:

❑   The data types available to us in our chosen database (SQL Server 7.0).

❑   Nulls and default values.

❑   Column constraints.

❑   Referential integrity.

❑   Indexes.

Data Types

When we create our tables we'll find that we must assign a data type to each column. Data types are determined by the characteristics of a column and specify what type of information can be stored in a column or variable. We need to choose the appropriate data type or we could end up having numerical data interpreted as text or vice versa.

Consider data such as zip codes and account numbers. A text data type would allow the entry of account numbers containing dashes or spaces. It would prevent the dropping of leading zeros, as the zip code 04901 would become 4901 if it were a numerical type. It would also also enable us to enter other types of postal codes that contain both numerals and letters.

There are several different data types used by SQL server, covering integers, money, time and characters (for text). These major data types have several types within the category to choose from, for better control. For example, if using integers, we have the choice of tinyint, smallint or int, depending on the type of integers we are working with. int is 4 bytes long and stores numbers from -2,147,483,648 through to 2,147,483,647. smallint is only 2 bytes long and stores numbers from -32,768 through to 32,767. tinyint is 1 byte, and stores numbers from 0 through to 255.

Some data types come with predefined lengths, like the integer types above. Others, such as char, require us to set a length. Choose the smallest data type or length that's the largest you'll ever need. From the integer example, if you're not going to use numbers higher than 150, tinyint will be the best choice.

The varchar data type is a variable-length data type, and is much slower, and uses more processor resources to process, than the char data type. Therefore, it shouldn't be used indiscriminately. If the data entries in a column are expected to be close to the same size, use char. If the entries are expected to vary considerably in size, as with URLs, use varchar, which does not pad the character string with extra spaces added to the end.

The following data types are the ones used in the `BigBank` database:

Data type	Description
char	Fixed-length non-Unicode character data with a maximum length of 8,000 characters.
datetime	Date and time data from January 1, 1753, to December 31, 9999, with an accuracy of three-hundredths of a second, or 3.33 milliseconds.
int	Integer (whole number) data from -2^{31} (-2,147,483,648) through $2^{31} - 1$ (2,147,483,647).
money	Monetary data values from -2^{63} (-922,337,203,685,477.5808) through $2^{63} - 1$ (+922,337,203,685,477.5807), with accuracy to a ten-thousandth of a monetary unit.
tinyint	Integer data from 0 through 255.
uniqueidentifier	A globally unique identifier (GUID).
varchar	Variable-length non-Unicode data with a maximum of 8,000 characters.

For completeness these are the rest of the data types to be found in SQL Server 7.0 (it is worth noting that data types, although similar, are not universal to all databases and if you work with another database you'll have to check the precise details):

Data type	Description
binary	Fixed-length binary data with a maximum length of 8,000 bytes.
bit	Integer data with either a 1 or 0 value.
decimal or numeric	Fixed precision and scale numeric data from $-10^{38} - 1$ through $10^{38} - 1$.
float	Floating precision number data from $-1.79E + 308$ through $1.79E + 308$.
image	Variable-length binary data with a maximum length of $2^{31} - 1$ (2,147,483,647) bytes.
nchar	Fixed-length Unicode data with a maximum length of 4,000 characters.
ntext	Variable-length Unicode data with a maximum length of $2^{30} - 1$ (1,073,741,823) characters.
nvarchar	Variable-length Unicode data with a maximum length of 4,000 characters.
real	Floating precision number data from $-3.40E + 38$ through $3.40E + 38$.

Table continued on following page

Data type	Description
smalldatetime	Date and time data from January 1, 1900, through June 6, 2079, with an accuracy of one minute.
smallint	Integer data from 2^{15} (-32,768) through 2^{15} - 1 (32,767).
smallmoney	Monetary data values from -214,748.3648 through +214,748.3647, with accuracy to a ten-thousandth of a monetary unit.
text	Variable-length non-Unicode data with a maximum length of 2^{31} - 1 (2,147,483,647) characters.
timestamp	A database-wide unique number.
varbinary	Variable-length binary data with a maximum length of 8,000 bytes.

Unique ID Creation Issues

The Identity feature of SQL Server 7.0 enables columns to contain system-generated values (an autonumber) that can uniquely identify each row within a table. The next identifier generated is based on the last identity value. SQL Server 7.0 starts the numbering from a given value (the **seed value**) and increases the value by a given amount (the **increment**) per inserted row. While identities provide an easy way to create unique IDs for an entity where no natural primary key can be identified, such as an invoice or customer number, identities tend to be slow when a large number of users are trying to insert records in a database table using incremental numbering.

We do have an alternative though, as SQL Server 7.0 lets us create unique IDs that do not require a database lookup and that scale better (but take up more storage –nothing is free). This new data type is called uniqueidentifier and is a **Globally Unique Identifier** (**GUID**) stored as a 16-byte binary string. To return a GUID when creating tables or inserting data using SQL scripts (a topic we discuss in Chapter 10), we use the NEWID() Transact-SQL function. We'll use the uniqueidentifier data type in the AccountHistory table in the case study.

NULLS and Default Values

To indicate an indeterminate value in a row we use a special value termed **NULL**. For example, we could have a table that has a column that tracks the gender of a customer. We may, however, decide that the customer doesn't have to supply us with gender information if they don't want to. Thus the gender column could contain either an M or F if we have the information, or be left empty if we don't. The "value" that the database attributes to that field is NULL. NULL values are not equal to each other or to any other non-NULL value.

If we specify that NULL is not an allowable value for a specific column (by having the Allow Nulls column unchecked during table design – we'll see this later), then we are specifying that a value for that column is always required. Updates or inserts that violate this requirement won't be allowed by the database. Requiring columns to contain data, by not allowing NULL, results in better performance because of the way SQL Server operates. It keeps a special bitmap in every row to indicate which nullable columns actually are NULL. It then needs to decode the bitmap every time the row is accessed. Additionally, allowing NULL adds complexity in application code, since we may need to add special logic to account for the case of NULL.

Instead of allowing NULL values in a table, we can insert default values for fields containing no data. For example, rather than allowing our gender column to contain NULL values to improve performance we could decide to create a non-nullable column and force it to have one of three values – M, F, or ?. We can have the latter option automatically inserted by using the Default Value field or by inserting default values using code in the VB project. The advantage of the former approach is that setting a default value on the server side means it can be easily changed at a later date.

Good defensive coding techniques would, however, mean if we are going to allow our application to insert a value for an unknown field, we should use validation techniques to ensure that the user chose to leave it blank, rather than forgot to enter data in the field (we'll look at validation approaches in Chapter 13). In the BigBank database, we allow NULLs for only one column (CounterPartyRef in the AccountHistory table) and every other column needs a value. The only column that uses a default value is the InvalidPasswordCnt column in the WROBACard table and there the default value is set using the Default Value field.

Column Constraints

A **column constraint** enforces certain behavior on a column by defining rules regarding the values allowed in columns. There are five types of column constraint in SQL Server 7.0:

❑   **Primary Key** – identifies the column(s) whose values uniquely identify a row.

❑   **Foreign Key** – identifies the relationships between tables.

❑   **Default** – specifies the value inserted into a column if no other value is supplied.

❑   **Unique** – enforces the uniqueness of the values in a set of columns..

❑   **Check** – limits the values that can be placed in a column.

So, placing a **primary key** constraint on a column (or set of columns) causes the column (or columns) to be the primary key for the table. A **unique** constraint is similar in that each entry in a column so constrained must be unique, but there can be more than one unique constraint per table. A **foreign key** constraint means each entry in the column must have a corresponding entry in the related column and the **check** constraint defines limits for field values (effectively giving some form of data validation). As we saw earlier, defining **default** values can be very useful in cases where we don't want NULL values.

Referential Integrity (RI)

Referential integrity is a system of rules to ensure that relationships between records in related tables are valid, and that we don't accidentally delete or change related data. If referential integrity is enforced a table cannot be deleted, or the primary key changed, as long as a foreign key exists that refers to that table. This ensures that we can't reference non-existent data and also that we don't get *orphaned* data which has no reference to it.

For example, in the database we construct, the BankAccount table cannot be deleted until the relationship between it and the AccountHistory table is broken, by removing the foreign key.

Indexes

An **index** is used in relational databases to provide fast access to data in the rows of a table, based on key values. They work like the index does in the back of, say, an encyclopedia – the key values are sorted in a given way, and once that key is located, another piece of information is released that allows the real data you want to be found.

There are two categories of index: clustered and non-clustered:

❑ In a **clustered index** the physical order of the rows in the table that the index is on is the same as the order of the key values. In our encyclopedia analogy, a clustered index would be the page numbers of the encyclopedia; the information in the publication is stored in the order of the page numbers.

❑ In a **non-clustered index** the logical order of the index does not match the physical order of the table rows and is more analogous to the keyword list at the back of the encyclopedia where finding the appropriate entry gives another value that lets you find the data.

As we'll see later, the case study database is set up with non-clustered indexes. The whole area of database indexes is quite complex and lies outside the scope of this book.

After generating our logical data design, and then thinking a little bit about the type of practical issues that we'll come across as we create our database, it's time to start using SQL Server 7.0.

Implementing the Database for WROBA

In this section we're going to run through the steps we need to take to create the database schema for the WROBA application using our logical design to guide us.

To create the schema, we're going to use a couple of different tools. To create the database, we'll use the SQL Server Enterprise Manager (a graphical user interface tool that provides functionality to manage SQL Server), while for actually working with the database we're going to work within the Visual Basic environment (although the same tasks can be performed using Enterprise Manager in a very similar way).

Try It Out – Creating the BigBank Database

1. Start SQL Server Enterprise Manager by selecting Start | Programs | Microsoft SQL Server 7.0 | Enterprise Manager.

2. Expand the view below the SQL server name and select the Databases node in the left-hand pane. If the server is not running, selecting it and attempting to expand the folder view will start the server automatically. This will cause a few seconds delay when expanding the folders.

3. To create a new database, right-click the Databases node and select New Database.

4. Type BigBank for the name of the new database, leave the options on their default settings, and click OK. After a couple of seconds we will have our new database.

5. Since we are going to work through the Visual Basic IDE to create the tables, Enterprise Manager can now be closed.

Adding Tables to the Database

The Data View window provides a visual interface to work with databases within Visual Basic. We are going to work with this to connect to our new BigBank database and add the tables we identified during the logical design phase.

To start with, we're going to add the BankAccount and AccountType tables that came out of thev normalization process.

Try It Out – Using Data View to Add Tables

1. Open Visual Basic and select Standard EXE from the New Project dialog.

2. Select View | Data View Window to open up the Data View. Then right-click on the Data Links node and select Add a Data Link...

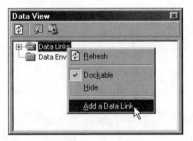

3. We now have a list of choices for the data we wish to connect to. Since we've just created a database in SQL Server, the obvious choice is Microsoft OLE DB Provider for SQL Server. Once highlighted click Next.

4. We now need to set up the connection. If the SQL Server 7.0 is locally installed type (local) as the server name, sa as the user and check Blank password. If the SQL server is not installed on your workstation, you'll need to alter the server name and user name/password as appropriate.

Once valid information has been entered, a list of the available databases will be available in the database combo box. Select BigBank, and then click OK.

At this point, a new node should appear in the Data View window, and be ready for renaming – here we're going to use WROBA.

5. Expand the WROBA node and after a few seconds a number of folders should appear. Right-click on Tables and select New Table .

6. Type in BankAccount as the table name and click on OK.

7. Enter the following column names and data types into the data design table. All columns used in the database will use the default settings for precision and scale and will have **Allow Nulls** *unchecked*, unless specified otherwise.

Design Table:BankAccount

Column Name	Datatype	Length	Precision	Scale	Allow Nulls	Default Value	Identity
AccountId	int	4	10	0			
AccountType	tinyint	1	3	0			
Balance	money	8	19	4			
DailyWithdrawalLimit	money	8	19	4			
DailyRemaining	money	8	19	4			
LastWithdrawalDate	datetime	8	0	0			
OverdraftLimit	money	8	19	4			

8. Our next task is to assign a primary key. To do this select the AccountID row and right-click and choose **Set Primary Key** to make this column the primary key of the table.

9. On finishing, simply close the design table window and click **Yes** when prompted to save the changes.

10. Our next job is to create the AccountType table. Just repeat steps 5 – 9 and create the table as indicated in the following screenshot:

Design Table:AccountType

Column Name	Datatype	Length	Precision	Scale	Allow Nulls	Default Value	Identity	I
AccountType	tinyint	1	3	0				
AccountTypeDesc	char	15	0	0				

The AccountTypeDesc data type uses a longer length than default to allow the use of longer account type descriptions. Before saving and closing this table, set the primary key to AccountType.

Since the new tables are persisted in SQL Server, there is no need to save this project at any time, but as we'll be continuing to work with the database for the rest of the chapter, there is no necessity to close the project yet. If you do close the project, unless you've specifically deleted the WROBA data link, when you re-open Visual Basic it should still be available for use.

That's all we need to know about creating tables. The information needed to create the remaining tables in the database is listed at the end of the next section. The next area of the physical design we're going to look at implementing is creating relationships between tables. As we know from our logical design, the BankAccount and AccountType tables we've just created have a relationship.

Creating Relationships between Tables

The Database Designer lets us create relationships between tables using database diagrams. We'll now use it to create the relationship between our two new tables.

Try It Out – Using the Database Designer to Create Relationships

1. Right-click on the Database Diagrams node and select New Diagram

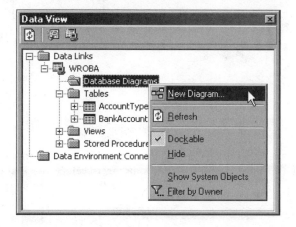

2. Expand the Table node and drag the BankAccount table from the Data View to the diagram, then repeat this for the AccountType table to give the following:

3. We can now create the foreign key relationship. Click on the gray area in front of the primary key of the AccountType table and drag it towards the AccountType column in the BankAccount table:

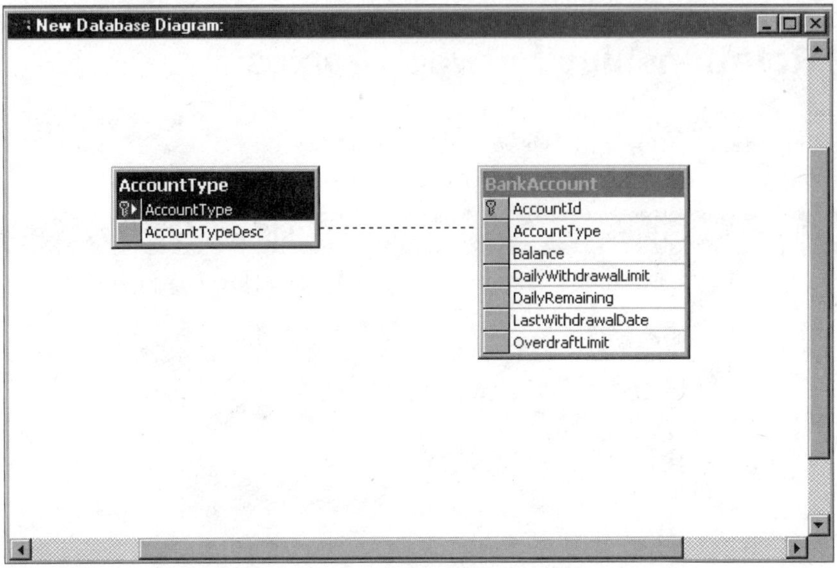

4. The Create Relationship dialog appears with the correct column identified in both tables. Should these not be correct, use the combo boxes to select the right columns (leave the three check boxes checked) then click on OK to create the relationship.

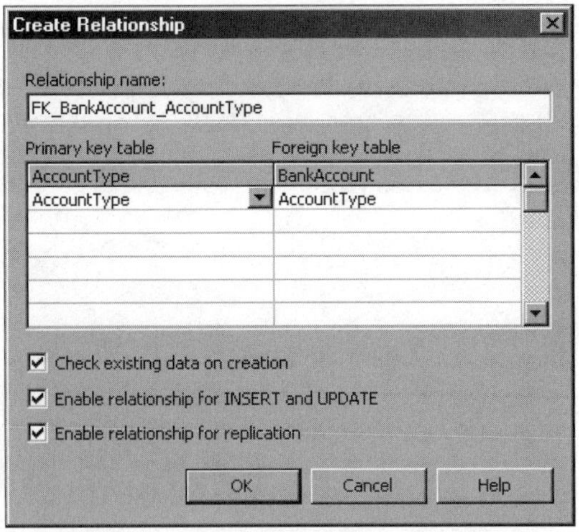

5. A thick line showing their relationship now connects the two tables. Right-clicking in the diagram enables various display options to be selected, such as whether to show relationship labels:

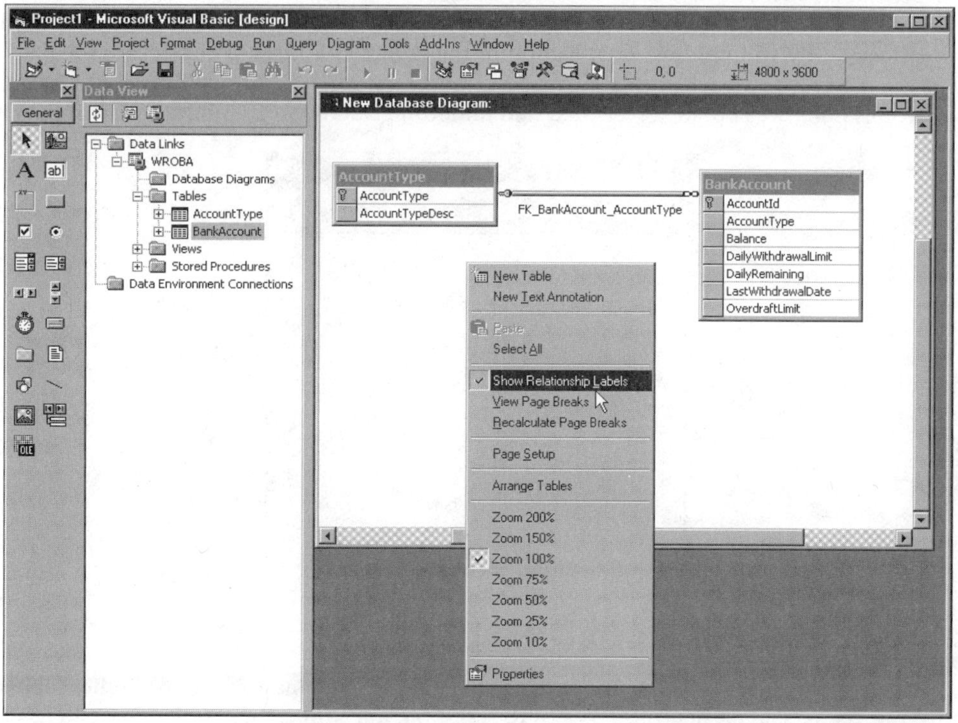

So we now have our foreign key relationship – the yellow key points to the table providing the foreign key, and the table at the opposite end of the connection (with the link) is the table that contains the foreign key.

6. The diagram can now be closed – agree to saving changes and give the diagram the name WROBA Diagram.

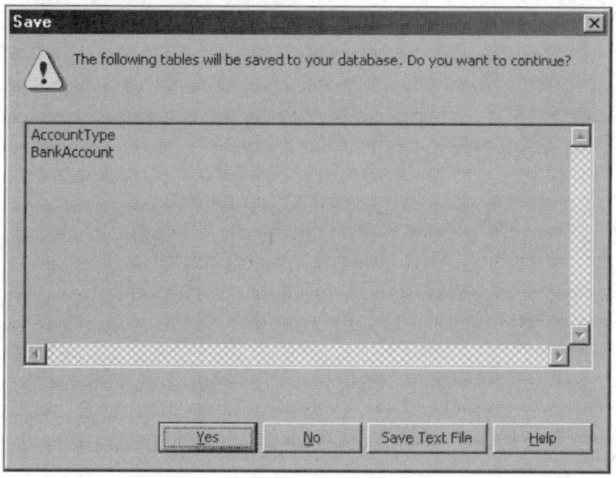

7. By creating relationships, we've made changes to the database, so on closing, we're prompted whether to save the changes. It's a good idea to save a text file before making the changes (to provide a record of the tables to which changes were made) by clicking on the **Save Text File** button. On returning to the save dialog, click on **Yes** to make the changes to the database. Choosing **No** will not save the diagram or the table's relationship changes to the database.

8. At this point we should see the diagram under the **Database Diagrams** node of the **Data Link**:

Completing the Physical Design

As we know from the logical design, the `BigBank` database contains a number of other tables and relationships. As we said earlier, there is a SQL script file that will create the database in its entirety. However, we think it's useful to list the tables here and highlight their relationships.

There are some general principles in this set of tables: except for the `CardxAccount` table, and the `TxLock` table, in which two columns are set as primary keys, only the *first* column in each table will be set as the primary key. And, barring one exception, the **Allow Nulls** box will be left unchecked for each column.

Try It Out – Finishing the BigBank Database

1. First off, we have the `WROBACard` table that holds password information. This is the only table that uses a default value. The `InvalidPasswordCnt` column acts as a counter and the value increments each time the user enters the wrong password when attempting to logon. The session is ended after five tries.

Column Name	Datatype	Length	Precision	Scale	Allow Nulls	Default Val
CardId	int	4	10	0		
Password	char	10	0	0		
InvalidPasswordCnt	tinyint	1	3	0		(0)

2. The `Bank` table is straightforward and identifies the bank at which the account is held:

Column Name	Datatype	Length	Precision	Scale	Allow Nulls	Default Value
BankId	smallint	2	5	0		
BankDesc	char	20	0	0		
BankDSN	varchar	250	0	0		

3. The `CardxAccount` table contains an `AccountType` column which enforces that a card can only be associated with one of each account type (Checking and Saving in our case study). Make sure you set both `CardId` and `AccountType` as primary keys. To do this, it is necessary to select both rows before setting the primary key.

Column Name	Datatype	Length	Precision	Scale	Allow Nulls	Default Value
CardId	int	4	10	0		
AccountType	tinyint	1	3	0		
AccountId	int	4	10	0		

4. We've already alluded to the `TxType` table during our discussion on normalization:

Column Name	Datatype	Length	Precision	Scale	Allow Nulls	Default Val
TxType	tinyint	1	3	0		
TxTypeDesc	char	15	0	0		

5. The `TXLock` table is used to prevent two users from logging in using the same card ID:

Column Name	Datatype	Length	Precision	Scale	Allow Nulls	Default Value
BankId	smallint	2	5	0		
CardId	int	4	10	0		

6. The `AccountHistory` table contains the only column in the database, `CounterPartyRef`, that allows the use of Nulls:

Design Table:AccountHistory

Column Name	Datatype	Length	Precision	Scale	Allow Nulls	Default Value	
TxId	uniqueidentifie	16	0	0			
AccountId	int	4	10	0			
TxDate	datetime	8	0	0			
TxType	tinyint	1	3	0			
TxDescription	char	40	0	0			
TxAmount	money	8	19	4			
CounterpartyRef	char	26	0	0	✓		

7. Lastly, we have the `Payee` table:

Design Table:Payee

Column Name	Datatype	Length	Precision	Scale	Allow Nulls	Default Value	
PayeeId	uniqueidentifie	16	0	0			
CardId	int	4	10	0			
PayeeDesc	char	30	0	0			
BankId	smallint	2	5	0			
AccountId	int	4	10	0			
DefaultAmount	money	8	19	4			
WROBACardId	int	4	10	0			

8. Once we've created all the tables, we then need to set the relationships between them. Open up the WROBA diagram by right-clicking on the **WROBA Diagram** node and selecting **Open**. Then set the following relationships between the tables, ensuring that the correct columns are selected.

Table to create relationships between	Column to use
AccountHistory and BankAccount	AccountId
AccountHistory and TxType	TxType
WROBACard and TxLock	CardId
WROBACard and CardxAccount	CardId
WROBACard and Payee	CardId
Bank and Payee	BankId
Bank and TxLock	BankId
BankAccount and CardxAccount	AccountId
AccountType and CardXAccount	AccountType

which should result in a database diagram as follows:

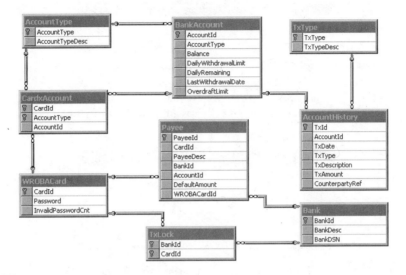

Of course, a database needs data to be useful. We can populate the database using either the SQL Server Enterprise Manager or Data View from within the Visual Basic IDE. The methods are similar in either program. Since we are working in Visual Basic's Data View currently, let's use it to add data to the AccountType table. Later in this book, you'll learn how to use SQL scripting to add data.

Try it Out: Populating a table

1. To enter data into a table, right click on the table name – AccountType – in the Data View window, and choose Open:

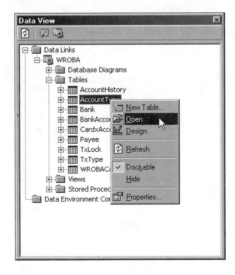

The table will open, ready for data entry:

```
Run Table: AccountType                    _ □ ×
   AccountType        AccountTypeDesc
▶  |
```

2. Enter the following data, pressing *Tab* to move to the next field. Close the table on finishing data entry. There is no need to specifically save the table, it's written to the database as the data is entered.

```
Run Table: AccountType                    _ □ ×
   AccountType        AccountTypeDesc
   0                  Administrator
   1                  Checking
▶  2                  Saving
*
```

There is no need to save the VB project. As we saw earlier, the tables will have been persisted to SQL Server, so next time Visual Basic is opened, the WROBA data link will be available for use.

Summary

In this chapter, we started to actually build the WROBA application and began work on the data tier. Our first task was to work out how we could approach the task of creating the database we required and, to this end, we discussed logical design, where the database was planned via analysis of business scenarios, and physical design, where the database was implemented.

During the logical design discussion, we looked at the concept of entities and entity relationships and developed a preliminary design for the database. We then refined our design through the process of normalization.

We then moved onto the physical design stage and looked at some of the issues surrounding practical database creation including the different data types available to us and the effect of using NULLs and default values.

Finally, we began the practical work and created the BigBank database using the Enterprise Manager utility in SQL Server 7.0. After creating the database, we then created the tables and relationships that form our data store by working through the Visual Basic IDE. Our last task was to start the work of populating the database.

In our next chapter we'll look at **Structured Query Language** (**SQL**) and see how that can help us out with database manipulation, table population, and with providing facilities to enable our application to retrieve and manipulate data.

If you really want to know far more about using SQL Server and Visual Basic we recommend *Beginning Visual Basic SQL Server 7.0, ISBN 1861003064*, also by *Wrox Press*.

10

Database II
SQL and Stored Procedures

In the previous chapter, we really got to grips with the construction of the database that supports our application. In this chapter, we're going to concern ourselves with how we can access and manipulate that data, and, if the need arises, alter the database itself.

The data tier, which we'll discuss in the next chapter, is concerned with communicating between the data store and the components in the business layer. Therefore, within this chapter we need to build an understanding of how we can provide the hooks into the database that the data tier will use, so we can programmatically query and manipulate the data in the database. Again, we're sticking our toes into a veritable lake of computing – the area of database administration and programming is just massive. But, even if you never intend to become a database guru, it's always useful to have some appreciation of what they do.

This chapter is split into two main sections. Firstly we'll look at **Structured Query Language** (**SQL**), and see how that language is used to query, manipulate and analyze databases. Secondly, we'll build on that understanding to see how SQL plays a crucial role within the WROBA application. In more detail, we'll be looking at:

- ❑   The basics of SQL

- ❑   How to create and manipulate database elements

- ❑   How to query and manipulate the data in the database

- ❑   What **stored procedures** are, and why they are so useful for us

- ❑   How stored procedures are used in the WROBA application

Without more ado, let's get down to the waterside.

Using SQL

SQL is an acronym for **Structured Query Language**, and is the industry standard language used to create, maintain, and query databases. Thus, in the context of our case study, we're going to have to learn a bit about SQL in order to be able to carry out the database operations necessary for our application.

> *Of course, there's more to SQL than what's covered here, but this should give you all the information you need for the case study. If you want to know more about using SQL with SQL Server, try Professional SQL Server 7.0 Programming, ISBN 1861002319, from Wrox.*

The standard version of SQL has been defined by the American National Standards Institute (ANSI), with the most recent version being known as ANSI SQL-92. This language can be used with all the major large databases like SQL Server and Oracle.

However, these databases may also support features that go beyond the standard, so the large databases have their own, slightly enhanced, versions of SQL. In the case of Microsoft's SQL Server, the SQL "dialect" is called **Transact-SQL** (**T-SQL**), whereas Oracle database servers support an extended language known as PL/SQL. The majority of the examples below use generic SQL, and should work with most database vendors.

SQL itself can be broken down into three sub-languages:

- ❑ **Data Definition Language** (**DDL**) – used to create, alter, or delete (drop) database objects like tables, fields, or indexes
- ❑ **Data Manipulation Language** (**DML**) – used to retrieve and manipulate the data in the database
- ❑ **Data Control Language** (**DCL**) – used to provide security for a database

In this chapter, we'll just be considering aspects of the first two sub-languages; the third lies beyond our limited encounter with SQL.

OK, so let's look at DDL.

Data Definition Language – DDL

As we said above, SQL uses Data Definition Language to create, alter, and drop database tables, fields, and indexes, so this section is divided into the following blocks:

- ❑ Creating tables
- ❑ Altering tables
- ❑ Deleting tables

We'll use these sections to introduce the basics of SQL.

Creating Tables

In SQL Server there are a number of ways to create tables without using SQL directly; we can use Wizards, or, as we saw in the previous chapter, we can work though the SQL Server 7 Enterprise Manager. We also saw how to create tables using the Data View window in Visual Basic 6, without even going into SQL Server 7.

In this chapter we'll be working with another of the utilities that comes with SQL Server 7 called **Query Analyzer**. One of the things this utility allows you to do is to write and execute SQL statements, to query and manipulate databases on your SQL Server installation.

Try It Out – Creating a Table

We'll start by creating a new table in our BigBank database.

1. First we need to launch the Query Analyzer, so select Start | Programs | Microsoft SQL Server 7.0 | Query Analyzer. It can also be launched from Enterprise Manager by selecting Tools | SQL Server Query Analyzer.

2. The first task is to connect to the correct installation of SQL Server (which will probably be the local one if you've installed it on your own system):

3. Next we need to select the database we wish to manipulate, so select BigBank from the drop-down list at the top right titled DB:

4. Let's add a table to the `BigBank` database that will allow us to record the gender of a hypothetical user. Enter the following code into the pane of the Query Analyzer:

```
CREATE TABLE Gender (
    UserId    INT       NOT NULL,
    AccountId INT       NOT NULL,
    Gender    CHAR (1) NOT NULL Default '?'
)
```

After entering the text, you can check the validity of the statement by clicking the **Parse** icon (blue check mark or *Ctrl + F5*), and execute it with the **Execute** icon (green triangle or *F5*). The lower pane should display confirmation that the statement was parsed or executed successfully (or information about where the errors are, if it was unsuccessful):

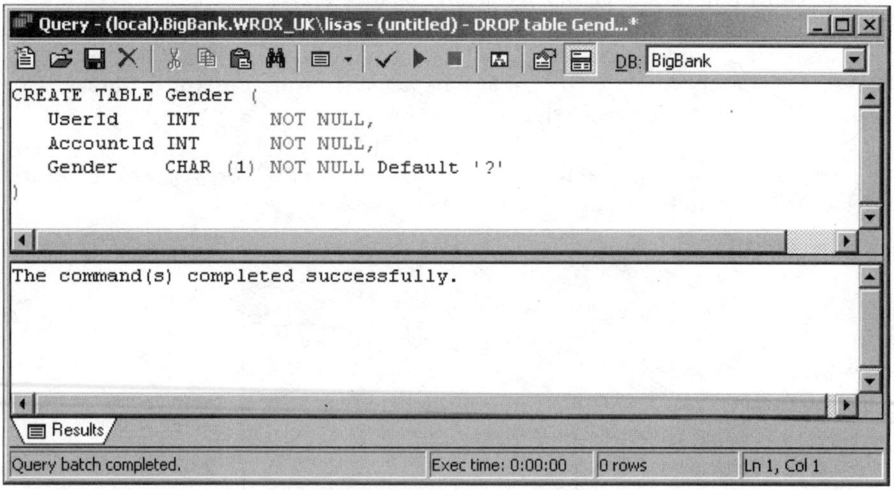

5. Once the command has completed successfully you can see what has happened by opening Enterprise Manager and drilling down to the **Tables** node of `BigBank`, where a new table – `Gender` – should be present. If you don't see it immediately you may have to press *F5* to refresh the view:

6. If you then right-click on the Gender table and select **Design Table** you'll see a familiar illustration of the table's design:

Column Name	Datatype	Length	Precision	Scale	Allow Nulls	Default Value
UserId	int	4	10	0		
AccountId	int	4	10	0		
Gender	char	1	0	0		('?')

How It Works

OK, so this little example doesn't exactly fit in with our carefully designed database. But real life being what it is, sometimes unforeseen needs arise, and this technique shows how we can programmatically change our database construction.

The last screen shot illustrates exactly what we've achieved – we've created a table called Gender with three fields (or columns as they're referred to in SQL Server) and have defined the column name and data type. We've also set a default value for one of the fields.

Let's dig into the SQL statement itself:

```
CREATE TABLE Gender (
    UserId    INT       NOT NULL,
    AccountId INT       NOT NULL,
    Gender    CHAR (1)  NOT NULL Default '?'
)
```

SQL uses case-insensitive keywords, but may use case-sensitive object names. In this chapter, all the SQL keywords are in capitals, and all the programmer-selected object names are in mixed case. So, in the SQL statement, CREATE TABLE, INT, and NOT NULL are all SQL keywords while the table name (Gender) and the column names (UserId, Gender, and AccountId) are object names.

SQL, unlike Visual Basic, doesn't require a line continuation character to break one line of SQL code into several lines, so many SQL programmers place the opening and closing parenthesis on separate lines as shown above. If the code doesn't work, it's usually easier to see errors if statements are written this way.

Technically, though, you can condense statements to one line per pair of parentheses if you want, and the Query Analyzer will still execute it quite happily:

```
CREATE TABLE Gender (UserId INT NOT NULL, AccountId INT NOT NULL, Gender CHAR (1)
NOT NULL Default '?')
```

Of course, this is just one specific case of table creation. Let's broaden things out by looking at the basic syntax of the CREATE TABLE SQL statement:

```
CREATE TABLE tablename ( <rowdefinition_1>, … ,<rowdefinition_n> )
```

Where *rowdefinition_x* is in the following format:

```
rowname datatype (length) [NOT] NULL
```

You should be familiar with the different data types that can be used in a database from our discussions in Chapter 9. Here, length is only required if *datatype* is a character type – other data types have a fixed length.

The brackets in [NOT] indicate that this keyword is optional. So, for example, we use either AccountId INT NOT NULL or AccountId INT NULL, depending on whether we wanted to allow NULLs or not. In our Try It Out, we define all our rows as NOT NULL:

```
    UserId    INT       NOT NULL,
    AccountId INT       NOT NULL,
    Gender    CHAR (1)  NOT NULL Default '?'
```

As we discussed in Chapter 9, there are performance advantages to be gained by using default values rather than just allowing columns to have null values. In this example we've assigned a default value of '?' to the column titled Gender.

Default values can be handled either by the SQL Server's **Default Value** column, or by inserting default values using code in your VB project. By setting the default value on the server side, you can easily change the value later if need be, by simply changing it in the table. If you allow your application to insert the default values, that requires changing the code and redeploying the application to change the values later.

If you allow your application to insert a value for an unknown field, you can use validation techniques to ensure the user chose to leave it blank, rather than forgot to enter data in the field.

Finally, notice that the entry in the Default Value column is ('?'). You use single quotes to identify text strings; the parenthesis will be added automatically.

SQL Scripts

In the above example, we've just typed in the SQL we want to use to create a table in our own database. However, just like any other language, we can save these statements (using the **Save** options in the **File** menu of Query Analyzer), and send them to other people so that they too can create similar tables in their databases.

These reusable chunks of code are known as **scripts**. The files associated with the case study that allow you to set up and populate the BigBank database automatically are a great example of such scripts (for example the Schema.sql file in Appendix A, which is concerned with the creation and configuration of the BigBank database).

Not only do scripts allow information to be transferred, they also allow database information to be retained. That means a database can be rebuilt if it's corrupted in any way.

Even if you created your database manually, the way we did with the BigBank database in Chapter 9, you can still create SQL scripts from the database. Let's see how this is done.

Try It Out – Creating SQL Scripts from an Existing Database

Let's take a look at the script that we'd need to recreate the BankAccount and Payee tables in our BigBank database.

1. In Enterprise Manager, select the BankAccount table of the BigBank database. Select **Tools | Database Scripting**. You'll see a screen like this, with the table we selected listed in the right-hand list box:

2. Select the Payee table in the left-hand list (Objects on BigBank), and click on the Add>> button, to transfer this table into the Objects to be scripted box. (If we wanted to Script All Objects, or all of one of a particular type of object, we could check the appropriate box).

3. Click the Formatting tab, and check Include descriptive headers in the script files.

4. Return to the General tab, and click the Preview button to see your script:

```
Object Scripting Preview                                              [x]

/****** Object:  Table [dbo].[BankAccount]   Script Date: 12/06/00 11:52:17 ******/
CREATE TABLE [dbo].[BankAccount] (
        [AccountId] [int] NOT NULL ,
        [AccountType] [tinyint] NOT NULL ,
        [Balance] [money] NOT NULL ,
        [DailyWithdrawalLimit] [money] NOT NULL ,
        [DailyRemaining] [money] NOT NULL ,
        [LastWithdrawalDate] [datetime] NOT NULL ,
        [OverdraftLimit] [money] NOT NULL
) ON [PRIMARY]
GO

/****** Object:  Table [dbo].[Payee]   Script Date: 12/06/00 11:52:18 ******/
CREATE TABLE [dbo].[Payee] (
        [PayeeId] [uniqueidentifier] NOT NULL ,
        [CardId] [int] NOT NULL ,
        [PayeeDesc] [char] (30) NOT NULL ,
        [BankId] [smallint] NOT NULL ,

        Copy        Save As...      Close
```

Here we can see the syntax that would create the two tables – as you can see, it's very similar to the code we just entered into Query Analyzer.

There are several things to note here:

❑ As mentioned earlier, SQL does not require a line continuation character like Visual Basic does, and, with one column per line, this statement is easy to read and understand.

❑ The /* and */ symbols are used to identify comments that are not meant to be executed.

❑ Many database vendors require you to use a **delimiter** between statements. This fragment of script contains two SQL statements that are separated with a delimiter: the word GO.

> **This is handy way to see the correct syntax for the SQL commands you would need to use to recreate something you built manually.**

5. Now click on the Save As... button, and save this script as `maketables.sql`.

6. Then go to Query Analyzer. Click File | Open, and navigate to the file you just created. The code will be loaded into Query Analyzer.

This way, it can be run by anyone else who wants to recreate the `BankAccount` and `Payeee` tables in their own databases.

Altering Tables

Of course, in the real world, nothing stays the same for long. What if we want to make changes to our database tables after we've created them? To modify a table by adding, changing or destroying a column, we can use the ALTER TABLE statement.

One particular use of this is to add further columns to an existing table. Say, for instance, we now want to add a column that monitors how long a user has been a customer of Big Bank.

Try It Out – Adding a Column to a Table

We'll add this new column to the Gender table that we created in our first Try It Out in this chapter.

1. Firstly we need to return to the Query Analyzer (ensuring that **BigBank** is still selected in the DB drop-down list). Delete any code that's in the Query window, and enter the following:

```
ALTER TABLE Gender ADD No_Of_Years_With_Bank INT NULL
```

Again, after entering the text, you can check the validity of the statement by clicking the **Parse** icon before executing it with the **Execute** icon.

2. After successful execution of the command, we can once again use the **Design Table** option in Enterprise Manager to view the amended table, which should look as follows:

Column Name	Datatype	Length	Precision	Scale	Allow Nulls	Default Value
UserId	int	4	10	0		
AccountId	int	4	10	0		
Gender	char	1	0	0		('?')
No_Of_Years_With_Bank	int	4	10	0	✓	

Note that this time we've used INT NULL in our SQL, so the **Allow Nulls** column is checked.

How It Works

So here, the general syntax of the ALTER TABLE command we're using is:

```
ALTER TABLE <table_name>
ADD COLUMN ( <rowdefinition> )
```

The ADD keyword can be replaced by either of the following:

❑ ALTER – To alter a column definition.

❑ DROP – To delete a column. Here, only the column name is required.

One thing to note is that when we use the ALTER TABLE command, we're only allowed to add columns that either accept NULL values or that have a default value defined.

This command can also be used to add constraints to a table – we saw why constraints are useful back in Chapter 9.

Try It Out – Adding Constraints to a Table

Let's test this with our Gender table. We'll make our UserID key into the primary key of the table, and the AccountID into a foreign key, that relates to the AccountID in our BankAccount table.

1. Delete all the code in the Query Analyzer, and add the following:

```
ALTER TABLE Gender
ADD CONSTRAINT PK_GENDER PRIMARY KEY (UserId),
    CONSTRAINT FK_GENDER FOREIGN KEY (AccountId) REFERENCES BankAccount
```

2. Parse and execute the command as usual, and view the table:

Column Name	Datatype	Length	Precision	Scale	Allow Nulls	Default Value
UserId	int	4	10	0		
AccountId	int	4	10	0		
Gender	char	1	0	0		('?')
No_Of_Years_With_Bank	int	4	10	0	✓	

UserID is now marked as the primary key.

We could actually have done this in our initial create statement, like so:

```
CREATE TABLE Gender (
    UserId INT NOT NULL CONSTRAINT PK_GENDER PRIMARY KEY,
    AccountId INT NOT NULL CONSTRAINT FK_GENDER FOREIGN KEY (AccountId)
                                        REFERENCES BankAccount,
    Gender CHAR (1) NOT NULL Default '?'
)
```

However, here, unless the table referenced by the foreign key constraint already exists, the statement will fail. That's why it's safest to add in constraints after the table has been created, and that's the method we've adopted in the case study scripts you can see in Appendix A.

While we're thinking about the case study again, there were a few constraints we didn't include when we set up the database in Chapter 9. These were the CHECK and UNIQUE constraints.

Try It Out – Adding CHECK and UNIQUE Constraints

As we encountered previously, a CHECK constraint is actually a logical check involving one or more columns. The UNIQUE constraint forces the PayeeDesc column to be unique.

There are a few columns in our database that we need to implement these constraints, so let's add them now.

1. Return to the Query Analyzer and make sure that **BigBank** is still selected in the **DB** drop-down list. Replace any code in the Query window with the following CHECK:

```
ALTER TABLE BankAccount ADD
   CONSTRAINT CK_BankAccount_Remaining
   CHECK (DailyRemaining <= DailyWithDrawalLimit)
GO
```

We're using the CHECK constraint to ensure that the daily available balance (DailyRemaining) hasn't exceeded the daily withdrawal limit, that is CHECK(DailyRemaining <= DailyWithDrawalLimit)

2. Then add the following UNIQUE constraints:

```
ALTER TABLE Payee ADD
   CONSTRAINT IX_Payee UNIQUE  NONCLUSTERED (PayeeDesc)
GO

ALTER TABLE AccountType ADD
   CONSTRAINT IX_AccountType UNIQUE NONCLUSTERED(AccountTypeDesc)
GO

ALTER TABLE Bank ADD
   CONSTRAINT IX_Bank UNIQUE NONCLUSTERED(BankDesc)
GO

ALTER TABLE TxType ADD
   CONSTRAINT IX_TxType UNIQUE NONCLUSTERED (TxTypeDesc)
GO
```

These UNIQUE constraints force the specified columns (PayeeDesc, AccountTypeDesc, BankDesc, and TxTypeDesc) to be unique. This prevents the user from, say, entering a payee's name and account information more than once.

3. Parse and Execute the code.

Deleting Tables

As we said previously, in relational database terminology removing or deleting an object from the database is called **dropping** the object. Since we don't really want the Gender table in our database, let's now remove it.

1. Back in Query Analyzer, delete the outstanding code, then enter and execute the following:

```
DROP TABLE Gender
```

2. Once the command has executed, the database structure will be back to its original state. You can check this through Enterprise Manager – but remember to refresh the window.

The DROP TABLE statement is very straightforward, but as you've just seen, will happily execute without checking for confirmation – so use carefully!

Now let's move on to the SQL commands used to deal with the data in the database.

Data Manipulation Language – DML

When the tables have been created, but before we can use them, we first need to be able to add data to them. After that, we need to be able to read, update, and delete this data. This section of the SQL language is termed the Data Manipulation Language, and here we'll be looking at:

- ❑ Adding data
- ❑ Modifying existing data
- ❑ Deleting data
- ❑ Retrieving data

There are examples of some of these actions in the case study script for populating the tables, but we will also make great use of such commands when we consider how to use the BigBank database within the WROBA application.

Adding Data

The first thing we need to do is to add some data to our tables.

If you're working through the book, you should already have populated the AccountType table through Enterprise Manager. If you haven't, you need to do it now – otherwise the following examples won't work, because of the relationships that exist between the tables.

1. Delete any code currently in Query Analyzer, then type in and execute the following code:

```
INSERT BankAccount (
    AccountId,
    AccountType,
    Balance,
```

```
    DailyWithdrawalLimit,
    DailyRemaining,
    LastWithdrawalDate,
    OverdraftLimit
)
VALUES (20000, 0,0,0,0,GETDATE(),0)
GO
INSERT BankAccount VALUES (20001, 1,254,500,500,GETDATE(), 500)
INSERT BankAccount VALUES (20002, 2,2376,500,500,GETDATE(),500)
INSERT BankAccount VALUES (20003, 1,-56,1000,40,GETDATE(),1500)
INSERT BankAccount VALUES (20004, 2,3236,500,340,GETDATE(),500)
INSERT BankAccount VALUES (20005, 2,236,500,100,GETDATE(),100)
GO
```

2. To inspect the BankAccount table after successful completion of the command, drill down to the table in Enterprise Manager, right-click on the table, and this time select **Open Table |
Return all rows**:

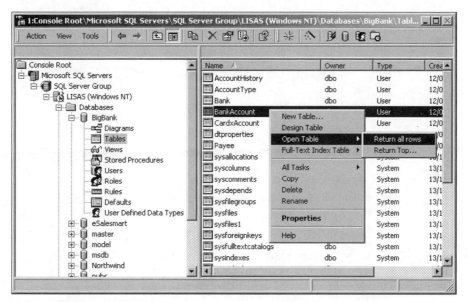

You should now see the following:

AccountId	AccountType	Balance	DailyWithdrawalLim	DailyRemaining	LastWithdrawalDat	OverdraftLimit
20000	0	0	0	0	12/06/00 16:25:15	0
20001	1	254	500	500	12/06/00 16:25:15	500
20002	2	2376	500	500	12/06/00 16:25:15	500
20003	1	-56	1000	40	12/06/00 16:25:15	1500
20004	2	3236	500	340	12/06/00 16:25:15	500
20005	2	236	500	100	12/06/00 16:25:15	100

How It Works

The INSERT statement is used to add data to a table – the table may be empty, or it may already contain data. For the INSERT to be successful, the data being added to the table must satisfy the constraints that apply to the table – if it doesn't, a database error occurs and the data isn't added.

The general INSERT statement has the following syntax:

```
INSERT <table_name> ( <column_1>,…, <column_n> )
VALUES ( < value_expression_1>, …, < value_expression_n>)
```

As you may recall (or if you don't, as you can check by looking at the table design through Enterprise Manager), the BankAccount columns have the following data types:

❑   The AccountId column: int.

❑   The AccountType column: tinyint.

❑   The LastWithdrawalDate column: datetime.

❑   The other columns have the money data type.

For all except the LastWithdrawalDate column, the data is just presented as an integer:

```
INSERT BankAccount (
    AccountId,
    AccountType,
    Balance,
    DailyWithdrawalLimit,
    DailyRemaining,
    LastWithdrawalDate,
    OverdraftLimit
)
VALUES (20000, 0,0,0,0,GETDATE(),0)
GO
```

The datetime value is more interesting, as that's set by a function: GETDATE(). There are several other functions available for use in SQL. We've already seen one that we use in our case study – NEWID(), which we mentioned in Chapter 9.

If a column exists in the table, but is not mentioned at all in the INSERT statement, then the default value for this column is inserted. If no default is specified for a column, then NULL is inserted. You need to take care when not specifying values for columns, as this may result in an error if this column has a NOT NULL constraint.

However, on large tables, listing every column name for every insert statement can be tedious. Here, a shortened version of the statement, containing the table name and data for each field, is enough:

```
INSERT BankAccount VALUES (20002, 2,2376,500,500,GETDATE(),500)
```

As we've shown above, it's a good idea to use the column names for the first insert, as a reminder of what columns exist in the database – getting the order of the values wrong will result in a database containing inaccurate information!

Before we move on, we'll need to populate a few more tables.

Try It Out – Populating the Rest of the Database

Enter the following into Query Analyzer (if you don't want to type it all by hand, you'll find this in a SQL script called `FillTables.sql` in the code download available from the Wrox web site).

1. First we'll add three cards to the `WROBACard` table:

```
INSERT [dbo].[WROBACard] (
    [CardId],
    [Password]
)
VALUES (
    10000,
    'Admin'
)
GO
```

```
INSERT [dbo].[WROBACard] (
    [CardId],
    [Password]
)
VALUES (
    10001,
    'Secret1'
)
GO
```

```
INSERT [dbo].[WROBACard] (
    [CardId],
    [Password]
)
VALUES (
    10002,
    'Secret2'
)
GO
```

2. Then add three banks to the `Bank` table:

```
INSERT [dbo].[Bank] (
    [BankId],
    [BankDesc],
    [BankDSN]
)
VALUES (
    1,
    'Big Bank',
    'DSN_Big_Bank'
)
GO
```

```
INSERT [dbo].[Bank] VALUES (2, 'Another Big Bank', 'DSN_Another_Big_Bank')
GO
```

```
INSERT [dbo].[Bank] VALUES (3, 'Small Bank', 'DSN_Small_Bank')
GO
```

3. Next, the CardxAccount table:

```
INSERT [dbo].[CardxAccount] (
    [CardId],
    [AccountType],
    [AccountId]
)
VALUES (
    10000,
    0,
    20000
)
GO
```

```
INSERT [dbo].[CardxAccount] VALUES (10001, 1, 20001)
GO
```

```
INSERT [dbo].[CardxAccount] VALUES (10001, 2, 20002)
GO
```

```
INSERT [dbo].[CardxAccount] VALUES (10002, 1, 20003)
GO
```

```
INSERT [dbo].[CardxAccount] VALUES (10002, 2, 20004)
GO
```

4. The TxType table:

```
INSERT [dbo].[TxType] (
    [TxType],
    [TxTypeDesc]
) VALUES (
    1,
    'TSF'
)
GO
```

```
INSERT [dbo].[TxType] (
    [TxType],
    [TxTypeDesc]
) VALUES (
    2,
    'BIL'
)
GO
```

5. And finally, we'll add one entry to the `Payee` table:

```
INSERT [dbo].[Payee] (
    [PayeeId],
    [CardId],
    [PayeeDesc],
    [BankId],
    [AccountId],
    [DefaultAmount],
    [WROBACardId]
) VALUES (
    '67FC28E6-6174-4684-8409-138CE36CED6C',
    10002,
    'Cecilia Poremsky',
    1,
    20003,
    100,
    10001
)
GO
```

6. Now execute all this. Your database should now be populated with enough data to let you fully use the case study's functionality.

The only thing to note here is that if any values were text strings, then the string is enclosed in single quotes. For example:

```
INSERT [dbo].[Bank] (
    [BankId],
    [BankDesc],
    [BankDSN]
)
VALUES (
    1,
    'Big Bank',
    'DSN_Big_Bank'
)
GO
```

Modifying Existing Data

Another important operation we're likely to want to attempt is that of changing the data we hold.

Try It Out – Updating Data

In our WROBA application, the balances of various accounts are going to be constantly changing, so let's modify the balance of one of the accounts.

1. Execute the following statement in Query Analyzer:

```
UPDATE BankAccount
SET Balance = 354
WHERE AccountId = 20001
```

2. Inspect the results by opening up the table and returning all the rows. You should see that the Balance column for AccountId 20001 has been changed from 254 to 354:

AccountId	AccountType	Balance	DailyWithdrawalLim	DailyRemaining	LastWithdrawalDat	OverdraftLimit
20000	0	0	0	0	12/06/00 16:25:15	0
20001	1	354	500	500	12/06/00 16:25:15	500
20002	2	2376	500	500	12/06/00 16:25:15	500
20003	1	-56	1000	40	12/06/00 16:25:15	1500
20004	2	3236	500	340	12/06/00 16:25:15	500
20005	2	236	500	100	12/06/00 16:25:15	100

How It Works

This is reasonably straightforward. The general syntax of UPDATE is:

```
UPDATE <table_name>
SET <column_1> = <value_expression_1>, …, <column_n> = <value_expression_n>
[WHERE <condition_1>
[ AND | OR condition_2 ]
…
[ AND | OR condition_n ]]
```

So, in our example, we just update one column (Balance) in the BankAccount table:

```
UPDATE BankAccount
SET Balance = 354
```

and we set the value_expression of this column to 354. However, we don't want to reset every row of the database – we need to specify which rows to apply the update to using WHERE.

The WHERE statement is optional, and can have as many conditions as we want. Here, we only specify the one condition:

```
AccountId = 20001
```

So we'll only update the Balance column for those rows with AccountID of 20001.

Deleting Data

Of course there may be times when we just wish to delete a whole set of data, for example, if one of our customers closes their account. We can do that via the DELETE statement.

Try It Out – Removing Data

Let's say we've just closed Account number 20005, so we need to remove the AccountId 20005 row from the BankAccount table.

1. Execute the following in Query Analyzer:

```
Delete BankAccount
WHERE AccountId = 20005
```

2. Once again we can check our results by inspecting the resulting table:

AccountId	AccountType	Balance	DailyWithdrawalLim	DailyRemaining	LastWithdrawalDat	OverdraftLimit
20000	0	0	0	0	12/06/00 16:25:15	0
20001	1	354	500	500	12/06/00 16:25:15	500
20002	2	2376	500	500	12/06/00 16:25:15	500
20003	1	-56	1000	40	12/06/00 16:25:15	1500
20004	2	3236	500	340	12/06/00 16:25:15	500

How It Works

The syntax for the DELETE statement is:

```
DELETE <table_name>
[WHERE <condition_1>
[ AND | OR condition_2 ]
...
[ AND | OR condition_n ]]
```

We only need to remove the one row from the BankAccount table: the one that satifies the condition AccountID = 20005:

```
Delete BankAccount
WHERE AccountId = 20005
```

And that's all there is to removing the data. Again note that this executes without giving you any chance to confirm it's what you want to do, so use it with care.

Now we've gained an appreciation of how to set up our database, let's move on to the subject of how to inspect the data we have in it. This is a large and, at points, tricky area, since we need to understand how to get data back from more than one table at a time.

Retrieving Data

The SELECT command is used to query a database and obtain the desired information. Let's have a look at the command in action.

Try It Out – Querying a Database

1. Enter and execute the following in Query analyzer:

```
SELECT * FROM BankAccount
GO

SELECT * FROM BankAccount
ORDER BY Balance
GO

SELECT Balance, OverdraftLimit
FROM BankAccount
WHERE AccountId = 20002
```

You should obtain the following screen, with the query results being shown in the lower pane of the Query Analyzer:

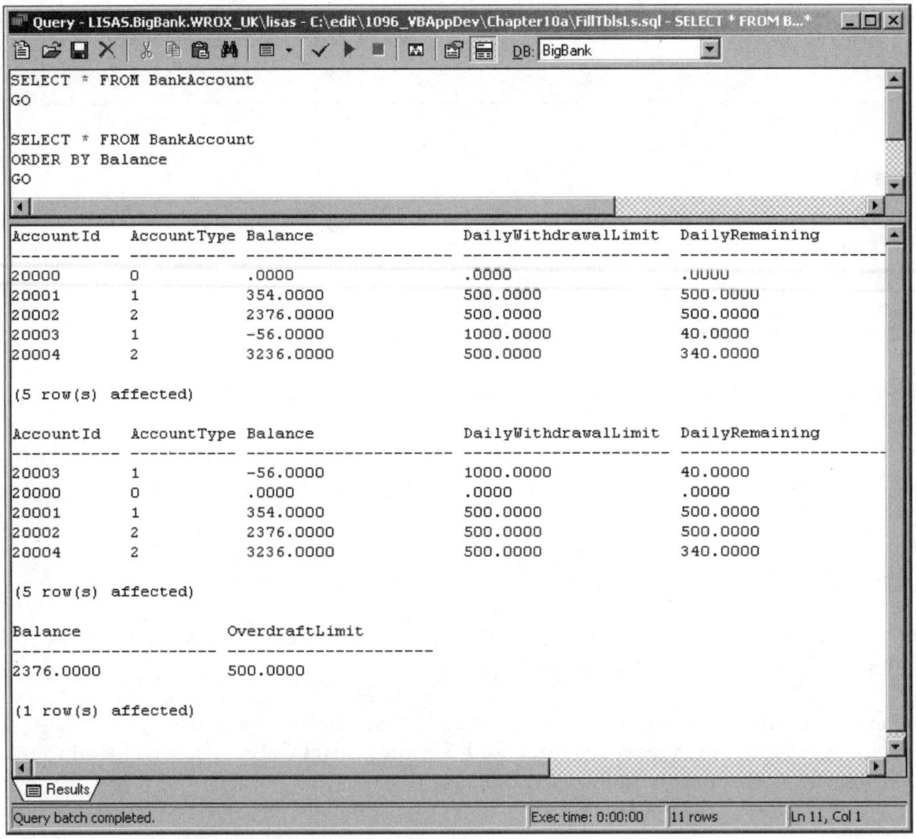

How It Works

In this one example we've seen a number of ways that the SELECT statement can be used (we'll be coming across more variations on this theme as the section progresses).

Firstly, we have:

```
SELECT * FROM BankAccount
GO
```

where the asterisk acts as a **wildcard**. This means that all the fields in the BankAccount table should be returned, which is what you can see in the first set of results in the lower pane of Query Analyzer. If the table was empty, then the SELECT statement would return nothing.

> *Use this wildcard with caution, especially in larger databases, since it will search every column and can result in slow data retrieval.*

The second statement defines an order in which the results should be displayed:

```
SELECT * FROM BankAccount
ORDER BY Balance
GO
```

And as you can see, the second block of results lists all the accounts ordered by the Balance column, with the lowest balance first.

Lastly, rather than select all the fields, we used a statement to retrieve selected fields (Balance and OverdraftLimit) from a particular row (the one where AccountID = 20002):

```
SELECT Balance, OverdraftLimit
FROM BankAccount
WHERE AccountId = 20002
```

Again, if no records in the table satisfy the conditions in the WHERE clause, then the SELECT statement returns nothing.

Also note that, although we've always used = (equal) conditions, you can actually use any mathematical operator in the conditions, including < (less than), > (greater than), <= (less than or equal to), and >= (greater than or equal to).

The general syntax for the SELECT statement can be represented as:

```
SELECT <column_1>, …, <column_n>
FROM <table_name>
[WHERE <condition_1>
[ AND | OR condition_2 ]
…
[ AND | OR condition_n ]]
[ ORDER BY <column_1> [ASC | DESC], …, <column_n> [ASC | DESC]]
```

The only thing about this we really need to explain is the ORDER BY clause. You can set a column to use for sorting order, and specify whether to sort in ascending (ASC) or descending (DESC) order. If ASC or DESC is not specified, the default is ascending. We've used this default in all our examples above.

We won't be going too much further into this query, since this is where things can get quite complex. Suffice to say, there are a number of other ways that we can modify our SELECT statements to increase the selectivity of our query. For example, we can use AND, OR, and NOT operators in the WHERE clause, and use extra clauses such as GROUP BY to gather returned rows into groups.

We've already mentioned that we should avoid using the wildcard. Optimization of queries is a subject of its own since we usually don't want to retrieve more information than we require. Firstly, on a user level we don't want to be bombarded with irrelevant information. Secondly, and more importantly, moving large amounts of data through a system can reduce the performance of both the client application and the network over which the data is being transferred.

Composing Queries

To help us compose, and look at the results of, SELECT statements we can use the Query Designer available through Enterprise Manager.

Try It Out – Using the Query Designer

1. To access the Query Designer, open a table (here we'll use BankAccount) from SQL Enterprise Manager by right-clicking on it and selecting Open Table | Return all rows.

   Note that if you ever want to select a table that already contains a lot of data, you may want to just return the top few rows via Return Top... instead.

2. From this, now familiar, screen, we need to select some additional panes. So, from the toolbar ensure that the Show/Hide Diagram Pane, Grid Pane, SQL Pane, and Results Pane buttons are all depressed (they're the second, third, fourth and fifth buttons in the following screen shot):

   That should give you the following:

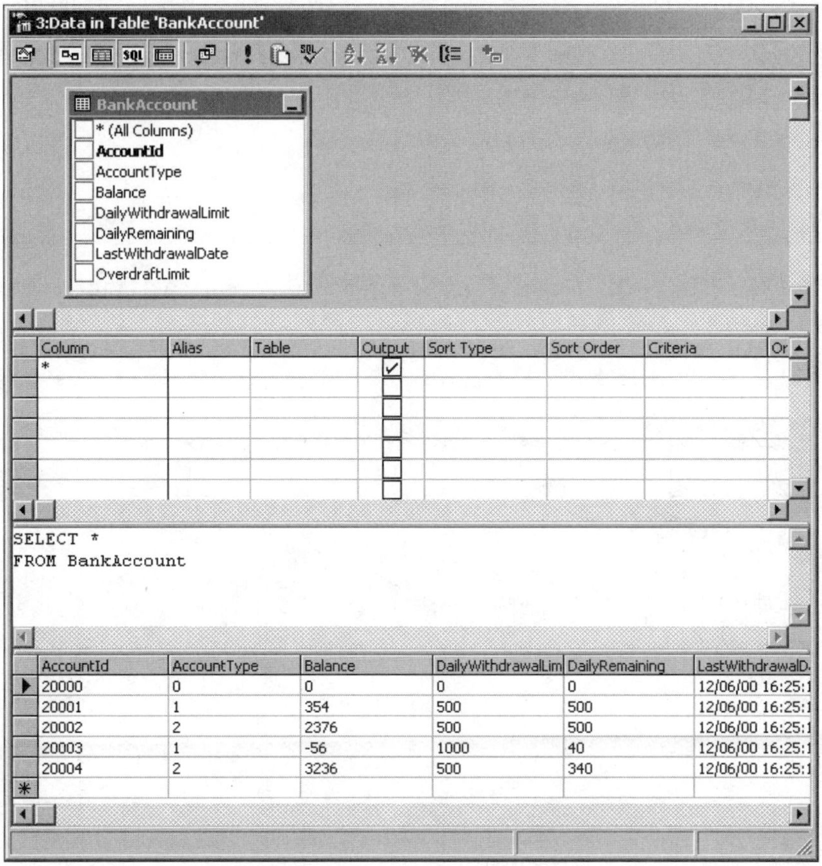

The four sections of this screen have the following uses:

❑ The top (Diagram) pane is a diagram of the tables that will be used in the query.

❑ The second (Grid) pane is a grid view of the columns chosen for the query. This allows you to enter criteria to determine what data to return – again, the mathematical operators that we referred to earlier can be used in the Criteria column. The Sort Type column allows you to select ascending or descending order.

❑ The third (SQL) pane writes out the SQL query in text format.

❑ The last (Results) pane shows the results.

So here we've automatically selected all the records from the BankAccount table.

3. In the Grid pane, uncheck the Output box for the "select all" wildcard (*). Then, in the Diagram pane, check the boxes for the AccountId, Balance, DailyWithdrawlLimit, DailyRemaining, LastWithdrawalDate, and OverdraftLimit columns.

4. In the AccountId row, type =20002 into the Criteria cell. The Grid pane should now look like this:

Column	Alias	Table	Output	Sort Type	Sort Order	Criteria	Or
AccountId		BankAccoun	✓			=20002	
Balance		BankAccoun	✓				
DailyWithdrawa		BankAccoun	✓				
DailyRemaining		BankAccoun	✓				
LastWithdrawall		BankAccoun	✓				
OverdraftLimit		BankAccoun	✓				

The corresponding SQL statement will be automatically generated in the SQL pane.

5. Click on the Verify SQL button and, on confirmation that the SQL statement is OK, select Run. This should yield the following, where the lower pane displays the new results:

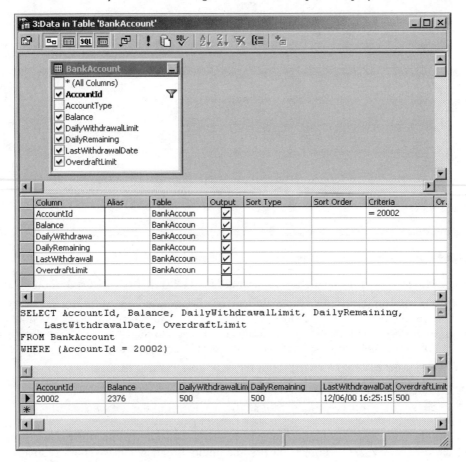

This is especially helpful when we use JOIN clauses, which we'll consider next.

Joins

Sometimes you want data from more than one table. This can be achieved by adding a **join clause** to the SELECT statement.

Joining of tables is something of an advanced SQL topic, and there are several different types of JOIN clause. However, since the most frequently used join – the INNER JOIN – is also the only join used within the WROBA case study, we can leave the other joins for more advanced texts.

The INNER JOIN (in some circumstances called the **equi-join**) is used to find exact matches in two tables (typically with a foreign key relationship). It specifies that only matching columns are returned.

Try It Out – Performing an INNER JOIN

1. If you've closed the Query Designer window since our last Try It Out, set it up as before by right-clicking on the BankAccount table and opening up the appropriate panes.

2. Add the AccountType table to the window by right-clicking in the Diagram pane and selecting Add table. Apart from showing the two tables, the upper pane will also show the relationship that we set up between the tables, and the inner join, indicated by a small square on the reference key:

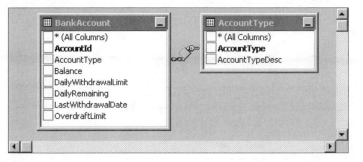

If the join is not visible, drag the column name AccountType from the BankAccount table to AccountType in the AccountType table.

3. Make sure that the wildcard (*) in the Grid pane is unchecked. Add a check to the AccountId and Balance columns in the BankAccount table, as well as one for AccountTypeDesc in the AccountType table:

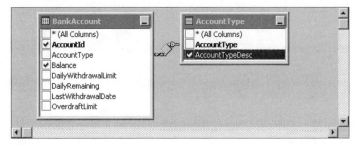

4. Verify and execute the SQL statement that's been generated. The Results pane should show:

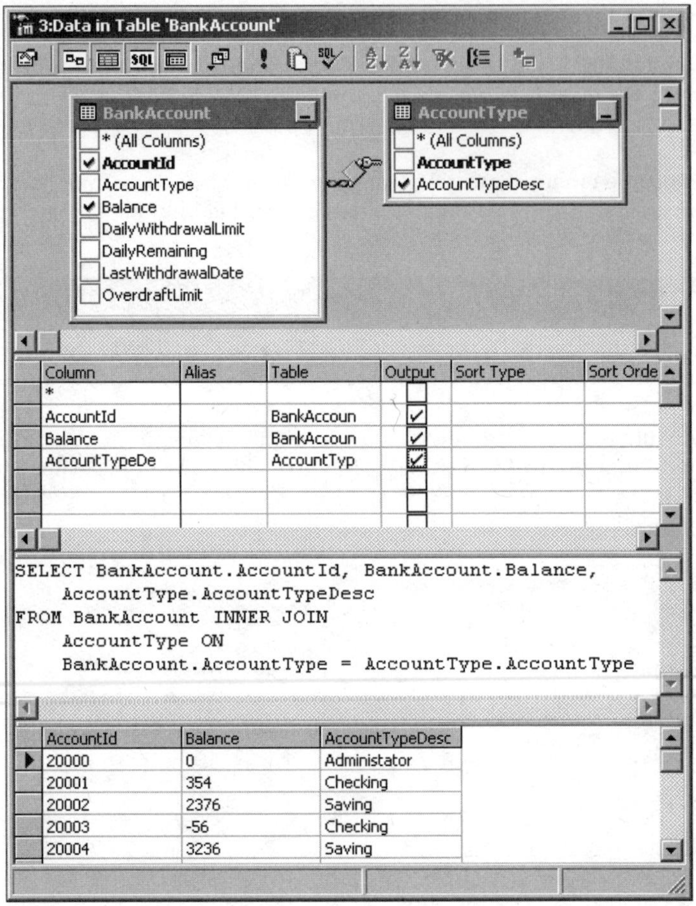

How It Works

We generated the following SQL statement:

```
SELECT BankAccount.AccountId, BankAccount.Balance,
    AccountType.AccountTypeDesc
FROM BankAccount INNER JOIN
    AccountType ON
    BankAccount.AccountType = AccountType.AccountType
```

When a match is found in the value of AccountType on both tables, the columns in the SELECT statement are joined together in the order listed in the SELECT statement.

We only asked for the `AccountID` and `Balance` columns from the `BankAccount` table, with the `AccountTypeDesc` column of the `AccountType` table. The relevant data from the original tables is:

BankAccount Table		
AccountId	AccountType	Balance
20000	0	0
20001	1	354
20002	2	2376
20003	1	-56
20004	2	3236

and:

AccountType Table	
AccountType	AccountTypeDesc
0	Administrator
1	Checking
2	Saving

And so the result of the `INNER JOIN` is:

AccountId	Balance	AccountTypeDesc
20000	0	Administator
20001	354	Checking
20002	2376	Saving
20003	-56	Checking
20004	3236	Saving

When a `SELECT` statement contains multiple tables, ambiguities may occur with column names, as two tables may contain a column with the same name. As you may have noticed in the code above, these ambiguities are resolved by prefacing the column name with the table name and a dot.

Alternatively, to make the statements easier to read, you can create a table name **alias**.

Aliases

Table name aliases are a word or abbreviation that you want to use to refer to a table. You might want to use aliases if you have long table names (like `BankAccount` and `AccountType`): you could instead use a short abbreviation (for instance `BA` and `AT`).

Aliases are defined in the FROM clause, using AS to assign the alias:

```
FROM BankAccount AS BA INNER JOIN
     AccountType AS AT
```

And we can use these aliases in a SELECT statement by prefacing the column names with our aliases (BA and AT). So the following means exactly the same as the SQL statement that we generated in our last Try It Out:

```
SELECT BA.AccountType, AT.AccountType
FROM BankAccount AS BA INNER JOIN
     AccountType AS AT ON
     BA.AccountType = AT.AccountType
```

Using AS is optional and the above code could also be expressed as:

```
SELECT BA.AccountType, AT.AccountType
FROM BankAccount BA INNER JOIN AccountType AT ON
     BA.AccountType = AT.AccountType
```

Column names can also be aliased in the same manner. And remember, you don't have to use aliases, but there are times where they're a welcome shortcut.

> *You may notice that Query Designer will create aliases for you (in the form of Exprn) if you use wildcards (*) as well as selecting specific columns for the query. To prevent this happening, you'll need to uncheck the Output column for the wildcard before checking any other columns, like we did in the Try It Outs.*

That's all the basic SQL we have time for. We're almost ready to put our new-found understanding of SQL to use in the case study, but first we have to get to grips with the concept of **stored procedures**.

Stored Procedures

Executing SQL commands from Query Analyzer is all well and good, but when we come to creating our WROBA application, we're going to want to execute these commands from within our VB code. We have two options on how to do this:

- ❑ We can manipulate the database directly from SQL commands in our Visual Basic components
- ❑ We can just send the database the data that it needs, and get it to execute some SQL command that we have previously stored on the database itself

This second option is the basic idea behind stored procedures.

> A *stored procedure* is a collection of SQL statements that are saved in the database.

These procedures can take **input parameters** (similar in concept to `ByVal` parameters in VB methods) and return **output parameters** (similar in concept to `ByRef` parameters in VB methods). We'll use these parameters to pass data to stored procedures from our VB code, and to return data back to the VB components.

As you'll find by the time we've finished looking at data services, stored procedures play a crucial role in our WROBA application. In fact, all the database querying and manipulation in the case study is done via stored procedures.

Why Use Stored Procedures?

So what advantages do we gain through using stored procedures on our database, instead of just issuing SQL statements from our VB code?

❑   For a start, using SQL statements as stored procedures allows you to make changes to the statements without having to redistribute them to the clients.

❑   They also reduce network traffic, since one call is made to the stored procedure on the server, rather than having the client send the code to the server for execution.

❑   If stored procedures use conditional logic, the server applies the logic and returns the final results to the client. This reduces the processing load on the client.

❑   Since the statements in stored procedures are pre-compiled, they provide faster performance for data processing. SQL statements sent from the client need to be compiled and optimized every time the server executes them. Stored procedures, on the other hand, are parsed and optimized when they are created, and remain in memory after the procedure is executed the first time. This reduces server load when the statements are being used repeatedly.

❑   They also provide increased security. We can grant a user permission to execute a stored procedure, but that user wouldn't necessarily have permission to execute the statements contained in that stored procedure directly.

What's more, stored procedures are extremely easy to create – so let's find out how it's done.

Try it Out – Creating a Stored Procedure from within Visual Basic

1.   Create a New Project in Visual Basic. Select Standard EXE as the project type.

2.   Open a data view window (View | Data View Window).

3. Right-click on Data Link and select Add a Data Link. From the list of OLE DB providers that pops up, select Microsoft OLE DB Provider for SQL Server:

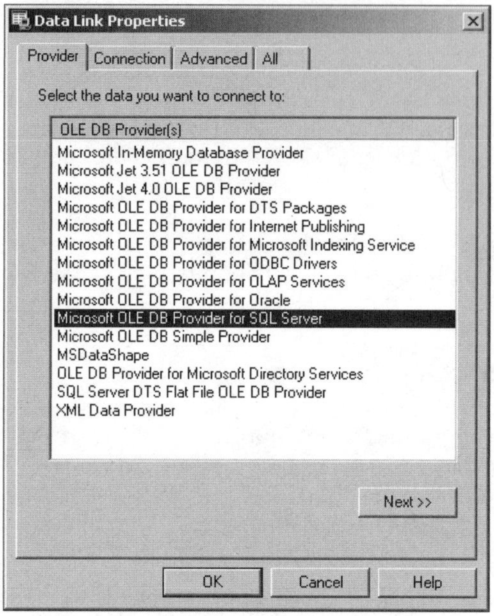

4. Then click on Next. In the Connection properties, type in the name of your server (you can use (local) if the server is your development PC), the user id and password. Select the BigBank database from the combo box:

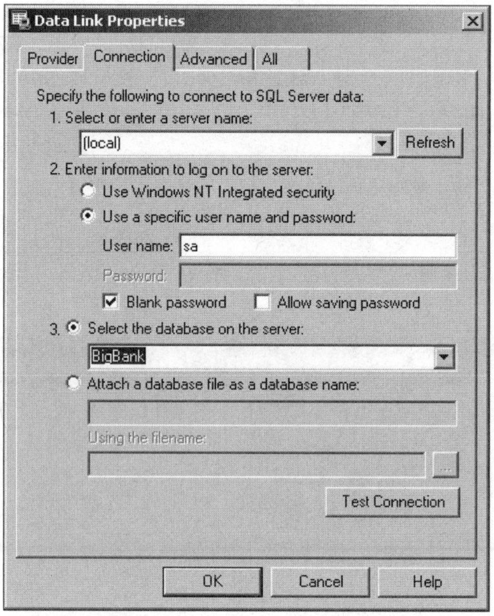

5. Next, click on **Test Connection** to ensure that you have entered the correct information:

And click **OK** twice to return to Visual Basic. Before we move on, rename the data link **WROBA** (right-click on **DataLink1** and select **Rename**).

6. Now expand the data link in the data view window, and right-click on **Stored Procedures**. Select **New Stored Procedure**.

7. Enter the following code in the code window that appears:

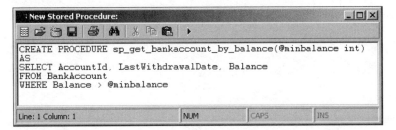

Looks like a SQL statement, doesn't it? The @ signifies an input parameter that will be assigned by the VB code at runtime. In this procedure, our parameter is called **minbalance**.

8. Click on the **Save to Database** icon (the third icon from the left), and close the code window. The new procedure should now appear in the list of the stored procedures:

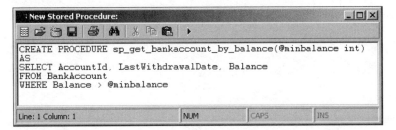

9. We'll be using this data link again in our Try It Outs, so leave VB open.

There's no need to save this project, as the stored procedure has been saved to the database. We'll learn how to use this stored procedure in our project later on.

You can also add stored procedures to your database using the Stored Procedure Wizard in Enterprise Manager (Tools | Wizards...). Alternatively, right-click on Stored Procedures in the database and choose Add New Stored Procedure, which is similar to using Data Link.

In this example, we've saved quite a simple SQL command, but we can use stored procedures to execute much more complicated statements.

Try It Out – A More Complex Stored Procedure

The following Try It Out illustrates how you can use stored procedures to encapsulate fairly complex logic, using IF statements to determine what happens if each condition is True or False.

1. Go back to Visual Basic, right-click on Stored Procedures and select New Stored Procedure again.

2. Enter the following code in the code window:

```
/****** Object:  Stored Procedure dbo.sp_update_BankAccount_Dec ******/
CREATE PROCEDURE sp_update_BankAccount_Dec
  (@AccountId_1            int,
   @TxAmount_2             money,
   @TxType_3               tinyint,
   @TxDescription_4        char(40),
   @CounterpartyRef_5      char(16),
   @ReturnValue            int output
  )

AS

DECLARE @today DATETIME

SELECT @today = GETDATE()

SELECT @ReturnValue = 3         -- Pessimistic default to UnknownError


IF (SELECT DATEDIFF(DAY, LastWithdrawalDate, @today)
    FROM BankAccount
    WHERE ( AccountId = @AccountId_1))
   > 0

BEGIN
-- LastWithdrawalDate is not current, reset the DailyRemaining
-- and the LastWithdrawalDate

   UPDATE BankAccount
   SET DailyRemaining      = DailyWithdrawalLimit,
       LastWithdrawalDate = @today
   WHERE ( AccountId = @AccountId_1)
END
```

```
IF (SELECT Balance + OverdraftLimit
    FROM BankAccount
    WHERE ( AccountId = @AccountId_1))
  < @TxAmount_2

    SELECT @ReturnValue = 2          -- NotEnoughFunds

ELSE

    BEGIN

    IF (SELECT DailyRemaining
        FROM BankAccount
        WHERE ( AccountId = @AccountId_1))
      < @TxAmount_2

        SELECT @ReturnValue = 1          -- DailyLimitExceeded

    ELSE

    BEGIN
        -- Withdraw
        UPDATE BankAccount
        SET Balance = Balance - @TxAmount_2,
            DailyRemaining = DailyRemaining - @TxAmount_2
        WHERE
          ( AccountId = @AccountId_1)

          -- Update AccountHistory
        INSERT INTO AccountHistory
                ( TxId,
                  AccountId,
                  TxDate,
                  TxType,
                  TxDescription,
                  TxAmount,
                  CounterpartyRef)
        VALUES
                ( NEWID(),
                  @AccountId_1,
                  @today,
                  @TxType_3,
                  @TxDescription_4,
                  - @TxAmount_2,
                  @CounterpartyRef_5)

        SELECT @ReturnValue = 0          -- Success
    END
END

RETURN @ReturnValue
```

3. Save it to the database.

We do a lot of work in this stored procedure, so let's take a look at exactly what it does in more detail.

How It Works

The sp_update_BankAccount_Dec procedure is used to determine if a customer can withdraw funds today, and if so, how much. It will then approve or deny the transaction.

This procedure is called from some Visual Basic code in the data layer of our WROBA application that we'll see later. We start by listing the five input parameters that we expect the VB code to supply, and one output parameter, which is what gets returned when the procedure has finished:

```
CREATE PROCEDURE sp_update_BankAccount_Dec
    (@AccountId_1          int,
     @TxAmount_2           money,
     @TxType_3             tinyint,
     @TxDescription_4      char(40),
     @CounterpartyRef_5    char(16),
     @ReturnValue          int output
    )
```

Notice that the output parameter, @ReturnValue, is characterized in the parameter list by the output keyword. The name of the return value is hard-coded in our VB, where we assume the following meanings for the return values:

- ❑   0 – Success – the transaction was successful.

- ❑   1 – DailyLimitExceeded – the customer's daily withdrawal limit has been exceeded.

- ❑   2 – NotEnoughFunds – the customer doesn't have enough funds for the transaction to proceed.

- ❑   3   UnknownError – some unknown error occurred.

The account that we're looking at is identified by the parameter @AccountId_1, which is assigned by the VB code that uses this stored procedure, based on the card number you enter at the start of the application.

The IF statement allows us to determine which statements to run – the general syntax is:

```
IF <condition>
   BEGIN
      <SQL Statements>
   END
ELSE
   BEGIN
      <SQL Statements>
   END
```

We compare the last withdrawal date to today's date (@today) in an IF statement:

```
IF (SELECT DATEDIFF(DAY, LastWithdrawalDate, @today)
   FROM BankAccount
   WHERE ( AccountId = @AccountId_1))
   > 0
```

DATEDIFF is a SQL function that returns the difference between the two dates in a specified unit of time – here we've asked for the difference in DAYs. If they are different, meaning this is the first attempt to withdraw funds today, we reset the daily withdrawal limit to the default:

```
BEGIN
    -- LastWithdrawalDate is not current, reset the DailyRemaining
    -- and the LastWithdrawalDate

    UPDATE BankAccount
    SET DailyRemaining      = DailyWithdrawalLimit,
        LastWithdrawalDate = @today
    WHERE ( AccountId = @AccountId_1)
END
```

Note the use of comments (--) here.

Also note that if LastWithdrawalDate is not current, then this stored procedure will reset the DailyRemaining and the LastWithdrawalDate, even if the withdrawal is refused (on the grounds of DailyLimitExceeded or NotEnoughFunds).

We then check the total available balance (that is, balance plus overdraft) against the amount of money the customer wants to withdraw (TxAmount_2 – again, this value is set by the VB code that calls the procedure), to see how much they have available to withdraw:

```
IF (SELECT Balance + OverdraftLimit
    FROM BankAccount
    WHERE ( AccountId = @AccountId_1))
    < @TxAmount_2
```

If the funds available are less than the transaction amount, we deny the transaction and set the return value equal to 2 (NotEnoughFunds):

```
SELECT @ReturnValue = 2        -- NotEnoughFunds
```

However, if the funds are there, we then check the transaction amount against the DailyRemaining balance (the daily withdrawal limit), to see if the customer has exceeded their daily limit:

```
IF (SELECT DailyRemaining
    FROM BankAccount
    WHERE ( AccountId = @AccountId_1))
    < @TxAmount_2
```

If they have, we deny the transaction and set the appropriate return value:

```
SELECT @ReturnValue = 1        -- DailyLimitExceeded
```

Otherwise, if they have enough funds and don't exceed their daily limit, we approve the transaction, and update the `BankAccount` and `AccountHistory` tables:

```
-- Withdraw
UPDATE BankAccount
SET Balance = Balance - @TxAmount_2,
    DailyRemaining = DailyRemaining - @TxAmount_2
WHERE
  ( AccountId = @AccountId_1)

    -- Update AccountHistory
INSERT INTO AccountHistory
            ( TxId,
              AccountId,
              TxDate,
              TxType,
              TxDescription,
              TxAmount,
              CounterpartyRef)
VALUES
            ( NEWID(),
              @AccountId_1,
              @today,
              @TxType_3,
              @TxDescription_4,
              - @TxAmount_2,
              @CounterpartyRef_5)

SELECT @ReturnValue = 0            -- Success
```

RETURN is used to output data back to the calling application:

```
RETURN @ReturnValue
```

And the stored procedure waits for the next transaction to call it.

As we mentioned earlier, a lot of the data services logic of our case study is contained in stored procedures, so let's take a look at the rest of them.

Adding the Remaining Stored Procedures to WROBA

In total, there are 35 stored procedures that we'll use in the case study. We can divide these into five broad categories:

- ❑ Stored procedures used to delete rows from tables.
- ❑ Stored procedures used to insert rows into tables.
- ❑ Stored procedures used to select rows.
- ❑ Stored procedures used to update tables.
- ❑ Stored procedures used to verify information.

We've already seen an example of the fourth category in our previous Try It Out (the `sp_udate_ BankAccount_Dec` procedure). But let's take a look at examples of the other four before we move on.

> In this chapter, we'll just give you a short description of each type of procedure, and show you one stored procedure from the case study that belongs to this category as an illustration. You'll find the complete list of stored procedures in Appendix A. You'll need to add all 35 of these procedures (following the steps in our last two Try It Outs) in order to implement the WROBA case study.

Type 1 – Procedures for Deleting Rows

The first type of stored procedure is used for deleting rows of account related information from tables. The administrator uses these to delete banks, accounts, WROBA cards and locks on the cards. Users access one to delete payee information.

Let's look at the stored procedure for deleting a lock on a card:

```
CREATE PROCEDURE sp_delete_TxLock
     (@BankId_1 smallint,
      @CardId_2 int)

AS DELETE TxLock

WHERE
     ( BankId = @BankId_1) and
     ( CardId = @CardId_2)
```

The client application passes two parameters to this procedure: one each for the `BankId` and `CardId`. We'll use both of these pieces of information to determine the correct row to delete. So while the other `DELETE` procedures use just one `WHERE` clause, this one uses two conditions: it deletes the row in the `TxLock` table that matches both the specified bank and card IDs.

Type 2 – Procedures for Inserting Rows

Another set of stored procedures are used to insert new rows into tables. As with the `DELETE`s, most of these are used by the administrator to add new banks, accounts and cards. Users just need one for adding payees.

The following `INSERT` example is used by the administrator to add a new account to the database. Except for variables representing the values, it looks like the `INSERT` SQL statements we learned about earlier.

```
Create Procedure sp_insert_BankAccount
     (@AccountId_1 int,
      @AccountType_2 tinyint,
      @Balance_3 money,
      @Limit_4 money,
      @Remaining_5 money,
      @LastDate_6 datetime,
      @Overdraft_7 money,
      @ReturnValue int output)
```

```
AS INSERT INTO BankAccount
    (AccountId,
     AccountType,
     Balance,
     DailyWithdrawalLimit,
     DailyRemaining,
     LastWithdrawalDate,
     OverdraftLimit)

VALUES
    (@AccountId_1,
     @AccountType_2,
     @Balance_3,
     @Limit_4,
     @Remaining_5,
     @LastDate_6,
     @Overdraft_7)

SET @ReturnValue = @@ERROR

RETURN    @ReturnValue
```

The input parameters are all the values we want to populate our new row with. We then simply INSERT a new row into the BankAccount table, specifying the names of the columns and the VALUES that we want inserted into those columns.

The single output value that we RETURN notifies the administrator whether the procedure was successful or not. The return value is determined by the value of @@ERROR.

> **@@ERROR** is one of the *global variables* that T-SQL provides – you can use these variables anywhere in your SQL commands. **@@ERROR** returns the error number of the last SQL statement executed, or 0 if no error occurred.

So if the row is added successfully, the administrator receives the result 0, indicating True or success. RETURN is always expressed as an integer.

Type 3 – Procedures for Selecting Rows

The select procedures used vary from simple SELECT statements (selecting columns from just one table), to those using JOINs to select data from different tables. Again, these are similar to the SELECT statements we saw earlier in the chapter – the only difference is that parameters are used to pass the values needed by the WHERE statement from the application to the procedure.

We'll just look at the most complicated of the select procedures: the one used to return account history for display in the Account History form. This form initially displays the five most recent transactions, displaying columns from the AccountHistory and TxType tables, and it's ordered by descending dates:

```
CREATE PROCEDURE sp_select_AccountHistory_By_AccountId (
    @AccountId_1 int,
    @MaxTxDate_2 datetime)

AS SELECT TOP 5
    AccountHistory.TxDate,
    TxType.TxTypeDesc,
    AccountHistory.TxDescription,
    AccountHistory.TxAmount,
    AccountHistory.CounterpartyRef

FROM AccountHistory INNER JOIN
    TxType ON AccountHistory.TxType = TxType.TxType

WHERE (AccountHistory.AccountId = @AccountId_1) AND
    (TxDate <=

        (SELECT MAX(TxDate)
        FROM AccountHistory
        WHERE (AccountHistory.AccountId = @AccountId_1) AND
            (TxDate < @MaxTxDate_2)))

ORDER BY AccountHistory.TxDate DESC
```

Note that we've got a SELECT statement nested inside a WHERE clause. In this SELECT, we extract the date of the most recent transaction (before a specified date, MaxTxDate) that's listed in the AccountHistory table for this account number. MAX is a SQL function that returns the row that has the maximum value for the specified column (in this case TxDate).

The first WHERE clause then matches against rows with the right AccountID and dates earlier than this MAX date. These are ordered by DESCending date, and the first five in the list are selected with the TOP function.

Type 5 – Procedures for Verifying Rows

The final type of stored procedures is used to verify accounts based on the CardId.

This particular one is used to verify that the account exists before transferring funds to it:

```
CREATE PROCEDURE sp_verify_BankAccount_By_CardId (
    @CardId_1 int,
    @ReturnValue int output)

AS SELECT @ReturnValue  = COUNT(BankAccount.AccountId)

FROM BankAccount

WHERE (BankAccount.AccountId = @CardId_1)

RETURN @ReturnValue
```

COUNT returns the number of rows that meet the qualifications of the query.

The @ReturnValue is passed back to the application, and if it's True (that is, more than one), the application allows the transfer to continue.

Summary

In this chapter we learned about using SQL to work with databases using two of SQL's sub-languages:

❑ Data Definition Language (DDL) to create, alter, or delete database objects such as tables or fields

❑ Data Manipulation Language (DML) to add, retrieve and manipulate the data in the database

We also learned:

❑ How to use SQL Server's Query Analyzer to create and alter tables, as well as add or change data within the tables

❑ How we can save SQL commands as scripts, which anyone can use to recreate our database objects

❑ How to use Query Designer to help us write and test SQL code

❑ How to create stored procedures, which we can use to save our SQL code actually on the database

And what's more, we've finished off the `BigBank` database we started building in Chapter 9, by adding some constraints and stored procedures. These stored procedures contain all of the code we need to query and manipulate the database in our case study.

> **Before you move on, make sure you've added all the stored procedures listed in Appendix A.**

So now we've got a fully functioning database, it's time to move on to creating the code that's going to use this database, in the Data Services Tier.

11

Data Access and ADO

In the previous chapter we finished looking at the database itself: now it's time to turn our attention to the "bottom" tier of our architecture – the data tier.

The data tier is concerned with communicating between the data store and the components in the business layer. So, within this chapter we need to build an understanding of how we can programmatically query and manipulate the data in the database – in our WROBA application, for example, we not only want to be able to view our account details, we also want to be able to pay bills, transfer money between accounts and so on.

Before we can get on to the case study itself, we need to learn a bit about the data access technology we use to move data from our data store into our VB application. You'll be familiar with the general coding approach, but the technology itself might be unfamiliar. So in this chapter we'll show you some simple examples to get you going before we embark on the case study coding.

More specifically, we're going to cover:

❑   An introduction to data access and **ActiveX Data Objects** (**ADO**)

❑   The major components of the ADO Object Model

❑   How to use ADO with Visual Basic to:

  ❑   Connect to a data source and retrieve data from it

  ❑   Use stored procedures on our database

  ❑   Implement error handling

So, let's look at what approaches we need to take to build an application that will allow us to get at the data inside our lovingly created database.

Data Access

As we mentioned back in Chapter 1, the part of the Windows DNA 2000 architecture that deals with information access is termed **Universal Data Access** (**UDA**). UDA is designed to provide access to information across the enterprise.

Like its predecessor, **Open Database Connectivity** (**ODBC**), Universal Data Access specifies the interfaces used to programmatically access a variety of data sources, from both the **provider**'s and the **consumer**'s perspective.

> **In this case, what Microsoft calls the provider is the application that provides data. The consumer is the application that connects to the provider, issues a command, and gets the data it needs. For example, the user tier in the case study is a data consumer.**

ODBC is extended by something called **OLE DB**. OLE DB and ODBC simplify data access across multiple platforms, and are intended as replacement for the slower and less capable **Data Access Objects** (**DAO**).

OLE DB provides COM-based applications with access data stored in various information sources. Note that we use the phrase "information sources" here – this is one of the main reasons we need OLE DB as opposed to ODBC. ODBC was created to access only **relational** databases, like Microsoft's Access and SQL Server. OLE DB, on the other hand, provides a conceptual model that can be used to access both relational and **non-relational** data sources – which includes directory services and messaging services like Microsoft Exchange Server.

So OLE DB is the underlying technology that provides us with access to our data. However, some languages, like Visual Basic and scripting languages, can't access OLE DB directly. That's why we need some sort of interface that sits between applications written in these languages and OLE DB.

Microsoft **ActiveX Data Objects** (**ADO**) is the COM-based **application-programming interface** (**API**) that's used to program OLE DB. Using this API you can access (or **consume** in UDA term) data in a data store though a vendor-specific OLE DB driver (the **provider**). Microsoft provides OLE DB providers for ODBC, SQL and most other data source types, allowing us to use ADO to programmatically access data stored in these sources.

What's more, because ADO is a COM component, it can be used from any COM-compliant language, including C++, Delphi or Java.

The following figure shows how all these technologies fit together:

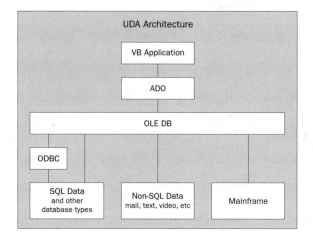

ADO provides the means for you to:

1. Connect to a data source.

2. Specify a command to gain access to the data source.

3. Execute the command.

4. If the command returns rows from a table, store these rows in a **cache** that you can easily examine, manipulate, or change.

5. If appropriate, update the data source with changes from the cache of rows.

6. Provide a general means to detect errors.

Typically, we'd employ all these steps in the programming model. However, ADO is flexible enough that we can do useful work by executing just part of this model.

The ADO Object Model

ADO 2.1 contains four collections and seven objects. We'll look at the most important of these in detail in this chapter – we'll concentrate on the areas of the topic we need to understand before we start to use it. Additionally, ADO 2.5 adds two new objects – Record and Stream – which needn't concern us here, as we'd only need them when working with a relational database.

> *Remember, either version of ADO will work with the case study; you only need to set the project references to the ADO version you have installed.*
>
> *You'll find a reference to the ADO objects and collections (and their associated methods, properties and events) in Appendix C.*

The following diagram illustrates the ADO object model – which should give you some idea of how the ADO objects are related:

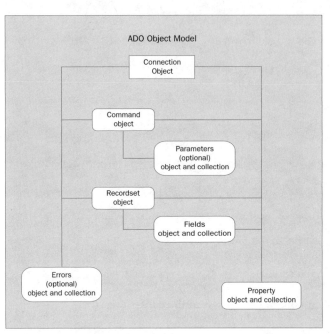

For our purposes, the most important objects that the ADO object model contains are the `Connection`, `Recordset`, and `Command` objects:

- ❑ The `Connection` object establishes connections with the database server.
- ❑ The `Command` object issues commands, such as queries and updates, to the database.
- ❑ The `Recordset` object allows you to view and work with the data returned.
- ❑ The `Field` object contains details about a single field (or column) in a recordset.

The properties of each of these objects are available through their `Properties` collections. A `Properties` collection contains one or more `Property` objects. In addition to returning the value and type for a property, the `Property` object provides attributes of a property, including whether or not the property is supported or required for this object, or can be read or written.

The Connection Object

The `Connection` object provides access to a database – that is, it provides a link or **active connection** between the application (consumer) and the data (provider).

To establish an active connection, we have to provide the information that's needed to connect to the database – the connection string – and invoke the `Open` method of the `Connection` object. The exact format of the connection string depends on the database provider. In this book we're using SQL Server as our database, so the following code opens a connection to the `BigBank` database using SQL.

This is a very basic way of connecting to the database. First we set the connection:

```
Dim cnnConnection As ADODB.Connection
Set cnnConnection = New Connection
```

then we provide the information needed to connect to the database:

```
cnnConnection.ConnectionString = "Provider=SQLOLEDB;" _
 & "Data Source=(local);Initial Catalog=BigBank;User Id=sa;Password=;" _
 & "Connect Timeout=3"
```

Here we're connecting to our SQL Server database called BigBank using the sa user ID and password.

And finally, we open the database:

```
cnnConnection.Open
```

Errors Collection

The Errors collection and Error object allow you to get information about an error when one occurs. The Errors collection doesn't exist on its own, and depends on the Connection object. For this reason, errors are always retrieved from the Connection object. It also stores warnings that don't stop code execution.

The Command Object

The Command object is used to issue commands (such as queries and stored procedures) to the database. The command language we need to use, and the features available, depend on the database provider. Again, the examples shown below will be those used with SQL.

The Command object can either open a new connection or use an existing one, depending on what you specify in the ActiveConnection property. If the ActiveConnection property references an existing Connection object, the Command object uses that connection. On the other hand, if the ActiveConnection property specifies a connection string, a new connection is established for the Command object.

> More than one Command object can use the connection from the same Connection object.

In the WROBA case study, we'll set ActiveConnection equal to a string equivalent to:

```
GetBank = "Provider=SQLOLEDB;" _
        & "Data Source=(local);" _
        & "Initial Catalog=BigBank;" _
        & "UID=sa;PWD=;" _
        & "Connect Timeout=3"
```

to provide the actual connection information. The connection is opened as needed:

```
Dim cmd As ADODB.Command

cmd.ActiveConnection = strDSN
```

When the procedure has finished accessing the database, the connection needs to be closed:

```
Clean_Up:
  Set cmd.ActiveConnection = Nothing
  Set cmd = Nothing
```

The Nothing keyword disassociates an object variable from the object, to release the memory and system resources that the object was using.

So here, we only keep the connection open as long as we need it – that is, while we perform whatever work we need to do. It's then closed immediately. This is in contrast to the Connection object, which gives us a permanent connection to the database.

We'll see in our Try It Outs later in the chapter how we can exeute commands using the Execute method of the Command object.

We'll see later how the WROBA case study uses the Command object to set the connection to the BigBank database.

The Parameters Collection

The Parameters collection consists of Parameter objects, which are used to provide parameter information and data for the Command object. The Parameters collection and Parameter object are unique to the Command object, and they're used to pass parameters into and out of stored queries and procedures.

We can add parameters to a collection manually using the CreateParameter and Append methods. First, we create a parameter. The CreateParameter method has the following syntax:

```
Set objParam = Cmd.CreateParameter (name, type, direction, size, value)
```

The name and value are obviously the name and value that we want the parameter we're creating to have. The type is the data type of the parameter, which can be any one of the ADO constants for specifying data types – we'll see these in the next section. The direction states whether the parameter is an input or output parameter, or both.

Then we add this to the collection:

```
cmd.Parameters.Append objParam
```

The case study uses parameters when querying the database using stored procedures. The following snippet of code is used when verifying the login information.

```
With cmd
  .Parameters.Append .CreateParameter(, adInteger, _
    adParamReturnValue)
  .Parameters.Append .CreateParameter("@CardId_1", _
    adInteger, adParamInput, 4, CardId)
  .Parameters.Append .CreateParameter("@Password_2", _
    adChar, adParamInput, 10, Password)
  .Parameters.Append .CreateParameter("@InvalidPasswordCnt_3", _
    adInteger, adParamOutput, 4)
End With
```

Data Types

When working with databases, you need to define the types of data each column uses. This is true of all databases and data access methods, including ADO.

In a previous chapter, we learned about the data types SQL uses. When we're using ADO to access data from our SQL databases, we need to use the constants that ADO uses to represent these data types.

For example, in our case study application we'll use the ADO `adInteger` data type that corresponds to SQL's `int` data type when accessing data using stored procedures:

```
Set GetAllPayees = m_objDBHelper.RunSPReturnRS( _
  strDSN, "sp_select_All_Payees", _
  Array("@CardId_1", adInteger, adSizeInteger, CardId))
```

The table below shows how the ADO data types correspond to the SQL Server data types:

SQL Server data type	ADO data type
binary	adBinary
bit	adBoolean
char	adChar
datetime	adDBTimeStamp
decimal	adDecimal
float	adDouble
image	adBinary
int	adInteger
money	adCurrency
nchar	adWChar
ntext	adWChar
numeric	adNumeric
nvarchar	adVarWChar
real	adSingle
smalldatetime	adDBTimeStamp
smallint	adSmallInt
smallmoney	adCurrency
sysname	adWChar
text	adChar
timestamp	adBinary
tinyint	adUnsignedTinyInt
uniqueidentifier	adGUID
varbinary	adBinary
varchar	adChar

The Recordset Object

The Recordset object allows you to add, update, delete, and scroll through records in the result set. The Recordset object has several methods that let us do this: we'll be using some of the most useful of these – the MoveNext and EOF (End Of File) properties – in our Try It Outs later in the chapter.

You can retrieve and update each record using the Fields collection and the Field object.

The Fields Collection

The Fields collection and Field object provide access to columns in the current record. We can use the Field object to compose a new record or change existing data, and then use the AddNew, Update, or UpdateBatch methods of the Recordset object to apply the new or changed data.

The Fields collection is the default collection of the Recordset object, so it isn't necessary to specify it. That is, we can access the AccountID field of a recordset called rstBankAccount using either:

```
rstBankAccount("AccountId")
```

or:

```
rstBankAccount.Fields("AccountId")
```

However, our BigBank case study doesn't use the Fields collection or Field objects to work with recordsets – it uses stored procedures instead.

Cursors

When you create a Recordset object, a **cursor** is automatically opened.

> Cursor is short for "*cur*rent *set of* records". A cursor is a database object used to manipulate data by rows instead of by sets. It indicates the current position in the result set.

As we've seen, the Recordset object represents the records in a table, or the records that result from running a query. If we're going to use the data we have in a recordset, we're going to need a way to mark our place in it, as well as control how we move through the records. Controlling access to the data we're working with is also crucial – we don't want to have two people trying to change the same data at the same time.

We can do all of this using three properties:

- ❑ CursorType
- ❑ CursorLocation
- ❑ LockType

Let's look at these topics in order.

Cursor Type

The **cursor type** specifies how you move through the recordset, whether you can update records, and whether you can view changes made on the database by any other users. There are four possible values:

❑ **Forward-only** – A forward-only cursor (adOpenForwardOnly) is the default cursor type. It creates a snapshot-type Recordset object – that is, a copy of a set of records as it exists at the time the snapshot is created – which isn't updateable. For the same reason, you won't be able to see changes made by others until another snapshot is taken. As its name gives away, the limitation is that you can only scroll forward through this type of recordset, but it is very efficient if you just need to traverse the records once.

❑ **Static** – The static cursor (adOpenStatic) is the same as a forward-only cursor, except you can move forward and backward through the records. As with forward-only, static cursors are snapshot-type Recordset objects, and you won't be able to see changes made by others after you created the recordset.

❑ **KeySet** – A keyset cursor (adOpenKeyset) initially just returns keys, and only gets the actual data when it's required. So, records added later by other users won't be visible, as you don't have the key for that record. And, if another user deletes a record, it will no longer be accessible to you – you only have the key pointing to the record, and both the record and key have now gone. However, because keyset brings in chunks of the recordset as you need them, changes made by other users to the *data* in an existing record *are* updated in your records as you move through the recordset.

❑ **Dynamic** – Unlike a static recordset, a dynamic recordset (adOpenDynamic) is regularly updated, so you can see all additions, updates and deletions made by other users. However, because it's always updating, it consumes the most resources.

Cursor Location

The **cursor location** defines where the recordset is located when it's created. There are two alternatives:

❑ A **client-side cursor** (adUseClient) is often used with distributed applications, because it can be disconnected from the database (a so-called **disconnected recordset**) to offload processing from the database server to the client. The WROBA case study uses client-side cursors.

They typically offer better performance for scrolling through or locating records. However, when we're using client-side cursors, all records that satisfy the query are returned when the recordset is opened. As a result, no matter what CursorType we selected, we'll really only have a static snapshot of what the data was when we opened the recordset. This means that we won't be able to see the changes made by other users while we're working with the data. The other drawback is the impact on network traffic, because all of the rows requested by the query have to be transferred to the client.

❑ A **server-side cursor** (adUseServer) supports keyset and dynamic cursor types, which expose the changes made by other users. However, they must maintain a connection to the database, which may impact database server performance. This is the default value of cursor location.

The table below summarizes the visibility on each cursor type:

Cursor Type	Client-Side / Server Side Use	Rowset Changes visible	Data changes visible
Forward-only	Client-side	No	No
Static	Client-side	No	No
Static	Server-side	No	No
Dynamic	Server-side	Yes	Yes
Keyset	Server-side	Only deletes updated rows	Yes

Lock Type

The lock type specifies what type of locks should be placed on records during editing.

> Locking is a database mechanism used to prevent data corruption in the event that more than one user attempts to update the same data simultaneously.

The four possible values are:

- ❑ **Read-only locking** (adLockReadOnly) – This is the default, and doesn't allow editing. You should stick to this default whenever possible because updateable recordsets require more resources. Our case study uses read-only locking.

- ❑ **Pessimistic locking** (adLockPessimistic) – Here the record locks at the data source while it is being edited. Pessimistic locking is the only way to be sure that your application reads the most current data, because one user can't change a record after another has begun editing it. However, this type of locking requires a permanent connection, so it can't be used for client-side recordsets. And since the lock is maintained until you've finished working with the recordset, you should use this lock type very sparingly.

- ❑ **Optimistic locking** (adLockOptimistic) – In this type of locking the record locks only when it is physically updated by calling the Update method. Optimistic locking can be used for both server and client-side recordsets. As the record is only locked when it's actually being updated, this is generally the most efficient lock type when it comes to resource management. However, the disadvantage is that you have no way of knowing whether other users have altered records while you've been editing them yourself.

- ❑ **Batch-optimistic locking** (adLockBatchOptimistic) – This lock type allows you to send multiple updates back to the database in a single batch. It's essentially the same as optimistic locking, except that all modified records are updated in one action – when the UpdateBatch method is called – instead of one at a time. This type of lock is most useful for client-side recordsets, as it lets you change multiple records on the client before committing them to the data store on the server in one go.

We can specify the cursor and lock types when we open a recordset with the Open method of the Recordset object, which has the following syntax:

```
Recordset.Open(Source, ActiveConnection, CursorType, LockType, Options)
```

where the *Options* tell us what our *Source* is: we'll generally use a Command object, like in the following example. As you can see from this code taken from the case study, we'll use the forward-only cursor type to move forward through a static (read-only) copy of the recordset.

```
rst.Open cmd, , adOpenForwardOnly, adLockReadOnly
```

Events

The concept of events was missing from RDO and DAO. However, ADO includes events for the Connection and Recordset objects in the programming model.

> **Events are notifications that certain operations are about to occur, or have already occurred.**

You can use events, in general, to efficiently orchestrate an application consisting of several asynchronous tasks (that is, one where data is transmitted intermittently instead of in a steady stream). There are two families of events: **connection** events and **recordset** events.

Connection events are issued when:

- ❑ Transactions on a connection begin, are committed, or rolled back.
- ❑ Commands execute.
- ❑ A connection is started or ended.

Recordset events are issued to report the progress of data retrieval; when you navigate through the rows and when any change is made within the entire recordset.

Events are processed by event handler routines, which are called before certain operations start or after they finish. Some events are paired, and these generally have matching names: in which case, the events called before an operation starts have names of the form Will<*event_name*> (Will events), and the events called after an operation concludes have names of the form <*event_name*>Complete (Complete events).

The remaining, unpaired events occur only after an operation concludes, and their names are not formed in any particular pattern; for example, Disconnect.

Now we have some of the background under our belts, let's have a go at using this technology.

Using ADO in Visual Basic

In this section we're going to build up a simple example that demonstrates a couple of the features of ADO we've already mentioned. Therefore, we're going to see:

❑ How to connect to data source and use a recordset.

❑ How to make use of Stored Procedures.

❑ How to handle errors.

Try It Out – Using ADO to Retrieve Data

So let's get started.

1. Create a new **Standard EXE** project in Visual Basic, and name it **RetrieveData**.

2. Set a reference to the ActiveX Data Objects Library by selecting **Project | References....** Then, depending on your system, select either **Microsoft ActiveX Data Objects 2.1 Library** or **Microsoft ActiveX Data Objects 2.5 Library**. Here we show the latter version, but as we discussed before, ADO 2.1 will do just fine:

3. Add a list box and two command buttons to the default form, as detailed below:

Object	Property	Value
Form	Name	frmMain
	BorderStyle	1 – Fixed Single
	Caption	Using ADO
	StartupPosition	1 – Center Owner
List Box	Name	lstAccount
Command Button	Name	cmdGetBalances
	Caption	&Get Balances
Command Button	Name	cmdExit
	Caption	E&xit

4. Now we need to add some code to the form. We'll start with the easy part – the **Exit** button:

```
Option Explicit

Private Sub cmdExit_Click()
   Unload Me
End Sub
```

5. And now for the **Get Balances** button. First we need to declare our variable types:

```
Private Sub cmdGetBalances_Click()

   Dim cnnConnection  As ADODB.Connection
   Dim rstBankAccount  As ADODB.Recordset
   Dim strQry       As String
   Dim lngRecCount   As Long
```

6. Then we'll set up the query using a SQL statement:

```
strQry = "SELECT * FROM BankAccount ORDER BY Balance"
```

7. Next, we'll set up the connection string to the SQL server, and open the connection. If your server isn't local, you'll need to replace (local) with your server name:

```
Set cnnConnection = New Connection

' In the following, you may need to change "(local)" to the
' name of your SQL Server
cnnConnection.ConnectionString = "Provider=sqloledb;" & _
                    "Data Source=(local);Initial Catalog=BigBank;" & _
                    "User Id=sa;Password=; "

cnnConnection.Open
```

397

8. In a moment, we'll create a function called `GetRecordSet` to get the account information we need from the database in the form of a recordset. For now, just add the code that loops through this recordset and fills the list box with the data we retrieved:

```
Set rstBankAccount = GetRecordSet(cnnConnection, strQry)

lngRecCount = rstBankAccount.RecordCount

If lngRecCount > 0 Then
  With lstAccount
    .Clear

    Do Until rstBankAccount.EOF
      .AddItem rstBankAccount!AccountId & " -- " & _
               rstBankAccount!LastWithdrawalDate & " $ " & _
               rstBankAccount!Balance
      rstBankAccount.MoveNext
    Loop

    rstBankAccount.Close
  End With
End If

cnnConnection.Close

Cleanup:
  ' Cleanup
  Set rstBankAccount = Nothing
  Set cnnConnection = Nothing

End Sub
```

When we've looped through all of the records, we close the ADO connection and set the recordset and connection variables to `Nothing`

9. And now, add the `GetRecordSet` function, which creates an empty recordset and populates it with the data that we want:

```
Private Function GetRecordSet(cnnConnection As ADODB.Connection, _
                             strQry As String) As ADODB.Recordset

  Dim rstRecords As ADODB.Recordset

  Set rstRecords = New ADODB.Recordset

  With rstRecords
    .CursorType = adOpenStatic
    .LockType = adLockReadOnly
    .CursorLocation = adUseClient
    .Source = strQry
    Set .ActiveConnection = cnnConnection

    .Open
  End With

  Set GetRecordSet = rstRecords

End Function
```

10. Save and run the project. Click on the **Get Balances** button, and after a short while, the list box should display the account numbers of the accounts in your database, along with the last withdrawal date and current balance for these accounts:

```
Using ADO                                    X

20000 -- 5/23/2000 12:51:27 PM $ 0
20003 -- 5/23/2000 12:51:27 PM $ 56
20001 -- 5/23/2000 12:51:27 PM $ 254
20002 -- 5/23/2000 12:51:27 PM $ 2376
20004 -- 5/23/2000 12:51:27 PM $ 3236




     Get Balances                    Exit
```

How It Works

Before we can perform any ADO operations, we have to establish a connection to our data source. The code to do this is contained in the `Click` event of our **Get Balances** button.

We do this by setting the connection string, `cnnConnection`, for a new `Connection` object:

```
Private Sub cmdGetBalances_Click()

   Dim cnnConnection  As ADODB.Connection

   Set cnnConnection = New Connection

   cnnConnection.ConnectionString = "Provider=sqloledb;" & _
                          "Data Source=(local);Initial Catalog=BigBank;" & _
                          "User Id=sa;Password=; "
```

and then issuing a call to the `Open` method:

```
   cnnConnection.Open
```

We also need a SQL query, to specify exactly which records we want returned from the database:

```
   strQry = "SELECT * FROM BankAccount ORDER BY Balance"
```

We're selecting all the records from the `BankAccount` table, and ordering them by the `Balance` column. As we don't specify otherwise, the accounts will be sorted in ascending order, with the lowest balance first. (Remember, if we wanted them in descending order, we'd have to specify the `DESC` keyword.)

We can now retrieve the data into a recordset, which we do using the `GetRecordSet` function. This takes our connection string and SQL query as parameters:

```
   Set rstBankAccount = GetRecordSet(cnnConnection, strQry)
```

Within the `GetRecordSet` function, we create the temporary recordset `rstRecords` to store the data:

```
Dim rstRecords As ADODB.Recordset

Set rstRecords = New ADODB.Recordset
```

We then use a `With` block to set the relevant properties for `rstRecords`:

```
With rstRecords
   .CursorType = adOpenStatic
   .LockType = adLockReadOnly
   .CursorLocation = adUseClient
   .Source = strQry
```

As we saw earlier, the constant `CursorType` determines the type of cursor that the provider should use when it opens the `Recordset` object – in this case we're using `adOpenStatic` to provide a static copy of our set of records, which we can scroll through in any direction.

The `LockType` property identifies the type of locks placed on records during editing. As we're not going to be making any changes here, we've used the default of read-only: `adLockReadOnly`.

We set the `CursorLocation` property to `adUseClient`, to indicate that we want the location of the cursor engine to be client-side.

Then we identify the record `Source` – which is the `strQry` that we set earlier.

Finally, the connection is set to use our connection string:

```
    Set .ActiveConnection = cnnConnection

   .Open
End With
```

And the resulting recordset is returned to the `cmdGetBalances_Click()` routine:

```
Set GetRecordSet = rstRecords
```

Back in the `cmdGetBalances_Click()` routine, we traverse this recordset using the `MoveNext` and EOF (end of file) methods:

```
Set rstBankAccount = GetRecordSet(cnnConnection, strQry)

...
   With lstAccount
     .Clear

     Do Until rstBankAccount.EOF
       .AddItem rstBankAccount!AccountId & " -- " & _
               rstBankAccount!LastWithdrawalDate & " $ " & _
               rstBankAccount!Balance
     rstBankAccount.MoveNext
   Loop
```

The EOF property becomes True when the end of the recordset is reached, therefore we can use it like this to loop through a recordset. The MoveNext method moves the current record position forward by one record at the end of each loop. So the loop executes until the current record position is after the last record (EOF) in the recordset object. The AddItem method then fills the list box with the data from the specified columns in the BackAccount table: AccountId, LastWithdrawalDate and Balance.

Of course, when we're done with a Connection, we have to call the Close method:

```
cnnConnection.Close
```

And to finish off, we clean up the mess we made:

```
Cleanup:
   ' Cleanup
   Set rstBankAccount = Nothing
   Set cnnConnection = Nothing
```

This Try It Out illustrates a simple way of retrieving data from a database using SQL queries. However, we can do pretty much the same thing by making use of stored procedures on the database.

Try It Out – Using ADO to call a Stored Procedure

This time, we'll get account numbers and balances from our banking database only if the balance is above $100. To do this, we'll make use of the stored procedure sp_get_bankaccount_by_balance that we created in the last chapter.

1. Return to the RetrieveData project we created above. To demonstrate how to use stored procedures, we're going to amend our project to use the sp_get_bankaccount_by_balance procedure that we created in the last chapter.

2. Modify the code as follows. The major change is the addition of an Enum statement, which sets the size of a variable szInteger to 4:

```
Option Explicit

Public Enum ESizeOfADOType
   szInteger = 4
End Enum


Private Sub cmdExit_Click()
   Unload Me
End Sub


Private Sub cmdGetBalances_Click()

Dim cnnConnection  As ADODB.Connection
Dim rstBankAccount  As ADODB.Recordset
Dim cmdStoredProc  As ADODB.Command
Dim lngRecCount    As Long
```

```
' one line of code deleted here

    Set cnnConnection = New Connection

    ' In the following, you may need to change "(local)" to the
    ' name of your SQL Server
    cnnConnection.ConnectionString = "Provider=sqloledb;" _
     & "Data Source=(local);Initial Catalog=BigBank;User Id=sa;Password=; "

    cnnConnection.Open

' another line of code deleted here

    lngRecCount = rstBankAccount.RecordCount

    If lngRecCount > 0 Then
      With lstAccount
        .Clear

        Do Until rstBankAccount.EOF
          .AddItem rstBankAccount!AccountId & " -- " & _
                   rstBankAccount!LastWithdrawalDate & " $ " & _
                   rstBankAccount!Balance
          rstBankAccount.MoveNext
        Loop

        rstBankAccount.Close
      End With
    End If

    cnnConnection.Close

Cleanup:
    ' Cleanup
    Set rstBankAccount = Nothing
    Set cnnConnection = Nothing

End Sub
```

Note that we've deleted two lines:

```
strQry = "SELECT * FROM BankAccount ORDER BY Balance"
```

and:

```
Set rstBankAccount = GetRecordSet(cnnConnection, strQry)
```

from our original code. You can also delete the `GetRecordSet` function – we won't be needing this any more.

3. Set the ADO `Command` and `Recordset` objects and specify a client-side cursor the following code after the command to open the connection:

```
cnnConnection.Open
```

```
' Set up ADO Objects object
Set cmdStoredProc = New ADODB.Command
Set rstBankAccount = New ADODB.Recordset
rstBankAccount.CursorLocation = adUseClient
```

4. We'll call the stored procedure using the `cmdStoredProc` object. Add this after the code in Step 3:

```
'Run the procedure
With cmdStoredProc
  .ActiveConnection = cnnConnection
  .CommandText = "sp_get_bankaccount_by_balance"
  .CommandType = adCmdStoredProc
```

5. Next we need to set the parameters used by the stored procedure query – here we set the `minbalance` variable to equal `100`. Complete the `With` block with the following code:

```
.Parameters.Append .CreateParameter ("@minbalance", _
                    adInteger, adParamInput, szInteger, 100)
                    ' 100 = Value of parameter

  rstBankAccount.Open cmdStoredProc, , adOpenForwardOnly, adLockReadOnly
End With

Set cmdStoredProc.ActiveConnection = Nothing
Set cmdStoredProc = Nothing
Set rstBankAccount.ActiveConnection = Nothing
```

The recordsets are then ready to be retrieved.

6. Run the form and click on the **Get Balances** button. The form should display the account numbers, last transaction date and balances for accounts that meet our constraints – namely that the balance is greater than $100:

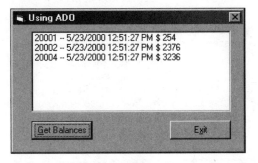

How It Works

As a reminder, the stored procedure we're using here, sp_get_bankaccount_by_balance, looks like this:

```
CREATE PROCEDURE sp_get_bankaccount_by_balance(@minbalance int)
AS
SELECT AccountId, LastWithdrawalDate, Balance
FROM BankAccount
Where Balance > @minbalance
```

We've already seen a lot of the code we use here, so we won't discuss it again. In fact, there's only one principal difference between the method we've used here and our earlier method of calling SQL statements: here, you may need to pass parameters. We've already seen how we can add parameters to a collection using the CreateParameter and Append methods of the Parameters collection – use the CreateParameter method to create a parameter, then Append the string to the parameter object.

The code to do this is quite straightforward. We begin by setting up the ADO objects:

```
Set cmdStoredProc = New ADODB.Command
Set rstBankAccount = New ADODB.Recordset
rstBankAccount.CursorLocation = adUseClient
```

We open the connection to SQL server, then the stored procedure is accessed:

```
With cmdStoredProc
    .ActiveConnection = cnnConnection
    .CommandText = "sp_get_bankaccount_by_balance"
    .CommandType = adCmdStoredProc
```

We have to tell the server that we're using a stored procedure, as well as which one. This is done using the CommandText and CommandType properties. CommandText contains the text of a command that you want to issue to the server – in this case, it's the name of the stored procedure we want to use. The CommandType signifies which type of command the CommandText property is referring to – here the value is adCmdStoredProc, so the server now knows to use a stored procedure called sp_get_bankaccount_by_balance.

We then create a parameter called @minbalance, and append it to the stored procedure:

```
.Parameters.Append .CreateParameter ("@minbalance", _
                    adInteger, adParamInput, szInteger, 100)
                 ' 100 = Value of parameter
```

We've specified that the parameter we're creating is an Integer type (adInteger), and that it's an input parameter to the command (adParamInput). We've also constrained the maximum length that the parameter can have with szInteger, which we defined earlier:

```
Public Enum ESizeOfADOType
   szInteger = 4
End Enum
```

So our parameter can't be longer than 4 characters. Finally, we set the value of the parameter to 100.

To finish off the With Block, we open the connection and retrieve the data into our `rstBankAccount` recordset:

```
    rstBankAccount.Open cmdStoredProc, , adOpenForwardOnly, adLockReadOnly
End With
```

Once the connection is opened and the recordset returned, the results of the SQL query (`AccountId` and `Balance` columns from accounts with balances greater than $100) are populated into the list box as before:

```
If lngRecCount > 0 Then
    With lstAccount
      .Clear

    Do Until rstBankAccount.EOF
      .AddItem rstBankAccount!AccountId & " -- " & _
                rstBankAccount!LastWithdrawalDate & " $ " & _
                rstBankAccount!Balance
      rstBankAccount.MoveNext
    Loop

    rstBankAccount.Close
    End With
End If
```

That's all there is to it.

Now we've got a handle on the basics of this technology – opening connections and using commands and recordsets. So let's now elaborate things by looking at how we can make use of error handling in such routines.

Try It Out – Using ADO Error Handling

For this exercise, we'll attempt to delete an account from the database. However, if the attempt fails, we'll display information that informs us what the error was.

1. Return to the `RetrieveData` project.

2. Add another command button to the form, name it `cmdDelete` and set its caption to **&Delete**:

3. Add the following code to the form:

```
Public Sub cmdDelete_Click()

  On Error GoTo VBError

  Dim cmd          As ADODB.Command
  Dim cnnConnection  As ADODB.Connection
  Dim strQry       As String
  Dim strID        As String

  strID = InputBox("Enter the Account ID to be deleted (blank for none)", _
                   "Delete an Account", "")
```

We've added an error handling statement – if the code finds an error, it will jump to the VBError statement that we'll add in a moment. We've also added an input box to the code, to get the number of the account that's going to be deleted.

4. Next, set up a query to the database. We'll delete the account that we enter into the input box:

```
If Len(strID) > 0 Then
  strQry = "DELETE BankAccount WHERE AccountId = " & strID
```

5. Add another error handling statement – this time, an error will cause the code to jump to the ADOError statement. As with the previous exercises, we open the connections to the database, retrieve the recordset and close the connection.

```
    On Error GoTo ADOError
    Set cnnConnection = New Connection

    ' In the following, you need may to change "(local)" to the
    ' name of your SQL Server
    cnnConnection.ConnectionString = "Provider=sqloledb;" & _
                                     "Data Source=(local);" & _
                                     "Initial Catalog=BigBank;" & _
                                     "User Id=sa;Password=; "

    cnnConnection.Open

    ' Set up Command object and Connection
    Set cmd = New ADODB.Command

    'Run the procedure
    With cmd
      .ActiveConnection = cnnConnection
      .CommandText = strQry
      .CommandType = adCmdText

      .Execute , , ADODB.adExecuteNoRecords
      Set .ActiveConnection = Nothing
    End With
  End If

Clean_Up:
  Set cmd = Nothing
  Set cnnConnection = Nothing

  Exit Sub
```

If no errors were found, the procedure ends at this point. However, if an error was found either in the VB code or with the ADO commands, the code jumps to the statements we'll provide for error handling.

6. Add the following error handling statements:

```
ADOError:  ' ADO error handler
  DisplayADOErrors cnnConnection
  GoTo Clean_Up

VBError:  ' Non-ADO error handler
  DisplayVBError
  GoTo Clean_Up

End Sub
```

7. If the error is with an ADO command, the `DisplayADOErrors` procedure is called, which displays a message box with information about the error:

```
Private Sub DisplayADOErrors(cnnConnection As ADODB.Connection)

  Dim errLoop  As ADODB.Error
  Dim strHelp  As String

  For Each errLoop In cnnConnection.Errors

    If errLoop.HelpFile = "" Then
      strHelp = " No Helpfile available"
    Else
      strHelp = " Helpfile: " & errLoop.HelpFile & _
                "; HelpContext: " & errLoop.HelpContext
    End If

  MsgBox "ADO Error #" & errLoop.Number & _
          vbCrLf & "Source: " & errLoop.Source & _
          vbCrLf & "SQL State: " & errLoop.SQLState & _
          "; Native Error: " & errLoop.NativeError & _
          vbCrLf & vbCrLf & "Description: " & errLoop.Description & _
          vbCrLf & vbCrLf & strHelp, _
          vbCritical, "ADO Error"

  Next errLoop

End Sub
```

8. If the error is with the Visual Basic section, this procedure displays a message box with information about the error:

```
Private Sub DisplayVBError()

  If CBool(Err) Then
   MsgBox "VB Error #" & Err.Number & _
          vbCrLf & "Source: " & Err.Source & _
          vbCrLf & vbCrLf & "Description: " & Err.Description, _
          vbCritical, "VB Runtime Error"
   Err.Clear
  End If

End Sub
```

9. Save and run the project. Click **Get Balance** to populate the form, then the **Delete** button. When prompted for an **Account ID**, enter **20001** as the account to delete.

10. When you try to delete account numbers that are used in the case study, an error occurs, and our error handler displays what's going on:

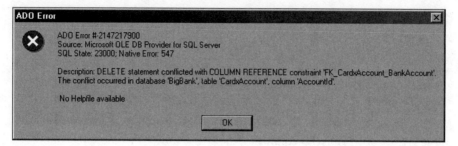

How It Works

The query string is set to equal the SQL statement for deleting accounts – the `StrID` is the **Account Id** that we entered into the input box form:

```
strQry = "DELETE BankAccount WHERE AccountId = " & strID
```

So when we enter account **20001**, the following statement is sent to the SQL sever via ADO after it's parsed:

```
DELETE BankAccount WHERE AccountId = 20001
```

We then make the connection to the SQL server and send the query string (`strQry`) we created:

```
'Run the procedure
With cmd
  .ActiveConnection = cnnConnection
  .CommandText = strQry
  .CommandType = adCmdText
```

We then execute the commands using the `Execute` method of the command object, and set the connection to nothing.

```
  .Execute , , ADODB.adExecuteNoRecords
  Set .ActiveConnection = Nothing
End With
```

The two commas in the `Execute` function represent optional parameters that we've not included: *RecordsAffected* (the number of records affected by the operation) and *Parameters* (any parameters we need to pass). The `adExecuteNoRecords` parameter is also optional, but we've used it here. This instructs ADO not to create a set of data records if there are no results returned – so specifying this parameter for the `Execute` method can improve the performance of the application.

As we're attempting to delete an account that's used in the case study, and is referenced by a foreign key, an ADO error is returned. As we learned in Chapter 9, this is because referential integrity rules won't allow the deletion.

Therefore, our code passes to our ADO error handler:

```
ADOError:  ' ADO error handler
  DisplayADOErrors cnnConnection
```

which calls the `DisplayADOErrors` routine. This simply loops through all the errors in the `Errors` collection. For each error found, we construct a string that describes what went wrong:

```
For Each errLoop In cnnConnection.Errors

  If errLoop.HelpFile = "" Then
    strHelp = " No Helpfile available"
  Else
    strHelp = " Helpfile: " & errLoop.HelpFile & _
              "; HelpContext: " & errLoop.HelpContext
  End If
```

And then we display the description in a message box:

```
MsgBox "ADO Error #" & errLoop.Number & _
        vbCrLf & "Source: " & errLoop.Source & _
        vbCrLf & "SQL State: " & errLoop.SQLState & _
        "; Native Error: " & errLoop.NativeError & _
        vbCrLf & vbCrLf & "Description: " & errLoop.Description & _
        vbCrLf & vbCrLf & strHelp, _
        vbCritical, "ADO Error"

Next errLoop
```

Summary

We haven't seen much of our case study in this chapter, but that's because it's important we get to grips with data access technology first. To that end, we've introduced ActiveX Data Objects, ADO.

We started by looking at the whole area of data access technology in a Microsoft environment, and covered more fully the Universal Data Access approach we introduced in Chapter 1. From there, we moved on to looking at what this means for you as a developer, and examined ADO in more detail.

We took a quick tour of the essential parts of the ADO Object Model. Then, to illustrate how ADO is used with Visual Basic, we tried out some examples involving:

❑   Connecting to a data source and retrieving data from our BigBank database.

❑   Using recordsets.

❑   Making use of stored procedures.

❑   How to handle errors.

Now we've got that basic VB data access programming under our belts, we can turn our attention to the WROBA case study again. In the next chapter, we're going to begin the job of coding the WROBA application: in particular, we'll be building the data services tier.

12

Data Services Tier

So, we've set up our data tier, and, in the previous chapter, we discussed the data access technology that we'll use to move data from our data store into our VB application. We now have all the information we need to be able to move on to coding the data tier of our WROBA application, which is concerned with communicating between the data store and the components in the business layer.

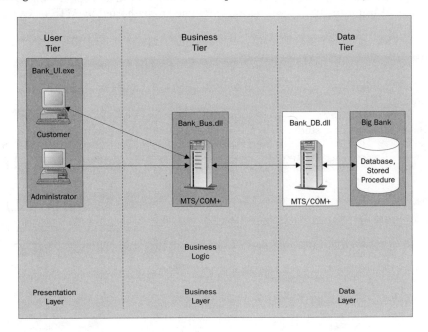

Our road map through this section will be as follows:

- ❑ A description of the Bank_DB project that provides our data access services
- ❑ Detailed coverage of the coding of the data services tier

All the way through our treatment of the case study, we'll be showing screen shots taken from a system running under Windows 2000. However, as we said at the outset of the book, the application we'll develop will also run under Windows 9x or NT 4.0.

Remember, all of the code in this and the following chapters can be found in the code download for the book, available from the Wrox web site at `http://www.wrox.com`.

Before we get down to some serious coding, here's a brief overview of exactly how our WROBA application code fits together.

The Stucture of WROBA

Although the WROBA case study groups the user, business, and data services tiers into one **application group**, all three tiers are really separate VB projects.

> *An application group is a way of collecting related VB projects so they load into VB at the same time and are visible together.*

The business and data services tiers are implemented as ActiveX DLL projects, which will not run as stand-alone applications. The user services tier application does run as a stand-alone Standard EXE project, but the DLLs for the two server tiers are designed to be hosted by MTS or COM+. Specifically, our projects are:

- ❑ `Bank_UI.exe` – the user services tier
- ❑ `Bank_Bus.dll` – the business service tier
- ❑ `Bank_DB.dll` – the data services tier

During the coding of the case study, we'll use a folder structure that emulates that of the code download:

The composition of the folders should be as follows:

- ❑ Bus – the business tier project and classes.
- ❑ Common – the code modules used in the data and business tiers.
- ❑ Distrib – the data and business tier DLLs, Bank_UI.exe, and files associated with compilation; the DLLs should be compiled to this folder.
- ❑ GUID – the DLLs from the Distrib folder are copied into this folder.
- ❑ UI – the user services tiers forms and modules.

The SQL folder isn't used during the book explicitly; in the download it contains the SQL scripts used to create and populate the BigBank database.

You'll find these SQL scripts, along with tables that summarize the purpose of every code module we use in this application, in Appendix A at the end of the book.

In Chapter 5, where we discussed MTS, we alluded to the positive and negative aspects of using MTS or COM+. This is a topic we'll revisit. For the moment, we'll just note that, to optimize performance, the WROBA case study only uses transactional processing where it is necessary.

An Aside – Visual Basic Project Groups

In fact, although the different tiers are constructed as different projects, one very useful way of working during development is to collect the WROBA components in a project group.

> A Visual Basic project group enables multiple projects to be open, and worked with, at the same time without running multiple instances of Visual Basic.

Since a distributed application is built from multiple ActiveX projects, it is important to be able to work with all these components in one development environment. Although we haven't actually begun the coding of our components, let's just step ahead of ourselves and look at how we may manipulate the final system on the local machine we're using for development.

As we pointed out above, the Bank_UI.exe is the only stand-alone unit. However, if you download the code from www.wrox.com and try loading just the Bank_UI.vbp file and running it, you'll get an error, because the ActiveX files are missing (the error message will say "Invalid Login", because the missing ActiveX files contain the information required to connect to the SQL Server for login verification).

If we had the complete WROBA project loaded, with the three project files as shown in the following screen shot, and then removed one, we would have received a message reminding us that the project being removed was referenced by one of the other projects in the group.

There is no special procedure to create project groups – just start with an ordinary project, and then add another project to it by selecting File | Add Project. Adding the second project creates a project group (with a .vbg extension). Other projects can then be added to the group. When we reopen the project group, all projects saved in the group will be loaded.

So, when we open up the Bank.vbg project group that comes with the code download of the case study, we'll actually open the three projects Bank_UI, Bank_Bus, and Bank_DB:

A project is not changed when it is included in a project group – the project can be opened individually, or included in another group. However, multiple copies of the same project cannot be included in a project group.

> **After a project group has been created, removing all but one project still keeps this single project wrapped in a project group.**

If you're working through the book and building your own version of the WROBA project, you may find it very helpful to work with the components in a project group.

Data Services Tier – The Bank_DB component

As we can see from our diagram of the WROBA application architecture, we're now turning our attention towards developing the Bank_DB component, which provides our data access services.

The code in the data tier is implemented in two code modules:

- ❑   MHelper
- ❑   MContext

and six class modules:

- ❑   Account
- ❑   Admin
- ❑   Bank
- ❑   BankLocator
- ❑   DBHelper
- ❑   Payees

The crucial thing to note here is that the MContext code module is used to encapsulate all the transactional functions; thus all the management of transactions is brought together in one place within the code. As we'll see later, the MHelper module holds the Enums for this project, as well as some data type conversion functions.

The class modules generally have specific tasks, such as locating banks and dealing with account manipulation. The exception is the DBHelper module, which is a helper class to aid with some of the repetitive coding encountered as we use ADO to communicate with the database.

We will see a recurring theme throughout this large section of coding. Most modules will start with constants for the module being set, and the DBHelper module being initialized. The methods in this module will then be used to execute stored procedures in the database. These stored procedures will be used to carry out all the retrieval and manipulation of the data we have in the BigBank database.

We can categorize the use of these stored procedures into two basic subsets:

- ❑   Row-returning – based upon SELECT statements
- ❑   Non row-returning – typically based upon UPDATE, INSERT, or DELETE statements

We'll see more of this as we run through the chapter.

After all that planning and designing let's finally take the plunge and start coding the WROBA data tier.

Try It Out – Creating the Bank_DB Project

1. Open up Visual Basic and create a new ActiveX DLL project called Bank_DB.

2. The project requires references setting to two libraries that aren't referenced by default in Visual Basic – the Microsoft ActiveX Data Objects Library and the MTS/COM+ Type Library.

At this point, the precise libraries you need to reference depends on your system configuration; in both cases select Project | References then:

❑ For Windows 2000 users select Microsoft ActiveX Data Objects 2.5 Library and COM+ Services Type Library.

❑ For Windows 9x or NT 4.0 users (without the updated ADO library) select Microsoft ActiveX 2.1 Library and Microsoft Transaction Server Type Library.

The screen shot here shows the references used under Windows 2000 but the code will work perfectly well under either system:

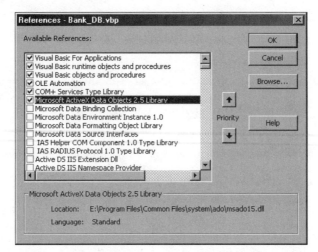

The WROBA case study code was created in Windows 2000 and references the COM+ Services Type Library. If you are running Windows NT 4, or even Windows 98 or Windows 95, an interesting thing happens with the reference to the COM+ Services Type Library. The library reference to the Windows 2000 COMSVCS.DLL (COM+ library) is automatically changed to a reference to MTXAS.DLL (the Windows NT, Windows 95 and Windows 98 MTS libraries) when the project is loaded into VB. You don't have to do anything to change that reference yourself – the library headers inform VB of the necessary change – but the MTS library must be installed in the system running the project for this to work.

The Bank_DB project does not reference the Bank_Bus ActiveX DLL we create in the next chapter, but the Bank_Bus project does reference the Bank_DB ActiveX DLL. To provide the DLL reference that the business services tier requires, we need to compile the Bank_DB project separately, then reference the resulting Bank_DB DLL in the references for the Bank_Bus project. We'll discuss the project compatibility compilation options that the project will require in the next section.

Try It Out – Setting the Project Properties

1. Open the Bank_DB project properties sheet (either via the Project menu or by right-clicking on the highlighted project in the Project Explorer window). Select the General tab and accept the default settings of no Startup Object, Upgrade ActiveX Controls and an Apartment Threaded model. No startup object is needed, because the DLL will not run as a stand-alone application.

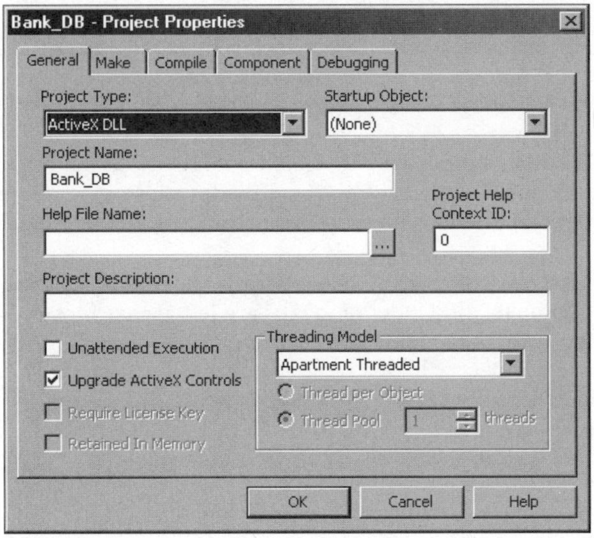

2. Next select the Make tab – set the application's title to Bank_DB and leave the check box for removing information about unused ActiveX controls checked. This tab is where the version information for the application is set. Standard version numbering practice is to number the first release version of an application as 1.0.0 (as shown here for the released case study component). Versions prior to release use a major version number of 0.

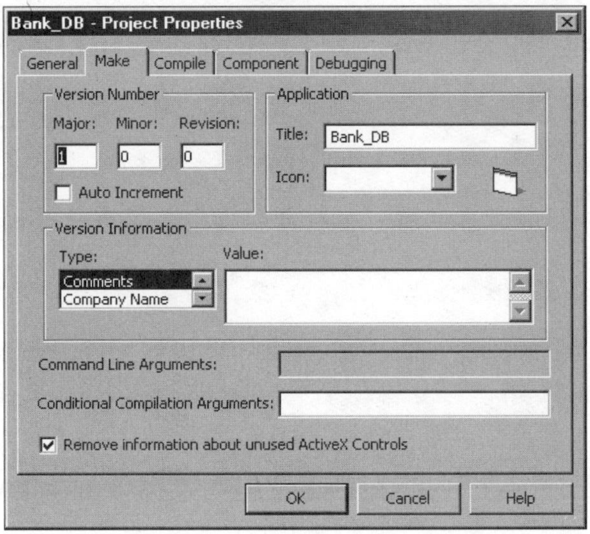

One recommendation is to start a project with a minor version number of 1, with a revision of 0. If the Auto Increment check box is checked, each compilation will increment the revision number by 1. When milestones are reached for deliverables or project features, reset the revision number to 0 and increment the minor version number. Using this procedure makes it easy to ensure that every member of the development and testing teams is working with the same code base. Even if you don't work as a member of a development team this is a good habit to get into, since it makes it easy to track different versions and revisions of your code base.

The use of Microsoft Visual Source Safe, which is included with Visual Basic 6 Professional and Enterprise Editions, is not discussed in this book. However, this is another tool that could prove very helpful if you're serious about application development. It creates a central repository for all the code and resources for a project, with check-in and check-out control that helps manage team projects. Thus, Visual Source Safe enables the revisions made to a project over the project's lifetime to be tracked. This version tracking provides a history of the project's code and resources, and enables previous versions of a project to be reverted to if necessary.

3. The last tab we have to concern ourselves with is the Component tab (in this project the settings for the Compile and Debugging tabs are left at their default settings and won't be discussed). Here we set the version compatibility of the project, how the project starts up, and decide whether the project will be a remote server. For ActiveX DLL projects the start mode settings are disabled, and when the time comes to use this project as a distributed component on the business services tier server, MTS or COM+ will provide the remote server capability; hence the Remote Server check box can be left unchecked.

The first time you compile the project, set the compatibility to Project Compatibility. After the project has been compiled to produce an ActiveX DLL, place a copy of the DLL in the GUID project subfolder that we previously created. Once this DLL is in place, change the project version compatibility to Binary Compatibility. Binary Compatibility is used to maintain compatibility with projects that have been compiled with references to the DLL.

Coding the Data Tier

Let's now move on to actual Visual Basic programming of the WROBA data tier component.

The MHelpers Module

The first module we're adding to the project is a code module to hold general enumerations for the Bank_DB project.

Try It Out – Coding the MHelpers Module

1. Create a new standard module via **Project | Add Module** and name it **MHelpers**.

2. The first task is to add the enumeration information:

```
Option Explicit

' Module in data tier

Public Enum EADODataSize
  adSizeCurrency = 8
  adSizeDateTime = 8
  adSizeInteger = 4
  adSizeSmallInt = 2
  adSizeBoolean = 1
  adSizetinyInt = 1
End Enum
```

3. Then we add two functions: `ConvertToString`, which converts a variant to a string, and `NullsToZero`, which converts NULL variants to zero:

```
Public Function ConvertToString(v As Variant) As String
' Converts a variant into a string. If the variant is null,
' it is converted to the empty string.

  If IsNull(v) Then
    ConvertToString = ""
  Else
    ConvertToString = CStr(v)
  End If
End Function
```

```
Public Function NullsToZero(v As Variant) As Variant
' Converts any Null variant to zero, otherwise it returns
' the existing value.

  If IsNull(v) Then
    NullsToZero = 0
  Else
    NullsToZero = v
  End If
End Function
```

The second code module we're going to look at here is crucial to the operation of the application – it encapsulates all the transactional functions and is shared by both the data services and the business services tiers.

The MContext Code Module

The UML class diagram for the MContext module is shown below. It's somewhat deceptively named, since MContext is really *not* a class module. However, a class diagram is still useful in discovering what functions and subs the module will require.

This diagram is used to generate the class template for the class, and then the template is filled in with the required code to implement the properties and methods. During the implementation phase, if it becomes necessary to add, remove, or change any of the properties and methods in the class, the round trip reverse engineering feature of the Visual Modeler software (discussed in Chapter 7) is used to update the class diagram. This iterative round tripping keeps the code and UML class diagrams in synch with each other. The calling arguments of the properties and methods of the class are not shown in this diagram, although display options in Visual Modeler enable you to do so.

The UML diagrams you'll see throughout the next few chapters were created with Visual Modeler during the modeling phase of the WROBA project. We used the Visual Modeler tool to create class diagrams and generate the class templates, because it's provided with Visual Basic Enterprise Edition. Class diagrams can be created with any modeling tool (or even with a drawing tool such as Corel Draw) and if the tool does not provide code generation, the templates for the classes can be created manually in VB.

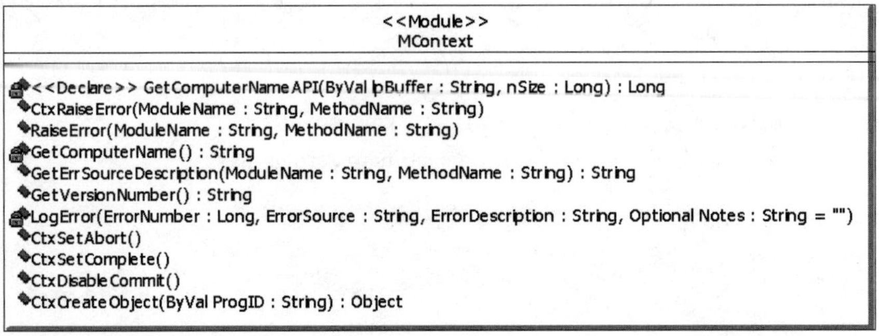

```
                        <<Module>>
                         MContext
─────────────────────────────────────────────────────────────
<<Declare>> GetComputerNameAPI(ByVal pBuffer : String, nSize : Long) : Long
CtxRaiseError(ModuleName : String, MethodName : String)
RaiseError(ModuleName : String, MethodName : String)
GetComputerName() : String
GetErrSourceDescription(ModuleName : String, MethodName : String) : String
GetVersionNumber() : String
LogError(ErrorNumber : Long, ErrorSource : String, ErrorDescription : String, Optional Notes : String = "")
CtxSetAbort()
CtxSetComplete()
CtxDisableCommit()
CtxCreateObject(ByVal ProgID : String) : Object
```

The class diagram shows the methods of the MContext code module. It also shows that a Declare statement was used to declare a Win32 API call.

Declare statements are used at the module level in a code or class module to reference external procedures in a DLL. In this case, the DLL is the Kernel32.DLL, which is part of the Win32 API, and the procedure is the GetComputerNameA procedure (which returns the name registered for the computer that the code is running on).

The Win32 API is the generic term used for the set of DLLs that are available in all 32-bit Windows systems. These DLLs provide procedures that are used for many common functions, such as returning the current computer name, current operating system version, local language, and many others that together make up a rich programming environment. Using these procedures enables you as a programmer to leverage existing system code and to avoid having to reinvent the wheel.

Try It Out – Coding the MContext Module

1. Create a new module (*not* a class module) called **MContext**.

2. The first job is to code the `Declare` statement:

```
Option Explicit

' Module shared by the business and data tiers

' Declaration for Win32 API function
Private Declare Function GetComputerNameAPI Lib "kernel32" Alias
"GetComputerNameA" (ByVal lpBuffer As String, nSize As Long) As Long
```

3. Next we have the `CtxRaiseError` method (which is only used in the data services tier):

```
Public Sub CtxRaiseError(ModuleName As String, MethodName As String)
' Change the transaction state, and raise an error.

  ' Set the default to disable transaction. Now unless someone
  ' does a SetComplete the transaction will abort.
  ' This is just like calling setabort, but has it doesn't destroy
  ' the Err object if we are in a transaction.
  CtxDisableCommit

  ' Log the error to the event for later use.
  LogError Err.Number, GetErrSourceDescription(ModuleName, _
      MethodName), Err.Description, "from CtxRaiseError"

  ' Raise an error to indate there was a problem.
  ' This will indicate that no one should do a SetComplete
  ' unless they can handle this error.
  '
  ' The following MsgBox code is for debugging purposes.
  ' It will permit a graceful way of acknowledging server side
  ' errors and enabling the client application to work after
  ' such an error. If you want to have the server side code
  ' terminate with a runtime error, comment out that and the
  ' Err.Clear and uncomment the Err.Raise statement.
  MsgBox "Error # " & Err.Number & vbCrLf & _
      GetErrSourceDescription(ModuleName, MethodName) & _
      vbCrLf & Err.Description
  Err.Clear
End Sub
```

4. For all other errors that occur in the business and data services tiers the `RaiseError` method is used:

```
Public Sub RaiseError(ModuleName As String, MethodName As String)
' Raise an error without changing the transaction state.

    ' Log the error to the event for later use.
    LogError Err.Number, GetErrSourceDescription(ModuleName, _
        MethodName), Err.Description, "From RaiseError"

    ' The following MsgBox code is for debugging purposes.
    ' It will permit a graceful way of acknowledging server side
    ' errors and enabling the client application to work after
    ' such an error. If you want to have the server side code
    ' terminate with a runtime error, comment out that and the
    ' Err.Clear and uncomment the Err.Raise statement.
    MsgBox "Error # " & Err.Number & vbCrLf & _
        GetErrSourceDescription(ModuleName, MethodName) & _
        vbCrLf & Err.Description
    Err.Clear
End Sub
```

5. The `GetComputerName` function uses a Win32 API call to return the name for the computer:

```
Private Function GetComputerName() As String
' Set or retrieve the name of the computer.

    Dim strBuffer As String
    Dim lngLen As Long

    ' Prepare a buffer for the return value
    strBuffer = Space$(255 + 1)
    lngLen = Len(strBuffer)
    If CBool(GetComputerNameAPI(strBuffer, lngLen)) Then
        GetComputerName = Left$(strBuffer, lngLen)
    Else
        GetComputerName = ""
    End If
End Function
```

6. The `GetErrSourceDescription` function creates an error string description that consists of the module and method or property where the error occurred and the computer name with the WROBA application version number:

```
Function GetErrSourceDescription(ModuleName As String, MethodName As String) As
String
' Returns an error message like:  "[Bank_DB.RangerZeroCurve]
' VerifyUser [on TOWW5391 version 5.21.176]"

    GetErrSourceDescription = Err.Source & vbNewLine & "<br>" & _
        "[" & ModuleName & "] " & MethodName & " [on " & _
        GetComputerName() & " version " & GetVersionNumber() & "]"
End Function
```

7. The `GetVersionNumber` function returns the version number of the running WROBA application:

```
Function GetVersionNumber() As String
' Returns the current DLL version number

    GetVersionNumber = App.Major & "." & App.Minor & "." & _
        App.Revision
End Function
```

8. The `LogError` method uses the application's log to store information about an error or event:

```
Private Sub LogError(ErrorNumber As Long, ErrorSource As String, ErrorDescription
As String, Optional Notes As String = "")
' This procedure logs an error to the system application log

    App.LogEvent vbNewLine & "An error has occured in this application." _
        & vbNewLine & "Error Number:" & ErrorNumber & vbNewLine & _
        vbNewLine & "Description:" & vbNewLine & ErrorDescription & _
        vbNewLine & vbNewLine & "Source: " & vbNewLine & ErrorSource _
        & vbNewLine & vbNewLine & "Notes: " & vbNewLine & Notes
End Sub
```

9. The `CtxSetAbort` method is called when an error is raised when a context is instantiated. It gets the current context for the transaction, and if it exists uses the context's `SetAbort` method to abort the transaction:

```
Public Sub CtxSetAbort()
' If the context exists, abort the transaction
    Dim objObjectContext As ObjectContext

    Set objObjectContext = GetObjectContext

    If Not (objObjectContext Is Nothing) Then
        objObjectContext.SetAbort
    End If

    Set objObjectContext = Nothing
End Sub
```

Placing the `SetAbort` and `SetComplete` actions in subroutines such as this is a good programming practice; it makes the routines easy to find, understand, and work with from a programming perspective, as well as easy to change.

10. The `CtxSetComplete` method is called after a transaction completes without an error. It gets the current context for the transaction, and if it exists uses the context's `SetComplete` method to commit the transaction:

```
Public Sub CtxSetComplete()
' If the context exists, complete the transaction
  Dim objObjectContext As ObjectContext

  Set objObjectContext = GetObjectContext

  If Not (objObjectContext Is Nothing) Then
     objObjectContext.SetComplete
  End If

  Set objObjectContext = Nothing
End Sub
```

11. The `CtxDisableCommit` method is called by the `CtxRaiseError` method, to disable committing a transaction if a context for the transaction exists:

```
Public Sub CtxDisableCommit()
' If the context exists, disable committing it
  Dim objObjectContext As ObjectContext

  Set objObjectContext = GetObjectContext

  If Not (objObjectContext Is Nothing) Then
     objObjectContext.DisableCommit
  End If

  Set objObjectContext = Nothing
End Sub
```

12. The `CtxCreateObject` method checks to see if there is a current context. If one exists, an instance of the module is created in that context. If no current context exists, an instance of the object is created with `CreateObject`:

```
Public Function CtxCreateObject(ByVal ProgID As String) As Object
' Create a transaction context with the ProgID string
  Dim objObjectContext As ObjectContext

  Set objObjectContext = GetObjectContext

  If Not (objObjectContext Is Nothing) Then
     Set CtxCreateObject = objObjectContext.CreateInstance(ProgID)
     Set objObjectContext = Nothing
  Else
     Set CtxCreateObject = CreateObject(ProgID)
  End If
End Function
```

As we'll see later, the `Transfer` class `MTSTransactionMode` property requires that a new context be created for every instance of `Transfer` that is created. When a new instance of the `Transfer` class is created with `CreateObject` a context is created for that object at the same time.

How It Works

`Declare Function GetComputerNameAPI` is used to name the procedure that is known to the Win32 API as `GetComputerNameA`. The name given to the procedure in the DLL does not have to be used; it can be given a more meaningful or user-friendly name by utilizing the `Alias` clause to link the defined name with a chosen name.

The library that contains the procedure is identified by the `Lib` clause, which in this case references the Kernel32 library:

```
Option Explicit

' Module shared by the business and data tiers

' Declaration for Win32 API function
Private Declare Function GetComputerNameAPI Lib "kernel32" Alias
"GetComputerNameA" (ByVal lpBuffer As String, nSize As Long) As Long
```

This simple example of the `Declare` statement enables us to make use of this external procedure in the Win32 API. `Declare` statements are used not only for referencing procedures in system DLLs such as Kernel32, but can be used to reference procedures in any DLL that is registered on the target computer.

Later we saw that the `GetComputerName` function uses this call to return the name for the computer. First a buffer is initialized to 256 spaces. The value for the number of spaces created in the buffer is the sum of the name length plus a terminating null, which marks the end of the string returned by the Win32 API call:

```
' Prepare a buffer for the return value
strBuffer = Space$(255 + 1)
lngLen = Len(strBuffer)
If CBool(GetComputerNameAPI(strBuffer, lngLen)) Then
   GetComputerName = Left$(strBuffer, lngLen)
Else
   GetComputerName = ""
End If
```

The `CtxRaiseError` method is used in the data services tier to handle an error that occurs in the method that parses arguments for the stored procedures in the database. It disables the transaction, which has the same result as directly aborting the transaction when `Err.Raise` is used in a production environment. Aborting the transaction in this way preserves the `Err` object if there is a current transaction. In the case study implementation, a message is displayed showing the error. In a production environment, when the code is running on a server, `Err.Raise` can be used to fire an error handler.

The `LogError` method is called to log an error message in the application log. The `RaiseError` message, used for all other errors, just logs the error using `LogError` and displays a message describing the error.

An interesting extension to the case study would be to change the `LogError` method to log the errors in a database rather than the application's log. We have a quick look at this option at the end of the chapter.

After implementing the two code modules, we'll address the class modules, starting with the `DBHelper` class module.

The DBHelper Class Module

Since much of the coding with ADO objects is repetitive, it makes sense to create a helper class to facilitate the creation of data tier functionality. This is what the `DBHelper` class does for us in the WROBA application.

Try It Out – Coding the DBHelper Class Module

1. Create a new class module via Project | Add Class Module, and rename it DBHelper.

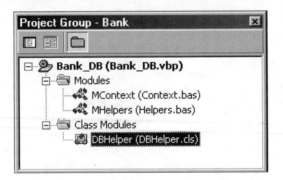

2. The next task is to set up the properties for the class. In the Properties window change the MTSTransactionMode property to 1 – NoTransactions. The other properties can be left unaltered.

3. In common with all the class modules in the WROBA application, we start off by ensuring we declare `Option Explicit`, comment the purpose of the class, and add a constant identifying the module name:

```
Option Explicit

' Class module in data tier
' Runs procedures stored in the database

Const MODULE_NAME As String = "Bank_DB.DBHelper"
```

4. Our first function, RunSPReturnRS, is used to return a recordset from a stored procedure:

```
Function RunSPReturnRS(ByVal ConnectionString As String, _
 ByVal StoredProcedureName As String, ParamArray ParameterArray() _
 As Variant) As ADODB.Recordset
' Run a stored procedure and return a recordset

 Dim rst As ADODB.Recordset
 Dim cmd As ADODB.Command

 On Error GoTo ErrorHandler

 ' Create the ADO objects
 Set rst = New ADODB.Recordset
 Set cmd = New ADODB.Command

 ' Init the ADO objects
 With cmd
  .ActiveConnection = ConnectionString
  .CommandText = StoredProcedureName
  .CommandType = adCmdStoredProc
 End With
 rst.CursorLocation = adUseClient

 ' Init the stored procedure parameters
 CollectParams cmd, ParameterArray

 ' Execute the stored procedure for readonly
 rst.Open cmd, , adOpenForwardOnly,adLockReadOnly

Clean_Up:
 ' Disconnect the recordset
 Set cmd.ActiveConnection = Nothing
 Set cmd = Nothing
 Set rst.ActiveConnection = Nothing

 ' Return the recordset
 Set RunSPReturnRS = rst
 Set rst = Nothing
 Exit Function

ErrorHandler:
 Set rst = Nothing
 RaiseError MODULE_NAME, "RunSPReturnRS(" _
  & StoredProcedureName & ", ...)"
 GoTo Clean_Up
End Function
```

5. This next function, `RunSP`, runs a stored procedure that does not return a recordset. It is used to run a stored procedure that updates, inserts, or deletes recordsets:

```
Function RunSP(ByVal ConnectionString As String, _
 ByVal StoredProcedureName As String, _
 ParamArray ParameterArray() As Variant)
' Run a stored procedure with no return value

 Dim cmd As ADODB.Command

 On Error GoTo ErrorHandler

 ' Create the ADO objects
 Set cmd = New ADODB.Command

 ' Init the ADO objects
 With cmd
   .ActiveConnection = ConnectionString
   .CommandText = StoredProcedureName
   .CommandType = adCmdStoredProc
 End With

 ' Init the stored procedure parameters
 CollectParams cmd, ParameterArray

 ' Execute the stored procedure without returning a recordset
 cmd.Execute , , adExecuteNoRecords

 ' Disconnect the recordset and clean up
Clean_Up:
 Set cmd.ActiveConnection = Nothing
 Set cmd = Nothing

 Exit Function

ErrorHandler:
 RaiseError MODULE_NAME, "RunSP(" & StoredProcedureName & _
   ", ...)"
 GoTo Clean_Up
End Function
```

6. Our next function, `RunSPReturnInteger`, is used to run a stored procedure that returns an integer:

```
Function RunSPReturnInteger(ByVal ConnectionString As String, _
 ByVal StoredProcedureName As String, _
 ParamArray ParameterArray() As Variant) As Long
' Run a stored procedure and return a value
' NOTE: The return type is a Long, which corresponds to the
' adInteger type selected for @ReturnValue
```

```
    Dim cmd As ADODB.Command

    On Error GoTo ErrorHandler

    ' Create the ADO objects
    Set cmd = New ADODB.Command

    ' Init the ADO objects
    With cmd
      .ActiveConnection = ConnectionString
      .CommandText = StoredProcedureName
      .CommandType = adCmdStoredProc
    End With

    CollectParams cmd, ParameterArray

    ' Assume the last parameter is outgoing
    cmd.Parameters.Append cmd.CreateParameter("@ReturnValue", _
      adInteger, adParamOutput, adSizeInteger)

    ' Execute without a resulting recordset
    cmd.Execute , , adExecuteNoRecords
    ' Pull out the "return value" parameter
    RunSPReturnInteger = cmd.Parameters("@ReturnValue").Value

    ' Disconnect the recordset, and clean up
Clean_Up:
    Set cmd.ActiveConnection = Nothing
    Set cmd = Nothing

    Exit Function

ErrorHandler:
    RunSPReturnInteger = -1
    Set cmd = Nothing
    RaiseError MODULE_NAME, "RunSPReturnInteger(" & _
      StoredProcedureName & ", ...)"
    GoTo Clean_Up
End Function
```

7. Lastly, we have the private `CollectParams` routine that extracts parameters from an array for use by the three methods we have just coded. Here the `Ubound` function is used to determine the upper limits of an array. The variant array is converted to an integer needed by the stored procedure:

```
Friend Sub CollectParams(ByRef cmd As ADODB.Command, _
  ParamArray ParamaterArray() As Variant)
' Convert a Variant array into a set of parameters for the
' stored procedure

  Dim vntParameterArray As Variant
  Dim vntParameter As Variant
```

431

```
Dim intParameterCnt As Integer
Dim intParameterArrayUBound As Integer
vntParameterArray = ParamaterArray(0)
intParameterArrayUBound = UBound(vntParameterArray)

' Loop through the array of parameters and collect
' the 4 required arguments for each parameter -
' Name, Data Type, Size, Value
For intParameterCnt = LBound(vntParameterArray) _
 To intParameterArrayUBound
 If UBound(vntParameterArray(intParameterCnt)) - _
  LBound(vntParameterArray(intParameterCnt)) = 3 Then
  ' Check for nulls.
  If VarType(vntParameterArray(intParameterCnt)(3)) = _
   vbString Then
   vntParameter = IIf(vntParameterArray(intParameterCnt)(3) _
    = "", Null, vntParameterArray(intParameterCnt)(3))
  Else
   vntParameter = vntParameterArray(intParameterCnt)(3)
  End If
  cmd.Parameters.Append cmd.CreateParameter( _
   vntParameterArray(intParameterCnt)(0), _
   vntParameterArray(intParameterCnt)(1), adParamInput, _
   vntParameterArray(intParameterCnt)(2), vntParameter)
 Else
  CtxRaiseError MODULE_NAME, "CollectParams(...): " _
   & "incorrect # of parameters"
 End If
Next intParameterCnt
End Sub
```

How It Works

This class contains three functions used to run stored procedures, and one procedure that converts Variant arrays to parameters for use with the stored procedures. We'll show examples of how these functions will be of help to us later, as we look at the rest of the data tier.

As we saw, the RunSPReturnRS function is used to return a recordset from a stored procedure. The exact stored procedure to use will be passed to the function at runtime by the variable StoredProcedureName. The function connects to our SQL Server database and collects the recordsets specified by the procedure calling this function.

The third function we coded, RunSPReturnInteger, which returns a single value from a stored procedure, is often used by the other class modules to verify that a bank, payee, or account exists.

Within this method, the argument adParamOutput (used within the ADO Command object CreateParameter method) is used to get data from a stored procedure:

```
' Assume the last parameter is outgoing
cmd.Parameters.Append cmd.CreateParameter("@ReturnValue", _
 adInteger, adParamOutput, adSizeInteger)
```

This parameter is used as data is being output from the command. If we wanted to send data to the stored procedure, we would have to use the adParamInput parameter. For bi-directional data flow, the adParamInputOutput argument would be used.

The three functions related to stored procedures all run very similar error handling routines: the module name, and the name of the property or method where the error occurred are passed to a public error method (RaiseError) in the MContext code module with the values of the arguments passed to the method or property. This can be illustrated by looking at this code snippet from the RunSPReturnRS function:

```
ErrorHandler:
 Set rst = Nothing
 RaiseError MODULE_NAME, "RunSPReturnRS(" _
  & StoredProcedureName & ", ...)"
 GoTo Clean_Up
End Function
```

This approach will become very familiar by the time we've finished coding all the data and business tier modules. Using a common error method makes it easy to implement different ways of displaying or logging errors that occur in projects that are running on servers. This can be of assistance during different phases of the project:

❑   During development, testing, and debugging messages can be displayed to signal errors.

❑   When the project is deployed, the error messages can then be replaced by error logging, either in the application's event log or in a dedicated error table in a database.

The error handling in the CollectParams method is somewhat different, as it utilizes the CtxRaiseError method relating to control of transactions:

```
    CtxRaiseError MODULE_NAME, "CollectParams(...): " _
     & "incorrect # of parameters"
```

How we use these helper functions in our data tier will become apparent as we code the rest of the class modules in the data tier.

The Account Class Module

The modeling phase of the WROBA project produced the following UML class diagram for the Account class module. The module contains just three main procedures which are concerned with adding funds to accounts, deleting funds from the accounts, and actually verifying the accounts.

```
        <<Class Module>>
           Account
MODULE_NAME : String = "Bank_DB.Account"
TXDESCRIPTION_SIZE : Integer = 40
COUNTERPARTYREF_SIZE : Integer = 16
txsSuccess = 0
txsUnknownError = 3

Class_Initialize()
Class_Terminate()
IncrementBalance()
DecrementBalance()
<<Get>> VerifyAccount()
<<Get>> VerifyAccount()
```

One thing to note is that this is the only class out of all of our core data services modules that actually requires transactions.

Let's consider the methods in the order they appear in the class diagram.

433

Try It Out – Coding the Account Module

1. Add a new class module to the project named Account, and here set the MTSTransactionMode property to 2 – RequiresTransactions. Leave the Persistable property unchanged at 0 – NotPersistable.

2. The module begins by setting constants needed by procedures and initializing DBHelper:

```
Option Explicit

' Class module in data tier

Const MODULE_NAME As String = "Bank_DB.Account"

' Sizes for strings in tables
Const TXDESCRIPTION_SIZE As Integer = 40
Const COUNTERPARTYREF_SIZE As Integer = 16

'These must match the enumerated values in Bank_Bus.Transfer
Const txsSuccess = 0
Const txsUnknownError = 3

Private m_objDBHelper As DBHelper
```

```
Private Sub Class_Initialize()
' Initialize the helper object to run stored procedures
    Set m_objDBHelper = CreateObject("Bank_DB.DBHelper")
End Sub
```

```
Private Sub Class_Terminate()
' Destroy the helper object
    Set m_objDBHelper = Nothing
End Sub
```

3. The IncrementBalance method uses the helper function RunSP to run a stored procedure called sp_update_BankAccount_Inc. Arrays are used to pass the data to the stored procedure so it can update the BankAccount table. The stored procedure adds the value of the parameter @TxAmount_2 to the Balance column:

```
Public Sub IncrementBalance(ByVal BankID As Integer, _
  ByVal AccountID As Long, ByVal Amount As Currency, _
  intTransactionType As Integer, Description As String, _
  CounterParty As String)
' Increment an account balance and log the transaction

  Dim objBankLocator As Bank_DB.BankLocator
  Dim strDSN As String

  On Error GoTo ErrorHandler

  ' Locate the selected bank and get the DSN for it
  Set objBankLocator = New Bank_DB.BankLocator
  strDSN = objBankLocator.GetBank(BankID)
```

```
   If strDSN <> "" Then
     ' If the bank exists run the stored procedure
    m_objDBHelper.RunSP strDSN, "sp_update_BankAccount_Inc", _
       Array("@AccountId_1", adInteger, adSizeInteger, AccountID), _
       Array("@TxAmount_2", adCurrency, adSizeCurrency, Amount), _
       Array("@TxType_3", adTinyInt, adSizetinyInt, _
       intTransactionType), Array("@TxDescription_4", adChar, _
       TXDESCRIPTION_SIZE, Description), Array("@CounterpartyRef_5", _
       adChar, 16, CounterParty)

     CtxSetComplete
   End If

Clean_Up:
   Set objBankLocator = Nothing
   Exit Sub

ErrorHandler:
   RaiseError MODULE_NAME, "IncrementBalance"
   GoTo Clean_Up
End Sub
```

4. The `DecrementBalance` function is very similar to the previous one, except this subtracts `@TxAmount_2` from the `Balance` column. Here the helper function `RunSPReturnInteger` is used to call the stored procedure `sp_update_BankAccount_Dec`:

```
Public Function DecrementBalance(ByVal BankID As Integer, _
   ByVal AccountID As Long, ByVal Amount As Currency, _
   ByRef intTransactionType As Integer, ByRef Description As String, _
   ByRef CounterParty As String) As Integer
' Decrement an account balance and log the transaction

   Dim objBankLocator As Bank_DB.BankLocator
   Dim strDSN As String

   On Error GoTo ErrorHandler

   ' Locate the selected bank and get the DSN for it
   Set objBankLocator = New Bank_DB.BankLocator
   strDSN = objBankLocator.GetBank(BankID)

   If strDSN <> "" Then
     ' If the bank exists run the stored procedure
     DecrementBalance = m_objDBHelper.RunSPReturnInteger( _
       strDSN, "sp_update_BankAccount_Dec", _
       Array("@AccountId_1", adInteger, adSizeInteger, _
       AccountID), Array("@TxAmount_2", adCurrency, _
       adSizeCurrency, Amount), Array("@TxType_3", _
       adTinyInt, adSizetinyInt, intTransactionType), _
       Array("@TxDescription_4", adChar, TXDESCRIPTION_SIZE, _
       Description), Array("@CounterpartyRef_5", adChar, 16, _
       CounterParty))
```

```
      CtxSetComplete
   Else
      DecrementBalance = txsUnknownError
   End If

Clean_Up:
   Set objBankLocator = Nothing
   Exit Function

ErrorHandler:
   RaiseError MODULE_NAME, "DecrementBalance"
   DecrementBalance = txsUnknownError
   GoTo Clean_Up
End Function
```

5. Lastly, in this module, we have the `VerifyAccount` property. This also uses the helper function `RunSPReturnInteger`, this time to call the stored procedure `sp_verify_BankAccount_By_CardId`:

```
Public Property Get VerifyAccount(ByVal BankID As Integer, _
   ByVal AccountID As Long) As Integer
' Verify that the selected account exists at the selected bank

   Dim objBankLocator As Bank_DB.BankLocator
   Dim strDSN As String

   On Error GoTo ErrorHandler

   ' Locate the selected bank and get the DSN for it
   Set objBankLocator = New Bank_DB.BankLocator
   strDSN = objBankLocator.GetBank(BankID)

   If strDSN <> "" Then
      ' If the bank exists run the stored procedure.
      ' Returns the count of accounts that have this AccountID
      VerifyAccount = m_objDBHelper.RunSPReturnInteger( _
         strDSN, "sp_verify_BankAccount_By_CardId", _
         Array("@AccountId_1", adInteger, adSizeInteger, _
         AccountID))
      CtxSetComplete
   Else
      VerifyAccount = 0 'Set to no accounts
   End If

Clean_Up:
   Set objBankLocator = Nothing
   Exit Property

ErrorHandler:
   RaiseError MODULE_NAME, "VerifyAccount"
   VerifyAccount = 0 'Set to no accounts
   GoTo Clean_Up
End Property
```

The Admin Class Module

In the UML class diagram for the `Admin` class module we can see two similarly named properties, `GetAccountType` and `GetAccountTypes`. As we'll see, `GetAccountType` is a row-returning routine, and returns only the account types for the current `CardId`. The `GetAccountTypes` property returns a recordset containing *all* the account types and account IDs.

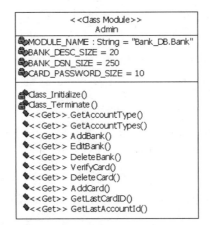

```
                <<Class Module>>
                     Admin
MODULE_NAME : String = "Bank_DB.Bank"
BANK_DESC_SIZE = 20
BANK_DSN_SIZE = 250
CARD_PASSWORD_SIZE = 10

Class_Initialize()
Class_Terminate()
<<Get>> GetAccountType()
<<Get>> GetAccountTypes()
<<Get>> AddBank()
<<Get>> EditBank()
<<Get>> DeleteBank()
<<Get>> VerifyCard()
<<Get>> DeleteCard()
<<Get>> AddCard()
<<Get>> GetLastCardID()
<<Get>> GetLastAccountId()
```

Try It Out – Coding the Admin Module

1. Add another class module to the project, and name it Admin. Set the MTSTransactionMode to 1 – NoTransactions and leave the Persistable property as 0 – NotPersistable.

2. As with the `Account` class, we start by setting constants and initializing the `DBHelper` module:

```
Option Explicit

Const MODULE_NAME As String = "Bank_DB.Bank"

Private m_objDBHelper As DBHelper

Private Const BANK_DESC_SIZE = 20
Private Const BANK_DSN_SIZE = 250
Private Const CARD_PASSWORD_SIZE = 10

Private Sub Class_Initialize()
' Initialize the helper object to run stored procedures
   Set m_objDBHelper = CreateObject("Bank_DB.DBHelper")
End Sub

Private Sub Class_Terminate()
' Destroy the helper object
   Set m_objDBHelper = Nothing
End Sub
```

3. Each WROBACard can have two bank accounts associated with it: one for Checking and one for Saving. The GetAccountType property returns a recordset of the account types for a specific CardId:

```
Public Property Get GetAccountType(ByVal BankID As Integer, _
  ByVal CardId As Long) As ADODB.Recordset

  Dim objBankLocator As Bank_DB.BankLocator
  Dim strDSN As String

  On Error GoTo ErrorHandler

  ' Locate the selected bank and get the DSN for it
  Set objBankLocator = New Bank_DB.BankLocator
  strDSN = objBankLocator.GetBank(BankID)

  ' Run the stored procedure. Return a recordset of all the
  ' account types that are listed for this CardID
  On Error Resume Next
  Set GetAccountType = m_objDBHelper.RunSPReturnRS( _
    strDSN, "sp_select_AccountType_By_CardId", _
    Array("@CardId_1", adInteger, adSizeInteger, CardId))

Clean_Up:
  Set objBankLocator = Nothing
  CtxSetComplete
  Exit Property

ErrorHandler:
  Debug.Print Err.Number
  RaiseError MODULE_NAME, "GetAccountType"
  GoTo Clean_Up
End Property
```

4. Next, we have the GetAccountTypes property. This returns all account types and account IDs, making use of the sp_select_accountType stored procedure:

```
Public Property Get GetAccountTypes(ByVal BankID As Integer) _
  As ADODB.Recordset

  Dim objBankLocator As Bank_DB.BankLocator
  Dim strDSN As String

  On Error GoTo ErrorHandler

  ' Locate the selected bank and get the DSN for it
  Set objBankLocator = New Bank_DB.BankLocator
  strDSN = objBankLocator.GetBank(BankID)

  ' Run the stored procedure. Return a recordset of all the
  ' account types and corresponding AccountID.
  On Error Resume Next
```

```
    Set GetAccountTypes = m_objDBHelper.RunSPReturnRS( _
      strDSN, "sp_select_AccountType")

Clean_Up:
  Set objBankLocator = Nothing
  CtxSetComplete
  Exit Property

ErrorHandler:
  Debug.Print Err.Number
  RaiseError MODULE_NAME, "GetAccountTypes"
  GoTo Clean_Up
End Property
```

5. We then have the AddBank property, which is used to add a new bank to the database. It uses the stored procedure sp_insert_Bank to insert new BankId, BankDesc, and BankDSN information to the Bank table:

```
Public Property Get AddBank(ByVal BankID As Integer, _
  ByVal NewBankId As Integer, ByVal Description As String, _
  DSN As String) As Boolean

  Dim objBankLocator As Bank_DB.BankLocator
  Dim lngReturn As Long
  Dim strDSN As String

  On Error GoTo ErrorHandler

  ' Locate the selected bank and get the DSN for it
  Set objBankLocator = New Bank_DB.BankLocator
  strDSN = objBankLocator.GetBank(BankID)

  ' Run the stored procedure. Insert a new bank in the table.
  On Error Resume Next
  lngReturn = m_objDBHelper.RunSPReturnInteger( _
    strDSN, "sp_insert_Bank", _
    Array("@BankId_1", adSmallInt, adSizeSmallInt, NewBankId), _
    Array("@BankDesc_2", adChar, BANK_DESC_SIZE, Description), _
    Array("@BankDSN_3", adVarChar, BANK_DSN_SIZE, DSN))

  If lngReturn = 0 Then
    AddBank = True
  Else
    AddBank = False
  End If

Clean_Up:
  Set objBankLocator = Nothing
  CtxSetComplete
  Exit Property
```

```
ErrorHandler:
  Debug.Print Err.Number
  RaiseError MODULE_NAME, "AddBank"
  GoTo Clean_Up
End Property
```

6. The next method we add, `EditBank`, works much like the previous property, except that it allows us to edit the bank information contained in the `Bank` table, instead of simply adding new information. This would be needed, for example, if a bank's name changed.

```
Public Property Get EditBank(ByVal BankID As Integer, _
  ByVal ChangeBankId As Integer, ByVal Description As String, _
  DSN As String) As Boolean

  Dim objBankLocator As Bank_DB.BankLocator
  Dim lngReturn As Long
  Dim strDSN As String

  On Error GoTo ErrorHandler

  ' Locate the selected bank and get the DSN for it
  Set objBankLocator = New Bank_DB.BankLocator
  strDSN = objBankLocator.GetBank(BankID)

  ' Run the stored procedure. Update the bank record.
  On Error Resume Next
  lngReturn = m_objDBHelper.RunSPReturnInteger( _
    strDSN, "sp_update_Bank", _
    Array("@BankId_1", adSmallInt, adSizeSmallInt, ChangeBankId), _
    Array("@BankDesc_2", adChar, BANK_DESC_SIZE, Description), _
    Array("@BankDSN_3", adVarChar, BANK_DSN_SIZE, DSN))

  If lngReturn = 0 Then
    EditBank = True
  Else
    EditBank = False
  End If

Clean_Up:
  Set objBankLocator = Nothing
  CtxSetComplete
  Exit Property

ErrorHandler:
  Debug.Print Err.Number
  RaiseError MODULE_NAME, "EditBank"
  GoTo Clean_Up
End Property
```

7. Next, we have the self-explanatory `DeleteBank` property – it's the last administrative feature for working with the `Bank` table:

```
Public Property Get DeleteBank(ByVal BankID As Integer, _
  ByVal ChangeBankId As Integer) As Boolean

  Dim objBankLocator As Bank_DB.BankLocator
  Dim lngReturn As Long
  Dim strDSN As String

  On Error GoTo ErrorHandler

  ' Locate the selected bank and get the DSN for it
  Set objBankLocator = New Bank_DB.BankLocator
  strDSN = objBankLocator.GetBank(BankID)

  ' Run the stored procedure. Update the bank record.
  On Error Resume Next
  lngReturn = m_objDBHelper.RunSPReturnInteger( _
    strDSN, "sp_delete_Bank", _
    Array("@BankId_1", adSmallInt, adSizeSmallInt, ChangeBankId))

  If lngReturn = 0 Then
    DeleteBank = True
  Else
    DeleteBank = False
  End If

Clean_Up:
  Set objBankLocator = Nothing
  CtxSetComplete
  Exit Property

ErrorHandler:
  Debug.Print Err.Number
  RaiseError MODULE_NAME, "DeleteBank"
  GoTo Clean_Up
End Property
```

8. The next four properties deal with administrative tasks for WROBACards. The first is `VerifyCard` to verify the card account using the stored procedure `sp_verify_CardAccount_By_CardId`:

```
Public Property Get VerifyCard(ByVal BankID As Integer, _
  ByVal CardId As Long) As Long
' Verify that the selected card account exists at the selected bank

  Dim objBankLocator As Bank_DB.BankLocator
  Dim strDSN As String

  On Error GoTo ErrorHandler
```

```
    ' Locate the selected bank and get the DSN for it
    Set objBankLocator = New Bank_DB.BankLocator
    strDSN = objBankLocator.GetBank(BankID)

    If strDSN <> "" Then
      ' If the bank exists run the stored procedure.
      ' Returns the count of accounts that have this AccountID
      VerifyCard = m_objDBHelper.RunSPReturnInteger( _
        strDSN, "sp_verify_CardAccount_By_CardId", _
        Array("@CardId_1", adInteger, adSizeInteger, _
        CardId))
      CtxSetComplete
    Else
      VerifyCard = 0 'Set to no accounts
    End If

Clean_Up:
    Set objBankLocator = Nothing
    Exit Property

ErrorHandler:
    RaiseError MODULE_NAME, "VerifyCard"
    VerifyCard = 0 'Set to no accounts
    GoTo Clean_Up
End Property
```

9. Secondly, we have a property that allows us to delete cards. This property does *not*, however, delete the account history for that card. It begins by using the stored procedure sp_select_AccountId_By_CardId to select the card we've requested for deletion. After the card is chosen, three stored procedures, sp_delete_CardxAccount, sp_delete_BankAccount, and sp_delete_WROBACard, are then executed:

```
Public Property Get DeleteCard(ByVal BankID As Integer, _
    ByVal CardId As Long) As Boolean

    Dim objBankLocator As Bank_DB.BankLocator
    Dim recAccountID As ADODB.Recordset
    Dim lngAccountID As Long
    Dim lngReturn As Long
    Dim strDSN As String

    On Error GoTo ErrorHandler
    DeleteCard = False

    ' Locate the selected bank and get the DSN for it
    Set objBankLocator = New Bank_DB.BankLocator
    strDSN = objBankLocator.GetBank(BankID)

    ' Run the stored procedure. Delete all the related records.
    ' Leave the AccountHistory records as an audit trail.
    On Error Resume Next
```

```
    Set recAccountID = m_objDBHelper.RunSPReturnRS( _
        strDSN, "sp_select_AccountId_By_CardId", _
        Array("@CardId_1", adInteger, adSizeInteger, CardId))

    Do While Not recAccountID.EOF
        lngAccountID = recAccountID!AccountID

        m_objDBHelper.RunSP strDSN, "sp_delete_CardxAccount", _
            Array("@AccountId_1", adInteger, adSizeInteger, lngAccountID)

        recAccountID.MoveNext
    Loop

    recAccountID.MoveFirst

    Do While Not recAccountID.EOF
        lngAccountID = recAccountID!AccountID

        m_objDBHelper.RunSP strDSN, "sp_delete_BankAccount", _
            Array("@AccountId_1", adInteger, adSizeInteger, lngAccountID)

        recAccountID.MoveNext
    Loop

    m_objDBHelper.RunSP strDSN, "sp_delete_WROBACard", _
        Array("@CardId_1", adInteger, adSizeInteger, CardId)

    DeleteCard = True

Clean_Up:
    Set objBankLocator = Nothing
    CtxSetComplete
    Exit Property

ErrorHandler:
    Debug.Print Err.Number
    RaiseError MODULE_NAME, "DeleteCard"
    GoTo Clean_Up
End Property
```

10. The third method in this series is used for adding new cards to the database. It might look long and complicated (as might the stored procedures it calls), but that's only because of the amount of data that needs inserting into the tables. Here three stored procedures are required during the method:

```
Public Property Get AddCard(ByVal BankID As Integer, _
    ByVal AccountType As Integer, ByVal InitialBalance As Currency, _
    ByVal DailyLimit As Currency, ByVal OverDraft As Currency, _
    ByVal Password As String, ByVal CardId As Long, _
    ByVal AccountID As Long) As Boolean
```

```
    Dim objBankLocator As Bank_DB.BankLocator
    Dim lngReturn As Long
    Dim strDSN As String

    On Error GoTo ErrorHandler
    AddCard = False

    ' Locate the selected bank and get the DSN for it
    Set objBankLocator = New Bank_DB.BankLocator
    strDSN = objBankLocator.GetBank(BankID)

    ' Run the stored procedure. Insert a new card in the
    ' related tables.
    On Error Resume Next
    lngReturn = m_objDBHelper.RunSPReturnInteger( _
      strDSN, "sp_insert_WROBACard", _
      Array("@CardId_1", adInteger, adSizeInteger, CardId), _
      Array("@BankDesc_2", adChar, CARD_PASSWORD_SIZE, Password), _
      Array("@InvalidPasswordCnt_3", adTinyInt, adSizetinyInt, 0))

    If lngReturn = 0 Then
      lngReturn = m_objDBHelper.RunSPReturnInteger( _
        strDSN, "sp_insert_BankAccount", _
        Array("@AccountId_1", adInteger, adSizeInteger, AccountID), _
        Array("@AccountType_2", adTinyInt, adSizetinyInt, AccountType), _
        Array("@Balance_3", adCurrency, adSizeCurrency, InitialBalance), _
        Array("@Limit_4", adCurrency, adSizeCurrency, DailyLimit), _
        Array("@Remaining_5", adCurrency, adSizeCurrency, DailyLimit), _
        Array("@LastDate_6", adDBTimeStamp, adSizeDateTime, Now), _
        Array("@Overdraft_7", adCurrency, adSizeCurrency, OverDraft))
    End If

    If lngReturn = 0 Then
      lngReturn = m_objDBHelper.RunSPReturnInteger( _
        strDSN, "sp_insert_CardxAccount", _
        Array("@Card_1", adInteger, adSizeInteger, CardId), _
        Array("@AccountType_2", adTinyInt, adSizetinyInt, AccountType), _
        Array("@AccountID_3", adInteger, adSizeInteger, AccountID))
    End If

    If lngReturn = 0 Then
      AddCard = True
    Else
      AddCard = False
    End If

Clean_Up:
  Set objBankLocator = Nothing
  CtxSetComplete
  Exit Property

ErrorHandler:
  Debug.Print Err.Number
  RaiseError MODULE_NAME, "AddCard"
  GoTo Clean_Up
End Property
```

11. The last method in the series of card related coding is the `GetLastCardID` property. As we'll see later, this is used by the `GenerateCardID` function in the `Admin` module of the business tier component, `Bank_Bus`. This returns the last card ID assigned, and the `GenerateCardID` function then increments the account number by one:

```
Public Property Get GetLastCardID(ByVal BankID As Integer) As Long
    Dim objBankLocator As Bank_DB.BankLocator
    Dim strDSN As String

    On Error GoTo ErrorHandler

    ' Locate the selected bank and get the DSN for it
    Set objBankLocator = New Bank_DB.BankLocator
    strDSN = objBankLocator.GetBank(BankID)

    ' Run the stored procedure. Return a recordset of all the
    ' account types that are listed for this CardID
    On Error Resume Next
    GetLastCardID = m_objDBHelper.RunSPReturnInteger( _
        strDSN, "sp_select_Last_CardId")

Clean_Up:
    Set objBankLocator = Nothing
    CtxSetComplete
    Exit Property

ErrorHandler:
    Debug.Print Err.Number
    RaiseError MODULE_NAME, "GetLastCardID"
    GoTo Clean_Up
End Property
```

12. Our last job for this module is to add a method that retrieves the last account ID assigned. This is used in much the same manner as the `GetLastCardID` property. After the information is retrieved, another function is used to increment the value by one when creating a new account:

```
Public Property Get GetLastAccountId(ByVal BankID As Integer) As Long
    Dim objBankLocator As Bank_DB.BankLocator
    Dim strDSN As String

    On Error GoTo ErrorHandler

    ' Locate the selected bank and get the DSN for it
    Set objBankLocator = New Bank_DB.BankLocator
    strDSN = objBankLocator.GetBank(BankID)

    ' Run the stored procedure. Return a recordset of all the
    ' account types that are listed for this CardID
    On Error Resume Next
    GetLastAccountId = m_objDBHelper.RunSPReturnInteger( _
        strDSN, "sp_select_Last_AccountId")
```

```
Clean_Up:
   Set objBankLocator = Nothing
   CtxSetComplete
   Exit Property

ErrorHandler:
   Debug.Print Err.Number
   RaiseError MODULE_NAME, "GetLastAccountId"
   GoTo Clean_Up
End Property
```

How It Works

Although each WROBACard can only have two bank accounts associated with it, there is an administration AccountType as well. The GetAccountType property returns a recordset of the account types for a specific CardId. As we'll see later, in Chapter 14, this is used by the function SeeIfAdmin in the main menu form to check for administrator rights. As we saw when we created the database, an AccountType value of 0 correlates to an administration account, and thus, if this value is returned, the user is logged on to the administrator screens.

This method is quite interesting as an example of a row returning routine where the use of the helper routine RunSPRetunRS from DBHelper reduces the coding effort to a minimum. The sp_select_BankAccount_By_CardId stored procedure uses a series of inner joins to join four tables to retrieve the bank accounts associated with the WROBA card:

```
CREATE PROCEDURE sp_select_BankAccount_By_CardId (
@CardId_1 int)
AS
SELECT BankAccount.AccountId, AccountType.AccountTypeDesc,
   BankAccount.Balance, BankAccount.DailyWithdrawalLimit,
   BankAccount.DailyRemaining,
   BankAccount.LastWithdrawalDate,
   BankAccount.OverdraftLimit
FROM BankAccount INNER JOIN
   CardxAccount ON
   BankAccount.AccountId = CardxAccount.AccountId INNER JOIN
   WROBACard ON
   CardxAccount.CardId = WROBACard.CardId INNER JOIN
   AccountType ON
   CardxAccount.AccountType = AccountType.AccountType
WHERE (WROBACard.CardId = @CardId_1)
```

The result of the query would be something like this:

AccountId	AccountTypeDesc	Balance	DailyWithdrawalLim	DailyRemaining	LastWithdrawalDate	OverdraftLimit
20000	Administrator	0	0	0	5/31/2000 6:23:35 PM	0
20001	Checking	254	500	500	5/31/2000 6:23:35 PM	500
20002	Saving	2376	500	500	5/31/2000 6:23:35 PM	500
20003	Checking	56	1000	40	5/31/2000 6:23:35 PM	1500
20004	Saving	3236	500	340	5/31/2000 6:23:35 PM	500

The stored procedure, sp_select_AccountType, used in the GetAccountTypes property is very simple; it selects the AccountType and AccountTypeDesc columns from the AccountType table:

```
SELECT AccountType, AccountTypeDesc
FROM AccountType
WHERE (AccountTypeDesc <> 'Administrator')
```

And returns the following data:

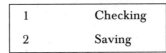

1	Checking
2	Saving

The administrator uses this when adding new cards, to display the types of customer accounts available (here just Checking or Saving). Since the administrator will not be adding more administrator accounts, we only need to have the Checking and Saving options returned.

Within the DeleteCard property, as we saw, three stored procedures are used. Each of these stored procedures is very basic, for instance the sp_delete_WROBACard procedure has the form:

```
Create PROCEDURE sp_delete_WROBACard(@CardId_1 int)
AS DELETE WROBACard
WHERE      ( CardId = @CardId_1)
```

Lastly, in this section let's pick apart some aspects of the lengthy AddCard method.

The first stored procedure is used to insert the data for a new card into the WROBACard table:

```
' Run the stored procedure. Insert a new card in the
' related tables.
On Error Resume Next
lngReturn = m_objDBHelper.RunSPReturnInteger( _
  strDSN, "sp_insert_WROBACard", _
  Array("@CardId_1", adInteger, adSizeInteger, CardId), _
  Array("@BankDesc_2", adChar, CARD_PASSWORD_SIZE, Password), _
  Array("@InvalidPasswordCnt_3", adTinyInt, adSizetinyInt, 0))
```

Then we insert data into the BankAccount table:

```
If lngReturn = 0 Then
  lngReturn = m_objDBHelper.RunSPReturnInteger( _
    strDSN, "sp_insert_BankAccount", _
    Array("@AccountId_1", adInteger, adSizeInteger, AccountID), _
    Array("@AccountType_2", adTinyInt, adSizetinyInt, AccountType), _
    Array("@Balance_3", adCurrency, adSizeCurrency, InitialBalance), _
    Array("@Limit_4", adCurrency, adSizeCurrency, DailyLimit), _
    Array("@Remaining_5", adCurrency, adSizeCurrency, DailyLimit), _
    Array("@LastDate_6", adDBTimeStamp, adSizeDateTime, Now), _
    Array("@Overdraft_7", adCurrency, adSizeCurrency, OverDraft))
End If
```

Finally, we insert the card and account numbers into the `CardxAcccount` table, as well as the account type. The card is then added to the database:

```
If lngReturn = 0 Then
  lngReturn = m_objDBHelper.RunSPReturnInteger( _
    strDSN, "sp_insert_CardxAccount", _
    Array("@Card_1", adInteger, adSizeInteger, CardId), _
    Array("@AccountType_2", adTinyInt, adSizetinyInt, AccountType), _
    Array("@AccountID_3", adInteger, adSizeInteger, AccountID))
End If

If lngReturn = 0 Then
  AddCard = True
Else
  AddCard = False
End If
```

The Bank Class Module

The UML class diagram for the `Bank` class is shown here. The module is used for interacting with the Bank, and facilitates tasks such as logging in, changing the password, and tracking attempts to logon as well as account history and balance.

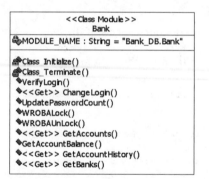

By now, you're probably getting familiar with the coding approach being used, with the calls to the `DBHelper` module methods addressing the ADO coding issues, and stored procedures in the database performing the retrieval and manipulation of the data.

Try It Out – Coding the Bank Module

1. Add another class module, name it Bank, and set the MTSTransactionMode to 1 – NoTransactions.

2. We begin with the usual constant setting and initialization. Note the importance of commenting to explain exactly what is going on at a particular point in code. Here the Enum listing correlates to data hard coded into the TxType table, and to ensure consistency needs to be kept synchronized:

```
Option Explicit

' Class module in data tier

Const MODULE_NAME As String = "Bank_DB.Bank"

' NOTE: THESE VALUES CORRESPOND
' TO ENTRIES IN THE TxType TABLE
' THIS ENUM AND THE TxType TABLE
' MUST BE KEPT SYNCHRONIZED!!!
Public Enum ETransactionType
  txTransfer = 1
  txBillPayment = 2
End Enum

Private m_objDBHelper As DBHelper

Private Sub Class_Initialize()
' Initialize the helper object to run stored procedures
   Set m_objDBHelper = CreateObject("Bank_DB.DBHelper")
End Sub

Private Sub Class_Terminate()
' Destroy the helper object
   Set m_objDBHelper = Nothing
End Sub
```

3. The VerifyLogin function is used to verify that the login credentials entered by the customer match with those on the database (as we'll see later, it is effectively used by the private function ValidateUser in the FLogin form via a pass through call in the business tier):

```
Public Function VerifyLogin(ByVal BankID As Integer, _
  ByVal CardId As Long, ByVal Password As String, _
  ByRef InvalidCount As Variant) As Boolean
' Verify the WROBA login

  Dim strUserInfo As String
  Dim objBankLocator As Bank_DB.BankLocator
  Dim strDSN As String
  Dim cmd As ADODB.Command

  On Error GoTo ErrorHandler

  ' Pessimistic assumption of login failure
  VerifyLogin = False
```

```
    ' Locate the selected bank and get the DSN for it
    Set objBankLocator = New Bank_DB.BankLocator
    strDSN = objBankLocator.GetBank(BankID)

    ' The following code directly runs the stored procedure.
    ' Set up Command and Connection objects
    Set cmd = CtxCreateObject("ADODB.Command")

    'Run the procedure
    cmd.ActiveConnection = strDSN
    cmd.CommandText = "sp_select_WROBACard_PwdCnt"
    cmd.CommandType = adCmdStoredProc

    ' Set up the parameters for the procedure call
    With cmd
      .Parameters.Append .CreateParameter(, adInteger, _
        adParamReturnValue)
      .Parameters.Append .CreateParameter("@CardId_1", _
        adInteger, adParamInput, 4, CardId)
      .Parameters.Append .CreateParameter("@Password_2", _
        adChar, adParamInput, 10, Password)
      .Parameters.Append .CreateParameter("@InvalidPasswordCnt_3", _
        adInteger, adParamOutput, 4)
    End With

    ' Execute the stored procedure directly
    cmd.Execute , , ADODB.adExecuteNoRecords

    If cmd.Parameters(0).Value <> 0 Then
      InvalidCount = cmd.Parameters(3).Value
      VerifyLogin = True
    End If

Clean_Up:
    Set objBankLocator = Nothing
    Set cmd.ActiveConnection = Nothing
    Set cmd = Nothing
    CtxSetComplete

    Exit Function

ErrorHandler:
    RaiseError MODULE_NAME, "VerifyLogin"
    GoTo Clean_Up
End Function
```

4. The `ChangeLogin` property facilitates the changing of passwords:

```
Public Property Get ChangeLogin(ByVal BankID As Integer, _
  ByVal CardId As Long, ByVal Password As String) As Boolean
' Verify the WROBA login

  Dim strUserInfo As String
  Dim objBankLocator As Bank_DB.BankLocator
  Dim strDSN As String
  Dim cmd As ADODB.Command

  On Error GoTo ErrorHandler

  ' Pessimistic assumption of failure
  ChangeLogin = False

  ' Locate the selected bank and get the DSN for it
  Set objBankLocator = New Bank_DB.BankLocator
  strDSN = objBankLocator.GetBank(BankID)

  ' The following code directly runs the stored procedure.
  ' Set up Command and Connection objects
  Set cmd = CtxCreateObject("ADODB.Command")

  'Run the procedure
  cmd.ActiveConnection = strDSN
  cmd.CommandText = "sp_update_WROBACard_Pwd"
  cmd.CommandType = adCmdStoredProc

  ' Set up the parameters for the procedure call
  With cmd
    .Parameters.Append .CreateParameter(, adInteger, _
      adParamReturnValue)
    .Parameters.Append .CreateParameter("@CardId_1", _
      adInteger, adParamInput, 4, CardId)
    .Parameters.Append .CreateParameter("@Password_2", _
      adChar, adParamInput, 10, Password)
  End With

  ' Execute the stored procedure directly
  cmd.Execute , , ADODB.adExecuteNoRecords

  If cmd.Parameters(0).Value = 0 Then
    ChangeLogin = False
  Else
    ChangeLogin = True
  End If

Clean_Up:
  Set objBankLocator = Nothing
  Set cmd.ActiveConnection = Nothing
  Set cmd = Nothing
  CtxSetComplete

  Exit Property

ErrorHandler:
  RaiseError MODULE_NAME, "ChangeLogin"
  GoTo Clean_Up
End Property
```

5. Next, we have the `UpdatePasswordCount` procedure that is used to increase the number stored in the `InvalidPasswordCnt` column of the `WROBACard` table each time the wrong password is entered. As we'll see when we cover the business logic, after five unsuccessful attempts to use invalid passwords the user is locked out of the database and the application ends:

```
Public Sub UpdatePasswordCount(ByVal BankID As Integer, _
  ByVal CardId As Long, ByVal InvalidCount As Integer)

    Dim objBankLocator As Bank_DB.BankLocator
    Dim strDSN As String

    On Error GoTo ErrorHandler

    ' Locate the selected bank and get the DSN for it
    Set objBankLocator = New Bank_DB.BankLocator
    strDSN = objBankLocator.GetBank(BankID)

    ' Run the stored procedure
    m_objDBHelper.RunSP strDSN, "sp_update_WROBACard_PwdCnt", _
      Array("@CardId_1", adInteger, adSizeInteger, CardId), _
      Array("@InvalidPasswordCnt_2", adTinyInt, adSizetinyInt, _
      InvalidCount)

Clean_Up:
  Set objBankLocator = Nothing
  CtxSetComplete
  Exit Sub

ErrorHandler:
  RaiseError MODULE_NAME, "UpdatePasswordCount"
  GoTo Clean_Up
End Sub
```

6. The next two properties we code concern the enabling and disabling of WROBA cards. Firstly, if a card is lost or stolen, or the account is closed, the administrator needs to have the facility to lock the card and stop that card from accessing the associated accounts:

```
Public Sub WROBALock(ByVal BankID As Integer, ByVal CardId As Long)

    Dim objBankLocator As Bank_DB.BankLocator
    Dim strDSN As String

    On Error GoTo ErrorHandler

    ' Locate the selected bank and get the DSN for it
    Set objBankLocator = New Bank_DB.BankLocator
    strDSN = objBankLocator.GetBank(BankID)

    ' Run the stored procedure
    m_objDBHelper.RunSP strDSN, "sp_insert_TxLock", _
      Array("@BankId_1", adSmallInt, adSizeSmallInt, BankID), _
      Array("@CardId_2", adInteger, adSizeInteger, CardId)
```

```
Clean_Up:
  Set objBankLocator = Nothing
  CtxSetComplete
  Exit Sub

ErrorHandler:
  Debug.Print Err.Number
  RaiseError MODULE_NAME, "WROBALock"
  GoTo Clean_Up
End Sub
```

7. All new cards are locked and need unlocking before use. Additionally, if the user does not properly exit the application, the card can remain locked. This method clears the rowset of the card that is locked, resulting in the card being unlocked and usable:

```
Public Sub WROBAUnLock(ByVal BankID As Integer, ByVal CardId As Long)

  Dim objBankLocator As Bank_DB.BankLocator
  Dim strDSN As String

  On Error GoTo ErrorHandler

  ' Locate the selected bank and get the DSN for it
  Set objBankLocator = New Bank_DB.BankLocator
  strDSN = objBankLocator.GetBank(BankID)

  ' Run the stored procedure
  m_objDBHelper.RunSP strDSN, "sp_delete_TxLock", _
    Array("@BankId_1", adSmallInt, adSizeSmallInt, BankID), _
    Array("@CardId_2", adInteger, adSizeInteger, CardId)

Clean_Up:
  Set objBankLocator = Nothing
  CtxSetComplete
  Exit Sub

ErrorHandler:
  RaiseError MODULE_NAME, "WROBAUnLock"
  GoTo Clean_Up
End Sub
```

8. We now need to code a number of methods that will allow us to access account information. First up, a method that obtains the accounts themselves:

```
Public Property Get GetAccounts(ByVal BankID As Integer, _
  ByVal CardId As Long) As ADODB.Recordset

  Dim objBankLocator As Bank_DB.BankLocator
  Dim strDSN As String
```

```
    On Error GoTo ErrorHandler

    ' Locate the selected bank and get the DSN for it
    Set objBankLocator = New Bank_DB.BankLocator
    strDSN = objBankLocator.GetBank(BankID)

    ' Run the stored procedure
    Set GetAccounts = m_objDBHelper.RunSPReturnRS(strDSN, _
      "sp_select_BankAccount_By_CardId", _
      Array("@CardId_1", adInteger, adSizeInteger, CardId))

Clean_Up:
    Set objBankLocator = Nothing
    CtxSetComplete
    Exit Property

ErrorHandler:
    Set GetAccounts = Nothing
    RaiseError MODULE_NAME, "GetAccounts"
    GoTo Clean_Up
End Property
```

9. One of the important parts of the application is its ability to display the account status information to a customer – the following method is used to enable this information to be retrieved from the `BigBank` database:

```
Public Sub GetAccountBalance(ByVal BankID As Integer, _
  ByVal AccountID As Long, ByRef AccountTypeDesc As Variant, _
  ByRef Balance As Variant, ByRef DailyRemaining As Variant, _
  ByRef OverdraftLimit As Variant)

  Dim objBankLocator As Bank_DB.BankLocator
  Dim strDSN As String
  Dim cmd As ADODB.Command

  On Error GoTo ErrorHandler

  ' Locate the selected bank and get the DSN for it
  Set objBankLocator = New Bank_DB.BankLocator
  strDSN = objBankLocator.GetBank(BankID)

  ' The following code directly runs the stored procedure.
  ' Set up Command and Connection objects
  Set cmd = New ADODB.Command

  ' Init the ADO objects & the stored proc parameters
  cmd.ActiveConnection = strDSN
  cmd.CommandText = "sp_select_BankAccount_By_AccountId"
  cmd.CommandType = adCmdStoredProc
```

```
      ' Add input parameters
      cmd.Parameters.Append cmd.CreateParameter("@AccountId_1", _
        adInteger, adParamInput, adSizeInteger, AccountID)

      ' Add output parameters
      cmd.Parameters.Append cmd.CreateParameter("@AccountTypeDesc_2", _
        adChar, adParamOutput, 15)
      cmd.Parameters.Append cmd.CreateParameter("@Balance_3", _
        adCurrency, adParamOutput)
      cmd.Parameters.Append cmd.CreateParameter("@DailyRemaining_4", _
        adCurrency, adParamOutput)
      cmd.Parameters.Append cmd.CreateParameter("@OverdraftLimit_5", _
        adCurrency, adParamOutput)

      ' Execute directly without a resulting recordset and
      ' pull out the return parameters
      cmd.Execute , , adExecuteNoRecords

      AccountTypeDesc = cmd.Parameters("@AccountTypeDesc_2").Value
      Balance = cmd.Parameters("@Balance_3").Value
      DailyRemaining = cmd.Parameters("@DailyRemaining_4").Value
      OverdraftLimit = cmd.Parameters("@OverdraftLimit_5").Value

      ' Disconnect the recordset, and clean up
Clean_Up:
      Set cmd.ActiveConnection = Nothing
      Set cmd = Nothing

      Set objBankLocator = Nothing
      CtxSetComplete
      Exit Sub

ErrorHandler:
      RaiseError MODULE_NAME, "GetAccountBalance"
      GoTo Clean_Up
End Sub
```

10. Similarly, data regarding the history of the account needs to be retrieved:

```
Public Property Get GetAccountHistory(ByVal BankID As Integer, _
      ByVal AccountID As Long, ByVal MaxTransactionDate As Date) _
      As ADODB.Recordset

      Dim objBankLocator As Bank_DB.BankLocator
      Dim strDSN As String

      On Error GoTo ErrorHandler

      ' Locate the selected bank and get the DSN for it
      Set objBankLocator = New Bank_DB.BankLocator
      strDSN = objBankLocator.GetBank(BankID)
```

```
    ' Run the stored procedure
    Set GetAccountHistory = m_objDBHelper.RunSPReturnRS(strDSN, _
      "sp_select_AccountHistory_By_AccountId", _
      Array("@AccountId_1", adInteger, adSizeInteger, AccountID), _
      Array("@MaxTxDate_2", adDBTimeStamp, adSizeDateTime, _
      MaxTransactionDate))

Clean_Up:
    Set objBankLocator = Nothing
    CtxSetComplete
    Exit Property

ErrorHandler:
    Set GetAccountHistory = Nothing
    RaiseError MODULE_NAME, "GetAccountHistory"
    GoTo Clean_Up
End Property
```

11. Lastly for this module, we need to add a method that will enable us to get hold of information about the banks we have in our network:

```
Public Property Get GetBanks(ByVal BankID As Integer) As ADODB.Recordset

    Dim objBankLocator As Bank_DB.BankLocator
    Dim strDSN As String

    On Error GoTo ErrorHandler

    ' Locate the selected bank and get the DSN for it
    Set objBankLocator = New Bank_DB.BankLocator
    strDSN = objBankLocator.GetBank(BankID)

    ' Run the stored procedure
    Set GetBanks = m_objDBHelper.RunSPReturnRS(strDSN, _
      "sp_select_Bank")

Clean_Up:
    Set objBankLocator = Nothing
    CtxSetComplete
    Exit Property

ErrorHandler:
    Set GetBanks = Nothing
    RaiseError MODULE_NAME, "GetBanks"
    GoTo Clean_Up
End Property
```

How It Works

Of interest in this module is the `UpdatePasswordCount` method, which is an example of a non-row returning procedure. The stored procedure used makes use of an UPDATE statement to update the invalid password count in the database if a user enters the wrong password:

```
CREATE PROCEDURE sp_update_WROBACard_PwdCnt
   (@CardId_1      int,
    @InvalidPasswordCnt_2      tinyint)

AS UPDATE WROBACard

SET InvalidPasswordCnt  = @InvalidPasswordCnt_2

WHERE
   ( CardId = @CardId_1)
```

Here the RunSP helper method is used. The arrays in the code send the CardId and the number of unsuccessful attempts to logon to the stored procedure, so the database can increment the count in the InvalidPasswordCount column:

```
' Run the stored procedure
m_objDBHelper.RunSP strDSN, "sp_update_WROBACard_PwdCnt", _
   Array("@CardId_1", adInteger, adSizeInteger, CardId), _
   Array("@InvalidPasswordCnt_2", adTinyInt, adSizetinyInt, _
   InvalidCount)
```

BankLocator Class Module

This module contains just one main procedure, so we're not showing the UML class diagram. However, the method may very well be considered as one of the most important ones in the project – the property to create the connection to the server and database.

Try It Out – Coding the BankLocator Module

1. Add another class module, name it BankLocator and, once again, set the MTSTransactionMode to 1 – NoTransactions. Here we only have a small amount of code to add, but as it's so important, we'll go through it in detail:

```
Option Explicit

' Class module in data tier

Const MODULE_NAME As String = "Bank_DB.BankLocator"

Private m_objDBHelper As DBHelper

Private Sub Class_Initialize()
' Initialize the helper object to run stored procedures
   Set m_objDBHelper = CreateObject("Bank_DB.DBHelper")
End Sub

Private Sub Class_Terminate()
' Destroy the helper object
   Set m_objDBHelper = Nothing
End Sub
```

```
Public Property Get GetBank(ByVal BankID As Long) As String

  On Error GoTo ErrorHandler

  Select Case BankID
  ' Only Big Bank is implemented for the case study
  Case 1 ' BankID for Big Bank
    ' We can use the native OLEDB provider for SQL Server

    GetBank = "Provider=SQLOLEDB;Data Source=(local);Initial" _
      & " Catalog=BigBank;User Id=sa;" _
      & "Password=;Connect Timeout=3"

    'Or the OLEDB provider for ODBC

    'GetBank = "Provider=MSDASQL;" _
      & "DRIVER=SQL Server;" _
      & "SERVER=(local);" _
      & "DATABASE=BigBank;" _
      & "UID=sa;PWD=;"

    ' Or you can use a DSN instead of a OLEDB connection string
    'GetBank = "DSN=MyWROBA"
  Case Else
    GetBank = ""
  End Select

Clean_Up:
  CtxSetComplete
  Exit Property

ErrorHandler:
  RaiseError MODULE_NAME, "GetBank"
  GoTo Clean_Up
End Property
```

How It Works

First off, we have the standard initialization routine, but after that we provide three separate ways of providing the GetBank connection string:

❑   Using the OLE DB provider for SQL Server

❑   Using the OLE DB provider for ODBC and the ODBC driver for SQL Server

❑   Using a DSN connection

The connection string options are entered in the preferred order, meaning connecting to the SQL server via the OLE DB provider is usually the best method, and using the DSN is the least desirable method. Thus in our code the second and third methods are commented out in code.

The OLE DB provider is the best method as it connects directly to the database and is thus quicker than connecting via ODBC (which, as we saw in the previous chapter, adds an extra layer to the architecture).

The DSN connection is the least desirable, since the client machines need the database set-up for the connection from the Data Source applet in the Control Panel. Naturally, your case may vary, and you may have a valid reason for using DSN.

> **You will need to remember to change the name of the Server or DSN string to the correct name. If the server software is running on your workstation, you can use (local) as the server name.**

The code `"UID=sa;PWD=;"` *stands for User ID, which here we have as* `sa` *(system administrator), and password, which we left blank. If your username is different, or you selected a password, it should be entered on this line.*

The Payees Class Module

We have one last class module to add – `Payees`. As we can glean from the class diagram, this one handles payee issues, including adding, editing, and deleting payees:

```
                  <<Class Module>>
                       Payees
  MODULE_NAME : String = "Bank_DB.Payees"
  PAYEEDESC_SIZE : Integer = 30
  PAYEEID_SIZE : Integer = 36
  UPDSUCCESS = 0
  UPDERROR = 1

  Class_Initialize()
  Class_Terminate()
   <<Get>> MatchPayee()
   <<Get>> InsertPayees()
   <<Get>> EditPayee()
   <<Get>> DeletePayee()
   <<Get>> GetAllPayees()
```

Try It Out – Coding the Payees Module

1. Add a class module called **Payees** to the project, and ensure the MTSTransactionMode property is 1 – NoTransactions. Add the following straightforward code:

```
Option Explicit

' Class module in data tier

Const MODULE_NAME As String = "Bank_DB.Payees"


' Size for strings in table
Const PAYEEDESC_SIZE As Integer = 30
Const PAYEEID_SIZE   As Integer = 36
```

```
Private m_objDBHelper As DBHelper

Private Const UPDSUCCESS = 0
Private Const UPDERROR = 1

Private Sub Class_Initialize()
' Initialize the helper object to run stored procedures
   Set m_objDBHelper = CreateObject("Bank_DB.DBHelper")
End Sub

Private Sub Class_Terminate()
' Destroy the helper object
   Set m_objDBHelper = Nothing
End Sub
```

2. Firstly, we add the functionality to enable the Payee table to be checked to see if any payees exist for that account already. If not (`lngPayees = 0`) then a payee can be created (`MatchPayee = True`). This is because each payee needs an account for the customer to transfer money to. If additional accounts are created from the administrator logon, new payees can be added – one for each new account.

```
Public Property Get MatchPayee(ByVal BankID As Integer, _
   ByVal CardId As Long) As Boolean

   Dim objBankLocator As Bank_DB.BankLocator
   Dim strDSN As String
   Dim lngPayees As Long

   On Error GoTo ErrorHandler
   MatchPayee = False

   ' Locate the selected bank and get the DSN for it
   Set objBankLocator = New Bank_DB.BankLocator
   strDSN = objBankLocator.GetBank(BankID)

   If strDSN <> "" Then
     lngPayees = m_objDBHelper.RunSPReturnInteger( _
       strDSN, "sp_verify_Payee_By_CardId", _
       Array("@CardId_1", adInteger, adSizeInteger, _
       CardId))
     If lngPayees = 0 Then
       MatchPayee = True
     End If
   End If

Clean_Up:
   Set objBankLocator = Nothing
   CtxSetComplete
   Exit Property

ErrorHandler:
   RaiseError MODULE_NAME, "MatchPayee"
   GoTo Clean_Up
End Property
```

3. We next have another series of methods, all to carry out self-explanatory operations. Firstly for adding new payees:

```
Public Property Get InsertPayees(ByVal PayeeDescription As String, _
   ByVal AccountID As Long, ByVal DefaultAmount As Currency, _
   ByVal BankID As Integer, ByVal CardId As Long, _
   ByVal WROBACardID As Long) As Long

   Dim objBankLocator As Bank_DB.BankLocator
   Dim strDSN As String

   On Error GoTo ErrorHandler

   ' Locate the selected bank and get the DSN for it
   Set objBankLocator = New Bank_DB.BankLocator
   strDSN = objBankLocator.GetBank(BankID)
   If strDSN <> "" Then
     On Error Resume Next
     ' Run the stored procedure
     InsertPayees = m_objDBHelper.RunSPReturnInteger( _
       strDSN, "sp_insert_Payee", _
       Array("@CardId_2", adInteger, adSizeInteger, CardId), _
       Array("@PayeeDesc_3", adChar, PAYEEDESC_SIZE, _
         PayeeDescription), _
       Array("@BankId_4", adSmallInt, adSizeSmallInt, BankID), _
       Array("@AccountId_5", adInteger, adSizeInteger, AccountID), _
       Array("@DefaultAmount_6", adCurrency, adSizeCurrency, _
         DefaultAmount), _
       Array("@WROBACardId_7", adInteger, adSizeInteger, WROBACardID))

     If InsertPayees > 0 Then InsertPayees = UPDERROR
   Else
     InsertPayees = UPDERROR
   End If


Clean_Up:
   Set objBankLocator = Nothing
   CtxSetComplete
   Exit Property

ErrorHandler:
   RaiseError MODULE_NAME, "InsertPayees"
   InsertPayees = UPDERROR
   GoTo Clean_Up
End Property
```

4. Secondly for editing payee information, (like changing the payment amount):

```
Public Property Get EditPayee(ByVal PayeeID As String, _
  ByVal PayeeDescription As String, ByVal DefaultAmount As Currency, _
  ByVal BankID As Integer) As Long

  Dim objBankLocator As Bank_DB.BankLocator
  Dim strDSN As String

  On Error GoTo ErrorHandler

  ' Locate the selected bank and get the DSN for it
  Set objBankLocator = New Bank_DB.BankLocator
  strDSN = objBankLocator.GetBank(BankID)

  If strDSN <> "" Then
    ' Run the stored procedure
    EditPayee = m_objDBHelper.RunSPReturnInteger( _
      strDSN, "sp_update_payee", _
      Array("@PayeeId_1", adChar, PAYEEID_SIZE, PayeeID), _
      Array("@PayeeDesc_2", adChar, PAYEEDESC_SIZE, _
        PayeeDescription), _
      Array("@DefaultAmount_3", adCurrency, adSizeCurrency, _
        DefaultAmount))
  Else
    EditPayee = UPDERROR
  End If

Clean_Up:
  Set objBankLocator = Nothing
  CtxSetComplete
  Exit Property

ErrorHandler:
  RaiseError MODULE_NAME, "EditPayee"
  EditPayee = UPDERROR
  GoTo Clean_Up
End Property
```

5. Thirdly, for removing payees from the database:

```
Public Property Get DeletePayee(ByVal PayeeID As String, _
  ByVal BankID As Integer, ByVal PayeeDescription As String) _
  As Long

  Dim objBankLocator As Bank_DB.BankLocator
  Dim strDSN As String

  On Error GoTo ErrorHandler
```

```
      ' Locate the selected bank and get the DSN for it
      Set objBankLocator = New Bank_DB.BankLocator
      strDSN = objBankLocator.GetBank(BankID)

      If strDSN <> "" Then
        ' Run the stored procedure
        DeletePayee = m_objDBHelper.RunSPReturnInteger( _
          strDSN, "sp_delete_payee", _
          Array("@PayeeId_1", adChar, PAYEEID_SIZE, PayeeID))
      Else
        DeletePayee = UPDERROR
      End If

Clean_Up:
    Set objBankLocator = Nothing
    CtxSetComplete
    Exit Property

ErrorHandler:
    RaiseError MODULE_NAME, "DeletePayee"
    DeletePayee = UPDERROR
    GoTo Clean_Up
End Property
```

6. Lastly for this module (and the data tier!) we have a method that returns a list of all payees – a function that means, in the user tier, the customer may be presented with a set of choices from which the payee's name can be selected:

```
Public Property Get GetAllPayees(ByVal BankID As Integer, _
    ByVal CardId As Long) As ADODB.Recordset

    Dim objBankLocator As Bank_DB.BankLocator
    Dim strDSN As String

    On Error GoTo ErrorHandler
    Set GetAllPayees = Nothing

    ' Locate the selected bank and get the DSN for it
    Set objBankLocator = New Bank_DB.BankLocator
    strDSN = objBankLocator.GetBank(BankID)

    ' Run the stored procedure. Return a recordset of all the payees
    ' that are in the table for this WROBA card
    On Error Resume Next
    Set GetAllPayees = m_objDBHelper.RunSPReturnRS( _
      strDSN, "sp_select_All_Payees", _
      Array("@CardId_1", adInteger, adSizeInteger, CardId))

Clean_Up:
    Set objBankLocator = Nothing
    CtxSetComplete
    Exit Property
ErrorHandler:
    RaiseError MODULE_NAME, "GetAllPayees"
    GoTo Clean_Up
End Property
```

Creating the ActiveX DLL

Our project now has all the modules needed and should look like this:

The `Bank_DB` project does not reference the `Bank_Bus` ActiveX DLL, but the `Bank_Bus` project does reference the `Bank_DB` ActiveX DLL, as we'll see in the next chapter.

To provide the DLL reference that the business services tier requires, we need to compile the `Bank_DB` project separately and then reference the resulting `Bank_DB` DLL in the references for the `Bank_Bus` project.

Try It Out – Creating Bank_DB.dll

1. Return to the `Bank_DB` project. The next step depends on what you have done so far. If you haven't yet compiled the project then it needs to be compiled (via **File | Make Bank_DB.dll**) with the **Version Compatibility** set to **Project Compatibility** (see the *Try It Out – Setting the Project Properties* section at the start of this section). After the project has been compiled to produce an ActiveX DLL, place a copy of the DLL in the GUID project subfolder (if you're using the folder system we suggest).

2. The next step (or the first step if you've already completed step 1) is to change the project version compatibility to **Binary Compatibility**. Binary Compatibility is used to maintain compatibility with projects that have been compiled with references to the DLL.

The DLL is now ready to be used in our next chapter when we code the business tier component.

The Bank_DB DLL as it now stands contains the core functionality of the case study as you'll find it if you download the files from the web site. However, before we finish this chapter, there's a bit of extra functionality that you might want to implement.

An Aside – Logging Errors

If you remember, back in Chapter 5 we created the CLogger component, which wrote logging information to a text file. At the end of that chapter, we pointed out that we should really be writing that information to a database, but at the time we didn't quite have the knowledge to do that. What we're going to do in this section is implement a similar kind of functionality, to log error information to the BigBank database.

> *Again, note that the information we show here is an enhancement to the WROBA case study, and has not been implemented in the code download. We do however think it's an interesting aside, and it shows the flexibility of the coding approach taken for the case study.*

As we have a database supporting our application, we have a resource manager we can easily leverage to support information logging and persist state information. To do this we're going to have to:

❑ Create a new table in the BigBank database

❑ Add a stored procedure to the database

❑ Add a class module, Logger, to the Bank_DB project

❑ Make a slight modification to the LogError method in the MContext module

So if you want to have a go at this ...

Try It Out – Using SQL Server for Logging Errors

First, we'll need to create a new table and a new stored procedure in our database. If you want to use a SQL script to do this, you'll find one called `Logger.sql` listed in Appendix A. It's also in the code download of the case study. If you use this script, you can skip straight ahead to point 5 of this Try It Out. Alternatively, create the table and stored procedure as follows:

1. Open up the SQL Server Enterprise Manager, and drill down to the BigBank database. Right-click on the Tables node, and select New Table…:

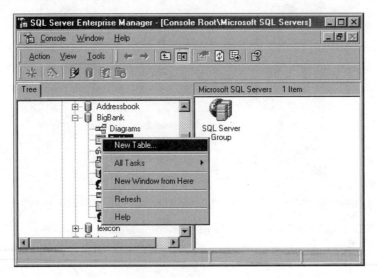

2. Name the new table ErrorLog and click OK:

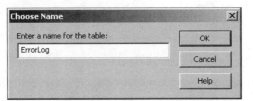

3. Add the following columns to the databse:

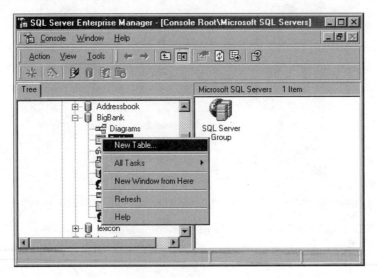

4. Close the table design view, right-click on Stored Procedures and chose New Stored Procedure. Type the following stored procedure into the window:

```
CREATE Procedure sp_insert_LogError
     (@ErrorDate_1 datetime,
      @ErrorNumber_2 int,
      @ErrorSource_3 varchar,
      @ErrorDescription_4 varchar,
      @Message_5 varchar)

AS INSERT INTO ErrorLog
     ( LogTime,
       ErrorNumber,
       ErrorSource,
       ErrorDescription,
       Message)

VALUES
     (@ErrorDate_1,
      @ErrorNumber_2,
      @ErrorSource_3,
      @ErrorDescription_4,
      @Message_5)
```

And click **OK** to add it to the database.

5. Next open up the `Bank_DB` project, and add a new class module. Name this class **Logger**.

6. Add the following code to this module:

```
Option Explicit

' Class module in data tier

Const MODULE_NAME As String = "Bank_DB.Logger"

' Size for strings in table
Const ERRSTRING_SIZE As Integer = 100

Private m_objDBHelper As DBHelper

Public Function LogError(ErrorNumber As Long, _
                         ErrorSource As String, _
                         ErrorDescription As String, _
                         Notes As String) As Boolean

  Dim objBankLocator As Bank_DB.BankLocator
  Dim strDSN As String

  ' Locate the selected bank and get the DSN for it
  Set objBankLocator = New Bank_DB.BankLocator
  strDSN = objBankLocator.GetBank(1)
```

```
' Run the stored procedure
m_objDBHelper.RunSP strDSN, "sp_insert_LogError", _
   Array("@ErrorDate_1", adDBTimeStamp, adSizeDateTime, Now), _
   Array("@ErrorNumber_2", adInteger, adSizeInteger, ErrorNumber), _
   Array("@ErrorSource_3", adVarChar, ERRSTRING_SIZE, ErrorSource), _
   Array("@ErrorDescription_4", adVarChar, ERRSTRING_SIZE, _
         ErrorDescription), _
   Array("@Message_5", adVarChar, ERRSTRING_SIZE, Notes)

   Set objBankLocator = Nothing

End Function
```

7. And make the following modifications to the `LogError` routine in the `MContext` module:

```
Private Sub LogError(ErrorNumber As Long, ErrorSource As String, _
                     ErrorDescription As String, _
                     Optional Notes As String = "")

   Dim objErrorLogger As Bank_DB.Logger
   Dim blnError As Boolean

   Set objErrorLogger = CtxCreateObject("Bank_DB.Logger")
   blnError = objErrorLogger.LogError(ErrorNumber, ErrorSource, _
                                      ErrorDescription, Notes)
   If Not blnError Then

      App.LogEvent vbNewLine & "An error has occured in this application," _
         & "could not log to database." & vbNewLine & "Error Number:" _
         & ErrorNumber & vbNewLine & vbNewLine & "Description:" _
         & vbNewLine & ErrorDescription & vbNewLine & vbNewLine _
         & "Source: " & vbNewLine & ErrorSource _
         & vbNewLine & vbNewLine & "Notes: " & vbNewLine & Notes

   End If

   CtxSetComplete
   Set objErrorLogger = Nothing

End Sub
```

8. Save your code and compile the DLL, as detailed in our last Try It Out.

How It Works

We created a new table in our `BigBank` database called `ErrorLog`, and a stored procedure called `sp_insert_LogError`. This procedure writes information about the error to the `ErrorLog` table, including the place and time it occurs, and the number and description of the error:

```
AS INSERT INTO ErrorLog
      ( LogTime,
        ErrorNumber,
        ErrorSource,
        ErrorDescription,
        Message)
```

This is the same information that we already pass into our `LogError` sub in `MContext`:

```
Private Sub LogError(ErrorNumber As Long, ErrorSource As String, _
                     ErrorDescription As String, _
                     Optional Notes As String = "")
```

In the `LogError` method, we added code to log the error from either the `RaiseError` method (for errors not under transactional control) or the `CtxRaiseError` method (for errors under transactional control) to the new `LogError` database table.

We first make a call to the `Logger` class:

```
Dim objErrorLogger As Bank_DB.Logger
Dim blnError As Boolean

Set objErrorLogger = CtxCreateObject("Bank_DB.Logger")
blnError = objErrorLogger.LogError(ErrorNumber, ErrorSource, _
                                   ErrorDescription, Notes)
```

In `Logger`, we define a constant `ERRSTRING_SIZE` as an Integer with a value of 100:

```
Private m_objDBHelper As DBHelper
```

This will be used to set the size of the strings written to the error log table to match the size established for the Varchar columns of the error log table.

We set up our connection as usual:

```
Dim objBankLocator As Bank_DB.BankLocator
Dim strDSN As String

' Locate the selected bank and get the DSN for it
Set objBankLocator = New Bank_DB.BankLocator
strDSN = objBankLocator.GetBank(1)
```

Notice that we use a constant of 1 to access the database connection string. This accesses the "home database", which is always given an account number of 1.

We then run the new stored procedure, passing it the error information it requires:

```
m_objDBHelper.RunSP strDSN, "sp_insert_LogError", _
   Array("@ErrorDate_1", adDBTimeStamp, adSizeDateTime, Now), _
   Array("@ErrorNumber_2", adInteger, adSizeInteger, ErrorNumber), _
   Array("@ErrorSource_3", adVarChar, ERRSTRING_SIZE, ErrorSource), _
   Array("@ErrorDescription_4", adVarChar, ERRSTRING_SIZE, _
         ErrorDescription), _
   Array("@Message_5", adVarChar, ERRSTRING_SIZE, Notes)
```

469

Back in `MContext`, if for some reason the call to the stored procedure didn't work (`blnError` is `false`), the information is written to the application log instead:

```
If Not blnError Then

    App.LogEvent vbNewLine & "An error has occured in this application," _
        & "could not log to database." & vbNewLine & "Error Number:" _
        & ErrorNumber & vbNewLine & vbNewLine & "Description:" _
        & vbNewLine & ErrorDescription & vbNewLine & vbNewLine _
        & "Source: " & vbNewLine & ErrorSource _
        & vbNewLine & vbNewLine & "Notes: " & vbNewLine & Notes

End If
```

Summary

We've covered a lot of ground in this chapter, but at the end of all that coding, what we have is a fully functional data services tier for our WROBA application, in the form of our data tier component `Bank_DB.dll`.

This first component introduced some very important points about the coding of the case study:

❑ Since hosting components in MTS or COM+ has a detrimental effect on performance, the WROBA case study only uses transactional processing where it is necessary

❑ The `MContext` code module is used to encapsulate all the transactional functions, and is used in both the data and the business tiers

❑ A common error handling method is used in many of the class modules, giving a uniform approach and considerable flexibility

In particular, we saw that in the WROBA case study, the coding of the ADO in the data tier is centralized in one class module (`DBHelper`) to minimize the amount of repetition involved in executing the stored procedures in the `BigBank` database. The other classes in the data tier have specific roles in the areas of functionality they deal with, and make use of the stored procedures to query and manipulate the data residing in the database.

We ended the chapter by having a look at a potential enhancement that we could make to the error handling in the case study.

Our next job is to code the business services tier of the WROBA application.

13

Business Services Tier

In this chapter we'll discuss the implementation of the **business services tier** of the WROBA application. This tier, very often referred to as the **middle tier,** is used as an intermediary to:

❑   Pass-through calls to the data services tier

❑   Process the business rules that were discovered when we analyzed the business requirements during the creation of the Use Cases and Use Case scenarios as project deliverables

❑   Return the data obtained from the data services tier to the user services tier

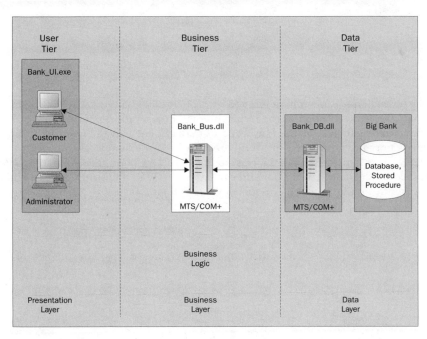

This chapter is divided into three main sections:

- ❑ An overview of the different types of methods used in the business tier
- ❑ A discussion of the implementation of the business tier
- ❑ Detailed coverage of the coding of the business tier

Once again the code contained in this chapter is all part of the WROBA case study that can be downloaded from `www.wrox.com`, so you don't have to type it all if you don't want to. However, this chapter will illustrate how to approach the coding of business components that are consistent, provide good error handling, and efficiently use transactional processing.

Business Services Tier Code Categories

Each method or property in the business services tier can be categorized as belonging to one of three areas:

1. **Pass-through** – In a database-driven application, the majority of public methods simply pass through to their equivalent data services tier methods. For example, the business component `Bank_Bus` method `Bank.UpdatePasswordCount` simply calls the `Bank_DB` `Bank.UpdatePasswordCount` method.

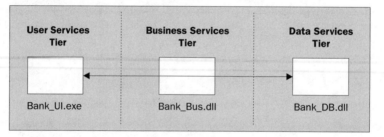

2. **Transformation** – Sometimes a method or property takes a recordset returned from the data services tier and reconfigures the results into either a simple numeric return value or a new recordset altogether. A method or property may also take a value returned from the data services tier and transform it into a different value. For example, the property `GetAccountType` in the `Admin` class of the `Bank_Bus` business component takes a string returned by the data services tier and evaluates it to see if the string indicates that the account is an administrative account. A Boolean value is then returned to the user services tier.

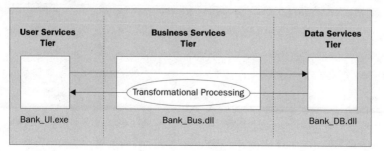

3. Logic – Sometimes a method contains hard-core business logic. For example, the properties `GetMaxBadTries`, `GetBankID`, and `GetCardID` in the `Bank` class of the `Bank_Bus` business component do not call the data services tier at all. All the processing in these properties is done within the business services tier, using the business rules that were discovered during the analysis phase of the project.

Methods that process the business logic of the application *may* call methods in the data services tier, but the business logic is processed entirely in the business services tier. So, if the bank decides that the number of login tries that can be attempted in one session should be changed, only the code in the business services tier that evaluates that business rule must be changed.

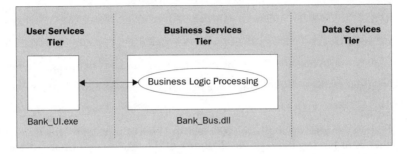

Understanding the differences among these business services tier code categories makes analyzing what the code in each method or property does relatively simple. In many ways, the code in the business services tier is the easiest code to analyze in the entire WROBA application. However, understanding what the code in the business services tier actually does requires an appreciation of the code in both the user services and data services tiers.

Business Services Tier Implementation

As we discovered in Chapter 5 on MTS, there are advantages, as well as disadvantages, to hosting the business services tier code in MTS or COM+. Although security can be enhanced, especially when using COM+, there are always trade-offs in software engineering. The use of MTS or COM+ imposes a performance penalty compared to running the code as a stand-alone executable, and the more **fine-grained** the code, the greater the performance penalty.

Fine-grained code is code that performs only one task, such as validating a login password. Somewhat less fine-grained code might validate both the login password and account number in one process. Since each time a component is given a context in MTS or COM+, and that context must be destroyed when the component terminates, each component that is placed under MTS or COM+ control exacts a performance penalty.

However, with carefully written code that transitions from one services tier to another as infrequently as possible, and uses transactional processing only where it is absolutely needed, the performance penalties can be lessened.

The code used in the business services tier in the WROBA case study was carefully written to provide a balance of performance with the best practices of component creation. All such code is a trade-off between creating the minimum functionality needed for the component and issues of performance.

In the WROBA application, the business services tier uses pass-through methods to delegate most of the work to the data services tier. The exceptions, noted previously, are data transformations and business rules processing. Transactional context management is provided by the MContext code module, which we encountered in the previous chapter. As we saw, this module encapsulates all the transactional functions and is used by both the business services tier and the data services tier.

The code in the business services tier is implemented in five classes. The classes are specialized for tasks such as locating banks, performing electronic funds transfers, working with administrative functions, and working with payees. We can summarize the functions of the class modules as follows:

- Admin class – Provides the functions to administer logins, passwords, banks, and card accounts.
- Bank class – Provides the functions to work with bank accounts and records.
- BankLocator class – Provides the function to locate a specific bank in the table of banks.
- Payees class – Provides the functions for retrieving, adding, deleting, and modifying payees.
- Transfer class – Provides the functions needed to transfer funds and pay bills.

The components for the business services tier are under MTS or COM+ control, but the only processes that are currently under *transactional* control are electronic funds transfers. This is done to minimize the performance penalties of hosting the code in MTS or COM+. This is an important point worth hammering home.

> **Putting all components under transactional control slows things down. When coding for MTS/COM+ follow the approach taken here and only use transactional control when necessary to maintain data integrity.**

All the properties or methods in the business services tier are written so that changing the business services tier project to implement as much transactional control as needed can be done simply by changing the properties of the appropriate components in the MTS Explorer, or for COM+, in the Component Services application (right-click on the component, select Properties and then the Transaction tab to reveal the different options).

OK, now we know what we're aiming at, let's start on the practical side of things.

Try It Out – Creating the Bank_Bus Project

1. Create a new Visual Basic ActiveX DLL project and save it as Bank_Bus.

2. The Bank_Bus project requires references setting to the same two additional libraries as for Bank_DB – the Microsoft ActiveX Data Objects Library and the MTS/COM+ Type Library:

   - For Windows 2000 users select Microsoft ActiveX Data Objects 2.5 Library and COM+ Services Type Library.
   - For Windows 9x or NT 4.0 users (without the updated ADO library) select Microsoft ActiveX Data Objects 2.1 Library and Microsoft Transaction Server Type Library.

Additionally, as we mentioned previously, the project also requires setting a reference to the Bank_DB ActiveX DLL, which provides the data services tier code. This reference is required because the methods and properties in the business services tier usually call corresponding methods and properties in the data services tier

Then, to set the reference to Bank_DB, select **Browse...**, navigate to the folder where the Bank_DB DLL is saved, highlight the folder, and select **Open**. The Bank_DB DLL will be added to the **Available References:** list and can be checked:

3. As we said previously, the MContext code module is shared between the business services and data services tiers. To add the MContext module to the project, select **Project | Add Module**, select the **Existing** tab, navigate to the **Common** folder (assuming the folder structure you're using is the same as the one we proposed previously), and **Open** the MContext.bas code module.

Try It Out – Setting the Project Properties

1. Setting the project properties is quite straightforward and effectively replicates the procedure for the Bank_DB component:

- ❑ On the **General** tab accept the default settings of no startup object, upgrade ActiveX controls, and an **Apartment Threaded** model.

- ❑ On the **Make** tab set the application's title to Bank_Bus, leave the check box for removing information about unused ActiveX controls checked, and set up the version information according to the convention you have selected to use for the Bank_DB project.

- ❑ Leave the settings for the **Compile** and **Debugging** tabs as their default settings.

- ❑ On the **Component** tab use the same methodology as previously – on compiling for the first time, set the compatibility to **Project Compatibility**. After the project has been compiled to produce an ActiveX DLL, place a copy of the DLL in the GUID project subfolder. Once this DLL is in place, change the project version compatibility to **Binary Compatibility** for subsequent recompilations.

Coding the Business Tier

Now the preliminary stuff is out of the way, it's time to implement and analyze the business services tier's code.

The Bank Class Module

The Bank class module is the first module we will examine in the business services tier. This class, like all the classes in the business services tier, is run under MTS/COM+ control, so the MTSTransactionMode property of the class will be set to 1 – NoTransactions. This indicates that the component does not support transactions and, when it is created, its object context is created without a transaction. As we'll see, this setting will be used for each class of the business services tier, with the exception of the Transfer class module.

If the business requirements change and transactions are required for this component later, either this property can be changed and the ActiveX DLL recompiled, or the transactional state of the component can be changed within MTS or COM+. Note that the transactional settings in MTS or COM+ take precedence over the compiled transactional properties; therefore, it is always worth checking the settings in MTS or COM+ to ensure that the transactional properties are set correctly when configuring the application.

The UML class diagram for the Bank class module is shown in the following diagram:

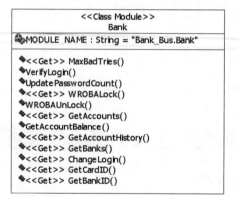

As we discuss how to code this module we'll cover all the properties and methods shown in the UML diagram.

Try It Out – Coding the Bank Class Module

1. Create a new class module via Project | Add Class Module, rename it Bank, and then in the Properties window change the MTSTransactionMode property to 1 – NoTransactions. Leave the Persistable property as 0 – NotPersistable:

2. The first property in the `Bank` class module is the `MaxBadTries` property which implements business logic:

```
Option Explicit

' Class module in business tier

Const MODULE_NAME As String = "Bank_Bus.Bank"

Public Property Get MaxBadTries() As Integer
    ' Count for maximum login failures before locking out the account
    MaxBadTries = 5
End Property
```

3. Next, we have the `VerifyLogin` method and the `ChangeLogin` property; the `VerifyLogin` method is used to verify that a valid login has occurred and the `ChangeLogin` property is used to verify that a change to the password for a login has occurred successfully. These are both examples of pass-through calls to the data services tier and neither method implements either business logic or transformational processing:

```
Public Function VerifyLogin(ByVal BankID As Integer, _
    ByVal CardID As Long, ByVal Password As String, _
    ByRef InvalidCount As Variant) As Boolean
' Verify a valid login

    Dim objBank As Bank_DB.Bank

    On Error GoTo ErrorHandler
```

```
      ' Create a transaction context for the DB call
      Set objBank = CtxCreateObject("Bank_DB.Bank")

      'Passthrough call to data tier
      VerifyLogin = objBank.VerifyLogin(BankID, CardID, _
         Password, InvalidCount)

      CtxSetComplete 'Commit the transaction

Clean_Up:
      Set objBank = Nothing
      Exit Function

ErrorHandler:
      RaiseError MODULE_NAME, "VerifyLogin(" & CStr(BankID) & _
         ", " & CStr(CardID) & ", " & Password & ")"
      GoTo Clean_Up
End Function

Public Property Get ChangeLogin(ByVal BankID As Integer, _
      ByVal CardID As Long, ByVal Password As String) As Boolean
' Verify a valid login

      Dim objBank As Bank_DB.Bank

      On Error GoTo ErrorHandler

      ' Create a transaction context for the DB call
      Set objBank = CtxCreateObject("Bank_DB.Bank")

      'Passthrough call to data tier
      ChangeLogin = objBank.ChangeLogin(BankID, CardID, Password)

      CtxSetComplete 'Commit the transaction

Clean_Up:
      Set objBank = Nothing
      Exit Property

ErrorHandler:
      RaiseError MODULE_NAME, "ChangeLogin(" & CStr(BankID) & _
         ", " & CStr(CardID) & ", " & Password & ")"
      GoTo Clean_Up
End Property
```

4. The `UpdatePasswordCount` method is a pass-through method used to update the `InvalidPasswordCnt` column in the `WROBACard` database table with the number of failed login attempts during the current session. The data in this column is used in conjunction with the value returned by the `MaxBadTries` property to determine when to disallow additional login attempts:

```
Public Sub UpdatePasswordCount(ByVal BankID As Integer, _
    ByVal CardID As Long, ByVal InvalidCount As Integer)
' Update the count of failed login attempts

    Dim objBank As Bank_DB.Bank
    On Error GoTo ErrorHandler

    Set objBank = CtxCreateObject("Bank_DB.Bank")

    'Passthrough call to data tier
    objBank.UpdatePasswordCount BankID, CardID, InvalidCount

    CtxSetComplete

Clean_Up:
    Set objBank = Nothing
    Exit Sub

ErrorHandler:
    RaiseError MODULE_NAME, "UpdatePasswordCount(" & CStr(BankID) _
        & ", " & CStr(CardID) & ", " & CStr(InvalidCount) & ")"
    GoTo Clean_Up
End Sub
```

5. The property and method that lock and unlock a card account are the WROBALock property
   and the WROBAUnlock method, which use pass-through calls to a corresponding property and
   method in the data services tier:

```
Public Property Get WROBALock(ByVal BankID As Integer, _
    ByVal CardID As Long) As Boolean
' Lock the account

    Dim objBank As Bank_DB.Bank

    On Error GoTo ErrorHandler

    Set objBank = CtxCreateObject("Bank_DB.Bank")

    ' Pessimistically assume failure...
    WROBALock = False

    'Passthrough call to data tier
    objBank.WROBALock BankID, CardID

    CtxSetComplete
    WROBALock = True

Clean_Up:
    Set objBank = Nothing
    Exit Property
```

```
ErrorHandler:
    Select Case Err.Number
    Case -2147217900
        Err.Clear
    Case Else
        RaiseError MODULE_NAME, "WROBALock(" & CStr(BankID) & _
            ", " & CStr(CardID) & ")"
    End Select
    GoTo Clean_Up
End Property
Public Sub WROBAUnLock(ByVal BankID As Integer, _
    ByVal CardID As Long)
' Unlock the account

    Dim objBank As Bank_DB.Bank

    On Error GoTo ErrorHandler

    Set objBank = CtxCreateObject("Bank_DB.Bank")

    'Passthrough call to data tier
    objBank.WROBAUnLock BankID, CardID

    CtxSetComplete

Clean_Up:
    Set objBank = Nothing
    Exit Sub

ErrorHandler:
    RaiseError MODULE_NAME, "WROBAUnLock(" & CStr(BankID) & _
        ", " & CStr(CardID) & ")"
    GoTo Clean_Up
End Sub
```

The WROBALock property initially assumes a failure to acquire a lock on the card account, and then sets the value of the property to True unless an error occurs in the property.

6. The GetAccounts property is another example of a pass-through call to the data services tier. It is used to return a recordset of the accounts (Saving or Checking) linked to the requested WROBA card account at the target bank:

```
Public Property Get GetAccounts(ByVal BankID As Integer, _
    ByVal CardID As Long) As ADODB.Recordset
' Get the accounts linked to this CardID

    Dim objBank As Bank_DB.Bank

    On Error GoTo ErrorHandler

    Set objBank = CtxCreateObject("Bank_DB.Bank")
```

```
    'Passthrough call to data tier
    Set GetAccounts = objBank.GetAccounts(BankID, CardID)

    CtxSetComplete

Clean_Up:
    Set objBank = Nothing
    Exit Property

ErrorHandler:
    RaiseError MODULE_NAME, "GetAccounts(" & CStr(BankID) & _
        ", " & CStr(CardID) & ")"
    GoTo Clean_Up
End Property
```

7. The `GetAccountBalance` method is a pass-through call to the data services tier that is used to return the current account description, balance, amount remaining in the daily withdrawal limit, and the account overdraft limit for the target account:

```
Public Sub GetAccountBalance(ByVal BankID As Integer, _
    ByVal AccountID As Long, ByRef AccountTypeDesc As Variant, _
    ByRef Balance As Variant, ByRef DailyRemaining As Variant, _
    ByRef OverdraftLimit As Variant)
' Get the balance for the AccountID account

    Dim objBank As Bank_DB.Bank

    On Error GoTo ErrorHandler

    Set objBank = CtxCreateObject("Bank_DB.Bank")

    'Passthrough call to data tier
    objBank.GetAccountBalance BankID, AccountID, AccountTypeDesc, _
        Balance, DailyRemaining, OverdraftLimit

    CtxSetComplete

Clean_Up:
    Set objBank = Nothing
    Exit Sub

ErrorHandler:
    RaiseError MODULE_NAME, "GetAccountBalance(" & CStr(BankID) _
        & ", " & CStr(AccountID) & ", ... " & ")"
    GoTo Clean_Up
End Sub
```

8. The `GetAccountHistory` property is a pass-through call to the data services tier that is used to return a recordset of the transactions for the requested account that are maintained in the database. This recordset is used to populate the data displayed when the user requests the history of a Saving or Checking account:

```
Public Property Get GetAccountHistory(ByVal BankID As Integer, _
   ByVal AccountID As Long, ByVal MaxTransactionDate As Date) _
   As ADODB.Recordset
' Get the transaction history for this AccountID

   Dim objBank As Bank_DB.Bank

   On Error GoTo ErrorHandler

   Set objBank = CtxCreateObject("Bank_DB.Bank")

   'Passthrough call to data tier
   Set GetAccountHistory = objBank.GetAccountHistory(BankID, _
      AccountID, MaxTransactionDate)

   CtxSetComplete
Clean_Up:
   Set objBank = Nothing
   Exit Property

ErrorHandler:
   RaiseError MODULE_NAME, "GetAccountHistory(" & CStr(BankID) _
      & ", " & CStr(AccountID) & ", " & CStr(MaxTransactionDate) & ")"
   GoTo Clean_Up
End Property
```

9. The GetBanks property is a pass-through call to the data services tier that returns a recordset of all the banks that are in the Bank table in the database:

```
Public Property Get GetBanks(ByVal BankID As Integer) As ADODB.Recordset
' Returns a recordset with all the banks in the Bank table
   Dim objBank As Bank_DB.Bank

   On Error GoTo ErrorHandler

   Set objBank = CtxCreateObject("Bank_DB.Bank")

   'Passthrough call to data tier
   Set GetBanks = objBank.GetBanks(BankID)

   CtxSetComplete

Clean_Up:
   Set objBank = Nothing
   Exit Property

ErrorHandler:
   RaiseError MODULE_NAME, "GetBanks(" & CStr(BankID) & ")"
   GoTo Clean_Up
End Property
```

10. The `GetCardID` and `GetBankID` properties are further examples of properties that implement the business logic of the application:

```
Public Property Get GetCardID(strCardID As String) As Long
   ' The 9 rightmost digits are the WROBA Card ID. The DB tables
   ' are set up for the case study to use only the rightmost
   ' 5 digits. To enable the use of 9 digits the tables must
   ' be changed to a different data type.
   GetCardID = CLng(Right$(strCardID, 9))
End Property

Public Property Get GetBankID(strCardID As String) As Integer
   ' The 3 leftmost digits are the Bank ID. The DB tables
   ' are set up for the case study to use only the rightmost
   ' 1 digit of those 3 digits. To enable the use of 3 digits
   ' the tables must be changed to a different data type.
    GetBankID = CInt(Left$(strCardID, 3))
End Property
```

How It Works

Since this is the first module we've coded in the business tier, we're going to go through some aspects of the code carefully. Don't be discouraged though, patterns of coding will quickly emerge and once we've got a good grounding in the general strategy the rest of the code in the chapter will look quite straightforward.

Firstly, let's see what we've got in this module by way of categories. There are three logic properties:

- ❑ MaxBadTries
- ❑ GetCardID
- ❑ GetBankID

and nine pass-through methods and properties:

- ❑ VerifyLogin
- ❑ ChangeLogin
- ❑ UpdatePasswordCount
- ❑ WROBALock
- ❑ WROBAUnlock
- ❑ GetAccounts
- ❑ GetAccountBalance
- ❑ GetAccountHistory
- ❑ GetBanks

We started off by setting up the `MaxBadTries` logic property; this is the only location in the whole application that maintains the maximum number of failed login attempts that can occur in one login session before the card account is locked for further access. If the business rules of the application change, the logic only has to be changed in this one place.

Next we coded the `VerifyLogin` method and the `ChangeLogin` property – these both return Boolean results to the calling procedure in the user services tier. The arguments passed to the property, and all but one of the arguments passed to the method, are passed `ByVal`:

```
Public Function VerifyLogin(ByVal BankID As Integer, _
    ByVal CardID As Long, ByVal Password As String, _
    ByRef InvalidCount As Variant) As Boolean


Public Property Get ChangeLogin(ByVal BankID As Integer, _
    ByVal CardID As Long, ByVal Password As String) As Boolean
```

The approach of using `ByVal` arguments minimizes the number of network trips required to execute the property and method, because these arguments are not changed in the business services tier code (the same methodology is also applied to the `UpdatePasswordCount` method). The `InvalidCount` Variant argument is passed `ByRef`, because its value is incremented by the data services tier and returned to the user services tier. The explicit `ByRef` argument modifier is used to clearly indicate that this argument can be modified in the method.

> *The default for Visual Basic arguments is `ByRef`, so using no argument modifier will produce the same results, but it won't be as clear when the source code is examined at a later date, so doing it this way is good coding practice.*

In contrast, the arguments that are used to return data to the `GetAccountBalance` pass-through method are passed `ByRef`, because they are changed by the code in the data services tier.

Many of the properties and methods in this class module, and indeed in all the components located in the business services tier, do not directly create objects for the components in the data services tier. Instead they use a public method in the `MContext` code module to do that, as we saw in the previous chapter. Prior to destroying the object, the acquired context is either set complete or aborted (if the context is under transactional control and an error occurs – only applicable to the `Transfer` class). This method of working with components in the data services tier is implemented so that transactional context control can be implemented at a later date with no code changes. So, for example, in the `VerifyLogin` method we have:

```
    ' Create a transaction context for the DB call
    Set objBank = CtxCreateObject("Bank_DB.Bank")

    'Passthrough call to data tier
    VerifyLogin = objBank.VerifyLogin(BankID, CardID, _
        Password, InvalidCount)

    CtxSetComplete 'Commit the transaction

Clean_Up:
    Set objBank = Nothing
    Exit Function
```

> *This approach makes it easy to implement transactions if they are required at a later date.*

The error handling in each method and property in each class in the business services tier uses similar code. The module name and property or method name where the error occurred are passed to a public error method `RaiseError` in the `MContext` code module with the values of the arguments passed to the method or property. This can be illustrated by looking at this code snippet from the `ChangeLogin` property:

```
ErrorHandler:
    RaiseError MODULE_NAME, "ChangeLogin(" & CStr(BankID) & _
        ", " & CStr(CardID) & ", " & Password & ")"
    GoTo Clean_Up
End Property
```

We saw in the previous chapter that using a common error handling method has great benefits in enabling us to implement different ways of displaying or logging errors – a great example being the enhanced error logging offered to us by the `CLogger` component.

To finish off this discussion let's have a look at the business logic implemented by the `GetCardID` and `GetBankID` properties. The `CardID` string argument of the `GetCardID` property is parsed into a Long variable, which is returned to the calling procedure in the user services tier. The business rules operating here are that the nine rightmost characters of the string are used to derive the numeric card ID. If the business rules are changed to use a different number of characters for the card ID number, then the logic is changed correspondingly.

The calling procedure has no knowledge of this logic; it uses whatever value is returned by the business logic.

Similarly, the `GetBankID` property uses the three leftmost characters of the string argument to derive a bank ID: thus, changes to the business rules for bank IDs only require changing this logic. Procedures in the user services tier that use this property have no knowledge of the business rules that are being applied: they use whatever value is returned by the `GetBankID` property.

The BankLocator Class Module

The `BankLocator` class module contains only one property, `GetBank`, so we're not showing a class diagram in this case. The property passes a call through to the data services tier to get the connection string or DSN for the target bank.

Try It Out – Coding the BankLocator Module

1. Create a new class module via Project | Add Class Module, rename it BankLocator, and then in the Properties window again change the MTSTransactionMode property to 1 – NoTransactions and ensure the Persistable property is left as 0 – NotPersistable.

2. The code for the method is shown below, and is analogous to the pass-through methods described previously.

```
Option Explicit

' Class module in business tier

Const MODULE_NAME As String = "Bank_Bus.BankLocator"
```

487

```
Public Property Get GetBank(ByVal BankID As Long) As String
' Returns the DSN string for the selected bank

    Dim objBankLocator As Bank_DB.BankLocator

    On Error GoTo ErrorHandler

    ' Create a context for the data tier BankLocator module
    Set objBankLocator = CtxCreateObject("Bank_DB.BankLocator")

    'Passthrough call to data tier
    GetBank = objBankLocator.GetBank(BankID)

    CtxSetComplete

Clean_Up:
    Set objBankLocator = Nothing
    Exit Property

ErrorHandler:
    RaiseError MODULE_NAME, "GetBank(" & CStr(BankID) & ")"
    GoTo Clean_Up
End Property
```

The Payees Class Module

The modeling phase of the project produced this UML class diagram for the Payees class module. All five properties are implemented as pass-through calls to the data services tier, so the code should be starting to have a very familiar appearance.

```
+-------------------------------------------+
|            <<Class Module>>               |
|                 Payees                    |
+-------------------------------------------+
| MODULE_NAME : String = "Bank_Bus.Payees"  |
+-------------------------------------------+
| <<Get>> MatchPayee()                      |
| <<Get>> InsertPayees()                    |
| <<Get>> EditPayee()                       |
| <<Get>> DeletePayee()                     |
| <<Get>> GetAllPayees()                    |
+-------------------------------------------+
```

Again, we'll consider the properties in the order they appear in the class diagram.

Try It Out – Coding the Payees Module

1. Once again add a new class module to the project, name it **Payees**, and then set the MTSTransactionMode property to 1 – NoTransactions and ensure the Persistable property is left as 0 – NotPersistable.

2. The `InsertPayees`, `EditPayee`, and `DeletePayee` properties return status values based on the success or failure of attempts to add a new payee, change information about an existing payee, and delete an existing payee respectively. To enhance the readability of the code an **Enum** is defined for success (0) or an error (1) in the update attempts. This `Enum`, `EUpdateStatus`, is used as the return type for these properties:

```
Option Explicit

' Class module in business tier

' In this module we are only concerned with success/failure
Public Enum EUpdateStatus
    UPDSUCCESS = 0
    UPDERROR = 1
End Enum
```

3. The `MatchPayee` property uses a pass-through call to the data services tier to verify that a selected payee card ID is present in the `Payees` table in the database. A Boolean value is returned:

```
Const MODULE_NAME As String = "Bank_Bus.Payees"

Public Property Get MatchPayee(ByVal BankID As Integer, _
    ByVal CardID As Long) As Boolean
' Check for matching payees in the Payee table

    Dim objBank As Bank_DB.Payees
    On Error GoTo ErrorHandler

    Set objBank = CtxCreateObject("Bank_DB.Payees")

    'Passthrough call to data tier
    MatchPayee = objBank.MatchPayee(BankID, CardID)

    CtxSetComplete

Clean_Up:
    Set objBank = Nothing
    Exit Property

ErrorHandler:
    RaiseError MODULE_NAME, "MatchPayee(" & CStr(BankID) & ", " _
        & CStr(CardID) & ")"
    GoTo Clean_Up
End Property
```

4. The next three properties follow the same format:

- ❑ The `InsertPayees` property returns a status value indicating the success or failure of an attempt to create a new payee and insert the record in the `Payees` table of the database.
- ❑ The `EditPayee` property returns a status value indicating the success or failure of an attempt to change information for an existing payee.
- ❑ The `DeletePayee` property returns a status value indicating the success or failure of an attempt to delete an existing payee.

489

```
Public Property Get InsertPayees(ByVal PayeeDescription As String, _
   ByVal AccountID As Long, ByVal DefaultAmount As Currency, _
   ByVal BankID As Integer, ByVal CardID As Long, _
   ByVal WROBACardID As Long) As EUpdateStatus
' Add a new payee

   Dim objBank As Bank_DB.Payees

   On Error GoTo ErrorHandler

   InsertPayees = EUpdateStatus.UPDERROR
   Set objBank = CtxCreateObject("Bank_DB.Payees")

   'Passthrough call to data tier
   InsertPayees = objBank.InsertPayees(PayeeDescription, _
      AccountID, DefaultAmount, BankID, CardID, WROBACardID)

   CtxSetComplete

Clean_Up:
   Set objBank = Nothing
   Exit Property

ErrorHandler:
   RaiseError MODULE_NAME, "InsertPayees(" & CStr(BankID) & ", " _
      & CStr(CardID) & ")"
   GoTo Clean_Up
End Property


Public Property Get EditPayee(ByVal PayeeID As String, _
   ByVal PayeeDescription As String, ByVal DefaultAmount As Currency, _
   ByVal BankID As Integer) As EUpdateStatus

   Dim objBank As Bank_DB.Payees

   On Error GoTo ErrorHandler

   EditPayee = EUpdateStatus.UPDERROR
   Set objBank = CtxCreateObject("Bank_DB.Payees")

   'Passthrough call to data tier
   EditPayee = objBank.EditPayee(PayeeID, PayeeDescription, _
      DefaultAmount, BankID)

   CtxSetComplete

Clean_Up:
   Set objBank = Nothing
   Exit Property

ErrorHandler:
   RaiseError MODULE_NAME, "EditPayee(" & CStr(BankID) & ", " _
      & PayeeDescription & ")"
   GoTo Clean_Up
End Property
```

```
   Public Property Get DeletePayee(ByVal PayeeID As String, _
      ByVal BankID As Integer, ByVal PayeeDescription As String) _
      As EUpdateStatus

      Dim objBank As Bank_DB.Payees
      Dim strDSN As String

      On Error GoTo ErrorHandler

      DeletePayee = EUpdateStatus.UPDERROR
      Set objBank = CtxCreateObject("Bank_DB.Payees")

      'Passthrough call to data tier
      DeletePayee = objBank.DeletePayee(PayeeID, BankID, _
         PayeeDescription)

      CtxSetComplete

Clean_Up:
      Set objBank = Nothing
      Exit Property

ErrorHandler:
      RaiseError MODULE_NAME, "DeletePayee(" & CStr(BankID) & ", " _
         & PayeeDescription & ")"
      GoTo Clean_Up
End Property
```

5. The `GetAllPayees` property, also implemented as a pass-through call to the data services tier, is used to return a recordset of all the existing payees in the `Payees` table of the database:

```
Public Property Get GetAllPayees(ByVal BankID As Integer, _
   ByVal CardID As Long) As ADODB.Recordset
'Get all payees for this bank

   Dim objBank As Bank_DB.Payees

   On Error GoTo ErrorHandler

   Set objBank = CtxCreateObject("Bank_DB.Payees")

   'Passthrough call to data tier
   Set GetAllPayees = objBank.GetAllPayees(BankID, CardID)

   CtxSetComplete

Clean_Up:
   Set objBank = Nothing
   Exit Property

ErrorHandler:
   RaiseError MODULE_NAME, "GetAllPayees(" & CStr(BankID) & ")"
   GoTo Clean_Up
End Property
```

The Transfer Class Module

As we noted earlier, the Transfer class module is the only class in the business services tier that currently implements a transactional context. Thus, here we'll set the MTSTransactionMode property to 4 – RequiresNewTransaction to force a new transactional context to be created each time the only property of the class is called from the user services tier. The Persistable property is left as 0 – NotPersistable. As there is only one property, TransferFunds, we won't present a class diagram.

Try It Out – Coding the Transfer Module

1. Create a new class module named Transfer, but this time change the MTSTransactionMode property to 4 – RequiresNewTransaction. Again the Persistable property should be left as 0 – NotPersistable.

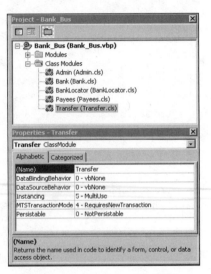

2. Although there's only one method in the module it's quite long, but once again we can see how clear, concise commenting of the code can significantly aid readability:

```
Option Explicit

' Class module in business tier

Const MODULE_NAME As String = "Bank_Bus.Transfer"

' NOTE: THESE VALUES CORRESPOND
' TO ENTRIES IN A DATABASE TABLE
' THIS ENUM AND THE TABLE MUST BE
' KEPT SYNCHRONIZED.
' SEE BANK_DB SOURCE FOR MORE DETAILS.
```

```
Public Enum ETransactionType
    txTransfer = Bank_DB.txTransfer
    txBillPayment = Bank_DB.txBillPayment
End Enum

' Return values enumeration for funds transfers
Public Enum ETransactionStatus
    txsSuccess = 0
    txsDailyLimitExceeded = 1
    txsNotEnoughFunds = 2
    txsUnknownError = 3
End Enum

Public Property Get TransferFunds(ByVal FromBankId As Long, _
    ByVal FromAccountId As Long, ByVal ToBankId As Long, _
    ByVal ToAccountId As Long, ByVal Amount As Currency, _
    ByVal enuTransactionType As ETransactionType, _
    ByVal Description As String) As ETransactionStatus
' Transfers funds from a source to a destination account

    Dim objFromAccount As Bank_DB.Account
    Dim objToAccount As Bank_DB.Account
    Dim ctxObjectContext As ObjectContext
    Dim enuTransactionStatus As ETransactionStatus
    Dim intCount As Integer

    On Error GoTo ErrorHandler

    ' Get a context object
    Set ctxObjectContext = GetObjectContext

    ' Verify that selected account exists before debiting
    ' the source account
    Set objToAccount = New Bank_DB.Account
    'Passthrough call to data tier
    intCount = objToAccount.VerifyAccount(ToBankId, ToAccountId)
    If intCount <> 0 Then
        ' If the account exists
        Set ctxObjectContext = GetObjectContext

        Set objFromAccount = New Bank_DB.Account

        'Passthrough call to data tier
        ' Debit source account
        enuTransactionStatus = objFromAccount.DecrementBalance( _
            FromBankId, FromAccountId, Amount, CInt(enuTransactionType), _
            Description, CStr(ToBankId) & "-" & CStr(ToAccountId))
        If enuTransactionStatus = txsSuccess Then
            Set objToAccount = CtxCreateObject("Bank_DB.Account")
            'Passthrough call to data tier
            ' Increment destination account
            objToAccount.IncrementBalance ToBankId, _
                ToAccountId, Amount, CInt(enuTransactionType), _
```

```
                    Description, CStr(FromBankId) & "-" & CStr(FromAccountId)
        Else
            ' If the debit failed abort the transaction
            If Not (ctxObjectContext Is Nothing) Then
                ctxObjectContext.SetAbort
            End If
        End If
    Else
        enuTransactionStatus = txsUnknownError
    End If

    TransferFunds = enuTransactionStatus

Clean_Up:
    Set objFromAccount = Nothing
    Set objToAccount = Nothing
    Set ctxObjectContext = Nothing
    Exit Property

ErrorHandler:
    RaiseError MODULE_NAME, "TransferFunds(" & CStr(FromBankId) & ", " _
        & CStr(FromAccountId) & ", " & CStr(ToBankId) & ", " & _
        CStr(ToAccountId) & ", " & CStr(Amount) & ", " & _
        CStr(enuTransactionType) & ", " & Description & ")"

    If Not (ctxObjectContext Is Nothing) Then
        ctxObjectContext.SetAbort
    End If

    TransferFunds = txsUnknownError
    GoTo Clean_Up
End Property
```

How It Works

The `Enum ETransactionType` is used to record the type of transaction for use in displaying the account history. This `Enum` corresponds to the `TxType` table in the database listing the implemented types of transactions (which are Transfer and Bill Payment). Any changes in this table will require a corresponding change in the `Enum` to keep the transaction types in synch with the table.

The `TransferFunds` property uses a different method to create an object context to the other properties and methods in the business services tier. The other properties and methods use the `CtxCreateObject` method of the `MContext` code module, whereas the `TransferFunds` property uses a direct call to the `GetObjectContext` method of the MTS/COM+ services library, which returns the current context for an object. This is done so that the code in the business services tier can control the creation of the context for the funds transfer:

```
    ' Get a context object
    Set ctxObjectContext = GetObjectContext
```

The MTSTransactionMode property setting of 4 – RequiresNewTransaction ensures that a new context is created. This method is used to ensure that the base class, (the class that calls the GetObjectContext method), can control the boundaries of the transaction and terminate the context by setting it equal to Nothing.

After a transactional context is acquired, a pass-through call is made to the data services tier to verify that the target account for the transaction exists:

```
'Passthrough call to data tier
intCount = objToAccount.VerifyAccount(ToBankId, ToAccountId)
```

The next pass-through call to the data services tier is made to debit the source account for the transaction. This call returns a transaction status code reflecting the success or failure of debiting the source account. If the debit action fails, the transaction status code provides the reason. The reasons for a debit transaction failure are coded as:

❑ Not enough funds

❑ Daily withdrawal limit exceeded

❑ Unknown error

If the debit transaction succeeds, the target account is credited with the amount debited from the source account. A failure of the debit transaction triggers an Abort action on the transaction. The result of the electronic funds transfer transaction is returned to the calling procedure in the user services tier:

```
If intCount <> 0 Then
    ' If the account exists
    Set ctxObjectContext = GetObjectContext

    Set objFromAccount = New Bank_DB.Account

    'Passthrough call to data tier
    ' Debit source account
    enuTransactionStatus = objFromAccount.DecrementBalance( _
        FromBankId, FromAccountId, Amount, CInt(enuTransactionType), _
        Description, CStr(ToBankId) & "-" & CStr(ToAccountId))
    If enuTransactionStatus = txsSuccess Then
        Set objToAccount = CtxCreateObject("Bank_DB.Account")
        'Passthrough call to data tier
        ' Increment destination account
        objToAccount.IncrementBalance ToBankId, _
            ToAccountId, Amount, CInt(enuTransactionType), _
            Description, CStr(FromBankId) & "-" & CStr(FromAccountId)
    Else
        ' If the debit failed abort the transaction
        If Not (ctxObjectContext Is Nothing) Then
            ctxObjectContext.SetAbort
        End If
    End If
Else
    enuTransactionStatus = txsUnknownError
End If
```

Last, but not least, we have the Admin class module.

The Admin Class Module

The UML class diagram for the Admin class module is shown in the following diagram. Note that the diagram shows the GeneratePassword, GenerateCardID, and GenerateAccountID methods with a padlock symbol at the left of the class diagram indicating that the methods are private to the Admin class module:

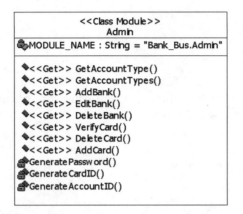

```
                <<Class Module>>
                     Admin
  MODULE_NAME : String = "Bank_Bus.Admin"

  <<Get>> GetAccountType()
  <<Get>> GetAccountTypes()
  <<Get>> AddBank()
  <<Get>> EditBank()
  <<Get>> DeleteBank()
  <<Get>> VerifyCard()
  <<Get>> DeleteCard()
  <<Get>> AddCard()
  GeneratePassword()
  GenerateCardID()
  GenerateAccountID()
```

As we'll see during the coding, all eight properties involve pass-through calls (but the GetAccountType property transforms the recordset returned by the call to the data services tier into a Boolean status value), while the three private methods encapsulate business logic. This is all getting quite familiar, so we run through this module quite quickly.

Try It Out – Coding the Admin Module

1. Once again we need a new class module, here named Admin, with the standard, for this DLL, properties of: 1 – NoTransactions for the MTSTransactionMode property and 0 – NotPersistable for the Persistable property.

2. The GetAccountType property is an example of a business services tier property that uses a pass-through call to the data services tier to return a String value to the business services tier. The String is evaluated to see if the logged in account is an administrative account. A Boolean result is returned to the user services tier, with the result set to True if the account is an administrative account:

```
Option Explicit

' Class module in business tier

Const MODULE_NAME As String = "Bank_Bus.Admin"

Public Property Get GetAccountType(ByVal BankID As Integer, _
    ByVal CardID As Long) As Boolean
' See if the CardID account is an Administrator account
' True is an Admin, False is not
    Dim objBank As Bank_DB.Admin
```

```
    Dim recAccounts As ADODB.Recordset

    On Error GoTo ErrorHandler
    GetAccountType = False

    ' Create a transaction context for the DB call
    Set objBank = CtxCreateObject("Bank_DB.Admin")

    'Passthrough call to data tier
    Set recAccounts = objBank.GetAccountType(BankID, CardID)

    CtxSetComplete 'Commit the transaction

    Do While Not recAccounts.EOF
        If Trim$(recAccounts!AccountTypeDesc) = "Administrator" Then
            GetAccountType = True
            Exit Do
        End If

        recAccounts.MoveNext
    Loop

Clean_Up:
    Set recAccounts = Nothing
    Set objBank = Nothing
  Exit Property

ErrorHandler:
    RaiseError MODULE_NAME, "GetAccountType(" & CStr(BankID) & _
        ", " & CStr(CardID) & ")"
    GoTo Clean_Up
End Property
```

3. The `GetAccountTypes` property is a pass-through call to the data services tier that returns a recordset of the types of card accounts (Saving or Checking) that are implemented in the WROBA card network. The account types are stored in a table in the database:

```
Public Property Get GetAccountTypes(ByVal BankID As Integer) _
    As ADODB.Recordset
    ' Get the account types.

    Dim objBank As Bank_DB.Admin

    On Error GoTo ErrorHandler

    Set objBank = CtxCreateObject("Bank_DB.Admin")

    'Passthrough call to data tier
    Set GetAccountTypes = objBank.GetAccountTypes(BankID)

    CtxSetComplete
```

```
Clean_Up:
   Set objBank = Nothing
   Exit Property

ErrorHandler:
   RaiseError MODULE_NAME, "GetAccountTypes(" & CStr(BankID) & ")"
   GoTo Clean_Up
End Property
```

4. The `AddBank` property uses a pass-through call to the data services tier to add a new bank to the WROBA card network. The `EditBank` property uses a pass-through call to the data services tier to save changes made to a bank's description or DSN to the `Banks` table in the database. The `DeleteBank` property uses a pass-through call to the data services tier to delete the selected bank from the `Banks` table in the database:

```
Public Property Get AddBank(ByVal BankID As Integer, _
   ByVal NewBankID As Integer, ByVal Description As String, _
   ByVal DSN As String) As Boolean

   Dim objBank As Bank_DB.Admin

   On Error GoTo ErrorHandler
   AddBank = False

   ' Create a transaction context for the DB call
   Set objBank = CtxCreateObject("Bank_DB.Admin")

   'Passthrough call to data tier
   AddBank = objBank.AddBank(BankID, NewBankID, Description, DSN)

   CtxSetComplete 'Commit the transaction

Clean_Up:
   Set objBank = Nothing
   Exit Property

ErrorHandler:
   RaiseError MODULE_NAME, "AddBank(" & CStr(NewBankID) & _
       ", " & Description & "," & DSN & ")"
   GoTo Clean_Up
End Property

Public Property Get EditBank(ByVal BankID As Integer, _
   ByVal ChangeBankID As Integer, ByVal Description As String, _
   ByVal DSN As String) As Boolean

   Dim objBank As Bank_DB.Admin

   On Error GoTo ErrorHandler
   EditBank = False

   ' Create a transaction context for the DB call
   Set objBank = CtxCreateObject("Bank_DB.Admin")
```

```
    'Passthrough call to data tier
    EditBank = objBank.EditBank(BankID, ChangeBankID, Description, DSN)

    CtxSetComplete 'Commit the transaction

Clean_Up:
    Set objBank = Nothing
    Exit Property

ErrorHandler:
    RaiseError MODULE_NAME, "EditBank(" & CStr(ChangeBankID) & _
        ", " & Description & "," & DSN & ")"
    GoTo Clean_Up
End Property

Public Property Get DeleteBank(ByVal BankID As Integer, _
    ByVal ChangeBankID As Integer) As Boolean

    Dim objBank As Bank_DB.Admin

    On Error GoTo ErrorHandler
    DeleteBank = False

    ' Create a transaction context for the DB call
    Set objBank = CtxCreateObject("Bank_DB.Admin")

    'Passthrough call to data tier
    DeleteBank = objBank.DeleteBank(BankID, ChangeBankID)

    CtxSetComplete 'Commit the transaction

Clean_Up:
    Set objBank = Nothing
    Exit Property

ErrorHandler:
    RaiseError MODULE_NAME, "DeleteBank(" & CStr(ChangeBankID) & ")"
    GoTo Clean_Up
End Property
```

5. The `VerifyCard` property uses a pass-through call to the data services tier to verify if a card account with the selected card ID exists in the database. The `DeleteCard` property uses a pass-through call to the data services tier to delete the selected card account from the database:

```
Public Property Get VerifyCard(ByVal BankID As Integer, _
    ByVal CardID As Long) As Boolean

    Dim objBank As Bank_DB.Admin
    Dim lngReturn As Long

    On Error GoTo ErrorHandler
    VerifyCard = False
```

```
    ' Create a transaction context for the DB call
    Set objBank = CtxCreateObject("Bank_DB.Admin")

    'Passthrough call to data tier
    lngReturn = objBank.VerifyCard(BankID, CardID)
    If lngReturn <> 0 Then
        VerifyCard = True
    End If

    CtxSetComplete 'Commit the transaction

Clean_Up:
    Set objBank = Nothing
    Exit Property

ErrorHandler:
    RaiseError MODULE_NAME, "VerifyCard(" & CStr(CardID) & ")"
    GoTo Clean_Up
End Property

Public Property Get DeleteCard(ByVal BankID As Integer, _
    ByVal CardID As Long) As Boolean

    Dim objBank As Bank_DB.Admin

    On Error GoTo ErrorHandler
    DeleteCard = False

    ' Create a transaction context for the DB call
    Set objBank = CtxCreateObject("Bank_DB.Admin")

    'Passthrough call to data tier
    DeleteCard = objBank.DeleteCard(BankID, CardID)

    CtxSetComplete 'Commit the transaction

Clean_Up:
    Set objBank = Nothing
    Exit Property

ErrorHandler:
    RaiseError MODULE_NAME, "DeleteCard(" & CStr(CardID) & ")"
    GoTo Clean_Up
End Property
```

6. The AddCard property uses a pass-through call to the data services tier to add a new card account to the database. To create the new properties required for a new card account the GenerateCardID, GenerateAccountID, and GeneratePassword private methods are used. The user can change the newly-generated default password later if they want to.

```
Public Property Get AddCard(ByVal BankID As Integer, _
    ByVal AccountType As Integer, ByVal InitialBalance As Currency, _
    ByVal DailyLimit As Currency, ByVal OverDraft As Currency, _
    ByRef CardID As String, ByRef Password As String) As Boolean

    Dim objBank As Bank_DB.Admin
    Dim lngCardID As Long
```

```
        Dim lngAccountID As Long
        Dim strPassword As String

        On Error GoTo ErrorHandler
        AddCard = False

        lngCardID = GenerateCardID(BankID)
        CardID = CStr(lngCardID)

        lngAccountID = GenerateAccountID(BankID)

        strPassword = GeneratePassword(lngAccountID)
        Password = strPassword

        ' Create a transaction context for the DB call
        Set objBank = CtxCreateObject("Bank_DB.Admin")

        'Passthrough call to data tier
        AddCard = objBank.AddCard(BankID, AccountType, InitialBalance, _
        DailyLimit, OverDraft, strPassword, lngCardID, lngAccountID)

        CtxSetComplete 'Commit the transaction

Clean_Up:
        Set objBank = Nothing
        Exit Property

ErrorHandler:
        RaiseError MODULE_NAME, "AddCard(" & CStr(BankID) & ")"
        GoTo Clean_Up
End Property
```

7. The `GenerateCardID`, `GenerateAccountID`, and `GeneratePassword` private methods
are examples of methods that implement business rules for the application.
`GeneratePassword` uses the rightmost four digits of the account ID argument, converted
into characters, and appends them to the word `secret`. The `GenerateCardID` and
`GenerateAccountID` methods use pass-through calls to the data services tier to get the
previous last card and account numbers respectively. They increment these numbers by 1,
and return the newly-generated card and account numbers to the calling property:

```
Private Function GeneratePassword(ByVal lngAccountID As Long) _
    As String
    ' This simple password is created by combining the word
    ' "secret" with the rightmost 4 digits of the AccountID
    GeneratePassword = "secret" & Right$(CStr(lngAccountID), 4)
End Function

Private Function GenerateCardID(ByVal BankID As Integer) As Long
' Generate a new CardID, which will be the previous last CardID + 1
    Dim objBank As Bank_DB.Admin

    On Error GoTo ErrorHandler
```

```
    ' Create a transaction context for the DB call
    Set objBank = CtxCreateObject("Bank_DB.Admin")

    'Passthrough call to data tier
    GenerateCardID = objBank.GetLastCardId(BankID)

    CtxSetComplete 'Commit the transaction

    GenerateCardID = GenerateCardID + 1

Clean_Up:
    Set objBank = Nothing
    Exit Function

ErrorHandler:
    RaiseError MODULE_NAME, "GenerateCardID(" & CStr(BankID) & ")"
    GoTo Clean_Up
End Function

Private Function GenerateAccountID(ByVal BankID As Integer) As Long
    ' Generate a new AccountID, which will be the previous
    ' last AccountID + 1

    Dim objBank As Bank_DB.Admin

    On Error GoTo ErrorHandler

    ' Create a transaction context for the DB call
    Set objBank = CtxCreateObject("Bank_DB.Admin")

    'Passthrough call to data tier
    GenerateAccountID = objBank.GetLastAccountId(BankID)

    CtxSetComplete 'Commit the transaction

    GenerateAccountID = GenerateAccountID + 1

Clean_Up:
    Set objBank = Nothing
    Exit Function

ErrorHandler:
    RaiseError MODULE_NAME, "GenerateAccountID(" & CStr(BankID) & ")"
    GoTo Clean_Up
End Function
```

Creating the ActiveX DLL

In the last chapter we talked about the need to compile the Bank_DB ActiveX DLL, as it is referenced by the business tier component. At this point, we have to compile the Bank_Bus ActiveX DLL to provide the appropriate reference for the user tier project, Bank_UI.exe, that we'll be constructing in the next two chapters.

We've seen that the compilation process is quite straightforward (select File | Make | Bank_Bus); however we should again point out that if the DLL is being compiled for the first time, the project properties Component tab should have Project Compatibility checked, then a copy of the DLL should be placed in the GUID subfolder. If the DLL has been compiled previously then re-compile it with the compatibility changed to Binary Compatibility.

Summary

In this chapter we looked at how the code in the business services tier is implemented. It quickly became obvious that most calls to the business services tier are pass-through calls, where the methods and properties in the business services tier call corresponding methods and properties in the data services tier. These calls are known as pass-through calls because the arguments to the business services tier methods and properties are passed through to the data services tier with no processing or decision making by the method or property in the business services tier.

The rest of the calls to the business services tier are transformation calls or logic calls. Transformation calls are where the business services method, or property, transforms the recordset returned by the data services tier and reconfigures the recordset into either an entirely new recordset, or a scalar value. Logic calls evaluate the arguments passed to them in accordance with the business logic of the application. These business rules are processed entirely within the business services tier, thereby centralizing all the business logic in the application at one location. Changing the business logic then becomes a matter of making the changes in one place, and deploying the changes to one or only a limited number of installations.

In the next chapter we'll start building the presentation or user tier.

14

User Tier I – Customer Services

Over the last couple of chapters we've covered an awful lot of ground in the implementation of the WROBA application; we've built our database and associated data handling procedures, we've built the data services tier and the business services tier, but as yet we still really don't have any way of seeing all that hard work in action. That's all going to change in this chapter as we start to build the **user services**, or **presentation**, tier of the application. As the chapter title suggests, this is only the start of the user tier discussion – in this chapter we only consider the logic that the customer interacts with.

It's important to remember that building an application from the top down usually means designing the user interface first. In this book, what looks like a bottom up approach has been taken by showing the database, business services, and data services tiers first. This was done so that we could acquaint ourselves with the necessary fundamentals of distributed application design, and does not indicate that these things are designed before the user interface. In fact, the *requirements* of the user interface and user services tier usually drive the components of the other services tiers.

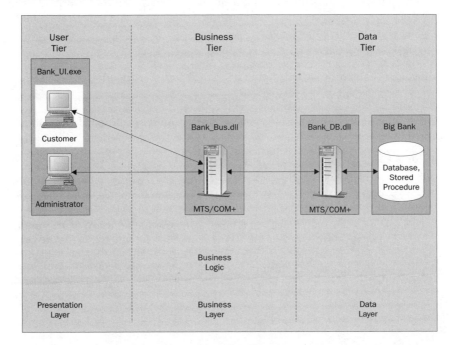

Here we're going to consider a bit of general technology – some of the fundamentals behind building a good **Graphical User Interfaces (GUI)** – before we move on to the case study itself.

A good GUI designer strives to create screens that are visually intuitive, easy to learn, and easy to navigate. Novice programmers often underestimate both the difficulty and the importance of GUI design. In this chapter, we'll introduce the topic of GUI design and highlight a few guiding principles to be followed in order to create screens that users will find appealing and useable.

Therefore, this chapter is composed of two main sections:

❑ An introduction to GUI design and implementation

❑ Implementation of the customer services section of the WROBA case study user services tier

Let's start by thinking about some of the basics of user interfaces.

GUI Design and Implementation

The first task in designing a GUI is to determine some basic facts:

❑ How will it be used and by whom?

❑ What will it be used for and how long will the user work in the interface – a few minutes to complete a task, or for hours each day?

Once the answers to these questions have been established, the following steps will be taken as part of the user interface design process:

❑ Task assignment – Each form will be responsible for enabling users to achieve defined tasks.

❑ Determination of form navigation – Forms should be easy to move around and between (if there are multiple forms within an application). This stage can be performed before any coding takes place – a storyboard of the whole UI is made, and a navigation hierarchy decided before diving into the code.

❑ Choice of control types – The form should be easy to use.

❑ Form layout – The form layout should be logical and user friendly.

❑ Menu definition – Pick menus that are appropriate for the application.

❑ Addition of visually appealing elements – Forms should be attractive without too much distracting clutter.

❑ Consistency – Windows applications are expected to have a have a consistent look and feel that makes it easier to learn to use them.

❑ Help element definition – To what degree is the application intuitive, or will the users need help?

Use Case Scenarios are used to assign tasks to a form. For example, in the WROBA application most Scenarios require one or two forms. Scenarios asking a question to which there is an answer-based action usually require two screens. For example, let's consider Scenario #6 from Chapter 6 where the customer wants to retrieve the account history of one of their accounts. The initial question is 'which account do you want to see recent transactions from?' and the associated form is:

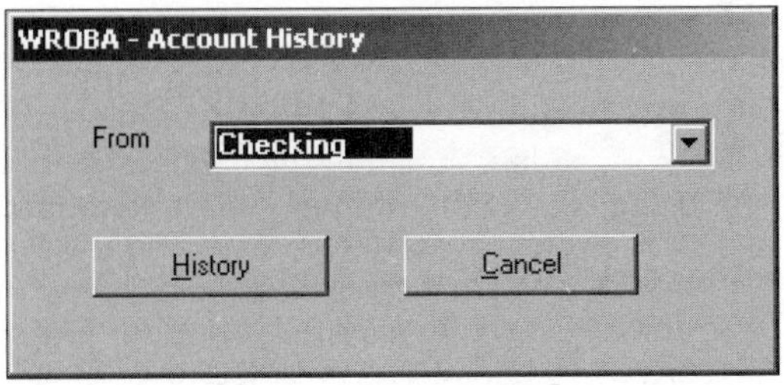

The answering action is 'here are the recent transactions for this account' and the screen is:

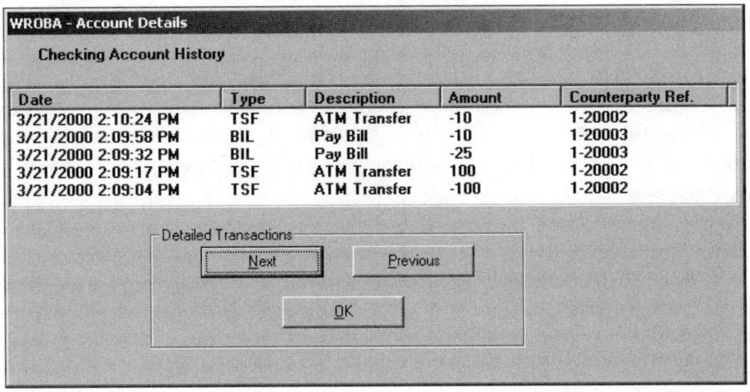

Other scenarios, such as the Login Scenario (Scenario #1), only require a single form, as we'll see later. Just to refresh our memories, the Customer Use Cases determined in Chapter 6 were:

Function	Use Case Scenario
Customer Login	1
Transfer Funds	2
Pay Bill	3
Add Payee	4
Edit Payee	5
Account History	6
Change Password	7

To collect information from the user, the proper Windows controls need to be used. Which one is chosen depends upon what the user will expect to be able to do; for instance, they may wish to:

- ❑ Modify data
- ❑ Select from mutually exclusive options – such as male or female
- ❑ Select more than one item simultaneously

As a recap the most commonly used controls are:

- ❑ **Command Button** – Used for action items like Exit. Command buttons can allow multiple actions, in which case ellipsis points shown in the caption, such as in Browse..., indicate that a dialog will result from the action, so more input will be required.

- ❑ **Radio Button** – Used for mutually exclusive multiple choices. In certain circumstances, it is worth considering the option of a *No Answer* response option for those cases where the user does not know (or chooses not to tell you) the answer.

- ❑ **Check Box** – Used for binary choices, like true/false or on/off. These are non-exclusive, so the user can pick as many as they wish.

- ❑ **Single Selection List Box** – A fixed size list box used to select a single item.

- ❑ **Drop-down List Box** – Used for a single selection; a guideline to keep in mind would be to limit it to a selection of between three to eight entries. (Two possible selections would normally be better suited to radio buttons, but more than three single selections generate a lot of clutter, so a drop down list box will most likely be a better use of space.)

- ❑ **List View** – May be used to get multiple selections, as it is used in the Banking application.

- ❑ **Combo Box** – an alternative to the drop-down list box. Combo boxes contain suggested items and, if the user wants, they can type in their own choice. List boxes force the user to select one of the items in the list.

- ❑ **Text Box** – Used for text entry.

Once the controls have been selected for the form, they need to be arranged in an aesthetically pleasing way; try to avoid cluttered screens and give the form a balanced look where empty spaces are spread equally across all the regions of the screen. It's always a good idea to get some feedback from the users themselves, if possible; remember the iterative approach!

Navigating between forms may be achieved by using menus. Defining the menus is usually fairly straightforward, as it is important to maintain consistency between the application being developed and standard Windows applications. Thus, a File menu should be first on the menu bar and a Help menu last. This makes learning to use the application easier, because the user is familiar with this menu layout.

Other good tactics are to make commonly used menu items easily accessible with associated keyboard shortcuts, and to try to avoid too many levels in cascading menus. After the menu structure has been added to the form, it's time to let your creativity loose to make the user interface more attractive. We will see a little later a few principles we can use here. Other items that may be added at this stage include toolbars, a status bar, and so on.

The final task should be to determine to what extent online help is needed. Online help may be provided simply by tool tips, or be somewhat more comprehensive. For simplicity, we haven't implemented any help within the WROBA application.

GUI Design Principles

In this section, we will consider ten principles that will help us create GUIs that are more appealing:

1. **Make the Interface Consistent**

Consistency is *very* important in user interface design. Computer magazines will give programs poor reviews for breaking the conventional way of doing things in Windows, such as requiring users to triple-click rather than double-click. This is because the program is not consistent with the way things are done in most Windows applications. Another area where we want to be consistent is within the program. In the banking application, for example, the buttons on all screens are the same size and positioned in a similar spot. This way, the application is more intuitive to use and has a more coherent look.

2. **Keep the User Interface Simple**

Unless there are special considerations for users with disabilities, avoid the excessive use of different colors or fonts, as well as bright colors and hard to read fonts. It's also very important to avoid cluttered screens. Later, in principle 7, we'll consider a technique to make complex screens more palatable to the user.

3. **Provide Flexibility**

Applications should empower the user to work any way they want to, and should avoid constraining the user. Users should only be disallowed from starting a second task before the first one is finished when the tasks are mutually dependant.

4. **Create Reversible or Cancelable Tasks**

Deep down, we're all afraid of making mistakes. This fear can be alleviated by allowing the user to undo operations in as many places as possible. Long tasks should be cancelable, so the user can back out without having to wait for the lengthy operation to finish.

5. **Trust the User**

The correct balance needs to be found between protecting the user from accidents and not trusting the user's wishes. When a user hits a Delete button, for example, they only need to be asked once whether to proceed with the action – for a durable operation like this, though, they should be given the chance to back out, in accordance with principle 4.

6. **Provide Meaningful Error Messages**

Try to be as specific as possible when providing error messages and tell the user what is required to remove the error condition. Rather than having an error message of Invalid password, it's better to have a message saying: A password must have at least three characters and at most eight. It may contain a-z, 0-9, and is case sensitive.

7. Use Progressive Disclosure for Complicated Forms

Principle 2 correctly states that simplicity is a good thing, but there are unavoidable cases where a lot of information must be collected from the user. The solution is **progressive disclosure**. Progressive disclosure lets the user deal with a small amount of information at a time. It could be considered, in one way, to be a cascading set of screens. Progressive disclosure can be implemented in a number of different ways, such as a using a More>> or Advanced>> button, using a tabbed form, or using a Wizard.

8. Give Visual Feedback

To let the user know what is happening on a form, or to show progress during a process, it is useful to give visual clues. Useful tactics here are to have status bars showing percentage task completion, labels indicating position on the form (for instance page x of y), or notes concerning the status of a record (such as <MODIFIED>).

9. Remember Preferences

Users often make the same choices repeatedly. They often want the form sized the same way, positioned on the same spot on the screen, files saved in the same location, columns in a grid sized the same way, etc. They will appreciate applications that remember these preferences. Other types of preferences involve regional settings, such as the date format and the currency symbol (perhaps even the presentation language could be considered under this heading), and one important task is to ensure an application works correctly regardless of the regional settings.

10. Test GUI Prototypes

The best way to find out if a user interface is intuitive is to demonstrate it to the user and collect their feedback. Better yet, give the application to a user and let them try to do the common tasks. Building a user interface prototype is a worthwhile exercise to collect user feedback. Such a user interface is a version of the program where all the program logic is hard-coded in a simplistic way. Typically, these prototypes do not access the database and trial data corresponding to database returns is also hard-coded.

To quickly summarize, a good GUI designer strives to create screens that look good, are easy to learn, and easy to navigate. After these basic points have been addressed, then the slightly more advanced functionality can be added – making it remember the user's last choices, its screen position, and so on. Part of making the GUI smarter is also disallowing user errors. This is called **form validation**. We'll take a look at this in the next section.

GUI Implementation Principles

It's best to try to use defensive coding techniques to eliminate the need to validate data. For example, controls such as a calendar control or list box will direct the user in their data entry and constrain them in their choice of data. Unfortunately, this isn't always possible, so there are points at which explicit coding has to be used to validate the data after it's been entered.

Form Validation

Form validation is the process of verifying the user input on a form; this can be achieved in two ways:

❑   **Field-level validation** – This involves checking for errors each time a single data item has been entered. Suppose a login form has two text boxes: one for first name, and one for last name (and the usual OK and Cancel command buttons). With field-level validation, if the user entered 123 as the first name, the program would report the error as the user left the First Name field, preventing the user from continuing until a valid name was entered (of course, here we are looking for a standard name involving letters not numbers).

❑   **Form-level validation** – Here checking for errors takes place after all input has been provided. With form-level validation, if the user enters 123 as the first name in our example, the program would allow the user to type in the last name. Only when the user clicked on OK would the error be reported.

Often both forms of validation are used. Typically, field-level validation is used for obvious mistakes (invalid input for which no database lookup is necessary) and form-level validation for violation of business rules. Implementation of form-level validation may involve choosing to catch the errors using exactly the same techniques that may be used to implement field-level validation. The only difference is that the error isn't reported directly, but the error message may be added to, say, a collection. Another way to store the error messages is to append them to a string. If, at the end of the checks, the string is not empty, then it can be displayed to the user.

Field-Level Validation in VB6

Before the introduction of Visual Basic 6, field level validation was implemented using the LostFocus event. Visual Basic 6 introduces an alternative to this technique with the Validate event and the accompanying CausesValidation property. The Validate event for a control triggers when the focus moves from that control to another control and both controls have their CausesValidation property set to True.

The Validate event has a Cancel parameter that can be set to True to prevent the focus from leaving the control where the error occurred. If using the Cancel parameter, we need to set the CausesValidation property to False for such things as Cancel buttons, otherwise clicking the Cancel button will cause validation to occur and if the value of the field is invalid, the focus will never move to the Cancel button, meaning there is no way out except with a valid entry.

Let's illustrate this by looking at that simple login example in more detail.

Try It Out – Field and Form Level Validation

1. Create a New Project in Visual Basic and select **Standard EXE** as the project type.

2. Rename the form `FMain` and add two text boxes (named `txtFirstName` and `txtLastName`), two labels, two command buttons (named `cmdOK` and `cmdCancel`), and a check box (named `chkFormLevel`):

The `CausesValidation` property should be set to `True` for all the controls except `cmdCancel` and `chkFormLevel` where it should be set to `False`.

3. Add the following code to `FMain`. The validation code testing first and last names is kept simple and only fires when you enter a numeric value.

```
Option Explicit

Private m_strErrorMsg      As String

Private Sub cmdOK_Click()
    ' See if the form level validation is enabled
    If chkFormLevel.Value = vbChecked Then
        ' If so, see if the error message string is empty
        If Len(m_strErrorMsg) Then ShowErrorMsg m_strErrorMsg
    End If
End Sub

Private Sub cmdCancel_Click()
    Unload Me
End Sub

Private Sub chkFormLevel_Click()
    ' Clear the form
    txtFirstName.Text = ""
    txtLastName.Text = ""

    m_strErrorMsg = ""
End Sub

Private Sub txtFirstName_Validate(Cancel As Boolean)
```

```
        'Check the text string for a numeric value
        'If numeric, jumpt to ErrorMsg sub
        If IsNumeric(txtFirstName.Text) Then
            ErrorMsg txtFirstName.Text _
                        & " is not a valid First Name!"

            'If the Form level box is not checked continue
            If chkFormLevel.Value <> vbChecked Then
                txtFirstName.SelStart = 0
                txtFirstName.SelLength = Len(txtFirstName.Text)
                Cancel = True
            End If
        End If
End Sub

Private Sub txtLastName_Validate(Cancel As Boolean)

    'Check the text string for a numeric value
    If IsNumeric(txtLastName.Text) Then
        ErrorMsg txtLastName.Text _
                    & " is not a valid Last Name!"

        'If the Form level box is not checked continue
        If chkFormLevel.Value <> vbChecked Then
            txtLastName.SelStart = 0
            txtLastName.SelLength = Len(txtLastName.Text)
            Cancel = True
        End If
    End If
End Sub

Private Sub ErrorMsg(strNewErrorMsg As String)

Dim strErrorMsg      As String

    'If the Form level box is checked,
    'use a variable to hold the error until
    'Ok button is pressed
If chkFormLevel.Value = vbChecked Then
        strErrorMsg = Trim$(m_strErrorMsg)
        If Len(strErrorMsg) > 0 Then
            strErrorMsg = strErrorMsg & vbCrLf
        End If
        m_strErrorMsg = strErrorMsg & strNewErrorMsg
    Else
    'If the Form level box is not checked,
    'show the error now, using ShowErrorMsg sub
        ShowErrorMsg strNewErrorMsg
    End If
End Sub

Private Sub ShowErrorMsg(strError As String)
    MsgBox strError, vbCritical + vbOKOnly, "Error!"
End Sub
```

4. Run the form and type 123 in the First Name or Last Name text box and tab to the next
selection. With the Form-Level box unchecked, the field is validated as we move to the next
field. Next check the Form-Level check box and see the form operation change to only
validating the entries after the OK button is pressed.

How It Works

The validation procedures check the text string entered. If it is numeric then an error message is returned. An alphanumeric string, such as "Me123" is valid, since validation is looking at the full string, not checking each character within the string.

```
Private Sub txtFirstName_Validate(Cancel As Boolean)
    If IsNumeric(txtFirstName.Text) Then
        ErrorMsg txtFirstName.Text _
                        & " is not a valid First Name!"
```

The `Cancel` parameter is set to `True`, holding focus on the invalid entry. If the `Cancel` parameter is not specified, it assumes the default of `False` and focus is lost.

```
        Cancel = True
```

As you move between text boxes, the contents are validated and if they are a string, the focus passes to the next control. If the text box contains a numeric value, focus remains on the text box, making it easy for the user to enter corrected data.

If the Form Level box is checked, the entries are not validated until the OK box is checked. Focus does not move to the invalid entry.

Now we've had a brief overview of some of the basics of GUI design, let's have a look at what the case study does, and how. As we go through the study we'll also see some of the compromises that were made because it's a case study and not a commercial application.

WROBA GUI and Customer Services

In this part of the chapter we're going to look at how the user services tier is constructed in the WROBA case study, and more specifically, the implementation of the user services tier that WROBA customers interact with (of course this is only part of the user tier; bank employees who carry out administrative duties on the application are also users).

Our discussion will cover:

- ❑ How the user tier is implemented in the WROBA case study and features of the coding of the customer functions
- ❑ The code and class modules used in the WROBA user services tier
- ❑ Logging into the WROBA application
- ❑ Setting up the customer main menu
- ❑ Implementation of the forms required to allow customers to view and administer their accounts
- ❑ Implementation of the forms required to allow customers to pay bills and transfer funds between accounts

WROBA GUI Implementation

As shown in the diagram at the head of the chapter, the User Tier has two actual interfaces – one for customers and one for administration. In the case study as currently implemented, the logic for both interfaces is contained in one project – Bank_UI.exe – which is the project that we'll be building over the next couple of chapters. In this chapter, we look at the forms in the project that customers will see and interact with, while in the next chapter we'll look at the forms associated with administration of the application.

The logic for the WROBA customer services forms follows the Use Cases and Use Case Scenarios that were detailed in Chapter 6 in Scenarios 1 – 7. The programming logic providing this functionality is distributed over all three tiers, with business logic in the business services tier and database access in the data services tier, as we may expect. Some business logic is contained in procedures stored in the database.

While many of the forms are specifically aimed at either customers or administrators there are just a few (like the login form and the operation status forms) that are seen in both interfaces. Additionally, there are three modules in the WROBA user tier that are used by all the forms (we'll discuss these shortly).

To appreciate the events that occur when login verification is received from the login screen by the main menu, let's have a look at an activity diagram for the process:

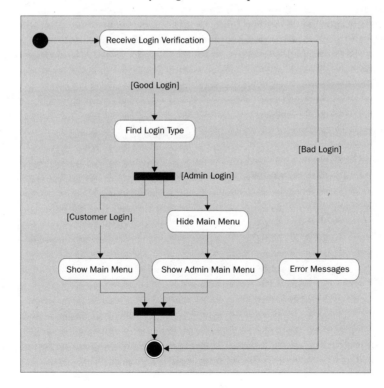

At the point login verification is received from the login screen there are two alternative paths:

❑ If the login verification is an error value, indicating a bad login, an error message is displayed.

❑ If the login is good, the type of login is determined and there are again two alternatives:

  ❑ If the login is a customer login, the main menu becomes operational.

  ❑ If the login is an administrative login, the main menu is hidden and the administrator's main menu is started (this will be discussed more in the next chapter).

The WROBA case study provides sample data consisting of two accounts with two potential logins:

❑ WROBA card number 001000010001, password Secret1

❑ WROBA card number 001000010002, password Secret2

Try It Out – Creating the Customer Logic Project

1. Begin by creating a new Standard EXE project and name it Bank_UI.

2. The Bank_UI project requires references set to the ActiveX Data Objects Libraries (either version 2.1 or 2.5 depending on your system configuration – the accompanying screen shot shows the situation for Windows 2000). Additionally, we also need to set a reference to the Bank_Bus ActiveX DLL, which provides the business services tier code. Again, you will need to navigate to the appropriate folder to locate the Bank_Bus DLL before being able to add the reference.

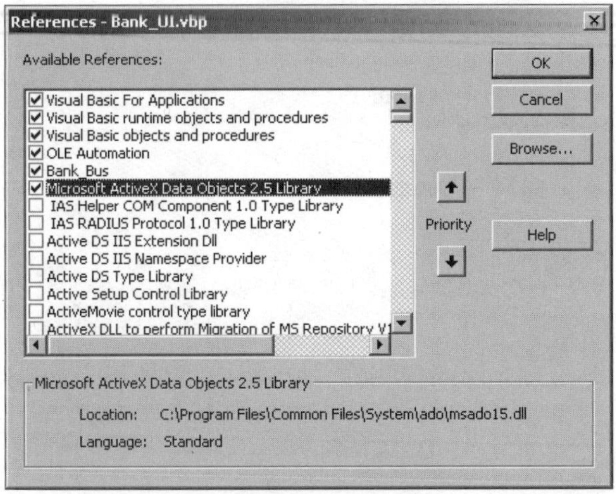

3. At this point in time we won't worry about the project properties, although later we'll need to set the Startup Object on the General tab (when we've built the form).

4. If you are coding Bank_UI.exe as part of a Project Group, then set this project as the project to start when the group is run for testing in the Visual Basic environment. To do this, highlight the project, right-click and select Set as Start Up.

After doing this, and when the code for the customer side of the Bank_UI project is in place, the case study can be tested in the Visual Basic environment. After seeing how the case study works, the administrative functions shown in the next chapter can be added – hence by the end of this chapter, we should be able to start to see the fruits of our labor.

The case study can be tested without placing the components for the business and data services under MTS or COM+ control (this is possible because of the way the case study is coded with context wrappers for the MTS objects). We'll see how to deploy the components for the business and data services tiers to MTS or COM+ later in this book.

Our first task in coding the user services tier is to add the shared code and class modules.

Shared Modules in the WROBA User Tier

There are three shared modules in the WROBA User Services Tier:

- ❑ The MMain code module contains procedures to instantiate and destroy the shared classes for the application. The StartWROBA and ExitWROBA procedures are called by methods of the FMainMenu form.

- ❑ The CPayeeInformation class module is used to maintain properties for payees when funds are transferred. These properties are used by more than one form, so a shared class is used to preserve the payee data in the user services tier.

- ❑ The SharedProperties class module contains public properties used throughout the user tier, such as the CardID and BankID for the logged in card account. It is also used to store results messages for account transactions.

Let's consider each of these modules in turn.

The MMain Code Module

MMain is called when the WROBA case study starts and when it exits. The following UML class diagram shows the methods and constants in the MMain code module. The class diagrams for the shared code and class modules were created using the Visual Modeler tool.

```
+--------------------------------------+
|            <<Module>>                |
|              MMain                   |
+--------------------------------------+
| ◈g_strAppTitle : String = "WROBA"    |
| ◈KEY_PREFIX : String = "Key="        |
+--------------------------------------+
| ✦StartWROBA()                        |
| ✦ExitWROBA()                         |
+--------------------------------------+
```

When the application starts, it calls StartWROBA to create the SharedProperties and CPayeeInformation classes, and it calls ExitWROBA to de-reference them when the application is exited. The StartWROBA procedure is called by the Form_Load procedure in the FMainMenu form. The ExitWROBA procedure is called from the event handler for the Exit command on the FMainMenu form, and sets the classes equal to Nothing to destroy them when the application is unloaded.

Try It Out – Coding the MMain Module

1. Create a new module, named **MMain** and add the following code:

```
Option Explicit

' Main module in the user tier

' Shared by all user tier modules. Provides communication between
' modules and stores last transaction status
Public g_objSharedProperties As SharedProperties

' Shared by all user tier modules. Provides communication between
' modules and stores payee information
Public g_objPayeeInformation As CPayeeInformation
```

2. Following the Public declarations of object variables for the shared classes, two global string constants are defined:

```
' Global string for title bar of forms in user tier
Public Const g_strAppTitle As String = "WROBA"

Public Const KEY_PREFIX As String = "Key="
```

3. StartWROBA and ExitWROBA create and destroy the instances of the shared CPayeeInformation and SharedProperties classes:

```
Public Sub StartWROBA()
' This procedure is executed when the application starts

    ' Create the global SharedProperties object
    Set g_objSharedProperties = New SharedProperties

    ' Create the global CPayeeInformation object
    Set g_objPayeeInformation = New CPayeeInformation
End Sub

Public Sub ExitWROBA()
    ' Clean up the global objects
    Set g_objSharedProperties = Nothing
    Set g_objPayeeInformation = Nothing
End Sub
```

The CPayeeInformation Class Module

The class module, CPayeeInformation, contains the Get and Let statements defining the property values used by the procedures that involve the payee. Classes such as CPayeeInformation are used to share data among different forms and classes because of their persistence during the application's lifetime.

Classes such as CPayeeInformation are defined at an early stage in the development of the application, and refined as the application is developed. As more detail is added to the code, such storage and message passing classes are iteratively refined by the addition of properties and methods.

The following class diagram shows the CPayeeInformation class module. Module level variables are indicated as being private to the module by the padlock symbols to the left of their names. Properties are indicated by the <<Get>> label, and the Init method is also shown:

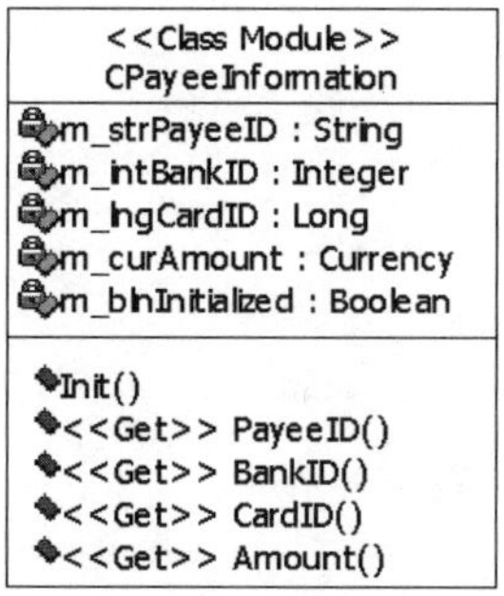

```
┌─────────────────────────────────┐
│      <<Class Module>>           │
│      CPayeeInformation          │
├─────────────────────────────────┤
│ 🔒m_strPayeeID : String          │
│ 🔒m_intBankID : Integer          │
│ 🔒m_lngCardID : Long             │
│ 🔒m_curAmount : Currency         │
│ 🔒m_blnInitialized : Boolean     │
├─────────────────────────────────┤
│ ◆Init()                         │
│ ◆<<Get>> PayeeID()              │
│ ◆<<Get>> BankID()               │
│ ◆<<Get>> CardID()               │
│ ◆<<Get>> Amount()               │
└─────────────────────────────────┘
```

Try It Out – Coding the CPayeeInformation Module

1. In this case, create a new *class* module, name it CPayeeInformation, and add the following code:

```
Option Explicit

' Class module in the user tier

' Module level variables
Private m_strPayeeID          As String
Private m_intBankID           As Integer
Private m_lngCardID           As Long
Private m_curAmount           As Currency

Private m_blnInitialized      As Boolean
```

2. An Init method is used to set all the property values with one call. The properties themselves are read-only.

```
Public Sub Init(ByVal PayeeID As String, ByVal BankID As Integer, _
    ByVal CardID As Long, ByVal Amount As Currency)
' Initialize the public properties of the class
' Called by other modules to set the property values

    m_strPayeeID = PayeeID
    m_intBankID = BankID
    m_lngCardID = CardID
    m_curAmount = Amount
```

```
    m_blnInitialized = True
End Sub

Public Property Get PayeeID() As String
' Read-only property

    ' Works within the development environment only
    ' Suspends execution if the class has not been initialized
    Debug.Assert (m_blnInitialized)

    PayeeID = m_strPayeeID
End Property

Public Property Get BankID() As Integer
' Read-only property

    ' Works within the development environment only
    ' Suspends execution if the class has not been initialized
    Debug.Assert (m_blnInitialized)

    BankID = m_intBankID
End Property

Public Property Get CardID() As Long
' Read-only property

    ' Works within the development environment only
    ' Suspends execution if the class has not been initialized
    Debug.Assert (m_blnInitialized)

    CardID = m_lngCardID
End Property

Public Property Get Amount() As Currency
' Read-only property

    ' Works within the development environment only
    ' Suspends execution if the class has not been initialized
    Debug.Assert (m_blnInitialized)

    Amount = m_curAmount
End Property
```

How It Works

The code that initializes the CPayeeInformation class calls the Init method and the values of the PayeeID, BankID, CardID, and Amount to pay are set. PayeeID is a string that contains the payee's description. These values are available to the code in other forms as Public properties, even though the form that initialized the class has gone out of scope. Shared classes are an alternative method to global variables for passing data and messages among forms and classes. Global variables are more prone to corruption and accidental reuse of their names than shared classes.

As an aid to debugging, m_blnInitialized is initialized as True after the other variables have been initialized and is used only during development to stop the execution of the code if the properties have not been initialized. The Debug.Assert statement will cause the code execution to stop if the expression is False. As long as the procedure Init has run and the class has been initialized, the expression will evaluate to True.

The SharedProperties Class Module

The SharedProperties class module code contains a large number of property variables that will be accessed by many of the procedures we'll be encountering over the forthcoming pages. The following class diagram shows the properties of the SharedProperties class. Notice that the Get (read) and Let (write) property definitions are shown separately.

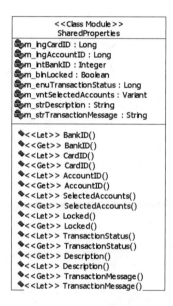

Try It Out – Coding the SharedProperties Module

1. Again create a new class module, name it SharedProperties, and add the following code:

```
Option Explicit

' Class module in the user tier

' Module level variables
Private m_lngCardID              As Long
Private m_lngAccountID           As Long
Private m_intBankID             As Integer
Private m_blnLocked             As Boolean
Private m_enuTransactionStatus  As Long
Private m_vntSelectedAccounts   As Variant
Private m_strDescription        As String
Private m_strTransactionMessage As String
```

2. The module level variables defined first are used internally in the class to read and write the property values. The next two definitions are for the `BankID` property that identifies the bank associated with the logged-in card account:

```
Public Property Get BankID() As Integer
    ' Property Get provides the Read portion of the property
    BankID = m_intBankID
End Property

Public Property Let BankID(ByVal intBankID As Integer)
    ' Property Let provides the Write portion of the property
    m_intBankID = intBankID
End Property
```

3. The `CardID` and `AccountID` of the logged-in card account are defined next as read/write properties:

```
Public Property Get CardID() As Long
    CardID = m_lngCardID
End Property

Public Property Let CardID(ByVal lngCardID As Long)
    m_lngCardID = lngCardID
End Property

Public Property Get AccountID() As Long
    AccountID = m_lngAccountID
End Property

Public Property Let AccountID(ByVal lngAccountID As Long)
    m_lngAccountID = lngAccountID
End Property
```

4. `SelectedAccounts` is a Variant property that is used to identify accounts that are selected for actions. A Variant is used so the data type is not constrained:

```
Public Property Get SelectedAccounts() As Variant
    SelectedAccounts = m_vntSelectedAccounts
End Property

Public Property Let SelectedAccounts(ByVal vntSelectedAccounts _
    As Variant)

    m_vntSelectedAccounts = vntSelectedAccounts
End Property
```

5. The Locked property is a Boolean value that is used to indicate whether a lock on an account has been granted. TransactionStatus is a Long that is one of the two ways that the results of a transaction are returned to the calling procedure.

```
Public Property Get Locked() As Boolean
    Locked = m_blnLocked
End Property

Public Property Let Locked(ByVal blnLocked As Boolean)
    m_blnLocked = blnLocked
End Property

Public Property Get TransactionStatus() As Long
    TransactionStatus = m_enuTransactionStatus
End Property

Public Property Let TransactionStatus(ByVal enuTransactionStatus _
    As Long)

    m_enuTransactionStatus = enuTransactionStatus
End Property
```

6. Description is a String property that is used for descriptive text such as bank names. TransactionMessage is another String, used to return result messages for transactions.

```
Public Property Get Description() As String
    Description = m_strDescription
End Property

Public Property Let Description(ByVal strDescription As String)
    m_strDescription = strDescription
End Property

Public Property Get TransactionMessage() As String
    TransactionMessage = m_strTransactionMessage
End Property

Public Property Let TransactionMessage(strMessage As String)
    m_strTransactionMessage = strMessage
End Property
```

Logging into the WROBA Application

When the application is started, the first screen presented to the user is the login screen. It's pretty basic; the user just needs to enter their card number and password and press Log In. The Main Menu form is actually the first to be loaded (and will be set as the startup object for the project), but it remains hidden until login is successful, so we will begin with looking at the login screen.

The following class diagram shows FLogin's methods. These methods are all Private to the form. The data that FLogin collects, and the login validation returned to the FMainMenu form, are passed in the properties of the SharedProperties class.

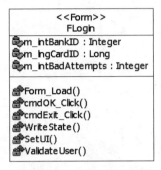

Try It Out – Implementing the FLogin Form

1. Add a new form to the project called FLogin and set it up as shown (remember to set the PasswordChar property for txtPassword to * to show the standard masked password):

2. First, we set up some variables and an Enum to define the possible login results, then we set up the Form_Load event. SetUI is called from the Load_Form sub to reset the number of attempted logins to zero and set the form and label captions. The bad login count is stored in the m_intBadAttempts variable. The user has five attempts to login correctly; this number is defined by the business logic in the business services tier. After the fifth failed attempt, the user receives a locked message and access is denied to the login screen. If the same account number is entered for each attempt, that card is also locked and the administrator needs to unlock it.

```
Option Explicit

' Form code in the user tier

Private m_intBankID As Integer
Private m_lngCardID As Long
Private m_intBadAttempts As Integer
```

```
Private Enum ELoginStatus
   lgnOK = 0
   lgnBad = 1
   lgnInUse = 2
   lgnLocked = 3
   lgnExit = 4
End Enum

Private Sub Form_Load()
   SetUI
End Sub

Private Sub SetUI()
   m_intBadAttempts = 0

   Me.Caption = g_strAppTitle
   lblTitle.Caption = "Login Screen"
End Sub
```

3. Next, we need to add the code for the button `Click` events. The `cmdOK_Click` procedure checks the logon status after calling the `ValidateUser` method. If the logon is locked after five tries, the `lgnLocked` case applies and access to the card is blocked. The `FStatus` form is displayed using the error message string provided if the card is locked or already in use. The return status of the login is written to the `TransactionStatus` property of the `SharedProperties` class. If the **Exit** button is clicked, an exit status code is written to `TransactionStatus`. `WriteUI` is called to save the `BankID` and `CardID` as `SharedProperties` properties.

```
Private Sub cmdOK_Click()
' Check for correct password
   Select Case ValidateUser(Trim$(txtCardID.Text), _
      Trim$(txtPassword.Text))

   Case lgnOK
      g_objSharedProperties.TransactionStatus = lgnOK
      WriteState ' Save the BankID and CardID
      Unload Me 'Go back to main menu

   Case lgnBad
      g_objSharedProperties.TransactionStatus = lgnBad
      MsgBox "Invalid Password, try again!", , _
         "Login - " & g_strAppTitle
      txtPassword.SetFocus
      ' Place the cursor at the end of the password entry
      SendKeys "{Home}+{End}"

   Case lgnLocked
      g_objSharedProperties.TransactionStatus = lgnLocked
      WriteState ' Save the BankID and CardID
      g_objSharedProperties.TransactionMessage = _
         "WROBA Card is locked." & vbCrLf & _
         "Please see the Administrator to unlock the card"
      Me.Hide
```

```
        FStatus.Show vbModal
        Me.Show vbModal

    Case lgnInUse
        g_objSharedProperties.TransactionStatus = lgnInUse
        WriteState ' Save the BankID and CardID
        g_objSharedProperties.TransactionMessage = _
            "WROBA Card is in use." & vbCrLf & _
            "Please try again later."

        Me.Hide
        FStatus.Show vbModal
        Me.Show vbModal
    Case Else
    End Select
End Sub

Private Sub cmdExit_Click()
' Exit the application
    g_objSharedProperties.TransactionStatus = lgnExit
    Unload Me
End Sub

Private Sub WriteState()
' Set the CardID and BankID to the global
' SharedProperties class object
    g_objSharedProperties.BankID = m_intBankID
    g_objSharedProperties.CardID = m_lngCardID
End Sub
```

4. Now we have to add the ValidateUser function to actually handle the logon and validation of the account number and password. The return status is first set to assume a failure (lgnBad), then verification is performed on the CardID string argument to check the length of the string and that it is a numeric value. Then a business services tier Bank object is instantiated:

```
Private Function ValidateUser(strCardId As String, _
    strPassword As String) As ELoginStatus

    Dim objBank As Bank_Bus.Bank
    Dim objBankLocator As Bank_Bus.BankLocator
    Dim intInvalidCount As Integer
    Dim blnValidateUser As Integer
    Dim intMaxBadTries As Integer
    Dim strBankDSN As String

    On Error GoTo ErrorHandler
    ' Pessimistic assumption that the login will fail
    ValidateUser = lgnBad

    If Len(strCardId) = 12 And IsNumeric(strCardId) Then
        blnValidateUser = False

        ' Prepare for call to business tier
        Set objBank = New Bank_Bus.Bank
```

5. The `GetCardID` and `GetBankID` business rules properties of the `Bank` component in the business services tier are called to parse the `CardID` and `BankID`. Even though the comments in the code show how these properties are parsed, the code in the user services tier actually knows nothing about these properties. Any changes made to the business rules won't require any changes to the user services tier code. The parsed `BankID` is then used as the argument for another call to the business services tier to locate the connection string for the selected bank:

```
' The 9 rightmost digits are the WROBA Card ID. This logic is
' maintained in the business layer
m_lngCardID = objBank.GetCardID(strCardId)


' The 3 leftmost digits are the Bank ID. This logic is
' maintained in the business layer
m_intBankID = objBank.GetBankID(strCardId)


' Prepare for call to business tier
Set objBankLocator = New Bank_Bus.BankLocator
' Find the selected bank. Code for the case study is
' implemented for only 1 bank. To add other banks, change
' the code in the Bank_DB.BankLocator class module in the
' Bank_DB project.
strBankDSN = objBankLocator.GetBank(m_intBankID)
```

6. If the bank is located, the maximum number of login attempts that are permitted is retrieved from the business services tier (another business rule that was discovered when the Use Case Scenario for a login was analyzed). Then an attempt to log in the user is made by calling the `VerifyLogin` method of the `Bank` component in the business services tier:

```
If Len(strBankDSN) > 0 Then
    ' If the bank exists and code is implemented to
    ' handle more banks.
    ' Call the business tier to find out the maximum
    ' allowable number of login attempts
    intMaxBadTries = objBank.MaxBadTries
    ' Call the login verification procedure in the
    ' business tier
    blnValidateUser = objBank.VerifyLogin(m_intBankID, _
        m_lngCardID, strPassword, intInvalidCount)
```

7. If the number of login attempts is less than the maximum allowed, the login result is checked for success and an attempt is made to acquire a lock on the WROBA card account by calling the `WROBALock` property. The results of the login attempt and the attempt to acquire the lock on the card account are written to the `Locked` property of the `SharedProperties` class. If the login attempt failed, the `UpdatePasswordCount` method of the `Bank` class in the business services tier is called to increment the number of failed login tries:

```
            If intInvalidCount = intMaxBadTries Then
                ' If the WROBA card is locked out the Administrator
        ' can unlock it using FAdminUnlock.
                ' During testing, delete the row referencing the
                ' WROBA card in the TxLock table. .
                ValidateUser = lgnLocked
            Else
                If blnValidateUser Then
                    m_intBadAttempts = 0
                    ' Attempt to get a lock on the WROBA card
                    If objBank.WROBALock(m_intBankID, m_lngCardID) Then
                        g_objSharedProperties.Locked = True
                        ValidateUser = lgnOK
                    Else
                        ' If the WROBA card is already in use or is
                        ' already locked out due to an unhandled error
                        ' or too many failed login attempts then report
                        ' the card is in use
                        ValidateUser = lgnInUse
                        g_objSharedProperties.Locked = True
                    End If
                Else
                    ' Validation failed
                    m_intBadAttempts = m_intBadAttempts + 1
                    If m_intBadAttempts < intMaxBadTries Then
                        ' Report failed login attempt
                        ValidateUser = lgnBad
                    Else
                        ' lock WROBA card
                        ValidateUser = lgnLocked
                    End If
                End If
                ' Call the business tier to update the number
                ' of login attempts
                objBank.UpdatePasswordCount m_intBankID, _
                m_lngCardID, m_intBadAttempts
            End If
        End If
    End If

    Clean_Up:
    Set objBank = Nothing
    Set objBankLocator = Nothing
    Exit Function

ErrorHandler:
    GoTo Clean_Up
End Function
```

How It Works

When the Log In button is clicked, the code verifies that the account and password are correct by calling a method in the business tier.

Remember, as set up, we have two valid customer logins for our application:

- ❑   WROBA card number 001000010001, password Secret1
- ❑   WROBA card number 001000010002, password Secret2

Once the details are verified, the user is allowed to progress to the next screen; the Main Menu. If the details fail verification, the user has four more chances to enter the correct account number and password before the session is ended and the card is locked out.

The Click event for the Log In button controls what happens during the verification of the account number and password. If the card is verified as OK, logon is approved and the card is locked to prevent others from logging on with the same card ID. Inserting the CardID into the database table called TxLock sets the lock. The remaining test cases are for failed logons, which would be the result of a bad password, a locked card (improper ending of the program, resulting in the lock key not being removed), or the card already being in use.

The actual verification is handled by the function ValidateUser. After the results from the login attempt are analyzed, they are written to properties in the SharedProperties class for use by the FMainMenu form.

In the cases of the function returning a value showing the card is accepted, in use, or locked, the WriteState method is called to allow variables in the global class SharedProperties to be set:

```
Private Sub WriteState()
' Set the CardID and BankID to the global
' SharedProperties class object
   g_objSharedProperties.BankID = m_intBankID
   g_objSharedProperties.CardID = m_lngCardID
End Sub
```

A feature of good GUI design we considered at the head of the chapter was that of giving visual feedback. We'll find a number of places through this chapter where we wish to alert the user to the success or failure of their activity (particularly for the transaction-based task we meet at the end of the chapter) so let's now consider the provision of dialogs to provide feedback.

Status Forms

After many of the procedures used in the case study are completed, resulting in success or failure, a form is displayed alerting the user of the status of the activity. The following two screen shots illustrate the types of status messages displayed by the status form FStatus:

WROBA - Operation Status

Operation successful.

OK

WROBA - Operation Status

Addition of this payee not allowed. Error.

OK

Try It Out – Implementing the FStatus Form

1. Add a new form to the project with the design shown above (controls labeled `lblStatus` and `cmdOK` as appropriate).

2. Add the following code:

```
Option Explicit

' Form code in the user tier

' Return values enumeration for transactions
Private Enum ETransactionStatus
    txsSuccess = 0
    txsDailyLimitExceeded = 1
    txsNotEnoughFunds = 2
    txsUnknownError = 3
End Enum

Private Sub cmdOK_Click()
    Unload Me
End Sub

Private Sub Form_Load()
    SetUI
End Sub
```

3. This bit of code displays the status messages, based on the value of the `TransactionStatus` property passed from the forms. The numeric `TransactionStatus` property is checked only if the string `TransactionMessage` property is empty (Null String).

```
Private Sub SetUI()
    Dim strMessage As String

    Me.Caption = g_strAppTitle & " - Operation Status"
    If g_objSharedProperties.TransactionMessage = "" Then
        Select Case g_objSharedProperties.TransactionStatus
        Case ETransactionStatus.txsSuccess
            strMessage = "Operation successful."
        Case ETransactionStatus.txsDailyLimitExceeded
            strMessage = "Daily limit exceeded."
        Case ETransactionStatus.txsNotEnoughFunds
            strMessage = "Not enough funds."
        Case ETransactionStatus.txsUnknownError
            strMessage = "Operation failed. Unknown error."
        Case Else
            strMessage = "Unknown error."
        End Select
    Else
        strMessage = g_objSharedProperties.TransactionMessage
    End If

    lblStatus.Caption = strMessage
End Sub
```

How It Works

The `SetUI` method controls what message is displayed in the dialog, determined by the actual code and form that calls the status form into focus. The string variable, `strMessage`, is created from the variables stored in `TransactionMessage` or `TransactionStatus` properties, and provides the caption text, displayed on the form using the label control, `lblStatus`.

Once the account has been validated, resulting in access allowed, the Main Menu is no longer hidden and can be viewed.

WROBA Customer Main Menu

The WROBA customer main menu provides four main menu items (File, Information, Transaction, and Help). As we'll find out during coding, the Information and Transaction menus are the ones that contain submenus that enable the customer to carry out various activities; we'll investigate those more closely later. The File and Help menus provide a way to exit the program and some limited information on the application. Their position on the form and the actions they reveal are what might be expected from any Windows application and thus this part of the form design fits in with the consistency aspect of GUI development we talked about earlier.

As we pointed out above, this is the form that is initially loaded on starting the application (and will be set as the startup object for the project). However, it is hidden until a successful login is obtained.

The form itself also contains a large list box that allows the customer to immediately view the status of their accounts after a successful login:

The menu for the `FMainMenu` form was generated by the Menu Editor, which is a Visual Basic tool that can be used for prototyping menus like this one. The objects that it creates have a `Click` event and expose properties that enable various options to be exercised, such as enabling or disabling menu items, or making those items visible or invisible. The Menu Editor is limited in the things that it can do; for example, it can't create a toolbar and it also has some quirks like not exposing a property to control its color. This latter foible can be worked around by changing the color of everything else in the form, but in production applications straight coding will probably be the best route to menu creation. Having said that, the Menu Editor does make an excellent prototyping tool, and a lot of the code written for the menus it creates can be reused in later stages of the application development process.

The following class diagram shows the methods of the `FMainMenu` form. The methods that start with mnu are the Click event handlers for the menu items.

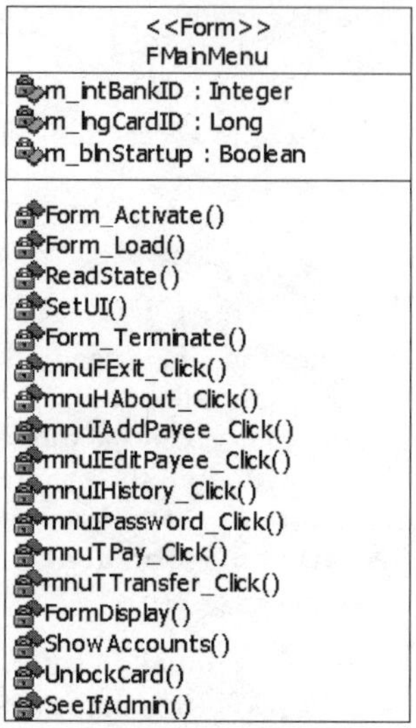

<<Form>>
FMainMenu
m_intBankID : Integer
m_lngCardID : Long
m_blnStartup : Boolean
Form_Activate()
Form_Load()
ReadState()
SetUI()
Form_Terminate()
mnuFExit_Click()
mnuHAbout_Click()
mnuIAddPayee_Click()
mnuIEditPayee_Click()
mnuIHistory_Click()
mnuIPassword_Click()
mnuTPay_Click()
mnuTTransfer_Click()
FormDisplay()
ShowAccounts()
UnlockCard()
SeeIfAdmin()

Let's now have a look at how to use the Menu Editor when we build the customer main menu form.

Try It Out – Building the Customer Main Menu Form

1. Add a new form to the project named `FMainMenu` and set up the label and listview controls as in the above figure (with the listview control named lvwAccounts).

2. With the focus on `FMainMenu`, choose Tools | Menu Editor... .

3. To start, we're going to add the top level File menu. When the Menu Editor opens, enter &File in the Caption: box, and mnuFile as the Name. The ampersand character sets the following key (here F) as the shortcut key for the menu item. Set the Index to 0. The result should look similar to the following screen shot:

Menu Editor
Caption: &File
Name: mnuFile
Index: 0
Shortcut: (None)
HelpContextID: 0
NegotiatePosition: 0 - None
Checked
Enabled
Visible
WindowList
OK
Cancel
Next
Insert
Delete
&File

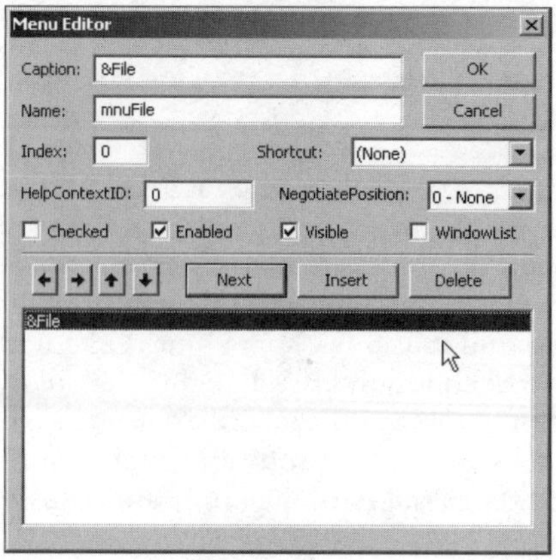

4. Click Next to enter the menu item and move down to the next line in the menu textbox; let's add the Exit second level menu control. Click the right arrow to indent the new menu item. Enter E&xit as the Caption, and mnuFExit as the Name. Set the Index to 0. The Menu Editor screen should look similar to the following figure. The left and right arrows are used to control the menu item level; indenting menu items makes them options under the previous menu item. It is possible (although unlikely that it would be desired in practice) to have up to five levels of submenus. The naming convention used starts all menu items with "mnu", followed by an initial indicating which menu the item is for. So, items for the File menu start with "mnuF".

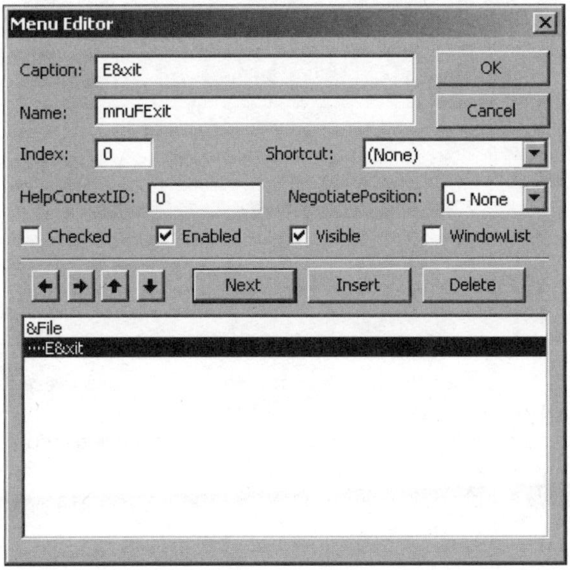

5. Press OK, and the form should have a File menu added with the Exit option revealed on clicking it.

6. On going to the code window for the form, the menu option Click events are exposed as the appropriate menu objects are selected. Writing code for these events enables a menu structure to be prototyped quickly.

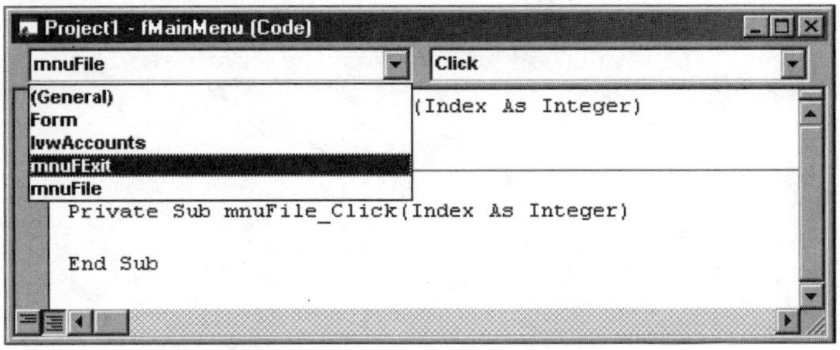

7. Now return to the menu editor; highlight the ...E&xit line, press Next, use the left arrow to remove the added indentation, and add the Information menu (without any options at this point in time). The name for the Information menu is mnuInformation, and it should have a caption of &Information.

8. Repeat this to add the Transaction menu (without options) and the Help menu (with the About option) to give:

Although the code in this form doesn't take advantage of it (because there are very few menu items), the `Click` event is passed an argument that is an index into the controls in the menu item. We can use a `Select Case` statement to handle the logic for the menu selection based on the index position of the control that was clicked. Code similar to this, which uses control arrays of command buttons to decide which command button was clicked, is used in many of the forms in the WROBA case study.

Now that the form has the correct appearance, we need to add the code to make it useful.

Try It Out – Adding Code to the Main Menu

1. The very first thing we'll do is to ensure this is the startup object for the `Bank_UI` project, so select **Project | Bank_UI Properties** and on the **General** tab go to the **Startup Object** combo box, select **FMainMenu** and **OK** the dialog.

2. Add the following code to the form to set module level variables and an `Enum` for the results of a login attempt. The results will be read from the `TransactionStatus` property of the `SharedProperties` class:

```
Option Explicit

' Form code in the user tier

Private m_frmCurrent As Form
Private m_intBankID As Integer
Private m_lngCardID As Long
Private m_blnStartup As Boolean
```

```
Private Enum ELoginStatus
    lgnOK = 0
    lgnBad = 1
    lgnInUse = 2
    lgnLocked = 3
    lgnExit = 4
End Enum
```

3. The `Form_Activate` method uses the `m_blnStartup` flag to determine whether the form has been activated as a result of the application starting up or as a result of focus being returned to the main menu form from some other form. This flag determines whether the current data for the user's accounts (Checking and Savings) are shown. Focus is then set to the form, and `SendKeys` is used to send a press of the *Alt* key to the menu. This is done to activate the menu, and because the menu generated by the Menu Editor does not show the underline under the menu shortcut keys unless *Alt* is pressed. The percent sign is used as a symbolic representation of the *Alt* key by the `SendKeys` function.

```
Private Sub Form_Activate()
    If m_blnStartup = False Then
        ShowAccounts
    Else
        m_blnStartup = False
    End If

    Me.SetFocus

    SendKeys "%", True ' Alt key to activate the menu
End Sub
```

4. Next we need to add code that loads and displays the Login form and decides whether or not to load the Administration menu form:

```
Private Sub Form_Load()
    Dim lngStatus As Long
    Dim blnAdmin As Boolean

    m_blnStartup = True
    StartWROBA

    Me.Hide
    FLogin.Show vbModal

    Select Case g_objSharedProperties.TransactionStatus

    Case ELoginStatus.lgnExit, ELoginStatus.lgnBad, _
            ELoginStatus.lgnInUse, ELoginStatus.lgnLocked
        ExitWROBA
        Unload Me

    Case ELoginStatus.lgnOK
        ReadState
        blnAdmin = SeeIfAdmin()
```

5. The following code controls the display of the user and administrative menu forms. If an administrative login has been provided, the FMainMenu form is hidden and the administrative menu form (FAdminMainMenu) is shown. In either case, the menu forms are shown modally. If the FAdminMainMenu form is shown, when it is exited the application is exited:

```
        If Not blnAdmin Then
            SetUI
            Me.Show vbModal
        Else
            Me.Hide
            FAdminMainMenu.Show vbModal
            ExitWROBA
            Unload Me
        End If
    End Select
End Sub
```

6. The following methods retrieve details for the logged in user, set the interface to show current account data, and set the module level form variable equal to Nothing to release the variable:

```
Private Sub ReadState()
' Get the BankID and selected accounts from the global
' SharedProperties class object
    m_intBankID = g_objSharedProperties.BankID
    m_lngCardID = g_objSharedProperties.CardID
End Sub

Private Sub SetUI()
    Me.Caption = g_strAppTitle
    ShowAccounts
End Sub

Private Sub Form_Terminate()
    Set m_frmCurrent = Nothing
End Sub
```

7. When the Exit menu item is chosen from the File menu the card account is unlocked, ExitWROBA (in the MMain code module) is called to destroy the shared classes, and the Main Menu form is unloaded. This exits the application when the startup form is closed:

```
Private Sub mnuFExit_Click(Index As Integer)
    UnlockCard
    ExitWROBA
    Unload Me
End Sub
```

8. The `Click` event handlers for the menu items (except for **Exit**) all follow the same pattern. The `FormDisplay` method is called, with the form to display as a calling argument to `FormDisplay`. This method hides the menu form and shows the requested form modally. When the displayed form is closed, the code resumes execution and shows the menu form again:

```
Private Sub mnuHAbout_Click(Index As Integer)
    FormDisplay FAbout
End Sub

Private Sub FormDisplay(FormToShow As Form)
    Me.Hide
    Set m_frmCurrent = FormToShow
    m_frmCurrent.Show vbModal
    Set m_frmCurrent = Nothing
    Me.Show vbModal
End Sub
```

9. These methods unlock the card account as part of exiting the application and check to see if a login was an administrative login. The `Admin` class of the business services tier is called to evaluate the login type:

```
Private Sub UnlockCard()
    Dim objBank As Bank_Bus.Bank

    Set objBank = New Bank_Bus.Bank

    objBank.WROBAUnLock m_intBankID, m_lngCardID

    Set objBank = Nothing
End Sub

Private Function SeeIfAdmin() As Boolean
    Dim objBank As Bank_Bus.Admin

    Set objBank = New Bank_Bus.Admin

    SeeIfAdmin = objBank.GetAccountType(m_intBankID, m_lngCardID)

    Set objBank = Nothing
End Function
```

10. As we saw, the main menu allows a customer to see the status of their accounts. This is achieved by the `ShowAccounts` method. An ADO recordset is returned by the business services tier that contains the current data for the accounts belonging to the logged in user. This recordset is returned to the business services tier by using a pass-through call to the data services tier, which gets the data from the database. The `GetAccounts` and `GetAccountBalance` properties are called to return the accounts and account data. The `listview` control on the menu form is filled with this account data:

537

```
Private Sub ShowAccounts()
    Dim objBank As Bank_Bus.Bank
    Dim recAccounts As ADODB.Recordset
    Dim objAccountListItem As MSComctlLib.ListItem
    Dim strAccountTypeDesc As String
    Dim curBalance As Currency
    Dim curDailyRemaining As Currency
    Dim curOverdraftLimit As Currency

    lvwAccounts.ListItems.Clear

    ' Prepare for call to business tier
    Set objBank = New Bank_Bus.Bank
    ' Retrieve the accounts
    Set recAccounts = objBank.GetAccounts(m_intBankID, m_lngCardID)

    If Not (recAccounts Is Nothing) Then
        Do While Not recAccounts.EOF ' Until end of recordset
            ' Display the data for each selected account
            objBank.GetAccountBalance m_intBankID, _
                recAccounts!AccountID, _
                strAccountTypeDesc, curBalance, _
                curDailyRemaining, curOverdraftLimit

            Set objAccountListItem = lvwAccounts.ListItems.Add(, _
                KEY_PREFIX & CStr(recAccounts!AccountID), _
                strAccountTypeDesc)
            objAccountListItem.SubItems(1) = curBalance
            objAccountListItem.SubItems(2) = curDailyRemaining
            objAccountListItem.SubItems(3) = curOverdraftLimit
            recAccounts.MoveNext ' Next row in recordset
        Loop
        lvwAccounts.Refresh
        lvwAccounts.Enabled = False
        Set recAccounts = Nothing
    End If

    Set objBank = Nothing
    Set objAccountListItem = Nothing
End Sub
```

How It Works

The first interesting thing to highlight is that the code in the Form_Activate event uses the
SendKeys method to send a message consisting of the *Alt* key, which is represented by the symbol for
the percent sign, to the menu. The *Alt* key activates the menu and highlights the File menu option.

```
SendKeys "%", True ' Alt key to activate the menu
```

One of the quirks of menus designed with the Menu Editor is that, unlike menus created in code, the
menu is not activated, and menu shortcut keys are not indicated by being underlined, unless the menu is
activated by pressing the *Alt* key. The SendKeys method is used here to activate the menu on startup.

The Form_Load method first calls the StartWROBA method of the MMain code module which instantiates SharedProperties and CPayeeInformation objects for use. It then hides the main menu form while the login form gets the necessary information (and as we have seen above the login form makes use of the SharedProperties object):

```
Private Sub Form_Load()
    Dim lngStatus As Long
    Dim blnAdmin As Boolean

    m_blnStartup = True
    StartWROBA

    Me.Hide
    FLogin.Show vbModal
```

If login is successful, the user is allowed to access the main menu and, based on the logon credentials (examined in the SeeIfAdmin method), the main menu determines if the user is an administrator or customer and loads the Administration menu if not a customer (the Administration menu will be discussed at length in the next chapter):

```
Case ELoginStatus.lgnOK
    ReadState
    blnAdmin = SeeIfAdmin()

    If Not blnAdmin Then
        SetUI
        Me.Show vbModal
    Else
        Me.Hide
        FAdminMainMenu.Show vbModal
        ExitWROBA
        Unload Me
    End If
```

If the login is OK, then the ReadState method is used to set the module level variables from the information contained in SharedProperties (which was provided through the login form):

```
Private Sub ReadState()
' Get the BankID and selected accounts from the global
' SharedProperties class object
    m_intBankID = g_objSharedProperties.BankID
    m_lngCardID = g_objSharedProperties.CardID
End Sub
```

Note that when the FAdminMainMenu form is exited, the code in this form restarts execution – at the ExitWROBA call. This call to a method in the MMain module ensures that the SharedProperties and CPayeeInformation objects are set to Nothing. This is an important point and the same approach is used to release all objects in the functions used within the code for the forms in the user tier.

For example, the SeeIfAdmin method starts with the variable declaration and object instantiation:

```
Dim objBank As Bank_Bus.Admin

Set objBank = New Bank_Bus.Admin
```

and ends with setting the object value to Nothing:

```
Set objBank = Nothing
```

This is to unload the objects from memory in preparation for the next call for that object to prevent **memory leaks**. When several object variables refer to the same object, memory and system resources used by the object are released only after all of them have been set to Nothing. Not doing this means new objects are created, using more memory and resources. Not releasing all objects can also result in the failure of an application to shut down completely, leaving it in memory.

If the account validates as a customer account, the SetUI method is called and this sets the caption of the form and calls the ShowAccounts method:

```
Private Sub SetUI()
    Me.Caption = g_strAppTitle
    ShowAccounts
End Sub
```

The ShowAccounts method shows the funds available to the customer; it works by making a call to the business tier requesting the information (for our purposes, we are connecting to the SQL Server database, using the Bank_Bus.Bank class) and populating the form with the account information.

When the user selects a menu option the Click event for that option is fired. This behavior is identical to the behavior of a command button. The code for the **Exit** menu unlocks the WROBA card (via the UnlockCard method), calls the clean up method, ExitWROBA, and then unloads the form and closes the application:

```
Private Sub mnuFExit_Click(Index As Integer)
    UnlockCard
    ExitWROBA
    Unload Me
End Sub
```

The code for the **About** menu option Click event calls the private FormDisplay method with the name of the form for that menu choice:

```
Private Sub mnuHAbout_Click(Index As Integer)
    FormDisplay FAbout
End Sub

Private Sub FormDisplay(FormToShow As Form)
    Me.Hide
    Set m_frmCurrent = FormToShow
    m_frmCurrent.Show vbModal
    Set m_frmCurrent = Nothing
    Me.Show vbModal
End Sub
```

The private `FormDisplay` method is passed a `Form` object as an argument, and displays that form modally. When the form is closed, it is set equal to `Nothing`, which destroys the form, and the `FMainMenu` form is shown again. The code that shows the `FMainMenu` form again is the line `Me.Show vbModal`. At this point the `FMainMenu` form is again waiting for user input. This is the same method that is used to display all the forms for Customer functions.

This type of sequence is typical in Windows applications, which are user and event driven. Most of the time an application is running it is waiting for user input in the form of a menu selection. The action selected by the menu item selection is performed, and then the application goes back to waiting for the next user input.

We've only coded two menu options at this point – we've seen what happens when the Exit option is selected, but the About option calls the `FAbout` form.

Try It Out – Adding the About WROBA screen

1. Every application needs an About screen and the WROBA application is no different, so add a new form to the project named `FAbout` and add the following code:

```
Option Explicit

Private Sub cmdOK_Click()
  Unload Me
End Sub

Private Sub Form_Load()
  SetUI
End Sub

Private Sub SetUI()
  Me.Caption = "About " & g_strAppTitle
  lblLabel.Caption = "WROBA 1.0" & vbCrLf & _
    "WRox Online Banking Application" & vbCrLf & _
    "Wrox Press"
End Sub
```

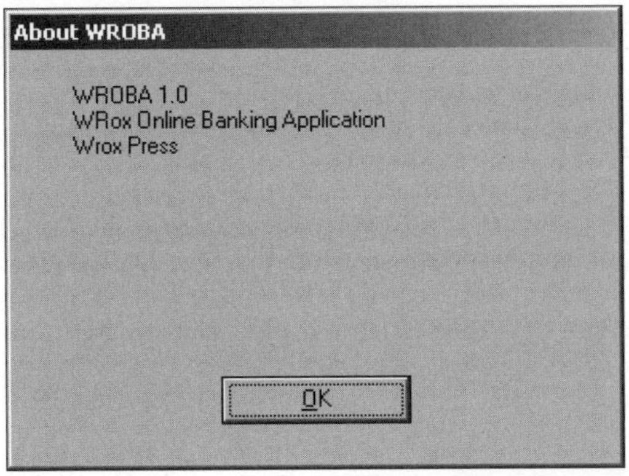

About WROBA

WROBA 1.0
WRox Online Banking Application
Wrox Press

OK

Now that the customer account information is loaded, they'll want to be able to carry out a variety of tasks – the first activities we'll consider (checking account history, administering payee accounts, and changing their password) are accessed via the Information menu.

WROBA Customer Information Menu

The Information menu contains four menu items: Account History, Add Payee, Edit Payee, and Change Password. These menu items were discovered when we analyzed the Use Case Scenarios earlier. The purpose of Account History should be obvious: the user selects this if they want to check the details of their account history. The Add and Edit Payee menus allow the user to set up electronic payments. In order to pay a bill, the bank needs to know what account to transfer the funds to; Add Payee allows the user to set this up. Edit Payee is used to change or correct information. The final menu item is for the user to change their password. We can represent the options available as follows:

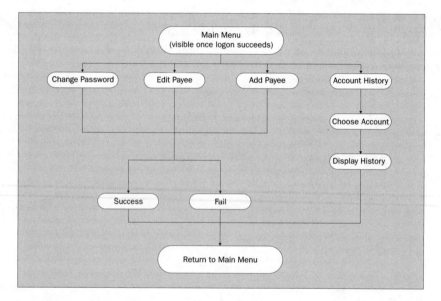

So, in this part of the chapter we'll be looking at how to implement the four menu options and seeing how we can:

- ❑ Display account details to customers
- ❑ Enable customers to add payees
- ❑ Enable customers to edit payees
- ❑ Enable customers to change their password

First though, we need to amend FMainMenu to add the appropriate options under this menu.

Try It Out – Adding the Information Menu Options

1. Return to the FMainMenu form, give it the focus and open up the Menu Editor. Highlight &Transaction and click Insert six times to add the appropriate number of lines. Next add the following caption/name pairs with appropriate indentation (one click of right button) and indices:

Menu Caption	Menu Name	Index
Account &History	mnuIHistory	0
–	mnuIDivider1	1
&Add Payees	mnuIAddPayee	2
&Edit Payees	mnuIEditPayee	3
–	mnuIDivider2	4
&Change Password	mnuIPassword	5

The hyphen character is used as a menu group separator.

2. Then add the following code for the Click events for the menu options:

```
Private Sub mnuIAddPayee_Click(Index As Integer)
    FormDisplay FPayee
End Sub

Private Sub mnuIEditPayee_Click(Index As Integer)
    FormDisplay FPayeeEdit
End Sub

Private Sub mnuIHistory_Click(Index As Integer)
    FormDisplay FHistory
End Sub

Private Sub mnuIPassword_Click(Index As Integer)
    FormDisplay FChangePassword
End Sub
```

The next job is to add and code each of the forms we can access through this set of options.

Displaying Account Details

Choosing Account History will engage us in a bit of progressive disclosure, as on selecting that option the customer will see the FHistory form that enables them to select which account they wish to see details of:

After making the selection they will then see the `FHistoryDetails` form, which has **Next** and **Previous** buttons that are activated if there are more than five transactions to display:

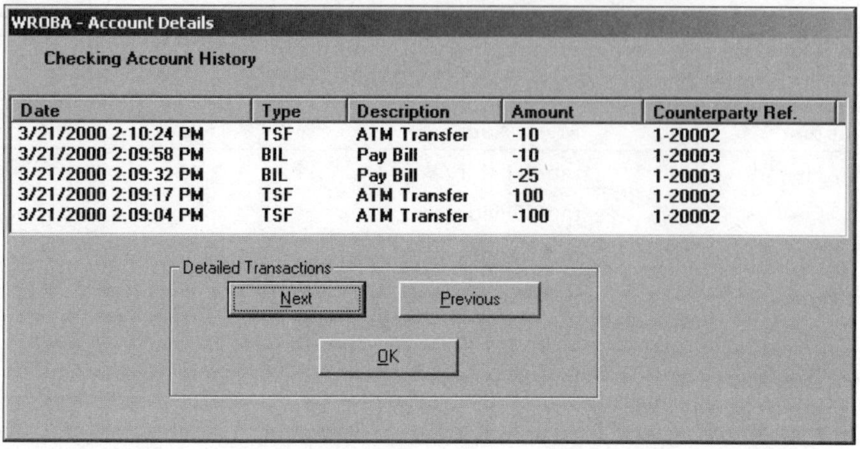

Date	Type	Description	Amount	Counterparty Ref.
3/21/2000 2:10:24 PM	TSF	ATM Transfer	-10	1-20002
3/21/2000 2:09:58 PM	BIL	Pay Bill	-10	1-20003
3/21/2000 2:09:32 PM	BIL	Pay Bill	-25	1-20003
3/21/2000 2:09:17 PM	TSF	ATM Transfer	100	1-20002
3/21/2000 2:09:04 PM	TSF	ATM Transfer	-100	1-20002

WROBA - Account Details

Checking Account History

Detailed Transactions

Next   Previous

OK

Note that this form may look as if it is straying from the standard Windows design principles we are used to. However, as long as our forms are consistent throughout our application, the user will be comfortable with their layout and, ultimately, with using them. After all, good design is all about using 'standards' as guidelines and yet still being a little creative!

The following class diagram shows the `FHistory` form's methods.

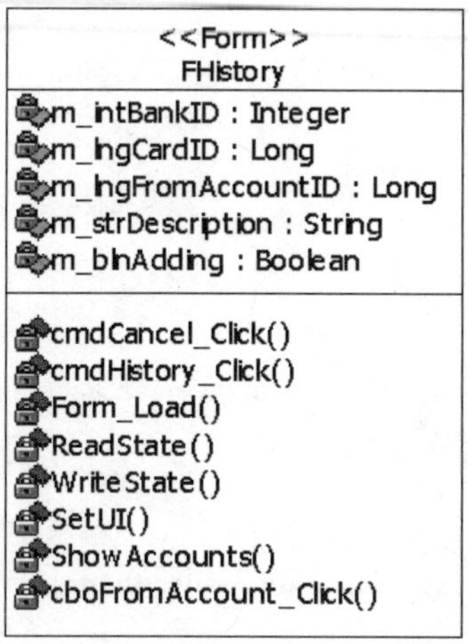

<<Form>> FHistory
m_intBankID : Integer
m_lngCardID : Long
m_lngFromAccountID : Long
m_strDescription : String
m_blnAdding : Boolean
cmdCancel_Click()
cmdHistory_Click()
Form_Load()
ReadState()
WriteState()
SetUI()
ShowAccounts()
cboFromAccount_Click()

Try It Out – Adding the Account History Related Forms

1. Add a new form named `FHistory` to the project and set it up as shown:

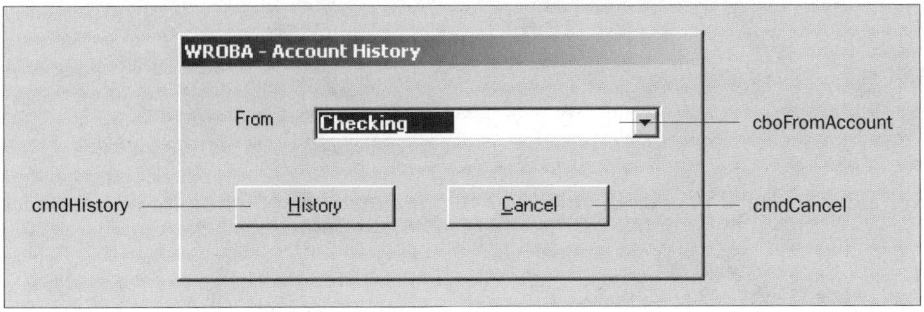

2. Next, we need to add code to the form; firstly we have the general form set up:

```
Option Explicit

' Form code in the user tier

Private m_intBankID As Integer
Private m_lngCardID As Long
Private m_lngFromAccountID As Long
Private m_strDescription As String
Private m_blnAdding As Boolean

Private Sub cmdCancel_Click()
   Unload Me
End Sub

Private Sub cmdHistory_Click()
   ' In development environment prints string to Immediate window
   Debug.Print "Account History"
   WriteState

   Me.Hide
   FHistoryDetails.Show vbModal

   Unload Me
End Sub

Private Sub Form_Load()
   ReadState
   SetUI
End Sub

Private Sub ReadState()
' Get the CardID and BankID from the global
' SharedProperties class object
   m_intBankID = g_objSharedProperties.BankID
   m_lngCardID = g_objSharedProperties.CardID
End Sub
```

```
Private Sub WriteState()
    g_objSharedProperties.AccountID = m_lngFromAccountID
    g_objSharedProperties.Description = m_strDescription
End Sub

Private Sub SetUI()
    Me.Caption = g_strAppTitle & " - Account History"
    ShowAccounts
End Sub
```

3. Secondly, we need to code the methods that populate the combo box with the accounts that are available to the customer:

```
Private Sub ShowAccounts()
    Dim objBank As Bank_Bus.Bank
    Dim recAccounts As ADODB.Recordset

    ' Prepare for call to business tier
    Set objBank = New Bank_Bus.Bank
    ' Retrieve the account history data as a recordset
    Set recAccounts = objBank.GetAccounts(m_intBankID, m_lngCardID)

    m_blnAdding = True
    Do While Not recAccounts.EOF ' Until end of recordset
        ' Add the data to the From combobox
        cboFromAccount.AddItem recAccounts!AccountTypeDesc
        cboFromAccount.ItemData(cboFromAccount.NewIndex) = _
            recAccounts!AccountID

        recAccounts.MoveNext
    Loop
    m_blnAdding = False

    If cboFromAccount.ListCount > 0 Then
        cboFromAccount.ListIndex = 0
    End If

    Set recAccounts = Nothing
    Set objBank = Nothing
End Sub

Private Sub cboFromAccount_Click()
    Dim lngListIndexSelection As Long

    If Not m_blnAdding Then
        lngListIndexSelection = cboFromAccount.ListIndex
        If lngListIndexSelection > -1 Then
            ' If there is a selection set the From AccountID
            m_lngFromAccountID = cboFromAccount. _
                ItemData(lngListIndexSelection)
            ' Save the account description
            m_strDescription = cboFromAccount.Text
        End If
    End If
End Sub
```

4. Now we need to add the second form (`FHistoryDetails`) to the project. Set it up as shown:

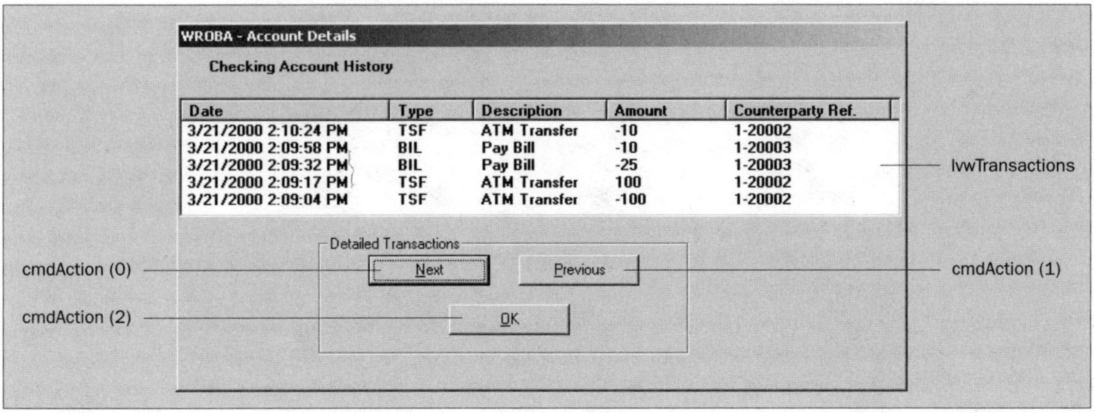

The buttons in the **Detailed Transactions** frame are set up as a command array. To do this just drag the controls onto the form as normal but give them the same name. Visual Basic 6 will then ask if a control array should be set up.

5. Add this code to the form:

```
Option Explicit

' Form code in the user tier

Private m_intBankID As Integer
Private m_lngAccountID As Long

Private m_intPageCnt As Integer
Private m_datMaxTransactionDate4Next As Date
Private m_datMaxTransactionDate4Prev() As Date

Private Enum EMenuActions
    eNext = 0
    ePrevious = 1
    eMainMenu = 2
End Enum

Private Sub Form_Load()
    ReadState
    SetUI
End Sub

Private Sub cmdAction_Click(intIndex As Integer)
' The command buttons are created as a control array and are
' addressed by index value
    Select Case intIndex
```

```
      Case eNext
         ' In development environment prints string to Immediate window
         Debug.Print "Next"
         m_intPageCnt = m_intPageCnt + 1
         ShowAccountHistory
      Case ePrevious
         Debug.Print "Previous"
         m_intPageCnt = m_intPageCnt - 1
         m_datMaxTransactionDate4Next = _
            m_datMaxTransactionDate4Prev(m_intPageCnt)
         If m_intPageCnt > 1 Then ReDim _
            Preserve m_datMaxTransactionDate4Prev(1 To _
            m_intPageCnt - 1) As Date
         ShowAccountHistory
      Case eMainMenu
         Debug.Print "Main Menu"
         m_intPageCnt = -1
      Case Else
      End Select

      If m_intPageCnt = -1 Then Unload Me
   End Sub

   Private Sub ReadState()
      ' Get the BankID and AccountID from the global
      ' SharedProperties class object
      m_intBankID = g_objSharedProperties.BankID
      m_lngAccountID = g_objSharedProperties.AccountID

      lblDescription = Trim(g_objSharedProperties.Description) & _
         " Account History"

      m_intPageCnt = 1
      m_datMaxTransactionDate4Next = Now
   End Sub

   Private Sub SetUI()
      Me.Caption = g_strAppTitle & " - Account Details"
      ShowAccountHistory
   End Sub
```

6. The ShowAccountHistory method shows the account history, moving between **Next** and **Previous**, and connects to the database to retrieve the data from the AccountHistory table. Add this code to the FhistoryDetails form.

```
Private Sub ShowAccountHistory()
   Dim bytAccountCnt As Byte
   Dim bytAccountMax As Byte
   Dim objBank As Bank_Bus.Bank
   Dim recTransactions As ADODB.Recordset
   Dim objAccountListItem As MSComctlLib.ListItem
```

```
' Keep datMaxTransactionDate, so we know what
' to do when we hit Previous
ReDim Preserve m_datMaxTransactionDate4Prev(1 To m_intPageCnt)
m_datMaxTransactionDate4Prev(m_intPageCnt) = _
   m_datMaxTransactionDate4Next

' Prepare for call to business tier
Set objBank = New Bank_Bus.Bank

Set recTransactions = objBank.GetAccountHistory(m_intBankID, _
   m_lngAccountID, m_datMaxTransactionDate4Next)

lvwTransactions.ListItems.Clear

' Anything to display?!
If Not recTransactions.BOF Then
   Do While Not recTransactions.EOF
      Set objAccountListItem = lvwTransactions.ListItems.Add(, _
         KEY_PREFIX & CStr(recTransactions!TxDate), _
        recTransactions!TxDate)
      objAccountListItem.SubItems(1) = _
         Trim$(recTransactions!TxTypeDesc)
      objAccountListItem.SubItems(2) = _
         Trim$(recTransactions!TxDescription)
      objAccountListItem.SubItems(3) = _
         recTransactions!TxAmount
      objAccountListItem.SubItems(4) = _
         Trim$(recTransactions!CounterpartyRef)

      recTransactions.MoveNext
   Loop

   lvwTransactions.Refresh

   ' Find out whether there are more transactions
   If recTransactions.EOF Then recTransactions.MovePrevious

   m_datMaxTransactionDate4Next = recTransactions!TxDate

   Set recTransactions = objBank.GetAccountHistory(m_intBankID, _
      m_lngAccountID, recTransactions!TxDate)

   If recTransactions.BOF Then
      cmdAction(eNext).Visible = False
   Else
      cmdAction(eNext).Visible = True
   End If

   If m_intPageCnt > 1 Then
      cmdAction(ePrevious).Visible = True
   Else
      cmdAction(ePrevious).Visible = False
```

```
            End If
      Else
          ' No transactions
          cmdAction(eNext).Visible = False
          cmdAction(ePrevious).Visible = False
      End If

      Set recTransactions = Nothing
      Set objBank = Nothing
      Set objAccountListItem = Nothing
   End Sub
```

How It Works

First, we use the `AccountHistory` form and the `ShowAccounts` procedure to populate the list box with the user's accounts. After the user selects the account they want to check the history details of, they click the **History** button and the `cmdHistory_Click` event shows the `HistoryDetails` form.

The code that handles the display of the **Next** and **Previous** buttons in the `HistoryDetails` form does it in a somewhat unusual manner for this type of form, by hiding and showing the **Next** and **Previous** buttons:

```
      If recTransactions.BOF Then
         cmdAction(eNext).Visible = False
      Else
         cmdAction(eNext).Visible = True
      End If

      If m_intPageCnt > 1 Then
         cmdAction(ePrevious).Visible = True
      Else
         cmdAction(ePrevious).Visible = False
      End If
   Else
      ' No transactions
      cmdAction(eNext).Visible = False
      cmdAction(ePrevious).Visible = False
   End If
```

A more common Windows behavior is to enable or disable buttons and menu items by graying them out. To do it this way, we would replace the **Visible** property with the **Enabled** property, for example:

```
   cmdAction(eNext).Enabled = False
```

The code that loads the listview control checks the returned recordset to see if the data pointer is at the beginning of the file (BOF). If it is, the recordset is empty and there are no records to display. If there are records, the recordset is traversed using the `MoveNext` method, and the data from each record is added to the listview control.

```
      ' Anything to display?!
      If Not recTransactions.BOF Then
         Do While Not recTransactions.EOF
            Set objAccountListItem = lvwTransactions.ListItems.Add(, _
               KEY_PREFIX & CStr(recTransactions!TxDate), _
            recTransactions!TxDate)
            objAccountListItem.SubItems(1) = _
               Trim$(recTransactions!TxTypeDesc)
            objAccountListItem.SubItems(2) = _
               Trim$(recTransactions!TxDescription)
            objAccountListItem.SubItems(3) = _
               recTransactions!TxAmount
            objAccountListItem.SubItems(4) = _
               Trim$(recTransactions!CounterpartyRef)

            recTransactions.MoveNext
      Loop
```

The Next and Previous buttons each display a screen of five items in the listview control, as mentioned earlier. Module level variable arrays m_datMaxTransactionDate4Prev and m_datMaxTransactionDate4Next are used to retain indexes for the transaction dates that delimit each page of data to display.

Next up are the payee screens. Let's start with the Add Payee dialog accessed via Information | Add Payee.

Adding a Payee

The form for adding a payee includes the card number of the payee, a "friendly name" for the description of the payee, the account that will be credited and the default amount. The user enters the card number (CardId) of the payee and presses the Validate button to verify that the card number is valid. The user then enters the name or description that identifies this payee. The card number and accounts for that card are acquired by using INNER JOINs to link data from the BankAccount, CardxAccount, and WROBACard tables in the BigBank database. The stored procedure sp_select_BankAccount_By_CardId is called from the data services tier to return this data.

The following class diagram shows the methods of the FPayee form:

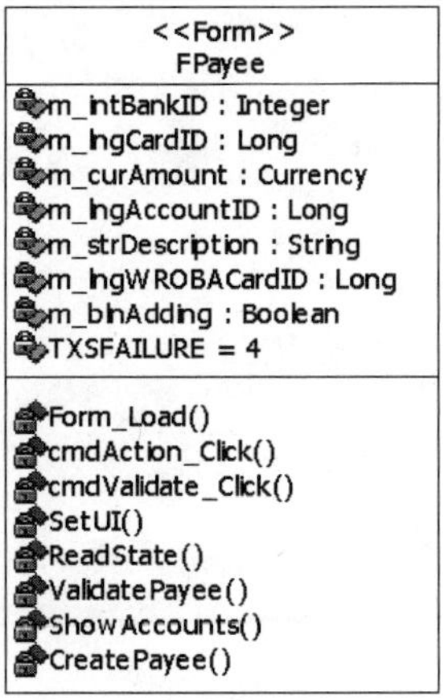

```
+---------------------------------------+
|              <<Form>>                 |
|               FPayee                  |
+---------------------------------------+
| m_intBankID : Integer                 |
| m_lngCardID : Long                    |
| m_curAmount : Currency                |
| m_lngAccountID : Long                 |
| m_strDescription : String             |
| m_lngWROBACardID : Long               |
| m_blnAdding : Boolean                 |
| TXSFAILURE = 4                        |
+---------------------------------------+
| Form_Load()                           |
| cmdAction_Click()                     |
| cmdValidate_Click()                   |
| SetUI()                               |
| ReadState()                           |
| ValidatePayee()                       |
| ShowAccounts()                        |
| CreatePayee()                         |
+---------------------------------------+
```

Try It Out – Implementing the FPayee Form

1. The new form `FPayee` should be set up as shown:

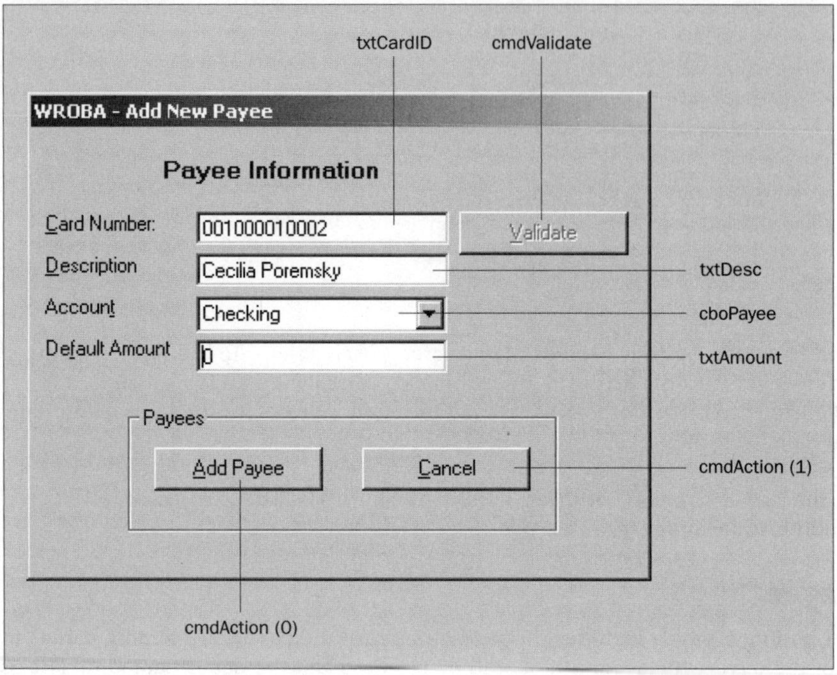

2. We begin by declaring the variables that will be used by the code in this form, and enter the `Load` and button `Click` procedures:

```
Option Explicit

' Form code in the user tier

Private m_intBankID As Integer
Private m_lngCardID As Long
Private m_curAmount As Currency
Private m_lngAccountID As Long
Private m_strDescription As String
Private m_lngWROBACardID As Long

Private m_blnAdding As Boolean

Private Enum EMenuActions
    eAddPayee = 0
    eMainMenu = 1
End Enum

Private Const TXSFAILURE = 4
```

```
Private Sub Form_Load()
  SetUI
  ReadState
End Sub

Private Sub cmdAction_Click(intIndex As Integer)
' The command buttons are created as a control array and are
' addressed by index value
  Select Case intIndex
  Case eAddPayee
      ' In development environment prints string to Immediate window
      Debug.Print "Add Payee"
      CreatePayee
      Me.Hide
      FStatus.Show vbModal
  Case eMainMenu
      Debug.Print "Main Menu"
  Case Else
  End Select

  Unload Me
End Sub

Private Sub cmdValidate_Click()
' Validate the new payee. If it is a valid entry in the DB,
' enable the Add command button
  If ValidatePayee(txtCardID.Text) = True Then
      cmdAction.Item(eAddPayee).Enabled = True
      cmdValidate.Enabled = False

      txtDesc.SetFocus
  Else
      MsgBox "Card Number for new Payee did not validate", , _
          g_strAppTitle
      cmdAction.Item(eAddPayee).Enabled = False
      cmdValidate.Enabled = True
  End If
End Sub
```

3.   The SetUI and ReadState methods perform the standard initializations, with the SetUI method also setting the initial state of the **Add** and **Validate** command buttons:

```
Private Sub SetUI()
  Me.Caption = g_strAppTitle & " - Add New Payee"
  ' Start out with the Validate command button enabled
  ' and the Add command button disabled
  cmdAction.Item(eAddPayee).Enabled = False
  cmdValidate.Enabled = True
End Sub

Private Sub ReadState()
' Get the CardID from the global
' SharedProperties class object
  m_lngWROBACardID = g_objSharedProperties.CardID
End Sub
```

4. This function is used in the validation process. It verifies that at least one account exists for the selected new payee by calling the `ShowAccounts` method, which returns `True` if at least one account is found:

```
Private Function ValidatePayee(strCardId As String) As Boolean
    Dim objBankLocator As Bank_Bus.BankLocator
    Dim objBank As Bank_Bus.Bank
    Dim strBankDSN As String

    On Error GoTo ErrorHandler
    ' Pessimistic assumption that the payee is not valid
    ValidatePayee = False

    ' Prepare for call to business tier
    Set objBank = New Bank_Bus.Bank

    ' CardID is 9 digits
    m_lngCardID = objBank.GetCardID(strCardId)

    ' BankID is 3 digits
    m_intBankID = objBank.GetBankID(strCardId)

    ' Prepare for call to business tier
    Set objBankLocator = New Bank_Bus.BankLocator
    ' Find the selected bank
    strBankDSN = objBankLocator.GetBank(m_intBankID)

    If Len(strBankDSN) > 0 Then
        ' The case study does not test to see if a new
        ' payee is already a payee. If the payee already
        ' exists an error is returned when an attempt is
        ' made to add the new payee.
        ValidatePayee = ShowAccounts()
    End If

Clean_Up:
    Set objBank = Nothing
    Set objBankLocator = Nothing
    Exit Function

ErrorHandler:
    ValidatePayee = False
    GoTo Clean_Up
End Function
```

5. Once the payee's `CardId` has been validated, the user is given a choice of accounts to transfer funds into. The `ShowAccounts` function handles this by retrieving a list of accounts. Finally, the payee is added to the database, using the `CreatePayee` function:

```
Private Function ShowAccounts() As Boolean
    Dim objBank As Bank_Bus.Bank
    Dim recAccounts As ADODB.Recordset

    ShowAccounts = False

    ' Prepare for call to business tier
    Set objBank = New Bank_Bus.Bank

    ' Retrieve recordset of accounts
    Set recAccounts = objBank.GetAccounts(m_intBankID, m_lngCardID)

    If Not (recAccounts Is Nothing) Then
        m_blnAdding = True
        Do While Not recAccounts.EOF ' Until end of recordset
            ' Populate the Payee combobox
            cboPayee.AddItem recAccounts!AccountTypeDesc
            cboPayee.ItemData(cboPayee.NewIndex) = recAccounts!AccountID

            recAccounts.MoveNext ' Next account
        Loop
        m_blnAdding = False

        If cboPayee.ListCount > 0 Then
            cboPayee.ListIndex = 0
            ShowAccounts = True ' Only if any payee accounts
        End If
    End If

    Set recAccounts = Nothing
    Set objBank = Nothing
End Function

Private Sub CreatePayee()
    Dim lngListIndex As Long
    Dim objBank As Bank_Bus.Payees
    Dim blnPayeeAllowed As Boolean

    lngListIndex = cboPayee.ListIndex
    If lngListIndex > -1 Then
        ' Payee AccountID
        m_lngAccountID = cboPayee.ItemData(lngListIndex)

        ' Prepare for call to business tier
        Set objBank = New Bank_Bus.Payees
        ' See if adding the new payee is permited
        blnPayeeAllowed = objBank.MatchPayee(m_intBankID, m_lngCardID)
        If blnPayeeAllowed = True Then
            ' Ensure a numeric result
```

```
              If txtAmount.Text = "" Or (Not IsNumeric(txtAmount.Text)) Then
                 txtAmount.Text = "0"
           End If
           ' Default payment amount
           m_curAmount = CCur(txtAmount.Text)

           If txtDesc.Text = "" Then txtDesc.Text = " "
              m_strDescription = txtDesc.Text

              g_objSharedProperties.TransactionMessage = ""

              g_objSharedProperties.TransactionStatus = _
                 objBank.InsertPayees(m_strDescription, _
                 m_lngAccountID, m_curAmount, m_intBankID, _
                 m_lngCardID, m_lngWROBACardID)
        Else
           g_objSharedProperties.TransactionMessage = _
              "Addition of this payee not allowed. Error."
        End If
     Else
        g_objSharedProperties.TransactionMessage = _
           "No payees selected. Error."
     End If

     Set objBank = Nothing
  End Sub
```

How It Works

When the FPayee form opens, the **Add** button is disabled and the **Verify** button is enabled. This is done in the SetUI method, where the **Add** button is addressed as a member of a control array of command buttons:

```
cmdAction.Item(eAddPayee).Enabled = False
cmdValidate.Enabled = True
```

The user enters a card account number for the new payee and then presses the **Verify** button. The Click event handler for this button calls the ValidatePayee method with the entered card account as a calling argument. ValidatePayee calls GetCardID and GetBankID in the business services tier to parse the card account for the new payee, and then locates the bank where the account is held.

```
m_lngCardID = objBank.GetCardID(strCardId)

m_intBankID = objBank.GetBankID(strCardId)

' Prepare for call to business tier
Set objBankLocator = New Bank_Bus.BankLocator
' Find the selected bank
strBankDSN = objBankLocator.GetBank(m_intBankID)
```

Finally, `ValidatePayee` calls the `ShowAccounts` method, which returns `False` if no accounts are found for this card account, and `True` if at least one account is found.

```
If Len(strBankDSN) > 0 Then
    ' The case study does not test to see if a new
    ' payee is already a payee. If the payee already
    ' exists an error is returned when an attempt is
    ' made to add the new payee.
    ValidatePayee = ShowAccounts()
End If
```

`ShowAccounts` retrieves a recordset containing any account (Checking or Savings) that exists for the specified card account and enters the description for the accounts in a combo box. When the user presses the **Add** button, the selected account is checked to see if it already exists as a payee.

```
blnPayeeAllowed = objBank.MatchPayee(m_intBankID, m_lngCardID)
```

If adding the payee is permitted, the description and default amount are verified and the new payee is added to the `Payee` table, with the result being written to the `TransactionStatus` Property of the `SharedProperties` class.

```
g_objSharedProperties.TransactionStatus = _
    objBank.InsertPayees(m_strDescription, _
    m_lngAccountID, m_curAmount, m_intBankID, _
    m_lngCardID, m_lngWROBACardID)
```

Editing Payee Information

Once a customer has a payee added, the payee details can be edited through selecting Information I Edit Payee. By now you will have noticed similarities in the methods of many of the forms. All of the forms use `Form_Load` to initialize the form, have `Set_UI` and `ReadState` methods to initialize the form's interface, read card account data from the `SharedProperties` class, and have methods to handle `Click` events from command buttons. The following class diagram shows the `FPayeeEdit` form's methods:

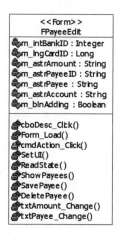

Try It Out – Implementing the FPayeeEdit form

1. Set up the `FPayeeEdit` form, as illustrated:

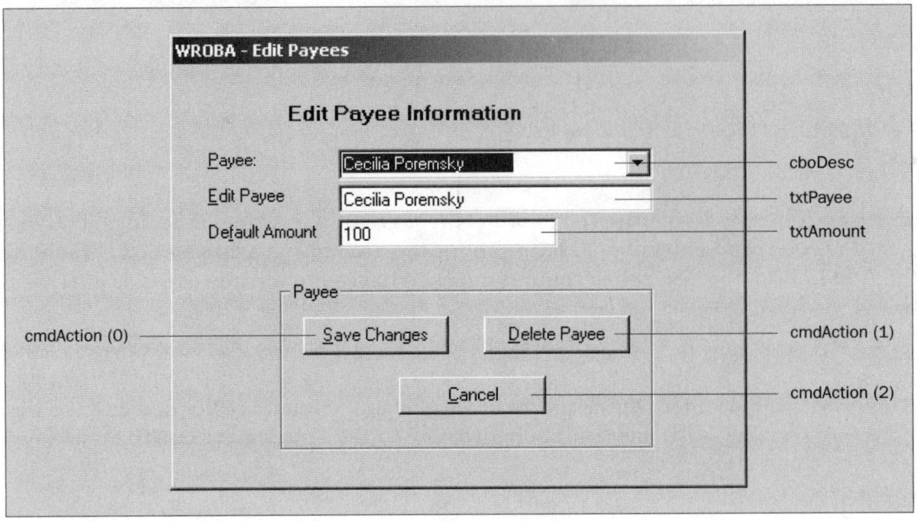

2. Then add the following code. By now, the following procedures should look fairly familiar:

```
Option Explicit

' Form code in the user tier

Private m_intBankID As Integer
Private m_lngCardID As Long

Private m_astrAmount() As String
Private m_astrPayeeID() As String
Private m_astrPayee() As String
Private m_astrAccount() As String

Private m_blnAdding As Boolean

Private Enum EMenuActions
    eSaveChanges = 0
    eDeletePayee = 1
    eMainMenu = 2
End Enum

Private Sub cboDesc_Click()
    Dim lngListIndex As Long

    If m_blnAdding = False And cboDesc.ListCount > 0 Then
        lngListIndex = cboDesc.ListIndex
        txtAmount.Text = m_astrAmount(lngListIndex)
        txtPayee.Text = m_astrPayee(lngListIndex)
```

```
      End If
   End Sub

   Private Sub Form_Load()
      Dim blnPayees As Boolean

      SetUI
      ReadState
      blnPayees = ShowPayees
      If blnPayees = False Then
         cmdAction(0).Enabled = False
         cmdAction(1).Enabled = False
      End If
   End Sub
```

The `Click` event handler for the command buttons handles the buttons as members of a
control array, calling the `SavePayee` method when the **Save** button is clicked, the
`DeletePayee` method when the **Delete** button is clicked, and exiting the form when the
Cancel button is clicked. `ReadState` is called by the `Form_Load` method, and reads the
`SharedProperties` class to find the values of the `CardID` and `BankID` properties. Most of
these forms follow this procedure when they are initialized.

3. Add the following code to the `FpayeeEdit` form:

```
Private Sub cmdAction_Click(intIndex As Integer)
' The command buttons are created as a control array and are
' addressed by index value
   Select Case intIndex
   Case eSaveChanges
      ' In development environment prints string to Immediate window
      Debug.Print "Save Payee Changes"
      SavePayee
      g_objSharedProperties.TransactionMessage = ""
      Me.Hide
      FStatus.Show vbModal
   Case eDeletePayee
      Debug.Print "Delete Payee"
      DeletePayee
      g_objSharedProperties.TransactionMessage = ""
      Me.Hide
      FStatus.Show vbModal
   Case eMainMenu
      Debug.Print "Cancel Payee Edit"
   Case Else
   End Select

   Unload Me
End Sub
```

559

```
Private Sub SetUI()
    Me.Caption = g_strAppTitle & " - Edit Payees"
End Sub

Private Sub ReadState()
' Get the CardID and BankID from the global
' SharedProperties class object
    m_lngCardID = g_objSharedProperties.CardID
    m_intBankID = g_objSharedProperties.BankID
End Sub
```

4. The following section of code retrieves the recordset of accounts for the `Payees` table, and adds the data to the `Payee` combo box and to module level arrays, which store the data:

```
Private Function ShowPayees() As Boolean
    Dim objBank As Bank_Bus.Payees
    Dim recPayees As ADODB.Recordset
    Dim strBuildAccount As String
    Dim lngIndex As Long

    On Error Resume Next
    ShowPayees = False

    ' Prepare for call to business tier
    Set objBank = New Bank_Bus.Payees

    ' Retrieve recordset of accounts
    Set recPayees = objBank.GetAllPayees(m_intBankID, m_lngCardID)

    If Not (recPayees.EOF) Then
        ShowPayees = True
        m_blnAdding = True
        lngIndex = 0
        Do While Not recPayees.EOF ' Until end of recordset
            ' Populate the Payee combobox
            strBuildAccount = CStr(recPayees!CardID)
            If Len(strBuildAccount) < 9 Then
                strBuildAccount = String$(9 - Len(strBuildAccount), "0") _
                    & strBuildAccount
            End If
            strBuildAccount = CStr(m_intBankID) & strBuildAccount
            If Len(strBuildAccount) < 12 Then
                strBuildAccount = String$(12 - Len(strBuildAccount), "0") _
                    & strBuildAccount
            End If

            ReDim Preserve m_astrAccount(lngIndex)
            m_astrAccount(lngIndex) = strBuildAccount

            ReDim Preserve m_astrPayee(lngIndex)
            m_astrPayee(lngIndex) = Trim$(recPayees!PayeeDesc)
            cboDesc.AddItem m_astrPayee(lngIndex)
```

```
                ReDim Preserve m_astrPayeeID(lngIndex)
                m_astrPayeeID(lngIndex) = CStr(recPayees!PayeeID)
                m_astrPayeeID(lngIndex) = Left$(m_astrPayeeID(lngIndex), _
                    Len(m_astrPayeeID(lngIndex)) - 1)
                m_astrPayeeID(lngIndex) = Right$(m_astrPayeeID(lngIndex), _
                    Len(m_astrPayeeID(lngIndex)) - 1)

                ReDim Preserve m_astrAmount(lngIndex)
                m_astrAmount(lngIndex) = CStr(recPayees!DefaultAmount)

                lngIndex = lngIndex + 1
                recPayees.MoveNext ' Next account
        Loop

        If cboDesc.ListCount > 0 Then
            cboDesc.ListIndex = 0
            txtPayee.Text = m_astrPayee(0)
            txtAmount.Text = m_astrAmount(0)
        End If
        m_blnAdding = False
    Else
        MsgBox "No payees to edit.", vbOKOnly, g_strAppTitle
    End If

    Set recPayees = Nothing
    Set objBank = Nothing
End Function
```

5. The following section shows the code to save changes to the payee data:

```
Private Sub SavePayee()
    Dim objBank As Bank_Bus.Payees
    Dim strPayeeID As String
    Dim strPayeeDesc As String
    Dim curAmount As Currency
    Dim lngListIndex As Long

    ' Ensure a numeric result
    If txtAmount.Text = "" Or _
       (Not IsNumeric(txtAmount.Text)) Then
           txtAmount.Text = "0"
    End If

    lngListIndex = cboDesc.ListIndex
    If lngListIndex > -1 Then
        strPayeeDesc = m_astrPayee(lngListIndex)
        strPayeeID = m_astrPayeeID(lngListIndex)
        curAmount = CCur(txtAmount.Text)

        ' Prepare for call to business tier
        Set objBank = New Bank_Bus.Payees
        g_objSharedProperties.TransactionStatus = _
```

```
            objBank.EditPayee(strPayeeID, strPayeeDesc, _
                curAmount, m_intBankID)
    Else
        g_objSharedProperties.TransactionStatus = _
            EUpdateStatus.updError
    End If

    Set objBank = Nothing
End Sub
```

6. Add the following code to enable us to delete a payee:

```
Private Sub DeletePayee()
    Dim objBank As Bank_Bus.Payees
    Dim strPayeeID As String
    Dim strPayeeDesc As String
    Dim lngListIndex As Long

    lngListIndex = cboDesc.ListIndex
    If lngListIndex > -1 Then
        strPayeeDesc = cboDesc.Text
        lngListIndex = cboDesc.ListIndex
        strPayeeID = m_astrPayeeID(lngListIndex)

        ' Prepare for call to business tier
        Set objBank = New Bank_Bus.Payees

        g_objSharedProperties.TransactionStatus = _
            objBank.DeletePayee(strPayeeID, m_intBankID, _
                strPayeeDesc)
    Else
        g_objSharedProperties.TransactionStatus = _
            EUpdateStatus.updError
    End If

    Set objBank = Nothing
End Sub

Private Sub txtAmount_Change()
  Dim lngListIndex As Long

    lngListIndex = cboDesc.ListIndex
    m_astrAmount(lngListIndex) = txtAmount.Text
End Sub

Private Sub txtPayee_Change()
    Dim lngListIndex As Long

    lngListIndex = cboDesc.ListIndex
    m_astrPayee(lngListIndex) = txtPayee.Text
End Sub
```

How It Works

When the form is loaded, the `Form_Load` method is executed, which calls the `ShowPayees` method. `ShowPayees` first instantiates a `Payees` class in the business services tier, and then retrieves a recordset containing all entries in the `Payees` table:

```
' Prepare for call to business tier
Set objBank = New Bank_Bus.Payees

' Retrieve recordset of accounts
Set recPayees = objBank.GetAllPayees(m_intBankID, m_lngCardID)
```

If the recordset isn't empty:

```
If Not (recPayees.EOF) Then
```

The recordset is traversed, constructing standard card account numbers from the `CardID` values in the recordset, and adding them to a module level array:

```
' Populate the Payee combobox
strBuildAccount = CStr(recPayees!CardID)
If Len(strBuildAccount) < 9 Then
    strBuildAccount = String$(9 - Len(strBuildAccount), "0") _
        & strBuildAccount
End If
strBuildAccount = CStr(m_intBankID) & strBuildAccount
If Len(strBuildAccount) < 12 Then
    strBuildAccount = String$(12 - Len(strBuildAccount), "0") _
        & strBuildAccount
End If

ReDim Preserve m_astrAccount(lngIndex)
m_astrAccount(lngIndex) = strBuildAccount
```

Then, the payee descriptions are added to the `Payee` combo box and to another module level array:

```
ReDim Preserve m_astrPayee(lngIndex)
m_astrPayee(lngIndex) = Trim$(recPayees!PayeeDesc)
cboDesc.AddItem m_astrPayee(lngIndex)
```

The `PayeeID` and `DefaultAmount` entries in the recordset are added to module level arrays, and the next record in the recordset is checked using the `MoveNext` method of the recordset:

```
ReDim Preserve m_astrPayeeID(lngIndex)
m_astrPayeeID(lngIndex) = CStr(recPayees!PayeeID)
m_astrPayeeID(lngIndex) = Left$(m_astrPayeeID(lngIndex), _
    Len(m_astrPayeeID(lngIndex)) - 1)
m_astrPayeeID(lngIndex) = Right$(m_astrPayeeID(lngIndex), _
    Len(m_astrPayeeID(lngIndex)) - 1)
```

563

```
        ReDim Preserve m_astrAmount(lngIndex)
        m_astrAmount(lngIndex) = CStr(recPayees!DefaultAmount)

        lngIndex = lngIndex + 1
        recPayees.MoveNext ' Next account
    Loop
```

If the Save button is clicked, the data for the currently selected payee is written to the Payees table using the EditPayee property of the Payees class in the business services tier. If the Delete button is clicked, the DeletePayee property of the Payees class in the business services tier is called. These properties in the business services tier pass through these calls to the data services tier for execution on the database.

Changing Passwords

The last item on the Information menu is Change Password. This has a familiar format:

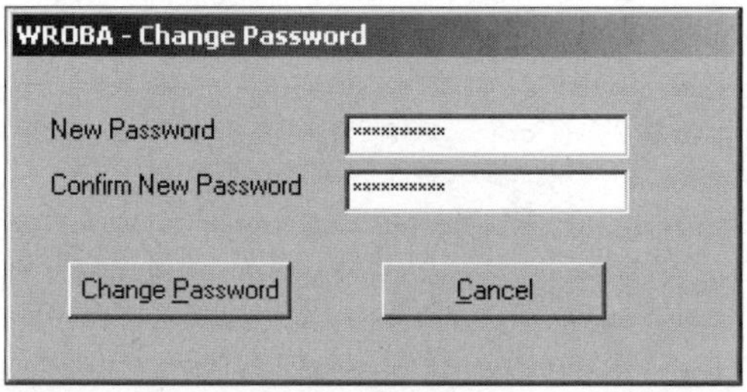

Try It Out – Implementing the FChangePassword Form

1. The FChangePassword form has controls, as shown above, with the self evident names; txtNewPassword, txtConfirmPassword, cmdChange, and cmdCancel.

2. We then need to add the following code:

```
Option Explicit

' Form code in the user tier

Private m_intBankID As Integer
Private m_lngCardID As Long

Private Enum ETransactionStatus
    txsSuccess = 0
    txsDailyLimitExceeded = 1
    txsNotEnoughFunds = 2
    txsUnknownError = 3
End Enum
```

```
Private Sub cmdCancel_Click()
   Unload Me
End Sub

Private Sub cmdChange_Click()
   ' In development environment prints string to Immediate window
   Debug.Print "Change Password"
   PasswordChange

   Me.Hide
   FStatus.Show vbModal

   Unload Me
End Sub

Private Sub Form_Load()
   ReadState
   SetUI
End Sub

Private Sub ReadState()
' Get the CardID and BankID from the global
' SharedProperties class object
   m_intBankID = g_objSharedProperties.BankID
   m_lngCardID = g_objSharedProperties.CardID
End Sub

Private Sub SetUI()
   Me.Caption = g_strAppTitle & " - Change Password"
End Sub

Private Sub PasswordChange()
   Dim objPassword As Bank_Bus.Bank
   Dim strNewPassword As String
   Dim strConfirmation As String
   Dim blnPasswordChanged As Boolean

   ' Check if the new password is the same as
   ' the confirmation for the new password
   strNewPassword = Trim$(txtNewPassword.Text)
   strConfirmation = Trim$(txtConfirmPassword.Text)
   If strNewPassword = strConfirmation _
      And strNewPassword <> "" Then

      ' Prepare for call to business tier
      Set objPassword = New Bank_Bus.Bank

      ' Change the password
      blnPasswordChanged = _
         objPassword.ChangeLogin(m_intBankID, _
         m_lngCardID, strNewPassword)
      If blnPasswordChanged Then
```

```
            g_objSharedProperties.TransactionMessage = _
                "Password changed."
        Else
            g_objSharedProperties.TransactionMessage = _
                "Password *not* changed. Unknown error."
        End If
    Else
        g_objSharedProperties.TransactionMessage = _
            "Password *not* changed. Unknown error."
    End If

    Set objPassword = Nothing
End Sub
```

How It Works

When the **Change Password** button is clicked, the `PasswordChange` method of the
`FChangePassword` form is called by the `Click` event handler for the button. This method first
verifies that the new password and new password verification are identical and not blank (Null String):

```
strNewPassword = Trim$(txtNewPassword.Text)
strConfirmation = Trim$(txtConfirmPassword.Text)
If strNewPassword = strConfirmation _
    And strNewPassword <> "" Then
```

If these conditions are met, the `ChangeLogin` property of the `Bank` class in the business services tier is
called to pass the new password to the data services tier. The new password is stored in the database for
future logins.

Of course, apart from viewing information, customers will want to be able to use the application for
moving money around; either between their accounts, or to pay off bills. These options are accessed
through the Transaction menu. It is to this that we now turn our attention.

WROBA Customer Transaction Menu

Here we only have two main options to code. These concern:

❑ Bill payment

❑ Money transfer between accounts

Here customers need to know if the transactions they've attempted to carry out have been successful or
not. In this context, the status forms we discussed earlier are extremely useful.

Of course, we do have to add the appropriate options and code to the `FMainMenu` form.

Try It Out – Adding the Transaction Menu Options

1. Return to the `FMainMenu` form, give it the focus, and open up the Menu Editor. Highlight **&Help**
and click **Insert** three times to add the appropriate number of lines. Next add the following
caption/name pairs, with appropriate indentation (one click of right button) and indices:

Menu Caption	Menu Name	Index
&Pay Bills	mnuTPay	0
–	mnuTDivider1	1
&Transfer Funds	mnuTTransfer	2

2. Then add the following code for the Click events for the options:

```
Private Sub mnuTPay_Click(Index As Integer)
    FormDisplay FPayBills
End Sub

Private Sub mnuTTransfer_Click(Index As Integer)
    FormDisplay FTransfer
End Sub
```

Next it's time to add some more new forms to the project, starting with the one for paying bills.

Paying Bills

Customers use the Pay Bills form to choose the Account to transfer the money from and the Payee to transfer it to. The form will display the default payment amount to be transferred (although the amount can be changed). The following class diagram shows the methods of the FPayBills form:

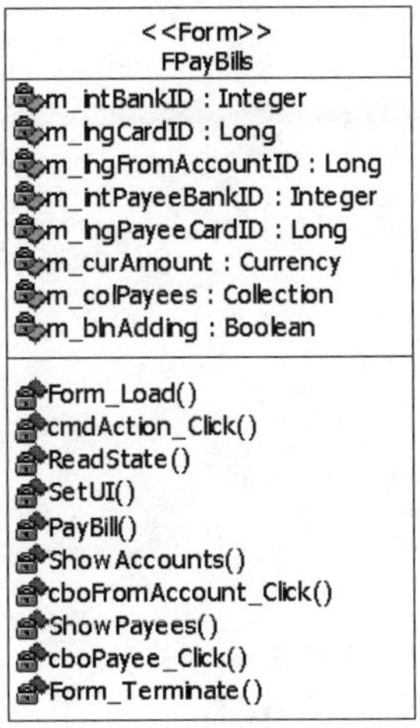

```
        <<Form>>
        FPayBills
─────────────────────────────
m_intBankID : Integer
m_lngCardID : Long
m_lngFromAccountID : Long
m_intPayeeBankID : Integer
m_lngPayeeCardID : Long
m_curAmount : Currency
m_colPayees : Collection
m_blnAdding : Boolean
─────────────────────────────
Form_Load()
cmdAction_Click()
ReadState()
SetUI()
PayBill()
ShowAccounts()
cboFromAccount_Click()
ShowPayees()
cboPayee_Click()
Form_Terminate()
```

Try It Out – Implementing the FPayBills Form

1. Set the `FPayBills` form up as shown:

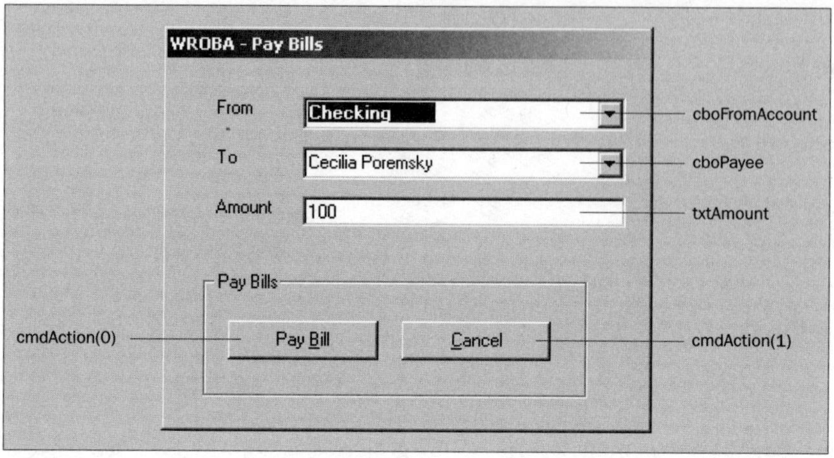

2. Add the following code to declare module level variables, the standard initialization methods, and the button `Click` event handler:

```
Option Explicit

' Form code in the user tier

Private m_intBankID As Integer
Private m_lngCardID As Long
Private m_lngFromAccountID As Long
Private m_intPayeeBankID As Integer
Private m_lngPayeeCardID As Long
Private m_curAmount As Currency
Private m_colPayees As Collection
Private m_blnAdding As Boolean

Private Enum EMenuActions
    ePayBill = 0
    eMainMenu = 1
End Enum

Private Sub Form_Load()
    ReadState
    SetUI
End Sub

Private Sub cmdAction_Click(intIndex As Integer)
' The command buttons are created as a control array and are
' addressed by index value
    Select Case intIndex
    Case ePayBill
```

```
                    ' In development environment prints string to Immediate window
                    Debug.Print "Pay Bill"
                    PayBill
                    g_objSharedProperties.TransactionMessage = ""
                    Me.Hide
                    FStatus.Show vbModal
                Case eMainMenu
                    Debug.Print "Main Menu"
                Case Else
                End Select

                Unload Me
        End Sub

        Private Sub ReadState()
        ' Get the CardID and BankID from the global
        ' SharedProperties class object
                m_intBankID = g_objSharedProperties.BankID
                m_lngCardID = g_objSharedProperties.CardID
        End Sub

        Private Sub SetUI()
                Dim blnPayees As Boolean

                Me.Caption = g_strAppTitle & " - Pay Bills"

                blnPayees = ShowAccounts
                If blnPayees = False Then
                    cmdAction(0).Enabled = False
                End If

                blnPayees = ShowPayees
                If blnPayees = False Then
                    cmdAction(0).Enabled = False
                End If
        End Sub
```

3. Add the code for the `PayBill` method, which is used to call the `TransferFunds` property of the `Transfer` class in the business services tier:

```
Private Sub PayBill()
        Dim objTransfer As Bank_Bus.Transfer

        ' Use the default payment amount if the Amount
        ' textbox is blank or nonnumeric
        If txtAmount.Text <> "" And _
            IsNumeric(txtAmount.Text) Then
                m_curAmount = CCur(txtAmount.Text)
        End If

        ' Prepare for call to business tier
        Set objTransfer = New Bank_Bus.Transfer
```

```
    ' Transfer the funds
    g_objSharedProperties.TransactionStatus = objTransfer. _
        TransferFunds(m_intBankID, m_lngFromAccountID, _
        m_intPayeeBankID, m_lngPayeeCardID, m_curAmount, _
        Bank_Bus.txBillPayment, "Pay Bill")

    Set objTransfer = Nothing
End Sub
```

4. The account information is retrieved from the database using the following code:

```
Private Function ShowAccounts() As Boolean
    Dim objBank As Bank_Bus.Bank
    Dim recAccounts As ADODB.Recordset

    On Error Resume Next
    ShowAccounts = False
    m_blnAdding = True

    ' Prepare for call to business tier
    Set objBank = New Bank_Bus.Bank

    ' Retrieve the accounts for the user as a recordset
    Set recAccounts = objBank.GetAccounts(m_intBankID, m_lngCardID)

    If Not (recAccounts.EOF) Then
        ShowAccounts = True
        ' If there are no accounts then EOF is True.
        Do While Not recAccounts.EOF ' Until end of recordset
            cboFromAccount.AddItem recAccounts!AccountTypeDesc
            cboFromAccount.ItemData(cboFromAccount.NewIndex) = _
                recAccounts!AccountID

            recAccounts.MoveNext ' Next account
        Loop
    End If

    If cboFromAccount.ListCount > 0 Then
        cboFromAccount.ListIndex = 0
        ' Initialize the From account
        m_lngFromAccountID = cboFromAccount.ItemData(0)
    End If
    m_blnAdding = False

    Set recAccounts = Nothing
    Set objBank = Nothing
End Function


Private Sub cboFromAccount_Click()
    Dim lngListIndexSelection As Long
```

```
      If Not m_blnAdding Then
          lngListIndexSelection = cboFromAccount.ListIndex
          If lngListIndexSelection > -1 Then
              ' Set the From AccountID from the ItemData
              ' property of the combobox
              m_lngFromAccountID = cboFromAccount. _
                  ItemData(lngListIndexSelection)
          End If
      End If
  End Sub
```

5. Once the account information is retrieved from the database, we need to get the payee information to populate the dropdown. The following code will achieve this:

```
Private Function ShowPayees() As Boolean
    Dim objBank As Bank_Bus.Payees
    Dim recPayees As ADODB.Recordset
    Dim objPayeeInformation As CPayeeInformation
    Dim lngItemData As Long

    On Error Resume Next
    ShowPayees = False
    lngItemData = 0

    ' Prepare for call to business tier
    Set objBank = New Bank_Bus.Payees

    ' Get all the current payees in a recordset
    Set recPayees = objBank.GetAllPayees(m_intBankID, m_lngCardID)

    If Not (recPayees.EOF) Then
        ShowPayees = True
        ' Create a collection object to act
        ' as a container for the payee data
        Set m_colPayees = New Collection

        m_blnAdding = True

        Do While Not recPayees.EOF ' Until end of recordset
            ' Populate the combobox with the payee descriptions
            cboPayee.AddItem recPayees!PayeeDesc
            ' Store an index number in the ItemData property
            cboPayee.ItemData(cboPayee.NewIndex) = lngItemData

            ' Create a CPayeeInformation class object
            Set objPayeeInformation = New CPayeeInformation

            ' Initialize the CPayeeInformation class object with
            ' the data from the payee in the recordset
            objPayeeInformation.Init CStr(recPayees!PayeeID), _
                recPayees!BankID, recPayees!AccountID, _
                recPayees!DefaultAmount
```

571

```
                    ' Add the CPayeeInformation class object
                    ' to the Collection container
                    m_colPayees.Add objPayeeInformation, "Key=" & _
                        CStr(lngItemData)

                    recPayees.MoveNext ' Next payee

                    lngItemData = lngItemData + 1 ' increment the index
                Loop

                If cboPayee.ListCount > 0 Then
                    cboPayee.ListIndex = 0
                    Set objPayeeInformation = m_colPayees.Item("Key=" & _
                        CStr(0))
                    txtAmount.Text = CStr(objPayeeInformation.Amount)
                    m_intPayeeBankID = objPayeeInformation.BankID
                    m_lngPayeeCardID = objPayeeInformation.CardID
                End If

                m_blnAdding = False
            Else
                MsgBox "No payees to pay.", vbOKOnly, g_strAppTitle
            End If


        Set objPayeeInformation = Nothing
        Set recPayees = Nothing
        Set objBank = Nothing
End Function
```

6. Add the following code to respond to a click in the combo box. This code takes the `CardID` and `BankID` data for the selected payee, and writes it to the `CPayeeInformation` class:

```
Private Sub cboPayee_Click()
    Dim lngListIndexSelection As Long
    Dim objPayeeInformation As CPayeeInformation
    Dim lngItemData As Long

    If Not m_blnAdding Then
        lngListIndexSelection = cboFromAccount.ListIndex
        If lngListIndexSelection > -1 Then
            lngItemData = cboPayee.ItemData(lngListIndexSelection)
            Set objPayeeInformation = m_colPayees.Item("Key=" & _
                CStr(lngItemData))
            m_intPayeeBankID = objPayeeInformation.BankID
            m_lngPayeeCardID = objPayeeInformation.CardID

            txtAmount.Text = CStr(objPayeeInformation.Amount)
        End If
    End If

    Set objPayeeInformation = Nothing
End Sub

Private Sub Form_Terminate()
    Set m_colPayees = Nothing
End Sub
```

How It Works

The user selects an account to be used as the source for the payment from the cboFromAccount combo box. This account can be either a Checking or a Savings account. When the Click event for the combo box fires, the module level variable m_blnAdding is checked to see if the event was fired during form initialization. If the event isn't caused by initialization, it is caused by the user clicking in the combo box. The ItemData property of the combo box is loaded with the AccountID of the accounts during initialization, and when the user selects the account the AccountID of the account is stored in a module level variable for later use:

```
If Not m_blnAdding Then
   lngListIndexSelection = cboFromAccount.ListIndex
   If lngListIndexSelection > -1 Then
      ' Set the From AccountID from the ItemData
      ' property of the combobox
      m_lngFromAccountID = cboFromAccount. _
        ItemData(lngListIndexSelection)
   End If
End If
```

This type of initialization check is used by many of the control Click event methods. When combo boxes, list boxes, listviews or other controls are loaded with data, they fire click events. Setting a module level Boolean flag variable to signal whether initialization is taking place or not is a standard technique for detecting this. If our Click event handlers have code that we don't want to run during initialization, we can use this technique to solve the problem.

Most of the remainder of the code for the FPayBills form is very familiar to us by now. But one part of the ShowPayees method is interesting. At the module level of the form, a collection variable was declared:

```
Private m_colPayees As Collection
```

This collection is instantiated in ShowPayees:

```
Set m_colPayees = New Collection

m_blnAdding = True
```

A loop is used to process each record in the recordset of payees linked to the logged-in user. A CPayeeInformation class object is created, and the data from the current record in the recordset is used to supply the arguments for the Init method of the CPayeeInformation class. The class is added to the m_colPayees collection, with an index key, so it can be located later on. The process is repeated until every record in the recordset has been added to the m_colPayees collection:

```
Do While Not recPayees.EOF ' Until end of recordset
    ' Populate the combobox with the payee descriptions
    cboPayee.AddItem recPayees!PayeeDesc
    ' Store an index number in the ItemData property
    cboPayee.ItemData(cboPayee.NewIndex) = lngItemData
```

```
                    ' Create a CPayeeInformation class object
                    Set objPayeeInformation = New CPayeeInformation

                    ' Initialize the CPayeeInformation class object with
                    ' the data from the payee in the recordset
                    objPayeeInformation.Init CStr(recPayees!PayeeID), _
                        recPayees!BankID, recPayees!AccountID, _
                        recPayees!DefaultAmount

                    ' Add the CPayeeInformation class object
                    ' to the Collection container
                    m_colPayees.Add objPayeeInformation, "Key=" & _
                        CStr(lngItemData)

                    recPayees.MoveNext ' Next payee

                    lngItemData = lngItemData + 1 ' increment the index
                Loop
```

The value of this technique is that it creates what essentially is a disconnected recordset of the payee information, which can be shared with other methods in the form without keeping a recordset open. This helps reduce network bandwidth use and also lowers the load on the business services, user services, and database servers. In this module, the Click event handler for the target account combo box, cboPayee, uses the collection to set module level variables with the CardID and BankID of the selected payee:

```
    Private Sub cboPayee_Click()
        Dim lngListIndexSelection As Long
        Dim objPayeeInformation As CPayeeInformation
        Dim lngItemData As Long

        If Not m_blnAdding Then
          lngListIndexSelection = cboFromAccount.ListIndex
          If lngListIndexSelection > -1 Then
            lngItemData = cboPayee.ItemData(lngListIndexSelection)
            Set objPayeeInformation = m_colPayees.Item("Key=" & _
                CStr(lngItemData))
            m_intPayeeBankID = objPayeeInformation.BankID
            m_lngPayeeCardID = objPayeeInformation.CardID

            txtAmount.Text = CStr(objPayeeInformation.Amount)
          End If
        End If

        Set objPayeeInformation = Nothing
    End Sub
```

The ItemData property of the combo box is used to provide the index for the selected payee. Then, the key field is assembled by adding the index to the string "Key=". This key is used to locate the selected payee in the m_colPayees collection. The module level variables for the CardID and BankID are used for the call to the business services tier to pay the bill by transferring funds from the source account to the target account.

```
' Prepare for call to business tier
Set objTransfer = New Bank_Bus.Transfer

' Transfer the funds
g_objSharedProperties.TransactionStatus = objTransfer. _
    TransferFunds(m_intBankID, m_lngFromAccountID, _
    m_intPayeeBankID, m_lngPayeeCardID, m_curAmount, _
    Bank_Bus.txBillPayment, "Pay Bill")
```

In addition to paying bills, customers can transfer funds between Checking and Saving accounts.

Transferring Funds

With only two accounts available to each user, it's possible to program the form to automatically select the account to which funds are going to be transferred after the From account has been selected:

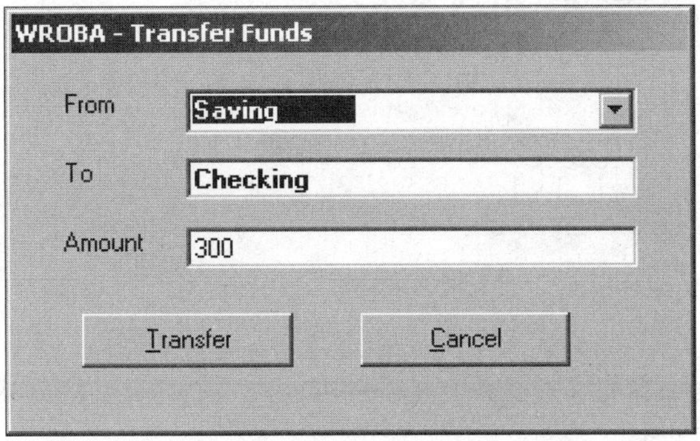

The following class diagram shows the methods for the FTransfer form:

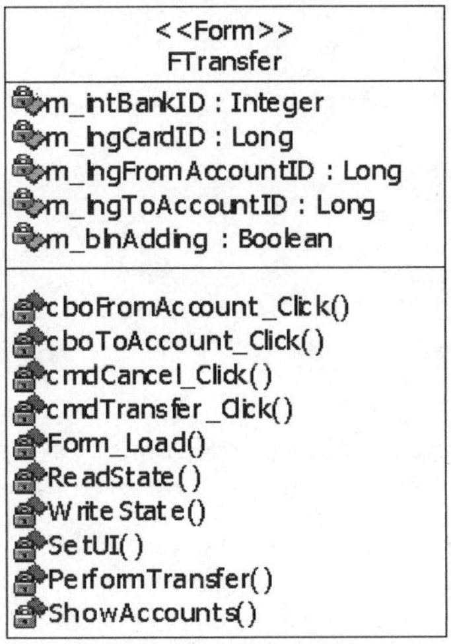

Try It Out – Implementing the FTransfer Form

1. The final customer form should be set up the same as in the previous form, with the controls named as in the previous form, except that, in this case, the middle combo box is called cboToAccount, and the buttons named cmdTransfer and cmdCancel respectively.

2. Enter the following module level declarations and the code for the From (source) account's Click event handler:

```
Option Explicit

' Form code in the user tier

Private m_intBankID As Integer
Private m_lngCardID As Long
Private m_lngFromAccountID As Long
Private m_lngToAccountID As Long
Private m_blnAdding As Boolean

Private Sub cboFromAccount_Click()
    Dim lngListIndexSelection As Long
    Dim lngListCount As Long
    Dim lngListIndexMax As Long

    If Not m_blnAdding Then
        If cboFromAccount.ListIndex > -1 Then
            ' If something is selected set the From account
            lngListIndexSelection = cboFromAccount.ListIndex
            lngListIndexMax = cboFromAccount.ListCount - 1

            ' Get the AccountID from the ItemData property of the combobox
            m_lngFromAccountID = cboFromAccount. _
                ItemData(lngListIndexSelection)

            If lngListIndexMax = 1 Then
                ' Special case - make the combobox invisible and
                ' make the underlying textbox visible
                txtToAccount.Visible = True
                cboToAccount.Visible = False

                If lngListIndexSelection = 0 Then
                    txtToAccount.Text = cboFromAccount.List(1)
                    m_lngToAccountID = cboFromAccount.ItemData(1)
                Else
                    txtToAccount.Text = cboFromAccount.List(0)
                    m_lngToAccountID = cboFromAccount.ItemData(0)
                End If
            Else
                m_lngToAccountID = 0
                txtToAccount.Visible = False

                m_blnAdding = True
                For lngListCount = 0 To lngListIndexMax
                    ' Populate the From combobox
```

```
              If lngListCount <> lngListIndexSelection Then
                  cboToAccount.AddItem cboFromAccount. _
                      List(lngListCount)
                  cboToAccount.ItemData(cboToAccount.NewIndex) = _
                      cboFromAccount.ItemData(lngListCount)
              End If
              Next lngListCount
              m_blnAdding = False

              cboToAccount.Visible = True
          End If
      End If
    End If
End Sub
```

3. Enter the code for the To (target) account's `Click` event handler, and the `Click` event handlers for the **Cancel** and **Transfer** buttons:

```
Private Sub cboToAccount_Click()
    If Not m_blnAdding Then
        If cboToAccount.ListIndex > -1 Then
            ' Set the To Account when the To combobox is clicked
            ' if something is selected
            m_lngToAccountID = CLng(cboToAccount. _
                ItemData(cboToAccount.ListIndex))
        End If
    End If
End Sub

Private Sub cmdCancel_Click()
    Unload Me
End Sub

Private Sub cmdTransfer_Click()
' In development environment prints string to Immediate window
    Debug.Print "Transfer"
    PerformTransfer
    g_objSharedProperties.TransactionMessage = ""

    Me.Hide
    FStatus.Show vbModal

    Unload Me
End Sub
```

4. Next, enter the code for the `Form_Load`, `ReadState`, `WriteState`, and `SetUI` methods:

```
Private Sub Form_Load()
    ReadState
    SetUI
End Sub
```

577

```
Private Sub ReadState()
' Get the CardID and BankID from the global
' SharedProperties class object
    m_intBankID = g_objSharedProperties.BankID
    m_lngCardID = g_objSharedProperties.CardID
End Sub

Private Sub WriteState()
' Save the CardID and BankID to the global
' SharedProperties class object
    g_objSharedProperties.BankID = m_intBankID
    g_objSharedProperties.CardID = m_lngCardID
End Sub

Private Sub SetUI()
    Me.Caption = g_strAppTitle & " - Transfer Funds"
    ShowAccounts
End Sub
```

5. The `PerformTransfer` method is the next code to add. This method makes the call to the business services tier to transfer the funds:

```
Private Sub PerformTransfer()
    Dim objTransfer As Bank_Bus.Transfer
    Dim curAmount As Currency

    ' Trap a blank Amount field
    If txtAmount.Text = "" Then txtAmount.Text = "0"

    ' Amount of money to transfer
    curAmount = CCur(txtAmount.Text)

    ' Prepare for call to business tier
    Set objTransfer = New Bank_Bus.Transfer

    ' Do the actual transfer
    g_objSharedProperties.TransactionStatus = _
        objTransfer.TransferFunds(m_intBankID, _
        m_lngFromAccountID, m_intBankID, m_lngToAccountID, _
        curAmount, Bank_Bus.txTransfer, "WROBA Transfer")

    Set objTransfer = Nothing
End Sub
```

6. Finally, enter the code for the `ShowAccounts` method, which is used to populate the From combo box:

```
Private Sub ShowAccounts()
    Dim objBank As Bank_Bus.Bank
    Dim recAccounts As ADODB.Recordset
```

```
    ' Prepare for call to business tier
    Set objBank = New Bank_Bus.Bank
    ' Return a recordset containing the selected accounts
    Set recAccounts = objBank.GetAccounts(m_intBankID, m_lngCardID)

    m_blnAdding = True
    Do While Not recAccounts.EOF ' Until end of recordset
        ' Populate the From combobox
        cboFromAccount.AddItem recAccounts!AccountTypeDesc
        cboFromAccount.ItemData(cboFromAccount.NewIndex) = _
            recAccounts!AccountID

        recAccounts.MoveNext ' Next recordset row
    Loop
    m_blnAdding = False

    If cboFromAccount.ListCount > 0 Then
        cboFromAccount.ListIndex = 0
    End If

    Set recAccounts = Nothing
    Set objBank = Nothing
End Sub
```

How It Works

The sequence of actions in transferring funds is very similar to the sequence of actions in paying bills. The major difference is the lack of a payee. The funds are being transferred from one account of the logged in user to the other. This simplifies the process and the code. Selecting the From (source) account automatically sets the To (target) account.

Clicking the Transfer button executes a call to the TransferFunds property of the Transfer class in the business services tier:

```
    ' Prepare for call to business tier
    Set objTransfer = New Bank_Bus.Transfer

    ' Do the actual transfer
    g_objSharedProperties.TransactionStatus = _
        objTransfer.TransferFunds(m_intBankID, _
        m_lngFromAccountID, m_intBankID, m_lngToAccountID, _
        curAmount, Bank_Bus.txTransfer, "WROBA Transfer")
```

The Transfer class in the business services tier uses MTS or COM+ to provide transactional control of the transfer of funds. The FTransfer form and the previous form, FPayBills, are the only forms that make calls to the business services tier that use transactional contexts.

Of course, we haven't done everything in this case study; one area we haven't touched on in this chapter is the provision of online help.

Summary

In this chapter, we saw how important it is to have a good GUI design, and also explored some of the basics that need to be considered when building a user interface. The GUI design principles we looked at were:

- ❑ Make the Interface Consistent
- ❑ Keep the User Interface Simple
- ❑ Provide Flexibility
- ❑ Create Reversible or Cancelable Tasks
- ❑ Trust the User
- ❑ Provide Meaningful Error Messages
- ❑ Use Progressive Disclosure for Complicated Forms
- ❑ Give Visual Feedback
- ❑ Remember Preferences
- ❑ Test GUI Prototypes

As part of the GUI design topic, we looked at field and form validation as a method of defensive coding. We saw how GUI design is used in the user services tier, and how to actually implement the WROBA user services tier.

The implementation of the WROBA user services tier uses two shared class modules, UserProperties and CPayeeInformation, to store data and messages. These classes provide data and message passing among the forms of the user services tier. The forms each implement one function that is derived from analysis of the Use Case scenarios for the case study. Each scenario is used to create a class diagram that serves as the template for the form code. The actions described by the scenarios also suggest the interface that each form requires, in accordance our GUI design principles.

Finally, we saw how each form for the customer functions of the user services tier was designed and coded. In our next chapter, we conclude the coding of the WROBA application by building the administration side of the user services tier.

15

User Tier II
Administration Services

In this chapter, we'll learn how the logic for the administration of WROBA cards and accounts is implemented. The administration logic parallels the logic used for customer accounts; it is distributed among the user services, business services and data services tiers. This chapter will look primarily at the implementation in the user services tier, with a few brief comments on how the code built here links to the components that are located in the business services and data services tiers.

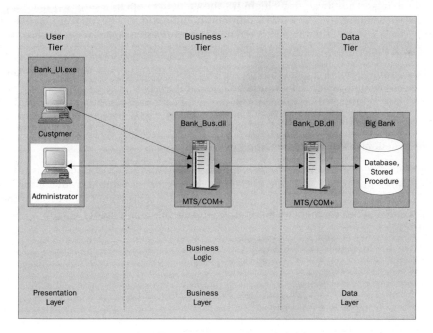

This is our last leg of constructing the WROBA application; we've completed our database, the data services tier, the business tier, and half of the user services tier. We've already learned all the general principles we need, so in this chapter we'll go straight into the case study. More specifically we'll:

- ❑ Outline the main features of the coding of the administration functions
- ❑ Set up the administration main menu
- ❑ Implement the forms required to administer activities relating to WROBA cards
- ❑ Implement the forms required to administer activities relating to banks
- ❑ Briefly overview the security considerations related to Visual Basic applications and distributed applications
- ❑ Review the WROBA implementation process

Again, all this code is contained within the web site download, but, as we work through this chapter, we'll see both how the design and analysis process led us to design these forms, and how to code them. All the way through the chapter we have highlighted areas where choices have been made about the operation of the case study, and where things could be done a little differently. Let's first look at some general aspects of this part of the application.

WROBA Administration

Administration of the WROBA project requires a different login to a standard login for WROBA customers. Supplying an administrator's login (as shown below) opens a different main menu to the main menu that a customer sees, and offers different menu options. The only forms that customers and administrators share are the initial login screen and the results message screen; the forms that provide the administrative functions are different to the customer forms.

If desired, the administration logic could be separated from the customer logic in the user services tier and made into a separate project. This would enable completely separate compilation and distribution of the customer and administration roles as separate applications. Separating the administrative logic into its own project and application provides stronger security to prevent someone from accidentally accessing the administrative functions. It would also enable separate development of the customer and administrative functions by different development teams.

The logic for WROBA administration follows the Use Cases and Use Case Scenarios for administration that were discovered in Chapter 6. The Use Case Scenarios for the administrative Use Cases are numbered as scenarios 8 to 14. Each one of these scenarios is represented by a form in the user services tier. Over the course of the chapter, we'll see all the forms that implement the administrative functions in the WROBA application.

WROBA Administration Code in Other Tiers

The administrative logic is distributed in the user services, business services, and data services tiers. This presents the same model as the customer logic. The database also implements services for the administration functions, in the form of stored procedures that are only used by the administrative logic. Over the course of this chapter, we'll see how calls to the database are done indirectly, by calls to the business services tier that are evaluated according to the business rules of the case study. The calls are then routed to the data services tier, where they are either executed by calls to stored procedures in the database or by directly executing SQL queries on the database.

If it was felt necessary to separate the customer and administrative user services logic, the forms that are specific to administration could be placed in a new VB EXE project with copies of the login (FLogin) and message results forms (FStatus), and the shared code module (MMain) and classes (CPayeeInformation and SharedProperties). The new administration project would need to have the startup object set to the FAdminMainMenu form, and some code in that form would have to be added to launch the login form.

Administration Logic Implementation

The login for an administrator is fixed with a WROBA card account number of 001000010000, and a password of Admin. The administrative login is shown in the following screenshot, although the password is masked with asterisks in place of the password characters:

The form used for the login is the same one used for a customer login, which we encountered in the last chapter. As we saw previously, there is no logic in the login form to determine whether the login is for a customer or an administrator; the login form only checks to see if the login is valid. This is in accordance with the design principles for distributed applications, where user interface and business logic objects are separated into independent code in separate tiers.

Let's look at the logical sequence of steps that are performed when the user services tier application (BankUI.exe) is started, by considering a couple of UML sequence and activity diagrams.

The following sequence diagram shows that when the user starts the WROBA application the main menu form (FMainMenu) is started. After some initialization the login screen (FLogin) is started. When the login validation is returned to the main menu the login screen is destroyed. If the login is an administrator's login, the administration main menu form (FAdminMainMenu) is started.

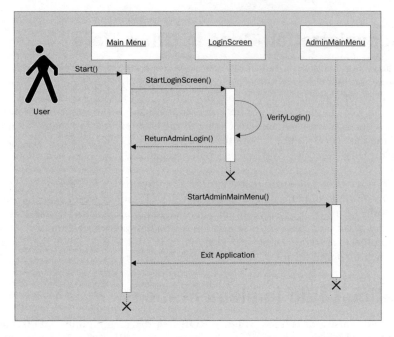

Let's now revisit the activity diagram covering the logic that is followed after a login is verified, from the point of view of the administration login:

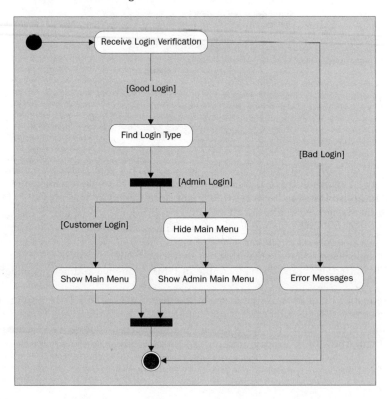

As we saw previously, if the login is an administrative login, the main menu is hidden and the administrator's main menu is started. When the command to exit the application is chosen in the administrator's main menu, the FAdminMainMenu form is destroyed and the main menu form exits the application after cleaning up the application objects.

The activity diagram indicates that the main menu is present in memory the entire time the application is running – if the login is an administrative login, the main menu is hidden before the administrator's main menu is started. This provides a common starting point for the application, and segregates the customer and administrative functions into two menu trees that are walled off from each other.

WROBA Administrator Main Menu

The administrator's main menu provides four menu items: File, Cards, Banks, and Help. This organization is similar to the menu organization for the customer main menu, and follows the general organization common to Windows menus. Windows applications always implement File and Help menus, which are used in this application to supply Exit and About menu items. The Cards and Banks menu selections initiate all the current administrative forms. We'll be looking at these in detail later in the chapter. The menu items in the Cards and Banks menus are derived from the Use Cases for Administrative functions that were discovered in Chapter 6, and are grouped by function into the Cards and Banks menus.

The Administrative Use Cases established in Chapter 6 were:

Function	Use Case Scenario
Admin Login	8
New Card	9
Delete Card	10
Unlock Card	11
Lock Card	12
New Bank	13
Edit Bank	14

The Administrator's login scenario is handled prior to the startup of the main menu for Administrators, in the main login logic. The remaining Administrative Use Case Scenarios can be grouped neatly into Use Cases that involve Cards and Use Cases that involve Banks, which then become the titles of main menu categories. The following screen shot shows the UML Class diagram that is used to create the template for the code in the Administrator Main Menu form:

```
              <<Form>>
            FAdminMainMenu
  m_intBankID : Integer
  m_lngCardID : Long

  Form_Load()
  SetUI()
  Form_Activate()
  ReadState()
  Form_Terminate()
  mnuBEdit_Click()
  mnuBNew_Click()
  mnuCDelete_Click()
  mnuCLock_Click()
  mnuCNew_Click()
  mnuCUnlock_Click()
  mnuFExit_Click()
  mnuHAbout_Click()
  FormDisplay()
  UnlockCard()
```

File Menu

The File menu has only one item implemented: Exit. Selecting this menu option destroys the administrator's main menu and returns an exit message to the application's main menu. The code in that form (FMainMenu) then destroys all global and module level objects and terminates the application. The code that exits the administrator's main menu is shown in the section on the main menu in this chapter.

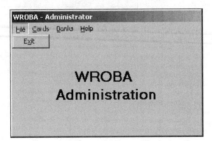

Help Menu

The Help menu has only one item implemented: About. Selecting this menu option displays the same About form that is displayed in the customer main menu.

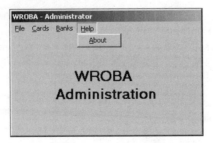

The WROBA administrator's main menu, as we've seen above, controls the program flow when an administrator is logged in. This menu is implemented by a form and is typical of Windows applications, which are event driven, since it just sits and waits for messages to be sent to it. This is in contrast to the procedural model, where menus are usually implemented as endless loops that are only exited by the user closing the application or an error. Before Windows became the dominant desktop environment, most applications written for DOS were implemented using a procedural model for their menus. Windows brought the event driven model into widespread use, and helped make it the most commonly used model today.

Try It Out – Implementing the Administration Main Menu

1. Open the Bank_UI project and choose **Project | Add Form** to add the Administration main menu form to the project. Name the form FAdminMainMenu.

2. Using the Menu Editor, as described in the previous chapter, set up the form (FAdminMainMenu) shown below in design mode, with four main menus (mnuFile, mnuCards, mnuBank, and mnuHelp respectively), and a label with the caption **WROBA Administration**:

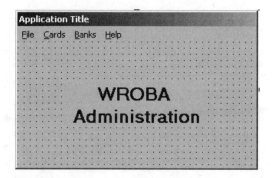

3. Add the following code to the form:

```
Option Explicit

' Form code in the user tier

Private m_frmCurrent As Form
Private m_intBankID As Integer
Private m_lngCardID As Long

Private Sub Form_Load()
    ReadState
    SetUI
End Sub

Private Sub SetUI()
    Me.Caption = g_strAppTitle & " - Administrator"
End Sub
```

```
Private Sub Form_Activate()
   Me.SetFocus
   SendKeys "%", True ' Alt key to activate the menu
End Sub

Private Sub ReadState()
' Get the BankID and selected accounts from the global
' SharedProperties class object
   m_intBankID = g_objSharedProperties.BankID
   m_lngCardID = g_objSharedProperties.CardID
End Sub

Private Sub Form_Terminate()
   Set m_frmCurrent = Nothing
End Sub
```

4. The form's Caption is set to **Application Title**, as are the captions for all the forms in the User Services Tier. The actual caption for each form is set at runtime in the SetUI method.

5. The next task is to return to the Menu Editor and add the menu choices for the **File** and **Help** menus (mnuFExit and mnuHAbout):

6. Then add the following code to the Click events for each menu, and the accompanying methods:

```
Private Sub mnuFExit_Click(Index As Integer)
   UnlockCard
   Unload Me
End Sub
```

```
Private Sub mnuHAbout_Click(Index As Integer)
    FormDisplay FAbout
End Sub

Private Sub FormDisplay(FormToShow As Form)
    Me.Hide
    Set m_frmCurrent = FormToShow
    m_frmCurrent.Show vbModal
    Set m_frmCurrent = Nothing
    Me.Show vbModal
End Sub

Private Sub UnlockCard()
    Dim objBank As Bank_Bus.Bank

    Set objBank = New Bank_Bus.Bank

    objBank.WROBAUnLock m_intBankID, m_lngCardID

    Set objBank = Nothing
End Sub
```

How It Works

When the FAdminMainMenu form loads, it reads the login IDs for the bank and the WROBA card. The ReadState method reads this information from the global class, SharedProperties. SharedProperties is initialized in the login screen code, if the login was verified.

```
Private Sub Form_Load()
    ReadState
    SetUI
End Sub

Private Sub ReadState()
' Get the BankID and selected accounts from the global
' SharedProperties class object
    m_intBankID = g_objSharedProperties.BankID
    m_lngCardID = g_objSharedProperties.CardID
End Sub
```

The SharedProperties class and methods that read and write to its properties were discussed in Chapter 7, in the sequence diagram for Use Case Scenario 1, and in the sample collaboration and object diagrams in that chapter. The set of UML diagrams for Use Case Scenario 2 in Chapter 8 also used this shared class. The coding of the class itself was covered in the previous chapter.

The code in the Form_Activate event uses the SendKeys method to send a message consisting of the *Alt* key, which is represented by the percentage symbol, to the menu. The *Alt* key activates the menu and highlights the File menu option.

```
Private Sub Form_Activate()
    Me.SetFocus
    SendKeys "%", True ' Alt key to activate the menu
End Sub
```

591

One of the quirks of menus designed with the Menu Editor is that, unlike menus created in code, the menu is not activated, and menu shortcut keys are not indicated by being underlined, unless the menu is activated by pressing the *Alt* key. The SendKeys method is used here to activate the menu on startup.

When the user selects a menu option the Click event for that option is fired. This behavior is identical to the behavior of a command button. The code for the **About** menu option Click event calls the private FormDisplay method with the name of the form for that menu choice:

```
Private Sub mnuHAbout_Click(Index As Integer)
    FormDisplay FAbout
End Sub

Private Sub FormDisplay(FormToShow As Form)
    Me.Hide
    Set m_frmCurrent = FormToShow
    m_frmCurrent.Show vbModal
    Set m_frmCurrent = Nothing
    Me.Show vbModal
End Sub
```

The private FormDisplay method is passed a Form object as an argument, and displays that form modally. When the form is closed, it is set to Nothing, which destroys the form, and the FAdminMainMenu form is shown again. The code that shows the FAdminMainMenu form again is the line Me.Show vbModal. At this point the FAdminMainMenu form is again waiting for user input. This is the same method that is used to display all the forms for Administrative functions, and we saw the same method of displaying forms used in the previous chapter for forms for the Customer portion of the User Services tier.

The code for the **Exit** menu option doesn't load a form to perform a task; it unlocks the WROBA card and then unloads the menu form.

```
Private Sub mnuFExit_Click(Index As Integer)
    UnlockCard
    Unload Me
End Sub
```

This restarts execution in the FMainMenu form (as we discussed in the previous chapter) on the line following:

```
FAdminMainMenu.Show vbModal
```

The lines following this in the FMainMenu form call the WROBAExit method of the code module and then unload the startup form, closing the application.

WROBA Administrator Cards Menu

The Cards menu enables the administrator to create a new card, delete a card, and lock or unlock a card. Cards have to be unlocked if the application crashes and does not exit by normal means. They might have to be locked if the card is suspended (perhaps because of theft of a card account's number and password).

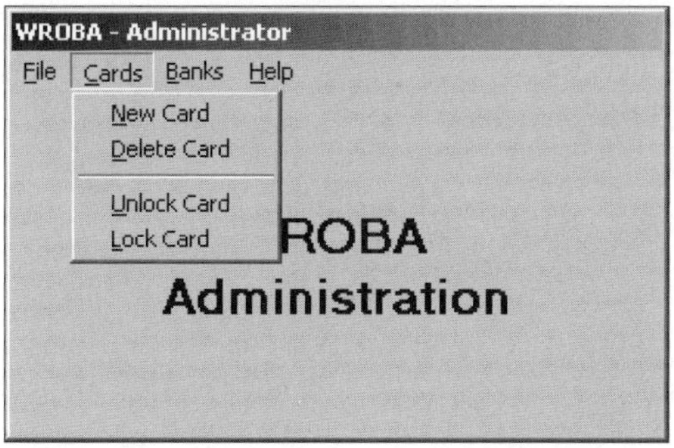

In this part of the chapter we'll be considering how to implement the following four activities:

❑   Adding Cards

❑   Deleting Cards

❑   Unlocking Cards

❑   Locking Cards

First, we need to amend FAdminMainMenu to provide the appropriate menu items.

Try It Out – Adding the Cards Submenu

1. Return to the Menu Editor and add the options shown in the following screenshot (mnuCNew, mnuCDelete, mnuCUnlock, and mnuCLock):

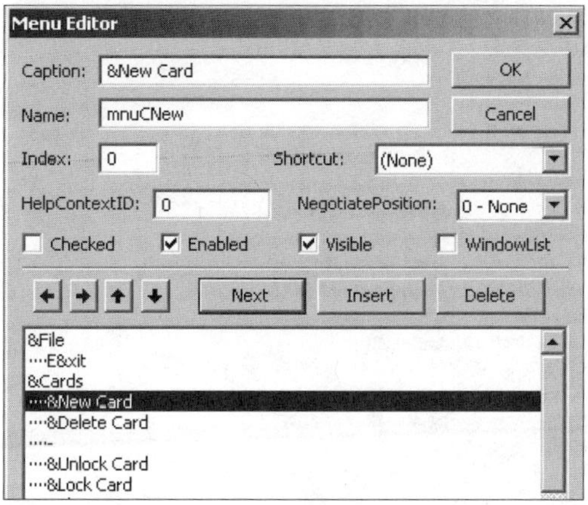

2. Then add the following code to handle the `Click` events for each option:

```
Private Sub mnuCDelete_Click(Index As Integer)
    FormDisplay FAdminDeleteCard
End Sub

Private Sub mnuCLock_Click(Index As Integer)
    FormDisplay FAdminLock
End Sub

Private Sub mnuCNew_Click(Index As Integer)
    FormDisplay FAdminNewCard
End Sub

Private Sub mnuCUnlock_Click(Index As Integer)
    FormDisplay FAdminUnlock
End Sub
```

This code uses the `FormDisplay` method to display the form for each menu choice modally. Of course, we now need to code each of these forms.

Adding a New WROBA Card

The `FAdminNewCard` form is used to create a new WROBA card account. The administrator chooses the account type (Saving or Checking) in a combo box. The account's initial balance, overdraft limit, and daily withdrawal limit are entered in text boxes. When the administrator adds the card, the system creates a new card account and account number, and generates a default password, as shown in the following screen shot. The customer can later change the password if they desire.

The following screen shot shows the UML Class diagram that was used to create the template for the code in the `FAdminNewCard` form:

```
       <<Form>>
      FAdminNewCard
─────────────────────────
 m_intBankID : Integer
─────────────────────────
 Form_Load()
 cmdAction_Click()
 ReadState()
 SetUI()
 ShowAccountTypes()
 CreateCard()
 EnsureNumeric()
```

Try It Out – Implementing the FAdminNewCard Form

1. Add a new form to the project. Name it `FAdminNewCard` and set it up as shown:

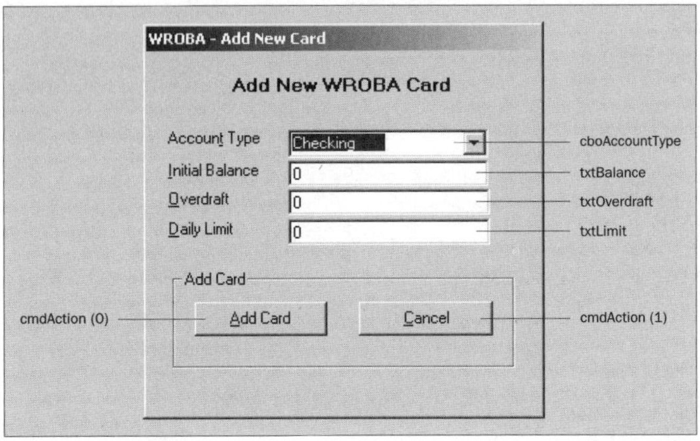

The **Add Card** and **Cancel** buttons are set up as a command array: to do this just give the controls the same name and Visual Basic 6 will automatically ask if a control array should be created. Create the **Add Card** button first, so the index numbers for the control array match the code that will be inserted.

2. Next add the following code to the form to provide the basic functionality for the form and the command buttons:

```
Option Explicit

' Form code in the user tier

Private m_intBankID As Integer

Private Enum EMenuActions
    eAddCard = 0
    eMainMenu = 1
End Enum

Private Sub Form_Load()
    ReadState
    SetUI
    ShowAccountTypes
End Sub

Private Sub cmdAction_Click(intIndex As Integer)
' The command buttons are created as a control array and are
' addressed by index value
    Select Case intIndex
    Case eAddCard
        ' In development environment prints string to Immediate window
        Debug.Print "Add Card"
        CreateCard
        Me.Hide
```

595

```
        FStatus.Show vbModal
    Case eMainMenu
        Debug.Print "Main Menu"
    Case Else
    End Select


    Unload Me
End Sub


Private Sub ReadState()
' Get the BankID from the global
' SharedProperties class object
    m_intBankID = g_objSharedProperties.BankID
End Sub


Private Sub SetUI()
    Me.Caption = g_strAppTitle & " - Add New Card"
End Sub
```

3. Next, we need to add code that fills the combo box, `cboAccountType`, with the available types of accounts:

```
Private Sub ShowAccountTypes()
    Dim objBank As Bank_Bus.Admin
    Dim recAccountTypes As ADODB.Recordset

    ' Prepare for call to business tier
    Set objBank = New Bank_Bus.Admin

    Set recAccountTypes = objBank.GetAccountTypes(m_intBankID)
    ' Populate the account type combobox
    Do While Not recAccountTypes.EOF
      cboAccountType.AddItem recAccountTypes!AccountTypeDesc
      cboAccountType.ItemData(cboAccountType.NewIndex) = _
        recAccountTypes!AccountType

      recAccountTypes.MoveNext ' Next account
    Loop

    cboAccountType.ListIndex = 0
    txtBalance.Text = "0"
    txtOverdraft.Text = "0"
    txtLimit.Text = "0"

    Set recAccountTypes = Nothing
    Set objBank = Nothing
End Sub
```

4. Of course, the form would be useless if we didn't have the code that actually allows us to add a new card, so add the following:

```
Private Sub CreateCard()
    Dim objBank As Bank_Bus.Admin
    Dim curBalance As Currency
    Dim curOverdraft As Currency
    Dim curLimit As Currency
    Dim intAccountType As Integer
    Dim lngListIndex As Long
    Dim blnResult As Boolean
    Dim strPassword As String
    Dim strNewCard As String

    lngListIndex = cboAccountType.ListIndex
    If lngListIndex > -1 Then
        ' Card account type
        intAccountType = cboAccountType.ItemData(lngListIndex)
    Else
        intAccountType = cboAccountType.ItemData(0)
    End If

    ' Ensure numeric results for the currency fields
    curBalance = CCur(EnsureNumeric(txtBalance.Text))
    curOverdraft = CCur(EnsureNumeric(txtOverdraft.Text))
    curLimit = CCur(EnsureNumeric(txtLimit.Text))

    ' Prepare for call to business tier
    Set objBank = New Bank_Bus.Admin

    blnResult = objBank.AddCard(m_intBankID, intAccountType, _
        curBalance, curLimit, curOverdraft, strNewCard, strPassword)

    If blnResult Then
        g_objSharedProperties.TransactionMessage = _
            "New WROBA card created." & vbCrLf & "Card ID: " _
            & strNewCard & vbCrLf & "Default Password: " & strPassword
    Else
        g_objSharedProperties.TransactionMessage = _
            "New WROBA card not created. Error."
    End If

    Set objBank = Nothing
End Sub

Private Function EnsureNumeric(strValue As String) As String
    ' Ensure a numeric result
    If strValue = "" Or (Not IsNumeric(strValue)) Then
        EnsureNumeric = "0"
    Else
        EnsureNumeric = strValue
    End If
End Function
```

How It Works

When the form loads, the BankID number is read from the SharedProperties class. Then the user interface for the form is instantiated. This private method just sets the form's caption, but it can be used for additional user interface features such as context sensitive messages, banners, dynamic images, and multimedia displays. All the administrative forms use the same methods to instantiate their working environments when they are loaded. If they need to store information for use in other forms, they store the data in properties of the SharedProperties class by calling the WriteState method. This data can include information about the machine state, such as transaction results, error codes, and error messages. It can also include user information, such as bank, card, or account (checking or saving) numbers.

The Click event handler for the control array for the **Add Card** and **Cancel** command buttons is passed an index number to indicate which button received the Click event:

```
Private Sub cmdAction_Click(intIndex As Integer)
' The command buttons are created as a control array and are
' addressed by index value
   Select Case intIndex
   Case eAddCard
       ' In development environment prints string to Immediate window
       Debug.Print "Add Card"
       CreateCard
       Me.Hide
       FStatus.Show vbModal
   Case eMainMenu
       Debug.Print "Main Menu"
   Case Else
   End Select

   Unload Me
End Sub
```

The **Add Card** command button calls the CreateCard method to add a new card and then displays the result in the FStatus form. The **Cancel** command button prints the name of the destination menu in the Immediate window of the debugger and unloads the FAdminNewCard form.

The private ShowAccountTypes method makes a call to the business services tier to get an ADO recordset of the available account types. This is done by instantiating an Admin class object in the Bank_Bus.DLL. The description of each account in the recordset and the code that represents that account type is stored to a combo box where the administrator chooses which type of card account to create.

```
Private Sub ShowAccountTypes()
    Dim objBank As Bank_Bus.Admin
    Dim recAccountTypes As ADODB.Recordset

    ' Prepare for call to business tier
    Set objBank = New Bank_Bus.Admin
```

```
     Set recAccountTypes = objBank.GetAccountTypes(m_intBankID)
     ' Populate the account type combobox
     Do While Not recAccountTypes.EOF
        cboAccountType.AddItem recAccountTypes!AccountTypeDesc
        cboAccountType.ItemData(cboAccountType.NewIndex) = _
           recAccountTypes!AccountType

        recAccountTypes.MoveNext ' Next account
     Loop

     cboAccountType.ListIndex = 0
     txtBalance.Text = "0"
     txtOverdraft.Text = "0"
     txtLimit.Text = "0"

     Set recAccountTypes = Nothing
     Set objBank = Nothing
  End Sub
```

This brings up another area where the application could be enhanced. Since there is no current implementation of a function to add a new account type to an existing card account, the WROBA application currently only supports Saving or Checking accounts.

The `CreateCard` method gathers the data from the form and validates the data by ensuring that the currency fields are currency values by using the following:

```
     ' Ensure numeric results for the currency fields
     curBalance = CCur(EnsureNumeric(txtBalance.Text))
     curOverdraft = CCur(EnsureNumeric(txtOverdraft.Text))
     curLimit = CCur(EnsureNumeric(txtLimit.Text))
```

The `Admin` class in the business services tier is called to create the card account and default account type and the result of the call is stored in the `TransactionMessage` property of the `SharedProperties` class for display to the administrator.

These messages are stored in the body of the code, which makes them difficult to convert to other languages. If internationalization, portability, or ease of change of the messages is of concern, a better approach is to store messages as constant strings in the declarations section of the forms, or in a project-wide resource file. A project-wide resource file that stores all the messages in the project can be changed for internationalization by changing which resource file the project is compiled with. These methods were not used in the WROBA case study because they make reading and following the code more difficult than the method chosen.

The `EnsureNumeric` function converts non-numeric values to 0; this is required to ensure that the numeric fields in the database are initialized correctly. A potential enhancement to the form would be to add a dialog box that would enable the administrator to cancel the creation of a new card, or issue an error message and loop back if any of the values are non-numeric, instead of just converting them to 0.

Deleting a WROBA Card

The card deletion form requires the validation of the existence of the card account before permitting card account deletion.

Thus, when the dialog is originally loaded, the Validate button is enabled with the Delete Card button disabled:

If the account validates, the situation is reversed:

This is an example of using the results of a transaction or application state to enable and disable controls. When the card account is deleted, only the AccountHistory table in the database retains records of this account. These rows in the AccountHistory table are retained to provide an audit trail of account transactions. The following UML Class diagram was used to create the template for the code in the FAdminDeleteCard form:

Try It Out – Implementing the FAdminDeleteCard Form

1. Add a new form to the project called `FAdminDeleteCard` and set it up as shown earlier, with the text box and upper command button controls named `txtCardID` and `cmdValidate` respectively. Again, the buttons relating to deleting the card form a control array (**Delete Card** – `cmdAction(0)`, **Cancel** – `cmdAction(1)`).

2. Firstly, we'll add the code that initializes the form and defines the use of the `cmdAction` buttons:

```
Option Explicit

' Form code in the user tier

Private m_intBankID As Integer
Private m_lngCardID As Long

Private Enum EMenuActions
    eDeleteCard = 0
    eMainMenu = 1
End Enum

Private Sub Form_Load()
    SetUI
End Sub

Private Sub cmdAction_Click(intIndex As Integer)
' The command buttons are created as a control array and are
' addressed by index value
    Select Case intIndex
    Case eDeleteCard
        ' In development environment prints string to Immediate window
        Debug.Print "Delete Card"
        CardDelete
        Me.Hide
        FStatus.Show vbModal
    Case eMainMenu
        Debug.Print "Main Menu"
    Case Else
    End Select

    Unload Me
End Sub

Private Sub SetUI()
    Me.Caption = g_strAppTitle & " - Delete WROBA card"
    ' Start out with the Validate command button enabled
    ' and the Delete command button disabled
    cmdAction.Item(eDeleteCard).Enabled = False
    cmdValidate.Enabled = True
End Sub
```

3. Secondly, we'll provide the code needed to validate the card number:

```
Private Sub cmdValidate_Click()
' Validate the card to delete. If it is a valid entry in the DB,
' enable the Delete command button
   If ValidateCard(txtCardID.Text) = True Then
      cmdAction.Item(eDeleteCard).Enabled = True
      cmdValidate.Enabled = False
   Else
      MsgBox "Card Number for deletion did not validate", , _
         g_strAppTitle
      cmdAction.Item(eDeleteCard).Enabled = False
      cmdValidate.Enabled = True
   End If
End Sub

Private Function ValidateCard(strCardId As String) As Boolean
   Dim objBankAdmin As Bank_Bus.Admin
   Dim objBank As Bank_Bus.Bank

   On Error GoTo ErrorHandler
   ' Pessimistic assumption that the card is not valid
   ValidateCard = False

   ' Prepare for call to business tier
   Set objBank = New Bank_Bus.Bank

   ' CardID is 9 digits
   m_lngCardID = objBank.GetCardID(strCardId)

   ' BankID is 3 digits
   m_intBankID = objBank.GetBankID(strCardId)

   ' Prepare for call to business tier
   Set objBankAdmin = New Bank_Bus.Admin
   ' Find the selected card
   ValidateCard = objBankAdmin.VerifyCard(m_intBankID, m_lngCardID)

Clean_Up:
   Set objBank = Nothing
   Set objBankAdmin = Nothing
   Exit Function

ErrorHandler:
   ValidateCard = False
   GoTo Clean_Up
End Function
```

4. Finally, we can provide the code needed to actually delete the card account:

```
Private Sub CardDelete()
   Dim objBank As Bank_Bus.Admin
   Dim blnDeleted As Boolean

   On Error GoTo ErrorHandler

   ' Prepare for call to business tier
   Set objBank = New Bank_Bus.Admin
   blnDeleted = objBank.DeleteCard(m_intBankID, m_lngCardID)

   If blnDeleted Then
      g_objSharedProperties.TransactionMessage = _
         "Card deleted"
   Else
      g_objSharedProperties.TransactionMessage = _
         "Card not deleted. Error"
   End If

Clean_Up:
   Set objBank = Nothing
   Exit Sub

ErrorHandler:
   g_objSharedProperties.TransactionMessage = _
      "Card not deleted. Error"
   GoTo Clean_Up
End Sub
```

How It Works

The administrator enters a card account number to delete, so the `SharedProperties` class is not read on loading this form, and the `FormLoad` event therefore only calls the `SetUI` method during its initializations. The `Click` event handler for the command button control array is similar to the event handler in many of the forms, using a `Select Case` construct to select which command button action to perform.

The `Click` event handler for the **Validate** command button calls the `ValidateCard` function and enables or disables the **Delete Card** command button, based on the return value from the function. The `SetUI` method in this form sets the enabled/disabled state of the command buttons as part of the form's initializations:

```
Private Sub SetUI()
   Me.Caption = g_strAppTitle & " - Delete WROBA card"
   ' Start out with the Validate command button enabled
   ' and the Delete command button disabled
   cmdAction.Item(eDeleteCard).Enabled = False
   cmdValidate.Enabled = True
End Sub
```

The `ValidateCard` function pessimistically assumes that the card validation will fail; so it initializes the return value of the function as `False`. It calls the `Bank` class in the business services tier to find the parsed bank and card numbers from the entered card account number. These numbers are parsed in properties in the business services tier so that, if changes are made to the business rules, the changes only have to be deployed to the server that runs the business services tier code, instead of to every administrator or user. After the numbers are parsed, the `Admin` class in the business services tier is called to validate the card account.

The card account is deleted with another call to the `Admin` class in the business services tier. The `TransactionMessage` property of the `SharedProperties` class is updated with a message based on the success or failure of the card account deletion, which is displayed by the `FStatus` form after the `CardDelete` method ends.

> *The code in the remaining menu options selected from the Cards menu follows the same pattern as the code for the previous menu options. The form is initialized by calling `ReadState` and `SetUI`, the action command buttons are validated, calls are made to the business tier for evaluation of business rules and for pass-through calls to the data service tier to make changes to the database. The differences are primarily in the specific properties and methods of classes in the business services tier that are called to perform the tasks. Therefore, we won't explain the code in detail for the remainder of the Cards menu section (although, of course, the comments within the code will provide effective documentation).*

Unlocking a WROBA Card

The Unlock Card menu option unlocks a card account that has been locked by an administrator or was left locked when the application terminated abnormally. The following UML Class diagram was used to create the template for the code in the `FAdminUnlock` form:

```
┌────────────────────────────────┐
│         <<Form>>               │
│        FAdminUnlock            │
├────────────────────────────────┤
│ m_intBankID : Integer          │
│ m_lngCardID : Long             │
├────────────────────────────────┤
│ Form_Load()                    │
│ cmdAction_Click()              │
│ cmdValidate_Click()            │
│ SetUI()                        │
│ ValidateCard()                 │
│ CardUnlock()                   │
└────────────────────────────────┘
```

Try It Out – Implementing the FAdminUnlock Form

1. Here we need to add a form to the project called `FAdminUnlock` and set it up as shown (apart from the caption changes, the control names are the same as for the `FAdminDeleteCard` form):

2. Add the following code to the form. This code should look very familiar by now, since it follows the same pattern as the previous forms, with methods to initialize the form and respond to `Click` events.

```
Option Explicit

' Form code in the user tier

Private m_intBankID As Integer
Private m_lngCardID As Long

Private Enum EMenuActions
    eUnLockCard = 0
    eMainMenu = 1
End Enum

Private Sub Form_Load()
    SetUI
End Sub

Private Sub cmdAction_Click(intIndex As Integer)
' The command buttons are created as a control array and are
' addressed by index value
    Select Case intIndex
    Case eUnLockCard
        ' In development environment prints string to Immediate window
        Debug.Print "Unlock Card"
        CardUnlock
        Me.Hide
        FStatus.Show vbModal
    Case eMainMenu
        Debug.Print "Main Menu"
    Case Else
    End Select

    Unload Me
End Sub

Private Sub cmdValidate_Click()
```

```
' Validate the card to unlock. If it is a valid entry in the DB,
' enable the Unlock command button
   If ValidateCard(txtCardID.Text) = True Then
       cmdAction.Item(eUnLockCard).Enabled = True
       cmdValidate.Enabled = False
   Else
       MsgBox "Card Number for unlock did not validate", , _
           g_strAppTitle
       cmdAction.Item(eUnLockCard).Enabled = False
       cmdValidate.Enabled = True
   End If
End Sub

Private Sub SetUI()
   Me.Caption = g_strAppTitle & " - Unlock WROBA card"
   ' Start out with the Validate command button enabled
   ' and the Unlock command button disabled
   cmdAction.Item(eUnLockCard).Enabled = False
   cmdValidate.Enabled = True
End Sub
```

3. Add the following code to the form to validate card numbers for the **Validate** button `Click` event:

```
Private Function ValidateCard(strCardId As String) As Boolean
    Dim objBankAdmin As Bank_Bus.Admin
    Dim objBank As Bank_Bus.Bank

    On Error GoTo ErrorHandler
    ' Pessimistic assumption that the card is not valid
    ValidateCard = False

    ' Prepare for call to business tier
    Set objBank = New Bank_Bus.Bank

    ' CardID is 9 digits
    m_lngCardID = objBank.GetCardID(strCardId)

    ' BankID is 3 digits
    m_intBankID = objBank.GetBankID(strCardId)

    ' Prepare for call to business tier
    Set objBankAdmin = New Bank_Bus.Admin
    ' Find the selected card
    ValidateCard = objBankAdmin.VerifyCard(m_intBankID, m_lngCardID)

Clean_Up:
    Set objBank = Nothing
    Set objBankAdmin = Nothing
    Exit Function

ErrorHandler:
    ValidateCard = False
    GoTo Clean_Up
End Function
```

4. Finally, add the code for the method that unlocks the card by calling the `WROBAUnlock` method in the business services tier code.

```
Private Sub CardUnlock()
    Dim objBank As Bank_Bus.Bank
    Dim blnUnlocked As Boolean

    On Error GoTo ErrorHandler
    ' Prepare for call to business tier
    Set objBank = New Bank_Bus.Bank
    objBank.WROBAUnLock m_intBankID, m_lngCardID

    g_objSharedProperties.TransactionMessage = _
        "Card unlocked"

Clean_Up:
    Set objBank = Nothing
    Exit Sub

ErrorHandler:
    g_objSharedProperties.TransactionMessage = _
        "Card not unlocked. Error"
    GoTo Clean_Up
End Sub
```

Locking a WROBA Card

The Lock Card menu option is used to lock a user out of logging into a card account. This might be to suspend the user's card privileges or to lock the card account while administrative maintenance is performed on the account. One limitation of the current implementation is if a user is logged into a card account when the lock is acquired, the lock is cleared when the user logs off the card account. One enhancement could be to check the current lock status of the card before the lock is acquired and notify the administrator that the card account is currently logged in.

The following UML Class diagram was used to create the template for the code in the `FAdminLock` form.

```
┌─────────────────────────────────┐
│         <<Form>>                 │
│         FAdminLock               │
├─────────────────────────────────┤
│ ⚑ m_intBankID : Integer          │
│ ⚑ m_lngCardID : Long             │
├─────────────────────────────────┤
│ ⚑ Form_Load()                    │
│ ⚑ cmdAction_Click()              │
│ ⚑ cmdValidate_Click()            │
│ ⚑ SetUI()                        │
│ ⚑ ValidateCard()                 │
│ ⚑ CardLock()                     │
└─────────────────────────────────┘
```

607

Try It Out – Implementing the FAdminLock Form

1. Here the new form is called `FAdminlock` and should be set up as shown (again, apart form the caption changes, the control names are the same as for the `FAdminDeleteCard` form):

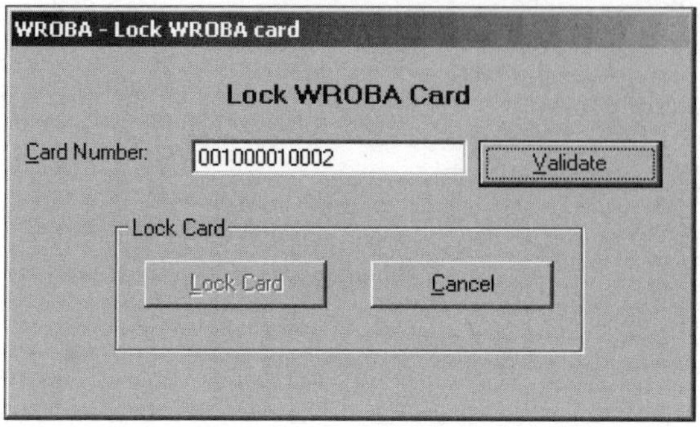

2. Add the code to the form for form initialization and the `Click` event handlers:

```
Option Explicit

' Form code in the user tier

Private m_intBankID As Integer
Private m_lngCardID As Long

Private Enum EMenuActions
    eLockCard = 0
    eMainMenu = 1
End Enum

Private Sub Form_Load()
  SetUI
End Sub

Private Sub cmdAction_Click(intIndex As Integer)
' The command buttons are created as a control array and are
' addressed by index value
    Select Case intIndex
    Case eLockCard
       ' In development environment prints string to Immediate window
       Debug.Print "Lock Card"
       CardLock
       Me.Hide
       FStatus.Show vbModal
    Case eMainMenu
       Debug.Print "Main Menu"
    Case Else
    End Select

    Unload Me
End Sub
Private Sub cmdValidate_Click()
' Validate the card to lock. If it is a valid entry in the DB,
' enable the Lock command button
```

```
      If ValidateCard(txtCardID.Text) = True Then
          cmdAction.Item(eLockCard).Enabled = True
          cmdValidate.Enabled = False
      Else
          MsgBox "Card Number for lock did not validate", , _
              g_strAppTitle
          cmdAction.Item(eLockCard).Enabled = False
          cmdValidate.Enabled = True
      End If
  End Sub

  Private Sub SetUI()
      Me.Caption = g_strAppTitle & " - Lock WROBA card"
      ' Start out with the Validate command button enabled
      ' and the Lock command button disabled
      cmdAction.Item(eLockCard).Enabled = False
      cmdValidate.Enabled = True
  End Sub
```

3. Next add the code for validating a card number:

```
Private Function ValidateCard(strCardId As String) As Boolean
    Dim objBankAdmin As Bank_Bus.Admin
    Dim objBank As Bank_Bus.Bank

    On Error GoTo ErrorHandler
    ' Pessimistic assumption that the card is not valid
    ValidateCard = False

    ' Prepare for call to business tier
    Set objBank = New Bank_Bus.Bank

    ' CardID is 9 digits
    m_lngCardID = objBank.GetCardID(strCardId)

    ' BankID is 3 digits
    m_intBankID = objBank.GetBankID(strCardId)

    ' Prepare for call to business tier
    Set objBankAdmin = New Bank_Bus.Admin
    ' Find the selected card
    ValidateCard = objBankAdmin.VerifyCard(m_intBankID, m_lngCardID)

Clean_Up:
    Set objBank = Nothing
    Set objBankAdmin = Nothing
    Exit Function

ErrorHandler:
    ValidateCard = False
    GoTo Clean_Up
End Function
```

The ValidateCard function could be removed from the forms in which it appears
(FAdminDeleteCard, FAdminUnlock, and FAdminLock) and placed in the MMain code
module. If we did this we'd have to remember to change the scope to Public from Private
so that the function is visible where it is needed.

609

4. Finally, add the code that locks the card by calling a property in the business services tier code:

```
Private Sub CardLock()
   Dim objBank As Bank_Bus.Bank
   Dim blnLocked As Boolean

   On Error GoTo ErrorHandler

   ' Prepare for call to business tier
   Set objBank = New Bank_Bus.Bank
   blnLocked = objBank.WROBALock(m_intBankID, m_lngCardID)

   If blnLocked Then
      g_objSharedProperties.TransactionMessage = _
         "Card locked"
   Else
      g_objSharedProperties.TransactionMessage = _
          "Card not locked. Error"
   End If

Clean_Up:
   Set objBank = Nothing
   Exit Sub

ErrorHandler:
   g_objSharedProperties.TransactionMessage = _
      "Card not locked. Error"
   GoTo Clean_Up
End Sub
```

WROBA Administrator Banks Menu

The **Banks** menu has two menu options (which we'll cover fully in the following sections):

- ❑ **New Bank** – which creates a new partner bank in the WROBACard network.

- ❑ **Edit Bank** – which enables the administrator to change the partner bank's description and DSN (data source name), or remove a bank from the WROBACard network.

DSNs, or connection strings, can be used to connect to a database. Of course, the first task is to add the appropriate menu options into FAdminMainMenu:

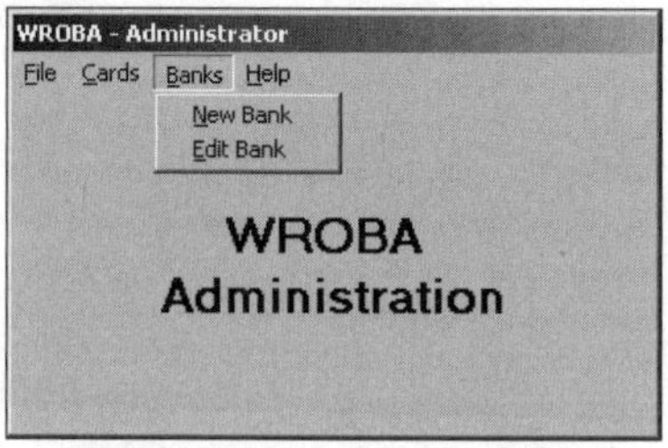

1. Open up the FAdminMainMenu form and, once the focus is on the form, open up the Menu Editor and add the options shown above using the names mnuBEdit and mnuBNew.

2. Add the following code for the Click events for the menu options:

```
Private Sub mnuBEdit_Click(Index As Integer)
    FormDisplay FAdminEditBank
End Sub

Private Sub mnuBNew_Click(Index As Integer)
    FormDisplay FAdminNewBank
End Sub
```

Adding a New Bank

The bank's description is purely textual. It is only for the purposes of bank identification to the administrator or customer, since internally the system uses a bank ID number. The present implementation uses only one bank, with a connection string that is hard coded into the BankLocator class module in the data services tier. Support for partner banks, which are other banks that are members of the WROBACard network, is not presently implemented.

Implementing support for more than one bank in the WROBACard network involves two problems, which are:

❑ How to acquire a connection string or DSN for the "home" bank – the bank database that the administrator or user is logging into

❑ How to acquire the connection string or DSN of the remote partner bank

The first problem can be solved by hard coding the connection string or DSN in the BankLocator module (as is presently done), defining a connection string or DSN constant in the declarations section of the BankLocator module, or storing the string in a resource file or in a table in the database that contains only the "home" bank's connection string or DSN.

The second problem can be solved by putting code in the Select Case statement in the BankLocator module to read the database table that contains the dataset of partner banks, and return the BankDSN column from the table based on matching the bank's ID number with the BankID column of the table. This solution can use the sp_select_bank stored procedure in the database to return a recordset containing the record of the selected bank's information.

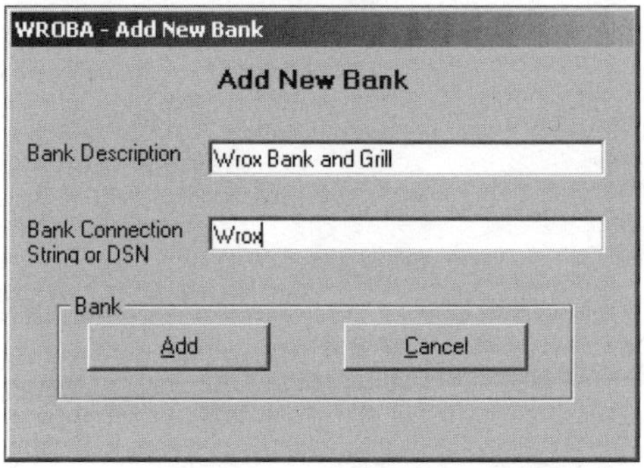

611

The following UML Class diagram was used to create the template for the code in the FAdminNewBank form:

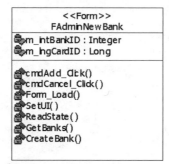

Try It Out – Implementing the FAdminNewBank Form

1. Add a new form to the project called FAdminNewBank and set it up as shown in the screenshot just shown, with the controls named txtDesc, txtDSN, cmdAdd, and cmdCancel as appropriate.

2. Our first job for this form is to put in the code associated with the loading of the form and the command buttons:

```
Option Explicit

' Form code in the user tier

Private m_intBankID As Integer
Private m_lngCardID As Long
Private m_recBanks As ADODB.Recordset

Private Sub cmdAdd_Click()
    ' In development environment prints string to Immediate window
    Debug.Print "Add Bank"
    CreateBank
    Me.Hide
    FStatus.Show vbModal
End Sub

Private Sub cmdCancel_Click()
    Debug.Print "Main Menu"
    Unload Me
End Sub

Private Sub Form_Load()
    ReadState
    SetUI
    GetBanks
End Sub
```

```
Private Sub SetUI()
  Me.Caption = g_strAppTitle & " - Add New Bank"
End Sub

Private Sub ReadState()
  ' Get the BankID from the global
   ' SharedProperties class object
   m_intBankID = g_objSharedProperties.BankID
End Sub
```

3. Next we need to implement the `GetBanks` method:

```
Private Sub GetBanks()
   Dim objBank As Bank_Bus.Bank

   Set objBank = New Bank_Bus.Bank
   Set m_recBanks = objBank.GetBanks(m_intBankID)

   Set objBank = Nothing
End Sub
```

4. Finally, we code the `CreateBank` method that will do all the hard work:

```
Private Sub CreateBank()
   Dim intBankID As Integer
   Dim strBankDesc As String
   Dim strDSN As String
   Dim objBank As Bank_Bus.Admin
   Dim blnBankAllowed As Boolean

   m_recBanks.MoveLast
   intBankID = (m_recBanks!BankID) + 1
   strBankDesc = txtDesc
   strDSN = txtDSN

   If strBankDesc <> "" And strDSN <> "" Then
      ' Prepare for call to business tier
      Set objBank = New Bank_Bus.Admin

      ' See if adding the new bank is successful
      blnBankAllowed = objBank.AddBank(m_intBankID, intBankID, _
         strBankDesc, strDSN)

      If blnBankAllowed Then
         g_objSharedProperties.TransactionMessage = _
            "New Bank added."
      Else
         g_objSharedProperties.TransactionMessage = _
            "Bank not added. Error."
      End If
   Else
      g_objSharedProperties.TransactionMessage = _
         "Bank not added. Error."
   End If

   Set objBank = Nothing
End Sub
```

613

How It Works

The Click events for the two command buttons in this form are handled by separate Click event handlers. In this form an indexed control array of command buttons isn't used to provide the Click event handler. We've done this simply to demonstrate another method of handling command button Click events. The FormLoad event in this form is also different to that in previous forms, as it is used to call the GetBanks method, which populates a module level ADO recordset of all the WROBACard member banks.

This GetBanks method uses the GetBanks property of the Bank class in the business services tier to return the recordset of WROBACard member banks. As we saw in Chapter 12, this property is a pass-through call to the data services tier, which in turn calls the sp_select_bank stored procedure in the database:

```
Private Sub GetBanks()
    Dim objBank As Bank_Bus.Bank

    Set objBank = New Bank_Bus.Bank
    Set m_recBanks = objBank.GetBanks(m_intBankID)

    Set objBank = Nothing
End Sub
```

The BankID argument for the GetBanks business services tier property is used in a pass-through call to the data services tier to locate a connection string to connect to the "home" bank's database.

The CreateBank method also uses a pass-through call to the Admin class module of the data services tier by way of the business services tier. The result message is displayed in the FStatus form based on the results of the call to the database.

Edit Bank

The Edit Bank menu option enables the administrator to change the description and connection string or DSN of the selected bank. The bank is selected in a combo box that is populated from an ADO recordset that contains the data for all the WROBACard member banks. This menu option also enables the administrator to remove a bank from the table of member banks. Be aware that, in this implementation of the case study, the delete action does *not* trigger a confirmation dialog box.

The following UML Class diagram was used to create the template for the code in the FAdminEditBank form:

```
        <<Form>>
      FAdminEditBank
━━━━━━━━━━━━━━━━━━━━━━━━
m_intBankID : Integer
m_lngAccountID : Long
m_blnAdding : Boolean
m_astrDesc : String
m_astrDSN : String
m_aintBankID : Integer
━━━━━━━━━━━━━━━━━━━━━━━━
cboSelect_Click()
cmdAction_Click()
Form_Load()
SetUI()
ReadState()
ShowBanks()
SaveBankChanges()
DeleteBank()
txtDesc_Change()
txtDSN_Change()
```

Try It Out – Implementing the FAdminEditBank Form

1. Add a new form named `FAdminEditBank` and set it up as shown:

Unlike the previous form, here we *do* use the familiar controls array of command buttons to respond to user input.

2. As usual, we need to declare some variables at the top of the code; here we declare the command buttons in an `Enum` to give meaningful names to their index values:

```
Option Explicit

' Form code in the user tier

Private m_intBankID As Integer
Private m_lngAccountID As Long
Private m_blnAdding As Boolean

Private m_astrDesc() As String
Private m_astrDSN() As String
Private m_aintBankID() As Integer

Private Enum EMenuActions
    eSaveChanges = 0
    eDeleteBank = 1
    eMainMenu = 2
End Enum
```

3. Our next task is to code for the `Click` event for the combo box:

```
Private Sub cboSelect_Click()
    Dim lngListIndex As Long

    If m_blnAdding = False And cboSelect.ListCount > 0 Then
        lngListIndex = cboSelect.ListIndex
        txtID.Text = Trim$(CStr(m_aintBankID(lngListIndex)))
        txtDesc.Text = Trim$(m_astrDesc(lngListIndex))
        txtDSN.Text = Trim$(m_astrDSN(lngListIndex))
    End If
End Sub
```

4. The `Click` event handler for the command buttons is implemented with a `Select Case` construct and the `FormLoad` event, `SetUI`, and `ReadState` methods are similar to those events and methods in the other forms in the user services tier:

```
Private Sub cmdAction_Click(Index As Integer)
    Select Case Index
    Case eSaveChanges
        ' In development environment prints string to Immediate window
        Debug.Print "Save Bank Changes"
        SaveBankChanges
        Me.Hide
        FStatus.Show vbModal
    Case eDeletebank
        Debug.Print "Delete Bank"
        DeleteBank
        Me.Hide
        FStatus.Show vbModal
    Case eMainMenu
        Debug.Print "Main Menu"
        Unload Me
    End Select
End Sub

Private Sub Form_Load()
    Dim blnBanks As Boolean

    ReadState
    SetUI
    blnBanks = ShowBanks
    If Not blnBanks Then
        cmdAction(0).Enabled = False
        cmdAction(1).Enabled = False
    End If
End Sub

Private Sub SetUI()
    Me.Caption = g_strAppTitle & " - Edit Banks"
End Sub
```

```
Private Sub ReadState()
    ' Get the BankID and AccountID from the global
    ' SharedProperties class object
    m_intBankID = g_objSharedProperties.BankID
    m_lngAccountID = g_objSharedProperties.AccountID
End Sub
```

5. The next piece of code to add is that which covers the ShowBanks function:

```
Private Function ShowBanks() As Boolean
    Dim objBank As Bank_Bus.Bank
    Dim recBanks As ADODB.Recordset
    Dim strBuildAccount As String
    Dim lngIndex As Long

    On Error Resume Next
    ShowBanks = False

    ' Prepare for call to business tier
    Set objBank = New Bank_Bus.Bank

    ' Retrieve recordset of banks
    Set recBanks = objBank.GetBanks(m_intBankID)

    If Not (recBanks.EOF) Then
        ShowBanks = True
        m_blnAdding = True
        lngIndex = 0
        Do While Not recBanks.EOF ' Until end of recordset
            ' Populate the Banks combobox

            ReDim Preserve m_astrDesc(lngIndex)
            m_astrDesc(lngIndex) = Trim$(recBanks!BankDesc)
            cboSelect.AddItem m_astrDesc(lngIndex)

            ReDim Preserve m_astrDSN(lngIndex)
            m_astrDSN(lngIndex) = Trim$(recBanks!BankDSN)

            ReDim Preserve m_aintBankID(lngIndex)
            m_aintBankID(lngIndex) = recBanks!BankID

            lngIndex = lngIndex + 1
            recBanks.MoveNext ' Next bank
        Loop

        If cboSelect.ListCount > 0 Then
            cboSelect.ListIndex = 0
            txtDesc.Text = m_astrDesc(0)
            txtDSN.Text = m_astrDSN(0)
            txtID = Trim$(CStr(m_aintBankID(0)))
        End If
        m_blnAdding = False
    Else
```

```
        MsgBox "No banks to edit.", vbOKOnly, g_strAppTitle
    End If

    Set recBanks = Nothing
    Set objBank = Nothing
End Function
```

6. Next we add the SaveBankChanges method:

```
Private Sub SaveBankChanges()
    Dim intChangeBankID As Integer
    Dim strBankDesc As String
    Dim strDSN As String
    Dim objBank As Bank_Bus.Admin
    Dim blnChangeAllowed As Boolean
    Dim lngListIndex As Long

    lngListIndex = cboSelect.ListIndex
    If lngListIndex > -1 Then
        intChangeBankID = m_aintBankID(lngListIndex)
        strBankDesc = m_astrDesc(lngListIndex)
        strDSN = m_astrDSN(lngListIndex)

        If strBankDesc <> "" And strDSN <> "" Then
            ' Prepare for call to business tier
            Set objBank = New Bank_Bus.Admin

            ' See if changing the bank is successful
            blnChangeAllowed = objBank.EditBank(m_intBankID, _
                intChangeBankID, strBankDesc, strDSN)

            If blnChangeAllowed = True Then
                g_objSharedProperties.TransactionMessage = _
                    "Bank changed."
            Else
                g_objSharedProperties.TransactionMessage = _
                    "Bank not changed. Error."
            End If
        Else
            g_objSharedProperties.TransactionMessage = _
                "Bank not changed. Error."
        End If
    Else
        g_objSharedProperties.TransactionMessage = _
            "Bank not changed. Error."
    End If

    Set objBank = Nothing
End Sub
```

7. And now we need to code the method that will allow us to delete a bank:

```
Private Sub DeleteBank()
   Dim objBank As Bank_Bus.Admin
   Dim intChangeBankID As Integer
   Dim lngListIndex As Long
   Dim blnDeleted As Boolean

   lngListIndex = cboSelect.ListIndex
   If lngListIndex > -1 Then
      intChangeBankID = m_aintBankID(lngListIndex)

      ' Prepare for call to business tier
      Set objBank = New Bank_Bus.Admin

      blnDeleted = objBank.DeleteBank(m_intBankID, intChangeBankID)
      If blnDeleted Then
         g_objSharedProperties.TransactionMessage = _
            "Bank deleted."
      Else
         g_objSharedProperties.TransactionMessage = _
            "Bank not deleted. Error."
      End If
   Else
      g_objSharedProperties.TransactionMessage = _
         "Bank not deleted. Error."
   End If

   Set objBank = Nothing
End Sub
```

8. To finish up, we need to add code that will update the module level string arrays, m_astrDesc and m_astrDSN, with the changed description and connection string or DSN:

```
Private Sub txtDesc_Change()
   Dim lngListIndex As Long

   lngListIndex = cboSelect.ListIndex
   m_astrDesc(lngListIndex) = txtDesc.Text
End Sub

Private Sub txtDSN_Change()
   Dim lngListIndex As Long

   lngListIndex = cboSelect.ListIndex
   m_astrDSN(lngListIndex) = txtDSN.Text
End Sub
```

619

How It Works

In this form the Click event for the combo box uses a module level Boolean variable to determine if the code is initializing the contents of the combo box or if the administrator has selected a bank to edit. If the Boolean variable m_blnAdding is False, the administrator has selected a bank, and the text box fields are filled with the selected bank's information. The m_blnAdding Boolean variable is set and cleared in the ShowBanks function, which we add later.

The ShowBanks function calls the Bank class module in the business services tier to get an ADO recordset containing the information for all the rows (member banks) in the Bank table in the database. If a recordset is returned that is not empty then the module level Boolean variable m_blnAdding is set to True. The recordset is tested for being empty by checking the position of the recordset pointer. If the newly returned recordset pointer is EOF (End of File), the recordset is empty:

```
' Retrieve recordset of banks
Set recBanks = objBank.GetBanks(m_intBankID)

If Not (recBanks.EOF) Then
    ShowBanks = True
    m_blnAdding = True
    lngIndex = 0
```

If the recordset isn't empty, it is used to populate the module level string arrays, m_astrDesc and m_astrDSN, and the module level integer array m_aintBankID. A loop is used to populate these arrays, with the loop exit triggered by reaching EOF in the recordset. The ReDim Preserve statement is used to increment the size of the arrays every pass through the loop while preserving the data that has already been loaded into the arrays:

```
Do While Not recBanks.EOF ' Until end of recordset
    ' Populate the Banks combobox

    ReDim Preserve m_astrDesc(lngIndex)
    m_astrDesc(lngIndex) = Trim$(recBanks!BankDesc)
    cboSelect.AddItem m_astrDesc(lngIndex)

    ReDim Preserve m_astrDSN(lngIndex)
    m_astrDSN(lngIndex) = Trim$(recBanks!BankDSN)

    ReDim Preserve m_aintBankID(lngIndex)
    m_aintBankID(lngIndex) = recBanks!BankID

    lngIndex = lngIndex + 1
    recBanks.MoveNext ' Next bank
Loop
```

The SaveBankChanges method calls the EditBank property in the Admin class module in the business services tier to save the changed bank information. This call is passed through to the Admin class module of the data services tier and a results message is stored in the TransactionMessage property of the SharedProperties class module and displayed by the FStatus form.

The DeleteBank method deletes the selected bank by using a pass-through call to the Admin class module of the business services tier. This call is passed to the Admin class module of the data services tier and the result message is stored in the SharedProperties TransactionMessage property for display in the FStatus form.

The first argument for the `SaveBankChanges` and `DeleteBank` properties is the bank ID of the "home" bank, the second argument is the bank ID of the bank that is to be changed or deleted.

These `m_astrDesc` and `m_astrDSN` arrays are initialized when the form is loaded, and updating them in memory ensures that, as the administrator selects different banks, the displayed information is always up to date. Changing the information in memory also saves network trips. The changed data is not committed to the database until the administrator clicks the **Save** command button.

By now the patterns of coding of many of the methods and functions used in these forms should be getting fairly familiar. Coding for database access is often repetitive and, if the code is similar enough, the methods and functions can be rewritten to be utility helper procedures in a code module. To do this, calling arguments are used to customize the operation of the helper procedure. It's a matter of judgement when to use such helper procedures.

The enhanced readability and componentization of the code must be balanced against not only the call overhead to the helper procedure (particularly when the procedure is called within a loop), but also the number of arguments that are needed to make the procedure universal. By the time such procedures are made universal, they often have so many arguments passed to them that they become unreadable and convoluted. My usual rule of thumb is that if more than half a dozen arguments are required for the setup of a helper function, then it usually pays not to make the helper function.

Congratulations on reaching this point: we've now completed the implementation of the administration logic in the user services tier.

Security

An application can participate in many different types and levels of security at the same time. Some of this security control is under the application's direction, but the majority is not. Entities that direct different levels of security control include operating systems, database servers, MTS/COM+, firewalls, and Web servers. Security of communications over public lines can be achieved with message encryption and signed messages.

The best sources of information about security implementations for products such as operating systems and servers are to be found within the documentation of the particular products that you happen to be using. As Visual Basic developers, we have to be aware of these things because, in many cases, we will have to implement them or program for them. In most cases this will require becoming familiar with supplying login information to various servers such as SQL Server and Windows NT or Windows 2000.

In this section we'll run through a very brief overview of some security considerations associated with:

- ❑ The WROBA application presentation tier
- ❑ The components of the application
- ❑ The operating system

First things first: let's have a look at what security we have explicitly defined for the application.

WROBA Security

WROBA has two defined security roles for users:

❑ Customer

❑ Administrator

The administrator role can only perform certain defined functions: add and remove customers (WROBA cards), add and remove banks, edit bank information, and lock and unlock customer accounts. In a commercial application the business requirements might call for other functions to be performed by administrators, such as the ability to make fund adjustments. Customers have no access to system administrative functions and the only administrative type functions customers can perform are adding, editing, and deleting payees, and changing their own passwords.

The WROBA application implements fairly typical security – it requires an ID and password to enable access to the financial records in the database. If more than a maximum number of failed logins occur, the card account is locked out. The security is relatively primitive, but typical of the security implemented for ATM cards, check cards, bank cards, and credit cards. More sophisticated security requirements can be enforced if they are needed. Some of the measures that could be added to improve security at the application level are:

❑ Passwords made to expire at set time intervals, and users prevented from reusing passwords they have previously used

❑ Encrypting the passwords and card IDs in the database

❑ Making passwords case sensitive

❑ Requiring passwords to be a mix of upper and lower case alpha and numeric characters

❑ Requiring a minimum password length of 8, 12, or 18 characters

❑ Assigning passwords generated by a random character generator, and not allowing the user to change them. This is user unfriendly but ensures that passwords are difficult to guess

These measures are all exterior access measures; they only have control of the application's presentation of data or access to data from within the application and can't control if a person accesses the data directly from the database or from some other application. Some control over that can be exercised by encrypting the data in the database, but that incurs a speed penalty when the data is encrypted and decrypted. Data requiring the highest security can be encrypted using 128-bit encryption for maximum security, despite the speed penalty.

The following sections will give a brief overview of other security measures that can be taken to secure the application's data.

Distributed Application Security

Distributing an application over a number of computers and servers has security implications because servers are often secured or guarded, and may be in different physical locations. If the only access to the data on a server is through an application, because there is no physical access to the server, then security is enhanced. When the business logic and data services tiers are placed on such servers, the application automatically inherits enhanced security.

During the discussion of MTS in Chapter 5 we saw that MTS can provide package level security by configuring the package's properties. Roles can be defined for user access to the package and those roles can be exported along with the package when it is moved or replicated to another server. This security is provided and enforced by the MTS server and the operating system. COM+ in Windows 2000 provides additional security options, such as security checks on individual components by assigned roles as well as on the packages that contain the components.

Additional Security

Within an organization, security is also provided by the operating system. System logins in Windows NT and Windows 2000 determine what rights the user has to run programs and see folders and their contents. These rights are determined by the role the login has been assigned by a system administrator and are maintained in **access control lists** (**ACL**). Windows 2000 adds the power of its **Active Directory** services to the security provided by Windows NT. Distributed logins in Windows 2000 can be configured to use Kerberos, an advanced authentication system that relies on encrypted key distribution. However, such topics lie outside the scope of this book.

> *For more information about how Windows 2000 implements Kerberos authentication, see the article* "Basic Overview of Kerberos Authentication in Windows 2000 " *in the Microsoft online KnowledgeBase:* `http://support.microsoft.com/support/kb /articles/q217/0/98.asp.`

> *Searching the Microsoft KnowledgeBase for security information about various Microsoft products can be done for U.S. English language searches from the search page at:* `http://search.support.microsoft.com/kb/c.asp?fr=0&SD=GN&LN=EN-US` *(substitute UK for US for searches in U.K. English).*

Database security can be configured for all the major databases such as SQL Server and Oracle. Security at the database level prevents unauthorized people or applications from even seeing that the data is there. Additional security can be provided on branches of internal networks as well as wide area networks by the configuration of software and/or hardware firewalls, switches, and routers. Security can also be provided by Web servers such as Internet Information Server (IIS).

> *For more information than you ever wanted to know about security on networks and over the Internet, I recommend reading Mastering Network Security, by Chris Brenton, published by Sybex, ISBN 0782123430.*

Reviewing the WROBA Implementation Process

Now we've finished the implementation of the WROBA case study, let's review our whole implementation process. The case study is a true n-tier distributed application that can easily scale to an enterprise level application. It implements user services, business services and data services tiers with code that can be run on one computer or be distributed on three or more computers. The database can be run on its own computer, and stored procedures in the database are used for efficient database access and manipulation. Security is implemented with passwords and ID numbers.

The design of the case study is extremely flexible, so the locations chosen for running `Bank_UI.EXE`, `Bank_Bus.DLL`, `Bank_DB.DLL`, and the `BigBank` database are the only considerations when running the case study on one or many computers. The use of MTS/COM+ to manage the components for the business services and data services tiers makes compilation of those components as Remote Servers unnecessary. No VB project options or sections of code have to be changed when the case study is moved from running as a desktop application on one computer to running as a network distributed application.

The implementation started with the Use Cases and Use Case Scenarios that were generated from the requirements for the project. Each scenario was used to create a form or class module in the User Services tier. The scenarios were analyzed to discover the methods and properties required by the classes and forms, and the forms were designed to operate from a menu structure consistent with Windows programs.

Business rules in the Use Case Scenarios were used for the logic of properties and methods in the business services tier. Business logic that involved manipulation of data in the database was implemented as stored procedures in the database. Initially, these stored procedures were just names of procedures for logical functions. Code for them was written later. Business logic that involved direct processing was implemented in the business services tier.

Access to the data stored in the database by the user services tier was implemented by using calls to the business services tier, which were passed on as pass-through, transformational or logical calls to the data services tier. The calls to the business services tier defined the methods and properties that were required by both the business services and data services tiers. These methods and properties were collected into related groups as class modules.

The data required for the case study was initially determined by the project requirements and the Use Case Scenarios. This data was organized into tables in the database. These initial tables were normalized to provide an efficient database organization. Finally, the stored procedures for the database were written to implement business rule processing in the database.

This implementation makes it possible not only for the application to scale well, but for its development to scale also. The implementation process that was followed applies just as well to a single programmer as to a large development team. The constraints of developing the case study in a book made it necessary to present the implementation out of order, but that was done to make distributed applications more understandable.

Summary

In this chapter we investigated how the administrative logic was implemented for WROBA. The distribution of the administrative components in the user services, business services, and data services tiers was analyzed, and the construction of the forms that make up the administrative logic in the user tier was explored. The user services administrative logic code was presented and examined. This chapter concluded with a brief summary of some of the security considerations and options for securing application data and program access.

In the next chapter we will look at the end phases of any software project: Testing, Deployment, and Maintenance.

16

Testing, Deployment, and Maintenance

In this chapter we will polish off the development process and prepare the application for release. The final stages of any cycle must ensure that the whole application works as intended, that the client can actually get to use the application, and that additional functionality can be added after release, if necessary. These final stages are called **testing**, **deployment**, and **maintenance**, respectively.

So, in this chapter we'll being looking at:

- ❑ Testing, which includes:
    - ❑ Test cases
    - ❑ Bug classifications
    - ❑ VB Project Groups

- ❑ Deployment, which includes:
    - ❑ Package and Deployment Wizard
    - ❑ Specifics on MTS and COM+ components

- ❑ Maintenance, which includes:
    - ❑ Compatibility
    - ❑ Changing Component Interfaces

Let's start with testing.

Testing

Earlier, we encountered unit testing; however, this only ensures that each component and stand-alone part works as it is supposed to. When all the parts of a project are completed, it is necessary to make sure that the parts work properly when they are fitted together; it's the interaction between the components that must now be rigorously tested to ensure that the system as a whole works as it should and is ready to be sent out to the general public.

This testing process is ongoing as part of the whole iterative development process. In a book, this is difficult to convey, but in each iteration of the process, testing is performed not only on individual components and interfaces, but also on the entire application. As the application draws closer to completion, testing becomes more detailed. Finally, when the code is complete, the final testing cycle begins. This cycle concentrates on fixing known bugs and making sure that no bugs that can be considered showstoppers are left unfixed.

Stabilizing Interim Milestones

An application is completed within the **Stabilizing Phase**. The goal of the Stabilizing Phase is to reach the Release milestone. This is the point at which we are ready to install the application on users' PCs (for internal applications), to release the product to manufacturing (for commercial applications), or to launch it on the Internet. There are six closely related interim milestones to the Stabilizing phase:

- ❑ Content Complete
- ❑ Bug Convergence
- ❑ Zero-Bug Release
- ❑ Code Freeze
- ❑ Release Candidate
- ❑ Golden Release

The first of these milestones, **Content Complete**, concerns user documentation and training materials, and is not relevant to us as programmers.

The next stabilization milestone, **Bug Convergence**, indicates that the number of new bug fixes is greater than the number of new bugs. As the project nears completion, this milestone should converge down to zero as no new bugs are introduced (hopefully, since fixing a bug can often cause new ones).

As its name implies, the **Zero-Bug Release** milestone is reached when all reproducible bugs have been fixed. This milestone is reached at the same time as the first important interim milestone: the **Code Freeze Milestone**. Code Freeze policy demands that absolutely no new functionality (however trivial) may be implemented at this point. The only changes that can be made are to fix unfixed bugs, or fix any that are subsequently discovered. The restriction on new functionality is enforced to avoid breaking existing code, which may cause considerable delays.

In early rounds of testing, an application will undergo testing by Testers on the development team. This first stage of testing is called **Alpha** testing. Later on, when the application is more stable and is closer to final release, the customers of the application and, possibly, selected outside testers work on **Beta** releases of the application. Applications from major developers such as Microsoft or Corel are often also tested, in the Beta stage, by corporate customers. These Beta releases are known as corporate preview tests.

The **Release Candidate Stage** is when the application is first judged to be ready for release; all required functionality has been implemented or postponed to a later release. This version is released to a wide range of beta testers for a final round of outside testing. Once any final bugs found during the beta test phase are fixed, the application goes gold, and is released to the public as a final version; hence the term **Golden Release**. And the development process can begin again, for a new and improved Version 2.

The following sections cover the steps working towards the Golden Release in greater detail.

Integration Testing

As you are working on creating and testing unit level modules, there comes a point in time where you need to know if your code works with the rest of the project code. This is called **Integration testing** and is a team responsibility. Integration testing verifies how the components of a system work together. Each unit has been tested and is working properly, so now the verification focuses on the interchange of data between the different components. As with unit testing, we would use breakpoints, watches, and a range of test inputs while running the code, to see if the results are what we would expect. Often, many errors are discovered during this phase, such as incorrectly planned data interchanges, or errors that have occurred because of misunderstandings (for example, was it planned to pass a value of 50% as 50 or as 0.5?). One example of this type of error occurred in the programming of the Mars Climate Orbiter: this failed because one NASA design team used Imperial measurements while the other team used Metric.

System Testing

After the system passes integration testing, it must undergo **System Testing**. In many organizations, a dedicated testing team performs system testing in a test lab. This may be the same team that does the integration testing, or it may include additional testers. System testing uses the Use Case Scenarios as the basis for a test plan. Each Scenario leads to one or more test cases. During the planning of test cases, an attempt is made to also cover exceptional cases, as well as invalid input. Let's look at planning test cases in a little more detail.

Creating Test Cases

The Use Case Scenarios are used as the starting point of creating test cases. When creating test cases, it is important to ensure that all business rules are checked. It is also a good idea to try the boundary values, such as a zero balance, or a withdrawal equal to the overdraft limit. Below is a sample test case for a Scenario of the Banking application:

Test Case for Scenario #2

❑ **Name**
Transfer Funds

❑ **Summary**
The scenario in this test case involves transferring funds from a savings account to a checking account and from a checking account to a savings account.

❑ **Assumptions**
None.

❑ **Pre Conditions**
User is logged on and selects "Transfer Funds".
For each account, check balance, daily remaining and overdraft limit.

❑ **Steps**

User	System
The user selects from which account (savings or checking) to transfer funds.	
	System selects the other account as the destination of the funds transfer.
The user puts in the amount of the funds transfer.	
The user initiates the transaction.	
	System debits the source account and credits the target account.

❑ **Business Rules**
The amount to be transferred must be smaller than or equal to the sum of the account balance and the overdraft limit.
The daily withdrawal limit must not be exceeded.

❑ **Post Conditions**
The "from" account is debited and the "to" account is credited with the amount selected by the user.

❑ **Exceptions**
The transaction is aborted with a "Not sufficient funds" message if the amount to be transferred is larger than the sum of the account balance and the overdraft limit.
The transaction is aborted with a "Daily limit exceeded" message if the daily withdrawal limit would have been exceeded.

Flow Diagram

This is the flow diagram to show what happens within the Transfer Funds scenario:

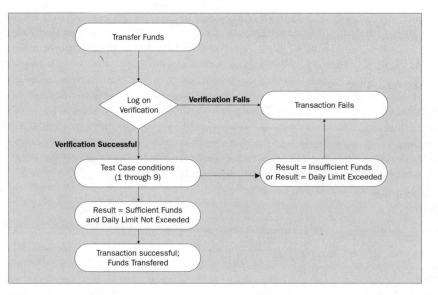

Test Cases

To try out these cases, tests would be created for all possible conditions. So, with test case #1, we would set the transfer amount to a few numbers less than the daily limit, a case where the amount was equal to the daily limit, and the same for the sum of the account balance and the overdraft, called the Available Balance. We would also try a test case where the transfer amount was 0. This combination of all conditions would be repeated for every test case. In cases where we derived many possible test cases, it would be necessary to use a test case generator (a program to automate the process of creating inputs for test cases).

1. Account Balance > 0; Transfer of funds < or = Daily Limit and < or = Available Balance = successful transaction

2. Account Balance > 0; Transfer of funds > Daily Limit = transaction failure

3. Account Balance > 0; Transfer of funds > Available Balance = transaction failure

The first condition tests that the Balance is greater than zero, and that the transfer request is less than or equal to the daily withdrawal limit and less than or equal to the available balance. This results in a successful completion of the transfer. The second condition fails because the transfer request is for more than the allowable daily limit. The third condition fails because the transfer request is greater than the Balance. In these final two conditions it is unnecessary to test for a condition other than the one that causes immediate failure.

4. Account Balance = 0; Transfer of funds < or = Daily Limit and < or = Overdraft Limit = successful transaction

5. Account Balance = 0; Transfer of funds > Daily Limit = transaction failure

6. Account Balance = 0; Transfer of funds > Overdraft Limit = transaction failure

If the balance is zero, then the transfer of funds needs to be less than or equal to the daily limit and less than or equal to the overdraft limit for the transaction to be completed successfully. Obviously, if the transfer request is for greater than the daily or overdraft limits, the transaction will fail.

7. Account Balance < 0; Transfer of funds < or = Daily Limit and < or = remaining Overdraft Limit (Available Balance) = successful transaction

8. Account Balance < 0; Transfer of funds > Daily Limit = transaction failure

9. Account Balance < 0; Transfer of funds > remaining Overdraft Limit (Available Balance)= transaction failure

Finally, if the balance is less than zero, the transaction amount is less than or equal to the daily withdrawal limit, and there are still sufficient funds left in the overdraft protection, then the transaction completes. Otherwise it fails, due to insufficient funds.

Let's move on to taking a look at how we should deal with bugs.

Severity and Priority Level Classifications

During testing, all bugs are classified according to severity and priority. This isn't just restricted to system testing; it is done throughout the Stabilizing Phase. Severity measures the effect of a bug on the system; priority measures how easily the bug can be reproduced.

Severity Level Definitions

❑   **Severity 1** – the bug causes the system to crash, hang, or stop working and requires either a warm or cold reboot to recover the system (a **warm reboot** means hitting *Ctrl + Alt + Del*, while a **cold reboot** means going for the power switch or reset button).

❑   **Severity 2** – the system has a major problem, which could cause the loss of data or work.

❑   **Severity 3** – the system has a minor problem, such as a discrepancy between the documentation and the actual operation.

❑   **Severity 4** – the system has a trivial problem, such as a spelling error. Severity 4 bugs also include suggestions and enhancements.

Priority Level Definitions

❑   **Priority 1** – high-priority bugs are completely reproducible, following a simple series of steps. These bugs must be fixed. It follows that severity 4 bugs are never classed as priority 1.

❑   **Priority 2** – these high-priority bugs are very reproducible, following a complex series of steps. These bugs should be fixed.

❑   **Priority 3** – these medium-priority bugs are only intermittently reproducible, through a convoluted series of steps. These bugs are fixed last and a product may ship with them.

❑   **Priority 4** – these low-priority bugs are very difficult to reproduce. Typically, these types of bugs are given very little attention.

Reaching the Release Candidate Milestone

The Release Candidate milestone is reached when the product has been tested and the following conditions have been met:

❑   No Severity 1 or 2 bugs that have been found are unfixed

❑   No Priority 1 or 2 bugs that have been found are unfixed

❑   All files to be shipped with the final product are included with this release

❑   No Severity 1 bugs have been found for a preset length of time

A Release Candidate is then submitted to final beta testing. A beta test is required because it is usually not possible to test a product on every type of hardware or in conjunction with every type of software. A similar set of priority and severity level bug criteria to the ones for a release candidate is used to determine when a product has reached the Golden Release: ideally, this is when all level 1, 2, or 3 bugs found during the Release Candidate testing stage have been corrected, although schedules or pressures from product marketing may exclude level 3 bugs from holding up Golden Release.

On larger projects, we may want to conduct additional beta tests before releasing the Release Candidate to outside beta testers. There may be more than one Release Candidate, depending on the results of testing the initial Release Candidate. These tests could also include an Alpha test. This would generally be an internal release, not unlike the integration and system testing mentioned earlier. Once the program is ready for wider testing, pre-release candidate beta versions may be released. As bugs are found and fixed, additional beta builds are released. Once we are satisfied that all major bugs (priority and severity levels 1, 2, and 3) have been fixed, the build called Release Candidate would be released for final testing.

Post-Mortem Review

After we have deployed the application, it is time to have a celebration. Then it's time to review how the project went. Discuss both the positive aspects and the areas where improvement is possible. Record this review in a document with recommendations for future projects.

Deployment

We reach the final milestone of the software development cycle, the Golden Release phase, when the application has all the required features and meets all the test criteria. As we saw earlier, a commercial application is then released to manufacturing to create the packages that will be sold on the shelves of the software stores. An in-house application, on the other hand, may be deployed through network distribution or a software deployment system such as SMS. Deployment over the Internet is another option. Whatever the means of distribution, an application needs to be deployed to the users' computers.

Deployment of a distributed application is, of course, more complex than deployment of a desktop application, as more than one computer is involved. In this section of the chapter, we will investigate how to use the **Package and Deployment Wizard** to distribute an application to users and install components on a server. We saw, back in Chapter 4, how to use this to create a simple setup file for a component. Now we will look in far more detail at how to use the Package and Deployment Wizard to create appropriate setup files for our distributed application. We will also look at how to deploy the MTS packages or COM+ applications that will be installed on the servers for the business and data services tiers. Finally, we will take a look at the new Windows Installer method of deploying and installing applications.

What is Deployment?

As we saw earlier, we may deploy our application through any of three channels:

- ❑ Using CD ROMs or floppy disks
- ❑ Through an intranet
- ❑ Via the Internet

Once we have decided the medium through which our application is to be distributed, we have to get the application into a suitable format. This can be particularly important if we wish to distribute the application on CD ROMs or floppy disks. It is likely that there will be more than one file in the application, and some of the files may be of considerable size. So, exactly how do we make sure that our application will fit neatly onto a number of floppy disk or CD ROMs? Well, one way to do this is to create a **package**. We'll explore how this can be done in the following section.

Using the Package and Deployment Wizard

The Package and Deployment Wizard is a VB utility that enables us to group the files needed to deploy an application into a **setup package**. The Wizard allows us to create either a traditional Windows install program, where we run a SETUP.EXE to install the application, or an Internet setup package, where our application is installed from a web page. The setup programs created by the Wizard also take care of installing and registering the support files needed by our application, such as the Visual Basic runtime files and any DLLs or ActiveX controls that may be required.

As implied by its name, the Wizard has two main functions: to group applications into packages and to deploy a setup package. A third function, which creates dependency files, will also help to create a Windows Installer package.

> A setup package is a set of files necessary to deploy an application, including supporting system DLLs, VB runtime libraries, data access components, and other files.

Creating a Project Package

We saw in Chapter 4 how we could use the Package and Deployment Wizard to deploy components. Here we will look in more detail at how we can use this Wizard to package and deploy our entire distributed application.

Try It Out – Loading the Package and Deployment Wizard

1. Create a New Project in Visual Basic. Select Standard as the project type. We just need this project as a way to access the Visual Basic IDE (Integrated Development Environment).

2. Select Package and Deployment Wizard from the Add-Ins menu.

3. If the Package and Deployment Wizard is not available, open up the Add-In Manager and select Package and Deployment Wizard. We saw how to use this in Chapter 4.

4. We'll create a small VB application using a Standard EXE project. Name the form for the project FMainMenu, and add the following code to this form:

```
Option Explicit

Private Sub Form_Load()
    MsgBox "Hello, World!", vbExclamation
End Sub
```

5. Set the project properties (Project | Project1 Properties). Rename the project HelloWorld, and set the startup object to FMainMenu.

6. Under the Make tab, it is a good idea to check Remove information about unused ActiveX Controls, as this will probably result in a smaller package. This setting removes information about controls that are in the Controls Toolbox, but not used or referenced in the project. If this check box is not checked, the information will remain in the project to enable the controls to be added at runtime.

7. Save the project as HelloWorld (it is necessary to save any project before using the Wizard).

8. Though the Wizard gives us the option of performing a compilation of the project, it is a good idea to compile the program before creating the package so that any errors can be corrected prior to running the Package and Deployment Wizard. If the project is compiled from the Wizard, any compilation errors cause the Wizard to terminate. Remember that to compile a project, select File | Make HelloWorld.exe.

9. Start the Wizard by clicking on **Package and Deployment Wizard** in the **Add-Ins** menu. If we have made changes to the project since it was last saved, we will be prompted to save the project. Select **Yes** to proceed.

10. This brings up the Wizard's main menu, from which we may create or deploy packages. As we can see, it is also possible to manage installation scripts from here. Installation scripts are automatically generated from the choices we make when we create a package or deploy a package. The button to **Manage Scripts** enables us to delete, copy, and rename existing scripts for the current project. The scripts themselves are editable in Notepad or any other text editor. In this exercise, we want to create a setup program, so select **Package**:

11. If the executable is not up-to-date (or does not exist), the Wizard will now prompt us to compile the program. In this case, select **Yes** to proceed. A series of dialogs will show us Visual Basic's progress as it compiles the program.

12. We then get the option to select the package type. For a **Standard EXE**, we get two choices: **Standard Setup Package** and **Dependency File**. A dependency file (which has a .DEP extension) lists all the files that are required to run a project. Dependency files are used by the Wizard to determine which support files are needed. We will see how dependency files are used for Windows Installer packages later in this chapter. To continue, select **Standard Setup Package** and click **Next**:

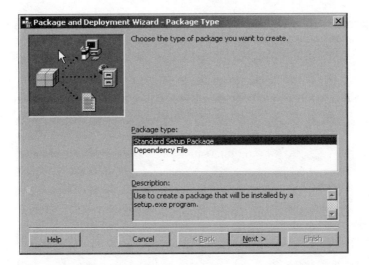

13. Next, select the directory where the Wizard will create your package. Select Next after you have selected an appropriate folder:

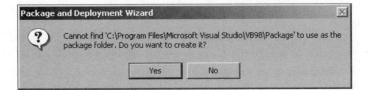

14. If our selection does not exist, we will receive a confirmation notice. Click Yes to create the folder:

15. If dependency information can't be found about files that are included or referenced in the project, we are presented with a dialog box telling us so. Here we can either proceed *without* the dependency, or permanently mark a particular file as having no dependencies.

16. Next comes the list of files included in our setup package. Here we can add extra files (such as a read me file, a user manual document, or a database file) to the package:

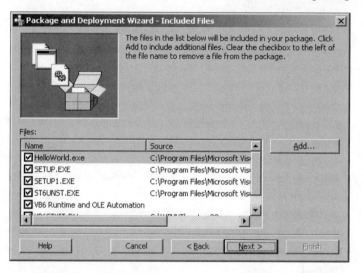

17. Next, we can determine the type of the package we require. If we choose to select multiple .CAB files (.CAB stands for cabinet file, the Microsoft standard compressed format used by the SETUP.EXE program), we can create installation floppy disks. However, for this exercise, select Single cab:

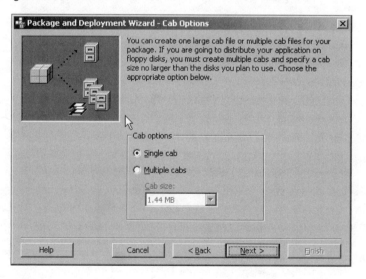

18. Next comes the application title that will be displayed during installation. Type in HelloWorld if it does not appear in the text box:

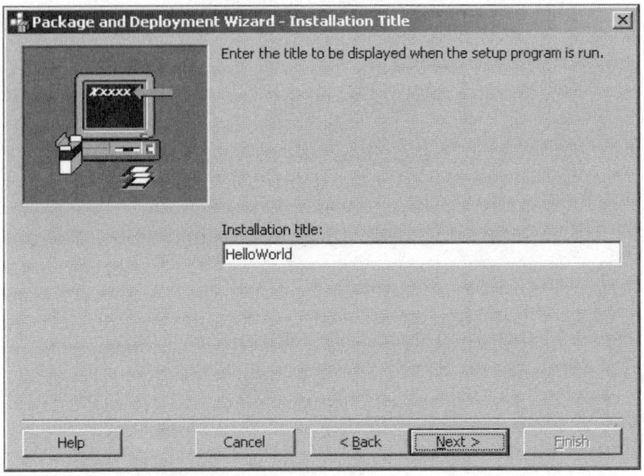

19. Click Next, and we are presented with a screen that allows us to determine how the application will be displayed in the Start menu. We saw how to use this back in Chapter 4.

20. If the Start Menu group is selected and we click the Properties button, the following dialog opens. This dialog enables us to choose to install the application and its group only for the logged in user (Private) or for all users with profiles on the computer (Common).

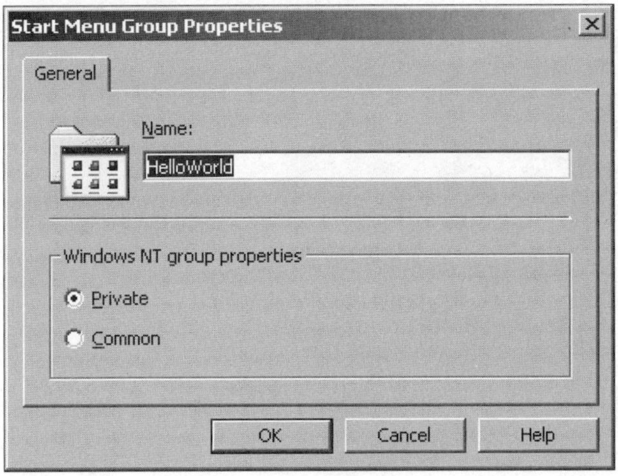

21. On the next screen, we see a list of the files and their default locations. We can change the location using symbolic names. For example, $(AppPath) is the directory that the user selected for the application. The $ symbol represents a macro that is interpreted by the setup program that the Package and Deployment Wizard provides. Symbolic folder names are provided that represent standard locations in Windows computers:

Symbolic Name	Standard Location
$(AppPath)	Application path (chosen in the P&D Wizard) – this default location can be changed by the user at installation time and is usually the best choice for non-system files
$(ProgramFiles)	Usually C:\Program Files
$(CommonFiles)	Usually C:\Program Files\Common Files
$(CommonFilesSys)	Usually C:\Program Files\Common Files – this indicates that the file is a system file and will not be uninstalled if the application is uninstalled
$(WinPath)	\Windows or \Winnt
$WinSysPath)	\Windows\System or \Winnt\System32
$(MSDAOPath)	Location for DAO (Data Access Components) files – should not be used for user files
$(Font)	Location where font files are installed

22. Next we get the option to mark files as shared. This option is used to indicate that the shared files should not be removed when un-installing this program if other programs are using those files. Shared files keep a count of how many programs use them and get removed only when the last program that uses them is removed.

23. And that is it. All that's left to do is to give the installation script a descriptive name. This name is used when maintaining scripts in the Wizard, and if we should want to change the application and use the P&D Wizard again, we can use this script to bypass most of the Wizard screens.

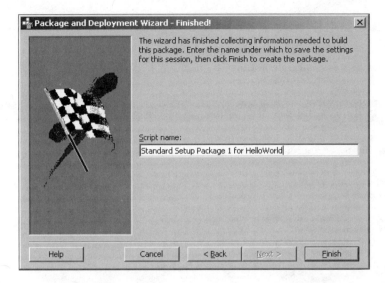

24. Click Finish, and the dialog will indicate the Wizard's progress while creating the package. When the Wizard is done, it will display a report:

HelloWorld.vbp - Packaging Report

The cab file for your application has been built as 'C:\Program Files\Microsoft Visual Studio\VB98\Package\HelloWorld.CAB'.

There is also a batch file in the support directory (C:\Program Files\Microsoft Visual Studio\VB98\Package\Support\HelloWorld.BAT) that will allow you to recreate the cab file in case you make changes to some of the files.

Save Report   Close

25. This report may be saved for reference. On closing the packaging report, we return to the Wizard main menu. We can close this at this point.

Deploying an Existing Package

After we have created a setup package, we can create setup disks, a setup CD, or a web page containing the setup program. This can also be done with the Wizard, as we will see in the following exercise.

Try It Out – Deploying a Package

1. If needed, open the `HelloWorld` project that we created in the previous exercise. Start the Wizard, but this time select the middle option: Deploy.

2. A list of existing packages is displayed. Select the package you created in the previous exercise and click on Next:

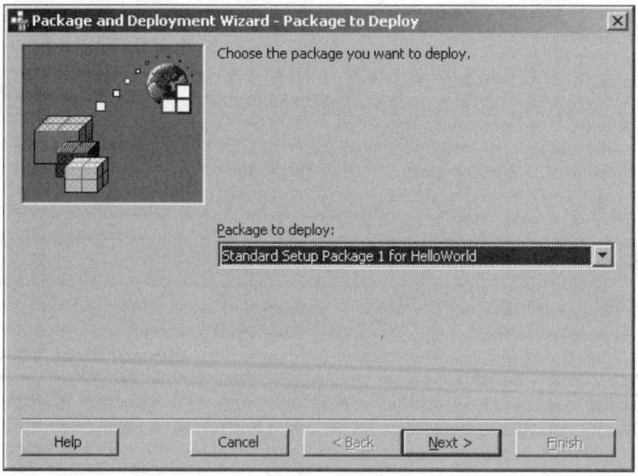

3. Next, we need to select whether to build a web page from which to distribute the software, or whether to use a directory to store the setup files (if you selected to build multiple cab files, then you also get the option to build floppy disks):

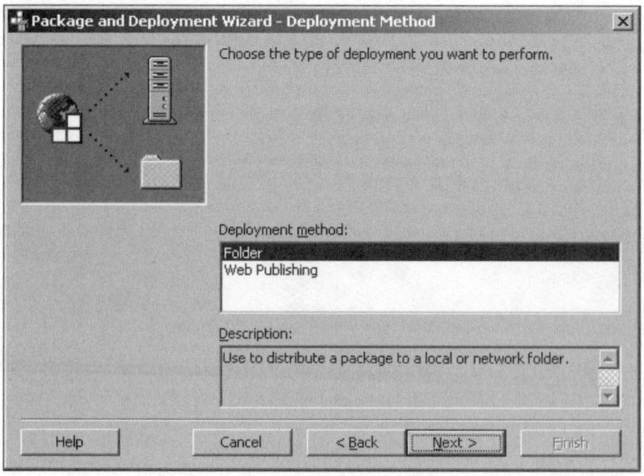

4. Select Folder and click on Next. Select the folder you want to deploy your package to. If the folder does not exist, we get the usual confirmation dialog (not unlike the one shown in the previous exercise).

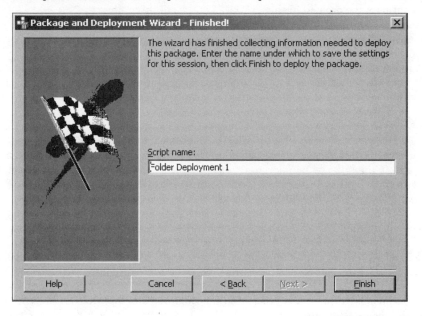

5. The last option is to save the script under a descriptive name:

6. Click Finish, and after a short while, we will see a report showing what was accomplished:

```
HelloWorld.vbp - Deployment Report                    _ □ ×

Copied C:\Program Files\Microsoft Visual Studio\VB98\Package\setup.exe
to C:\Program Files\Microsoft Visual Studio\VB98
Copied C:\Program Files\Microsoft Visual
Studio\VB98\Package\SETUP.LST to C:\Program Files\Microsoft Visual
Studio\VB98
Copied C:\Program Files\Microsoft Visual
Studio\VB98\Package\HelloWorld.CAB to C:\Program Files\Microsoft
Visual Studio\VB98




                                    Save Report        Close
```

7. Close this report, exit the Wizard, and close the Visual Basic IDE.

8. To install the application, we can now run the SETUP.EXE program located in the directory we selected in Step 3.

The deployment package created in this exercise consists of three files: SETUP.EXE, SETUP.LST, and HelloWorld.CAB, located in the same folder. These are the same three files that were created during the exercise on creating a package. So why create a deployment package? Usually a package is created on the developer's computer or a network folder used by a development team. A deployment package is usually used to deploy these files to a folder used to deploy the installation package, often on a network drive that is accessible to all the users in a company. This keeps the deployed package separate from the package the developers work with. Deployment is also used to deploy an application to a Web page or to create floppy disks, as mentioned earlier.

Under the folder in which you stored the package, a subfolder named Support is created by the Package and Deployment Wizard. This contains all the files used in the package. These files are used with a .BAT file, which is also in the Support folder, to reconstruct the .CAB file if it is damaged or deleted. Running this .BAT file from a command prompt or from the Start | Run dialog box re-creates the original .CAB file created when the Package and Deployment Wizard was used to create the package.

If the deployment is done from a network folder that the users of the application have access to, the deployment package can be assembled in this folder. A recommendation is to build the deployment package in a local folder and copy the package to the network folder. The users can then install the application by running the SETUP.EXE program from the network folder.

When the deployment is distributed, we must distribute all three files that were created: Setup.LST, Setup.EXE, and the .CAB file that contains the files to be installed. These files can be placed in a Zip, or other, compressed file for distribution in one file, and extracted to the user's local hard drive for installation.

Deploying MTS and COM+ Components

Deploying MTS packages and COM+ applications consists of two types of deployment:

- ❑ The server applications must be deployed on the business and data services tiers
- ❑ The proxy components must be installed on the client computers

These two types of deployment are different, but neither one requires any changes to the code, or any recompilation of components.

Proxy components intercept calls to a remote component, and redirect them to the server where the components are running. The client doesn't know where the components are located: DCOM redirects the calls transparently. Component stubs running on the server receive the remote calls and direct them to the server as if they were the original components. When these components are running under MTS or COM+ on a remote computer, the proxies are created by the process of exporting packages or applications from MTS or COM+.

It is likely that administrators will install the Bank_Bus.DLL business services tier and Bank_DB.DLL data services tier components on their respective servers. This enables the administrator to configure roles and the security for the packages in MTS or COM+.

We have several options for installing MTS and COM+ components:

- ❑ We can install components into MTS or COM+ from a distribution package similar to the one we created earlier in this chapter
- ❑ We can install a package or application created by another server running MTS or COM+
- ❑ We can also automate the installation into MTS or COM+ using scripts or VB

To install the DLLs manually on a server, we need to create empty packages in MTS Explorer, or Component Services for COM+, and add the DLLs to the packages. The administrator then defines roles, users in those roles, and security for the package and the roles. We learned about this in Chapter 5.

We also saw back in Chapter 5 how we can export MTS packages and COM+ applications as either server or client components. The major difference between the two is the executable output that's created:

- ❑ MTS creates an EXE file that installs the package on the target computer or server
- ❑ COM+ creates an MSI file, the new Windows Installer file, to install the application in COM+ on the client or server

When the package or application is created for a client, stubs are created for the components that are being exported. These stubs are registered on the client computer when the package or application is installed by the .EXE (or .MSI) file that MTS (or COM+) created.

We can manually import these packages to the target client using the MTS or COM+ MMC interfaces (using the Install pre-built packages in the package/application installation Wizard). The following example shows us how we can install DLLs and COM+ applications programmatically from VB.

Try It Out – Installing the Code for the Data and Business Services Tiers

1. First, open the Component Services administration application (MTS Explorer in Windows NT). Double click the **My Computer** icon and the **COM+ Applications** tree in the left pane of Component Services (open the **Packages Installed** folder in MTS Explorer).

2. Click on the **Action** toolbar button and select **New | Application** (select **File | New** in MTS Explorer) to create a new Application (a new Package in MTS). The COM Applications Wizard opens (Package Wizard in MTS). Click **Next** to go past the opening screen in the Application Wizard.

3. Select **Create an Empty Application** (**Create an Empty Package** in MTS).

4. Name the Application **BigBank Business Services** and check the check box to make the Application a Server Application (in MTS just name the Package **BigBank Business Services**).

5. Select **Interactive User** as the Account used to log in for a COM+ Application.

6. Click **Finish** and the new empty Application or Package is created.

7. Expand the **COM+ Applications** tree to show the **BigBank Business Services** Application and expand that to show the **Components** folder. Right-click on the **Components** folder for the **BigBank Business Services Application** and select **New | Component**. This opens the COM Component Install Wizard. (For MTS, double-click your way to the **Components** folder of the new Package and select **File | New** to open the **Install Components Wizard**.)

8. Select **Install New Component(s)**, navigate to where `Bank_Bus.DLL` is stored, and select it.

9. Press **Finish** and the components are installed into COM+ or MTS.

10. Repeat Steps 2 to 9, but create an Application (or Package) named **BigBank Data Services** and add `Bank_DB.DLL` to it. Component Services should now look something like this:

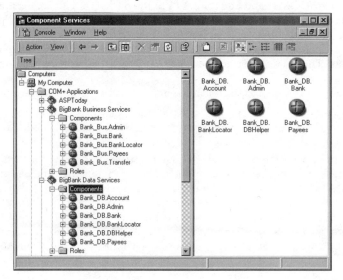

If you have Component Services (or MTS Explorer) open at the same time as Windows Explorer, we can drag and drop the DLLs into the Applications or Packages where they are being installed. Just drag the DLL into the Components folder of the Application or Package and it will be installed automatically.

Of course, for installation on production servers the components for the business services and data services tiers would be installed on different servers. We'll now take a look at how we could automate the process of importing our application components.

Automating the Import of MTS/COM+ Packages

We can automate the import of MTS components using VB code. Exporting can also be automated, although we won't be doing that in this chapter. In fact, any administrative function in MTS or COM+ can be automated using a script or VB code.

We'll start off by setting up VB to use the relevant type libraries it needs.

Try It Out – Creating the VB Project

1. Create a new Standard EXE application, and name it ImportPackage.

2. Name the form FImport. Place a command button on the form, name it cmdImport, and set the Caption to &Import:

3. We'll need a reference to either the MTS 2.0 Admin Type Library (MTXADMIN.DLL) for MTS, or to the COM+ 1.9 Admin Type Library (COMADMIN.DLL) for COM+.

The following sections show the code used to import packages to MTS or applications to COM+.

Importing MTS Components

The MTS 2.0 Admin Type Library provides four objects we can use for administering MTS from VB:

- ❑ The Catalog object
- ❑ The CatalogCollection object
- ❑ The CatalogObject object
- ❑ The ComponentUtil object

All the MTS administration we'll do involves using catalogs.

> **An MTS catalog is a data store that contains information about MTS components, packages, and roles.**

We'll see how to use these objects in the following code, which creates two new packages in MTS: BigBank Business Services and BigBank Data Services. We can use this to deploy our Bank_Bus and Bank_DB components. If the business and data services DLLs are being installed on separate servers, obviously, we only need to use the code appropriate for that server.

Try It Out – Importing MTS Components

The code gets the collection of packages in MTS and adds new packages for the business and data services tiers. After the package names are set, the packages are saved. The DLLs for the Packages are then installed in the Packages using the InstallComponent method.

In the following code, the source DLLs for the Packages are stored in the file path:

- ❑ C:\My Documents\Wrox\MTS\Bank_Bus.DLL
- ❑ C:\My Documents\Wrox\MTS\Bank_DB.DLL

You'll need to change the paths to match the location of your component DLLs.

Add the following code to the project we just created.

1. First we need to create a Catalog object, which contains the components in MTS. The Packages CatalogCollection of the Catalog object is instantiated, and then we call the Populate method of the CatalogCollection object, to fill the collection with its components. Add the following code to the form we just created.

```
Private Sub cmdImport_Click()
    ' Create MTS Packages and install components

    ' Create the catalog object
    Dim objCatalog As New MTSAdmin.Catalog
    Dim objPackages As MTSAdmin.CatalogCollection
    Dim objNewPack As MTSAdmin.CatalogObject
    Dim objComponents As MTSAdmin.CatalogCollection
    Dim objUtil As MTSAdmin.ComponentUtil
    Dim strNewPackID As String

    On Error GoTo ImportError

    ' Get the packages collection
    Set objPackages = objCatalog.GetCollection("Packages")
    objPackages.Populate
```

2. A new package is added to the `Packages` collection and is named `BigBank Business Services`. The `Key` value for the newly created Package is saved to a string for later use. Then the Package is saved:

```
' Add a new package to the packages collection
Set objNewPack = objPackages.Add
strNewPackID = objNewPack.Key
objNewPack.Value("Name") = "BigBank Business Services"
objPackages.SaveChanges
```

3. A new `CatalogCollection` is instantiated for the `ComponentsInPackage` Collection that belongs to the newly added `BigBank Business Services` Package. Then the `GetUtilInterface` method is called to get a handle to the `InstallComponent` method. The `InstallComponent` method is called to install the `Bank_Bus.DLL` component into the `BigBank Business Services` Package. Then the changes are saved:

```
' Add a new component to the package
Set objComponents = objPackages.GetCollection( _
"ComponentsInPackage", strNewPackID)

' Install components.
Set objUtil = objComponents.GetUtilInterface
objUtil.InstallComponent _
    "C:\My Documents\Wrox\MTS\Bank_Bus.DLL", "", ""

' Commit the changes to the components
objComponents.SaveChanges
```

4. The same set of steps is followed to add a `BigBank Data Services` Package and add the `Bank_DB.DLL` component to it. Then all objects are set to `Nothing` to release them. This code would be changed to install the components for either the business or data services tier when the components are installed and running on different servers.

```
' Add another new package to the packages collection
Set objNewPack = objPackages.Add
strNewPackID = objNewPack.Key
objNewPack.Value("Name") = "BigBank Data Services"
objPackages.SaveChanges

' Add a new component to the package
Set objComponents = objPackages.GetCollection( _
"ComponentsInPackage", strNewPackID)

' Install components.
Set objUtil = objComponents.GetUtilInterface
objUtil.InstallComponent _
    "C:\My Documents\Wrox\MTS\Bank_DB.DLL", "", ""

' Commit the changes to the components
objComponents.SaveChanges
```

649

```
ImportExit:
    Set objCatalog = Nothing
    Set objPackages = Nothing
    Set objNewPack = Nothing
    Set objComponents = Nothing
    Set objUtil = Nothing

    Unload Me
    Exit Sub

ImportError:
    MsgBox "Error: " & Err.Description & vbCrLf & "Error # " _
                    & Err.Number, vbCritical

    GoTo ImportExit
End Sub
```

5. On running the form, the bank components should be installed; this can be checked in MTS Explorer.

Importing COM+ Applications

We've already learned that when an application is exported from COM+, it's exported to an MSI file. MSI files are compressed installation packages that are executed by the MSI.EXE application. To manually install a COM+ application packaged in an MSI file, we can execute the MSI file. This will create a new application in COM+, and add the components of the application automatically.

However, if we wish, we can also use automation to import an MSI-packaged application. We'll need to use the COMAdminCatalog object, which is the root object for COM+ administration. The following code uses the InstallApplication method of the COMAdminCatalog object to install the MSI file. This creates a new application in COM+, and installs the required components in that application.

As we will see, importing into COM+ is a lot simpler than importing into MTS. Just as with the MTS code, the COM+ code will need to be modified to only install the components for one service's tier when the business and data services tier code is running on different servers.

Try It Out – Importing COM+ Components

1. Ensure that you have created the appropriate MSI files (see Chapter 5 for how to do this).

2. Enter the following code into the form that we created earlier, ensuring that the path and filenames for your MSI files are correct:

```
Private Sub cmdImport_Click()
    ' Import COM+ packages
    Dim objCatalog As COMAdminCatalog

    On Error GoTo ImportError
```

```
      ' Open a session with the catalog
      ' Instantiate a COMAdminCatalog object
      Set objCatalog = New COMAdminCatalog

      ' These MSI files will automatically install the Packages
      ' into the COM+ services on their respective servers
      ' when they are run.

      ' The next lines will import the Packages into COM+ services
      objCatalog.InstallApplication _
          "C:\Temp\BigBank Business Services.MSI"

      objCatalog.InstallApplication _
          "C:\Temp\BigBank Data Services.MSI"

   ImportExit:
      Set objCatalog = Nothing

      Unload Me
      Exit Sub

   ImportError:
      MsgBox "Error: " & Err.Description & vbCrLf & "Error # " _
                    & Err.Number, vbCritical

      GoTo ImportExit
   End Sub
```

3. On running the form, the bank components will be installed; this can be checked in Component Services.

The Windows Installer

The Windows Installer, introduced with Office 2000, is now the preferred method of distributing and installing applications on Windows computers. This method uses an installer program that resides on the user's computer to install the compressed components of the MSI installation package. The MSI file types are associated with this installer, so that it's executed when the MSI file is run. There are versions of the installer program available for developers to install, if necessary, for Windows 95/98 and Windows NT/2000.

The tool to create an MSI installation package, Visual Studio Installer 1.0, is available for download on the MSDN (Microsoft Developer Network) for owners of Visual Basic Professional and Enterprise editions. It is also possible to download Visual Studio Installer at:

`http://www.msdn.microsoft.com/vstudio/downloads/vsi/default.asp`

Visual Studio Installer is also available on CD, which can be ordered from the same web page. MSDN Universal subscribers can get Visual Studio Installer from the Windows 2000 Developer Readiness Kit CD, Disc 8 of the Office Test Platform and Development Tools group. Additional information with a FAQ (Frequently Asked Questions) section and a guided tour of Visual Studio Installer are also available at the MSDN Web page.

Another web page with a download of tools for and documentation about creating, using, and modifying Windows Installer files is at:

```
http://www.microsoft.com/msdownload/platformsdk/WinInst.htm
```

This download installs the Orca tool for examining and editing the contents of MSI and component MSM files, with samples and documentation.

There are still bugs to be worked out with the Visual Studio Installer, and the documentation needs more explanation, and better VB examples, but there's no doubt that the Windows Installer will become the preferred method of deployment for applications in the near future.

So, we've now finished our application, and made it available to the intended audience. What happens after that? We still have a responsibility to maintain the solution we provide. This is covered in the next section.

Maintenance

In business, and in software development, the only constant is change. Deployment of an application is not the end of the development efforts, just the end of the initial phase. New business requirements, updated features, and bug fixes will lead to requests for changes to the deployed application. In this section, we will look at:

- ❑ How to make changes to components during development
- ❑ How to make changes to components in production
- ❑ How to change the interface of a component in production

Deployed Application Maintenance

We investigated the creation, debugging, and deploying of the components that run in our application earlier in the book; now we'll take a look at how to maintain our application.

What happens when we want to upgrade applications? This is something that we could well need to do at some point in time, maybe to add new functionally, or change a feature based on user feedback.

Maintaining the application means creating upgraded components that can be deployed with as little disruption as possible to the users. Deploying a single component should not require redeploying all the components in the program; only the one that was changed should need to be redeployed. However, it is important to strive to maintain component compatibility between old and new versions. This can, in the long run, save a lot of trouble.

There are three compatibility options available:

- ❑ Binary compatibility
- ❑ Project compatibility
- ❑ No compatibility

We looked at these back in Chapter 12. When people talk about version compatibility, they're usually referring to binary compatibility. It's important, when deploying a new component for an application, that it is configured for compatibility.

Changing Component Interfaces

Changing component interfaces is only a problem when an application has been deployed, as we would tend to use project compatibility during the development phase. The problem with deployed components is further aggravated by the possibility that more than one application may use the component – we don't want to have to update all the different client applications that use the component at the same time.

One solution is to create a new component that uses the old component, using a technique known as interface inheritance, which we encountered in Chapter 4. Another solution is to add new properties and methods to later versions of the component, and retain the entire interface of the original component.

> *Interface inheritance* is when a class inherits the interface, but not the implementation, of another class. With interface inheritance, the derived class ignores implementation changes in the base class.

Try It Out – Changing Component Interfaces (Part 1)

1. Create a new project in Visual Basic: select **ActiveX DLL** as the project type.

2. Change the name of the class to `BankAccount`, then add the following code to the class:

```
Option Explicit

Private m_curBalance As Currency

Public Sub Deposit(Amount As Currency)
    m_curBalance = m_curBalance + Amount
End Sub

Public Sub WithDraw(Amount As Currency)
    m_curBalance = m_curBalance - Amount
End Sub

Public Property Get Balance() As Currency
    Balance = m_curBalance
End Property
```

3. Name this project `SimpleBank`, and compile and save it.

4. Now we need to create a test harness. Create another new project, and this time select **Standard EXE** as its type.

5. Name the project TestBankAccount. Then go to Project | References and add a reference to the SimpleBank component:

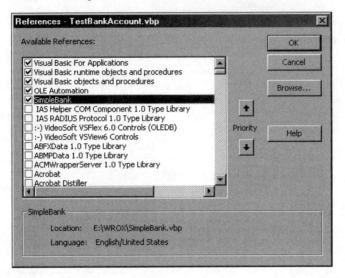

and press OK.

6. Add a label, a text box, and three command buttons to the form. Set the properties as in the table below:

Control	Property	Value
Form	Name	FTestAccount
	BorderStyle	1 – Fixed Single
	Caption	Bank Account Test Harness
	StartupPosition	1 – Center Owner

Control	Property	Value
Label	Name	lblBalance
	Caption	Balance: ???
Text Box	Name	txtAmount
	Text	1000
Command Button	Name	cmdDeposit
	Caption	Deposit
Command Button	Name	cmdWithdraw
	Caption	Withdraw
Command Button	Name	cmdExit
	Caption	Exit

7. Add the following code to the form:

```
Option Explicit

Private m_objBankAccount As SimpleBank.BankAccount

Private Sub Form_Load()
    Set m_objBankAccount = New SimpleBank.BankAccount
    UpdateUI
End Sub

Private Sub Form_Terminate()
    Set m_objBankAccount = Nothing
End Sub

Private Sub cmdExit_Click()
    Unload Me
End Sub

Private Sub cmdDeposit_Click()

    Dim curAmount As Currency

    If IsNumeric(txtAmount.Text) Then
        curAmount = CCur(txtAmount.Text)
        ' Call the SimpleBank.Deposit method
        m_objBankAccount.Deposit (curAmount)
        UpdateUI
    Else
        ErrMsgBox "Please enter a number!"
        txtAmount.SetFocus
        txtAmount.SelStart = 0
        txtAmount.SelLength = Len(txtAmount.Text)
    End If

End Sub
```

655

```
Private Sub cmdWithdraw_Click()

   Dim curAmount As Currency

   If IsNumeric(txtAmount.Text) Then
      curAmount = CCur(txtAmount.Text)
      ' Call the SimpleBank.WithDraw method
      m_objBankAccount.WithDraw (curAmount)
      UpdateUI
   Else
      ErrMsgBox "Please enter a number!"
      txtAmount.SetFocus
      txtAmount.SelStart = 0
      txtAmount.SelLength = Len(txtAmount.Text)
   End If
End Sub
```

```
Private Sub UpdateUI()
   lblBalance.Caption = "Balance = " & CStr(m_objBankAccount.Balance)
   Me.Refresh
End Sub
```

```
Private Sub ErrMsgBox(strMessage As String)
   MsgBox strMessage, vbExclamation, "Error!"
End Sub
```

8. Save and run the project. Press the **Deposit** and **Withdraw** buttons, and the balance should change accordingly.

However, this version of our project allows us to enter negative numbers in the text box, so we can withdraw using the **Deposit** button and deposit using the **Withdraw** button. It also allows us to withdraw more than our balance. Let's fix the deficiencies of this application by changing the component interface.

Try It Out – Changing Component Interfaces (Part 2)

1. Create a new project in Visual Basic, and select **ActiveX DLL** as the project type. Name this project SimpleBank2.

2. Set a reference to the SimpleBank DLL in the **Project | References** dialog.

3. Once again, name the class BankAccount. Using inheritance, we will create the improved rudimentary bank account class used in the previous exercise. The Implements keyword is used to add the implementation inheritance of the SimpleBank class. To do this, add the following code to the class:

```
Option Explicit

Implements SimpleBank.BankAccount

Dim m_objBankAccount As SimpleBank.BankAccount

' New class methods with enhanced functionality
Public Function Deposit(Amount As Currency) As Boolean
    Deposit = (Amount >= 0)
    If Deposit Then BankAccount_Deposit Amount
End Function

Public Function WithDraw(Amount As Currency) As Boolean
    WithDraw = (Amount >= 0) And (BankAccount_Balance >= Amount)
    If WithDraw Then BankAccount_WithDraw Amount
End Function

Public Property Get Balance() As Currency
    Balance = BankAccount_Balance
End Property

Private Sub Class_Initialize()
    Set m_objBankAccount = New SimpleBank.BankAccount
End Sub

Private Sub Class_Terminate()
    Set m_objBankAccount = Nothing
End Sub

Private Property Get BankAccount_Balance() As Currency
    BankAccount_Balance = m_objBankAccount.Balance
End Property

Private Sub BankAccount_Deposit(Amount As Currency)
    m_objBankAccount.Deposit Amount
End Sub

Private Sub BankAccount_WithDraw(Amount As Currency)
    m_objBankAccount.WithDraw Amount
End Sub
```

4. Compile and save the project.

5. Now we'll recreate the test harness used in the previous exercise, using the compiled DLL rather than the project.

6. Open the test harness for SimpleBank (TestBankAccount.vbp) that we created in the previous exercise.

7. Under Project | References, change the reference from SimpleBank to SimpleBank2.

657

8. Modify the code in the form as follows:

```
Option Explicit

Private m_objBankAccount As SimpleBank2.BankAccount

Private Sub Form_Load()
    Set m_objBankAccount = New SimpleBank2.BankAccount
    UpdateUI
End Sub

Private Sub Form_Terminate()
    Set m_objBankAccount = Nothing
End Sub

Private Sub cmdExit_Click()
    Unload Me
End Sub

Private Sub cmdDeposit_Click()
Dim curAmount As Currency

    If IsNumeric(txtAmount.Text) Then
        curAmount = CCur(txtAmount.Text)
        If m_objBankAccount.Deposit(curAmount) Then
            UpdateUI
        Else
            ErrMsgBox "Deposit failed!"
        End If
    Else
        ErrMsgBox "Please enter a number!"
        txtAmount.SetFocus
        txtAmount.SelStart = 0
        txtAmount.SelLength = Len(txtAmount.Text)
    End If
End Sub

Private Sub cmdWithdraw_Click()
Dim curAmount As Currency

    If IsNumeric(txtAmount.Text) Then
        curAmount = CCur(txtAmount.Text)
        If m_objBankAccount.WithDraw(curAmount) Then
            UpdateUI
        Else
            ErrMsgBox "Withdraw failed!"
        End If
    Else
        ErrMsgBox "Please enter a number!"
        txtAmount.SetFocus
        txtAmount.SelStart = 0
        txtAmount.SelLength = Len(txtAmount.Text)
    End If
End Sub
```

```
Private Sub UpdateUI()
   lblBalance.Caption = "Balance = " & CStr(m_objBankAccount.Balance)
   Me.Refresh
End Sub

Private Sub ErrMsgBox(strMessage As String)
   MsgBox strMessage, vbExclamation, "Error!"
End Sub
```

9. Change the project name to `TestBankAccount2`, and save the form and the project under different filenames (**File | Save Project As**). Run this project to test the enhancements made.

10. So far this is similar to the previous exercise. The difference is that the first test harness still works, using the old `SimpleBank.DLL`. Let us try this out. Open the first test harness (`TestBankAccount`) created in this exercise and make sure it still runs.

The techniques shown in this section are crucial to be able to change the interface of components shared by more than one application. The new component reuses the implementation of the old component, but deploying the new component will not break existing applications using the older version. The real power of this technique becomes apparent when we make a change to the old component that does not break the interface.

Try It Out – Changing Component Interfaces (Part 3)

1. Open the `SimpleBank` ActiveX component created in Part 1.

2. Create a GUID directory and copy the ActiveX DLL into this directory. Using the **Project Properties** dialog, set the project to **Binary Compatibility** on the **Component** tab:

3. Change the code in the `BankAccount` class to deduct a $0.25 transaction fee for both deposits and withdrawals:

```
Option Explicit

Private m_curBalance As Currency

Public Sub Deposit(Amount As Currency)
    m_curBalance = m_curBalance + Amount - 0.25
End Sub

Public Sub WithDraw(Amount As Currency)
    m_curBalance = m_curBalance - Amount - 0.25
End Sub

Public Property Get Balance() As Currency
    Balance = m_curBalance
End Property
```

4. Save and compile this project.

5. Open the test harness for `SimpleBank.DLL` created in Part 1 (`TestBankAccount`). Run the project. As you can see, because of binary compatibility, the project automatically uses the new version of `SimpleBank.DLL`.

6. Open the test harness for `SimpleBank2.DLL` created in Part 2 (`TestBankAccount2`). Run the project. As we can see, because we used inheritance, this project also automatically uses the new version of `SimpleBank.DLL`.

The last project shows why we would want to use inheritance when creating components that break compatibility; that way, we automatically get the enhancements to the original components.

How It Works

By using inheritance, the version of the program that breaks compatibility will work with the new DLLs and the older version will continue to work because the DLLs it requires remain installed. Each version of the program will call the proper version of the DLL.

Version Numbering

This screen shot shows the **Make** tab for the **Project Properties** of our `Bank_UI` project. This is where we can set the **Version Number** of the project:

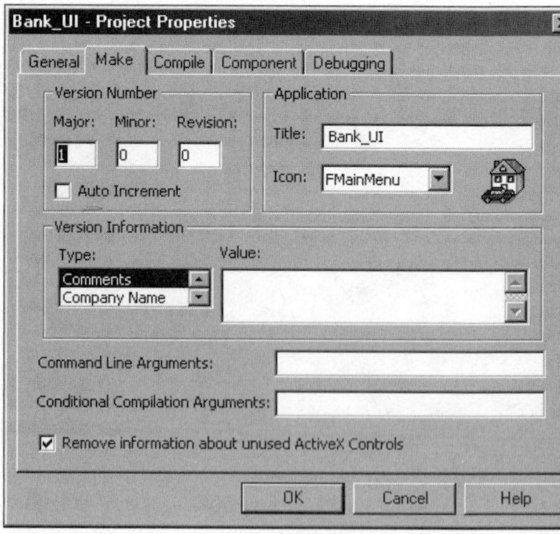

The three text boxes let us set the Major, Minor, and Revision numbers.

We need to change the **major** version number if we have:

❑ Changed a data type that is used by an existing function

❑ Changed a function in the interface, for example, if we've added or removed a parameter

❑ Add callbacks that are called by existing functions

These changes are major changes because they break compatibility with the previous version of the component.

We'd need to change the **minor** version number if we:

❑ Haven't changed any existing functions or added new functions to the interface

❑ Added type definitions or constants that are not used by existing functions

❑ Added callbacks that are not called by any existing functions or if the new callbacks follow any existing functions

Generally, our goal is to maintain upward compatibility among versions. This means we want our modifications to require only minor version number changes. We can maintain compatibility when we add new data types that aren't used by existing functions, and when we add new functions without changing the interface for existing functions.

Revisions are used when we make small changes to the application, and the changes are either to an unreleased component or none of the minor version number changing conditions applies to the changes. If the Auto Increment check box is checked, then each time we compile the project the revision number is automatically incremented by 1.

Visual SourceSafe

Visual SourceSafe (**VSS**) is a source code management tool included with Visual Studio for tracking all file types within a project. This includes text, graphics, sound, and video files, as well as programming files.

VSS saves the files to a database, which can either be local or on a network drive. When we add a file to VSS, the file is backed up in the database and changes that have been made to the file are saved. This means that we can recover an older version at any time. Others can see the latest version of any file, make changes, and save a new version in the database. The database can be used to recover older versions if compatibility is broken or if mistakes have been made.

VSS can be set to be installed as a management tool for individual use or for team use. Files can be checked in and out of the database, and when a file is checked out, no other developer can check out the same file. This prevents conflicting sets of changes being made to a file. When builds of a project are released, the versions of all files included in the build can be set so the build can be reconstructed later if necessary, even if changes have been made to the files that make up the build.

When Visual Studio is installed, we are given the option of installing VSS. If VSS is installed, it can be added it to the Tools menu in VB by using the Add-In Manager. This adds a SourceSafe menu item to the Tools menu. This enables us to check files in to and out of VSS, to add projects to VSS control, and to run VSS.

Summary

This chapter has covered a number of topics related to the final phases of software development: testing, deployment and maintenance.

At the beginning of the chapter, we looked at the types of testing that are carried out at the end of a project. At the team level, this is achieved through integration testing, and at the product level, through system testing. We also explored some of the debugging tools Visual Basic offers. As we reach higher levels of testing, we can begin to test the Use Case Scenarios that our project is based on, using the program's interface and controls. In an ideal world, the project isn't finished until no bugs exist. In the real world, the severity of any remaining bugs is the determining factor when making the decision to release a program.

We've also looked at how to create setup packages to deploy an application. We saw how to use the Package and Deployment Wizard to create packages, and how the same Wizard can then be used to deploy this package.

We also investigated how to export and import MTS Packages and COM+ Applications to deploy the business and data services tier DLLs, and how to automate the import of Packages or Applications using VB code. Finally, we took a look at the new Windows Installer method of deploying applications.

After a program is deployed, we still have a responsibility to maintain it. In this chapter we have seen techniques that will enable us to enhance components that are in production without breaking the applications that use them. Even when the job of actually creating the application is over, the hard work doesn't stop!

In the next chapter, we'll broaden our horizons by exploring how we can adapt the WROBA application so that it can be accessed over the Internet.

17

Web-Enabling the WROBA Application

You'd have to have been living on a desert island for the past five years not to have noticed the growth in interest surrounding the Internet and the impact that it has had on the business community, who now have a new way to communicate and interact with their customers. Today, if we were to roll our WROBA application out into the real world, our customers would expect access to a Web site allowing them to check balances, pay bills, and transfer funds, just as they can with the application we've built thus far.

So, one of the first tasks we may face as a programmer supporting our application is to answer a call from the client saying WROBA meets the initial specifications, but the world has changed and they now want the application upgraded and **Web-enabled**.

To get the terminology right from the outset, we're going to refer to the application as it stands now as the **desktop** version. In this chapter, we'll be building the **online** version. Thanks to the distributed design we've used up until this point, Web-enabling our application will be surprisingly easy. As you know, we already have a tier implementing the business logic, and a tier enabling access to the underlying data that drives the application, so all we have to do is create a new user services, or presentation, tier for our online application, alongside our existing presentation tier for our desktop application.

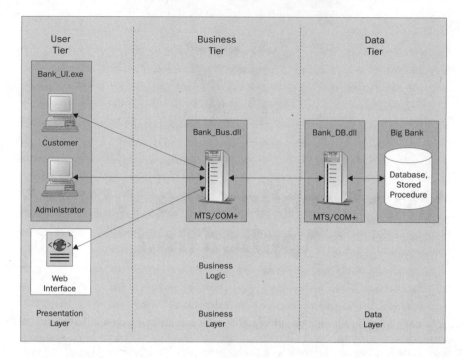

Programming for the Web is a vast and extremely fast moving area of computer technology – one that we can only hope to lightly touch on in this chapter so our aims are quite limited. Firstly, we want to show how the good design and coding of our desktop application means that we can easily adapt WROBA to operate in a new environment, and secondly, how accessible the world of Web technology is to Visual Basic programmers. Therefore, in this chapter we're going to:

❑   Introduce the topic of Web development and look at **Hypertext Markup Language** (**HTML**)

❑   Examine what technology we need to build dynamic Web pages rather than static ones

❑   Start to Web-enable the WROBA application

Again, the code contained in the chapter will be present in the download available at www.wrox.com. Since we are only skating over the surface of this topic, if the chapter does fire your enthusiasm we'd like to suggest you try (depending on your system) either *Beginning Active Server Pages 2.0*, *ISBN 1-861001-34-7* or *Beginning Active Sever Pages 3.0*, *ISBN 1-861003-38-2* (both from *Wrox Press*) for more details.

Web Development

For those of us who haven't done any work developing Web sites before, we're going to kick off with an introduction to getting a **Web server** running and how to work with Hypertext Markup Language (HTML) – the language of the Web.

The Web Server

A web site is powered by a web server, a special piece of software running on a computer connected to either the Internet or a private network that *serves* Web pages down to Web browsers (such as Internet Explorer or Netscape Navigator). These pages are typically formatted using a language called HTML. When the browser receives an HTML file, it interprets the HTML and displays (or *renders*) the page on the screen. If the HTML page contains references to images, the browser makes separate requests to the server for each image until the entire page is displayed as the original designer intended.

Setting up your own Web server is a two-fold process. Firstly, it is necessary to obtain and install the relevant software. Secondly, it is essential to make sure that the server that you serve your pages from is accessible to the audience. We'll cover both those points in the following two sections.

Web Server Software

Later in this chapter, we're going to be using a Microsoft technology called **Active Server Pages** (**ASP**) to drive the new user services (presentation) tier of our application. For this reason, you'll need to get hold of the specific Microsoft Web server for your platform:

❑ **Windows 95 and 98** – You'll need **Personal Web Server** (**PWS**). Windows 95 users will have to download and install the latest version of this from `http://www.microsoft.com/`. Windows 98 users can find PWS on their original installation disc. PWS is only available as part of the Windows NT 4 Option Pack, so you'll need to install this whole package.

❑ **Windows NT 4.0 Workstation and Server** – You'll need to download and install the Windows NT 4 Option Pack from `http://www.microsoft.com/`. On Workstation, this will install **Peer Web Server** (**PWS**). On Server, this will install the **Internet Information Server**, or **IIS**, version 4.0

❑ **Windows 2000 Professional, Server, and Advanced Server** – **Internet Information Services** (**IIS**), version 5.0, is included on your installation disks. If you haven't already installed the components, use the Add/Remove Programs applet on Control Panel to install the components.

Configuring both PWS and IIS can be a complicated process, so throughout this chapter we're going to be leveraging the settings in the default configuration.

Getting Connected

The slightly trickier aspect of getting your Web server configured is making sure that your chosen audience has access to it. Today, we tend to describe a Web site's audience in one of three ways:

❑ **Intranet** – accessible only to people within a single organization

❑ **Extranet** – accessible to people within an organization, and also accessible to selected business partners external to that organization

❑ **Internet** – accessible to anyone connected to the Internet

Be careful when referring to these three audiences of intranet, extranet, and Internet; only Internet has an initial capital letter, as it's a proper name.

If you're just playing around with Web development and you have your Web server installed on the computer that you're going to be developing on, connectivity is a straightforward matter. Accessing network services on your local computer doesn't require establishing any connections, so you'll find that everything should work just fine.

To access the Web server on your machine, use the name `localhost` in the browser **Address** box, like this: `http://localhost/`. The name `localhost` resolves to the IP address 127.0.0.1, which is defined in the TCP/IP specifications as an IP address that always refers to your local machine, irrespective of what its actual IP address may be. In a properly configured Windows network, the machine name is also resolvable to an IP address, so it is possible to use `http://MyMachineName/`.

Be careful not to include any domain identifiers, such as `.com` or `.co.uk` in the name.

If you're trying to get connectivity to other members of your team, it is necessary to examine the structure of your network. Luckily, if you're a small organization without an Information Services (IS) or Information Technology (IT) department, chances are that the development server on your network is accessible to everyone else on your network. If it isn't, it will probably be necessary to install the TCP/IP protocol (although, if you have Web and e-mail access, this is probably already installed). However, if your organization has an IS or IT department, they can probably iron out such problems for you! However, addressing the technicalities of different types of network configuration lies outside the scope of this chapter.

If your ultimate goal is to make your server accessible to partners, or to the general public, things get fairly complex. If this is the case, you'll maybe have to do some more research into the topic, or seek advice from someone more experienced in the field.

We'll turn now to creating a very simple HTML document, which we'll access through our Web server.

"Hello, world!" in HTML

To make a Web server work, it is first necessary to nominate a directory on your server into which the files that we wish to access may be placed. By default, when PWS or IIS is installed, it nominates a folder on the server into which files that we want to access through the server may be stored. This folder is usually located at c:\inetpub\wwwroot. However, because your systems administrator may have changed this folder from its default, we need to use the PWS/IIS tools to find the root folder in order to make sure the examples in this chapter work. Follow the instructions for your specific operating system. Once this has been done, we can move on to constructing a basic HTML page.

Windows 2000 Server and Windows 2000 Professional

To find the folder of the default Web site in Windows 2000, select **Start | Programs | Administrative Tools | Internet Services Manager**. It may, however, be necessary to access IIS via the Control Panel. In this case, select **Start | Settings | Control Panel**, then select **Administrative Tools**, and from there, select **Internet Services Manager**. This should start the IIS management console.

Expand out the server object, select and right-click on **Default Web Site**. Select **Properties** and opt for the **Home Directory** tab. The **Local Path** edit box gives us the location of the folder. This is the root folder in which any files that we want to access via our Web server must be stored:

Windows NT

To find the folder of the default Web site in Windows NT Server, open up Internet Service Manager under Start | Programs | Windows NT 4.0 Option Pack | Microsoft Internet Information Server. The path of the default Web site will be found under the Home Directory tab:

Windows 95/98

To find the folder of the default Web site in Windows 95 and 98, open up Personal Web Manager by selecting Start | Microsoft Personal Web Server | Personal Web Manager. Click the Start button. At this point, the default directory should be displayed, as shown:

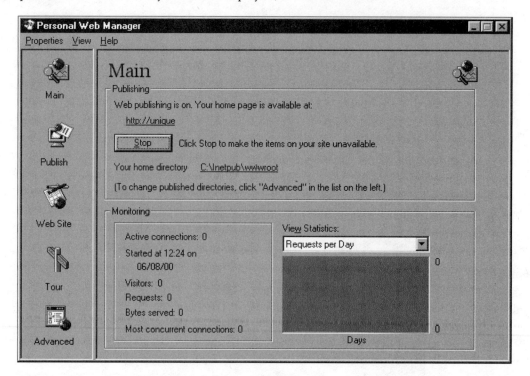

In order to change the default directory, select Advanced. This will take you through to a screen in which changing the default is a fairly straightforward matter.

A Basic HTML Page

Creating an HTML page is simplicity itself. All that is needed is a text editor and some knowledge of HTML **tags**. These tags determine how a browser will present – or render – our HTML page. In this book, we'll just be skimming the surface of HTML. Although it is a very simple language to learn and use, its popularity has seen the available functionality grow to the stage where creating a complicated page can be reasonably difficult.

To learn more about HTML, try *Instant HTML Programmers Reference, HTML 4.0 Edition*, *ISBN 1-861001-56-8* also published by *Wrox Press*.

Let's take a look at using HTML tags.

An HTML tag starts with a "less-than" sign and ends with a "greater-than" sign. Here's an example:

```
<b>
```

The <b> tag is used to tell the browser that everything that comes after it should be displayed in bold text. So, if we want to write the word "Hello" in bold, we'd write something like this:

```
<b>Hello
```

Correct HTML syntax requires that most tags be "closed". This is how the browser is informed that we'd like to return to normal text. In fact, with certain tags, unless we specifically close them, the browser will not know how to render a page. In some such circumstances, browsers will hang! To end a tag, we repeat the tag name, but prefixed with a forward slash, like this:

```
<b>Hello</b>
```

So, to write the word "Hello" in bold and the word "world" in normal text, we might write:

```
<b>Hello,</b> world!
```

This would give us the result:

Hello, world!

Although this is an example of how some HTML tags work, it's not an example of an HTML page. A *page* must comprise of <html>, <head>, and <body> tags, all of which must be properly positioned and closed, like this:

```
<html>
    <head>
    </head>
    <body>
    </body>
</html>
```

The indentation we've used there is optional, but the order of the tags is not. Every HTML page comprises a "head" section and a "body" section. The head section is used to define certain features of the page as a whole (most of which we won't see in this chapter), whereas the body section contains the bulk of the page data.

Try It Out – Creating an HTML Page

1. To create an HTML page, we need a basic text editor such as Notepad. Open this now and enter this code:

```
<html>
  <head>
      <title>My First Web Page</title>
  </head>
  <body>
      <b>Hello</b>, world!
  </body>
</html>
```

2. Save the file in the root folder as `HelloWorld.html`.

3. Open the browser, and navigate to this URL:

```
http://localhost/HelloWorld.html
```

4. At which point, we'll see something like this:

We have now created a *very* basic HTML page and accessed it through our Web server. Before moving on to discuss dynamic Web pages, we'll take a look at a few other useful HTML tags.

Some Other HTML Tags

Later in this chapter, we'll use tags for controlling:

❑ Line Breaks

❑ Fonts

❑ Tables

❑ Forms

Let's look in a little more detail at how these are used.

Line Breaks

The line break tag, `<br>`, tells the browser to start a new line. Here's an example:

```html
<html>
    <head>
        <title>My Second Web Page</title>
    </head>
    <body>
        <b>Hello</b>,<br>world!
    </body>
</html>
```

Notice that it's not necessary to start a new line in the code itself. The browser will ignore any carriage returns and virtually all tabs and spaces in the text of the document itself. Notice also that it is not necessary to close the break tag.

Fonts

To change the font in which text is displayed, we use the <font> tag. This is actually one of the more complicated tags to use.

To determine the type or size of the font that we want to use, we include **attributes** within the tags. Tags can contain any number of attributes, and one of the wonderful things about HTML is that it will ignore anything it doesn't instantly understand. This means that we can put in any tags we like – whether they have any effect depends on the specification of the tag.

The <font> tag can, among other things, contain a reference to the font size, the font face, and color. Here's an example of a font tag that sets a larger font size:

```
<font size=5>This is a BIG font</font>
```

The <font> tag was never designed to allow fonts to be specified in point sizes, mainly due to the different scaling specifications on different platforms; PC, Mac, UNIX, etc. However, recent advances in Web technology have made this possible.

Nonetheless, usability experts recommend that we do not use explicit font sizes in our documents, as this prevents the pages from being used by people who require larger font sizes. Using the <font> tag allows the user to change the font sizes using an option on their browser, effectively making all of the text larger or smaller, as required. Using explicit font sizes prevents this option from working, limiting them to the size specified by the designer.

Tables

Tables can be reasonably complicated, but we'll be using them in a fairly straightforward way in this chapter.

A table is made up of table rows, and a table row is made up of table cells. We can then render anything we like in each cell. A table is started and ended with a <table> tag. A row is started and ended with a <tr> tag. And a cell is started and ended with a <td> tag, where <td> stands for "table data". Here's some HTML code that will render a simple table:

```
<html>
    <head>
        <title>My First Table</title>
    </head>
    <body>
        <table border=1>
            <tr>
                <td><b>Dogs</b></td>
                <td>Disraeli</td>
                <td>Cheerio</td>
            </tr>
            <tr>
                <td><b>Cat</b></td>
                <td>Tina</td>
                <td>Willow</td>
            </tr>
        </table>
    </body>
</html>
```

673

This is what our code will generate:

Forms

The final HTML feature we'll be using in this chapter is the form. To properly understand forms, we need to have an understanding of the ASP code that we'll be using to handle the forms when the user submits them. However, we'll be looking at creating ASP code in detail a little later. In the first instance, think of ASP pages as being such that they can process information that is sent to them.

Forms allow users to enter information onto an HTML page. This information can then be passed to the server for appropriate kinds of processing.

A `<form>` tag has to have an attribute that specifies the page that will be used to handle the form input. For example, in the following code, the attribute specifies that the information entered in the form will be sent to a page called `ThisIsThePageThatHandlesTheForm.asp`:

```
<form action="ThisIsThePageThatHandlesTheForm.asp">
   ...
</form>
```

We can specify that a form should contain boxes into which user input may be typed. The following code will generate such a box and accept the user's name:

```
<form action="ThisIsThePageThatHandlesTheForm.asp">
<b>Enter your name:</b> <input type=input name=YourName>
</form>
```

A form should have a submit button. This enables the user to submit information once it is entered in the form box.

```
<form action="ThisIsThePageThatHandlesTheForm.asp">
<b>Enter your name:</b> <input type=input name=YourName>
<br>
<input type=submit>
</form>
```

This will generate a simple form like this:

A form can have drop-down select lists made up of different options:

```
<form action="ThisIsThePageThatHandlesTheForm.asp">
<b>Enter your name:</b> <input type=input name=YourName>
<br>
<b>Select your best friend:</b>
<select name=BestFriend>
    <option>Alex</option>
    <option>Darren</option>
    <option>Edward</option>
</select>
<br>
<input type=submit>
</form>
```

As we can see, this will create a form with a drop-down menu containing a list of possible best friends:

Finally, a form can have hidden values that can be used to determine what the form is all about:

```
<form action="ThisIsThePageThatHandlesTheForm.asp">
<b>Enter your name:</b> <input type=input name=YourName>
<br>
<b>Select your best friend:</b>
<select name=BestFriend>
   <option>Alex</option>
   <option>Darren</option>
   <option>Edward</option>
</select>
<br>
<input type=hidden name=MyHiddenValue value=27>
<input type=submit>
</form>
```

The use of forms will become clearer as we work through the parts of the chapter that deal with them. We'll now turn to a far more interesting topic: how to create *dynamic* Web pages.

Dynamic Web Sites

If we look at a sample of popular Web sites, we'll notice that most of them are a mix of unchanging, **static** content, and active, **dynamic** content. This is indicative of the evolution of the Web over the past few years from a technology that was based on the ideas of sharing documents to a technology that powers online applications. In the early days of the Internet, Web sites usually consisted of a static collection of documents. Whatever the type of site, the only activity the server had to undertake was to send static pages directly to the visitor's browser. As server-side technology has become more sophisticated, we've seen a move away from static sites towards more dynamic sites. These have made possible the expansion of online services and e-commerce that we've witnessed in recent years.

Typically, the proportion of dynamic pages to static pages determines whether we consider that site to be a **Web site** or a **Web application**. For example, www.Wired.com, the popular news site, has a large number of static pages containing information about interesting technical news topics, and a number of pages for searching through its archives. As most of the visitors to www.Wired.com are interested in reading the static news pages, we consider www.Wired.com to be a Web *site*.

On the other hand, consider www.Amazon.com. The majority of visitors to this site use search tools to find exactly what they want, and each product page has dynamic components that examine warehouse levels, customer comments, and so on. Like most e-commerce sites, we consider www.Amazon.com to be a Web *application*.

Online banking applications are also classic examples of Web applications, which is why we say that the thing we build in the remainder of this chapter is a Web *application*, not a Web *site*.

Active Server Pages

Over the past few years, there have been a number of technologies designed to allow developers to build dynamic Web applications. These stemmed from a technology called **Common Gateway Interface** (**CGI**). Today, one of the fastest growing dynamic Web technology architectures is Microsoft's **Active Server Pages** (**ASP**).

ASP 3.0 is the latest version of ASP. This is supplied as standard with IIS 5.0, which is packaged with all versions of Windows 2000. Windows NT, Windows 95, and Windows 98 users can enjoy ASP 2.0. There are no fundamental differences between version 2.0 and version 3.0. In this respect, the changes have been evolutionary rather than revolutionary. So we can follow through this chapter whether we have version 2.0 or 3.0 at our disposal.

ASP works on the principle of building an HTML template for a page into which is embedded code that will *dynamically* generate more HTML code. This generated code is the dynamic content of a page.

One important thing to understand about ASP is that it's all processed at the server, as opposed to on the client. One problem with client-side scripting is that, as most dynamic Web sites need access to databases and other resources, each browser would have to be able to communicate with these resources, and this constitutes a security risk. Additionally, the browser would have to have the capability to understand the code, which, given the myriad of available browsers out there, is an arduous task. Using server-side scripting means that our site will be compatible with different sorts of browser. Also, it means that our resources can be properly secured.

In order for ASP to interpret our files, they must have .asp extensions, rather than .htm or .html extensions. We'll see why this is a little later.

Whenever an ASP file is processed, ASP seeks out the **ASP tags**, <% and %>, which distinguish the ASP code from the HTML. These tags tell ASP that it's time to execute some code, rather than send the HTML code straight to the browser. For example, if we wished to create a message saying "Welcome back to WROBA, George", where "George" is the name of the logged in user, we could write:

```
Welcome back to WROBA, <%=FirstName%>
```

In this case, the name "George" is stored elsewhere in the system. What we're doing with this code is extracting that value and inserting it into the HTML code, which is then returned to the browser. This has turned our static site into a dynamic site.

The equal sign is used to tell ASP to process whatever's in the ASP tag and send it back to the browser. Usually, script embedded into ASP pages is written in VBScript. This is a simplified version of Visual Basic. As we'll see in a little while, ASP can also support JScript and other languages.

In our above example, we've assumed that a variable called FirstName has already been defined, and we just want to pass that specific value back to the browser. However, we can ask ASP to process more complex directives:

```
The total of your order is: <%= SubTotal + 6.95 + (SubTotal * .075) %>
```

677

This will return, as we might expect, the *result* of the given equation.

Whenever text is returned to the browser, it can include HTML tags in the following way:

```
Welcome back, <%= "<b>" & FirstName & "</b>" %>
```

This will instruct the browser to present the contents of the `FirstName` variable in bold.

ASP can also process blocks of code. These may include many features that we are familiar with in ordinary VB such as `For...Next` loops. In this way, VBScript shares many features with more powerful programming languages, unlike HTML.

Let's take a look at how we can put together a very simple ASP page.

Try It Out – Creating an ASP Page

In this example, we use the ASP built-in `Response` object to pass HTML to the browser. We'll be looking at built-in objects a little later.

ASP pages are simple text files stored on your server, much like normal HTML pages. The easiest way to create a basic ASP page is to use Notepad.

1. Open up Notepad.

2. Add this code to the page:

```
<HTML>
    <HEAD>
    <TITLE>ASP Hello World</TITLE>
    </HEAD>
<BODY>
    Hello, world!
    <br><br>

    <!-- Add the date... -->
    <% =Now() %>
    <br><br>

    <!-- Count to five... -->
    <%
        For n = 1 to 5
            Response.Write n & "<br>"
        Next
    %>
</BODY>
</HTML>
```

3. Save the page into the root folder of your server as `HelloWorld.asp`.

4. To view the page, open your Web browser and use the **Address** bar to navigate to `http://localhost/HelloWorld.asp`. Our page should look like this:

How It Works

When IIS or PWS receives a request for a page ending in `.asp` it knows it has to pass that page on to the ASP processor. We look at the way in which this happens in the next section.

Once the ASP processor has the file, it simply has to execute the code contained within the ASP tags. The first of these tags uses the = directive to specify that the result of the Now() function is to be returned to the browser. The Now() function is a built-in VBScript function that returns the current date and time.

Immediately after this, ASP encounters another set of tags. This time, the tags contain a loop from 1 to 5. On each iteration, the loop passes the current value of n down to the browser.

The Internals of ASP

ASP itself is actually a **Common Gateway Interface** (**CGI**) program used by IIS or PWS whenever a request for a file with a `.asp` extension is received. Internally, ASP is accessed through a technology called **Internet Server Application Programming Interface** (**ISAPI**). This too is a form of CGI, which is why we call ASP a CGI program. Let's take a look at how this works.

If IIS or PWS receives a request for a file that typically does not need processing, such as an HTML file, text file, or image file, all that happens is that the bytes that make up that file are sent straight to the browser. If, on the other hand, the file needs some server-side processing to be performed on it, such as having a list of account balances added, the Web server has to pass the request on to another piece of software that has the capability to do this processing. The Web server also passes on a reference to a conduit that can be used by the processing software to pass the HTML to the browser.

The first technology to do this was called CGI, and this technology is still in use today. ASP has been developed from CGI, essentially turning what used to be a pretty tricky technology to use into something more accessible. Microsoft's first attempt at achieving this came in the form of **ISAPI**, but this still proved difficult to use. Subsequently, they bolted ASP onto ISAPI, making it significantly easier to write dynamic Web sites.

ASP is dependent on another Microsoft technology, called **Active Scripting**, to interpret and execute the code embedded in pages. This converts VBScript (and JavaScript and other scripting languages) into COM calls.

Active Scripting is also used in Internet Explorer and **Windows Script Host**. Windows Script Host enables us to build a file containing commands written in any of the languages that Active Scripting supports, and, because it is powered by Active Scripting, it acts as an ActiveX component and can therefore make calls to any other ActiveX component. One of the powerful things about this technology is that script engines can be plugged into it to extend the set of languages that can be used with Active Scripting and, therefore, with ASP. Usually, Active Scripting is installed along with the engine that powers VBScript and the engine that powers JScript.

Central to Active Scripting is COM technology. As we've already seen, COM powers the vast majority of Microsoft technologies. The use of COM in Active Scripting means that all of the components in our business tier can be called from script code embedded in ASP pages.

This diagram illustrates how these technologies integrate to support a Web-enabled application:

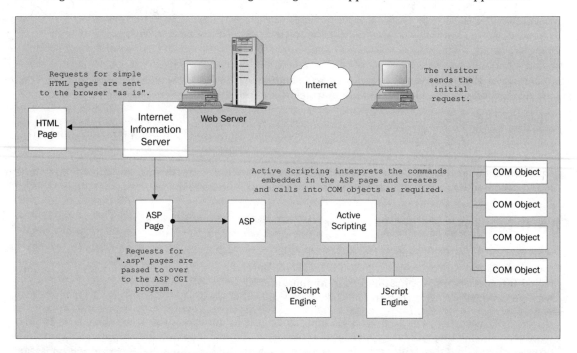

As we can see, central to the whole operation is IIS. This receives requests over the Internet from visitors and is responsible for making sure that they receive the information they request. IIS examines the request to determine the kind of file required. If it's a file that doesn't require any processing, it can be accessed and sent directly to the visitor's browser.

If an ASP page request is detected, the page name is passed over to the ASP processor. Along with this request is provided a conduit down which ASP can send HTML back to the visitor through IIS.

The ASP processor works through the page from top to bottom. Whenever it locates an ASP tag, the code embedded into the tag is passed over to an Active Scripting engine. As we mentioned before, the vast majority of ASP is developed using VBScript, but any of the scripting engines supported by Active Scripting can be used.

The ASP processor also passes references to the five ASP intrinsic objects (`Request`, `Response`, `Server`, `Application`, and `Session`) to the Active Scripting engine. These references point to COM objects, the lifetimes of which are handled by Active Scripting.

The scripting engines can also pass requests for different COM objects (such as the business objects we've already built) over to Active Scripting.

This arrangement of technologies makes ASP an extremely powerful Web development platform. Although this has been a very cursory overview of the complexities of the ASP processor and its associated technologies, a broad idea of how these technologies integrate is essential to a better understanding of how to construct Web based applications.

The Built-in Objects

The two essential requirements of a CGI program are the ability to translate a page request into a format that can access information from a database, and the ability to translate information from a database into a format that can be handled by Web browsers. ASP provides for both of these requirements using *built-in* objects. These are COM objects that are always available to the code embedded in the ASP page. We met the `Response` object a little while ago, but let's take a look at all five objects:

- ❑ `Response` – provides access to the conduit that sends data back to the browser; it can also redirect the user to other URLs.

- ❑ `Request` – provides information on the request that was made, including data entered into form fields, and information on the server environment.

- ❑ `Session` – provides access to a connectionless session manager. We'll look at this in more detail later on.

- ❑ `Server` – provides access to server utilities.

- ❑ `Application` – provides access to information shared between all parts of the Web application.

We'll look at these objects in more detail, and then move on to developing more complex ASP pages. If you need more information about these objects, Appendix D contains in-depth reference material.

Response Object

In order to use any of these objects, all we have to do is call them by name. The `Response` object sends HTML text, cookies, and other content back to the browser or other user agent (we will look at cookies a little later). Its `Write` method is the most commonly used call in ASP. This sends text back to the visitor's browser, in the following way:

```
<% Response.Write "Hello, world!" %>
```

The equivalent plain HTML text for this call is:

```
Hello, world!
```

Request Object

The `Request` object is most commonly used for accessing information about requests. For instance, it may be used to access the URL of the current page in the following way:

```
The URL of this page is:<br>
<% Response.Write Request.ServerVariables("script_name") %>
```

The `Request` object supports the following collections:

- ❑ `Form` – a list of the values entered into a form that is to be processed by a page
- ❑ `QueryString` – a list of the values attached to the end of the URL of the page
- ❑ `ServerVariables` – a list of helpful information about the server and browser environments
- ❑ `Cookies` – a list of cookies (more on cookies later)
- ❑ `ClientCertificate` – a list of properties associated with the client certificate used when a page is accessed over a secure connection (we won't be concerned with this in this chapter)

It is possible to ask the `Request` object to search through all five of its collections with a single call. This is useful for situations where we may not know if the variable we want is in the `Request.Form` or in the `Request.QueryString` collection. To do this, we simply make the call without specifying a collection, like this:

```
My card number is <%= Request("cardnumber") %>
```

However, the `Request` object should only be used in this shorthand manner in particular types of circumstances, as there is a performance impact associated with having to search through all five of the collections.

Session Object

The `Session` object provides a way of holding information about a specific visitor to a Web site. This is known as **state** information. This information can include names, account numbers, dates of birth; in short, anything you want. This is because ASP provides a completely free-form way of associating state information with a user session.

For example, the following code can be used to store a Bank ID number in the session object:

```
Session("BankID") = intBankID
```

Later, we will see in detail how the session object is used.

Server Object

The `Server` object provides some useful helper functions for ASP developers. Its most common function is to create COM objects. For example, to create a COM object called `objMyObject`, we could use the following code:

```
Set objMyObject = Server.CreateObject("MyApplication.MyObject")
```

Another example of a method available in the `Server` object is `MapPath`. This derives the physical path (the path corresponding to the actual directory location of a file) of a particular Web path (the *virtual* path which is given in the URL). For example, this code returns the physical path of the root of the Web server:

```
Response.Write "This Web server is at: " & Server.MapPath("/")
```

Application Object

Similar to the `Session` object, the `Application` object provides an ad hoc method for storing information about an application. Unlike the `Session` object, where variables are only visible to pages used in the session, `Application` variables are available to each and every page. A common use of the `Application` variables is to store the location of the database or databases used with the application. For example, the following code can be used to store the OLE DB connection string to the database:

```
Application("DBString") = "Driver=SQL Server;
                          UID=sa;pwd=;Database=WROBA;Server=localhost"
```

Later, whenever we need to connect to the database, we can use this code:

```
Set objConn = Server.CreateObject("ADODB.Connection")
objConn.Open Application("DBString")Calling Business Objects
```

As we've mentioned, Active Scripting is heavily integrated with COM. For instance, if we want to create an instance of our `Bank` object, we could use this code:

```
<% Set objBank = Server.CreateObject("Bus_Bank.Bank")
```

In the next section we'll see how we can turn that call into a launch pad for Web-enabling WROBA.

Web-Enabling WROBA

In this section we're going to start putting together the code we need to Web-enable WROBA.

> *We're not going to implement the administrative tools. Rather, we're going to concentrate on implementing the tools a typical user of the site may require.*

To Web-enable the customer services side of the WROBA application, we're going to cover:

❑ Customer login and authentication

❑ Presentation of customer accounts

❑ Presentation of account history

❑ Fund transfer

❑ Additional tasks to complete the movement of WROBA to being a full Web-enabled application

Authentication

Our first job is to authenticate the user coming into the site. Our goal is to present the user with a login form the first time they visit the site and use the existing VerifyLogin method on the Bank_Bus.Bank object to authenticate entry to the site based on the card number and password they supply. Remember, our goal here is to add new presentation tier code and leave the business tier code well alone. This fits in with our whole approach to 3-tier development.

In our example, we're going to wrap all of the functionality of WROBA into a single ASP page. It's not typical to find an entire Web application written in a single file, but we've chosen this method because of the simplicity of the functionality required by the WROBA application and to make following this example that little bit easier. In real-world ASP development, expect to find a single ASP page for each major application function, for example one page for signing on a customer, one page for presenting account information and history, one page for providing account transfer forms, etc.

For our Web interface to be able to interact with the Bank application properly, it is necessary either to have our VB Bank project running, by opening Visual Basic and running the application from there, or to have it fully installed, by having the appropriate DLLs compiled and registered.

> *Windows 2000 users might encounter certain problems when running the ASP interface. If you experience either an ASP 0178 error, or a 'Version' not found error, then you'll need to give the IUSR account permissions using the DCOMCNFG.EXE utility, making sure you add both Default Access Permissions and Default Launch Permissions for IUSR under the Default Security tab. If needed, more detailed instructions can be found at:*
> *http://support.microsoft.com/support/kb/articles/Q192/1/52.asp*

Try It Out – Creating a Login Form

1. Create a new file called default.asp and save it in the folder into which we earlier put our "Hello, world!" example.

2. Add this basic HTML code to default.asp. This provides the framework used by all HTML pages:

```
<%
    Option Explicit
%>
<html>
    <head>
        <title>Wrox Online Banking Application</title>
    </head>
    <body>
        <font size=3><b>Welcome to WROBA</b></font>
    </body>
</html>
```

As in Visual Basic, it is common to use `Option Explicit` in VBScript. This puts the language into a mode where any variables we want to use have to be explicitly defined.

3. This same page is going to be used whether a user is logged in or not, so our first job is to establish if the user is logged on and, if not, present them with an appropriate form. Insert the highlighted code at the appropriate place into `default.asp`:

```
<%
    Option Explicit
%>
<html>
    <head>
    <title>Wrox Online Banking Application</title>
    </head>
    <body>
    <font size=3><b>Welcome to WROBA</b></font>
    <%
        ' Are we logged in?
        If IsEmpty(Session("BankID")) Then
    %>

        <!-- Create a login form... -->
        <form action="default.asp" method=post>

            <!-- Add the controls to the form... -->
            Card Number: <input type=text name=cardnumber><br>
            Password: <input type=password name=password><br>
            <input type=submit value="Login">
            <input type=hidden name="processlogin" value=1>

            <!-- End the form... -->
        </form>
    <% Else %>
    <% End If %>
    </body>
</html>
```

4. If we look at that ASP page now, we'll see something like this, although, of course, at this point it will not yet do anything:

How it Works

The trick with our authentication routine is to check to see if the user is already logged into the application and, if not, present the form. At the moment, we haven't written the code to present the accounts list if they are logged in, and we haven't written the code to process the login once the Login button is pressed, but we'll move on to these issues very soon.

We use the `Session` built-in ASP object to determine if the user has already been through the process of authenticating himself. As we saw earlier, the Session object provides a way of holding information about a specific visitor to a Web site.

In order to ensure scalability and to keep server load down to manageable levels, Web servers are designed to be **connectionless**. What this means is that whenever a browser requests a page, a connection to the server is established, but the instant the server sends the last byte to the browser, the connection is removed. The next time that the same browser requests a page from that same Web server, the Web server has no way of knowing that the two distinct requests are actually part of one whole session, where a session is a sequence of interactions with the server from the same individual.

ASP provides a simple session manager for handling sessions on single server installations. The first time a user visits a site, the user's **cookies** are examined for an entry starting with the text `ASPSESSIONID`. A cookie is a small text file (limited to 4kb of data) stored on the hard drive of the client, which contains information about the user. Cookies may be dropped from a server down onto a user's computer. ASP uses cookies to associate sessions with a browser. The `ASPSessionID` entry points to an encrypted value that represents a unique user session held in IIS's or PWS's memory on the server. This encrypted value is known as a **token**. Each time a request comes through, this token is examined and, from this, the session ID can be identified. As a known ID can now be associated with a request, extra information can be associated with this ID. In our case, we're going to hang a Bank ID and Card ID off the session.

The ASP Session has a lifespan (also known as a **timeout**) of 20 minutes from the last activity. This provides a neat way of adding security to an application. For example, in a situation where someone is signed onto an online banking application, if there has been no page request for 20 minutes, the session will be destroyed and the user will thus be automatically signed off.

In the following diagram, the Web server maintains an internal table of sessions. Each of these sessions is identified by a unique integer ID. When Alex first visits the site, the next session number is allotted to him, in this case, 27. Rather than sending the integer 27 straight to the user's browser, ASP returns an encrypted token. The bank ID and card ID are hung off the session so that, on subsequent page requests, the server is able to use the token to find out Alex's bank ID and card ID.

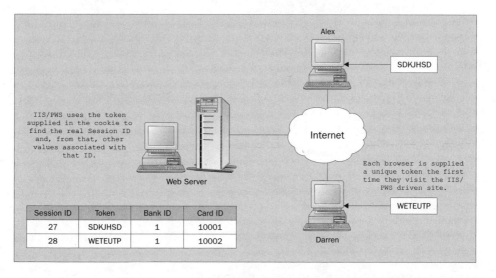

Session ID	Token	Bank ID	Card ID
27	SDKJHSD	1	10001
28	WETEUTP	1	10002

Try It Out – Authenticating the User

We'll now turn to look at how we can set up our ASP page so that users can log into the application through it.

1. Add the highlighted code to the top and middle of default.asp as appropriate:

```
<%
Option Explicit
```

```
    ' We'll be using these variables...
    Dim objBank, strProblem
    Dim lngCardID, intBankID, intInvalidCount

    ' Do we want to process the login?
    If Request("processlogin") <> "" Then

        ' Create an instance of the Bank...
        Set objBank = Server.CreateObject("Bank_Bus.Bank")

        ' Do we have a valid card?
        strProblem = ""
        If Len(Request("cardnumber")) = 12 Then
            ' Is the card number all numeric?
            If IsNumeric(Request("cardnumber")) Then
                ' Get hold of the card id and bank id...
                lngCardID = objBank.GetCardID(Request.Form("cardnumber"))
                intBankID = objBank.GetBankID(Request.Form("cardnumber"))
```

```
                        ' Verify the user...
                        If objBank.VerifyLogin(intBankID, lngCardID, _
                            Request("password"), intInvalidCount) = True Then

                            ' Sign them in the logic...
                            Session("BankID") = intBankID
                            Session("CardID") = lngCardID

                        Else
                            strProblem = _
                            "Your password does not appear to be valid."
                        End if

                    Else
                        strProblem = "Enter only numbers into the card number."
                    End If

                Else
                    strProblem = _
                        "You must enter exactly 12 digits for the card number."
                End If

        End If
%>
<html>
    <head>
    <title>Wrox Online Banking Application</title>
    </head>
    <body>

    <font size=3><b>Welcome to WROBA</b></font>

    <%
        ' Are we logged in?
        If IsEmpty(Session("BankID")) Then
    %>

        <!-- Create a login form... -->
        <form action="default.asp" method=post>

        <%
         ' Did we have a problem?
        If strProblem <> "" Then
            Response.Write "<font color=#800000>"
            Response.Write strProblem
            Response.Write "</font>"
        End If
        %>
        <!-- Add the controls to the form... -->
        Card Number: <input type=text name=cardnumber><br>
        Password: <input type=password name=password><br>
        <input type=submit value="Login">
        <input type=hidden name="processlogin" value=1>

        <!-- End the form... -->
        </form>

    <% Else %>
    <% End If %>

    </body>
</html>
```

How It Works

When the Login button is pressed, `default.asp` is requested again, but this time the form information will contain a hidden field called `processlogin`, which indicates that we came from within the form, rather than from outside of the page. That is, it indicates that we are submitting information from the page, rather than merely accessing the page.

Effectively, what we're trying to do throughout the process of Web-enabling the application is to replicate the functionality of the presentation tier. If we look back to the private `ValidateUser` function on the `FLogin` form that we put together when building the presentation tier, we can see that it goes through a process of checking the card number, deriving the actual Bank ID and Card ID numbers from that ID, and then passing the details over to the `Bank_Bus.Bank` object for validation. In our ASP-based presentation tier, we have to do the same things.

Throughout this code, we've ensured that we check the values that are supplied. This is good basic programming practice. We performed these same validation procedures in the presentation code for the desktop version of our application. Whenever a problem is encountered with the entered values, a message is added to the `strProblem` variable. If we can't log the user onto the application because problems occurred, the form is redisplayed and the contents of `strProblem` are displayed to inform the user what type of error has occurred.

Let's look at the code in a little more detail.

First, an instance of the `Bank_Bus.Bank` object is created:

```
Set objBank = Server.CreateObject("Bank_Bus.Bank")
```

After this, we validate the basics of the card details and then ask the `Bank` object to derive the Bank ID and Card ID:

```
    ' Get hold of the card id and bank id...
lngCardID = objBank.GetCardID(Request.Form("cardnumber"))
intBankID = objBank.GetBankID(Request.Form("cardnumber"))
```

This call asks the `Request` object to examine its `Form` collection.

In this case, the `cardnumber` and `password` have been passed through as form variables.

A query string is a set of key and value pairs tacked onto the end of the URL to supply extra information to the page. In this example, our server is called "Beetle". Currently, our page request looks like this:

```
http://Beetle/default.asp
```

However, we can add extra query string variables to the page, like this:

```
http://Beetle/default.asp?action=view&id=20001
```

689

This new request contains two query string variables: one is called `action`, which has a value of `view`, and one is called `id`, which has a value of `20001`. This is very similar to the way form variables are passed through. In our example, we have one called `cardnumber` and one called `password`. The `METHOD` attribute of the `FORM` tag is set to `POST`. This means that variables have to be passed through into the `Request.Form` collection. However, we could set the `METHOD` attribute to `GET`. If we did this, our variables would be passed through the query string, like this:

```
/default.asp?cardnumber=001000010001&password=secret1
```

Typically, the `POST` method is used for forms because it enables us to pass more information than we can using `GET`. This is because the entire query string has a limited length. Additionally, using `POST` makes it harder for other people to access passwords, as it doesn't appear in the address bar of the browser.

In real world applications, it's common to find a technology called **Secure Socket Layer** (**SSL**) being used. This encrypts data as it passes between server and browser ensuring that it cannot be intercepted.

Once we have the ID, we call the `VerifyLogin` method. If this is successful, we set the `BankID` and `CardID` values in the Session. Otherwise we send an error message to the `strProblem` variable.

```
If objBank.VerifyLogin(intBankID, lngCardID, Request("password"), _
            intInvalidCount) = True Then

    ' Sign them in the logic...
    Session("BankID") = intBankID
    Session("CardID") = lngCardID

Else
    strProblem = "Your password does not appear to be valid."
End if
```

Now we've allowed the customer to login, we'd better make sure they have something to see, so our next job is to present the status of their accounts to them.

Presenting Accounts and Creating a Menu

Web usability studies have shown that Web applications work better as flat pages with links, rather than having the bundles of user interface widgets, such as menus and windows, commonly found in desktop applications. This means that it would be better, in developing our online application, not to try to merely make a replica of the desktop presentation.

After users have logged into our desktop application, they are presented with a list of their accounts. We want to duplicate this functionality. In our version, however, we'll present each account name as a hotlink that the user can click on to view his or her account history.

Try It Out – Presenting the Account List

1. Add the highlighted code to `default.asp`:

```
<%
    ' Are we logged in?
    If IsEmpty(Session("BankID")) Then
%>

    <!-- Create a login form... -->
    <form action="default.asp" method=post>
    <%
        ' Did we have a problem?
        If strProblem <> "" Then
            Response.Write "<font color=#800000>"
            Response.Write strProblem
            Response.Write "</font>"
        End If
    %>
    <!-- Add the controls to the form... -->
        Card Number: <input type=text name=cardnumber><br>
        Password: <input type=password name=password><br>
        <input type=submit value="Login">
        <input type=hidden name="processlogin" value=1>

        <!-- End the form... -->
    </form>

<% Else %>

    <% ' What activity do we want to undertake?
    Select Case Request("action") %>

        <% Case Else %>
        <table cellspacing=0 cellpadding=2 border=1>
        <tr><td colspan=4><b>Your Accounts</b></td></tr>
        <tr><td>Name</td>
        <td>Balance</td>
        <td>Daily Remaining</td>
        <td>Overdraft Limit</td></tr>
        <%
            ' Get a list of the accounts...
            Dim rsAccounts
            Set objBank = Server.CreateObject("Bank_Bus.Bank")
            Set rsAccounts = objBank.GetAccounts(Session("BankID"), _
                    Session("CardID"))
            Do While Not rsAccounts.EOF

                ' Render the account...
                Response.Write "<tr>"
                Response.Write "<td><a href="""
```

```
            Response.Write Request.ServerVariables("script_name") & _
                "?action=view&id=" & rsAccounts("accountid")
            Response.Write """>"
            Response.Write rsAccounts("AccountTypeDesc")
            Response.Write "</a></td>"
            Response.Write "<td>" & _
                rsAccounts("Balance") & "</td>"
            Response.Write "<td>" & _
                rsAccounts("DailyRemaining") & "</td>"
            Response.Write "<td>" & _
                rsAccounts("OverdraftLimit") & "</td>"
            Response.Write "</tr>"


        ' Next...
        rsAccounts.MoveNext
        response.write "<br>"


        Loop
            rsAccounts.Close
            Set rsAccounts = Nothing
        %>
        </table>
    <br><br>

    <% End Select %>
```

```
    <% End If %>
```

How it Works

As mentioned before, the Request built-in object provides access to detailed information about the request that caused the ASP page to be processed. The first call we make in the modified code is:

```
<% ' What activity do we want to undertake?
    Select Case Request("action") %>
```

Notice how we use the Request object to search through all five of the collections. As we'll see later, this allows us to pass the action variable through both form variables and query string variables, thus giving us maximum flexibility.

As we work through this chapter, we'll be reusing this page. In reusing it, we will pass through different action values in order to get the page to perform a variety of functions, such as presenting account lists, transferring funds, and so on.

If the action string is either blank or not understandable, as the default, account information will be displayed. This is done through use of the Case Else statement.

After this is performed, we display the headings for the table, before moving on to create an instance of the Bank_Bus.Bank object. The GetAccounts method of this object is passed the Bank ID and Card ID. These had been stored in the Session object back when the user logged on:

```
Dim rsAccounts
Set objBank = Server.CreateObject("Bank_Bus.Bank")
Set rsAccounts = objBank.GetAccounts(Session("BankID"), _
        Session("CardID"))
```

Once the business tier has done its work to get the accounts back, all we have to is present them:

```
Do While Not rsAccounts.EOF

  ' Render the account...
  Response.Write "<tr>"
  Response.Write "<td><a href="""
  Response.Write Request.ServerVariables("script_name") & _
     "?action=view&id=" & rsAccounts("accountid")
  Response.Write """>"
  Response.Write rsAccounts("AccountTypeDesc")
  Response.Write "</a></td>"
  Response.Write "<td>" & _
     rsAccounts("Balance") & "</td>"
  Response.Write "<td>" & _
     rsAccounts("DailyRemaining") & "</td>"
  Response.Write "<td>" & _
     rsAccounts("OverdraftLimit") & "</td>"
  Response.Write "</tr>"

  ' Next...
  rsAccounts.MoveNext
  response.write "<br>"

Loop
```

We've turned the account name into a hyperlink and tacked a query string onto the end that re-enters the page.

The `Request.ServerVariables("script_name")` call then returns the URL that is used to access this page. This is a neat ASP trick that has the consequence that if the page is renamed, the script continues working as normal.

In order to gain a better understanding of how the query string is manipulated, try logging in with the card number 001000010001, using the password secret1, and looking at the accounts:

If we hover the mouse over the Checking and Saving links, two URLs can be seen:

/default.asp?action=view&id=20001
/default.asp?action=view&id=20002

You will probably find that you have more text before the /default.asp. This represents the *explicit* path to the page, including the protocol and server name. In constructing our Internet interface, we'll mainly be interested in the values for action and id.

Now that we've displayed the account summary, we can move on to displaying the account history.

Viewing the Account History

To do this, all we have to do is create the code to call the appropriate business tier objects.

Try It Out – Viewing Account History

1. Add this code to default.asp, immediately before the Case Else statement we built a moment ago:

```
<% ' What activity do we want to undertake?
   Select Case Request("action") %>
```

```
<% Case "view" %>
<table cellspacing=0 cellpadding=2 border=1>
<tr> <td colspan=5><b>Transaction History</b></td></tr>
<tr><td>Date</td>
<td>Type</td>
<td>Description</td>
<td>Amount</td>
<td>Counterparty</td></tr>
<%
Dim rsTransactions
Set objBank = Server.CreateObject("Bank_Bus.Bank")
Set rsTransactions = objBank.GetAccountHistory(Session("BankID"), _
        Request("id"), Now)
Do While Not rsTransactions.EOF

    ' Render the transaction...
    Response.Write "<tr>"
    Response.Write "<td>" & rsTransactions("TxDate") & "</td>"
    Response.Write "<td>" & rsTransactions("TxTypeDesc") & "</td>"
    Response.Write "<td>" & rsTransactions("TxDescription") & "</td>"
    Response.Write "<td>" & rsTransactions("TxAmount") & "</td>"
    Response.Write "<td>" & _
        rsTransactions("CounterpartyRef") & "</td>"
    Response.Write "</tr>"

' Next
rsTransactions.MoveNext
```

```
      Loop
         rsTransactions.Close
         Set rsTransactions = Nothing
      %>
      </table>

<!-- add a link to go back... -->
<br>
<a href="<%=Request.ServerVariables("script_name")%>">Back</a>

<% Case Else %>
```

How It Works

The code used to display a list of the transactions is not wildly different to the code we used to present the account list. All we do is call the `GetAccountHistory` method of the `Bank_Bus.Bank` object instead of calling the `GetAccounts` method:

```
Set rsTransactions = objBank.GetAccountHistory(Session("BankID"), _
          Request("id"), Now)
```

In order to construct this call, we take the Bank ID from the `Session` object and the ID value from the `Request` collection. We use the generic `Request` call, rather than requesting a specific collection, as this enables us to reuse the same call from within a form, or from a link, as we've done in this example.

Here's what our example account history for the Checking account looks like:

Transferring Funds

Up until this point, all we've done is provide ways of viewing account information stored in the database. In this section, we'll be providing a way of transferring money between accounts.

Try It Out – Transferring Funds

1. The first thing we need to do is add a link to the home page that provides access to the transfer form. Add the highlighted code to `default.asp`, at the end of the code we wrote earlier in the chapter to present the list of accounts:

```
' Get a list of the accounts...
Dim rsAccounts
Set objBank = Server.CreateObject("Bank_Bus.Bank")
Set rsAccounts = objBank.GetAccounts(Session("BankID"), _
        Session("CardID"))
Do While Not rsAccounts.EOF

  ' Render the account...
  Response.Write "<tr>"
  Response.Write "<td><a href="""
  Response.Write Request.ServerVariables("script_name") & _
      "?action=view&id=" & rsAccounts("accountid")
  Response.Write """>"
  Response.Write rsAccounts("AccountTypeDesc")
  Response.Write "</a></td>"
  Response.Write "<td>" & _
      rsAccounts("Balance") & "</td>"
  Response.Write "<td>" & _
      rsAccounts("DailyRemaining") & "</td>"
  Response.Write "<td>" & _
      rsAccounts("OverdraftLimit") & "</td>"
  Response.Write "</tr>"

  ' Next...
  rsAccounts.MoveNext
  response.write "<br>"

Loop
rsAccounts.Close
Set rsAccounts = Nothing
%>
</table>
<br><br>
<a href="<%=Request.ServerVariables("script_name")%>?action=transfer">Transfer
Funds</a><br>
```

2. In this bit of functionality, we're going to need a helper function to add the list of accounts to a list in the form. Add this code to the very bottom of the ASP page:

```
</body>
</html>

<%
  Sub AddAccountList
```

```
      Dim objBank, rsAccounts
      Set objBank = Server.CreateObject("Bank_Bus.Bank")
      Set rsAccounts = objBank.GetAccounts(Session("BankID"), _
                Session("CardID"))
      Do While Not rsAccounts.EOF

        ' Render...
        Response.Write "<option value="""
        Response.Write rsAccounts("AccountId")
        Response.Write """>"
        Response.Write rsAccounts("AccountTypeDesc")
        Response.Write "</option>"

        ' Next
        rsAccounts.MoveNext

      Loop
      rsAccounts.Close
      Set rsAccounts = Nothing
      Set objBank = Nothing

    End Sub
%>
```

3. Next, we need to add code that will present the form. In this section, we're not going to add the code that actually performs the transfer. We'll do that in a moment. Add this code immediately above the code we wrote earlier to display account history:

```
<% ' What activity do we want to undertake?
Select Case Request("action") %>
```

```
    <% Case "transfer" %>
    <b>Transfer Funds</b><br><br>
    <% If Request.Form("source") = "" Or Request.Form("target") = "" Then %>

    <!-- Present the transfer form -->
    <form action="<%=Request.ServerVariables("script_name")%>" method=post>
    Transfer from: <select name=source>
    <option value="">(Select)</option>
    <% AddAccountList %>
    </select><br>
    Transfer to: <select name=target>
    <option value="">(Select)</option>
    <% AddAccountList %>
    </select><br>
    Amount: <input type=text name="amount" value="0"><br>
    <input type=submit value="Transfer">
    <input type=hidden name="action" value="<%=Request("action")%>">
    </form>

    <% Else
    End If %>
```

```
    <% Case "view" %>
```

697

How It Works

We should now be able to access both our Saving and Checking account details, like this:

The way we determine whether to display the transfer form is by checking the form variables to see if both a source account and target account have been selected. If the user submits the form without having selecting one value from each of these lists, or if the user has just clicked on the **Transfer Funds** link, we simply display the fields. Likewise, if the user selects just one account, rather than two, we redisplay the form to ask them to try again.

The `select` tag instructs the browser to render a drop down list. We use the `AddAccountList` helper function to add the accounts to the list. The HTML that this function generates looks like this:

```
<option value=10001>Checking</option>
```

Notice how we're embedding the account ID directly into the `OPTION` tag itself. This means that when the user submits the form we simply check the `source` and `target` form variables to derive the exact IDs of the accounts we're interested in. We've also added a `TEXT` input field to capture the amount of the transfer.

The last line to draw attention to here is:

```
<input type=hidden name="action" value="<%=Request("action")%>">
```

This line puts the current `action` value back into the form variables. This means that when the user clicks the **Transfer** button, the `Select Case` statement at the top of the page properly routes the user back through to the transfer form.

The form should now look like this:

Of course, we haven't yet written any of the code to perform the actual transfer! Let's do this now.

Try It Out – Performing the Transfer

1. In the last section, we wrote code to check the values of the source and target form variables. Add the following code to the second half of the If statement that we wrote there:

```
<% Else
```

```
    ' We'll need these...
    Dim dblAmount

    ' Reset the problem string...
    strProblem = ""

    ' Did we specify two distinct accounts?
    If Request.Form("source") <> Request.Form("target") Then

        ' Try and convert the amount...
        dblAmount = 0
        On Error Resume Next
        dblAmount = CDbl(Request.Form("amount"))
        On Error Goto 0

        ' Did we get a proper amount?
    If dblAmount = 0 Then
        strProblem = "You must specify an amount to transfer."
    End If

    Else
        strProblem = "You must specify two separate accounts."
    End If
```

```
    ' Did we pass validation OK?
    If strProblem = "" Then

        ' Transfer the money...
        Dim objTransfer, intResult
        Set objTransfer = Server.CreateObject("Bank_Bus.Transfer")
        intResult = objTransfer.TransferFunds(Session("BankID"), _
        Request.Form("source"), Session("BankID"), _
        Request.Form("target"), dblAmount, 1, "WROBA Transfer")

        ' Render the results...
        Response.Write "<b>Result:</b> " & GetResultString(intResult)
        Response.Write "<br><br>"

        ' Render a button to go back...
        Response.Write "<a href="""
        Response.Write Request.ServerVariables("script_name")
        Response.Write """>Back</a>"

    Else
        Response.Write "<b>Funds could not be transferred...</b><br>"
        Response.Write strProblem
    End If
```

```
End If %>
```

2. We also need to add this helper function. This will send a human-readable string to users to tell them what happened when the transfer was attempted. Add this code to the bottom of default.asp, just above the AddAccountList function:

```
Function GetResultString(intResult)
    Select Case intResult
    Case 0
        GetResultString = "Success"
    Case 1
        GetResultString = "Transfer failed: Daily limit exceeded"
    Case 2
        GetResultString = "Transfer failed: Not enough funds"
    Case Else
        GetResultString = "Transfer failed: Unknown Error (" & intResult & ")"
    End Select
End Function
```

```
Sub AddAccountList
```

How It Works

Once we have determined that a request to transfer funds has been received, we need to validate the request. Our first validation job is to make sure two discrete accounts were specified:

```
If Request.Form("source") <> Request.Form("target") Then
    ...
Else
    strProblem = "You must specify two separate accounts."
End If
```

In the development of the desktop version, the check is not an issue as the UI contains logic to swap out this potentially invalid selection. In Web development, if we want to maximize our audience reach, we do not have this luxury, so we perform a check here.

The second check we do is to make sure the value we have is valid. We do this by using the VBScript `CDbl` function. This function will produce an error if anything is wrong, so we use VBScript's fairly basic error handling to skip over an error if one occurs:

```
' Try and convert the amount...
dblAmount = 0
On Error Resume Next
dblAmount = CDbl(Request.Form("amount"))
On Error Goto 0

' Did we get a proper amount?
If dblAmount = 0 Then
  strProblem = "You must specify an amount to transfer."
End If
```

If no value was specified, 0 was explicitly specified, or a value that could not be converted into a double was specified, we throw an error specifying that a specific amount must be specified.

Providing we've passed all of this validation, it's time to create an instance of the `Bank_Bus.Transfer` object and ask it to perform the actual transfer:

```
' Transfer the money...
Dim objTransfer, intResult
Set objTransfer = Server.CreateObject("Bank_Bus.Transfer")
intResult = objTransfer.TransferFunds(Session("BankID"), _
    Request.Form("source"), Session("BankID"), _
    Request.Form("target"), dblAmount, 1, "WROBA Transfer")
```

Thanks to our distributed design, that's all we have to do to perform the transfer! It's virtually the same call as made by the desktop application.

The last stage in the transfer is to capture and interpret the return value from the `TransferFunds` call. This is what the `GetResultString` method is for:

```
Response.Write "<b>Result:</b> " & GetResultString(intResult)
Response.Write "<br><br>"
```

This should bring up a page that indicates that funds have been transferred successfully:

Other Functionality

At this point, we should have a clear idea of how to go about building this alternative presentation layer for our application. Completing the duplication of the entire application presentation layer requires more of the same, so we won't be drilling into each of the additional functions here. It should be a reasonably straightforward exercise to put the rest together yourself.

Here's a list of the functionality that we haven't yet included:

- ❑ Change password
- ❑ Add and edit payees
- ❑ Pay bills

We haven't touched at all on how to develop the administrative side of the application, so here's a list of the work that has to be done there:

- ❑ Add and delete cards
- ❑ Lock and unlock cards
- ❑ Add and edit banks

Summary

In this chapter, we've had two main teaching aims. Firstly, we wished to show how effective 3-teir (or n-teir) tier design and coding can be beneficial when developing and adapting an application for use in different areas. Within the scope of this book the choice was made to show how a new user services or presentation tier could be grafted onto the application – in this case, to make the application accessible to those using the Web. Secondly, we wanted to introduce the topic of Web programming and development. Web programming is an exploding field of computing and every programmer will come into contact with aspects of it sooner or later. In this chapter, we hope we've shown how interesting the subject is, and, equally importantly, how easy it is to get going in Web development if you've got a bit of Visual Basic knowledge.

Within the chapter, we've had a lightening introduction to the world of Web development. We've considered the type of languages and programming approaches that would enable us to present dynamic content to the Web user. During this discussion, we introduced both Hypertext Markup Language (HTML) and Active Server Pages (ASP). In the discussion of ASP we saw how VBScript could be used as the scripting language within the ASP tags and thus how easily accessible this technology is to Visual Basic programmers.

Once we'd got a bit of technology under our belts we moved onto Web-enabling the WROBA application (or rather a substantial part of the customer services side of the application). At this point, the benefit of the 3-tier architecture we adopted for the application became obvious as we reproduced the functionality of the desktop version by merely coding a new user services, or presentation, tier that leveraged the existing business and data services tiers. Thus, the effort in developing the upgraded application was kept to a minimum – an achievement that is beneficial to the client and the programmer. We finished the chapter off by pointing out what other tasks were remaining in order to fully Web-enable the WROBA application.

In the next chapter, we're really going to bring in the cutting edge of application development by introducing **eXtensible Markup Language**. This technology is going to become very important in the field of distributed and Web-enabled applications, and as an application developer, it's a language you're going to want to know about.

Inter-Application Communication Using XML

At some point during the lifetime of a successful application, there is a chance it will have to be enabled for data exchange between itself and another application. We might have written the perfect banking application, capable of managing *every* function needed by the bank we've been commissioned by, only to find that our bank merges with another company, who are also happy with *their* system. Our application will need to be able to communicate with the other system. Also, the banking world being what it is, the two banks might well join one of the large banking networks, and you'll have to enable more information communication between the two smaller applications and the central applications for the banking network. During the course of a successful application's lifetime, it is more than likely that data will have to be exchanged between it and another application, which could feasibly be in another location as well.

The topic of inter-application communication is the basis of our second chapter concerned with enhancing and expanding the capabilities of the WROBA application beyond the original specification. In fact, there are two key ideas that arise when data must be shared between two applications – the format of the message, and the transport mechanism moving the information. In this chapter we introduce the topic of **XML (eXtensible Markup Language)** to address the first of these issues. A discussion of transport mechanisms lies outside the scope of this book.

As befits the last chapter in the book, we're now moving on to a fairly advanced topic; one that is at the cutting edge of application development. In this chapter we're going to introduce the topic of XML and show why and how it could be used in relation to the WROBA application. The subject of XML is rapidly expanding, and in this chapter we are going to confine our treatment of the subject quite rigidly to its potential utility in the context of our enterprise application.

In this chapter we're going to look at:

- ❑   What is XML
- ❑   XML structure
- ❑   Using XML in Visual Basic Applications
- ❑   Using XML with the WROBA application
- ❑   Some further considerations related to this topic

Incidentally, don't think XML is a bit too esoteric for you to worry about at the moment – Microsoft is beginning to use XML wherever possible; SQL Server 2000 will support XML and Windows DNA 2000 is going to make heavy use of XML. This technology is going to be huge in the next decade!

If you wish to expand your knowledge of XML, an appropriate place to go to next is *Beginning XML*, *ISBN 1-861003-41-2*, also from *Wrox Press*. Let's start by examining just what we mean when we refer to XML.

What is XML?

XML (eXtensible Markup Language) is, as implied by its name, a markup language that looks similar to HTML. Markup languages use **tags**, or markers, to denote the beginning and end of sections in a block of text. However, what XML and HTML do with these tags is very different. With HTML, for example, there may be tags to mark the beginning and end of a section of text that should be italicized; in XML these markers would be used to denote, or describe, a piece of data – for example, a part number.

For example, and HTML file may contain the following:

```
<H1>Screwdriver types</H1>
<UL>
    <LI>Flathead
    <LI>Phillips
    <LI>Robertson
    <LI>Torx
</UL>
```

This would appear in a web browser like this:

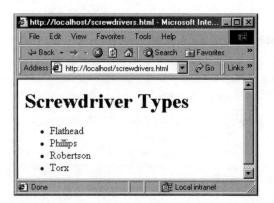

However, this does not tell us anything about the *data* contained in those lines, just how it should be presented in a browser. Due to the proximity of the list items and the title, a relationship can be inferred. But this does highlight an issue about HTML – HTML describes the formatting of the message, but doesn't say anything about the data in the message.

The same message formatted with XML might look like:

```
<Tool type="manual">Screwdriver Types
  <subtypes>
    <subtype description="flat" partNum="234">Flathead</subtype>
    <subtype description="cross" partNum="4562">Phillips</subtype>
    <subtype description="square" partNum="3245">Robertson</subtype>
    <subtype description="star" partNum="2123">Torx</subtype>
  </subtypes>
</Tool>
```

Just as with HTML, XML uses tags to mark information. However, in XML the tags identify the data. This could be made to look the same as the HTML version (using a technology known as Cascading Style Sheets, which we won't be discussing here). The crucial thing about the example is that the tags in the XML are not some type of standard; they are user defined (hence the use of the word eXtensible in the name XML).

> **XML looks very similar to HTML but has a vital difference: the developer defines their own set of tags.**

While XML and HTML look similar, in that both use the now familiar `<tag>value</tag>` syntax, there are some notable differences.

The most important difference between XML and HTML is the thing they are formatting. HTML was designed to format pages of information; XML, on the other hand, was designed to describe data.

The difference seems subtle, but is easily demonstrated.

Applying XML

Let's consider an Internet search. When searching for a word or phrase, a search engine doesn't know what is meant – more specifically, it doesn't know the context of the search term. For example, if we went to a search engine and searched for "Darwin", our results would very probably include references to Charles Darwin and Darwin, Australia, as well as personal home pages for people with either a first, or last, name of Darwin, and other Darwin related pages.

There is no way for us to tell the search engine which of those we want before the search is done by just using the term "Darwin" (of course, we could put more detail into our search term, but that would wreck the example!). This is because the only way that the city Darwin can be isolated from the scientist Darwin is by context. If the Internet used XML instead, the context could be identified. For example, a page on the city Darwin might have the following excerpt:

```
<country>Australia
   <city>Darwin</city>
</country>
```

While one on the scientist could be identified with the following excerpt:

```
<firstname>Charles</firstname>
<lastname>Darwin</lastname>
```

Search engines could then allow us to define whether we are looking for a city or a first name/last name. Of course, this person may not be the scientist Charles Darwin, but another man with the same name. So, an even better way of pinpointing the scientist Charles Darwin is with the following excerpt:

```
<firstname>Charles</firstname>
<lastname>Darwin</lastname>
<occupation>Scientist</occupation>
```

Again, this would bring us closer, but it still may not be the actual person we want. Adding more detail and more tags can allow us to pinpoint more closely the thing we are looking for. Of course, for this to work perfectly, everybody would have to use the same tags.

Another major difference between XML and HTML is that XML is much more rigorous. That is, it has more rules that define legitimate XML documents.

These rules include:

Rule	Description
Case-sensitivity	Tags in XML are case-sensitive; firstname is considered to be a different tag from FirstName and firstName.
Quoted attributes	If a tag has an attribute (see Elements and Attributes, below), the attribute's value must be surrounded by quotes. For example, <Name first="Charles" last="Darwin"></Name>.
No standalone tags	HTML has a number of standalone tags (i.e. those that don't have a closing tag), such as <P>, or <HR>. These are not allowed in XML. Instead, these must be used in combination with a closing tag (for example </P>), or using the equivalent XML standalone tag, which includes a closing forward slash character, such as .
Errors	If an error is encountered in an HTML document, it will just be ignored. However, if an error is encountered in an XML document, it is a problem, and, as a result, the XML document may not execute correctly.

As we've already seen, unlike HTML, XML does not have a defined set of available tags. Instead, as it is used to define data, each type of document defines the appropriate tags. Any two programs that know how to create and read these tags can then use the documents to communicate. The list of available tags may be defined:

❑ Informally – two programs share the list of tags, but don't require that they all be present without any additional tags.

❑ Formally – the available tags are defined, and documents must restrict themselves to tags on the list.

> **Remember, the set of tags used in an XML document is user defined.**

So, what is XML?

> *XML is a language that allows for the creation of tags, or markers, that may be applied to data to further define the context of the data. It is open, and extensible, in that it does not limit the user to a pre-defined set of tags, but still remains strict in the way those tags may be used. These sets of tags define a language.*

XML Structure

XML is composed primarily of tags. However, there are other items that can make up XML documents. These items include, among others, **attributes**, **processing instructions**, and **comments**. Note that the term 'XML documents' is used throughout this chapter to refer to actual files, as well as blocks of information in memory that will be passed between applications.

For the purpose of discussion, let's look at a simple XML document and examine its component parts:

```xml
<?xml version="1.0"?>
<!DOCTYPE order SYSTEM "order.dtd">
<order>
    <completed />
    <employee>Mary Jones</employee>
    <client>Stuff R Us</client>
    <trackingnumber>12345<trackingnumber>
    <salesdetails>1
       <salesdetail>
        <item>098</item>
        <value>50</value>
        <quantity>5</quantity>
      <salesdetail/>
    </salesdetails>
    <salespayments>1
       <salespayment>250</salespayment>
    </salespayments>
</order>
```

As described above (and as we can see from the example) XML looks very much like HTML. One can easily scan the document, finding tags that define data such as an order, sales details, and payments.

Our discussion of XML structure can be divided into two main areas:

❑   Elements and Attributes

❑   Document Type Definition (DTD) and Schemas

Elements and Attributes

The vast majority of XML is composed of **elements** and **attributes**.

Elements

Elements are the main components used in a document. Typically, they are used to describe the objects in the document. In the sample listing, `<order>`, `<salesdetails>`, `<salesdetail>`, `<salespayments>`, and `<salespayment>` (with the associated text and closing tags) are all elements. They often represent the same types of structures that become objects in a Visual Basic application.

The names given to the elements in a document are used to identify these objects later. There must be one, *and only one*, element that contains all the other elements in an XML document. This is similar to the `<HTML>` element in a web page. This element is termed the **root element**. In the above document, the root element is `<order>`. All the other elements are termed **children** of the root element. They in turn may have child elements of their own. Elements that follow this rule, and the following rules, are termed **well-formed** documents.

> **Elements are the most important part of an XML document. They define the main objects described in an XML document.**

One important point to notice about the sample document is that there is no overlap between the end of one element and the beginning of another. This is an area of XML that is more specific than HTML. For example, this fragment contains overlapping elements, and is therefore *not* well-formed XML:

```
<order>
<salesdetails>
</order>
</salesdetails>
```

As the `order` element is closed before the `salesdetails` element, this is not proper XML. A subtler example using legitimate (albeit sloppy) HTML code is:

```
<strong><i>some text that appears bold and italic</strong></i>
```

If the above content were included in an XML document, it would not be properly formed.

As we saw previously, each element must be closed. Usually, this means that there must be a closing tag for each element. The closing tag for an element uses the same name as the start tag, but begins with a slash – in our example consider the `<salesdetails>` `</salesdetails>` pairing.

There are times when there is no need to add a closing tag; for example, when the tag does not contain any information, as in the `<completed/>` element. When this occurs, the element is usually described as being **standalone**, or **empty**, and it *must* end with the characters `/>`.

Finally, an element may contain text. This text appears between the start tag and the closing tag, and is often considered the *value* for that element. In the sample code, an example of this is:

```
<salesdetail>250<salesdetail>
```

Another, more common, example can be seen in the following XML, where the text in the `FirstName` and `LastName` elements is the text for the element:

```
<employee id="12345">
   <FirstName>John</FirstName>
   <LastName>Bull</FirstName>
</employee>
```

Attributes

Attributes typically define the *properties* of an element, that is, they typically modify the element somehow. They exist within the start tag of an element, and consist of name-value pairs. These name-value pairs have the syntax:

```
name="value"
```

All values must appear in quotes. In addition, like element names, attribute names are case-sensitive. Consider the following sample document:

```
<? xml version="1.0" ?>
<employees>
   <employee id="smithj" hireDate="4/1/80">
      <firstName>John</firstName>
      <lastName>Smith</lastName>
      <salary currencyID="CA">20000</salary>
   <employee>
</employees>
```

In it there are a variety of attributes, including `id`, `hireDate`, and `currencyID`.

We should draw attention to differences in opinion among developers at this point. In one camp are the developers who feel strongly that an XML document should be composed of *only* elements. Then there are those who feel that any non-object property should be defined using attributes, and that elements should be reserved for objects. For example, in the above XML document, `firstName` and `lastName` could be considered non-object properties. This is because they do not have any child properties themselves. However, `salary` and `employee` would be considered object properties, as they do have their own children.

Still others believe in a hybrid approach, where most items are defined using elements (for example, unique keys, or Boolean values), with only a few items using attributes.

All three of these are legitimate approaches; your choice should depend on personal preference, partner needs (that is, if you are using an existing document format) or ease of preparation. However, it should be noted that something that you define as a property now might turn out to need children later. Therefore, when in doubt, use elements whenever possible.

DTD and Schemas

When using XML to communicate between applications, if the applications are both controlled by the same person, things are quite straightforward – that person can decide on the format of the information and ensure that the sending program doesn't send information to the receiving program that cannot be processed. However, we cannot make the same assumptions when communicating with an application written by someone else. As XML allows us to define our own tags, we need a way to share the format we have used to markup our data so that others can understand it too. For situations such as these a **Document Type Definition** (**DTD**) should be used.

DTD

A **Document Type Definition** (**DTD**) defines the expected structure of elements and attributes. In an application, a parser can then **validate** the document against the DTD, raising an error if it does not match the expected structure.

In our opening example the DTD is referred to in the second line:

```
<!DOCTYPE order SYSTEM "order.dtd">
```

> **DTDs are used to define a language for the message – they describe the format of the expected document.**

There are a wide number of existing languages that have been defined using DTDs. These languages include a wide variety of special purpose message formats for a variety of purposes. One such example is **MathML** (Mathematics Markup Language), which is used to describe mathematical notation.

> **Links to this standard, and many others, are available at the XML catalogue located at: http://www.xml.org.**

A DTD is written – and individual developers can write their own – in a syntax borrowed from another, older, markup language, **Standard Generalized Markup Language** – **SGML** – which was the forerunner of HTML and XML. This is stored either within the document or separately in an external file which has the extension .dtd.

The definition describes the elements and attributes that may be used in an XML file that supports that document type. For example, the following is a DTD that might be used in a human resources application to define an employee:

```
<!ELEMENT Employee ( FirstName?, LastName, Address?, Phone? )>
<!ELEMENT FirstName EMPTY>
<!ELEMENT FirstName EMPTY>
<!ELEMENT LastName EMPTY>
<!ELEMENT Address ( Street?, City? )>
<!ELEMENT Street EMPTY>
<!ELEMENT Street EMPTY>
<!ELEMENT City EMPTY>
<!ELEMENT Phone EMPTY>
```

If a document has been declared to use a specific DTD, only those elements defined in the DTD should be used in the document. If an XML document is well-formed (we'll see the criteria for this in a moment) *and* only uses elements defined in the DTD, it is said to be **valid**.

A complete DTD may be quite lengthy, as each type of element or attribute that may be used in the document must be defined, along with the rules on how often and where they may appear. The following is an example of an XML document that complies with the above DTD:

```
<? xml version="1.0" ?>
<!DOCTYPE Employee SYSTEM "employee.dtd">
<Employee>
  <FirstName>Bruce</FirstName>
  <LastName>Wayne</LastName>
  <Address>
    <Street>123 Any Drive</Street>
    <City>Gotham</City>
  </Address>
  <Phone>2125551212</Phone>
</Employee>
```

While DTDs were part of the original XML specification, a number of companies have complained about certain shortcomings:

❑   DTDs are not written in XML syntax

❑   There is no way to define the data types or other information about the elements and attributes using DTDs

One emerging standard, **XML Schemas**, serves to solve these problems.

Schemas

XML Schemas are an alternative means of defining a language in XML, similar to DTDs. However, XML Schemas are written in XML. This allows the use of other XML tools to create and process a schema. In addition, schemas allow for the definition of data types and sizes when defining a document type. The following is a simple XML Schema definition that is comparable to the DTD defined above:

```
<schema>

  <element name="Employee" type="EmployeeType">

  <complexType name="EmployeeType">
    <element name="FirstName" type="string">
    <element name="LastName" type="string" minOccurs="1">
    <element name="Address" type="AddressType">
    <element name="Phone" type="PhoneType">
  </complexType>

  <complexType name="AddressType">
    <element name="Street" type="string">
    <element name="City" type="string">
  </complexType>

  <simpleType name="PhoneType" base="string">
    <pattern value="/(d{3}) d{3}-d{4}"/>
  </simpleType>

</schema>
```

It should be noted that while the traditional plural of schema is schemata, the use of the more recent "schemas" has become standard in this area and therefore will be used here.

XML Structure – Summary

To summarize, the base rules that define a good XML document include:

❑ All named items, such as `order`, `clientid`, etc. are **case-sensitive**. This includes elements, attributes, document type, and so on. For example, `clientid` would be considered different to `ClientID` and `clientID`. This is often one of the first *harsh lessons* learned when switching to XML.

❑ All elements must either have a closing tag, or use the standalone tag format (`<tag/>`).

❑ There must be a single root element in a document.

❑ All other elements must be nested correctly inside the root element.

❑ There should be no overlapped elements in the document.

❑ All attributes must have the value in quotes. In the sample document, this includes `clientid="smithj"` and `filenumber="0001"`, among others.

❑ Any given attribute may only appear once for any given element.

If a document supports all the above rules, it is defined as **well-formed**. If it also complies with the supplied DTD or schema, it is termed **valid**. Validating XML parsers will perform this check when loading the document.

Using XML in Visual Basic Applications

Now that we've looked at what XML looks like, there still remains one major question before we can examine, in detail, how to use XML in Visual Basic applications. That question is: "Why should we use XML in our Visual Basic applications?"

There are a number of different possibilities for the format we could use for our message, apart from XML – alternatives being formats like comma-delimited text files and binary formats such as objects. However, XML does have some significant factors in its favor:

❑ **XML is supported by all platforms** – XML parsers are available for just about every operating system and hardware platform. They can be used from almost every programming language, including Visual Basic, Java, C/C++, Python, and Perl. Binary formats, such as objects, restrict the developer to a single development language and often a single operating system.

❑ **XML is plain text** – This is actually both a benefit and weakness of XML. The benefit is that you, I, or a computer can look at it and make sense of it, but the flip side of this is that anyone can have a go and edit your XML, thereby bypassing any security and auditing procedures. All text message formats (XML, comma-delimited, and fixed-width column) share these strengths and weaknesses. In addition, text-based formats, like XML, are larger than binary formats (although it is possible to encrypt or compress them, but we won't deal with these topics in this chapter).

❑ **XML is self-describing** – This seems related to the above, but it goes further than XML just being in plain text. As each element or attribute is named, one can easily understand the importance of values in an XML file. In contrast, understanding the significance of a column in a comma-delimited file that contains the number 52 is difficult, while the significance in an XML file of <unitprice>52</unitprice> is more obvious.

❑ **Tools are widely available** – Microsoft ships an XML parser with Internet Explorer 5.x. In addition, the same parser is available for free download for those who do not use that browser. Other platforms and environments also include, or make available, free or inexpensive parsers. This means that it is possible to select the "best of breed" solution. Other message formats, especially the binary formats, do not support such a broad range of tools. Only the other text formats support as many tools for processing.

❑ **Adding XML support to a Visual Basic application is easy** – While this may seem to be a frivolous reason to use XML, it isn't. If adding XML support to an application were difficult, there would be far less justification to use it. Due to its simplicity, it is relatively easy to add XML support to an application, without requiring a great deal of extra programming effort, or dramatically changing the application. Again, the other text formats share this feature, as do ADO recordsets and PropertyBags.

Of the choices, therefore, it seems that only XML supports all the positive features of the message formats. It provides an easy, extensible, and rich format to communicate within, or between, applications.

Before we go on to discuss the **Document Object Model** (**DOM**), let's quickly see how XML fits into the 3-tier architecture we've been working with throughout the book.

XML and 3-Tier Architectures

While XML is a very powerful and rich tool for any application development, it is much more potent in multi-tier applications.

There are two broad ways that XML can fit into n-tier architectures:

❑ **Between tiers** – XML can be used as the data format of the messages passed between the tiers of an application. In this function, XML provides a simple, more or less lightweight, message.

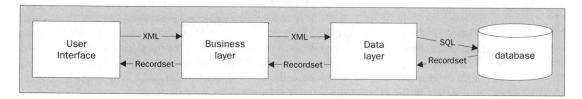

❑ **Between applications** – XML can, as explained already, be used as a message format between applications, especially if those applications reside on other platforms or are written in other programming languages.

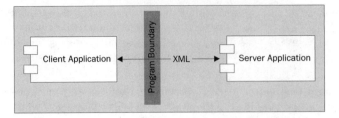

XML can easily fit into any Visual Basic development, whether it is used only as an inter-application communication format, or for both inter- and intra-application communication.

Using XML to communicate between applications has tradeoffs, as does any architecture decision. Whether the benefits of using XML as a communication medium are worth the shortcomings is a decision that must be made on an application-by-application basis, based on the needs of the application.

In general, however, the risks are greatly outweighed by the benefits when communicating with systems written on differing platforms, or where a common communication channel (such as DCOM – see our brief discussion in Chapter 4) is not available. It also provides a number of benefits, even when all the applications involved are written in Visual Basic.

Inter-application use of XML does increase complexity, as now the two applications must create and parse XML to communicate. This adds additional code, and the possibility of errors being introduced into the application. In addition, it slightly reduces the overall performance of the application, as messages must usually be converted to and from XML.

However, the actual complexity and performance costs of using XML are actually quite small. The complexity can be managed, either through the use of standard routines to perform common tasks, or through the creation of helper components that perform common tasks.

Other benefits of using XML include:

❑   **Platform/language independence** – As XML is simple text, it can be passed to other languages for processing. There is no possibility of losing part of the message due to one application not being able to understand the message (for example, some languages may impose a restriction on the size of numeric data types).

❑   **Less coupling** – Coupling describes the *tightness* of the association between two applications or components. It is generally considered bad; it implies that changes to one component's methods or parameters require changes to any client applications (usually requiring a re-install). By using XML as the message format, it is possible to *extend* the message without having to replace all the client applications. Existing applications will use the data from the XML document that they expect without causing errors, while newer applications will understand and use all the data. However, if the message is *altered*, that is, some of the elements and/or attributes are changed, this could prevent the client application from reading the message.

Now we've looked at the structure of XML, and how and where it can be used in our applications, let's now look at how we can handle it programmatically.

The Document Object Model

To prevent an explosion of strategies for working with XML documents, the W3C (World Wide Web Consortium – the body responsible for overseeing standards for Internet technologies) has released a recommendation for a standard **Document Object Model** (**DOM**) that describes the programmatic interface for an XML document. That is, the standard defines how an application is to navigate and manipulate the content of the document. More correctly, the standard DOM defines the interfaces that should be used to work with the document. Software developers are then responsible for creating implementations of these interfaces to be used by various programming languages.

Although outside the scope of this book, it should be noted that, while there are Document Object Models for both XML and HTML, the two are different. The DOM for HTML defines the structure of HTML documents, including some of the key elements that make up web pages, such as images, forms, tables, headings, and so on. The DOM for XML defines the abstract structure of XML documents and it is this one we'll be looking at now.

At the basis of the DOM are the objects that map to the important sections of an XML document. This is a topic that we don't want to go into in too much detail, just enough to allow you to have an appreciation of the code we present later in the chapter.

The structure of the DOM is based on the idea of a tree of **nodes** for a small XML document. The structure of the full DOM may have unlimited levels.

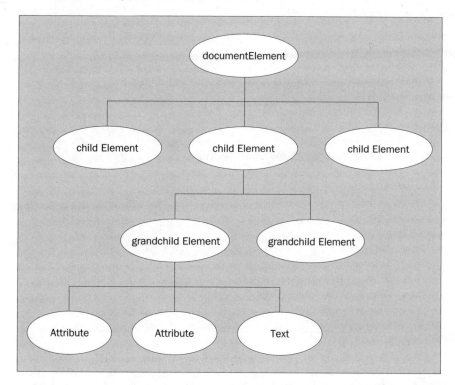

Each node in the tree represents an Element, Attribute, or other part of an XML document. XML also includes `NodeList` and `NamedNodeMap` collections. These are used to represent collections of `Node` objects, similar to the `Collection` object in Visual Basic. However, each has a specific purpose.

The `NodeList` object is an ordered collection; we retrieve `Node` objects from the collection by a numeric index. The `NamedNodeMap`, in contrast, returns the `Node` objects by name. The DOM outlines how these collections are returned to the user. The DOM also defines the functionality required to create, update, and delete `Node` objects. Finally, the DOM outlines a standard set of error messages that an implementation should return when processing errors occur.

Microsoft has announced full support for the W3C XML standards (and the development of IE5 follows the W3C DOM recommendation). However, to extend the functionality for the DOM, the Microsoft implementation of this standard – the MSXML component – has additional objects, methods, and properties. Since we are just presenting an introduction to this technology, and as this book deals primarily with development in a Microsoft environment, we are going to ignore this complexity and just look at the DOM in terms of the MSXML component.

The MSXML Component

Microsoft has distributed an XML parser since version 4.0 of Internet Explorer, but that version was not compliant with the DOM. However, with the release of Internet Explorer 5.0, a newer, DOM-compliant version was released. This version was also made available for free download from `http://msdn.microsoft.com/xml`.

When using MSXML in VB applications, the first task is to add MS XML Version 2.0 to the project references, by selecting the Microsoft XML, version 2.0 component from the References dialog:

As you can see from the above figure, there are other versions of XML available (version 3.0 was made available just as this chapter was being written). Throughout this chapter, whenever we suggest loading version 2.0 of MSXML, in fact, any version after version 2.0 could be loaded. The newer versions of the library are backwards compatible with version 2.0.

As shown in the accompanying figure of the MSXML type library in the Object Browser, the MSXML library contains a large number of classes. However, many of these are interfaces that represent the various types of nodes in an XML document. Each of these inherits a number of features from the IXMLDOMNode class.

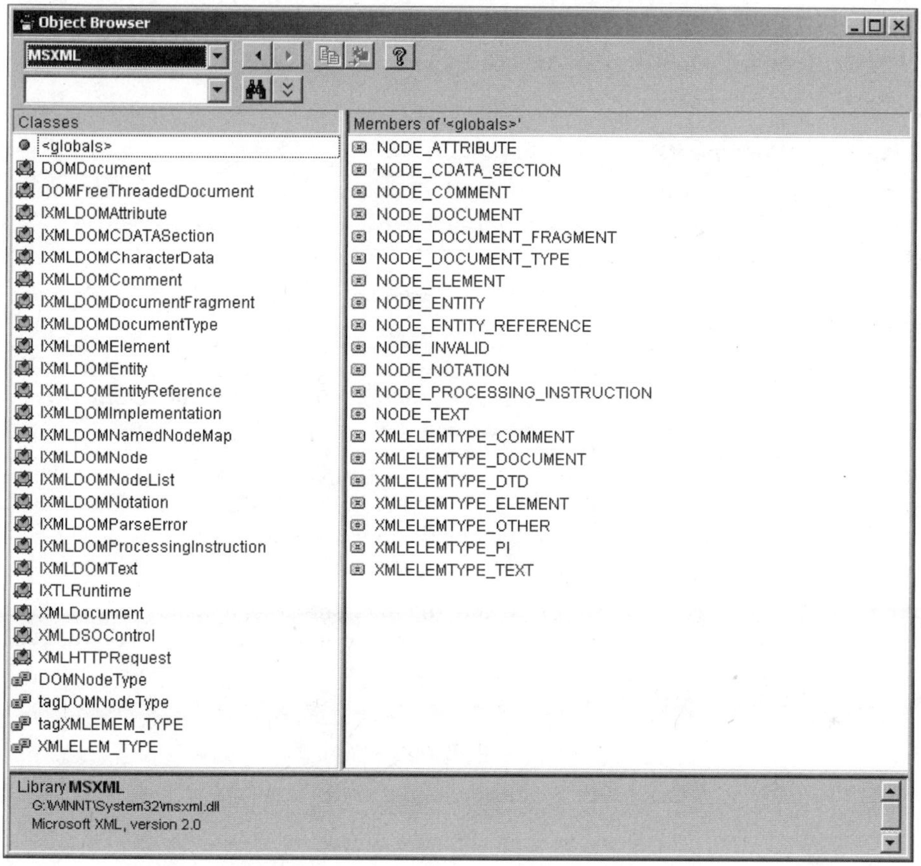

In addition, the MSXML component contains classes that provide backwards compatibility with the pre-DOM version that came with Internet Explorer 4.0 (the XMLDocument class).

OK, let's examine the MSXML component in more detail and highlight some aspects of the object model that we'll come across when we begin coding.

Objects, Methods, and Properties in the MSXML Component

The aspects of the object model listed in this section are highly selective and are only aimed at giving the background required for the code we build later.

In fact, we are concentrating on two particular areas:

❑ The routines that allow a developer to read and query the contents of an XML document. The document may either be an actual file, or a string containing XML. Once loaded, the DOM automatically parses the XML into the tree of nodes, through which the developer can navigate, using the methods of the individual nodes.

❑ The methods that allow the developer to quickly and easily create the Node objects and add them into the document.

Document (IXMLDOMDocument)

The Document object is the root object for an XML document. It contains all the methods and properties related to creating nodes and is responsible for loading the XML document and containing all the other objects.

Method/Property	Comments
appendChild	Adds a node to document. When creating a document from scratch, this node becomes the root node for the document; otherwise it adds a child node to the current one.
async	Boolean flag that identifies whether the DOMDocument will load all the contents of the document before continuing (False), or if the program will continue while the document continues loading (True – the default). Generally, set this to False to make coding simpler.
createNode	Allows for the creation of any node type, including Elements and Attributes. Returns a generic Node object. However, if the type of node being created is known, use one of the specific methods (such as createElement, or createAttribute) instead.
createElement	Creates a new element-type node.
createAttribute	Creates a new attribute-type node.
load	Loads the contents of a file containing XML into the DOM.
loadXML	Loads the contents of a string containing XML into the DOM.
parsed	Boolean flag that identifies if the entire document was parsed correctly.
parseError	Contains information about the section causing any parsing errors if the document could not be parsed completely.
xml	Returns the contents of the document, formatted as XML.

Node (IXMLDOMNode)

The generic interface supported by all node types. It contains methods and properties related to handling the contents of the node.

Method/Property	Comments
appendChild	Adds a child node to the current node.
attributes	Collection of the attributes of this node (see IXMLDOMNamedNodeMap).
baseName	The name of the node (excluding any Namespace information provided).
childNodes	Collection of the child nodes of this node (see IXMLDOMNodeList).
hasChildNodes	Boolean flag that identifies if this node has any children.
text	Assigns a value to the node.
nodeName	The name of the node (including any Namespace information if provided).
nodeType	An enumeration that defines the type of the node (such as Element, Attribute, etc.).
nodeValue	The value of the node.
xml	Returns the contents of this node (including children) formatted as XML.

Element (IXMLDOMElement)

This interface represents an element-type node. It contains all the methods of IXMLDOMNode as well as some element-specific ones. Here we're just concerned with one method.

Method/Property	Comments
setAttribute	Creates a new Attribute for this element, assigning it the appropriate value.

Attribute (IXMLDOMAttribute)

This interface represents an attribute-type node. Contains all the methods of IXMLDOMNode as well as some attribute-specific ones.

NodeList (IXMLDOMNodeList)

This is a collection of nodes that are indexed by position. In addition to the methods below, this collection supports For Each.

Method/Property	Comments
length	The number of nodes in the node list.
item	Default property – used to retrieve nodes from the node list.
nextNode	Returns the next node in the list.
reset	Resets the position for nextNode back to the first node in the list.

NamedNodeMap (IXMLDOMNamedNodeMap)

A collection of nodes that are indexed by name. In addition to the methods below, this collection supports For Each.

Method/Property	Comments
length	The number of nodes in the collection.
item	Default property – used to retrieve nodes from the collection.
nextNode	Returns the next node in the list.
reset	Resets the position for nextNode back to the first node in the list.
getNamedItem	Returns an item from the collection by name.

Now we're through with the reference material let's see how to use XML in a practical context.

Using XML with the WROBA Application

There are two main situations where our WROBA case study could potentially use XML:

- ❑ To communicate with other applications. This may be to request additional information; for example, it may need to request information on a client's bank account at another bank. This is the case when we use ATMs of banks other than our own. Alternately, the application may provide an XML response at the request of another application.

- ❑ As a format for communication between the layers, instead of ADO recordsets. This would allow the application to communicate with systems that are not able to read ADO recordsets: for example, a Unix system.

In this section we're going to address the first of these situations and build an application (the Network Application) that will communicate with the WROBA application (more specifically, with the business layer of the application) using XML. It will represent an application that might run as part of a central multi-bank network. This application will allow for the querying of account balances, and for the transfer of money between accounts.

The Network Application

The Network Application will be composed of three parts, as shown in this screen shot of the application group:

We can summarise the components of the application as follows:

- ❑ Bank_XML – An XML translation component that communicates with the bank business layer. This component will receive queries from the network application, and submit them to the business layer for processing.

- ❑ Network_Bus – The business layer for the application. This component composes XML requests, and translates the response into a format to be used by the user interface.

- ❑ Network_UI – The user interface allows the user to query an associated bank for a client's accounts, and to transfer money between two accounts.

Try It Out – Creating Bank_XML

1. Create an ActiveX DLL project and name it Bank_XML.

2. Add references to the Bank_Bus component of the WROBA application, Microsoft XML, version 2.0 (or later), and Microsoft ActiveX Data Objects, 2.1 (or later) type libraries.

3. Add a Standard module to the project. Rename the module modXMLHelper. This module will contain routines that will be used to make handling XML easier.

4. Add a routine that will be used to add new Elements to the DOM:

```
Public Function AddElement(ByVal DOM As MSXML.DOMDocument, _
     ByVal ElementName As String, _
     Optional ByVal ElementValue As String, _
     Optional ByVal Parent As MSXML.IXMLDOMElement) _
     As MSXML.IXMLDOMElement

  Dim oNode As MSXML.IXMLDOMElement

  Set oNode = DOM.createElement(ElementName)
  If Len(ElementValue) > 0 Then
     oNode.Text = ElementValue
  End If

  If Not Parent Is Nothing Then
     Call Parent.appendChild(oNode)
  Else
     Call DOM.appendChild(oNode)
  End If

  Set AddElement = oNode

End Function
```

5. Add a routine to the module that will be used to add new Attributes to the DOM:

```
Public Sub AddAttribute(ByVal AttributeName As String, _
                        ByVal AttributeValue As String, _
                        ByVal Parent As MSXML.IXMLDOMElement)
    Call Parent.setAttribute(AttributeName, AttributeValue)
End Sub
```

6. Rename the `Class1` class module to `Accounts`.

7. Create a routine, in the class module, that uses the above two functions to use the DOM to create the XML, returning the XML as a string:

```
Private Function SaveAccountsXML(ByVal BankID As Long, _
        ByVal ClientID As Long, ByVal Data As ADODB.Recordset) As String
    Dim oDOM As MSXML.DOMDocument
    Dim oNode As MSXML.IXMLDOMElement
    Dim oChild As MSXML.IXMLDOMElement
    Dim oField As ADODB.Field

    'Saves a list of accounts for a given user in the form:

    On Error GoTo ERR_SaveAccountsXML

    Set oDOM = New MSXML.DOMDocument

    'create the root (bank) node
    Set oNode = AddElement(oDOM, "bank")

    'add the ID attribute
    Call AddAttribute("id", BankID, oNode)

    'add the client node
    Set oNode = AddElement(oDOM, "client", , oNode)

    'and its ID attribute
    Call AddAttribute("id", ClientID, oNode)

    'we'll create an 'accounts' element to contain all the account entries
    Set oNode = AddElement(oDOM, "accounts", , oNode)

    'and now for the recordset
    With Data
        .MoveFirst

        Do Until .EOF
            Set oChild = AddElement(oDOM, "account", , oNode)

            For Each oField In .Fields
                Call AddAttribute(oField.Name, oField.Value, oChild)
            Next
```

```
            .MoveNext
        Loop

    End With

    SaveAccountsXML = oDOM.xml

EXIT_SaveAccountsXML:
Exit Function

ERR_SaveAccountsXML:
    Select Case Err.Number
        Case Else
            MsgBox "Error saving XML: " & vbCrLf & Err.Description, _
                vbExclamation & "Error: " & Err.Number
            Resume ERR_SaveAccountsXML
    End Select
    Resume 0
End Function
```

8. Add a routine to get the list of accounts for a client. The routine should take an XML string representing a query of the form:

```
<request type="GetAccounts"><bankid>1</bankid><clientid>10001</clientid></request>
```

The routine should return a string (the XML response). Add the following code to the Accounts class:

```
Public Function GetAccounts(ByVal Query As String) As String
    Dim oRS As ADODB.Recordset
    Dim oDOM As MSXML.DOMDocument
    Dim oBank As Bank_Bus.Bank
    Dim lBankID As Long
    Dim lClientID As Long
    Dim sXML As String

    On Error GoTo ERR_GetAccounts

    'need to retrieve the information from the Query
    Set oDOM = New MSXML.DOMDocument
    With oDOM
        .async = False
        Call .loadXML(Query)
        If .parsed Then
            'double check the type of query
            If .documentElement.getAttribute("type") = "GetAccounts" Then
                lBankID = CLng(.getElementsByTagName("bankid").Item(0).Text)
                lClientID = CLng(.getElementsByTagName("clientid").Item(0).Text)
            End If
        End If
```

```
      End With

      'access the bank
      Set oBank = New Bank_Bus.Bank
      Set oRS = oBank.GetAccounts(lBankID, lClientID)

      If Not oRS Is Nothing Then
         'convert it to XML
         sXML = SaveAccountsXML(lBankID, lClientID, oRS)
         GetAccounts = sXML

      Else
         MsgBox "Could not get the accounts", vbInformation, _
                  "Account not available"
      End If

EXIT_GetAccounts:
Exit Function

ERR_GetAccounts:
   Select Case Err.Number
      Case Else
         MsgBox "Error retrieving account list: " _
            & vbCrLf & Err.Description, vbExclamation, "Error: " _
            & Err.Number
         Resume EXIT_GetAccounts
   End Select

   Resume 0

End Function
```

9. Add a second routine that will transfer funds between two accounts. The format of the query for this will be:

```
<request type="TransferFunds">
   <from>
      <bank>1</bank>
      <account>20001</account>
   </from>
   <to>
      <bank>1</bank>
      <account>20002</account>
   </to>
   <quantity>500</quantity>
</request>
```

The routine should return a string representing the results of the transfer. That is, one of the Transaction Status messages (**Success, Not Enough Funds, Daily Limit Exceeded, Unknown Error**). Add the following code to the Accounts class:

```
Public Function TransferFunds(ByVal Query As String) As String

    Dim oDOM As MSXML.DOMDocument
    Dim sReturn As String
    Dim oBank As Bank_Bus.Transfer
    Dim eReturn As Bank_Bus.ETransactionStatus

    Dim lFromBank As Long
    Dim lFromAccount As Long
    Dim lToBank As Long
    Dim lToAccount As Long
    Dim cQuantity As Currency

    On Error GoTo ERR_TransferFunds
    'need to retrieve the information from the Query
    Set oDOM = New MSXML.DOMDocument
    With oDOM
        .async = False
        Call .loadXML(Query)
        If .parsed Then
          'double check the type of query
          If .documentElement.getAttribute("type") = "TransferFunds" Then
              lFromBank = CLng(.getElementsByTagName("bank").Item(0).Text)
              lFromAccount = _
                  CLng(.getElementsByTagName("account").Item(0).Text)

              lToBank = CLng(.getElementsByTagName("bank").Item(1).Text)
              lToAccount = CLng(.getElementsByTagName("account").Item(1).Text)

              cQuantity = CCur(.getElementsByTagName("quantity").Item(0).Text)
          End If
        End If

    End With

    'access the bank
    Set oBank = New Bank_Bus.Transfer
    eReturn = oBank.TransferFunds (lFromBank, lFromAccount, _
            lToBank, lToAccount, cQuantity, _
            txTransfer, "Transferred by Credit bureau")

    sReturn = TransactionStatusDesc(eReturn)

EXIT_TransferFunds:
    TransferFunds = sReturn
Exit Function

ERR_TransferFunds:
    Select Case Err.Number
        Case Else
            MsgBox "Error transferring funds: " & vbCrLf & Err.Description, _
                    vbExclamation, "Error: " & Err.Number
            Resume EXIT_TransferFunds
    End Select
```

```
       Resume 0

   End Function

   Private Function TransactionStatusDesc(ByVal TransactionStatus _
              As Bank_Bus.ETransactionStatus) As String
      Dim sReturn As String

      'converts the status to a string
      Select Case TransactionStatus
         Case txsSuccess
            sReturn = "Success"
         Case txsDailyLimitExceeded
            sReturn = "Daily Limit Exceeded"
         Case txsNotEnoughFunds
            sReturn = "Not Enough Funds"
         Case txsUnknownError
            sReturn = "Unknown error occurred"
         Case Else
            'will never happen
      End Select

      TransactionStatusDesc = sReturn

   End Function
```

10. Save and compile the project.

Now we create the business component for the network application:

Try It Out – Creating Network_Bus

1. Create an ActiveX DLL project and name it `Network_Bus`.

2. Add References to the `Bank_XML`, Microsoft XML, version 2.0 (or later), and Microsoft ActiveX Data Objects 2.1 (or later) type libraries.

3. Add the `modXMLHelper` module (created above) to the project.

4. Rename the `Class1` class module to `Accounts`.

5. Add a routine that creates an XML request to query for client balances. The routine should take the `BankID` and `ClientID` and return an ADO recordset. Note that the recordset will need to be created from the XML.

```
Public Function AccountBalances(ByVal BankID As Long, _
              ByVal ClientID As Long) As ADODB.Recordset
   Dim oBank As Bank_XML.Accounts
   Dim oDOM As MSXML.DOMDocument
   Dim oNode As MSXML.IXMLDOMElement
```

```
        Dim colNodes As MSXML.IXMLDOMNodeList
        Dim oRS As ADODB.Recordset
        Dim sResponse As String

        On Error GoTo ERR_AccountBalances

        'build the request
        Set oDOM = New MSXML.DOMDocument
        Set oNode = AddElement(oDOM, "request")
        Call AddAttribute("type", "GetAccounts", oNode)
        Call AddElement(oDOM, "bankid", BankID, oNode)
        Call AddElement(oDOM, "clientid", ClientID, oNode)

        'send the request to the Bank
        Set oBank = New Bank_XML.Accounts
        sResponse = oBank.GetAccounts(oDOM.xml)

        'convert the response to a recordset (for example only, _
              not really required)
        If Len(sResponse) > 0 Then
           Set oDOM = New MSXML.DOMDocument
           Call oDOM.loadXML(sResponse)

           Set oRS = New ADODB.Recordset
           'add the fields of interest to the new recordset
           Call BuildRecordset(oRS)

           Call oRS.Open
           'add the records defined in the <accounts> section
           Set colNodes = oDOM.getElementsByTagName("account")
           Call AddRecords(oRS, colNodes)
        End If

EXIT_AccountBalances:
    'return the new recordset
    Set AccountBalances = oRS
Exit Function

ERR_AccountBalances:
    Select Case Err.Number
       Case Else
          MsgBox "Error retrieving account balances." & vbCrLf_
                 & Err.Description, vbExclamation, "Error: " & Err.Number
          Resume EXIT_AccountBalances
    End Select

    Resume 0
End Function

Private Sub BuildRecordset(ByRef Data As ADODB.Recordset)
    'adds the appropriate fields to a closed, but created recordset
```

```
      'the only fields we really want are:
      '    AccountTypeDesc
      '    Balance="234"
      With Data.Fields
         Call .Append("AccountID", adInteger)
         Call .Append("Account", adVarChar, 15)
         Call .Append("Balance", adCurrency)
      End With

End Sub

Private Sub AddRecords(ByRef Data As ADODB.Recordset, _
         ByVal Records As MSXML.IXMLDOMNodeList)
   Dim oNode As MSXML.IXMLDOMElement
   Dim iCount As Integer
   Dim lID As Long
   Dim sAccount As String
   Dim cBalance As Currency

   'adds a number of XML nodes to a recordset

   For iCount = 0 To Records.length - 1
      Set oNode = Records.Item(iCount)
      With oNode
         lID = CLng(.getAttribute("AccountId"))
         sAccount = Trim$(.getAttribute("AccountTypeDesc"))
         cBalance = .getAttribute("Balance")
      End With

      Call Data.AddNew(Array("AccountID", "Account", "Balance"), _
              Array(lID, sAccount, cBalance))
   Next

End Sub
```

6. Add a routine that creates an XML request to transfer funds between two accounts. The routine should take the two BankIDs, the two AccountIDs, and a quantity to transfer. It should return a string that describes the result (such as Success, Insufficient funds, etc.).

```
Public Function TransferFunds(ByVal FromBankID As Long, _
             ByVal FromAccountID As Long, _
             ByVal ToBankID As Long, ByVal ToAccountID As Long, _
             ByVal Quantity As Currency) As String

   Dim oDOM As MSXML.DOMDocument
   Dim oRoot As MSXML.IXMLDOMElement
   Dim oChild As MSXML.IXMLDOMElement
   Dim oBank As Bank_XML.Accounts
   Dim sResult As String

   'Calls Bank_Bus (via XML) to transfer funds, _
        returns a string representing the result
```

```
    On Error GoTo ERR_TransferFunds

    'build the request
    Set oDOM = New MSXML.DOMDocument
    Set oRoot = AddElement(oDOM, "request")
    Call AddAttribute("type", "TransferFunds", oRoot)

    'add the 'from' account information
    Set oChild = AddElement(oDOM, "from", , oRoot)
    Call AddElement(oDOM, "bank", FromBankID, oChild)
    Call AddElement(oDOM, "account", FromAccountID, oChild)

    'add the 'to' account information
    Set oChild = AddElement(oDOM, "to", , oRoot)
    Call AddElement(oDOM, "bank", ToBankID, oChild)
    Call AddElement(oDOM, "account", ToAccountID, oChild)

    'add the quantity
    Call AddElement(oDOM, "quantity", Quantity, oRoot)

    'send the request to the bank
    Set oBank = New Bank_XML.Accounts

    'retrieve the result
    sResult = oBank.TransferFunds(oDOM.xml)

EXIT_TransferFunds:
    TransferFunds = sResult
Exit Function

ERR_TransferFunds:
    Select Case Err.Number
        Case Else
            MsgBox "Error retrieving account balances." _
                    & vbCrLf & Err.Description, _
                    vbExclamation, "Error: " & Err.Number
            Resume EXIT_TransferFunds
    End Select

    Resume 0
End Function
```

Now that we've completed the Network_Bus component, we can turn our attention to constructing the user interface.

Try It Out – Creating Network_Bus

1. Create a new Standard EXE project, naming it Network_UI.

2. Add a Reference to the Network_Bus and ActiveX Data Objects 2.1 type libraries.

731

3. Add the Microsoft DataGrid component to the Toolbox. This can be done by right-clicking anywhere on the toolbox and selecting **Components**. This will present a list of optional extra tools, from which we want to select **Microsoft Datagrid Control 6.0 (OLEDB)**.

4. Rename the form as `frmReport` and add controls and labels (with the appropriate captions and text) to the form, as shown below (the DataGrid, `dbgView`, should have the property **AllowUpdate** set to **False**):

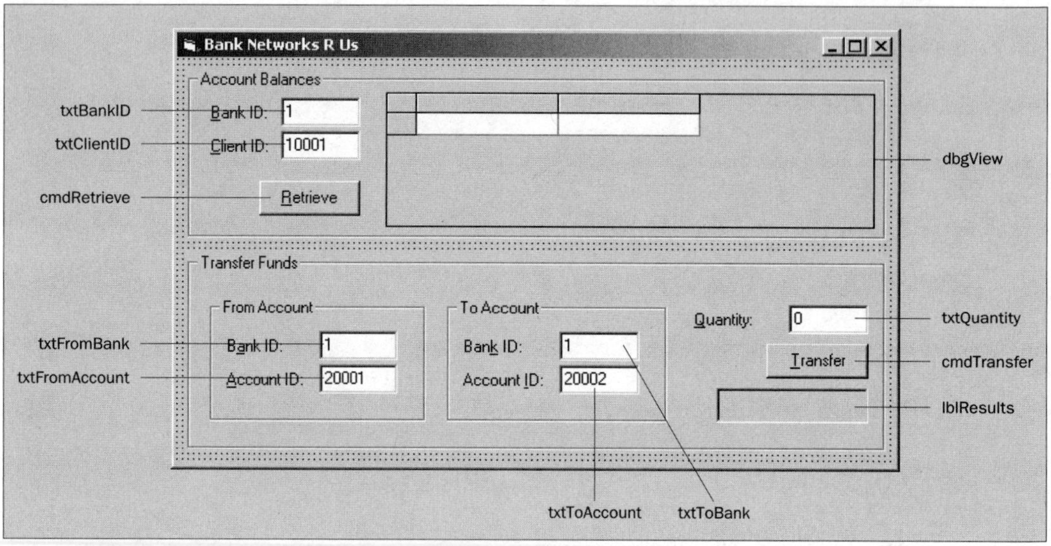

5. Declare a private variable of the type `Network_Bus.Accounts` in the General Declarations section of the form. Add code to create a new instance of this class in the `Load` event of the Form, and set it to `Nothing` when the application ends:

```
Private oAccounts As Network_Bus.Accounts

Private Sub Form_Load()
    Set oAccounts = New Network_Bus.Accounts
End Sub

Private Sub Form_Unload(Cancel As Integer)
    Set oAccounts = Nothing
End Sub
```

6. Add an event handler that will retrieve a recordset when the `cmdRetrieve` button is clicked. Use this recordset as the DataSource for the DataGrid control.

```
Private Sub cmdRetrieve_Click()
    Dim oRS As ADODB.Recordset

    Set oRS = oAccounts.AccountBalances(txtBankID.Text, txtClientID.Text)
```

```
    If Not oRS Is Nothing Then
        Set dbgView.DataSource = oRS
    End If

End Sub
```

7. Add an event handler that will transfer funds when the `cmdTransfer` button is clicked. Display the result in the `lblResult` label.

```
Private Sub cmdTransfer_Click()

    lblResults.Caption = ""
    lblResults.Caption = oAccounts.TransferFunds(txtFromBank.Text, _
                        txtFromAccount.Text, txtToBank.Text, _
                        txtToAccount.Text, txtQuantity.Text)

End Sub
```

8. Compile and run all three components.

If you do not have the Banking application fully installed on your machine, then it will be necessary to open it (in a second instance of VB) and run it from there.

Enter a valid `BankID` and `ClientID` (the defaults should be valid, if you haven't deleted them previously) and retrieve the list of accounts. Enter valid `BankID`s and `AccountID`s, and transfer funds. If it returns Success, retrieve the list of accounts again to see the change:

How It Works

Admittedly, this is a lengthy example. Indeed, it essentially recreates the business component created earlier! However, this was done to show how the Bank application could be modified to use XML to communicate with another application that can submit requests to our bank; in this case, that of a banking network.

There are three new components to this project group: a user interface, the business layer of the banking network application, and a third component that communicates with the business layer of the sample application. For brevity, we won't examine all the code in the three projects, but only that which is particularly significant.

Notice that the user interface does not know that XML is involved, and that it is rather simple. The `Network_Bus` component isolates the code required to create the XML requests, and process the XML responses. Similarly, the `Bank_XML` component masks the change from the business layer. However, the code in this component could easily have been added to the original `Bank_Bus` component, allowing it to directly accept XML requests.

Let's begin by examining the two routines used in the `Network_Bus` and `Bank_XML` projects.

The `AddElement` routine is responsible for adding new elements to the DOM. It takes an instance of the DOM to add to, the name of the element, and, optionally, a parent to add the new element to. If no parent is supplied, the new element becomes the root element for the document.

The `AddAttribute` routine is responsible for adding new attributes to an element of the DOM. It takes the name and value of the new attribute, and the element to add the attribute to.

The `Bank_XML` project represents an addition to the Bank application that we've been looking at throughout this book. It adds to the existing program, to allow the application to communicate via XML instead of Recordsets. As described above, this code could have been part of the original business layer. This component receives an XML request for an action, reads it, and then calls the `Bank_Bus.Bank` component to perform the task. It then takes the data returned from the `Bank` component and converts it to XML.

An example of this is the `GetAccounts` routine. This serves to retrieve the accounts held at a bank by a client. It is a wrapper around the bank's `GetAccounts` routine, and expects to receive an XML request of the form:

```
<request type="GetAccounts">
  <bankid>1</bankid>
  <clientid>10001</clientid>
</request>
```

First, the routine confirms that the request is of the correct format (by requesting the `type` attribute of the document element). Next, it retrieves the expected data. That is, the `bankid` and `clientid` variables from the XML. Third, it uses this information to retrieve a Recordset from the business layer of the Bank application. As pointed out above, the code before and after this section could have been built into the original business layer. Finally, once the Recordset has been retrieved, it is converted into XML, just as we did in the earlier example in Creating Bank_XML, with the DOM.

The `Network_Bus` component is similar to the `Bank_XML` component. It represents the business layer for a hypothetical banking network application. When it needs to retrieve information, however, it does not directly query a database. Instead, it communicates with the `Bank_XML` component via XML to retrieve the information. Initially, it builds a request (using the format described above) and passes it to the `Bank_XML` application. Once it receives the XML, it then converts it into an ADO Recordset. Obviously, this is not necessary, as this component could have simply returned the XML. The conversion was done to allow the user interface to use data binding. The conversion from XML to a Recordset is done using the two procedures, `BuildRecordset` and `AddRecords`. `BuildRecordset` creates a standalone Recordset containing the appropriate fields, and `AddRecords` adds each of the accounts contained in the XML document to the Recordset. The `TransferFunds` routine is similar, albeit longer.

Finally, the benefit of using component architecture is shown in the user interface project. Notice just how little code is required to retrieve information. Remember that the information could be retrieved across a network. The programmer using the `Network_Bus` component simply creates a new instance, and calls the appropriate method.

Further Considerations

Although the scope of this chapter is limited to an introduction to XML, we feel it would be appropriate to give a brief overview of some additional areas, which you may want to investigate further.

Transferring XML to Other Applications

Right at the start of the chapter we indicated that the sharing of data involved consideration of the format of the information being transferred and the transport mechanism itself. While we're not going to examine data transfer methods in detail, as a Visual Basic developer using XML, some of the more straightforward strategies to implement include:

❑ **Direct communication** – The simplest way to pass information is to do it directly: one application calls a method on another application, passing a message request. It does, however, need two programs using the same communications channel – for Visual Basic this would be COM/DCOM.

❑ **Microsoft Message Queue Server (MSMQ)** – As we saw in Chapter 1, MSMQ one of the tools associated with Windows DNA.

❑ **HyperText Transfer Protocol (HTTP)** – This protocol is used to transfer information over the Internet. In this strategy, a client application would communicate with a server application running on a Web server (for example, an ASP application).

❑ **Simple Object Access Protocol (SOAP)** – A relatively recent development. It is based on HTTP, but involves the use of a specific XML message format and specific headers present in the request to, and the response from, the server. SOAP adds a standard communication method to the XML scenario over HTTP, and is currently attracting a lot of interest as it allows businesses to participate in a standard approach.

Other XML Standards

If you're going to get serious about XML, there are a number of standards that you should be aware of:

❑ **XSLT (eXtensible Stylesheet Language Transformation)** – A standard for transforming XML into other formats (such as HTML, plain text, SQL, or another XML document, which is supported by a DTD different to that of the original document).

❑ **XPath** – The XML standard for selecting sections of an XML document.

❑ **XLink** – An emerging standard to create a syntax for linking information (could be thought of as a more powerful version of the HTML anchor tag).

❑ **XHTML (eXtensible Stylesheet Language Transformation)** – A revision of HTML that follows the more rigorous rules of XML; it was designed to ensure future HTML documents are also valid XML documents and additionally allow for the extension of HTML.

BizTalk

The Microsoft led **BizTalk** initiative (www.biztalk.org) involves a drive to create an XML framework for businesses to communicate data. In addition to the framework (the schema used for BizTalk messages), there is software (the BizTalk server is a server application that facilitates message delivery) and a library of document types (containing XML schemas defining standard types of business communication such as purchase orders). This initiative is aimed at enabling companies to simplify their **business-to-business (B2B)** communications, and will become increasingly important as e-commerce grows.

Summary

Most applications either *must* communicate with other applications, or would be improved by being able to. By providing a standard mechanism and message format, XML greatly simplifies the development needed to add this feature. XML gives the distributed application developer a tool that allows for the definition of data, while allowing the data to be self-describing.

In this chapter, we have taken a brief look at the history of XML. We have seen how it has become a very important standard that allows for the creation, processing and querying of data. The importance of XML will only continue to increase as more and more developers explore its features.

We have seen the structure of XML documents, and have seen the most important characteristics that all XML documents share. Elements and Attributes are used to define most XML documents. Through the creation of a set of standard Elements and Attributes, we can define a language. Once defined, other companies or partners can use that language to communicate with our company's applications. To solidify this relationship, you may want to create a Document Type Definition (DTD) or Schema that defines the structure of your documents.

Creating an XML document by hand is laborious and error-prone. Avoiding having to do laborious and error-prone tasks are two of many reasons we use computers. Using a program to create and read XML documents as a communication method allows the application to reach out and communicate with applications wherever they may reside, on any platform they may reside on.

XML is a moving set of standards. Once we have learned one, we quickly discover that there are many more lying in wait for us. However, each of the newer standards highlights the significance and consistency of XML. Most of the new standards simply add a new language (using either a DTD or Schema) to XML (often simply a few specific Elements and Attributes) rather than changing the standard.

So, why should we use XML for inter-application communication? We should use it for the following reasons:

- ❑ XML gives us a platform-neutral communication message.

- ❑ XML documents are simple, yet self-describing and infinitely hierarchical.

- ❑ All of the major vendors are producing tools and add-ons for supporting development with XML.

- ❑ Using XML opens up a wide range of possible strategies for communicating with other applications.

- ❑ XML is actually quite simple and fun to explore and program with.

The WROBA Application

In this appendix, we're going to list the remaining code that makes up the WROBA case study we've been building throughout this book. You'll find more details about exactly what this code does and how to use it in the relevant chapters in the book.

> **All of the code in this appendix is available for download from the Wrox web site at http://www.wrox.com.**

We'll present the project in a similar order to the way it's built in the book – that is, from the bottom up. The code we list falls into three broad categories:

- ❑ The SQL scripts that build the BigBank database on SQL Server
- ❑ The stored procedures that we need to add to the database to encapsulate our data services logic
- ❑ A summary of the Visual Basic code modules that make up the Bank project

Creating the BigBank Database – SQL Scripts

We'll present three SQL scripts here:

- ❑ Schema.sql – which builds the BigBank database, including all tables and the constraints on those tables
- ❑ FillTables.sql – which populates the finished database
- ❑ Logger.sql (optional) – which lets us add error logging functionality to the application

After running the first two of these scripts, you should have a database in the same state as the one that we build in Chapter 9 and 10.

Running the SQL Scripts

We cover SQL syntax, and what SQL scripts are and how to use them, in more detail in Chapter 10.

Before you can run them, you'll have to set up a new database in SQL Server called `BigBank`. Refer to the **Try It Out – Creating the BigBank Database** in Chapter 9 for instructions on how to do this.

To run the scripts, all you actually have to do is:

- ❑ Either type the code into the text editor of your choice, or download the files from the Wrox web site, and save the scripts somewhere on your machine
- ❑ Open SQL Server Query Analyzer (Start | Programs | Microsoft SQL Server 7.0 | Query Analyzer)
- ❑ Connect to your SQL Server
- ❑ Click on File | Open, navigate to the SQL script you want and click Open
- ❑ The code should be loaded into the Query window for you
- ❑ Select the BigBank database in the drop-down list in the top right
- ❑ Click Parse to check the code, and Execute to run it

Building the Database – Schema.sql

We recommend that you actually build the database manually, following the instructions in Chapters 9 and 10. However, if you'd prefer to get to work more quickly, the following script will build the database for you. This creates the tables and adds the necessary constraints.

```
/****** Object:  Login Builtin\Administrators ******/
IF NOT EXISTS (SELECT * FROM master..syslogins
    WHERE name = N'Builtin\Administrators')
        exec sp_grantlogin N'Builtin\Administrators'
        exec sp_defaultdb N'Builtin\Administrators', N'master'
        exec sp_defaultlanguage N'Builtin\Administrators', N'us_english'
GO


/****** Object:  Login Builtin\Administrators ******/
exec sp_addsrvrolemember N'Builtin\Administrators', sysadmin
GO
```

```
/****** Object:  Table [dbo].[AccountHistory] ******/
CREATE TABLE [dbo].[AccountHistory] (
    [TxId] [uniqueidentifier] NOT NULL ,
    [AccountId] [int] NOT NULL ,
    [TxDate] [datetime] NOT NULL ,
    [TxType] [tinyint] NOT NULL ,
    [TxDescription] [char] (40) NOT NULL ,
    [TxAmount] [money] NOT NULL ,
    [CounterpartyRef] [char] (26) NULL
) ON [PRIMARY]
GO
```

```
/****** Object:  Table [dbo].[AccountType] ******/
CREATE TABLE [dbo].[AccountType] (
   [AccountType] [tinyint] NOT NULL ,
   [AccountTypeDesc] [char] (15) NOT NULL
) ON [PRIMARY]
GO


/****** Object:  Table [dbo].[Bank] ******/
CREATE TABLE [dbo].[Bank] (
   [BankId] [smallint] NOT NULL ,
   [BankDesc] [char] (20) NOT NULL ,
   [BankDSN] [varchar] (250) NOT NULL
) ON [PRIMARY]
GO


/****** Object:  Table [dbo].[BankAccount] ******/
CREATE TABLE [dbo].[BankAccount] (
   [AccountId] [int] NOT NULL ,
   [AccountType] [tinyint] NOT NULL ,
   [Balance] [money] NOT NULL ,
   [DailyWithdrawalLimit] [money] NOT NULL ,
   [DailyRemaining] [money] NOT NULL ,
   [LastWithdrawalDate] [datetime] NOT NULL ,
   [OverdraftLimit] [money] NOT NULL
) ON [PRIMARY]
GO


/****** Object:  Table [dbo].[CardxAccount] ******/
CREATE TABLE [dbo].[CardxAccount] (
   [CardId] [int] NOT NULL ,
   [AccountType] [tinyint] NOT NULL ,
   [AccountId] [int] NOT NULL
) ON [PRIMARY]
GO


/****** Object:  Table [dbo].[Payee] ******/
CREATE TABLE [dbo].[Payee] (
   [PayeeId] [uniqueidentifier] NOT NULL ,
   [CardId] [int] NOT NULL ,
   [PayeeDesc] [char] (30) NOT NULL ,
   [BankId] [smallint] NOT NULL ,
   [AccountId] [int] NOT NULL ,
   [DefaultAmount] [money] NOT NULL ,
   [WROBACardId] [int] NOT NULL
) ON [PRIMARY]
GO


/****** Object:  Table [dbo].[TxLock]  ******/
CREATE TABLE [dbo].[TxLock] (
   [BankId] [smallint] NOT NULL ,
   [CardId] [int] NOT NULL
) ON [PRIMARY]
GO
```

```
/****** Object:  Table [dbo].[TxType] ******/
CREATE TABLE [dbo].[TxType] (
   [TxType] [tinyint] NOT NULL ,
   [TxTypeDesc] [char] (15) NOT NULL
) ON [PRIMARY]
GO
```

```
/****** Object:  Table [dbo].[WROBACard] ******/
CREATE TABLE [dbo].[WROBACard] (
   [CardId] [int] NOT NULL ,
   [Password] [char] (10) NOT NULL ,
   [InvalidPasswordCnt] [tinyint] NOT NULL
) ON [PRIMARY]
GO
```

```
ALTER TABLE [dbo].[AccountHistory] WITH NOCHECK ADD
   CONSTRAINT [PK_AccountHistory] PRIMARY KEY  NONCLUSTERED
   (
      [TxId]
   ) ON [PRIMARY]
GO
```

```
ALTER TABLE [dbo].[AccountType] WITH NOCHECK ADD
   CONSTRAINT [PK_AccountType] PRIMARY KEY  NONCLUSTERED
   (
      [AccountType]
   ) ON [PRIMARY] ,
   CONSTRAINT [IX_AccountType] UNIQUE  NONCLUSTERED
   (
      [AccountTypeDesc]
   ) ON [PRIMARY]
GO
```

```
ALTER TABLE [dbo].[Bank] WITH NOCHECK ADD
   CONSTRAINT [PK_Bank] PRIMARY KEY  NONCLUSTERED
   (
      [BankId]
   ) ON [PRIMARY] ,
   CONSTRAINT [IX_Bank] UNIQUE  NONCLUSTERED
   (
      [BankDesc]
   ) ON [PRIMARY]
GO
```

```
ALTER TABLE [dbo].[BankAccount] WITH NOCHECK ADD
   CONSTRAINT [PK_BankAccount] PRIMARY KEY  NONCLUSTERED
   (
      [AccountId]
   ) ON [PRIMARY] ,
   CONSTRAINT [CK_BankAccount_Remaining] CHECK ([DailyRemaining] <=
[DailyWithDrawalLimit])
GO
```

```
ALTER TABLE [dbo].[CardxAccount] WITH NOCHECK ADD
   CONSTRAINT [PK_CardxAccount] PRIMARY KEY  NONCLUSTERED
   (
      [CardId],
      [AccountType]
   ) ON [PRIMARY]
GO

ALTER TABLE [dbo].[Payee] WITH NOCHECK ADD
   CONSTRAINT [PK_Payee] PRIMARY KEY  NONCLUSTERED
   (
      [PayeeId]
   ) ON [PRIMARY] ,
   CONSTRAINT [IX_Payee] UNIQUE  NONCLUSTERED
   (
      [PayeeDesc]
   ) ON [PRIMARY]
GO

ALTER TABLE [dbo].[TxLock] WITH NOCHECK ADD
   CONSTRAINT [PK_TxLock] PRIMARY KEY  NONCLUSTERED
   (
      [BankId],
      [CardId]
   ) ON [PRIMARY]
GO

ALTER TABLE [dbo].[TxType] WITH NOCHECK ADD
   CONSTRAINT [PK_TxType] PRIMARY KEY  NONCLUSTERED
   (
      [TxType]
   ) ON [PRIMARY] ,
   CONSTRAINT [IX_TxType] UNIQUE  NONCLUSTERED
   (
      [TxTypeDesc]
   ) ON [PRIMARY]
GO

ALTER TABLE [dbo].[WROBACard] WITH NOCHECK ADD
   CONSTRAINT [DF_ATMCard_InvalidPasswordCnt] DEFAULT (0) FOR
[InvalidPasswordCnt],
   CONSTRAINT [PK_ATMCard] PRIMARY KEY  NONCLUSTERED
   (
      [CardId]
   ) ON [PRIMARY]
GO

ALTER TABLE [dbo].[AccountHistory] ADD
   CONSTRAINT [FK_AccountHistory_BankAccount] FOREIGN KEY
   (
      [AccountId]
   ) REFERENCES [dbo].[BankAccount] (
      [AccountId]
   ),
   CONSTRAINT [FK_AccountHistory_TxType] FOREIGN KEY
   (
      [TxType]
   ) REFERENCES [dbo].[TxType] (
      [TxType]
   )
GO
```

743

```sql
ALTER TABLE [dbo].[BankAccount] ADD
    CONSTRAINT [FK_BankAccount_AccountType] FOREIGN KEY
    (
        [AccountType]
    ) REFERENCES [dbo].[AccountType] (
        [AccountType]
    )
GO
```

```sql
ALTER TABLE [dbo].[CardxAccount] ADD
    CONSTRAINT [FK_CardxAccount_AccountType] FOREIGN KEY
    (
        [AccountType]
    ) REFERENCES [dbo].[AccountType] (
        [AccountType]
    ),
    CONSTRAINT [FK_CardxAccount_ATMCard] FOREIGN KEY
    (
        [CardId]
    ) REFERENCES [dbo].[WROBACard] (
        [CardId]
    ),
    CONSTRAINT [FK_CardxAccount_BankAccount] FOREIGN KEY
    (
        [AccountId]
    ) REFERENCES [dbo].[BankAccount] (
        [AccountId]
    )
GO
```

```sql
ALTER TABLE [dbo].[TxLock] ADD
    CONSTRAINT [FK_TxLock_Bank] FOREIGN KEY
    (
        [BankId]
    ) REFERENCES [dbo].[Bank] (
        [BankId]
    ),
    CONSTRAINT [FK_TxLock_WROBACard] FOREIGN KEY
    (
        [CardId]
    ) REFERENCES [dbo].[WROBACard] (
        [CardId]
    )
GO

SET QUOTED_IDENTIFIER  ON    SET ANSI_NULLS  ON
GO
```

Resetting the Database to its Initial State

If you look at the Schema.sql script that comes with the code download, you'll find the following SQL commands at the head of the file. These commands are actually designed to let you re-run the script and reset the database to its original state, if you've changed it in any way.

The first block of commands removes the foreign key constraints we've added to the database. We need to do this before we can delete any tables, because SQL Server won't allow you to drop tables that have foreign keys:

```
ALTER TABLE [dbo].[BankAccount] DROP CONSTRAINT FK_BankAccount_AccountType
GO


ALTER TABLE [dbo].[CardxAccount] DROP CONSTRAINT FK_CardxAccount_AccountType
GO


ALTER TABLE [dbo].[TxLock] DROP CONSTRAINT FK_TxLock_Bank
GO


ALTER TABLE [dbo].[AccountHistory] DROP CONSTRAINT FK_AccountHistory_BankAccount
GO


ALTER TABLE [dbo].[CardxAccount] DROP CONSTRAINT FK_CardxAccount_BankAccount
GO


ALTER TABLE [dbo].[AccountHistory] DROP CONSTRAINT FK_AccountHistory_TxType
GO


ALTER TABLE [dbo].[CardxAccount] DROP CONSTRAINT FK_CardxAccount_ATMCard
GO


ALTER TABLE [dbo].[TxLock] DROP CONSTRAINT FK_TxLock_WROBACard
GO
```

The next block of statements removes any stored procedures that we might have added (the stored procedures themselves are listed later in this appendix):

```
/****** Object:  Stored Procedure dbo.sp_delete_Bank ******/
IF EXISTS (SELECT * FROM sysobjects
          WHERE id = object_id(N'[dbo].[sp_delete_Bank]') and
              OBJECTPROPERTY(id, N'IsProcedure') = 1)
drop procedure [dbo].[sp_delete_Bank]
GO


/****** Object:  Stored Procedure dbo.sp_delete_BankAccount ******/
IF EXISTS (SELECT * FROM sysobjects
          WHERE id = object_id(N'[dbo].[sp_delete_BankAccount]') and
              OBJECTPROPERTY(id, N'IsProcedure') = 1)
drop procedure [dbo].[sp_delete_BankAccount]
GO
```

```
/****** Object:  Stored Procedure dbo.sp_delete_CardxAccount ******/
IF EXISTS (SELECT * FROM sysobjects
          WHERE id = object_id(N'[dbo].[sp_delete_CardxAccount]') and
                OBJECTPROPERTY(id, N'IsProcedure') = 1)
drop procedure [dbo].[sp_delete_CardxAccount]
GO


/****** Object:  Stored Procedure dbo.sp_delete_payee ******/
IF EXISTS (SELECT * FROM sysobjects
          WHERE id = object_id(N'[dbo].[sp_delete_payee]') and
                OBJECTPROPERTY(id, N'IsProcedure') = 1)
drop procedure [dbo].[sp_delete_payee]
GO


/****** Object:  Stored Procedure dbo.sp_delete_TxLock ******/
IF EXISTS (SELECT * FROM sysobjects
          WHERE id = object_id(N'[dbo].[sp_delete_TxLock]') and
                OBJECTPROPERTY(id, N'IsProcedure') = 1)
drop procedure [dbo].[sp_delete_TxLock]
GO


/****** Object:  Stored Procedure dbo.sp_delete_WROBACard ******/
IF EXISTS (SELECT * FROM sysobjects
          WHERE id = object_id(N'[dbo].[sp_delete_WROBACard]') and
                OBJECTPROPERTY(id, N'IsProcedure') = 1)
drop procedure [dbo].[sp_delete_WROBACard]
GO


/****** Object:  Stored Procedure dbo.sp_insert_Bank ******/
IF EXISTS (SELECT * FROM sysobjects
          WHERE id = object_id(N'[dbo].[sp_insert_Bank]') and
                OBJECTPROPERTY(id, N'IsProcedure') = 1)
drop procedure [dbo].[sp_insert_Bank]
GO


/****** Object:  Stored Procedure dbo.sp_insert_BankAccount ******/
IF EXISTS (SELECT * FROM sysobjects
          WHERE id = object_id(N'[dbo].[sp_insert_BankAccount]') and
                OBJECTPROPERTY(id, N'IsProcedure') = 1)
drop procedure [dbo].[sp_insert_BankAccount]
GO


/****** Object:  Stored Procedure dbo.sp_insert_CardxAccount ******/
IF EXISTS (SELECT * FROM sysobjects
          WHERE id = object_id(N'[dbo].[sp_insert_CardxAccount]') and
                OBJECTPROPERTY(id, N'IsProcedure') = 1)
drop procedure [dbo].[sp_insert_CardxAccount]
GO


/****** Object:  Stored Procedure dbo.sp_insert_Payee ******/
IF EXISTS (SELECT * FROM sysobjects
          WHERE id = object_id(N'[dbo].[sp_insert_Payee]') and
                OBJECTPROPERTY(id, N'IsProcedure') = 1)
drop procedure [dbo].[sp_insert_Payee]
GO
```

```
/****** Object:  Stored Procedure dbo.sp_insert_TxLock ******/
IF EXISTS (SELECT * FROM sysobjects
          WHERE id = object_id(N'[dbo].[sp_insert_TxLock]') and
                OBJECTPROPERTY(id, N'IsProcedure') = 1)
drop procedure [dbo].[sp_insert_TxLock]
GO


/****** Object:  Stored Procedure dbo.sp_insert_WROBACard ******/
IF EXISTS (SELECT * FROM sysobjects
          WHERE id = object_id(N'[dbo].[sp_insert_WROBACard]') and
                OBJECTPROPERTY(id, N'IsProcedure') = 1)
drop procedure [dbo].[sp_insert_WROBACard]
GO


/****** Object:  Stored Procedure dbo.sp_select_AccountHistory_By_AccountId
******/
IF EXISTS (SELECT * FROM sysobjects WHERE
          id = object_id(N'[dbo].[sp_select_AccountHistory_By_AccountId]')
          and OBJECTPROPERTY(id, N'IsProcedure') = 1)
drop procedure [dbo].[sp_select_AccountHistory_By_AccountId]
GO


/****** Object:  Stored Procedure dbo.sp_select_AccountId_By_CardId ******/
IF EXISTS (SELECT * FROM sysobjects
          WHERE id = object_id(N'[dbo].[sp_select_AccountId_By_CardId]')
                and OBJECTPROPERTY(id, N'IsProcedure') = 1)
drop procedure [dbo].[sp_select_AccountId_By_CardId]
GO


/****** Object:  Stored Procedure dbo.sp_select_AccountType ******/
IF EXISTS (SELECT * FROM sysobjects
          WHERE id = object_id(N'[dbo].[sp_select_AccountType]') and
                OBJECTPROPERTY(id, N'IsProcedure') = 1)
drop procedure [dbo].[sp_select_AccountType]
GO


/****** Object:  Stored Procedure dbo.sp_select_AccountType_By_CardId ******/
IF EXISTS (SELECT * FROM sysobjects
          WHERE id = object_id(N'[dbo].[sp_select_AccountType_By_CardId]')
                and OBJECTPROPERTY(id, N'IsProcedure') = 1)
drop procedure [dbo].[sp_select_AccountType_By_CardId]
GO


/****** Object:  Stored Procedure dbo.sp_select_All_Payees ******/
IF EXISTS (SELECT * FROM sysobjects
          WHERE id = object_id(N'[dbo].[sp_select_All_Payees]') and
                OBJECTPROPERTY(id, N'IsProcedure') = 1)
drop procedure [dbo].[sp_select_All_Payees]
GO


/****** Object:  Stored Procedure dbo.sp_select_Bank ******/
IF EXISTS (SELECT * FROM sysobjects
          WHERE id = object_id(N'[dbo].[sp_select_Bank]') and
                OBJECTPROPERTY(id, N'IsProcedure') = 1)
drop procedure [dbo].[sp_select_Bank]
GO
```

```
/****** Object:  Stored Procedure dbo.sp_select_Bank_By_BankId ******/
IF EXISTS (SELECT * FROM sysobjects
            WHERE id = object_id(N'[dbo].[sp_select_Bank_By_BankId]') and
                OBJECTPROPERTY(id, N'IsProcedure') = 1)
drop procedure [dbo].[sp_select_Bank_By_BankId]
GO


/****** Object:  Stored Procedure dbo.sp_select_BankAccount_By_AccountId ******/
IF EXISTS (SELECT * FROM sysobjects WHERE
            id = object_id(N'[dbo].[sp_select_BankAccount_By_AccountId]') and
            OBJECTPROPERTY(id, N'IsProcedure') = 1)
drop procedure [dbo].[sp_select_BankAccount_By_AccountId]
GO


/****** Object:  Stored Procedure dbo.sp_select_BankAccount_By_CardId ******/
IF EXISTS (SELECT * FROM sysobjects
            WHERE id = object_id(N'[dbo].[sp_select_BankAccount_By_CardId]')
                and OBJECTPROPERTY(id, N'IsProcedure') = 1)
drop procedure [dbo].[sp_select_BankAccount_By_CardId]
GO


/****** Object:  Stored Procedure dbo.sp_select_Last_AccountId ******/
IF EXISTS (SELECT * FROM sysobjects
            WHERE id = object_id(N'[dbo].[sp_select_Last_AccountId]')
                and OBJECTPROPERTY(id, N'IsProcedure') = 1)
drop procedure [dbo].[sp_select_Last_AccountId]
GO


/****** Object:  Stored Procedure dbo.sp_select_Last_CardId ******/
IF EXISTS (SELECT * FROM sysobjects
            WHERE id = object_id(N'[dbo].[sp_select_Last_CardId]')
                and OBJECTPROPERTY(id, N'IsProcedure') = 1)
drop procedure [dbo].[sp_select_Last_CardId]
GO


/****** Object:  Stored Procedure dbo.sp_select_PayeeByCardId ******/
IF EXISTS (SELECT * FROM sysobjects
            WHERE id = object_id(N'[dbo].[sp_select_PayeeByCardId]')
                and OBJECTPROPERTY(id, N'IsProcedure') = 1)
drop procedure [dbo].[sp_select_PayeeByCardId]
GO


/****** Object:  Stored Procedure dbo.sp_select_WROBACard_PwdCnt ******/
IF EXISTS (SELECT * FROM sysobjects
            WHERE id = object_id(N'[dbo].[sp_select_WROBACard_PwdCnt]')
                and OBJECTPROPERTY(id, N'IsProcedure') = 1)
drop procedure [dbo].[sp_select_WROBACard_PwdCnt]
GO


/****** Object:  Stored Procedure dbo.sp_update_Bank ******/
IF EXISTS (SELECT * FROM sysobjects
            WHERE id = object_id(N'[dbo].[sp_update_Bank]')
                and OBJECTPROPERTY(id, N'IsProcedure') = 1)
drop procedure [dbo].[sp_update_Bank]
GO
```

```
/****** Object:  Stored Procedure dbo.sp_update_BankAccount ******/
IF EXISTS (SELECT * FROM sysobjects
          WHERE id = object_id(N'[dbo].[sp_update_BankAccount]')
              and OBJECTPROPERTY(id, N'IsProcedure') = 1)
drop procedure [dbo].[sp_update_BankAccount]
GO


/****** Object:  Stored Procedure dbo.sp_update_BankAccount_Dec ******/
IF EXISTS (SELECT * FROM sysobjects
          WHERE id = object_id(N'[dbo].[sp_update_BankAccount_Dec]')
              and OBJECTPROPERTY(id, N'IsProcedure') = 1)
drop procedure [dbo].[sp_update_BankAccount_Dec]
GO


/****** Object:  Stored Procedure dbo.sp_update_BankAccount_Inc ******/
IF EXISTS (SELECT * FROM sysobjects
          WHERE id = object_id(N'[dbo].[sp_update_BankAccount_Inc]')
              and OBJECTPROPERTY(id, N'IsProcedure') = 1)
drop procedure [dbo].[sp_update_BankAccount_Inc]
GO


/****** Object:  Stored Procedure dbo.sp_update_payee ******/
IF EXISTS (SELECT * FROM sysobjects
          WHERE id = object_id(N'[dbo].[sp_update_payee]')
              and OBJECTPROPERTY(id, N'IsProcedure') = 1)
drop procedure [dbo].[sp_update_payee]
GO


/****** Object:  Stored Procedure dbo.sp_update_WROBACard_Pwd ******/
IF EXISTS (SELECT * FROM sysobjects
          WHERE id = object_id(N'[dbo].[sp_update_WROBACard_Pwd]')
              and OBJECTPROPERTY(id, N'IsProcedure') = 1)
drop procedure [dbo].[sp_update_WROBACard_Pwd]
GO


/****** Object:  Stored Procedure dbo.sp_update_WROBACard_PwdCnt ******/
IF EXISTS (SELECT * FROM sysobjects
          WHERE id = object_id(N'[dbo].[sp_update_WROBACard_PwdCnt]')
              and OBJECTPROPERTY(id, N'IsProcedure') = 1)
drop procedure [dbo].[sp_update_WROBACard_PwdCnt]
GO


/****** Object:  Stored Procedure dbo.sp_verify_BankAccount_By_CardId ******/
IF EXISTS (SELECT * FROM sysobjects
          WHERE id = object_id(N'[dbo].[sp_verify_BankAccount_By_CardId]')
              and OBJECTPROPERTY(id, N'IsProcedure') = 1)
drop procedure [dbo].[sp_verify_BankAccount_By_CardId]
GO
```

```
/****** Object:  Stored Procedure dbo.sp_verify_CardAccount_By_CardId ******/
IF EXISTS (SELECT * FROM sysobjects
          WHERE id = object_id(N'[dbo].[sp_verify_CardAccount_By_CardId]')
                and OBJECTPROPERTY(id, N'IsProcedure') = 1)
drop procedure [dbo].[sp_verify_CardAccount_By_CardId]
GO


/****** Object:  Stored Procedure dbo.sp_verify_Payee_By_CardId ******/
IF EXISTS (SELECT * FROM sysobjects
          WHERE id = object_id(N'[dbo].[sp_verify_Payee_By_CardId]')
                and OBJECTPROPERTY(id, N'IsProcedure') = 1)
drop procedure [dbo].[sp_verify_Payee_By_CardId]
GO


/****** Object:  Table [dbo].[AccountHistory] ******/
IF EXISTS (SELECT * FROM sysobjects
          WHERE id = object_id(N'[dbo].[AccountHistory]')
                and OBJECTPROPERTY(id, N'IsUserTable') = 1)
drop table [dbo].[AccountHistory]
GO
```

Then we can remove the tables:

```
/****** Object:  Table [dbo].[AccountType] ******/
IF EXISTS (SELECT * FROM sysobjects
          WHERE id = object_id(N'[dbo].[AccountType]')
                and OBJECTPROPERTY(id, N'IsUserTable') = 1)
drop table [dbo].[AccountType]
GO


/****** Object:  Table [dbo].[Bank] ******/
IF EXISTS (SELECT * FROM sysobjects
          WHERE id = object_id(N'[dbo].[Bank]')
                and OBJECTPROPERTY(id, N'IsUserTable') = 1)
drop table [dbo].[Bank]
GO


/****** Object:  Table [dbo].[BankAccount] ******/
IF EXISTS (SELECT * FROM sysobjects
          WHERE id = object_id(N'[dbo].[BankAccount]')
                and OBJECTPROPERTY(id, N'IsUserTable') = 1)
drop table [dbo].[BankAccount]
GO


/****** Object:  Table [dbo].[CardxAccount] ******/
IF EXISTS (SELECT * FROM sysobjects
          WHERE id = object_id(N'[dbo].[CardxAccount]')
                and OBJECTPROPERTY(id, N'IsUserTable') = 1)
drop table [dbo].[CardxAccount]
GO
```

```
/****** Object:  Table [dbo].[Payee] ******/
IF EXISTS (SELECT * FROM sysobjects
          WHERE id = object_id(N'[dbo].[Payee]')
                and OBJECTPROPERTY(id, N'IsUserTable') = 1)
drop table [dbo].[Payee]
GO


/****** Object:  Table [dbo].[TxLock] ******/
IF EXISTS (SELECT * FROM sysobjects
          WHERE id = object_id(N'[dbo].[TxLock]')
                and OBJECTPROPERTY(id, N'IsUserTable') = 1)
drop table [dbo].[TxLock]
GO


/****** Object:  Table [dbo].[TxType] ******/
IF EXISTS (SELECT * FROM sysobjects
          WHERE id = object_id(N'[dbo].[TxType]')
                and OBJECTPROPERTY(id, N'IsUserTable') = 1)
drop table [dbo].[TxType]
GO


/****** Object:  Table [dbo].[WROBACard] ******/
IF EXISTS (SELECT * FROM sysobjects
          WHERE id = object_id(N'[dbo].[WROBACard]')
                and OBJECTPROPERTY(id, N'IsUserTable') = 1)
drop table [dbo].[WROBACard]
GO
```

We're now in a position to rebuild the database.

Note that when you run the Schema.sql *script for the first time you may get some error messages because the foreign key constraints that you're removing don't exist.*

Populating the Tables – FillTables.sql

This script will populate the database tables with enough data to make the database fully functional.

If you work through the chapters in the book, you'll populate the AccountType table manually in Chapter 9, and the BankAccount table using Query Analyzer in Chapter 10. This data is not highlighted in the following listing – if you've already added it, you only need to add the additional highlighted code. We add the highlighted data to the database in the **Try It Out – Populating the Rest of the Database** in Chapter 10.

```
INSERT [dbo].[AccountType] (
    [AccountType],
    [AccountTypeDesc]
)
VALUES (
    0,
    'Administrator'
)
GO
```

```
INSERT [dbo].[AccountType] (
    [AccountType],
    [AccountTypeDesc]
)
VALUES (
    1,
    'Checking'
)
GO

INSERT [dbo].[AccountType] (
    [AccountType],
    [AccountTypeDesc]
)
VALUES (
    2,
    'Saving'
)
GO

INSERT [dbo].[WROBACard] (
    [CardId],
    [Password]
)
VALUES (
    10000,
    'Admin'
)
GO

INSERT [dbo].[WROBACard] (
    [CardId],
    [Password]
)
VALUES (
    10001,
    'Secret1'
)
GO

INSERT [dbo].[WROBACard] (
    [CardId],
    [Password]
)
VALUES (
    10002,
    'Secret2'
)
GO
```

```
INSERT [dbo].[Bank] (
   [BankId],
   [BankDesc],
   [BankDSN]
)
VALUES (
   1,
   'Big Bank',
   'DSN_Big_Bank'
)
GO
INSERT [dbo].[Bank] VALUES (2, 'Another Big Bank', 'DSN_Another_Big_Bank')
GO
INSERT [dbo].[Bank] VALUES (3, 'Small Bank', 'DSN_Small_Bank')
GO
```

```
INSERT BankAccount (
   AccountId,
   AccountType,
   Balance,
   DailyWithdrawalLimit,
   DailyRemaining,
   LastWithdrawalDate,
   OverdraftLimit
)
VALUES (20000, 0,0,0,0,GETDATE(),0)
GO
INSERT BankAccount VALUES (20001, 1,254,500,500,GETDATE(), 500)
INSERT BankAccount VALUES (20002, 2,2376,500,500,GETDATE(),500)
INSERT BankAccount VALUES (20003, 1,-56,1000,40,GETDATE(),1500)
INSERT BankAccount VALUES (20004, 2,3236,500,340,GETDATE(),500)
INSERT BankAccount VALUES (20005, 2,236,500,100,GETDATE(),100)
GO
```

```
INSERT [dbo].[CardxAccount] (
   [CardId],
   [AccountType],
   [AccountId]
)
VALUES (
   10000,
   0,
   20000
)
GO
INSERT [dbo].[CardxAccount] VALUES (10001, 1, 20001)
GO
INSERT [dbo].[CardxAccount] VALUES (10001, 2, 20002)
GO
INSERT [dbo].[CardxAccount] VALUES (10002, 1, 20003)
GO
INSERT [dbo].[CardxAccount] VALUES (10002, 2, 20004)
GO
```

```
INSERT [dbo].[TxType] (
    [TxType],
    [TxTypeDesc]
) VALUES (
    1,
    'TSF'
)
GO

INSERT [dbo].[TxType] (
    [TxType],
    [TxTypeDesc]
) VALUES (
    2,
    'BIL'
)
GO
```

```
INSERT [dbo].[Payee] (
    [PayeeId],
    [CardId],
    [PayeeDesc],
    [BankId],
    [AccountId],
    [DefaultAmount],
    [WROBACardId]
) VALUES (
    '67FC28E6-6174-4684-8409-138CE36CED6C',
    10002,
    'Cecilia Poremsky',
    1,
    20003,
    100,
    10001
)
GO
```

Error Logging – Logger.sql

The following script creates an optional additional table and stored procedure that you'll need if you want to implement the error logging functionality we describe in Chapter 12. Again, the code at the head of this file is there in case you want to reset the database to its original state after you've changed something.

```
IF EXISTS (SELECT * FROM sysobjects
          WHERE id = object_id(N'[dbo].[sp_insert_LogError]')
              and OBJECTPROPERTY(id, N'IsProcedure') = 1)
drop procedure [dbo].[sp_insert_LogError]
GO

IF EXISTS (SELECT * FROM sysobjects
          WHERE id = object_id(N'[dbo].[ErrorLog]')
              and OBJECTPROPERTY(id, N'IsUserTable') = 1)
drop table [dbo].[ErrorLog]
GO
```

```
CREATE TABLE [dbo].[ErrorLog] (
    [LogTime] [datetime] NULL ,
    [ErrorNumber] [int] NULL ,
    [ErrorSource] [varchar] (100) NULL ,
    [ErrorDescription] [varchar] (100) NULL ,
    [Message] [varchar] (100) NULL
) ON [PRIMARY]
GO


SET QUOTED_IDENTIFIER  ON    SET ANSI_NULLS  ON
GO
```

```
/****** Object:  Stored Procedure dbo.sp_insert_LogError    Script Date: 6/14/2000
******/
CREATE Procedure sp_insert_LogError
    (@ErrorDate_1 datetime,
     @ErrorNumber_2 int,
     @ErrorSource_3 varchar,
     @ErrorDescription_4 varchar,
     @Message_5 varchar)

AS INSERT INTO ErrorLog
    ( LogTime,
      ErrorNumber,
      ErrorSource,
      ErrorDescription,
      Message)

VALUES
     (@ErrorDate_1,
      @ErrorNumber_2,
      @ErrorSource_3,
      @ErrorDescription_4,
      @Message_5)

GO
SET QUOTED_IDENTIFIER  OFF    SET ANSI_NULLS  ON
GO
```

Stored Procedures

As we mentioned in Chapter 10 where we introduced the concept of stored procedures, the procedures that we use in the WROBA application can be categorized as follows:

- Stored procedures used to delete rows
- Stored procedures used to insert rows into tables
- Stored procedures used to select rows
- Stored procedures are used to update tables
- Stored procedures used to verify information

Refer to Chapter 10 for instructions on how to save these stored procedures to the BigBank database.

Stored Procedures to Delete Rows

```
Create Procedure sp_delete_Bank
  (@BankId_1 smallint,
   @ReturnValue int output)

AS DELETE Bank

WHERE  (BankId = @BankId_1)

SET @ReturnValue = @@ERROR

RETURN @ReturnValue
```

```
Create PROCEDURE sp_delete_BankAccount(@AccountId_1 int)

AS DELETE BankAccount

WHERE ( AccountId = @AccountId_1)
```

```
Create PROCEDURE sp_delete_CardxAccount(@AccountId_1 int)

AS DELETE CardxAccount

WHERE ( AccountId = @AccountId_1)
```

```
CREATE Procedure sp_delete_payee
  (@PayeeId_1    char(36),
   @ReturnValue  int output)
AS  DELETE Payee
WHERE  (PayeeId = @PayeeId_1)

SET @ReturnValue = @@ERROR

RETURN @ReturnValue
```

Note – we discuss the following stored procedure, `sp_delete_TxLock`, *in Chapter 10.*

```
CREATE PROCEDURE sp_delete_TxLock
  (@BankId_1    smallint,
   @CardId_2    int)

AS DELETE TxLock

WHERE
  ( BankId    = @BankId_1) and
  ( CardId    = @CardId_2)
```

```
Create PROCEDURE sp_delete_WROBACard(@CardId_1 int)

AS DELETE WROBACard

WHERE    ( CardId = @CardId_1)
```

Stored Procedures to Insert Rows into Tables

```
Create Procedure sp_insert_Bank
  (@BankId_1 smallint,
   @BankDesc_2 char(20),
   @BankDSN_3 varchar(250),
   @ReturnValue int output)

AS INSERT INTO Bank
  ( BankId,
   BankDesc,
   BankDSN)

VALUES
  (@BankId_1,
   @BankDesc_2,
   @BankDSN_3)

SET @ReturnValue = @@ERROR

RETURN    @ReturnValue
```

Note – we discuss the following stored procedure, `sp_insert_BankAccount`, *in Chapter 10.*

```
Create Procedure sp_insert_BankAccount
  (@AccountId_1 int,
   @AccountType_2 tinyint,
   @Balance_3 money,
   @Limit_4 money,
   @Remaining_5 money,
   @LastDate_6 datetime,
   @Overdraft_7 money,
   @ReturnValue int output)

AS INSERT INTO BankAccount
  (AccountId,
   AccountType,
   Balance,
   DailyWithdrawalLimit,
   DailyRemaining,
   LastWithdrawalDate,
   OverdraftLimit)

VALUES
  (@AccountId_1,
   @AccountType_2,
   @Balance_3,
   @Limit_4,
   @Remaining_5,
   @LastDate_6,
   @Overdraft_7)

SET @ReturnValue = @@ERROR

RETURN    @ReturnValue
```

```
Create Procedure sp_insert_CardxAccount
  (@CardId_1 int,
   @AccountType_2 tinyint,
   @AccountId_3 int,
   @ReturnValue int output)

AS INSERT INTO CardxAccount
  (CardId,
   AccountType,
   AccountId)

VALUES
  (@CardId_1,
   @AccountType_2,
   @AccountId_3)

SET @ReturnValue = @@ERROR

RETURN    @ReturnValue
```

```
CREATE PROCEDURE sp_insert_Payee
  (@CardId_2 int,
   @PayeeDesc_3 char(30),
   @BankId_4 smallint,
   @AccountId_5 int,
   @DefaultAmount_6 money,
   @WROBACardId_7 int,
   @ReturnValue int output)

AS INSERT INTO Payee
  (PayeeId,
   CardId,
   PayeeDesc,
   BankId,
   AccountId,
   DefaultAmount,
   WROBACardId)

VALUES
  (NewID(),
   @CardId_2,
   @PayeeDesc_3,
   @BankId_4,
   @AccountId_5,
   @DefaultAmount_6,
   @WROBACardId_7)

SET @ReturnValue = @@ERROR

RETURN    @ReturnValue
```

```
CREATE PROCEDURE sp_insert_TxLock
  (@BankId_1    smallint,
   @CardId_2    int)

AS INSERT INTO TxLock
  (BankId, CardId)

VALUES
  ( @BankId_1, @CardId_2)
```

```
CREATE Procedure sp_insert_WROBACard
  (@CardId_1 int,
   @Password_2 char(10),
   @InvalidPasswordCnt_3 tinyint,
   @ReturnValue int output)

AS INSERT INTO WROBACard
  (CardId,
   Password,
   InvalidPasswordCnt)

VALUES
  (@CardId_1,
   @Password_2,
   @InvalidPasswordCnt_3)

SET @ReturnValue = @@ERROR

RETURN    @ReturnValue
```

Stored Procedures to Select Rows

Note – we discuss the following stored procedure, sp_select_AccountHistory_ By_AccountID, in Chapter 10.

```
CREATE PROCEDURE sp_select_AccountHistory_By_AccountId (
    @AccountId_1 int,
    @MaxTxDate_2 datetime)
AS
SELECT TOP 5 AccountHistory.TxDate, TxType.TxTypeDesc,
    AccountHistory.TxDescription, AccountHistory.TxAmount,
    AccountHistory.CounterpartyRef
FROM AccountHistory INNER JOIN
    TxType ON AccountHistory.TxType = TxType.TxType
WHERE (AccountHistory.AccountId = @AccountId_1) AND
    (TxDate <=
        (SELECT MAX(TxDate)
        FROM AccountHistory
        WHERE (AccountHistory.AccountId = @AccountId_1) AND
            (TxDate < @MaxTxDate_2)))
ORDER BY AccountHistory.TxDate DESC
```

```
Create PROCEDURE sp_select_AccountId_By_CardId (@CardId_1 int)
AS SELECT CardxAccount.AccountId
FROM CardxAccount INNER JOIN
     WROBACard ON
     CardxAccount.CardId = WROBACard.CardId
WHERE (WROBACard.CardId = @CardId_1)

--RETURN @@ROWCOUNT
```

```
Create Procedure sp_select_AccountType

As SELECT AccountType, AccountTypeDesc

FROM AccountType

WHERE (AccountTypeDesc <> 'Administrator')     .
```

```
CREATE Procedure sp_select_AccountType_By_CardId(@CardId_1 int)

As SELECT AccountTypeDesc

FROM AccountType INNER JOIN
     CardxAccount ON
     AccountType.AccountType = CardxAccount.AccountType

WHERE (CardxAccount.CardId = @CardId_1)
```

```
CREATE PROCEDURE sp_select_All_Payees (@CardId 1 int)

AS

SELECT PayeeId, CardId, PayeeDesc, BankId, AccountId, DefaultAmount,
       WROBACardId

FROM Payee

WHERE (WROBACardId = @CardId_1)
```

```
CREATE PROCEDURE sp_select_Bank AS
SELECT BankId, BankDesc, BankDSN
FROM Bank
ORDER BY BankId
```

```
CREATE PROCEDURE sp_select_Bank_By_BankId (
@BankId_1 int)
AS
SELECT BankDesc, BankDSN
FROM Bank
WHERE (BankId = @BankId_1)
```

```
CREATE PROCEDURE sp_select_BankAccount_By_AccountId (
    @AccountId_1 int,
    @AccountTypeDesc_2 char(15) out,
    @Balance_3 money out,
    @DailyRemaining_4 money out,
    @OverdraftLimit_5 money out)
AS
-- NOTE: If LastWithdrawalDate is not current, then this
-- stored procedure will reset the DailyRemaining
-- and the LastWithdrawalDate.

DECLARE @today DATETIME

SELECT @today = GETDATE()

IF (SELECT DATEDIFF(DAY, LastWithdrawalDate, @today)
    FROM BankAccount
    WHERE ( AccountId    = @AccountId_1))
    > 0
BEGIN
   UPDATE BankAccount
     SET  DailyRemaining    = DailyWithdrawalLimit,
          LastWithdrawalDate    = @today
     WHERE ( AccountId    = @AccountId_1)
END

SELECT
    @AccountTypeDesc_2 = AccountType.AccountTypeDesc,
    @Balance_3 = BankAccount.Balance,
    @DailyRemaining_4 = BankAccount.DailyRemaining,
    @OverdraftLimit_5 = BankAccount.OverdraftLimit
FROM BankAccount INNER JOIN
    AccountType ON
    BankAccount.AccountType = AccountType.AccountType
WHERE (BankAccount.AccountId = @AccountId_1)
```

```
CREATE PROCEDURE sp_select_BankAccount_By_CardId (
@CardId_1 int)
AS
SELECT BankAccount.AccountId, AccountType.AccountTypeDesc,
    BankAccount.Balance, BankAccount.DailyWithdrawalLimit,
    BankAccount.DailyRemaining,
    BankAccount.LastWithdrawalDate,
    BankAccount.OverdraftLimit
FROM BankAccount INNER JOIN
    CardxAccount ON
    BankAccount.AccountId = CardxAccount.AccountId INNER JOIN
    WROBACard ON
    CardxAccount.CardId = WROBACard.CardId INNER JOIN
    AccountType ON
    CardxAccount.AccountType = AccountType.AccountType
WHERE (WROBACard.CardId = @CardId_1)

--RETURN @@ROWCOUNT
```

```
Create PROCEDURE sp_select_Last_AccountId(@ReturnValue int output)
AS SELECT @ReturnValue = MAX(AccountId)
FROM CardxAccount
```

```
Create PROCEDURE sp_select_Last_CardId(@ReturnValue int output)
AS SELECT @ReturnValue = MAX(CardId)
FROM WROBACard
```

```
CREATE Procedure sp_select_PayeeByCardId
    (@CardId_1    int)

AS SELECT
    PayeeId,
    PayeeDesc,
    BankId,
    AccountId,
    DefaultAmount

FROM Payee

WHERE (CardId =  @CardId_1)
```

```
CREATE PROCEDURE sp_select_WROBACard_PwdCnt (
@CardId_1 int,
@Password_2 char(10),
@InvalidPasswordCnt_3 tinyint output)
AS
SELECT @InvalidPasswordCnt_3 = InvalidPasswordCnt
FROM WROBACard
WHERE CardId = @CardId_1
AND Password = @Password_2

return @@ROWCOUNT     -- 0 means not found, 1 means it matched
```

Stored Procedures to Update Tables

```
Create PROCEDURE sp_update_Bank
   (@BankId_1 smallint,
    @BankDesc_2 char(20),
    @BankDSN_3 varchar(250),
    @ReturnValue int output)

AS UPDATE Bank

SET  BankDesc = @BankDesc_2,
        BankDSN = @BankDSN_3

WHERE
    (BankId = @BankId_1)

SET @ReturnValue = @@ERROR

RETURN @ReturnValue
```

```
CREATE PROCEDURE sp_update_BankAccount
  (@AccountId_1    int,
   @Balance_2    money,
   @DailyRemaining_3    money)

AS UPDATE BankAccount

SET  Balance    = @Balance_2,
     DailyRemaining    = @DailyRemaining_3

WHERE
  (AccountId    = @AccountId_1)
```

Note – we discuss the following stored procedure, `sp_update_BankAccount_Dec`, *in Chapter 10.*

```
CREATE PROCEDURE sp_update_BankAccount_Dec
  (@AccountId_1    int,
   @TxAmount_2    money,
   @TxType_3    tinyint,
   @TxDescription_4    char(40),
   @CounterpartyRef_5    char(16),
   @ReturnValue int output

-- NOTE 1: The name of the @ReturnValue parameter is hardcoded
-- in a VB method in the data layer and MUST NOT be changed.
-- NOTE 2:The following meaning for the return values are
-- assumed in the business layer:
   -- Success = 0;
   -- DailyLimitExceeded = 1;
   -- NotEnoughFunds = 2;
   -- UnknownError = 3.
-- NOTE 3: If LastWithdrawalDate is not current, then this
-- stored procedure will reset the DailyRemaining
-- and the LastWithdrawalDate, even if the withdrawal
-- is refused (DailyLimitExceeded or NotEnoughFunds).
)

AS

DECLARE @today DATETIME

SELECT @today = GETDATE()

SELECT @ReturnValue = 3          -- Pessimistic default to UnknownError

IF   (SELECT DATEDIFF(DAY, LastWithdrawalDate, @today)
     FROM BankAccount
     WHERE ( AccountId    = @AccountId_1))
   > 0
BEGIN
   -- LastWithdrawalDate is not current, reset the DailyRemaining
   -- and the LastWithdrawalDate

   UPDATE BankAccount
```

```
        SET   DailyRemaining    = DailyWithdrawalLimit,
            LastWithdrawalDate   = @today
        WHERE ( AccountId    = @AccountId_1)
    END

    IF   (SELECT Balance + OverdraftLimit
          FROM BankAccount
          WHERE ( AccountId    = @AccountId_1))
        < @TxAmount_2

        SELECT @ReturnValue = 2           -- NotEnoughFunds

    ELSE

    BEGIN

        IF     (SELECT DailyRemaining
                FROM BankAccount
                WHERE ( AccountId    = @AccountId_1))
            < @TxAmount_2

            SELECT @ReturnValue = 1          -- DailyLimitExceeded

        ELSE

        BEGIN
            -- Withdraw
            UPDATE BankAccount
            SET    Balance        = Balance - @TxAmount_2,
                DailyRemaining    = DailyRemaining - @TxAmount_2
            WHERE
            ( AccountId    = @AccountId_1)

            -- Update AccountHistory
            INSERT INTO AccountHistory
            ( TxId,
            AccountId,
            TxDate,
            TxType,
            TxDescription,
            TxAmount,
            CounterpartyRef)
            VALUES
            ( NEWID(),
            @AccountId_1,
            @today,
            @TxType_3,
            @TxDescription_4,
            - @TxAmount_2,
            @CounterpartyRef_5)

            SELECT @ReturnValue = 0          -- Success
        END
    END

    RETURN @ReturnValue
    CREATE PROCEDURE sp_update_BankAccount_Inc
    (@AccountId_1     int,
    @TxAmount_2      money,
```

```
@TxType_3      tinyint,
    @TxDescription_4     char(40),
    @CounterpartyRef_5     char(16))

AS

UPDATE BankAccount
SET   Balance         = Balance + @TxAmount_2
WHERE
   ( AccountId     = @AccountId_1)

INSERT INTO AccountHistory
   (TxId,
    AccountId,
    TxDate,
    TxType,
    TxDescription,
    TxAmount,
    CounterpartyRef)

VALUES
   (NEWID(),
    @AccountId_1,
    GETDATE(),
    @TxType_3,
    @TxDescription_4,
    @TxAmount_2,
    @CounterpartyRef_5)
```

```
CREATE Procedure sp_update_payee
   (@PayeeId_1    char(36),
    @PayeeDesc_2    char(30),
    @DefaultAmount_3    money,
    @ReturnValue   int output)

AS UPDATE Payee

SET   PayeeDesc = @PayeeDesc_2,
   DefaultAmount = @DefaultAmount_3

WHERE   ( PayeeId    = @PayeeId_1)

SET @ReturnValue = @@ERROR

RETURN  @ReturnValue
```

```
CREATE PROCEDURE sp_update_WROBACard_Pwd (
@CardId_1 int,
@Password_2 char(10))
AS
UPDATE WROBACard SET Password = @Password_2
WHERE CardId = @CardId_1

return @@ROWCOUNT      -- 0 means not found, 1 means it matched
```

765

```
CREATE PROCEDURE sp_update_WROBACard_PwdCnt
   (@CardId_1     int,
    @InvalidPasswordCnt_2      tinyint)

AS UPDATE WROBACard

SET  InvalidPasswordCnt    = @InvalidPasswordCnt_2

WHERE
   ( CardId    = @CardId_1)
```

Stored Procedures to Verify Information

Note – we discuss the following stored procedure, sp_verify_BankAccount_By_CardID, in Chapter 10.

```
CREATE PROCEDURE sp_verify_BankAccount_By_CardId (
@CardId_1 int,
@ReturnValue int output
)
AS
SELECT @ReturnValue  = COUNT(BankAccount.AccountId)
FROM BankAccount
WHERE (BankAccount.AccountId = @CardId_1)
RETURN @ReturnValue
```

```
Create PROCEDURE sp_verify_CardAccount_By_CardId (@CardId_1 int,@ReturnValue int
output)
AS
SELECT @ReturnValue  = COUNT(CardId)
FROM WROBACard
WHERE (CardId = @CardId_1)
RETURN @ReturnValue
```

```
CREATE PROCEDURE sp_verify_Payee_By_CardId (@CardId_1 int, @ReturnValue int
output)
AS
SELECT CardId
FROM Payee
WHERE (CardId = @CardId_1)

SET @ReturnValue = @@ROWCOUNT      -- 0 means not found, 1 means it matched

RETURN @ReturnValue
```

The Visual Basic Project

You'll find the complete VB code listings for this case study interspersed throughout the book. We discuss this code in detail in the relevant chapters.

We've now covered the data services tier of our application. The code modules that make up the Bank project fall into three projects corresponding to our three remaining tiers:

- ❑ The data services tier – Bank_DB.dll

- ❑ The business services tier – Bank_Bus.dll

- ❑ The user services tier – BankUI.exe

These fit together like this:

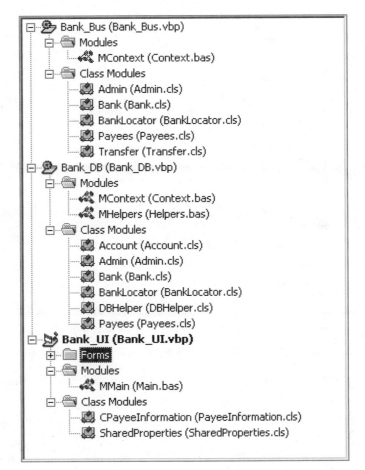

We also have 18 forms that make up our user interface, as follows:

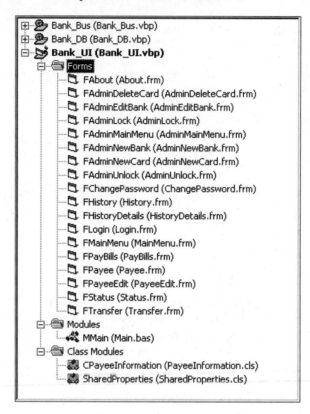

The following tables summarize what each of these does.

Bank_DB

The Bank_DB component provides the data access services for our application:

Module Type	Name	Filename	Description
Standard	MContext	Context.bas	A module shared by the business and data tiers: encapsulates all the transactional functions for the project.
Standard	MHelpers	Helper.bas	Holds general enumerations and data type conversion functions for the Bank_DB project.
Class	Account	Account.cls	Implements methods to add and delete funds from accounts, and verify accounts: the only class in this project to require transactions.

Module Type	Name	Filename	Description
Class	Admin	Admin.cls	Implements two properties that return the account types for a current CardID and for all account IDs.
Class	Bank	Bank.cls	Used to interact with the Bank: deals with tasks such as logging in, changing the password, tracking account history and balance.
Class	BankLocator	BankLocator.cls	Implements the property to create the connection to the server and database.
Class	DBHelper	DBHelper.cls	A helper class to facilitate the creation of data tier functionality.
Class	Payees	Payess.cls	Used to deal with payees, including adding, editing, and deleting payees.

We cover building this project in Chapter 12.

In addition to the classes listed above, in Chapter 12 we also show you how to add the optional Logger class (Logger.cls) to implement error logging to the database.

Bank_Bus

The Bank_Bus component provides the code used in the business services tier of our application. All the classes in this tier are run under MTS control.

Module Type	Name	Filename	Description
Standard	MContext	Context.bas	A module shared by the business and data tiers: encapsulates all the transactional functions for the project.
Class	Admin	Admin.cls	Contains properties implemented as pass-through calls to the data tier and business logic dealing with administrative functionality.

Table continued on following page

Module Type	Name	Filename	Description
Class	Bank	Bank.cls	Contains properties and methods implemented as pass-through calls to the data services tier and business logic dealing with functionality such as verifying and changing passwords, locking and unlocking WROBA cards, and getting account information.
Class	BankLocator	BankLocator.cls	Passes a call through to the data services tier to get the connection to the server and database.
Class	Payees	Payees.cls	Contains properties implemented as pass-through calls to the data tier, dealing with functionality related to payees.
Class	Transfer	Transfer.cls	The only class in this project that currently implements a transactional context: contains business logic needed to implement financial transactions.

We cover building this project in chapter 13.

Bank_UI

This contains the code for the user services tier, which lets customers and bank administrators interact with the application:

Module Type	Name	Filename	Description
Standard	MMain	Main.bas	The main module, which creates the SharedProperies object when the application starts and removes it when the application closes.

Module Type	Name	Filename	Description
Class	CPayee Information	Payee Information.cls	Contains the Let and Get statements for the property values used by the procedures that involve the payee.
Class	Shared Properties	Shared Properties.cls	Contains Let and Get statements for property variables used throughout the application.
Form	FAbout	About.frm	The About screen, which gives users information about the application.
Form	FAdmin DeleteCard	Admin DeleteCard.frm	Used by administrators to validate and then delete an existing WROBA card account.
Form	FAdmin EditBank	Admin EditBank.frm	Used by administrators to change existing details about a bank.
Form	FAdminLock	AdminLock.frm	Used by administrators to lock a WROBA card account.
Form	FAmin MainMenu	Admin MainMenu.frm	The main menu for WROBA administrators.
Form	FAdmin NewBank	Admin NewBank.frm	Used by administrators to add details about a new bank.
Form	FAdmin NewCard	Admin NewCard.frm	Used by administrators to create a new WROBA card account.
Form	FAdmin Unlock	AdminUnlock.frm	Used by administrators to unlock a WROBA card account that has been locked by an administrator, or was left locked when the application terminated abnormally.
Form	FChange Password	Change Password.frm	Allows the user to change their password.

Table continued on following page

Module Type	Name	Filename	Description
Form	FHistory	History.frm	Enables customers to select which account they want to see details of in the FHistoryDetails form.
Form	FHistory Details	History Details.frm	Displays details of five previous transactions for the account selected in the FHistory form.
Form	FLogin	Login.frm	The login form for the application, where the user enters their card number and password.
Form	FMainMenu	MainMenu.frm	The main menu for WROBA customers.
Form	FPayBills	PayBills.frm	Allows customers to pay bills to their payees.
Form	FPayee	Payee.frm	Used to add details of a new payee.
Form	FPayeeEdit	PayeeEdit.frm	Used to edit details of an existing payee.
Form	FStatus	Status.frm	Used to inform the user of the status of some activity (whether it failed or succeeded).
Form	FTransfer	Transfer.frm	Allows customers to transfer funds between their Checking and Saving accounts and vice versa.

We deal with the customer side of this project in Chapter 14, and the administrative side in Chapter 15.

Installing and Configuring MTS

Microsoft Transaction Server 2.0 is available in the Windows NT 4.0 Option Pack, which is included with both the Professional and Enterprise editions of Visual Studio 6.0. It is located on CD-ROM #2 inside the NTOptPk folder. This folder contains an x86 folder, which in turn contains three subfolders: Win.95, Winnt.srv, and Winnt.wks. These folders contain the installation files for Windows 95/98, Windows NT Server, and Windows NT Workstation, respectively:

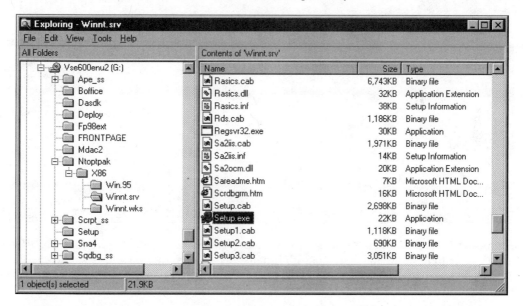

The Windows NT 4.0 Option Pack is also available for download at
http://www.microsoft.com/ntserver/nts/downloads/. However, be
warned: it's a 27 MB download.

To install Microsoft Transaction Server, launch `Setup.exe` from the appropriate subdirectory.

> **If you are running Windows NT Service Pack 4 or later, you will be warned that the Option Pack has not been tested on that service pack. Click on Yes to continue. After installation, you should reinstall the service pack you were running in order to restore versions of DLLs that were replaced by the Windows NT 4.0 Option Pack.**

A welcome screen listing the components that are included in the Windows NT 4.0 Option Pack will be displayed:

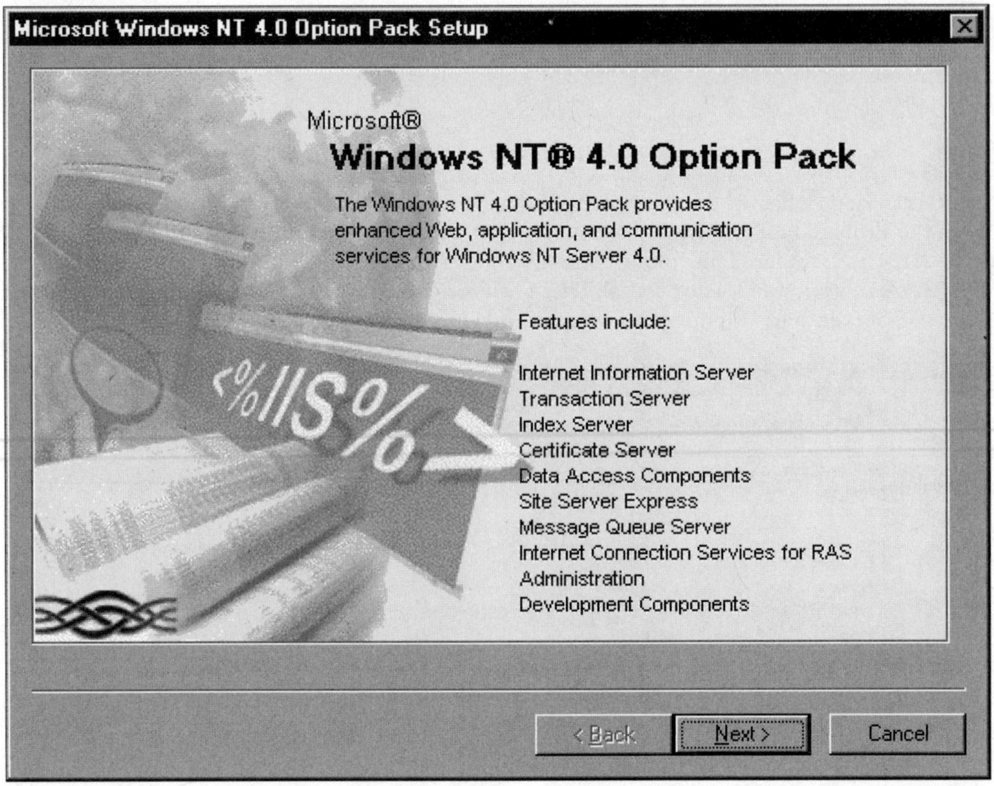

Click on **Next** to continue. You will be shown a license agreement. After you have read it, click on **Accept** to agree to its terms and continue with installation. The next screen allows you to choose a minimal, typical, or custom installation. Both a minimal and a typical installation install Internet Information Server. Since we are only interested in Transaction Server, click on **Custom** here:

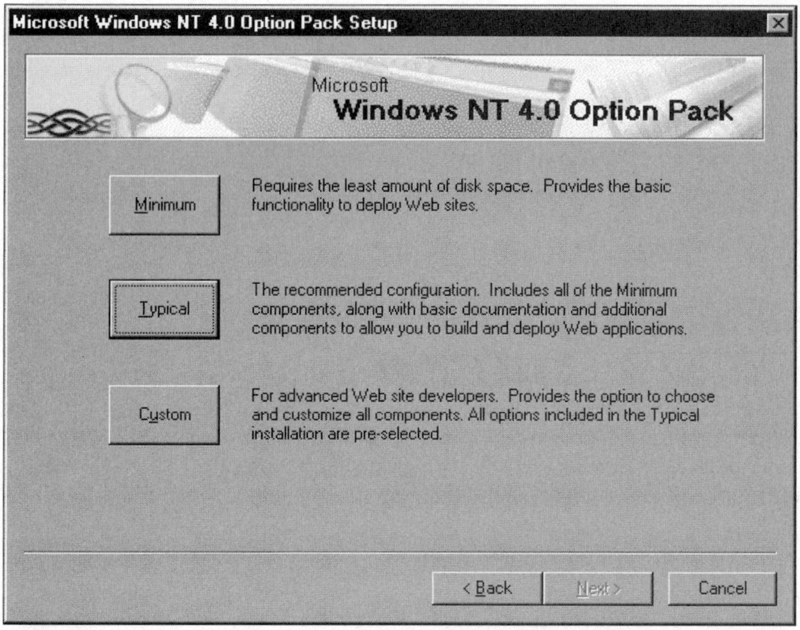

Microsoft Windows NT 4.0 Option Pack Setup

Microsoft
Windows NT 4.0 Option Pack

Minimum — Requires the least amount of disk space. Provides the basic functionality to deploy Web sites.

Typical — The recommended configuration. Includes all of the Minimum components, along with basic documentation and additional components to allow you to build and deploy Web applications.

Custom — For advanced Web site developers. Provides the option to choose and customize all components. All options included in the Typical installation are pre-selected.

< Back   Next >   Cancel

The next screen allows you to choose the parts of the option pack you would like to install. The components that are installed during a typical installation are selected by default:

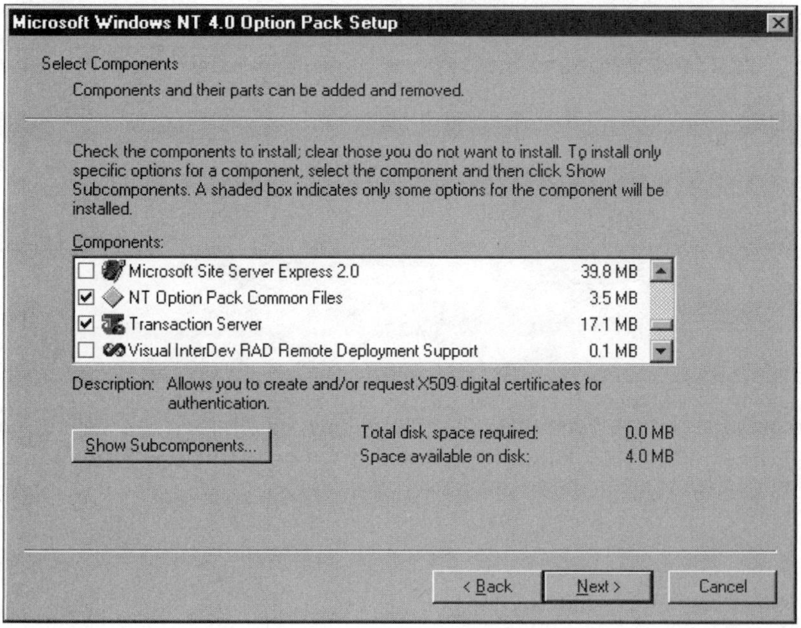

Microsoft Windows NT 4.0 Option Pack Setup

Select Components

Components and their parts can be added and removed.

Check the components to install; clear those you do not want to install. To install only specific options for a component, select the component and then click Show Subcomponents. A shaded box indicates only some options for the component will be installed.

Components:

	Component	Size
☐	Microsoft Site Server Express 2.0	39.8 MB
☑	NT Option Pack Common Files	3.5 MB
☑	Transaction Server	17.1 MB
☐	Visual InterDev RAD Remote Deployment Support	0.1 MB

Description: Allows you to create and/or request X509 digital certificates for authentication.

Show Subcomponents...

Total disk space required: 0.0 MB
Space available on disk: 4.0 MB

< Back   Next >   Cancel

The only components required for running Microsoft Transaction Server are:

- ❑ Microsoft Data Access Components
- ❑ Microsoft Management Console
- ❑ NT Option Pack Common Files
- ❑ Transaction Server

> **If you are already running Internet Information Server 4.0, some of these components will already be installed on the computer.**

Feel free to clear the check box of any other components you don't wish to install. You will also want to install all of the components of Transaction Server. Either click in the Transaction Server check box twice, or select Transaction Server and click on Show Subcomponents.... By default, the Transaction Server Development components are not selected. Click to select them:

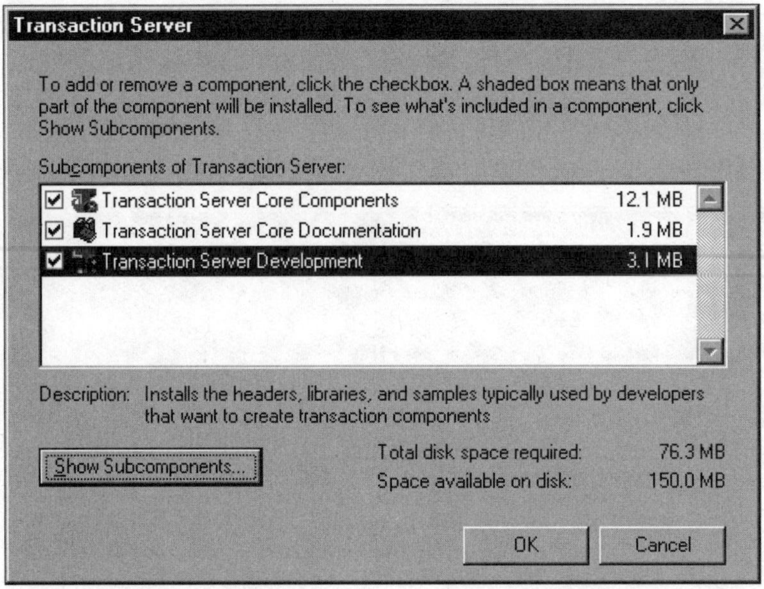

The Transaction Server Development components include the libraries you will need to call from Visual Basic. They also include a Visual Basic add-in you can use to update the MTS package with the latest version of your component as you make changes:

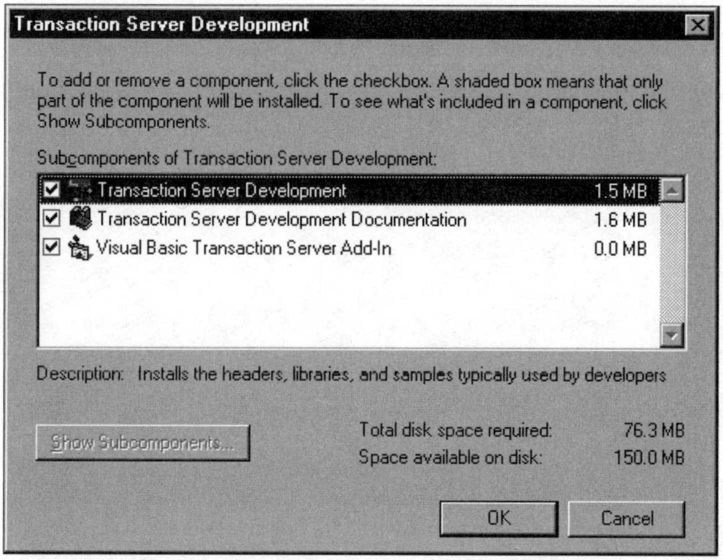

Once you have finished selecting the subcomponents you'd like to install, close all of the subcomponent dialogs by clicking on OK and click on Next to continue the installation. If you are only installing Transaction Server and the components it depends on, you will next be asked to choose a destination for the Transaction Server files:

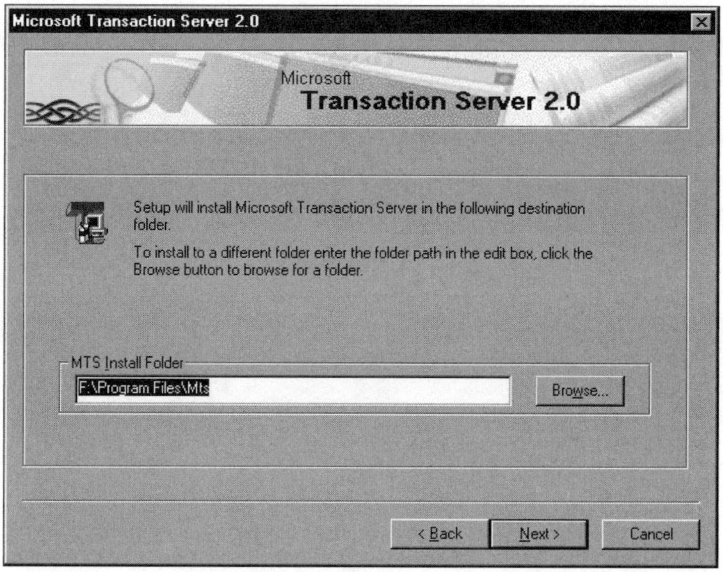

Once you have selected a destination, click on Next to continue. When MTS is installed, it automatically defaults to Local administration where MTS is configured by default to allow administration for the interactive user (the user that is currently logged on to the machine). If you want to enable remote administration, you should select the option button labeled Remote and then enter a login ID and password for an administrator account:

779

Setup will copy the appropriate files to your computer. You will need to restart after the files have been copied.

Recordset

Recordset.AddNew([*FieldList As Variant*], [*Values As Variant*])
Recordset.Cancel
Recordset.CancelBatch([*AffectRecords As AffectEnum*])
Recordset.CancelUpdate
Recordset = *Recordset*.Clone([*LockType As LockTypeEnum*])
Recordset.Close
CompareEnum = *Recordset*.CompareBookmarks(*Bookmark1 As Variant,_
                                              Bookmark2 As Variant*)
Recordset.Delete(*AffectRecords As AffectEnum*)
Recordset.Find(*Criteria As String*, [*SkipRecords As Long*], _
                [*SearchDirection As SearchDirectionEnum*], [*Start As Variant*])
Variant = *Recordset*.GetRows(*Rows As Long*, [*Start As Variant*], [*Fields As Variant*])
String = *Recordset*.GetString(*StringFormat As StringFormatEnum*, [*NumRows As Long*], _
                                 [*ColumnDelimeter As String*], [*RowDelimeter As String*], _
                                 [*NullExpr As String*])
Recordset.Move(*NumRecords As Long*, [*Start As Variant*])
Recordset.MoveFirst
Recordset.MoveLast
Recordset.MoveNext
Recordset.MovePrevious
Recordset = *Recordset*.NextRecordset([*RecordsAffected As Variant*])
Recordset.Open([*Source As Variant*], [*ActiveConnection As Variant*], _
                 [*CursorType As CursorTypeEnum*], [*LockType As LockTypeEnum*], _
                 [*Options As Long*])
Recordset.Requery([*Options As Long*])
Recordset.Resync([*AffectRecords As AffectEnum*], [*ResyncValues As ResyncEnum*])
Recordset.Save([*Destination As Variant*], [*PersistFormat As PersistFormatEnum*])
Recordset.Seek(*KeyValues As Variant, SeekOption As SeekEnum*)
Boolean = *Recordset*.Supports(*CursorOptions As CursorOptionEnum*)
Recordset.Update([*Fields As Variant*], [*Values As Variant*])
Recordset.UpdateBatch([*AffectRecords As AffectEnum*])

Stream

Stream.Cancel
Stream.Close
Stream.CopyTo(*DestStream As Stream*, [*CharNumber As Long*])
Stream.Flush
Stream.LoadFromFile(*FileName As String*)
Stream.Open([*Source As Variant*], [*Mode As ConnectModeEnum*], _
              [*Options As StreamOpenOptionsEnum*], [*UserName As String*], _
              [*Password As String*])
Variant = *Stream*.Read([*NumBytes As Long*])
String = *Stream*.ReadText([*NumChars As Long*])
Stream.SaveToFile(*FileName As String*, *Options As SaveOptionsEnum*)
Stream.SetEOS
Stream.SkipLine
Stream.Write(*Buffer As Variant*)
Stream.WriteText(*Data As String*, [*Options As StreamWriteEnum*])

ASP 2.0 and ASP 3.0 Object Model

This appendix offers a handy reference to the Active Server Pages **object model**, covering ASP 2.0 and ASP 3.0, and in each case provides the properties, methods and events for the object, along with their collections.

> Objects, methods and properties added in ASP 3.0 are shown *italicized*.

Objects

Name	Description
Application	The Application object holds information about currently active sessions.
ASPError	The *ASPError* object provides a range of detailed information about the last error that occurred in ASP.
Request	The Request object makes available to the script all the information that the client provides when requesting a page or submitting a form.
Response	The Response object is used to access the response that is being sent back to the client. It also provides a series of methods that are used to create the returned page.
Server	The Server object provides a series of methods and properties that are useful in scripting with ASP.
Session	The Session object provides a repository for storing variables and object references that are available just to the pages that the visitor opens during the lifetime of the session.
ObjectContext	Used to manage transactions when using MTS.

The Application Object

Each application is represented by an instance of the Application object. This object stores variables and objects for application-scope usage. It also holds information about any currently-active sessions.

Collections

Collections	Description
Contents	Contains all of the items added to the application through script commands.
StaticObjects	Contains all of the objects added to the application with the <OBJECT> tag.

Methods

Methods	Description
Contents.Remove ("variable_name")	Removes a named variable from the Application.Contents collection.
Contents.RemoveAll()	Removes all variables from the Application.Contents collection.
Lock()	Prevents other clients from modifying application properties.
Unlock()	Allows other clients to modify application properties.

You cannot remove variables from the Application.StaticObjects collection at run-time.

Events

Events	Description
onStart	Occurs when a page in the application is first referenced.
onEnd	Occurs when the application ends, that is, when the web server is shut down.

The ASPError Object

The ASPError object is new in ASP 3.0, and is available through the GetLastError method of the Server object. It provides a range of detailed information about the last error that occurred in ASP.

Properties

Property	Description
ASPCode	*Integer.* The error number generated by IIS.
ASPDescription	*Integer.* A detailed description of the error if it is ASP-related.
Category	*String.* Indicates the source of the error: for example, ASP itself, the scripting language, or an object.
Column	*Integer.* The character position within the file that generated the error.
Description	*String.* A short description of the error.
File	*String.* The name of the file that was being processed when the error occurred.
Line	*Integer.* The number of the line within the file that generated the error.
Number	*Integer.* A standard COM error code.
Source	*String.* The actual code, where available, of the line that caused the error.

The Request Object

Together, the Request object and the Response object form the 'conversational mechanism' of ASP. The Request object is responsible for controlling how the user sends information to the server. Using the Request object, the server can obtain information about what the user wants – either explicitly (for example, through programmed ASP code) or implicitly (for example, through the HTTP headers).

Collections

Collections	Description
ClientCertificate	Client certificate values sent from the browser. Read Only.
Cookies	Values of cookies sent from the browser. Read Only.
Form	Values of form elements sent from the browser. Read Only.
QueryString	Values of variables in the HTTP query string. Read Only.
ServerVariables	Values of the HTTP and environment variables. Read Only.

Properties

Property	Description
TotalBytes	Specifies the number of bytes the client is sending in the body of the request. Read Only.

Methods

Method	Description
BinaryRead (count)	Used to retrieve *count* bytes of data sent to the server as part of the POST request. This method *cannot* be used successfully if the ASP code has already referenced the Request.Form collection; likewise, the Request.Form collection *cannot* be successfully accessed if you have used the Binaryread method.

The Response Object

The Response object is responsible for sending the server's output to the client. In this sense, the Response object is the counterpart to the Request object: the Request object gathers information from both the client and the server, and the Response object sends, or resends, the information to the client by writing to the HTTP data stream.

Collections

Collection	Description
Cookies	Values of all the cookies to send to the browser. Each member is Write Only.

The Response object provides a range of properties that can be read (in most cases) and modified to tailor the response:

Properties

Properties	Description
Buffer = True|False	*Boolean.* Read/Write. Determines whether the page is to be buffered until complete.
CacheControl "setting"	*String.* Read/Write. Determines whether proxy servers are allowed to cache the output generated by ASP.
Charset = "value"	*String.* Read/Write. Appends the name of the character set to the content-type header.

Properties	Description
ContentType "MIME-type"	*String*. Read/Write. HTTP content type (for example, "Text/HTML") for the response.
Expires minutes	*Number*. Read/Write. Number of minutes between caching and expiry, for a page cached on the browser.
ExpiresAbsolute #date[time]#	*Date/Time*. Read/Write. Explicit date and/or time of expiry for a page cached on a browser.
IsClientConnected	*Boolean*. Read Only. Indicates whether the client has disconnected from the server.
PICS ("PICS-label-string")	*String*. Write Only. Adds the value of a PICS label to the pics-label field of the response header.
Status = " code message"	*String*. Read/Write. Value of the HTTP status line returned by the server.

Methods

Methods	Description
AddHeader ("name", "content")	Adds or changes a value in the HTML header.
AppendToLog ("string")	Adds text to the web server log entry for this request.
BinaryWrite (SafeArray)	Sends text to the browser without character-set conversion.
Clear()	Erases any buffered HTML output.
End()	Stops processing the page and returns the current result.
Flush()	Sends buffered output immediately.
Redirect("url")	Instructs the browser to connect to a different URL.
Write ("string")	Writes variable values, strings, etc. to the current page as a string.

The Response interface elements can be divided into groups, like this:

Response Items	Description
Write, BinaryWrite	Insert information into a page.
Cookies	Sends cookies to the browser.
Redirect	Redirects the browser.
Buffer, Flush, Clear, End	Buffer the page as it is created.

Table continued on following page

807

Response Items	Description
Expires, ExpiresAbsolute, ContentType, AddHeader, Status, CacheContol, PICS, Charset	Set the properties of a page.
IsClientConnected	Checks the client connection.

The Server Object

The main use of the Server object is to create components.

Properties

Property	Description
ScriptTimeout	Length of time a script can run before an error occurs.

Methods

Methods	Description
CreateObject ("identifier")	Creates an instance of an object or server component.
Execute ("url")	Stops execution of the current page and transfers control to the page specified in "url". After that page has finished execution, control passes back to the original page and execution resumes at the statement after the Execute method call.
GetLastError()	Returns a reference to an ASPError object that holds details of the last error that occurred within the ASP processing.
HTMLEncode ("string")	Applies HTML encoding to the specified string.
MapPath ("url")	Converts a virtual path into a physical path.
Transfer ("url")	Stops execution of the current page and transfers control to the page specified in "url". Unlike the Execute method, execution does not resume in the original page, but ends when the new page has completed executing.
URLEncode ("string")	Applies URL encoding, including escape chars, to a string.

The Session Object

The Session object is used to keep track of an individual browser as it navigates through your web site.

Collections

Collections	Description
Contents	Contains all of the items added to the session through script commands.
StaticObjects	Contains all of the objects added to the session with the <OBJECT> tag.

Properties

Properties	Description
CodePage	Sets the codepage that will be used for symbol mapping.
LCID	Sets the locale identifier.
SessionID	Returns the session identification for this user.
Timeout	Sets the timeout period for the session state for this application, in minutes.

Methods

Methods	Description
Contents.Remove ("variable_name")	Removes a named variable from the Session.Contents collection.
Contents.RemoveAll()	Removes all variables from the Session.Contents collection.
Abandon	Destroys a Session object and releases its resources.

You *cannot* remove variables from the Session.StaticObjects collection at run-time.

Events

Events	Description
onStart	Occurs when the server creates a new session.
onEnd	Occurs when a session is abandoned or times out.

The ObjectContext Object

When we use MTS (Microsoft Transaction Server) to manage a transaction, we have the functionality within our script to commit (or to abort) the transaction. This functionality is provided by the ObjectContext object.

Methods

Methods	Description
SetComplete	Declares that the script knows no reason for the transaction not to complete. If all participating components call SetComplete then the transaction will complete. SetComplete overrides any previous SetAbort method that has been called in the script.
SetAbort	Aborts a transaction initiated by an ASP.

Events

Events	Description
OnTransactionCommit	Occurs after a transacted script's transaction commits.
OnTransactionAbort	Occurs if the transaction is aborted.

Index

A Guide to the Index

The index is arranged hierarchically, in alphabetical order, with symbols preceding the letter A. Most second-level entries and many third-level entries also occur as first-level entries. This is to ensure that users will find the information they require however they choose to search for it.

Symbols

1NF (first normal form), databases, 316, 317-18
2NF (second normal form), databases, 316, 319
3NF (third normal form), databases, 316, 319-20
3-tier applications, 11-12
  business tier, **473-503**
  data tier, 10, **12, 413-70**
  user tier, 10, **12, 199, 583-690**
    administration, **583-625**
    customer services, **505-80**
    GUIs, **506-14**
  XML, **715-16**

A

ACID test, transactions, 140-41
ACLs (access control lists), 623
Activate method, ObjectControl interface, MTS, 164
activations, 246
Active Scripting, 680, 681
Active Server Pages
  See "ASP".
ActiveX controls, 100-101
ActiveX Data Objects
  See "ADO".
ActiveX DLLs
  See "DLLs".
ActiveX documents, 100
ActiveX servers, 100-101, 116-20
  error handling, **117-18**
  in-process servers
    See "DLLs".
  out-of-process servers, **101**
    threads, **108-9**
activity diagrams, 251, 253, **303-4**
actors, 199, 237, 238, 245
Add Argument dialogue, Method Builder window, Class Builder Utility, 72
Add Class Module dialogue, 46
Add Procedure dialogue, 51-53
Add-In Manager, Visual Modeler, 260-61

administration, user tier, 583-625
  login form, **585-87**
  security, **621-23**
ADO (ActiveX Data Objects), 385-410
  cursors, **392-95**
    location, **393-94**
    lock types, **394-95**
    types of cursor, **393**
  data types, **391**
  error handling, **405-9**
  object model, **387-95**
    Command object, 388, **389-91**
    Connection object, **388-89**
    events, **395**
    Field object, **388**
    Recordset object, 388, **392**
  requirements for this book, **21-22**
  stored procedures, **401-5**
  Visual Basic and ADO, **396-409**
aliases, tables, databases, 369-70
alpha testing, 628
ALTER TABLE statement, SQL, 351-53
analysis workflow, RUP, 34
apartments, 107, 108
application model, MSF, 32
Application object, ASP, 681, 683
applications, 8-13
  3-tier applications, **11-12**
  availability, **10, 231-32**
  business tier, **473-503**
  client/server applications, **10-11**
  coupling, **716**
  data tier, 10, **12, 413-70**
  DCOM, **133-36**
  deployment, **633-52**
  distributed applications, **10-13, 275-77**
    secuirty, **622-23**
  enterprise applications, **8**
  extensibility, **230**
  implementation process, **623-24**
  maintainability, **229-30**
  maintenance, **652-61**
  n-tier applications, **12-13**

applications (continued)
performance, **224-29**
  bandwidth, **225-28**
  barriers to performance, **229**
  capacity, **227**
  hardware, **228**
  response times, **228**
  transactions, **225**
reliability, **9**
scalability, **9, 230-31**
security, **232, 621-23**
testing an application, **82-88, 628-33**
  bugs, **632**
  integration testing, **629**
  milestones, **26, 628**
  priority levels, bugs, **632**
  release candidate stage, **632-33**
  severity levels, bugs, **632**
  stabilization phase, **628-29**
  system testing, **629**
  unit testing, **82-88**
user tier, 10, **12, 199, 583-690**
  administration, **583-625**
  customer services, **505-80**
  GUIs, **506-14**
web sites, **665-703**
AppServer object, MTS, 164-66
GetObjectContext method, **165**
SafeRef method, **165-66**
arguments, methods, 72
artifacts, RUP, 34
ASP (Active Server Pages), 16, 17, 677-83
IIS and ASP, 679
objects, **681-83**
pages, **678-79**
PWS and ASP, 679
tags, **677**
asp file name extension, 679
Debug.**Assert statements, 83**
asynchronous method calls, 286
atomicity, transactions, 140
Attribute object, XML, 721
attributes, databases, 312-13
attributes, tags, HTML, 673
attributes, tags, XML, 711
attributes, visibility, 242
authentication, web sites, 684-90
login forms, **684-87**
availability, applications, 10, 231-32

B

b tag, HTML, 671
bandwidth, 225-27
DCOM, 134
peak requirements, **227-28**
barriers to performance, 229
base classes, 243
batch-optimistic locking, cursors, ADO, 394
beta releases, 628
binary compatibility, 111-13
COM, **93**
binary standards, 92
binding, 59, 79

BizTalk initiative, 735
black-box tools, 41
body tag, HTML, 671
br tag, HTML, 672
breakpoints, 83-85
bug convergence milestone, 628
bugs
Debug.Assert statements, **83**
priority levels, **632**
severity levels, **632**
zero bug release milestone, 628
See also "testing".
business modeling workflow, RUP, 34
business objects, 290
business requirements, 14, 196-201
business tier, 12, 473-503
ByRef keyword, 49-50
ByVal keyword, 49-50

C

CanBePooled method, ObjectControl interface, MTS,
164
capacity, 227
cardinality, relationships, 243
CDbl function, VBScript, 701
CGI (Common Gateway Interface), 679
check boxes, 508
CHECK constraint, SQL, 353
Class Builder Utility, 68-75
Class Module Builder window, **69-70**
Event Builder window, **73-74**
Method Builder window, **72-73**
  Add Argument dialogue, **72**
Property Builder window, **70-71**
class diagrams, 33, **241-44**, 252, **293-99**
creating a class diagram, Visual Modeler, **293-95**
class inheritance, 274
Class Module Builder window, Class Builder Utility,
69-70
Class Wizard, Visual Modeler, 255-60
methods, **257-58**
properties, **258**
classes, 44, 45-57
base classes, 243
creating a class, **45-47**
  Add Class Module dialogue, **46**
  Visual Modeler, **254-60**
events, **41**
  adding an event to a class, **66-68**, 73-74
  Initialize, Terminate events, **54-55**, 278
instances
  See "objects".
methods, **40**, 59-60
  adding a method to a class, **53-54**, 72-73, 295
properties, **40**, 47-53, 59-60
  adding a property to a class, **48-49**, 70-71
  enumerated properties, **63-65**
  Get, Let, Set routines, **49-51**
client/server applications, 10-11
ClientCertificate collection, Request object, ASP, 682
clients, 10
hardware, **228**

client-side cursors, ADO, 393
CLogger class, 167-79, 184-89, 465
clustered indexes, databases, 328
code freeze milestone, 628
Code Generation Wizard, Visual Modeler, 261-66
collaboration diagrams, 245, 247-48, 253, 302-3
    See also "sequence diagrams".
column constraints, databases, 327
columns, tables, databases, 351-52
COM (Component Object Model), 16, 17, 91-136, 680
    ActiveX controls, 100-101
    ActiveX documents, 100
    ActiveX servers, 100-101, 116-20
    DCOM, 132-36
    DLLs, 92, 116
        creating a DLL, 101-6, 418-19, 464-65
        instances, 114-20
        properties, 419-20
    instancing, 113
    interfaces, 94-100
    Package and Deployment Wizard, 122-28
    regsvr32.exe file, 121-22
    threads, 106-9
        apartments, 107
    unattended execution, 109
    version compatibility, 109-13
        binary compatibility, 93, 111-13
        GUIDs, 110-11
        project compatibility, 111
COM+, 18, 150-54
    IObjectContext interface, 166
    packages, 190-92
        deploying a package, 645-52
    requirements for this book, 21, 22
    transactional control, 476
    type libraries, 153-54
combo boxes, 508
command buttons, 508
Command object, ADO, 388, 389-91
    Parameters collection, 390
Common Gateway Interface (CGI), 679
compatibility
    See "version compatibility".
component based development, 33
component diagrams, 249, 252
    creating a component diagram, Visual Modeler,
        268-70
components, 273-89
    class inheritance, 274
    COM, 91-136
        ActiveX controls, 100-101
        ActiveX servers, 100-101, 116-20
        DLLs, 92, 101-6, 116
    containment, 279-80
    coupling, 716
    DCOM, 132-36
        creating a component, 135-36
    deploying a component, 645-52
    distributed applications, 275-77
    generalization, 280-84
    instances, 278
    interface inheritance, 281
    interfaces, 94-100, 274
    logical design, 274

MTS, 142, 154-60
    importing a component, 647
    own/contain rules, 285-86
    ownership, 277-79
    physical design, 274
    registering a component, 120-32
        regsvr32.exe file, 121-22
        Visual Component Manager, 128-32
    threads, 106-9
    unattended execution, 109
    usage, 284
    version compatibility, 109-13
composite primary keys, databases, 317
composition, 242-43, 277
configuration and change management workflow, RUP,
    35
Connection object, ADO, 388-89
    Errors collection, 389
    events, 395
consistency, transactions, 140-41
constraints, tables, databases, 352-53
contained/container classes, 242
containment relationships, 243
containment, components, 279-80
content complete milestone, 628
Context object, MTS, 143, 161-63
    DisableCommit method, 162
    EnableCommit method, 162
    SetAbort method, 162, 181-82
    SetComplete method, 162, 181-82
context wrappers, 143
ContextInfo object, COM+, 163
contravariance, 287
controls, GUIs, 508
cookies, 686
Cookies collection, Request object, ASP, 682
coupling, 716
coverage analysis, 83-85
Create Relationship dialog, 334-35
CreateObject method, 58
cursors, ADO, 392-95
    location, 393-94
    lock types, 394-95
    types of cursor, 393
customer services, user tier, 505-80
    GUIs, 506-14
        controls, 508
        form validation, 511-14

D

Data Definition Language (DDL), 344-54
    scripts, 349-50
data layers, 10, 12
data links, 330-31
Data Manipulation Language (DML), 354-70
data tier, 10, 12, 413-70
data types
    databases, 324-26
        ADO, 391
    Variant data type, 79
Data View window, 330-33

databases, 309-40
  ADO, 385-410
    cursors, 392-95
    error handling, 405-9
    object model, 387-95
    stored procedures, 401-5
  attributes, 312-13
  column constraints, 327
  connecting to a database, 330-31
  creating a database, 328-29
  data types, 324-26
    ADO, 391
  denormalization, 320
  diagrams, 333-36, 339
  entities, 311-16
  identifiers, 314
  indexes, 328
  logical design, 309-23
  normalization, 316-20
    first normal form (1NF), 316, 317-18
    second normal form (2NF), 316, 319
    third normal form (3NF), 316, 319-20
  NULL values, 326-27
  physical design, 323-28
  referential integrity, 327
  relationships, 314-16, 333-36
  schemas, 323-24
  SQL, 343-82
    DDL, 344-54
    DML, 354-70
    scripts, 349-50
    stored procedures, 370-81
  tables
    adding a table, 331-33
    aliases, 369-70
    altering a table, 351-53
    columns, 351-52
    constraints, 352-53
    creating a table, 345-49
    data, 354-70
    deleting a table, 353-54
    joins, 367-69
    rows, 379-81
DATEDIFF function, SQL, 377
DCOM (Distributed COM), 132-36
DDL (Data Definition Language), 344-54
  scripts, 349-50
Deactivate method, ObjectControl interface, MTS, 164
Debug.Assert statements, 83
debugging
  See "testing".
default web sites, 668-70
DELETE statement, SQL, 361
delimiters, SQL, 350
denormalization, databases, 320
deployment, 633-52
  COM+, 645-52
  MTS, 645-52
  Package and Deployment Wizard, 634-44
deployment diagrams, 249-50, 252
  creating a deployment diagram, Visual Modeler,
    266-68
deployment workflow, RUP, 35
design model diagrams, UML, 302-4
design process model, MSF, 32

design workflow, RUP, 34
destructors, 246
development
  See "software development process".
diagrams, databases, 333-36, 339
diagrams, UML, 236-52, 291-304
  activity diagrams, 251, 253, 303-4
  class diagrams, 241-44, 252, 293-99
  collaboration diagrams, 245, 247-48, 253, 302-3
  component diagrams, 249, 252
  deployment diagrams, 249-50, 252
  domain model diagrams, 291
  instance diagrams, 248
  interaction diagrams
    See "collaboration diagrams", "sequence diagrams".
  object diagrams, 248-49, 252
  package diagrams, 252, 253, 301-2
  sequence diagrams, 245-47, 253, 299-302
  statechart diagrams, 250, 253, 303
  use case diagrams, 237-41, 253
DisableCommit method, Context object, MTS, 162
distributed applications, 10-13, 275-77
  security, 622-23
Distributed COM (DCOM), 132-36
Distributed Transaction Coordinator (DTC), 142
dll file name extension, 101
DLLs (Dynamic Link Libraries), 92, 101-120
  creating a DLL, 101-6, 418-19, 464-65
  instances, 113-20
  properties, 419-20
  threads, 106-9
    apartments, 107
  unattended execution, 109
  version compatibility, 109-13
    binary compatibility, 93, 111-13
    GUIDs, 110-11
    project compatibility, 111
DML (Data Manipulation Language), 354-70
DNA
  See "Windows DNA".
Document object, XML, 720
document type definitions (DTDs), 712-13
documents, ActiveX, 100
DOM (document object model), XML, 717-22
  Attribute object, 721
  Document object, 720
  Element object, 721
  NamedNodeMap object, 722
  Node object, 721
  NodeList object, 721
domain model diagrams, UML, 291
DROP TABLE statement, SQL, 353-54
drop-down list boxes, 508
DTC (Distributed Transaction Coordinator), 142
DTDs (document type definitions), 712-13
dynamic binding, 59
dynamic cursors, ADO, 393
Dynamic Link Library
  See "DLL".
dynamic web sites, 676-83

E

early binding, 59
Element object, XML, 721
elements, XML, 710-11
EnableCommit method, Context object, MTS, 162
encapsulation, 12, 41
    COM, **93**
enterprise applications, 8
enterprise architecture model, MSF, 30
Enterprise Manager, SQL Server, 328-29
    Query Analyzer, **345-49**
    Query Designer, **364-66**
entities, databases, 311-16
    attributes, **312-13**
    identifiers, **314**
    link entities, 316
    relationships, **314-16**
enumerated properties, 63-65
environment workflow, RUP, 35
Err object, 117
errors
    ActiveX servers, **117-18**
    ADO, **405-9**
    logging errors, **465-70**
Errors collection, Connection object, ADO, 389
Event Builder window, Class Builder Utility, 73-74
events, 41
    ADO, **395**
    adding an event to a class, **66-68**
        Class Builder Utility, **73-74**
    firing an event, 66
    Initialize event, **54-55**, 278
    RaiseEvent keyword, **66**
    Terminate event, **54-55**, 278
    WithEvents keyword, **66**, 67, 286
execution paths, 83
extend relationships, 239
extensibility, applications, 230
extension points, 239
extranets, 667

F

fat client applications, 11
Field object, ADO, 388
field-level validation, 511-14
Fields collection, Recordset object, ADO, 392
first normal form (1NF), databases, 316, 317-18
flow diagrams, 630
font tag, HTML, 673
foreign keys, databases, 314, 327
Form collection, Request object, ASP, 682, 689, 690
form tag, HTML, 674-76
    login forms, **684-87**
    method attribute, 690
form validation, 511-14
form-level validation, 511, 512-14
forward-only cursors, ADO, 393
FROM statement, SQL, 370

G

generalization, components, 280-84
generalize relationships, 239, 243
Get routines, 49
GetObjectContext method, AppServer object, MTS, 165
global multi-use components, 113
global scope, 43-44
global single use components, 113
global visibility, 242
GUIDs (Globally Unique Identifiers), 110-11, 326
GUIs (graphical user interfaces), 506-14
    controls, **508**
    design principles, **509-10**
    form validation, **511-14**

H

hardware, 228
head tag, HTML, 671
HTML (Hypertext Markup Language)
    fonts, **673**
    forms, **674-76**
        login forms, **684-87**
    line breaks, **672**
    pages, **670-72**
    tables, **673-74**
    tags, **670-71**
        attributes, **673**
    XML vs HTML, **707**
html tag, 671
HTTP (Hypertext Transfer Protocol), 735
    POST method, 690

I

IDE (Integrated Development Environment), 46
identifiers, databases, 314
IF statement, SQL, 376
If statement, VB, 83
IIS (Internet Information Server), 16, 17, 667
    ASP and IIS, 679
Immediate window, 87-88
implementation inheritance
    See "generalization".
implementation process, 623-24
implementation workflow, RUP, 35
include relationships, 238-39
indexes, databases, 328
inheritance
    class inheritance, **274**
    implementation inheritance
        See "generalization".
    interface inheritance, **281**
Init method, 54
Initialize event, 54-55, 278
INNER JOIN statement, SQL, 367
in-process servers
    See "DLLs".

input parameters, stored procedures, SQL, 371
INSERT statement, SQL, **354-59**, 379-80
instance diagrams, 248
instances, **113**
  classes
    See "objects".
  components, **278**
    DLLs, **114-20**
Integrated Development Environment (IDE), **46**
integration testing, **629**
interaction diagrams
  See "collaboration diagrams", "sequence diagrams".
interception, MTS, **143**
interface inheritance, 281
interfaces, **94**, 242, **274**, 290
  changing an interface, **653-60**
  COM, **95-100**
Internet, 667
Internet Server Application Programming Interface (ISAPI), 679
interoperability, **227**
intranets, 667
intrinsic objects, 40
IObjectContext interface, COM+, 166
IP addresses, 668
ISAPI (Internet Server Application Programming Interface), 679
isolation, transactions, **141**
iterative development methodologies, 29-36
  MSF, **30-33**
    application model, **32**
    design process model, **32**
    enterprise architecture model, **30**
    process model, **31**
    risk management model, **32**
    TCO (total cost of ownership) model, **32**
    team model, **30-31**
  RUP, **33-36**
    artifacts, **34**
    workflows, **34-35**

J

joins, tables, databases, 367-69
junction tables, 316

K

keys, databases, **314**, 327
keyset cursors, ADO, **393**

L

late binding, **59**
Let routines, 49
library routines, 92
lifelines, 246
lifetime, objects, 44
  MTS, **181-82**
link entities, databases, 316

Liskov substitution principle, 286
list views, 508
local hosts, 668
location transparency, COM, 93
lock types, cursors, ADO, **394-95**
Logger component, **154-56**
logical design, **289-90**
  components, **274**
  databases, **309-23**
    denormalization, **320**
    entities, **311**
    normalization, **316-20**
login forms
  administration, **585-87**
  customer services, **523-29**
  HTML, **684-87**
loops, **81-82**

M

maintainability, applications, 229-30
maintenance, **652-61**
many-to-many relationships, 315-16
MapPath method, Server object, ASP, 683
membership, components, 278
memory
  leaks, **540**
  releasing memory, **60-61**
Menu Editor, **531-34**
messages, participants, 246
method attribute, form tag, HTML, 690
Method Builder window, Class Builder Utility, **72-73**
  Add Argument dialogue, **72**
methods, **40**, 59-60, 61-63
  adding a method to a class, **53-54**
    Class Builder Utility, **72-73**
    Visual Modeler (VM), **257-58**, 295
  arguments, 72
  calling a method, 246
  Init method, 54
  visibility, **242**
Microsoft Solutions Framework (MSF), 13, 15, **30-33**
Microsoft Management Console (MMC), 144-45, 189-90
Microsoft Message Queue Server (MSMQ), **16**, **17**
Microsoft Transaction Server
  See "MTS".
middle tiers
  See "business services tiers".
mil specs (military specifications), **26**
milestones, **26**, 628
MMC (Microsoft Management Console), 144-45, 189-90
module level scope, **43**
module level visibility, 242
MSF (Microsoft Solutions Framework), 13, 15, **30-33**
  application model, **32**
  design process model, **32**
  enterprise architecture model, **30**
  process model, **31**
  risk management model, **32**
  TCO (total cost of onwership) model, **32**
  team model, **30-31**

MSMQ (Microsoft Message Queue Server), 16, 17
MSXML component, 718-22
    See also "DOM".
MTS (Microsoft Transaction Server), 16, 17, 139-93
    COM+, 150-54
    components, 142, 154-60
        deploying a component, 189-93, 645-52
        importing a component, 647
        instances, 158
    interception, 143
    objects, 142, 160-66
        AppServer object, 164-66
        Context object, 143, 161-63
        lifetime, 181-82
        ObjectControl interface, 164
        SecurityProperty object, 163
        state, 179-89
    packages, 145-48
        exporting a package, 189-90
        importing a package, 192-93
    requirements for this book, 21, 22
    roles, 148
    transaction modes, 157-60
    transactional control, 476
    transactions, 140-41, 149-50
    type libraries, 153-54
multiplicity, relationships, 243
multi-tasking, 107
multi-thread processing, 107, 108
multi-use components, 113

N

NamedNodeMap object, XML, 722
network trips, 275
New Database Diagram window, 333-36
New keyword, 58, 278
Node object, XML, 721
NodeList object, XML, 721
nodes, XML DOM, 717
non-clustered indexes, databases, 328
normalization, databases, 316-20
    first normal form (1NF), 316, 317-18
    second normal form (2NF), 316, 319
    third normal form (3NF), 316, 319-20
Now function, VBScript, 679
n-tier applications, 12-13
NULL values, databases, 326-27

O

Object Browser, 75-78
object diagrams, 248-49, 252
object orientated programming, 39-88
    classes, 44, 45-57
    components, 273-89
        COM, 91-136
    containment, 279-80
    encapsulation, 41
    generalization, 280-84

inheritance
    class inheritance, 274
    interface inheritance, 281
interfaces, 94, 242, 274, 290
    changing an interface, 653-60
    COM, 95-100
optimization, 78-82
own/contain rules, 285-86
ownership, 277-79
polymorphism, 287-88
usage, 284
object variables, 57-58
ObjectContext object
    See "Context object".
ObjectControl interface, MTS, 164
objects, 40-44
    ADO, 387-95
    ASP, 681-83
    binding, 59, 79
    business objects, 290
    creating an object, 58-59, 61-63
    destroying an object, 60-61
    events, 41
        adding an event to a class, 66-68, 73-74
        Initialize, Terminate events, 54-55, 278
    lifetime, 44
    methods, 40, 59-60, 61-63
        adding a method to a class, 53-54, 72-73, 295
    MTS, 142, 160-66
    properties, 40, 47-53, 59-60, 61-63
        adding a property to a class, 48-49, 70-71
        enumerated properties, 63-65
        Get, Let, Set routines, 49-51
    references to objects, 78-79
    scope, 42-44
    state, 41-42
    With construct, 80-81
    XML, 718-22
    See also "classes".
ODBC (Open Database Connectivity), 386
OLAP (online analytical processing), 323
OLE DB, 386-87
OLTP (online transaction processing), 323
one-to-many relationships, 315
one-to-one relationships, 315
OOP
    See "object orientated programming".
operators, 199
optimistic locking, cursors, ADO, 394
optimization, 78-82
Option Explicit statement, 48
out-of-process servers, 101
    threads, 108-9
output parameters, stored procedures, SQL, 371
own/contain rules, 285-86
owners, 199
ownership relationships, 242
ownership, components, 277-79

P

Package and Deployment Wizard, 122-28, 634-44
package diagrams, 252, 253, 301-2
packages, 145
  COM+, 190-92
  deploying a package, 642-44
  importing a package, 647
  MTS, 145-48
    exporting a package, 189-90
    importing a package, 192-93
pages, ASP, 678-79
pages, HTML, 670-72
parallel development, 12
Parameters collection, Command object, ADO, 390
parameters, procedures, 49-50
parameters, stored procedures, SQL, 371
participants, 245-46
  messages, 246
peak bandwidth requirements, 227-28
performance, applications, 224-29
  bandwidth, 225-27
    peak requirements, 227-28
  barriers to performance, 229
  capacity, 227
  hardware, 228
  response times, 228
  transactions, 225
pessimistic locking, cursors, ADO, 394
physical design
  components, 274
  databases, 323-28
    column constraints, 327
    data types, 324-26
    indexes, 328
    NULL values, 326-27
    referential integrity, 327
    schemas, 323-24
polymorphism, 287-88
portability, COM, 93
POST method, HTTP, 690
presentation tier
  See "user tier".
primary keys, databases, 314, 327
  composite primary keys, 317
priority levels, bugs, 632
private components, 113
procedure-level scope, 43
procedures
  Add Procedure dialogue, 51-53
  parameters, 49-50
process model, MSF, 31
processes, 106
project compatibility, COM, 111
project groups, 415-16
project management workflow, RUP, 34
project packages, 634-41
properties, 40, 47-53, 59-60, 61-63
  accessing a property, 80
  adding a property to a class, 48-49
    Class Builder Utility, 70-71
    Visual Modeler, 258
  enumerated properties, 63-65
  Get, Let, Set routines, 49-51

Property Builder window, Class Builder Utility, 70-71
public non-creatable components, 113
PWS, 667
  ASP and PWS, 679

Q

Query Analyzer, SQL Server, 345-49
Query Designer, SQL Server, 364-66
query strings, 689
QueryString collection, Request object, ASP, 682

R

radio buttons, 508
RaiseEvent keyword, 66
Rational Software, 236
Rational Unified Process
  See "RUP".
read-only locking, cursors, ADO, 394
Recordset object, ADO, 388, 392
  cursors, 392-95
  events, 395
  Fields collection, 392
recursive messages, 246
references to objects, 78-79
referential integrity, databases, 327
regsvr32.exe file, 121-22
relational databases, 309
relationships, databases, 314-16
release candidate stage, 629, 632-33
reliability, applications, 9
Request object, ASP, 681, 682, 692
  collections, 682
requirements workflow, RUP, 34
resource managers, 183-84
Response object, ASP, 678, 681-82
  Write method, 681
response times, 228
return messages, 246
RETURN statement, SQL, 378
risk management model, MSF, 32
roles, MTS, 148
root elements, XML, 710
rows, tables, databases
  deleting a row, 379
  inserting a row, 379-80
  selecting a row, 380-81
  verifying a row, 381
RUP (Rational Unified Process), 33-36
  artifacts, 34
  workflows, 34-35

S

SafeRef method, AppServer object, MTS, 165-66
scalability, applications, 9, 230-31
schemas, databases, 323-24
schemas, XML, 713-14
scope, 42-44, 242
scripts, SQL, 349-50
second normal form (2NF), databases, 316, 319
Secure Socket Layer (SSL), 690
security, 232, 621-23
    distributed applications, 622-23
SecurityProperty object, MTS, 163
SELECT statement, SQL, 361-66, 380-81
select tag, HTML, 698
sequence diagrams, 33, 245-47, 253, 299-302
    See also "collaboration diagrams".
Server object, ASP, 681, 683
    MapPath method, 683
servers, 10
    ActiveX servers, 100-101, 116-20
        errors, 117-18
    hardware, 228
    in-process servers
        See "DLLs".
    out-of-process servers, 101
        threads, 108-9
    web servers, 666-70, 686
        ASP, 16, 17, 677-83
        IIS, 16, 17, 667
        Windows, 667, 668-70
server-side cursors, ADO, 393
ServerVariables collection, Request object, ASP, 682
Session object, ASP, 681, 682, 686
Set keyword, 58
Set routines, 50-51
SetAbort method, Context object, MTS, 162, 181-82
SetComplete method, Context object, MTS, 162, 181-82
severity levels, bugs, 632
Simple Object Access Protocol (SOAP), 735
simple aggregation, 243
single selection list boxes, 508
single use components, 109, 113
single-threaded applications, 107, 108
SOAP (Simple Object Access Protocol), 735
software development process, 13-14, 25-36
    iterative development methodologies, 29-36
        MSF, 30-33
        RUP, 33-36
    mil specs, 26
    waterfall method, 26-29
SQL (Structured Query Language), 343-82
    DDL, 344-54
    DML, 354-70
    scripts, 349-50
    stored procedures, 370-81
        ADO, 401-5
        creating a stored procedure, 371-74
        parameters, 371
SQL Server, 16, 18
    connecting to SQL Server, 345
    data types, 324-26
    Enterprise Manager, 328-29
        Query Analyzer, 345-49
        Query Designer, 364-66

requirements for this book, 21, 22
SSL (Secure Socket Layer), 690
stabilization phase, 628-29
state information, web sites, 682
state, objects, 41-42
    MTS, 179-89
statechart diagrams, 33, 250, 253, 303
static binding, 59
static cursors, ADO, 393
stored procedures, SQL, 370-81
    ADO, 401-5
    creating a stored procedure, 371-74
    parameters, 371
submit buttons, HTML, 674
synchronous method calls, 286
system boundaries, 238
system testing, 629

T

table tag, HTML, 673-74
tables, databases
    adding a table, 331-33
    aliases, 369-70
    altering a table, 351-53
    columns, 351-52
    constraints, 352-53
    creating a table, 345-49
    data
        adding data, 354-59
        deleting data, 360-61
        modifying data, 359-60
        retrieving data, 361-70
    deleting a table, 353-54
    joins, 367-69
    relationships, 333-36
    rows
        deleting a row, 379
        inserting a row, 379-80
        selecting a row, 380-81
        verifying a row, 381
tags, ASP, 677
tags, HTML, 670-71
    attributes, 673
tags, XML, 706
TCO (total cost of onwership) model, MSF, 32
td tag, HTML, 673
team model, MSF, 30-31
Terminate event, 54-55, 278
test cases, 629-31
test workflow, RUP, 35
testing, 82-88, 628-33
    bugs, 632
    integration testing, 629
    milestones, 26, 628
    release candidate stage, 632-33
    stabilization phase, 628-29
    system testing, 629
    unit testing, 82-88
        Debug.Assert statements, 83
        breakpoints, 83-85
        Immediate window, 87-88
        message boxes, 88
        Watches window, 86-87

text boxes, 508
thin client applications, **11**
third normal form (3NF), databases, 316, 319-20
threads, 106-9
   apartments, **107**, **108**
   out-of-process servers, **108-9**
   single-threaded applications, **107**, **108**
tiers
   3-tier applications, **11-12**
      XML, **715-16**
   business tier, **473-503**
   data tier, 10, **12**, **413-70**
   n-tier applications, **12-13**
   user tier, 10, **12**, **199**, **583-690**
      administration, **583-625**
      customer services, **505-80**
      GUIs, **506-14**
timeouts, ASP, 686
tokens, ASP, 686
total cost of onwership (TCO) model, MSF, 32
tr tag, HTML, 673
transaction modes, MTS, 157-60
transactional control, 476
TransactionContext object, 159
transactions, 140-41, 225
   ACID test, **140-41**
   MTS, **149-50**
type libraries, 153-54

U

UDA (Universal Data Access), 16, 18, 386-87
UML (Unified Modeling Language), 33, **235-71**, **290-304**
   composition, 277
   diagrams, **236-52**, **291-304**
      activity diagrams, **251**, 253, 303-4
      class diagrams, **241-44**, 252, 293-99
      collaboration diagrams, **245**, **247-48**, 253, 302-3
      component diagrams, **249**, 252
      deployment diagrams, **249-50**, 252
      domain model diagrams, 291
      object diagrams, **248-49**, 252
      package diagrams, **252**, 253, 301-2
      sequence diagrams, **245-47**, 253
      statechart diagrams, **250**, 253, 303
      use case diagrams, **237-41**, 253
   use cases, 291
UML web site, 14, 236
unattended execution, 109
UNIQUE constraint, SQL, 353
unit testing, 82-88
   breakpoints, **83-85**
   Debug.Assert statements, **83**
   Immediate window, **87**
   message boxes, **88**
   Watches window, **86-87**
Universal Data Access (UDA), 16, **18**, **386-87**
UPDATE statement, SQL, 360
usage relationships, 244
usage, components, 284
use case diagrams, 33, 201-2, 203-5, **237-41**, 253
use case relationships, 238-39
   extend relationships, **239**
   generalize relationships, **239**, *243*
   include relationships, **238-39**

use case scenarios, 201, **205-23**, **237**, 247
   test cases, **629-31**
use cases, 33, **201-2**, 291
user interfaces, 12
user tier, 10, **12**, **583-690**
   administration, **583-625**
      security, **621-23**
   authentication, **684-90**
      login forms, **523-29**, **585-87**, **684-87**
   customer services, **505-80**
   GUIs, **506-14**
      controls, **508**
      form validation, **511-14**
users, 199
uses relationships, 238

V

object **variables**, **57-58**
Variant data type, 79
version compatibility, 109-13
   binary compatibility, **111-13**
      COM, **93**
   GUIDs, **110-11**
   project compatibility, **111**
version numbers, 660-61
visibility, 242
Visual Basic (VB)
   ADO and Visual Basic, **396-409**
   Class Builder Utility, **68-75**
      Class Module Builder window, **69-70**
      Event Builder window, **73-74**
      Method Builder window, **72-73**
      Property Builder window, **70-71**
   classes, **44**, **45-57**
   components, **273-89**
      COM, **91-136**
   IDE, **46**
   Immediate window, **87-88**
   interfaces, **94**, 242, **274**, 290
      COM, **95-100**
   Menu Editor, **531-34**
   Object Browser, **75-78**
   optimization, **78-82**
   Package and Deployment Wizard, **122-28**, **634-44**
   project groups, **415-16**
   requirements for this book, **21**
   version compatibility, **109-13**
      binary compatibility, **93**, **111-13**
      GUIDs, **110-11**
      project compatibility, **111**
   Watches window, **86-87**
   XML and Visual Basic, **714-22**
Visual Component Manager, 128-32
Visual Modeler (VM), 254-70
   Add-In Manager, **260-61**
   class diagrams, **293-95**
      methods, 295
   Class Wizard, **255-60**
      methods, **257-58**
      properties, 258
   Code Generation Wizard, **261-66**
   component diagrams, **268-70**
   deployment diagrams, **266-68**
VSS (Visual SourceSafe), 661

W

Watches window, 86-87
waterfall method, 26-29
web servers
    See under "servers".
web sites, 665-703
    authentication, 684-90
        login forms, 684-87
    default web sites, 668-70
    dynamic web sites, 676-83
WHERE statement, SQL, 360
wildcards, 363
Windows
    requirements for this book, 21
    web servers, 667, 668-70
        IIS, 16, 17, 667
Windows DNA, 15-18
Windows Installer, 651-52
Windows Script Host, 680
With construct, 80-81
WithEvents keyword, 66, 67, 286
workflows, RUP, 34-35
Wrapper object, 160
Write method, Response object, ASP, 681
WROBA (Wrox Online Banking Application), 18-20,
    195-232, 414-16
    ActiveX servers, 116-20
    administration, 584-621
    availability, 231-32
    Bank_Bus component (business tier), 476-503
        Admin class, 496-502
        Bank class, 478-87
        BankLocator class, 487-88
        Payees class, 488-91
        Transfer class, 492-95
    Bank_DB component (data tier), 417-70
        Account class, 433-36
        Admin class, 437-48
        Bank class, 448-57
        BankLocator class, 457-59
        DBHelper class, 428-33
        MContext module, 422-28
        MHelpers module, 421-22
        Payees class, 459-63
        properties, 419-20
    Bank_UI component (user tier), 515-79, 584-621
        CPayeeInformation class, 69-75, 517, 518-21
        FAbout form, 541-42
        FAdminDeleteCard form, 600-604
        FAdminEditBank form, 614-21
        FAdminLock form, 607-10
        FAdminMainMenu form, 587-92, 593-94, 610-11
        FAdminNewBank form, 611-14
        FAdminNewCard form, 594-99
        FAdminUnlock form, 604-7
        FChangePassword form, 564-66
        FHistory form, 543-51
        FHistoryDetails form, 544, 547-51
        FLogin form, 523-29
        FMainMenu form, 531-41, 542-43, 566-67
        FPayBills form, 567-75
        FPayee form, 551-57
        FPayeeEdit form, 557-64
        FStatus form, 529-31
        FTransfer form, 575-79
        MMain module, 517-18
        SharedProperties class, 45-47, 517, 521-23
    Bank_XML component, 723-28
    customer services, 515-79
    database, 310-340
        AccountHistory table, 338
        Bank table, 337
        BankAccount table, 332
        CardxAccount table, 337
        creating the database, 328-29
        logical design, 321-22
        normalization, 317-20
        Payee table, 322, 338
        stored procedures, 378-81
        TXLock table, 337
        TxType table, 337
        WROBACard table, 336
    default.asp file, 683-702
    design goals, 202
    implementation process, 623-24
    Network_Bus component, 723, 728-31
    Network_UI component, 723, 731-34
    security, 232, 622-23
    use case diagrams, 203-5
    use case scenarios, 207-23
    vision statement, 202
    web site, 683-702
        authentication, 684-90

X

XHTML (Extensible Stylesheet Language
    Transformation), 735
XLink, 735
XML (Extensible Markup Language), 705-36
    3-tier applications and XML, 715-16
    attributes, 711
    DOM (document object model), 717-22
        Attribute object, 721
        Document object, 720
        Element object, 721
        NamedNodeMap object, 722
        Node object, 721
        NodeList object, 721
    DTDs (document type definitions), 712-13
    elements, 710-11
    HTML vs XML, 707
    MSXML component, 718-22
    schemas, 713-14
    Visual Basic and XML, 714-22
XPath, 735
XSLT (Extensible Stylesheet Language
    Transformation), 735

Z

zero bug release milestone, 628

Computer Book Publishers

NB. If you post the bounce back card below in the UK, please send it to:

Wrox Press Ltd., Arden House, 1102 Warwick Road,
Acocks Green, Birmingham B27 6BH. UK.

WROX
PROGRAMMER TO PROGRAMMER™

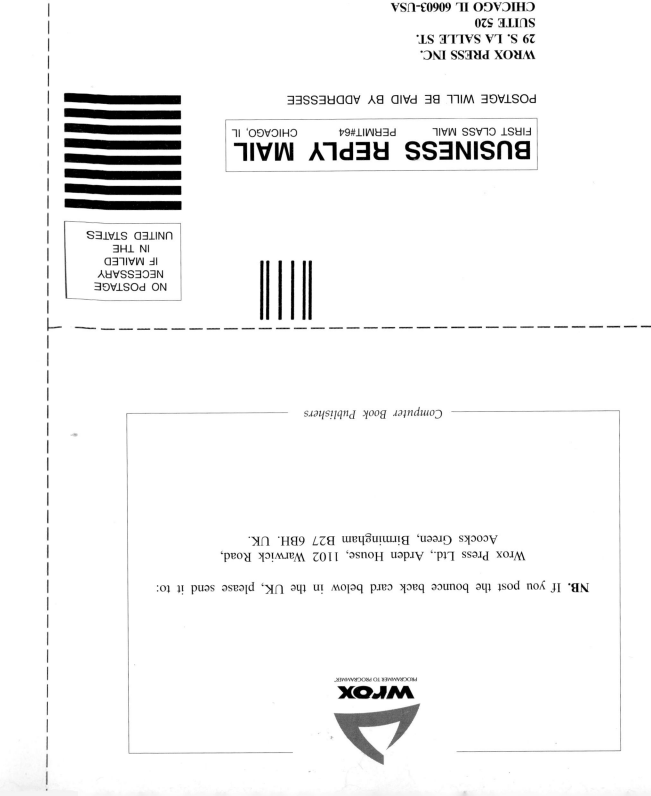

wrox

PROGRAMMER TO PROGRAMMER™

Wrox writes books for you. Any suggestions, or ideas about how you want information given in your ideal book will be studied by our team. Your comments are always valued at Wrox.

Free phone in USA 800-USE-WROX
Fax (312) 893 8001

UK Tel. (0121) 687 4100   Fax (0121) 687 4101

Beginning Visual Basic Application Development - Registration Card

Name _____

Address _____

_____

_____

City _____ State/Region _____

Country _____ Postcode/Zip _____

E-mail _____

Occupation _____

How did you hear about this book? _____

☐ Book review (name) _____

☐ Advertisement (name) _____

☐ Recommendation _____

☐ Catalog _____

☐ Other _____

Where did you buy this book? _____

☐ Bookstore (name) _____ City _____

☐ Computer Store (name) _____

☐ Mail Order _____

☐ Other _____

What influenced you in the purchase of this book?

☐ Cover Design

☐ Contents

☐ Other (please specify) _____

How did you rate the overall contents of this book?

☐ Excellent   ☐ Good

☐ Average   ☐ Poor

What did you find most useful about this book? _____

What did you find least useful about this book? _____

Please add any additional comments. _____

What other subjects will you buy a computer book on soon? _____

What is the best computer book you have used this year? _____

Note: This information will only be used to keep you updated about new Wrox Press titles and will not be used for any other purpose or passed to any other third party.

1096

Check here if you DO NOT want to receive support for this book ☐ 1096